ATTITUDES AREN'T FREE
A CALL TO ACTION

Volume II

Editors:

JAMES E. PARCO
DAVID A. LEVY
DAPHNE DEPORRES
ALFREDO SANDOVAL

Published by Enso Books, 2023.

Attitudes Aren't Free: A Call to Action (Volume II)
A peer-reviewed publication.

Cover art: Design by vadimrysev. Licensed for publication by iStock (1317602552).

ISBN: 978-0-98-947761-1 (hardcover)
LCCN: 2010282390

Editors:
Parco, James E., 1968-
Levy, David A., 1964-
DePorres, Daphne, 1957-
Sandoval, Alfredo, 1959-

10 9 8 7 6 5 4 3 2

Published in the United States of America

First volume published in 2010 under ISBN 978-0982018569.

Enso Books, USA
www.ensobooks.com
For more information, contact sales@ensobooks.com

Dedication

We dedicate this volume to the collective memory of all those whom we've lost to COVID-19 since the global pandemic began in March 2020.

At the time of publication, more than 1,250,000 Americans lost their lives to this disease. For the sake of comparison, the United States lost approximately 620,000 citizens during the American Civil War (1861-1865) and approximately 617,000 citizens across all major wars during the 20th Century (WWI, WWII, Korean War and Vietnam War).

CONTENTS

"It's a helluva thing for the Pentagon to feel like it has to issue a statement that it is supporting the Constitution." – Scott Pelly, *60 Minutes*, 17 January 2021

SECTION I: THE NATIONAL DEBATE, CIRCA 2020–2021

SECTION II: AN INSTITUTIONAL DIALOGUE

SECTION III: INDIVIDUAL PERSPECTIVES—
BEARING WITNESS

SECTION IV: SOCIAL POLICY PERSPECTIVES

∾ Introduction ∽

A CALL TO ACTION

When Attitudes Aren't Free: Thinking Deeply about Diversity in the US Armed Forces was published in 2010, we never imagined that a second volume would be necessary. Our assumption at the time was that we would have been farther along the path toward the resolution of the social policy issues that divided us at the time. We believed that with the progress that Congress had made with the repeal of "Don't Ask, Don't Tell" (DADT) as yet another step forward in the American odyssey, and that we would look back in a decade and see Attitudes Aren't Free (volume I) as sort of a "time capsule" for diversity in the US Armed Forces circa 2010. Unfortunately, that is not where we find ourselves today and to that end, we concluded that a second volume to Attitudes Aren't Free was in order. However in a second volume, we felt it necessary to define the national political context in light of the previously unthinkable January 6, 2021 Capitol Insurrection ignited by a sitting Commander-in-Chief that we believe will have an indelible impact on the fabric of the American society for the decades to come. We also wanted to capture the institutional dialogue pertaining to race and ethnicity, the current social policy topic that has come to the forefront of the conversation through the emergence of the #BlackLivesMatter movement. To that end, we also wanted to hear from servicemembers through testimonies of their lived experiences in how the national, institutional and organizational cultures impacted them while on active duty. Finally, we included some current academic research social policy perspectives with respect to the Armed Services of the United States with guidance on how best to continue to build upon the progress that we have made as a society further develop a more inclusive military that illustrates America at its best. Despite the repeal of DADT being welcome change in 2010, critics continue to argue that other areas such as race, gender, and religion have not received the attention necessary and that more works needs to be done. *This is the Call to Action.*

When it comes to race, the main theme within the following pages of this volume, one has to wonder if we if things might even be worse now than they were over a decade ago for minority servicemembers. This is not a supposition. In fact, there is significant evidence supporting this notion contained in the 2020 Air Force Inspector General Department of the Air Force: Report of Inquiry (S8918P) Independent Racial Disparity Review (see Appendix for the full report). We have included the full text of this report at the end of the volume for readers to see for themselves the very words of leaders within the Department of Defense that attest to the empirical evidence that racial disparities are currently prevalent in the US Air Force, corroborated by accounts of the service members' experiences that follow. Although this report is specific to the Air Force, one can only imagine that the other services (Army, Navy, Coast Guard and Marines), are in a similar situation, at best. Although not stated specifically, this report also provides a *Call to Action*.

Our goal in bringing the publication to press is simply point out that there is still work to do, since issues of diversity and inclusion remain ever present. Attitudes Aren't Free: A Call to Action (volume II) offers a lens through which to view the fabric of diversity within the US Armed Forces as we embark on the third decade of the 21st century. Inherent in the narrative that latently weaves through every chapter in this volume is an implicit assumption: All human beings have a right to thrive. In the US military this is critical as the US military's mission of "providing military forces to deter war and ensure our nation's security" requires each member to be able to operate at their full potential. We can not overstate the importance of this assumption, and we are asking every leader within the US armed services, be it military or civilian, officer or enlisted, active or guard/reserve, to reflect on their individual leadership philosophies and ask themselves if they also hold such an assumption. Do you?

To clarify this assumption, it is important to understand what we mean by the much overused term, thrive. We have defined thriving as a positive and energizing state that emerges when individual and system needs are fulfilled within the symbiotic relationship that exists between the individual and the organization. Thriving, as it relates to the US Armed Forces, is largely about creating an environment that allows organizational members to maximize their potential in a way that is energizing rather than depleting and is geared towards helping the US Military accomplish its mission. Anything short of that should be considered unacceptable considering the high stakes.

So you might ask yourself, what does an environment that allows its members to thrive look like? Based on our exploration of the literature, particularly that of Self-Determination Theory, as well as exploratory work conducted by members of our editorial team at the US Air Force Academy, we offer a lens that consists of three elements: Belonging, Efficacy, and Agency. As you read the chapters in this volume, we ask that you please remain mindful to what each author is communicating to the reader these important human needs.

Consider for a moment how often you think about your own race or gender on a daily basis. When asked, most people report very infrequently to not at all if they are members of the majority demographics within their units. However, for those who are different in terms of race or gender, their answers are starkly different as they report they constantly are reminded of their difference. Regardless of your own race or gender, we ask that you reflect and contemplate what it feels like when you do not feel that you fit in, or, when you do not feel that you belong within a particular group or organization. Specifically, what does it feel like when you do not feel that you have the tools, training, or skills to do what you have been asked to employ? Also, ask yourself what it feels like when you are micro-managed, over-controlled, or have little voice to address your concerns. Finally, ask yourself what the impact on productivity, well-being, retention, and mission accomplishment is when these critical psychological needs are not met in suffi-cient quantities. To help readers along their own individual journeys to become the best leader that he or she can be, we have included reflection questions at the end of the Section III chapters. These questions are meant to help readers think about the needs of belonging, efficacy, and agency in concrete ways. By working on the issues these questions raise, we hope you will help us create environments where all organizational members can thrive.

Attitudes Aren't Free: A Call to Action (Volume II) is structured differently from Attitudes Aren't Free: Thinking Deeply About Diversity in the US Armed Forces (now, Volume I) which has more than 40,000 copies in circulation today. Whereas Volume I organized sections around the various social policy issues and included chapters written by leading experts and activists across the spectrum of perspectives to showcase the range of attitudes and beliefs present within the organizational culture, circa 2010. Volume II takes a different approach by orga-nizing the narrative around the societal, organization and individual levels for readers to better understand the gaps and provides a *Call to Action* for leaders to make inclusion a cornerstone for the next generation of military leaders.

Our hope is that you, the reader, after reading some or all of the pages that follow, that you are *called to action*. We feel strongly that the voices in this volume need and deserve to be heard in order to bring the attention to ongoing injus-tices and inequality in our Armed Forces. It hasn't been easy to get to this point. During the process of bringing this book to press, attempts by those who would wish to have these voices silenced have been made repeatedly to derail this work and to silence these voices. We could not let this happen and it has only furthered our collective resolve.

Section I

The National Debate, Circa 2020-2021

Attitudes Aren't Free: Thinking Deeply About Diversity in the US Armed Forces (Volume I) was originally published in 2010 by Air University Press. At that time, it emerged as a novel work which recognized the polarization of perspectives on critical social policy issues within the political discussions involving the US Armed Services on the key topical areas of race, gender, religion, sexuality. At the time, the most pressing debate focused on the military's ban on openly serving gay service members know as "Don't Ask, Don't Tell" (DADT).

Now, just more than a decade later, the political landscape has changed in ways that many of us could not have imagined. First, DADT was repealed in 2011, but almost immediately, political activists and elected officials turned their attention to the transgender ban. Transgender service members had not been considered as part of the DADT policy repeal, and thus, policy ambiguity remained for this class of American soldiers, sailors, airmen and Marines. Political and military leaders struggled for nearly a decade as to what the most appropriate policy for transgender service members should be, ranging from a complete prohibition, to a back-and-forth series of allowance and disallowance between 2019 and 2021. More on this in Section IV.

Second, gender equality had become a key policy issue for the armed forces starting with the 1976 law that allowed female cadets to attend the service academies. Sexual harassment had also been an issue within the rank and file of the armed services, but with women starting to attend the academies, greater political attention became focused on it. The issue of sexual harassment in the US military finally came to the forefront of the political realm in 2006 when the Tilly Report was briefed to Congress, which was entitled "Sexual Assault and Violence Against Women in the Military and the Academies." Since then, with a renewed commitment by senior military leaders, the armed services has worked tirelessly to overcome such deplorable behaviors within military units, but it has not been an easy problem to resolve. As the military is, by definition, a microcosm of American society, it came as no real surprise in 2017 when the #MeToo movement took hold across the country, almost overnight. Social media witnessed women coming forward by the hundreds that ultimately gave rise to an 2017 report in The Washington Post that claimed approximately half of all American

1

women surveyed claimed they had been victim to inappropriate sexual advances within the organizations where they worked, with nearly every respondent indicating that such behavior went unpunished, even after being reported. Although this movement did not focus on the military, everyone within the rank and file understood, the military was certainly not exempt. Much work remains.

Third, and probably most recently, has been what historians will likely determine to be a third "great awakening" on race in America, following the first with Reconstruction (1860s) and the second with the Civil Rights Movement (1960s). This third great awakening on race erupted in May following the on-camera murder of a Black American, George Floyd at the hands of a former Minneapolis Police Officer, which set the stage for a type of discussion on diversity that few people reading this essay have witnessed in his/her/their lifetime. Overnight, the #BlackLivesMatter movement came to the forefront of the political and civil discourse and remains an active dialogue today. Although race has been a critical issue of political discussion since the American Civil War in the 1860s, we are now at a new moment of dialogue, reconciliation and policy change to ensure equity of opportunity for all ethnic groups.

Make no mistake. None of these dialogues are going to go away anytime soon and all are worthy of intense conversation where we all try to understand the perspectives of others and work to find common ground to ensure an equitable society for the generations that will follow us. We are truly living in epic times, but despite all of the narratives that emerged, none has been more astounding or more threatening to the American concept of democracy than that which transpired with the events leading up to, during and after the 2020 US Presidential election in November 2020, and the Capitol Insurrection that followed on January 6, 2021. In Section I, we have printed select transcripts and memos made by military and political leaders at the highest levels of government that illustrate their unobstructed perspectives. We do not feel the need to summarize, analyze or critique them here in this introduction. The chapters that follow clearly speak for themselves articulating the individual perspectives that are unadulterated and pure. However, because this manuscript is being published amidst the aftermath of an era of history that has yet to be written, it is simply too soon to draw any conclusions.

However, the following chapters, taken together, provide a narrative of what will likely become one of the most telling case studies describing the core of the American democracy, and moreover, what the future for our the country, which we all love so dearly, may hold. As a society, we have walked up to a precipice and now must bear witness to our next steps as we plot a course forward to support and defend our way of life, against all enemies, foreign and domestic. This forever shall be our collective charge as defenders of the American ideal.

Winston Churchill once remarked "You can always count on the Americans to do the right thing after they have tried everything else." Let us hope this wisdom holds true, yet again....

CHAPTER 1

EULOGY FOR REPRESENTATIVE JOHN LEWIS

Barack H. Obama
Forty-Fourth President of the United States (2008–2016)
30 July 2020
Atlanta, Georgia

James wrote to the believers, "Consider it pure joy, my brothers and sisters, whenever you face trials of many kinds, because you know that the testing of your faith produces perseverance. Let perseverance finish its work so that you may be mature and complete, lacking nothing."

It is a great honor to be back in Ebenezer Baptist Church, in the pulpit of its greatest pastor, Dr. Martin Luther King Jr., to pay my respects to perhaps his finest disciple—an American whose faith was tested again and again to produce a man of pure joy and unbreakable perseverance—John Robert Lewis.

To those who have spoken to Presidents Bush and Clinton, Madam Speaker, Reverend Warnock, Reverend King, John's family, friends, his beloved staff, Mayor Bottoms—I've come here today because I, like so many Americans, owe a great debt to John Lewis and his forceful vision of freedom.

Now, this country is a constant work in progress. We were born with instructions: to form a more perfect union. Explicit in those words is the idea that we are imperfect, that what gives each new generation purpose is to take up the unfinished work of the last and carry it further than anyone might have thought possible.

John Lewis—the first of the Freedom Riders, head of the Student Nonviolent Coordinating Committee, youngest speaker at the March on Washington, leader of the march from Selma to Montgomery, member of Congress representing the people of this state and this district for thirty-three years, mentor to young people, including me at the time, until his final day on this earth—he not only embraced that responsibility, but he made it his life's work.

Which isn't bad for a boy from Troy. John was born into modest means—that means he was poor—in the heart of the Jim Crow South to parents who picked somebody else's cotton. Apparently, he didn't take to farm work. On days when he was supposed to help his brothers and sisters with their labor, he'd hide under the porch and make a break for the school bus when it showed up. His mother, Willie Mae Lewis, nurtured that curiosity in this shy, serious child. "Once you learn something," she told her son, "once you get something inside your head, no one can take it away from you."

As a boy, John listened through the door after bedtime as his father's friends complained about the Klan. One Sunday as a teenager, he heard Dr. King preach on the radio. As a college student in Tennessee, he signed up for Jim Lawson's workshops on the tactic of nonviolent civil disobedience. John Lewis was getting something inside his head, an idea he couldn't shake that took hold of him—that nonviolent resistance and civil disobedience were the means to change laws, but also change hearts, and change minds, and change nations, and change the world.

So he helped organize the Nashville campaign in 1960. He and other young men and women sat at a segregated lunch counter, well-dressed, straight-backed, refusing to let a milkshake poured on their heads, or a cigarette extinguished on their backs, or a foot aimed at their ribs, refused to let that dent their dignity and their sense of purpose. And after a few months, the Nashville campaign achieved the first successful desegregation of public facilities in any major city in the South.

John got a taste of jail for the first, second, third . . . well, several times. But he also got a taste of victory. And it consumed him with righteous purpose. And he took the battle deeper into the South.

That same year, just weeks after the Supreme Court ruled that segregation of interstate bus facilities was unconstitutional, John and Bernard Lafayette bought two tickets, climbed aboard a Greyhound, sat up front, and refused to move. This was months before the first official Freedom Rides. He was doing a test. The trip was unsanctioned. Few knew what they were up to. And at every stop, through the night, apparently the angry driver stormed out of the bus and into the bus station. And John and Bernard had no idea what he might come back with or who he might come back with. Nobody was there to protect them. There were no camera crews to record events. You know, sometimes we read about this and kind of take it for granted. Or at least we act as if it was inevitable. Imagine the courage of two people Malia's age, younger than my oldest daughter, on their own, to challenge an entire infrastructure of oppression.

John was only twenty years old. But he pushed all twenty of those years to the center of the table, betting everything, all of it, that his example could challenge centuries of convention, and generations of brutal violence, and countless daily indignities suffered by African Americans.

Like John the Baptist preparing the way, like those Old Testament prophets speaking truth to kings, John Lewis did not hesitate—he kept on getting on board buses and sitting at lunch counters, got his mug shot taken again and again, marched again and again on a mission to change America.

Spoke to a quarter million people at the March on Washington when he was just twenty-three.

Helped organize the Freedom Summer in Mississippi when he was just twenty-four.

At the ripe old age of twenty-five, John was asked to lead the march from Selma to Montgomery. He was warned that Governor Wallace had ordered troopers to use violence. But he and Hosea Williams and others led them across that bridge anyway. And we've all seen the film and the footage and the photographs, and President Clinton mentioned the trench coat, the knapsack, the book to read, the apple to eat, the toothbrush—apparently jails weren't big on such creature comforts. And you look at those pictures and John looks so young and he's small in stature. Looking every bit that shy, serious child that his mother had raised, and yet, he is full of purpose. God put perseverance in him.

And we know what happened to the marchers that day. Their bones were cracked by billy clubs, their eyes and lungs choked with tear gas—as they knelt to pray, which made their heads even easier targets, and John was struck in the skull. And he thought he was going to die, surrounded by the sight of young Americans gagging, and bleeding, and trampled, victims in their own country of state-sponsored violence.

And the thing is, I imagine initially that day, the troopers thought that they had won the battle. You can imagine the conversations they had afterward. You can imagine them saying, "Yeah, we showed them." They figured they'd turned the protesters back over the bridge, that they'd kept, that they'd preserved a system that denied the basic humanity of their fellow citizens. Except this time, there were some cameras there. This time, the world saw what happened, bore witness to Black Americans who were asking for nothing more than to be treated like other Americans. Who were not asking for special treatment, just the equal treatment promised to them a century before, and almost another century before that.

When John woke up and checked himself out of the hospital, he would make sure the world saw a movement that was, in the words of Scripture, "hard pressed on every side, but not crushed; perplexed but not in despair; persecuted, but not abandoned; struck down, but not destroyed." They returned to Brown Chapel, a battered prophet, bandages around his head, and he said, "More marchers will come now." And the people came. And the troopers parted. And the marchers reached Montgomery. And their words reached the White House—and Lyndon Johnson, son of the South, said "We shall overcome," and the Voting Rights Act was signed into law.

The life of John Lewis was, in so many ways, exceptional. It vindicated the faith in our founding, redeemed that faith—that most American of ideas, that idea that any of us ordinary people without rank or wealth or title or fame can somehow point out the imperfections of this nation, and come together, and challenge the status quo, and decide that it is in our power to remake this country that we love until it more closely aligns with our highest ideals. What a radical ideal. What a revolutionary notion. This idea that any of us, ordinary people, a young kid from Troy can stand up to the powers and principalities and say no this isn't right, this isn't true, this isn't just. We can do better. On the battlefield of justice,

Americans like John, Americans like the Reverends Lowery and C.T. Vivian—two other patriots that we lost this year—liberated all of us that many Americans came to take for granted.

America was built by people like them. America was built by John Lewises. He as much as anyone in our history brought this country a little bit closer to our highest ideals. And someday, when we do finish that long journey toward freedom, when we do form a more perfect union—whether it's years from now, or decades, or even if it takes another two centuries—John Lewis will be a founding father of that fuller, fairer, better America.

And yet, as exceptional as John was, here's the thing: John never believed that what he did was more than any citizen of this country can do. I mentioned in the statement the day John passed, the thing about John was just how gentle and humble he was. And despite this storied, remarkable career, he treated everyone with kindness and respect because it was innate to him—this idea that any of us can do what he did if we are willing to persevere.

He believed that in all of us there exists the capacity for great courage, that in all of us there is a longing to do what's right, that in all of us there is a willingness to love all people, and to extend to them their God-given rights to dignity and respect. So many of us lose that sense. It's taught out of us. We start feeling as if, in fact, that we can't afford to extend kindness or decency to other people. That we're better off if we are above other people and looking down on them, and so often that's encouraged in our culture. But John always saw the best in us. And he never gave up, and never stopped speaking out because he saw the best in us. He believed in us even when we didn't believe in ourselves. As a Congressman, he didn't rest; he kept getting himself arrested. As an old man, he didn't sit out any fight; he sat in, all night long, on the floor of the United States Capitol. I know his staff was stressed.

But the testing of his faith produced perseverance. He knew that the march is not yet over, that the race is not yet won, that we have not yet reached that blessed destination where we are judged by the content of our character. He knew from his own life that progress is fragile, that we have to be vigilant against the darker currents of this country's history, of our own history, with their whirlpools of violence and hatred and despair that can always rise again.

Bull Connor may be gone. But today we witness with our own eyes police officers kneeling on the necks of Black Americans. George Wallace may be gone. But we can witness our federal government sending agents to use tear gas and batons against peaceful demonstrators. We may no longer have to guess the number of jelly beans in a jar in order to cast a ballot. But even as we sit here, there are those in power doing their darnedest to discourage people from voting—by closing polling locations, and targeting minorities and students with restrictive ID laws, and attacking our voting rights with surgical precision, even undermining the postal service in the run-up to an election that is going to be dependent on mailed-in ballots so people don't get sick.

Now, I know this is a celebration of John's life. There are some who might say we shouldn't dwell on such things. But that's why I'm talking about it. John Lewis devoted his time on this earth fighting the very attacks on democracy and what's best in America that we are seeing circulate right now.

He knew that every single one of us has a God-given power. And that the fate of this democracy depends on how we use it; that democracy isn't automatic, it has to be nurtured, it has to be tended to; we have to work at it, it's hard. And so he knew it depends on whether we summon a measure, just a measure, of John's moral courage to question what's right and what's wrong and call things as they are. He said that as long as he had breath in his body, he would do everything he could to preserve this democracy. That as long as we have breath in our bodies, we have to continue his cause. If we want our children to grow up in a democracy—not just with elections, but a true democracy, a representative democracy, a big-hearted, tolerant, vibrant, inclusive America of perpetual self-creation—then we are going to have to be more like John. We don't have to do all the things he had to do because he did them for us. But we have got to do something. As the Lord instructed Paul, "Do not be afraid, go on speaking; do not be silent, for I am with you, and no one will attack you to harm you, for I have many in this city who are my people." Everybody's just got to come out and vote. We've got all those people in the city but we can't do nothing.

Like John, we have got to keep getting into that good trouble. He knew that nonviolent protest is patriotic—a way to raise public awareness, put a spotlight on injustice, and make the powers that be uncomfortable.

Like John, we don't have to choose between protest and politics; it is not an either-or situation, it is a both-and situation. We have to engage in protests where that is effective but we also have to translate our passion and our causes into laws and institutional practices. That's why John ran for Congress thirty-four years ago.

Like John, we have got to fight even harder for the most powerful tool we have, which is the right to vote. The Voting Rights Act is one of the crowning achievements of our democracy. It's why John crossed that bridge. It's why he spilled his blood. And by the way, it was the result of Democratic and Republican efforts. President Bush, who spoke here earlier, and his father, both signed its renewal when they were in office. President Clinton didn't have to because it was the law when he arrived, so instead he made a law that made it easier for people to register to vote.

But once the Supreme Court weakened the Voting Rights Act, some state legislatures unleashed a flood of laws designed specifically to make voting harder, especially, by the way, state legislatures where there is a lot of minority turnout and population growth. That's not necessarily a mystery or an accident. It was an attack on what John fought for. It was an attack on our democratic freedoms. And we should treat it as such.

If politicians want to honor John, and I'm so grateful for the legacy of work of all the Congressional leaders who are here, but there's a better way than a statement calling him a hero. You want to honor John? Let's honor him by revitalizing the law that he was willing to die for. And by the way, naming it the John Lewis Voting Rights Act—that is a fine tribute. But John wouldn't want us to stop there, trying to get back to where we already were. Once we pass the John Lewis Voting Rights Act, we should keep marching to make it even better.

By making sure every American is automatically registered to vote, including former inmates who've earned their second chance.

By adding polling places, and expanding early voting, and making Election Day a national holiday, so if you are someone who is working in a factory, or you are a single mom who has got to go to her job and doesn't get time off, you can still cast your ballot.

By guaranteeing that every American citizen has equal representation in our government, including the American citizens who live in Washington, DC, and in Puerto Rico. They are Americans.

By ending some of the partisan gerrymandering—so that all voters have the power to choose their politicians, not the other way around.

And if all this takes eliminating the filibuster—another Jim Crow relic—in order to secure the God-given rights of every American, then that's what we should do.

And yet, even if we do all this—even if every bogus voter suppression law was struck off the books today—we have got to be honest with ourselves that too many of us choose not to exercise the franchise, that too many of our citizens believe their vote won't make a difference, or they buy into the cynicism that, by the way, is the central strategy of voter suppression—to make you discouraged, to stop believing in your own power.

So we are also going to have to remember what John said: "If you don't do everything you can to change things, then they will remain the same. You only pass this way once. You have to give it all you have." As long as young people are protesting in the streets, hoping real change takes hold, I'm hopeful, but we cannot casually abandon them at the ballot box. Not when few elections have been as urgent, on so many levels, as this one. We cannot treat voting as an errand to run if we have some time. We have to treat it as the most important action we can take on behalf of democracy.

Like John, we have to give it all we have.

I was proud that John Lewis was a friend of mine. I met him when I was in law school. He came to speak and I went up and I said, "Mr. Lewis, you are one of my heroes. What inspired me more than anything as a young man was to see what you and Reverend Lawson and Bob Moses and Diane Nash and others did." And he got that kind of—aw shucks, thank you very much.

The next time I saw him, I had been elected to the United States Senate. And I told him, "John, I am here because of you." On Inauguration Day in 2008, 2009, he was one of the first people that I greeted and hugged on that stand. I told him, "This is your day too."

He was a good and kind and gentle man. And he believed in us—even when we don't believe in ourselves. It's fitting that the last time John and I shared a public forum was on Zoom. I am pretty sure that neither he nor I set up the Zoom call because we didn't know how to work it. It was a virtual town hall with a gathering of young activists who had been helping to lead this summer's demonstrations in the wake of George Floyd's death. And afterward, I spoke to John privately, and he could not have been prouder to see this new generation of activists standing up for freedom and equality, a new generation that was intent on voting and protecting the right to vote—in some cases, a new generation running for political office.

I told him, all those young people, John—of every race and every religion, from every background and gender and sexual orientation—John, those are your children. They learned from your example, even if they didn't always know it. They had understood, through him, what American citizenship requires, even if they had only heard about his courage through the history books.

"By the thousands, faceless, anonymous, relentless young people, Black and White . . . have taken our whole nation back to those great wells of democracy which were dug deep by the founding fathers in the formulation of the Constitution and the Declaration of Independence."

Dr. King said that in the 1960s. And it came true again this summer.

We see it outside our windows, in big cities and rural towns, in men and women, young and old, straight Americans and LGBTQ Americans, Blacks who long for equal treatment and Whites who can no longer accept freedom for themselves while witnessing the subjugation of their fellow Americans. We see it in everybody doing the hard work of overcoming complacency, of overcoming our own fears and our own prejudices, our own hatreds. You see it in people trying to be better, truer versions of ourselves.

And that's what John Lewis teaches us. That's where real courage comes from. Not from turning on each other, but by turning toward one another. Not by sowing hatred and division, but by spreading love and truth. Not by avoiding our responsibilities to create a better America and a better world, but by embracing those responsibilities with joy and perseverance and discovering that in our beloved community, we do not walk alone.

What a gift John Lewis was. We are all so lucky to have had him walk with us for a while, and show us the way.

God bless you all. God bless America. God bless this gentle soul who pulled it closer to its promise.

CHAPTER 2

2020 Vice Presidential Acceptance Speech

Kamala Harris
Forty-Ninth Vice President (Elect) of the United States of America
7 November 2020
Wilmington, Delaware

Congressman John Lewis wrote before his passing: "Democracy is not a state. It is an act." And what he meant was that America's democracy is not guaranteed. It is only as strong as our willingness to fight for it, to guard it and never take it for granted. And protecting our democracy takes struggle. It takes sacrifice. But there is joy in it, and there is progress. Because we the people have the power to build a better future.

And when our very democracy was on the ballot in this election, with the very soul of America at stake, and the world watching, you ushered in a new day for America.

To our campaign staff and volunteers, this extraordinary team—thank you for bringing more people than ever before into the democratic process and for making this victory possible. To the poll workers and election officials across our country who have worked tirelessly to make sure every vote is counted—our nation owes you a debt of gratitude as you have protected the integrity of our democracy.

And to the American people who make up our beautiful country, thank you for turning out in record numbers to make your voices heard.

And I know times have been challenging, especially the last several months—the grief, sorrow, and pain, the worries and the struggles. But we have also witnessed your courage, your resilience, and the generosity of your spirit.

For four years, you marched and organized for equality and justice, for our lives, and for our planet. And then, you voted. And you delivered a clear message. You chose hope and unity, decency, science, and yes, truth.

You chose Joe Biden as the next President of the United States of America. And Joe is a healer, a uniter, a tested and steady hand, a person whose own experience of loss gives him a sense of purpose that will help us, as a nation, reclaim our own sense of purpose. And a man with a big heart who loves with abandon. It's his love for Jill, who will be an incredible first lady. It's his love for Hunter, Ashley, and his grandchildren, and the entire Biden family. And while I first knew Joe as vice president, I really got to know him as the father who loved Beau, my dear friend, who we remember here today.

And to my husband, Doug; our children, Cole and Ella; my sister, Maya; and our whole family—I love you all more than I can ever express. We are so grateful to Joe and Jill for welcoming our family into theirs on this incredible journey. And to the woman most responsible for my presence here today—my mother, Shyamala Gopalan Harris, who is always in our hearts.

When she came here from India at the age of nineteen, she maybe didn't quite imagine this moment. But she believed so deeply in an America where a moment like this is possible. And so, I'm thinking about her and about the generations of women—Black women, Asian, White, Latina, Native American women who throughout our nation's history have paved the way for this moment tonight. Women who fought and sacrificed so much for equality, liberty, and justice for all, including the Black women, who are often, too often overlooked, but so often prove that they are the backbone of our democracy. All the women who worked to secure and protect the right to vote for over a century: one hundred years ago with the Nineteenth Amendment, fifty-five years ago with the Voting Rights Act, and now, in 2020, with a new generation of women in our country who cast their ballots and continued the fight for their fundamental right to vote and be heard.

Tonight, I reflect on their struggle, their determination, and the strength of their vision—to see what can be, unburdened by what has been. And I stand on their shoulders. And what a testament it is to Joe's character that he had the audacity to break one of the most substantial barriers that exists in our country and select a woman as his vice president.

But while I may be the first woman in this office, I will not be the last, because every little girl watching tonight sees that this is a country of possibilities. And to the children of our country, regardless of your gender, our country has sent you a clear message: Dream with ambition, lead with conviction, and see yourselves in a way that others may not, simply because they've never seen it before, but know that we will applaud you every step of the way.

And to the American people: No matter who you voted for, I will strive to be a vice president like Joe was to President Obama—loyal, honest, and prepared, waking up every day thinking of you and your family.

Because now is when the real work begins. The hard work. The necessary work. The good work. The essential work to save lives and beat this pandemic. To rebuild our economy so it works for working people. To root out systemic racism in our justice system and society. To combat the climate crisis. To unite our country and heal the soul of our nation.

And the road ahead will not be easy. But America is ready, and so are Joe and I.

We have elected a president who represents the best in us. A leader the world will respect and our children can look up to. A commander in chief who will respect our troops and keep our country safe. And a president for all Americans.

CHAPTER 3

SAVE AMERICA

Donald J. Trump
Forty-Fifth President of the United States of America (2017–2021)
6 January 2021
The White House
Washington, DC

The media will not show the magnitude of this crowd. Even I, when I turned on today, I looked, and I saw thousands of people here, but you don't see hundreds of thousands of people behind you because they don't want to show that. We have hundreds of thousands of people here, and I just want them to be recognized by the fake news media. Turn your cameras please and show what's really happening out here because these people are not going to take it any longer. They're not going to take it any longer. Go ahead. Turn your cameras, please. Would you show? They came from all over the world, actually, but they came from all over our country. I just really want to see what they do. I just want to see how they covered. I've never seen anything like it. But it would be really great if we could be covered fairly by the media. The media is the biggest problem we have as far as I'm concerned, single biggest problem—the fake news and the big tech.

Big tech is now coming into their own. We beat them four years ago. We surprised them. We took them by surprise, and this year, they rigged an election. They rigged it like they've never rigged an election before. By the way, last night, they didn't do a bad job either, if you notice. I'm honest. I just, again, I want to thank you. It's just a great honor to have this kind of crowd and to be before you. Hundreds of thousands of American patriots are committed to the honesty of our elections and the integrity of our glorious republic. All of us here today do not want to see our election victory stolen by emboldened radical left Democrats, which is what they're doing, and stolen by the fake news media. That's what they've done and what they're doing. We will never give up. We will never concede; it doesn't happen. You don't concede when there's theft involved.

Our country has had enough. We will not take it anymore, and that's what this is all about. To use a favorite term that all of you people really came up with, we will stop the steal. Today I will lay out just some of the evidence proving that we won this election, and we won it by a landslide. This was not a close election. I say sometimes jokingly, but there's no joke about it, I've been in two elections. I won them both, and the second one I won much bigger than the first. Almost 75 million people voted for our campaign, the most of any incumbent president by far in the history of our country, 12 million more people than four years ago. I was told by the real pollsters—we do have real pollsters. They knew that we were going to do well, and we were going to win. What I was told: if I went from 63 million—which we had four years ago—to 66 million, there was no chance of losing. Well, we didn't go to 66. We went to 75 million and they say we lost. We didn't lose.

By the way, does anybody believe that Joe had 80 million votes? Does anybody believe that? He had 80 million computer votes. It's a disgrace. There's never been anything like that. You could take third world countries. Just take a look, take third world countries. Their elections are more honest than what we've been going through in this country. It's a disgrace. It's a disgrace. Even when you look at last night, they're all running around like chickens with their heads cut off with boxes. Nobody knows what the hell is going on. There's never been anything like this. We will not let them silence your voices. We're not going to let it happen. Not going to let it happen.

Crowd: Fight for Trump! Fight for Trump! Fight for Trump!

Thank you. I'd love to have—if those tens of thousands of people would be allowed—the military, the secret service, and we want to thank you, and the police law enforcement. Great, you're doing a great job. But I'd love it if they could be allowed to come up here with us. Is that possible? Can you just let them come up, please?

Rudy, you did a great job. He's got guts. You know what? He's got guts, unlike a lot of people in the Republican party. He's got guts, he fights. He fights, and I'll tell you.

Thank you very much, John. Fantastic job. I watched. That's a tough act to follow, those two. John is one of the most brilliant lawyers in the country, and he looked at this and he said, "What an absolute disgrace that this could be happening to our Constitution." He looked at Mike Pence, and I hope Mike is going to do the right thing.

I hope so. I hope so because if Mike Pence does the right thing, we win the election. All he has to do. This is from the number one or certainly one of the top constitutional lawyers in our country. He has the absolute right to do it.

We're supposed to protect our country, support our country, support our Constitution, and protect our Constitution. States want to revote. The States got defrauded. They were given false information. They voted on it. Now they want to recertify. They want it back. All Vice President Pence has to do is send it back to the States to recertify and we become president, and you are the happiest people.

I just spoke to Mike. I said, "Mike, that doesn't take courage. What takes courage is to do nothing. That takes courage," and then we're stuck with a president who lost the election by a lot, and we have to live with that for four more years. We're just not going to let that happen.

Many of you have traveled from all across the nation to be here, and I want to thank you for the extraordinary love. That's what it is. There's never been a movement like this ever, ever for the extraordinary love for this amazing country and this amazing movement. Thank you.

Crowd: "We love Trump! We love Trump! We love Trump!"

By the way, this goes all the way back past the Washington Monument. Do you believe this? Look at this. Unfortunately, they gave the press the prime seats. I can't stand that. No, but you look at that behind. I wish they'd flip those cameras and look behind you. That is the most amazing sight. When they make a mistake, you get to see it on television. Amazing, amazing, all the way back. Don't worry. We will not take the name off the Washington Monument. We will not. Cancel culture. They wanted to get rid of the Jefferson Memorial, either take it down or just put somebody else in there. I don't think that's going to happen. It damn well better not. Although with this administration, if this happens, it could happen. You'll see some really bad things happen.

They'll knock out Lincoln too, by the way. They've been taking his statue down, but then we signed a little law. You hurt our monuments, you hurt our heroes, you go to jail for ten years and everything stopped. Did you notice that? It stopped. It all stopped.

They could use Rudy back in New York City. Rudy, they could use you. Your city is going to hell. They want Rudy Giuliani back in New York. We'll get a little younger version of Rudy. Is that okay, Rudy?

We're gathered together in the heart of our nation's Capitol for one very, very basic and simple reason: to save our democracy. Most candidates on election evening—and of course this thing goes on so long, they still don't have any idea what the votes are. We still have congressional seats under review. They have no idea. They've totally lost control. They've used the pandemic as a way of defrauding the people in a proper election. But when you see this and when you see what's happening, number one, they all say, "Sir, we'll never let it happen again." I said, "That's good, but what about eight weeks ago?" They try and get you to go. They say, "Sir, in four years, you're guaranteed." I said, "I'm not interested right now. Do me a favor, go back eight weeks. I want to go back eight weeks. Let's go back eight weeks." We want to go back, and we want to get this right because we're going to have somebody in there that should not be in there and our country will be destroyed, and we're not going to stand for that.

For years, Democrats have gotten away with election fraud, and weak Republicans, and that's what they are. There's so many weak Republicans. We have great ones—Jim Jordan and some of these guys. They're out there fighting the House. Guys are fighting, but it's incredible. Many of the Republicans, I helped them get in. I helped them get elected. I helped Mitch get elected. I could name twenty-four of them, let's say. I won't bore you with it, and then all of a sudden you have something like this. It's like, "Gee, maybe I'll talk to the president sometime later." No, it's amazing. The weak Republicans, they're pathetic Republicans, and that's what happens. If this happened to the Democrats, there'd be hell all over the country going on. There'd be hell all over the country. But just remember this. You're stronger, you're smarter. You've got more going than anybody, and they try and demean everybody having to do with us, and you're the real people. You're the people that built this nation. You're not the people that tore down our nation.

The weak Republicans, and that's it. I really believe it. I think I'm going to use the term "the weak Republicans." You got a lot of them, and you got a lot of great ones, but you got a lot of weak ones. They've turned a blind eye even as Democrats enacted policies that chipped away our jobs, weakened our military, threw open our borders, and put America last. Did you see the other day where Joe Biden said, "I want to get rid of the America first policy." What's that all about, get rid of ...? How do you say, "I want to get rid of America first?" Even if you're going to do it, don't talk about it. Unbelievable what we have to go through, what we have to go through. And you have to get your people to fight. If they don't fight, we have to primary the hell out of the ones that don't fight. You primary them. We're going to let you know who they are. I can already tell you, frankly.

But this year, using the pretext of the China virus and the scam of mail-in ballots, Democrats attempted the most brazen and outrageous election theft. There's never been anything like this. It's a pure theft in American history, everybody knows it. That election, our election was over at ten o'clock in the evening. We're leading Pennsylvania, Michigan, Georgia by hundreds of thousands of votes, and then late in the evening or early in the morning, boom, these explosions of bullshit, and all of a sudden, all of a sudden it started to happen.

Don't forget when Romney got beat. Romney. I wonder if he enjoyed his flight in last night? But when Romney got beaten, he stands up like you're more typical. Well, I'd like to congratulate the victor, the victor. Who was the victor, Mitt? I'd like to congratulate. They don't go and look at the facts. Now I don't know. He got slaughtered probably; maybe it was okay. Maybe that's what happened. But we look at the facts, and our election was so corrupt that in the history of this country, we've never seen anything like it. You can go all the way back. America is blessed with elections. All over the world they talk about our elections. You know what the world says about us now? They say we don't have free and fair elections, and you know what else? We don't have a free and fair press.

Our media is not free. It's not fair. It suppresses thought. It suppresses speech, and it's become the enemy of the people. It's become the enemy of the people. It's the biggest problem we have in this country. No third world countries would even attempt to do what we caught them doing, and you'll hear about that in just a few minutes. Republicans are constantly fighting—like a boxer with his hands tied behind his back. It's like a boxer, and we want to be so nice. We want to be so respectful of everybody, including bad people. We're going to have to fight much harder, and Mike Pence is going to have to come through for us. If he doesn't, that will be a sad day for our country because you're sworn to uphold our Constitution.

Now it is up to Congress to confront this egregious assault on our democracy. After this, we're going to walk down and I'll be there with you. We're going to walk down. We're going to walk down any one you want, but I think right here. We're going to walk down to the Capitol, and we're going to cheer on our brave senators and congressmen and women. We're probably not going to be cheering so much for some of them because you'll never take back our country with weakness. You have to show strength, and you have to be strong.

We have come to demand that Congress do the right thing and only counts the electors who have been lawfully slated, lawfully slated. I know that everyone here will soon be marching over to the Capitol building to peacefully and patriotically make your voices heard. Today we will see whether Republicans stand strong for integrity of our elections, but whether or not they stand strong for our country. Our country has been under siege for a long time, far longer than this four-year period. We've set it on a much straighter course, a much . . . I thought four more years. I thought it would be easy. We created—Four more years, I thought it would be easy. We created the greatest economy in history. We rebuilt our military. We got you the biggest tax cuts in history. We got you the biggest regulation cuts. There's no president—whether it's four years, eight years, or in one case more—got anywhere near the regulation cuts. It used to take twenty years to get a highway approved. Now we're down to two. I want to get it down to one, but we're down to two. And it may get rejected for environmental or safety reasons, but we got it down to safety.

We created Space Force. Look at what we did. Our military has been totally rebuilt. So we create Space Force, which in and of itself is a major achievement for an administration. And with us, it's one of so many different things.

Right to try. Everybody knows about right to try. We did things that nobody ever thought possible. We took care of our vets. Our vets: the VA now has the highest rating—91 percent—the highest rating that it's had from the beginning, 91 percent approval rating. Always you watch the VA, when it was on television. Every night people living in a horrible, horrible manner. We got that done. We got accountability done. We got it so that now in the VA, you don't have to wait for four weeks, six weeks, eight weeks, four months to see a doctor. If you can't get a doctor, you go outside, you get the doctor, you have them taken care of. And we pay the doctor. And we've not only made life wonderful for so many people, we've saved tremendous amounts of money—far secondarily, but we've saved a lot of money.

And now we have the right to fire bad people in the VA. We had 9,000 people that treated our veterans horribly. In primetime, they would not have treated our veterans badly. But they treated our veterans horribly. And we have what's called the VA Accountability Act. And the Accountability [Act] says if we see somebody in there that doesn't treat our vets well, or they steal, they rob, they do things badly, we say, "Joe, you're fired. Get out of here." Before you couldn't do that. You couldn't do that before.

So we've taken care of things. We've done things like nobody's ever thought possible. And that's part of the reason that many people don't like us, because we've done too much, but we've done it quickly. And we were going to sit home and watch a big victory. And everybody had us down for a victory. It was going to be great. And now we're out here fighting. I said to somebody I was going to take a few days and relax after our big electoral victory. Ten o'clock, it was over. But I was going to take a few days.

And I can say this, since our election, I believe, which was a catastrophe, when I watch, and even these guys knew what happened, they know what happened. They're saying, "Wow, Pennsylvania's insurmountable. Wow, Wisconsin, look at the big leads we had." Even though the press said we were going to lose Wisconsin by 17 points. Even though the press said Ohio is going to be close; we set a record. Florida's going to be close; we set a record. Texas is going to be close. Texas is going to be close; we set a record. And we set a record with the Hispanic, with the Black community. We set a record with everybody.

Today, we see a very important event, though, because right over there, right there, we see the event going to take place. And I'm going to be watching, because history is going to be made. We're going to see whether or not we have great and courageous leaders or whether or not we have leaders that should be ashamed of themselves throughout history, throughout eternity; they'll be ashamed. And you know what? If they do the wrong thing, we should never, ever forget that they did. Never forget. We should never, ever forget. With only three of the seven states in question, we win the presidency of the United States.

And by the way, it's much more important today than it was twenty-four hours ago. Because I spoke to David Perdue, what a great person, and Kelly Loeffler, two great people, but it was a setup. And I said, "We have no back line anymore." The only back line, the only line of demarcation, the only line that we have is the veto of the President of the United States. So this is now what we're doing, a far more important election than it was two days ago.

I want to thank the more than 140 members of the House. Those are warriors. They're over there working like you've never seen before—studying, talking, actually going all the way back, studying the roots of the Constitution, because they know we have the right to send a bad vote that was illegally got. They gave these people bad things to vote for and they voted, because what did they know? And then when they found out a few weeks later . . .

Again, it took them four years to revise history. And the only unhappy person in the United States, single most unhappy is Hillary Clinton because she said, "Why didn't you do this for me four years ago? Why didn't you do this for me four years ago? Change the votes! Ten thousand in Michigan. You could have changed the whole thing!" But she's not too happy. You notice you don't see her anymore. What happened? Where is Hillary? Where is she?

But I want to thank all of those congressmen and women. I also want to thank our thirteen most courageous members of the US Senate: Senator Ted Cruz, Senator Ron Johnson, Senator Josh Hawley, Kelly Loeffler. And Kelly Loeffler, I'll tell you, she's been so great. She works so hard. So let's give her and David a little special hand, because it was rigged against them. Let's give her and David . . . Kelly Loeffler, David Perdue. They fought a good race. They never had a shot. That equipment should never have been allowed to be used, and I was telling these people don't let them use this stuff. Marsha Blackburn, terrific person. Mike Braun, Indiana. Steve Daines, great guy. Bill Hagerty, John Kennedy, James Lankford, Cynthia Lummis. Tommy Tuberville, to the coach. And Roger Marshall. We want to thank them, senators that stepped up, we want to thank them.

I actually think though it takes, again, more courage not to step up. And I think a lot of those people are going to find that out. And you better start looking at your leadership because the leadership has led you down the tubes. "We don't want to give $2,000 to people. We want to give them $600." Oh, great. How does that play politically? Pretty good? And this has nothing to do with politics. But how does it play politically? China destroyed these people. We didn't destroy. China destroyed them, totally destroyed them. We want to give them $600, and they just wouldn't change. I said, "Give them $2,000. We'll pay it back. We'll pay it back fast. You already owe 26 trillion. Give them a couple of bucks. Let them live. Give them a couple of bucks!"

And some of the people here disagree with me on that. But I just say, look, you got to let people live. And how does that play, though? Okay, number one, it's the right thing to do. But how does that play politically? I think it's the primary reason, one of the primary reasons; the other was just pure cheating. That was the super primary reason. But you can't do that. You got to use your head.

As you know, the media is constantly asserting the outrageous lie that there was no evidence of widespread fraud. You ever see these people? "While there is no evidence of fraud . . ." Oh, really? Well, I'm going to read you pages. I hope you don't get bored listening to it. Promise? Don't get bored listening to it, all those hundreds of thousands of people back there. Move them up, please. Yeah. All these people don't get bored. Don't get angry at me because you're going to get bored because it's so much. The American people do not believe the corrupt fake news anymore. They have ruined their reputation.

But it used to be that they'd argue with me; I'd fight. So I'd fight, they'd fight. I'd fight, they'd fight. Boop-boop. You'd believe me, you'd believe them. Somebody comes out. They had their point of view; I had my point of view. But you'd have an argument. Now what they do is they go silent. It's called suppression. And that's what happens in a communist country. That's what they do. They suppress. You don't fight with them anymore, unless it's a bad . . . they have a little bad story about me. They'll make it ten times worse and it's a major headline.

But Hunter Biden, they don't talk about him. What happened to Hunter? Where's Hunter? Where is Hunter? They don't talk about him.

Now watch . . . all the sets will go off. Well, they can't do that because they get good ratings. The ratings are too good. Now where is Hunter? And how come Joe was allowed to give a billion dollars of money to get rid of the prosecutor in Ukraine? How does that happen? I'd ask you that question. How does that happen? Can you imagine if I said that? If I said that, it would be a whole different ball game.

And how come Hunter gets three and a half million dollars from the mayor of Moscow's wife, and gets hundreds of thousands of dollars to sit on an energy board even though he admits he has no knowledge of energy, and millions of dollars up front? And how come they go into China and they leave with billions of dollars to manage? "Have you managed money before?" "No, I haven't." "Oh, that's good. Here's about 3 billion."

No, they don't talk about that. No, we have a corrupt media. They've gone silent. They've gone dead. I now realize how good it was if you go back ten years. I realized how good, even though I didn't necessarily love 'em, I realized how good it was, like a cleansing motion. But we don't have that anymore. We don't have a fair media anymore. It's suppression, and you have to be very careful with that. And they've lost all credibility in this country.

We will not be intimidated into accepting the hoaxes and the lies that we've been forced to believe over the past several weeks. We've amassed overwhelming evidence about a fake election. This is the presidential election. Last night was a little bit better because of the fact that we had a lot of eyes watching one specific state, but they cheated like hell anyway.

You have one of the dumbest governors in the United States. And when I endorsed him, I didn't know this guy. At the request of David Perdue—he said, "A friend of mine is running for governor, what's his name." And you know the rest. He was in fourth place, fifth place. I don't know. He was way . . . He was doing poorly. I endorsed him. He went like a rocket ship and he won.

And then I had to beat Stacey Abrams with this guy, Brian Kemp. I had to beat Stacey Abrams and I had to beat Oprah—used to be a friend of mine. I was on her last show. Her last week she picked the five outstanding people. I don't think she thinks that anymore. Once I ran for president, I didn't notice there were too many calls coming in from Oprah. Believe it or not, she used to like me, but I was one of the five outstanding people.

And I had a campaign against Michelle Obama and Barack Hussein Obama against Stacey. And I had Brian Kemp—he weighs 130 pounds. He said he played offensive line in football. I'm trying to figure that . . . I'm still trying to figure that out. He said that the other night, "I was an offensive lineman." I'm saying, "Really? That must've been a really small team." But I look at that and I look at what's happened, and he turned out to be a disaster. This stuff happens.

Look, I'm not happy with the Supreme Court. They love to rule against me. I picked three people. I fought like hell for them; one in particular I fought. They all said, "Sir, cut him loose. He's killing us." The senators, very loyal senators. They're very loyal people. "Sir, cut him loose. He's killing us, sir. Cut him loose, sir." I must've gotten half of the senators. I said, "No, I can't do that. It's unfair to him. And it's unfair to the family. He didn't do anything wrong. They're made-up stories." They were all made-up stories. He didn't do anything wrong. "Cut him loose, sir." I said, "No, I won't do that." We got him through. And you know what?

They couldn't give a damn. They couldn't give a damn. Let them rule the right way, but it almost seems that they're all going out of their way to hurt all of us, and to hurt our country . . . to hurt our country.

I read a story in one of the newspapers recently how I control the three Supreme Court justices. I control them. They're puppets. I read it about Bill Barr, that he's my personal attorney. That he'll do anything for me. And I said, "It really is genius," because what they do is that, and it makes it really impossible for them to ever give you a victory, because all of a sudden Bill Barr changed, if you hadn't noticed. I like Bill Barr, but he changed, because he didn't want to be considered my personal attorney. And the Supreme Court, they rule against me so much. You know why? Because the story is I haven't spoken to any of them, any of them, since virtually they got in. But the story is that they're my puppet. That they're puppets, and now that the only way they can get out of that—because they hate that, it's not good on the social circuit—and the only way they get out is to rule against Trump. So let's rule against Trump, and they do that. So I want to congratulate them.

But it shows you the media's genius. In fact, probably, if I was the media, I'd do it the same way. I hate to say it. But we got to get them straightened out. Today, for the sake of our democracy, for the sake of our Constitution, and for the sake of our children, we lay out the case for the entire world to hear. You want to hear it?

Crowd: Yes!

In every single swing state, local officials, state officials—almost all Democrats—made illegal and unconstitutional changes to election procedures without the mandated approvals by the state legislatures, that these changes paved the way for fraud on a scale never seen before. And I think we'd go a long way outside of our country when I say that.

So just in a nutshell, you can't make a change on voting for a federal election unless the state legislature approves it. No judge can do it. Nobody can do it; only a legislature. So as an example, in Pennsylvania or whatever, you have a Republican legislature, you have a Democrat mayor, and you have a lot of Democrats all over the place. They go to the legislature, the legislature laughs at them. Says, "We're not going to do that." They say, "Thank you very much." And they go and make the changes themselves. They do it anyway. And that's totally illegal. That's totally illegal. You can't do that.

In Pennsylvania, the Democrat Secretary of State and the Democrat State Supreme Court justices illegally abolished the signature verification requirements just eleven days prior to the election. So think of what they did: No longer is there signature verification. Oh, that's okay. We want voter ID by the way. But no longer is there signature verification, eleven days before the election! They say, "We don't want it." You know why they don't want it? Because they want to cheat. That's the only reason. Who would even think of that? We don't want to verify a signature?

There were over 205,000 more ballots counted in Pennsylvania. Now think of this. You had 205,000 more ballots than you had voters. Where did they come from? You know where they came from? Somebody's imagination. Whatever they needed. So in Pennsylvania you had 205,000 more votes than you had voters! And the number is actually much greater than that now. That was as of a week ago. And this is a mathematical impossibility, unless you want to say it's a total fraud. So Pennsylvania was defrauded.

Over 8,000 ballots in Pennsylvania were cast by people whose names and dates of birth match individuals who died in 2020 and prior to the election. Think of that. Dead people! Lots of dead people—thousands. And some dead people actually requested an application. That bothers me even more. Not only are they voting, they want an application to vote. One of them was twenty-nine years ago died. It's incredible.

Over 14,000 ballots were cast by out-of-state voters. So these are voters that don't live in the state. And by the way, these numbers are what they call outcome determinative. Meaning, these numbers far surpass . . . I lost by a very little bit. These numbers are massive. Massive.

More than 10,000 votes in Pennsylvania were illegally counted, even though they were received after Election Day. In other words, "They were received after Election Day, let's count them anyway!" And what they did in many cases is they did fraud. They took the date and they moved it back, so that it no longer is after Election Day.

And more than 60,000 ballots in Pennsylvania were reported received back. They got back before they were ever supposedly mailed out. In other words, you got the ballot back before you mailed it!

They were supposedly mailed out. In other words, you got the ballot back before you mailed it, which is also logically and logistically impossible. Think of that one. You got the ballot back. Let's send the ballots. Oh, they've already been sent. But we got the ballot back before they were sent. I don't think that's too good.

Twenty-five thousand ballots in Pennsylvania were requested by nursing home residents, all in a single giant batch—not legal. Indicating an enormous illegal ballot harvesting operation. You're not allowed to do it. It's against the law.

The day before the election, the state of Pennsylvania reported the number of absentee ballots that had been sent out. Yet this number was suddenly and drastically increased by 400,000 people. It was increased. Nobody knows where it came from by 400,000 ballots. One day after the election, it remains totally unexplained. They said, "Well, we can't figure that." Now that's many, many times what it would take to overthrow the state. Just that one element. Four hundred thousand ballots appeared from nowhere, right after the election.

By the way, Pennsylvania has now seen all of this. They didn't know because it was so quick. They had a vote, they voted, but now they see all this stuff. It's all come to light. Doesn't happen that fast. And they want to recertify their votes. They want to recertify. But the only way that can happen is if Mike Pence agrees to send it back.

Mike Pence has to agree to send it back. And many people in Congress want it sent back. Let's say you don't do it. Somebody says, "Well, we have to obey the

Constitution." And you are, because you're protecting our country and you're protecting the Constitution, so you are. But think of what happens. Let's say they're stiffs and they're stupid people. And they say, "Well, we really have no choice." Even though Pennsylvania and other states want to redo their votes, they want to see the numbers. They already have the numbers. Go very quickly and they want to redo their legislature because many of these votes were taken, as I said, because it wasn't approved by their legislature. That in itself is illegal. And then you have the scam, and that's all of the things that we're talking about.

But think of this: if you don't do that, that means you will have a President of the United States for four years, with his wonderful son.

You will have a president who lost all of these states, or you will have a president, to put it another way, who was voted on by a bunch of stupid people who lost all of these things. You will have an illegitimate president, that's what you'll have. And we can't let that happen.

These are the facts that you won't hear from the fake news media. It's all part of the suppression effort. They don't want to talk about it. They don't want to talk about it. In fact, when I started talking about that, I guarantee you a lot of the television sets and a lot of those cameras went off—and that's a lot of cameras back there. A lot of them went off, but these are the things you don't hear about. You don't hear what you just heard. And I'm going to go over a few more states. But you don't hear it by the people who want to deceive you and demoralize you and control you—big tech, media.

Just like the suppression polls that said we're going to lose Wisconsin by 17 points; well, we won Wisconsin. They don't have it that way because they lose just by a little sliver. But they had me down the day before—Washington Post, ABC poll—down 17 points. I called up a real pollster. I said, "What is that?" "Sir, that's called a suppression poll. I think you're going to win Wisconsin, sir." I said, "But why don't they make it four or five points?" "Because then people vote, but when you're down 17, they say, 'Hey, I'm not going to waste my time. I love the president, but there's no way.'" Despite that, we won Wisconsin—you'll see. But that's called suppression because a lot of people, when they see that, it's very interesting. This pollster said, "Sir, if you're down three, four, or five, people vote. When you go down 17, they say, 'Let's go and have dinner, and let's watch the presidential defeat tonight on television, darling.'"

And just like the radical left tries to blacklist you on social media, every time I put out a tweet, even if it's totally correct, totally correct, I get a flag. I get a flag. And they also don't let you get it out. On Twitter, it's very hard to come on to my account. It's very hard to get out a message. They don't let the message get out nearly like they should, but I've had many people say, "I can't get on your Twitter." I don't care about Twitter. Twitter is bad news. They're all bad news. But you know what? If you want to get out a message and if you want to go through big tech, social media, they are really—if you're a conservative, if you're a Republican, if you have a big voice—I guess they call it shadow ban. Shadow ban. They shadow ban you, and it should be illegal. I've been telling these Republicans to get rid of Section 230.

And for some reason, Mitch and the group, they don't want to put it in there. And they don't realize that that's going to be the end of the Republican party as we know it. But it's never going to be the end of us—never. Let them get out. Let the weak ones get out. This is a time for strength.

They also want to indoctrinate your children in school by teaching them things that aren't so. They want to indoctrinate your children. It's all part of the comprehensive assault on our democracy and the American people to finally standing up and saying, "No." This crowd is again a testament to it. I did no advertising. I did nothing. You do have some groups that are big supporters. I want to thank that Amy and everybody. We have some incredible supporters, incredible, but we didn't do anything. This just happened.

Two months ago, we had a massive crowd come down to Washington. I said, "What are they there for?" "Sir, they're there for you." We have nothing to do with it. These groups, they're forming all over the United States.

And we got to remember, in a year from now, you're going to start working on Congress. And we got to get rid of the weak congresspeople, the ones that aren't any good, the Liz Cheneys of the world; we got to get rid of them. We got to get rid of them. She never wants a soldier brought home. I've brought a lot of our soldiers home. I don't know, some like it. They're in countries that nobody even knows the name. Nobody knows where they are. They're dying. They're great, but they're dying. They're losing their arms, their legs, their face. I brought them back home, largely back home—Afghanistan, Iraq.

Remember I used to say in the old days, "Don't go into Iraq. But if you go in, keep the oil." We didn't keep the oil. So stupid. So stupid, these people. And Iraq has billions and billions of dollars now in the bank. And what did we do? We get nothing. We never get. But we do actually; we kept the oil here. We did good. We got rid of the ISIS caliphate. We got rid of plenty of different things that everybody knows and the rebuilding of our military in three years. People said it couldn't be done. And it was all made in the USA, all made in the USA. Best equipment in the world.

In Wisconsin, corrupt Democrat-run cities deployed more than five hundred illegal, unmanned, unsecured drop boxes, which collected a minimum of 91,000 unlawful votes. It was razor thin, the loss. This one thing alone is much more than we would need, but there are many things.

They have these lockboxes, and they pick them up and they disappear for two days. People would say, "Where's that box?" They disappeared. Nobody even knew where the hell it was.

In addition, over 170,000 absentee votes were counted in Wisconsin without a valid absentee ballot application. So they had a vote, but they had no application. And that's illegal in Wisconsin. Meaning those votes were blatantly done in opposition to state law. And they came 100 percent from Democrat areas, such as Milwaukee and Madison—100 percent.

In Madison, 17,000 votes were deposited in so-called human drop boxes. You know what that is, right? Where operatives stuff thousands of unsecured ballots into duffel bags on park benches across the city in complete defiance of cease and desist letters from state legislature. The state legislature said, "Don't do it." They're the only ones that could approve it. They gave tens of thousands of votes.

They came in in duffel bags. Where the hell did they come from?

According to eyewitness testimony, postal service workers in Wisconsin were also instructed to illegally backdate approximately 100,000 ballots. The margin of difference in Wisconsin was less than 20,000 votes. Each one of these things alone wins us the state—great state, we love the state, we won the state.

In Georgia, your secretary of state—I can't believe this guy's a Republican. He loves recording telephone conversations. I thought it was a great conversation personally, so did a lot of other . . . people love that conversation, because it says what's going on. These people are crooked. They're 100 percent, in my opinion, one of the most corrupt—between your governor and your secretary of state. And now you have it again last night, just take a look at what happened, what a mess. And the Democrat party operatives entered into an illegal and unconstitutional settlement agreement that drastically weakened signature verification and other election security procedures.

Stacey Abrams, she took them to lunch, and I beat her two years ago with a bad candidate, Brian Kemp. But the Democrats took the Republicans to lunch because the secretary of state had no clue what the hell was happening . . . unless he did have a clue. That's interesting. Maybe he was with the other side. But we've been trying to get verifications of signatures in Fulton County. They won't let us do it. The only reason they won't is because we'll find things in the hundreds of thousands. Why wouldn't they let us verify signatures in Fulton County? Which is known for being very corrupt. They won't do it. They go to some other county where you would live. I said, "That's not the problem. The problem is Fulton County"—home of Stacey Abrams. She did a good job. I congratulate her, but it was done in such a way that we can't let this stuff happen.

We won't have a country if it happens. As a result, Georgia's absentee ballot rejection rate was more than ten times lower than previous levels. Because the criteria was so off, forty-eight counties in Georgia with thousands and thousands of votes rejected zero ballots. There wasn't one ballot. In other words, in a year in which more mail-in ballots were sent than ever before, and more people were voting by mail for the first time, the rejection rate was drastically lower than it had ever been before. The only way this can be explained is if tens of thousands of illegitimate votes were added to the tally; that's the only way you could explain it. By the way, you're talking about tens of thousands. If Georgia had merely rejected the same number of unlawful ballots as in other years, there should have been approximately 45,000 ballots rejected, far more than what we needed to win, just over 11,000.

They should find those votes. They should absolutely find that just over 11,000 votes—that's all we need. They defrauded us out of a win in Georgia, and we're not going to forget it. There's only one reason the Democrats could possibly want to eliminate signature matching, oppose voter ID, and stop citizenship confirmation.

Are you in citizenship? You're not allowed to ask that question. Because they want to steal the election.

The radical left knows exactly what they're doing. They're ruthless, and it's time that somebody did something about it. And Mike Pence, I hope you're going to stand up for the good of our Constitution and for the good of our country. And if you're not, I'm going to be very disappointed in you. I will tell you right now.

I'm not hearing good stories. In Fulton County, Republican poll watchers were ejected, in some cases, physically from the room under the false pretense of a pipe burst.

Water main burst, everybody leave. Which we now know was a total lie. Then election officials pull boxes—Democrats—and suitcases of ballots out from under a table. You all saw it on television, totally fraudulent. And illegally scanned them for nearly two hours totally unsupervised. Tens of thousands of votes, as that coincided with a mysterious vote dump of up to 100,000 votes for Joe Biden, almost none for Trump. Oh, that sounds fair. That was at 1:34 a.m.

The Georgia Secretary of State and pathetic governor of Georgia . . . although he says I'm a great president. I sort of maybe have to change. He said the other day, "Yes, I disagree with the president, but he's been a great president." Oh, good. Thanks. Thank you very much. Because of him and others. Brian Kemp, vote him the hell out of office, please.

Well, his rates are so low, his approval rating now, I think it just reached a record low.

They've rejected five separate appeals for an independent and comprehensive audit of signatures in Fulton County. Even without an audit, the number of fraudulent ballots that we've identified across the state is staggering. Over 10,300 ballots in Georgia were cast by individuals whose names and dates of birth match Georgia residents who died in 2020 and prior to the election. More than 2,500 ballots were cast by individuals whose names and dates of birth match incarcerated felons in Georgia prison—people who are not allowed to vote. More than 4,500 illegal ballots were cast by individuals who do not appear on the state's own voter rolls. Over 18,000 illegal ballots were cast by individuals who registered to vote using an address listed as vacant, according to the postal service. At least 88,000 ballots in Georgia were cast by people whose registrations were illegally backdated.

Each one of these is far more than we need. Sixty-six thousand votes in Georgia were cast by individuals under the legal voting age. And at least 15,000 ballots were cast by individuals who moved out of the state prior to the November 3rd election. They say they moved right back. They move right back. Oh, they moved out. They moved right back. Okay. They miss Georgia that much. I do. I love Georgia, but it's a corrupt system.

Despite all of this, the margin in Georgia is only 11,779 votes. Each and every one of these issues is enough to give us a victory in Georgia—a big, beautiful victory. Make no mistake, this election was stolen from you, from me, and from the country. And not a single swing state has conducted a comprehensive audit to remove the illegal ballots. This should absolutely occur in every single contestant state before the election is certified.

In the state of Arizona, over 36,000 ballots were illegally cast by noncitizens. Two thousand ballots were returned with no address. More than 22,000 ballots were returned before they were ever supposedly mailed out. They returned, but we haven't mailed them yet. Eleven thousand six hundred more ballots and votes were counted more than there were actual voters. You see that? So you have more votes again than you have voters.

One hundred fifty thousand people registered in Maricopa County after the registration deadline. One hundred three thousand ballots in the county were sent for electronic adjudication with no Republican observers.

In Clark County, Nevada, the accuracy settings on signature verification machines were purposely lowered before they were used to count over 130,000 ballots. If you signed your name as Santa Claus, it would go through. There were also more than 42,000 double votes in Nevada. Over 150,000 people were hurt so badly by what took place. And 1,500 ballots were cast by individuals whose names and dates of birth match Nevada residents who died in 2020, prior to the November 3rd election. More than 8,000 votes were cast by individuals who had no address and probably didn't live there. The margin in Nevada is down at a very low number. Any of these things would have taken care of the situation. We would have won. Any of these things would have taken care of the situation. We would have won Nevada also. Every one of these we're going over, we win.

In Michigan, quickly, the secretary of state—a real great one—flooded the state with unsolicited mail-in ballot applications sent to every person on the rolls, in direct violation of state law. More than 17,000 Michigan ballots were cast by individuals whose names and dates of birth matched people who were deceased. In Wayne County—that's a great one; that's Detroit—174,000 ballots were counted without being tied to an actual registered voter. Nobody knows where they came from. Also in Wayne County, poll watchers observed canvassers re-scanning batches of ballots over and over again, up to three or four or five times. In Detroit, turnout was 139 percent of registered voters. Think of that. So you had 139 percent of the people in Detroit voting. This is in Michigan—Detroit, Michigan.

A career employee of the city of Detroit testified under penalty of perjury that she witnessed city workers coaching voters to vote straight Democrat, while accompanying them to watch who they voted for. When a Republican came in, they wouldn't talk to him. The same worker was instructed not to ask for any voter ID and not to attempt to validate any signatures if they were Democrats. She also was told to backdate ballots received after the deadline and reports that thousands and thousands of ballots were improperly backdated. That's Michigan.

Four witnesses have testified under penalty of perjury that after officials in Detroit announced the last votes had been counted, tens of thousands of additional ballots arrived without required envelopes. Every single one was for a Democrat. I got no votes.

At 6:31 a.m., in the early morning hours after voting had ended, Michigan suddenly reported 147,000 votes. An astounding 94 percent went to Joe Biden, who campaigned brilliantly from his basement. Only a couple of percentage points went to Trump.

Such gigantic and one-sided vote dumps were only observed in a few swing states, and they were observed in the states where it was necessary. You know what's interesting? President Obama beat Biden in every state other than the swing states where Biden killed him. But the swing states were the ones that mattered. There were always just enough to push Joe Biden barely into the lead. We were ahead by a lot, and within the number of hours we were losing by a little.

In addition, there is the highly troubling matter of Dominion voting systems. In one Michigan county alone, 6,000 votes were switched from Trump to Biden, and the same systems are used in the majority of states in our country. Senator William Ligon, a great gentleman, chairman of Georgia Senate Judiciary Subcommittee, Senator Ligon, highly respected on elections has written a letter describing his concerns with Dominion in Georgia.

He wrote, and I quote, "The Dominion voting machines employed in Fulton County had an astronomical and astounding 93.67 percent error rate"—it's only wrong 93 percent of the time. "In the scanning of ballots requiring a review panel to adjudicate or determine the voter's interest, in over 106,000 ballots out of a total of 113,000." Think of it, you go in and you vote and then they tell people who you're supposed to be voting for. They make up whatever they want. Nobody's ever even heard. They adjudicate your vote. They say, "Well, we don't think Trump wants to vote for Trump. We think he wants to vote for Biden. Put it down for Biden." The national average for such an error rate is far less than 1 percent and yet you're at 93 percent. "The source of this astronomical error rate must be identified to determine if these machines were set up or destroyed to allow for a third party to disregard the actual ballot cast by the registered voter."

The letter continues, "There is clear evidence that tens of thousands of votes were switched from President Trump to former Vice President Biden in several counties in Georgia. For example, in Bibb County, President Trump was reported to have 29,391 votes at 9:11 p.m. Eastern time. While simultaneously Vice President Joe Biden was reported to have 17,213. Minutes later, just minutes, at the next update, these vote numbers switched with President Trump going way down to 17,000 and Biden going way up to 29,391." And that was very quick, a 12,000 vote switch, all in Mr. Biden's favor.

So, I mean, I could go on and on about this fraud that took place in every state, and all of these legislatures want this back. I don't want to do it to you because I love you and it's freezing out here, but I could just go on forever. I can tell you this . . .

Speaker from the crowd: "We love you. We love you. We love you. We love you. We love you. We love you. We love you. We love you."

So when you hear, when you hear, "While there is no evidence to prove any wrongdoing," this is the most fraudulent thing anybody's . . . This is a criminal enterprise. This is a criminal enterprise and the press will say, and I'm sure they won't put any of that on there because that's no good. Do you ever see, "While there is no evidence to back President Trump's assertion," I could go on for another hour reading this stuff to you and telling you about it. There's never been anything like it.

Think about it, Detroit had more votes than it had voters. Pennsylvania had 205,000 more votes than it had voters. I think that's almost better than dead people, if you think, right? More votes than they had voters, and many other states are also.

It's a disgrace that in the United States of America, tens of millions of people are allowed to go vote without so much as even showing identification. In no state is there any question or effort made to verify the identity, citizenship, residency, or eligibility of the votes cast. The Republicans have to get tougher. You're not going to have a Republican party if you don't get tougher. They want to play so straight, they want to play so, "Sir, yes, the United States, the Constitution doesn't allow me to send them back to the states." Well, I say, "Yes, it does because the Constitution says you have to protect our country and you have to protect our Constitution and you can't vote on fraud." And fraud breaks up everything, doesn't it?

When you catch somebody in a fraud, you're allowed to go by very different rules. So I hope Mike has the courage to do what he has to do. And I hope he doesn't listen to the RINOs and the stupid people that he's listening to. It is also widely understood that the voter rolls are crammed full of noncitizens, felons, and people who have moved out of state and individuals who are otherwise ineligible to vote.

Yet Democrats oppose every effort to clean up their voter rolls. They don't want to clean them up; they are loaded. And how many people here know other people that when the hundreds of thousands and then millions of ballots got sent out, got three, four, five, six, and I heard one who got seven ballots. And then they say, "You didn't quite make it, sir." We won. We won in a landslide. This was a landslide.

They said, "It's not American to challenge the election." This is the most corrupt election in the history, maybe of the world. You know, you could go to third world countries, but I don't think they had hundreds of thousands of votes and they don't have voters for them. I mean, no matter where you go, nobody would think this. In fact, it's so egregious, it's so bad that a lot of people don't even believe it. It's so crazy that people don't even believe it. It can't be true. So they don't believe it. This is not just a matter of domestic politics, this is a matter of national security.

So today, in addition to challenging the certification of the election, I'm calling on Congress and the state legislatures to quickly pass sweeping election reforms, and you better do it before we have no country left. Today is not the end. It's just the beginning.

With your help over the last four years, we built the greatest political movement in the history of our country, and nobody even challenges that. I say that over and over, and I never get challenged by the fake news, and they challenge almost everything we say. But our fight against the big donors, big media, big tech, and others is just getting started. This is the greatest in history. There's never been a movement like that. You look back there all the way to the Washington Monument. It's hard to believe.

We must stop the steal and then we must ensure that such outrageous election fraud never happens again, can never be allowed to happen again. But we're going forward. We'll take care of going forward. We got to take care of going back. Don't let them talk, "Okay, well we promise." I've had a lot of people [say], "Sir, you're at 96 percent for four years." I said, "I'm not interested right now. I'm interested in right there."

With your help we will finally pass powerful requirements for voter ID. You need an ID to cash your check. You need an ID to go to a bank, to buy alcohol, to drive a car. Every person should need to show an ID in order to cast your most important thing—a vote. We will also require proof of American citizenship in order to vote in American elections. We just had a good victory in court on that one, actually.

We will ban ballot harvesting and prohibit the use of unsecured drop boxes to commit rampant fraud. These drop boxes are fraudulent. They disappear and then all of a sudden they show up. It's fraudulent. We will stop the practice of universal, unsolicited mail-in balloting. We will clean up the voter rolls that ensure that every single person who cast a vote is a citizen of our country, a resident of the state in which they vote, and their vote is cast in a lawful and honest manner. We will restore the vital civic tradition of in-person voting on election day so that voters can be fully informed when they make their choice. We will finally hold big tech accountable, and if these people had courage and guts, they would get rid of Section 230, something that no other company, no other person in America, in the world has.

All of these tech monopolies are going to abuse their power and interfere in our elections, and it has to be stopped. And the Republicans have to get a lot tougher and so should the Democrats. They should be regulated, investigated, and brought to justice under the fullest extent of the law. They're totally breaking the law.

Together we will drain the Washington swamp and we will clean up the corruption in our nation's capital. We have done a big job on it, but you think it's easy; it's a dirty business. It's a dirty business. You have a lot of bad people out there. Despite everything we've been through, looking out all over this country and seeing fantastic crowds, although this I think is our all-time record—I think you have 250,000 people, 250,000.

Looking out at all the amazing patriots here today, I have never been more confident in our nation's future. Well, I have to say we have to be a little bit careful. That's a nice statement, but we have to be a little careful with that statement, if we allow this group of people to illegally take over our country. Because it's illegal when the votes are illegal, when the way they got there is illegal, when the states that vote are given false and fraudulent information. We are the greatest country on earth and we are headed, and were headed, in the right direction.

You know, the wall is built, we're doing record numbers at the wall. Now they want to take down the wall. Let's let everyone flow in. Let's let everybody flow in.

We did a great job on the wall. Remember the wall? They said it could never be done. One of the largest infrastructure projects we've ever had in this country, and it's had a tremendous impact and we got rid of catch and release, we got rid of all of the stuff that we had to live with. But now the caravans, they think Biden's getting in. The caravans are forming again. They want to come in again and rip off our country. Can't let it happen.

As this enormous crowd shows, we have truth and justice on our side. We have a deep and enduring love for America in our hearts. We love our country. We have overwhelming pride in this great country, and we have it deep in our souls. Together we are determined to defend and preserve government of the people, by the people, and for the people.

Our brightest days are before us, our greatest achievements still wait. I think one of our great achievements will be election security, because nobody until I came along had any idea how corrupt our elections were. And again, most people would stand there at nine o'clock in the evening and say, "I want to thank you very much," and they go off to some other life. But I said, "Something's wrong here. Something's really wrong. Can't have happened." And we fight. We fight like hell, and if you don't fight like hell, you're not going to have a country anymore.

Our exciting adventures and boldest endeavors have not yet begun, my fellow Americans, for our movement, for our children, and for our beloved country. And I say this, despite all that's happened, the best is yet to come.

So we're going to, we're going to walk down Pennsylvania Avenue. I love Pennsylvania Avenue, and we're going to the Capitol and we're going to try and give . . . The Democrats are hopeless. They're never voting for anything, not even one vote. But we're going to try and give our Republicans—the weak ones, because the strong ones don't need any of our help—we're going to try and give them the kind of pride and boldness that they need to take back our country.

So let's walk down Pennsylvania Avenue. I want to thank you all. God bless you and God bless America. Thank you all for being here; this is incredible. Thank you very much. Thank you.

CHAPTER 4

VICE PRESIDENT COMMENTS FOLLOWING THE US CAPITOL INSURRECTION

Michael R. Pence
Forty-Eighth Vice President of the United States of America
(2017–2021)

6 January 2021
The Capitol
Washington, DC

I want to thank the federal, state, and local law enforcement. The violence was quelled. The Capitol is secured and the people's work continues. We condemn the violence that took place here in the strongest possible terms. We grieve the loss of life in these hallowed halls, as well as the injuries suffered by those who defended our Capitol today. And we will always be grateful to the men and women who stayed at their posts to defend this historic place. To those who wreaked havoc in our Capitol today, you did not win. Violence never wins. Freedom wins, and this is still the people's house.

And as we reconvene in this chamber, the world will again witness the resilience and strength of our democracy, for even in the wake of unprecedented violence and vandalism at this Capitol, the elected representatives of the people of the United States have assembled again on the very same day to support and defend the Constitution of the United States. So may God bless the lost, the injured, and the heroes forged on this day. May God bless all who serve here and those who protect this place. And may God bless the United States of America.

Let's get back to work.

CHAPTER 5

US Department of Justice Update on Capitol Attack

Michael Sherwin
US Attorney, District of Washington

Steven D'Antuono
FBI Assistant Director-in-Charge, Washington Field Office

Ashan Benedict
Special Agent-in-Charge, ATF Office, Washington, DC

15 January 2021
Washington, DC

Michael Sherwin, US Attorney for the District of Washington: Okay. So, hello everyone. It's Mike Sherwin here. So, a quick update with where we're at in terms of prosecution and the investigation, then I'll turn it over to my colleagues here with the Bureau and ATF. So, as of this morning, eight o'clock a.m., we have currently 175 open investigations [crosstalk 00:13:58] that are subjects that we're currently looking at related to the violence in the Capitol. That would include cases of violence outside the Capitol, and also on the Capitol grounds, and also inside the Capitol.

As related to those 275 open investigations, we anticipate that that's going to grow easily past three hundred probably by the end of the day, and then exponentially increase into the weekend and next week. So again, as of eight a.m. this morning, in terms of cases, prosecutions, we've opened ninety-eight criminal cases in terms of criminal cases that have been filed. And the majority of those cases are federal felony cases. So, I think I tried to articulate this earlier this week that initially we were looking to fix, find, and charge the low-hanging fruit, the individuals that we could easily round up and charge. A great bulk of those were misdemeanor cases.

But as the investigation continues, as the days and weeks progress, we're looking at more significant federal felony charges. And that's exactly what we're doing in partnership with our local and federal partners. So, some of the cases that I think I want to just highlight, that are emblematic of what we're trying to do here are the following. In terms of trying to really focus on some of the violent offenders, both inside and outside the Capitol, some of these cases include Mr. Peter Stager. This was the individual of Arkansas. He was charged with a federal felony and arrested yesterday in Arkansas.

And this was the individual, I think that's really the height of hypocrisy, that was beating an MPD officer with a flagpole. And at the other end of that flagpole was attached the American flag. And look, as a veteran, I found that case even more egregious, the act of just, again, the hypocrisy of Mr. Stager's actions. Another case focusing on violence that was . . . Mr. Stager's case was balanced on law enforcement, and we're specifically focusing on that. But also, unfortunately, as this case goes on, we're seeing indications that law enforcement officers, both former and current, maybe have been off-duty and participating in this riot activity.

And I think as we said earlier, we don't care what your profession is, who you are, who you're affiliated with. If you were conducting or engaged in criminal activity, we will charge you and you will be arrested. And that's exactly what we're doing. For example, yesterday two off-duty Rocky Mountain Virginia police officers were charged federally and arrested in Virginia for their participation in the rioting at the Capitol.

Another case of interest that also came up was Robert Sanford out of Pennsylvania. Again, I think this is another case, the height of hypocrisy. Mr. Sanford is a retired firefighter and he was charged with a federal felony with attacking MPD officers. He actually threw a fire extinguisher at them and hit one in the head. Now, there's some confusion. This is unrelated to the death of the CP officer that perished, that died, unfortunately, during these riots. But again, this is just another indication of our aggressiveness to try to find and charge immediately the most egregious actors.

A final note here before I turn it over to my colleagues. We believe, and we're hopeful, and we believe that these cases are having impact. Over the past few days we've had several people, given the way we're charging these cases and what we're charging them with, these federal felonies, have self-reported and turned themselves in with attorneys. And we encourage the public to do that. And we believe that we'll continue as the investigation goes on. So at this point, I'm going to turn over the discussion to my colleagues at the FBI.

Steven D'Antuono, FBI Assistant Director-in-Charge of the Washington Field Office:

This is Steven D'Antuono. I'm the assistant director in charge of the Washington field office for the FBI. We are here to provide an update on our progress in the investigation of last week's siege of the Capitol. I want to assure you that an enormous amount of work has been done in the past nine days. We are making progress on all fronts: the pipe bomb case, the rioting and violence investigation, and the death of the US Capitol Police Officer Brian Sicknick.

This is a large puzzle with so many pieces. We are working diligently to put those pieces together. We continue to work closely with our partners in the DC US Attorney's office, as well as with other law enforcement partners here and across the country. I wanted to take this opportunity to thank them for their partnership and collaboration and tracking down, arresting, and charging those responsible for the Capitol riots. FBI personnel continue to work day and night gathering evidence, sharing intelligence, working with federal prosecutors to bring charges.

To date, we've identified more than 270 suspects involved in criminal activity in and around the Capitol. The FBI has arrested more than forty subjects, and with the help of our partners around the country, more than one hundred individuals have been taken into custody. We are methodically following all the leads to identify those responsible and hold them accountable. The American people have played a critical role in assisting us with these efforts. On behalf of the FBI and our law enforcement partners, I want to thank the American people for your incredible outpouring of tips to help us bring these perpetrators to justice. We are continuing to review them all and we ask that you keep them coming.

In the past week alone, we've received nearly 140,000 photos and videos from the public. To those of you who took part in the violence, here's something you should know. Every FBI field office in the country is looking for you. As a matter of fact, even your friends and family are tipping us off. So, you might want to consider turning yourself in, instead of wondering when we're going to come knocking on your door, because we will. If you have tips, no matter how small, please contact 1-800-CALL-FBI or submit photos and videos to fbi.gov/uscapitol. That's Capitol with an O. Your tips are helping us investigate people on a variety of federal charges.

Today, I want to focus on a particular egregious charge: assault on a law enforcement officer. Law enforcement officers risk their lives each and every day to protect the rights of the American people. Investigating violent assault on these offices is a priority for the FBI and our partners. You attack one of us, you attack us all. And as acting US Attorney, Mike Sherwin just stated, we arrested several first subjects on these charges. One was Peter Stager, as he mentioned, of Arkansas, who was captured on video using an American flag, the symbol of our democracy, to repeatedly strike down a DC metropolitan police officer, who was dragged down the Capitol steps and forced into a prone position by a large group of rioters. Also, like Mike said was arrested, Robert Sanford, a retired Pennsylvania firefighter who is alleged to have struck three officers with a fire extinguisher ... with a fire extinguisher. And these are just two examples of this brutal assault on law enforcement this week. We are working with the Metropolitan Police Department and the US Capitol Police to identify and investigate all of these and other violent attacks on those who are doing their duty to protect the very symbol of our democracy, the US Capitol. The tips we have received from the public have been critical in furthering these investigations. You can see photos of additional suspects of assault on a law enforcement officer, and help us find them by viewing our seeking information posters at www.fbi.gov.

This is an unprecedented incident. If this investigation was a football game, we'd still be in the first quarter. So let this be a reminder. The full force of the FBI is investigating the heinous acts we saw last week, and we will leave no stone unturned until we locate and apprehend anyone who participated in the violence. Thank you.

All right. Now speaking as Ashan Benedict from the ATF, the Alcohol, Tobacco and Firearms Washington, DC, field office, where he is the special agent in charge.

Ashan Benedict, Special Agent-in-Charge, ATF Washington, DC, Office:

Good afternoon, everybody. So ATF's been sitting on the Inaugural Committee for months now, and we routinely support every inauguration in Washington, DC, working with Capitol Police, Secret Service, FBI, and MPD to coordinate. Just to back up to January 6, ATF responded to the explosive devices on that day, working with Capitol Police and FBI to secure that scene. As that was unfolding, we ended up supporting the US Capitol Police, our brothers and sisters in uniform, during the day of the riots there. We are jointly investigating the pipe bombs and the Molotov cocktails with the FBI and the US Capitol Police, and that investigation is currently ongoing. Following up on the events of January 6 and the overall planning with the inauguration, we have special agents, explosive specialists, bomb technicians, K-9 units, and our Special Response Team, all assigned and deployed in and around Washington, DC, working with Secret Service, Capitol Police, and our MPD partners moving forward. Firearms: I ask anybody who's coming in the district to be very cognizant of the laws of the district regarding firearms. Anybody who violates federal law as it pertains to firearms possession, or firearms trafficking, or the use of firearms, they will be investigated by the ATF, and prosecuted by the US Attorney's Office. So please, folks, be mindful of the laws on the books and act smartly.

We're asking for the public's assistance to provide information on illegal possession of firearms and explosives related to this event, any other events, or in the regular course of business. They can contact any one of the ATF field offices around the country, or call ATF at 888-ATF-BOMB. They can also report anonymously through an ATF app called Report It. Finally, I hope this coming week is safe, and lawful, and free of these challenges that we've faced on the 6th. And we stand ready to protect the nation's capitol, and work with our partners to ensure the transition and tradition of a peaceful transition of power here in Washington, DC. Thank you.

All right. Thank you all for those brief remarks. And operator, we'll open it up now for questions, please.

Q&A with the Panel of Presenters
Operator:

We will now begin the question-and-answer session. If you do have a question, please press star then one on your touch tone phone. If you're using a speaker-phone, please pick up your handset before pressing the keys. Please note that you will be limited to one question today. Our first question will come from Alex Mallin with ABC News.

Alex Mallin:

Hi there. I'm just wondering if you can confirm that there are currently thirty-seven suspects that are being looked at into the investigation of Officer Brian Sicknick's death. And separately from that, several lawmakers in the past couple of days have come forward and raised concerns about their colleagues, fellow lawmakers, potentially other people in the Congress, staffers, being involved in potentially assisting some of the rioters that we saw. Has that become a part of this investigation yet?

Steve D'Antuono:

So I'll address your first question first, obviously. The Officer Sicknick case is an ongoing investigation, and we are looking at everything and anyone that is involved in that matter. And then as for your . . . Oh, sorry, this is Steve D'Antuono, the ADIC of FBI, the [inaudible 00:26:59] WFO. And then the second part, the second question, is the women and men of the FBI, we'll leave no stone unturned. We are looking at every piece of this puzzle. It's a very large puzzle, as you can imagine. And we're taking every piece that we possibly can and finding every piece to put that puzzle together, to give us a true picture of what happened on that day, on the 6th, before the 6th, and after the 6th.

Operator:

Our next question comes from Kevin Johnson with USA Today.

Kevin Johnson:

Hi, good afternoon. In an earlier filing, I believe late yesterday, y'all indicated that there was strong evidence that lawmakers were targeted for capture or for assassination. Can you talk a little bit about whether that applies beyond the case of Mr. Chansley?

Mike Sherwin:

Sure, I'll address that. This is Mike Sherwin, the US Attorney here in DC. So, first of all, I want to start right off the bat by saying there is no direct evidence at this point of kill-capture teams and assassination, but let me add to that. Look, as we tried to describe here, the cases are all being charged here in DC, and with our law enforcement partners. And what makes this case in particular unprecedented and unusual and extremely complex is the fact that after the event, obviously thousands of people went back to their home districts. And that has complicated things, obviously, because we've had to locate them with our law enforcement partners. After they're charged, we need to work with other districts to not only find these people, but have initial appearances in districts across the United States. There were appearances in two districts, I believe you're making reference to, I believe Texas and Arizona.

And at some of those hearings, there were other prosecutors that may be a disconnect, that may be adding information that's not directly related to what we have. So I want to just reiterate what I have already stated. And on that basis, yes, in terms of complex cases, looking for these organized groups, I think I've stated this before, we have specialized prosecutors here working with specialized counterterrorism investigators, looking at these type of organization for these most egregious acts. But right now, again, we don't have any direct evidence of kill-capture teams.

Operator:

Our next question comes from Katie Benner with The New York Times.

Katie Benner:

Hi, thanks so much. This is a question for either the US Attorney or the ADIC. We've seen images of people wearing clothing that seemed to identify them as members of groups, like the Proud Boys or other militia groups. We've seen neo-Nazi garb. Can you say which extremist groups you've been able to identify at the Capitol so far, and can you characterize the impact that those extremist groups have had on the investigation? Could you characterize the impact they've had by being in the mix at the rally that day and as part of the attack? And have you seen any coordination within these groups to come to DC in a coordinated way to disrupt Congress last week?

Mike Sherwin:

So Katie, I'll start that question and then I'll turn it over to my colleagues here at the Bureau. So look, you're right. If you look at social media, you could see a lot of affiliation with some of the protest activity, some of the rioting activity, and it runs the whole gamut of different groups from soup to nuts, A to Z. But right now, look, we're not going to label anything because everything's on the table in terms of the extremist groups. But look, I think the evidence speaks for itself. These guys have labeled themselves. I mean Mr. Kevin Seefried labeled himself when he was walking through the Capitol with the Stars and Bars, and Mr. Robert Packer labeled himself when he was with the Camp Auschwitz shirt in the Capitol. So we're not going to try to label these people. We'll let them label themselves with the evidence. But all of these extremist groups are being looked at in terms of their participation at the Capitol.

Steve, do you have anything to add?

Steve D'Antuono:

Yeah. So I would just add the fact that we're looking at this as a riot case. We're looking at everything we can, and we're focusing on people who broke the law. I just can't stress enough of a wide broad scope that this investigation has.

Operator:

Our next question comes from Catherine Herridge with CBS News.

Catherine Herridge:

Thanks for taking my questions. My first question is for Mr. Sherwin. We're ten days into this. What does the evidence tell us about premeditation? And secondly, for Mr. Benedict, did the pipe bombs at the RNC and the DNC fail to explode? Thank you.

Mike Sherwin:

Okay. So to try address that, Catherine. So look, initially, the initial tranche of arrests are all very reactive-type cases where we had violence on police officers, destruction of property within the Capitol, and trespassing and violence outside the Capitol grounds. Those were the initial reactive, quick-hit cases. Trying to reiterate again, look, there are bread crumbs of organization in terms of maybe what was taking place outside of the Capitol and inside, with perhaps some type of communication with core groups of people ingressing into the Capitol, and some coordinated activity of individuals within the Capitol. And that is a tier-one top priority for both the US Attorney's office and our federal law enforcement partners to see, again, whether there was this overarching command and control, and whether there were these organized, there was this overarching command and control. And whether there were these organized teams that were organized to breach the Capitol, and then perhaps try to accomplish some type of a mission inside the Capitol. But that is ongoing. And again, I think this is going to take weeks, if not months, to find out the actual motivations of some of those groups.

Sean?

Sean Benedict:

Excuse me. Sean Benedict. Answering your question, I can confirm that devices did not explode by the Capitol on that day. They were rendered safe by law enforcement, and we mitigated the risk to the public. And the components are currently being analyzed.

Operator:

Our next question comes from Sarah Lynch with Reuters.

Sarah Lynch:

Yeah, hi, I was hoping you could provide a little bit more update about what you might be looking at with regard to public employees and government employees that might have been involved. As some of these cases have come out, there's been more information about strange things happening with Capitol police, where one person gave someone a hug and said, "It's your house now," and let the person in. I also was wondering, there's been some talk and chatter online about whether any congressional members may have played a role. And I was wondering if you can say whether you are looking to see if any lawmakers may have aided and abetted the rioters getting into the building. Thanks.

Steve D'Antuono:

This is Steve D'Antuono of the FBI. This is a large puzzle, and we're looking at every piece of the puzzle that we can possibly put on the table to put the picture together. And the men and women of the FBI are not leaving any stone unturned.

Mike Sherwin:

And I'm sorry, this is Mike Sherwin. I just want to add to what Steve was saying. And I apologize, at the beginning I think I may have misspoke. As of eight a.m. this morning, we have ninety-eight current cases in which we have charged, the majority of those are federal felony cases. And as, again, of nine a.m. this morning, we have 275 open subject files, which we think will be well over three hundred by the end of the day.

Operator:

Our next question will come from Patricia Milton with CBS News.

Patricia Milton:

Yes, for Mr. Sherwin. Of those arrested, are there any cooperation being given where they're providing a fuller picture for you and more evidence?

Mike Sherwin:

In short sum? Yes. Again, I think the quick efforts of law enforcement and our prosecutors to charge and quickly arrest a great number of these rioters has had a significant impact. We have had several people, based upon people that have already been charged, that have, on their own, self-reported. In some instances with defense attorneys, to not only turn themselves in but to provide information about others. Which is extremely beneficial and makes our cases move much more quickly. And it helps provide intelligence to the FBI and other partners so we could charge additional people.

So yes, people are coming forward. Now, looking into the nuts and bolts, we're not cutting deals with anyone. Even if people are self- reporting, they will be held accountable. But obviously we encourage those people to self-report because they could usually, at the end of the day, perhaps get some benefit that other people do not, if they do not cooperate with law enforcement.

So again, reiterating what the FBI and ATF said, there are hotlines out there. If you know someone involved, or if you are involved, it behooves you to turn yourselves in for a variety of reasons.

Operator:

Our next question will come from Sadie Gurman with Wall Street Journal.

Sadie Gurman:

Hi there. Hoping that you can clarify whether you've been able to definitively determine how Officer Sicknick died. And secondly, there's been a lot of chatter and a lot of memos and bulletins sent out about the general landscape of threat possibilities ahead of the inauguration. But I'm wondering if you can kind of describe what you're seeing, and whether you're seeing any evidence of specific, credible threats to come in the next few days.

Steve D'Antuono:

The Officer Sicknick case is an ongoing investigation, and we're still pursuing all leads and avenues on that.

Operator:

The conference has now concluded. Thank you for attending today's presentation. You may now disconnect.

CHAPTER 6

CLOSING ARGUMENT FOR THE SECOND IMPEACHMENT OF PRESIDENT DONALD J. TRUMP

Representative Steny H. Hoyer
House Majority Leader, 117th Congress of the
United States of America
13 January 2021
The Capitol
Washington, DC

This is a troubled time, a sad time. Is a time where all of us have stood almost to a person and lamented the violence and the assault on this Capitol and the assault on democracy itself. It was right to do that, but this impeachment ought to be put in the perspective of what the Republican chair of the Republican conference said it was. She said the President of the United States summoned the mob, assembled the mob, and lit the flame of that attack. There has never been, she said, a greater betrayal by a President of the United States of this office, of his office and his oath to the Constitution. That is why we are here today. That is why we are here today just a week before that president, at the request of the American people, will leave office.

And the issue is what do we do? The 433 of us, I believe who are here, do on behalf of the American people do respond to what Representative Cheney described happened on the 6th of January? A mob assembled by, summoned by, and then spoken to, to light the flame of the attack to stop the steal, as we sat here exercising our constitutional duty, and to his great credit, the Vice President of the United States, following the Constitution of the United States of America, notwithstanding [the] fact that he was opportuned by the president not to do so.

That mob sent by the president to stop the steal did so for a few hours, not the steal, but the constitutional duty that we had. And so we ask ourselves, what do we do? What is our responsibility? What should we say? In light of only the Civil War as an analogy. That doesn't mean there haven't been demonstrations in

Washington before and demonstrations throughout this country before, but it is the first and only physical presence other than the 9/11 attack on this nation, which came from abroad and had a plane aimed at our Capitol dome. This attack was not from abroad. It was, as Liz Cheney said, summoned, assembled, and inflamed by the President of the United States of America, who—in Liz Cheney said—words that there has never been a greater betrayal by a President of the United States of his office and his oath to the constitution.

I pride myself as a member of this Congress who for forty years has worked in a bipartisan fashion with many of your leaders and do to this day, but are we to remain silent in the face of Liz Cheney's saying this was the greatest betrayal of the duty of the President of the United States in history? Are we just staying silent? Will we not stand up and say, this is not acceptable. And I'm speaker for four years. Donald Trump has made no effort to hide his ambitions or his lacking of Republican principles.

Not our principles, but the principles that Abraham Lincoln was just quoted as having said. Your president, our president has never displayed those in the four years he's been President of United States. He has allowed little constraint on his worst inclinations. His desire for autocracy and glorification of violence have not been tempered, but rationalized, rationalized by those who sought to profit financially and politically from their proximity to power. Upon the foundations of virtue, reason, and patient wisdom laid down by George Washington as our first president, Donald Trump has constructed a glass palace of lies, fear-mongering, and sedition.

Last Wednesday on January 6th, 2021, the nation and the world watched it shatter to pieces. There can be no mistaking any longer the kind of man sitting in the Oval Office or his intentions and capabilities. The curtain has been pulled back [on] the office to which he was elected, could not temper or reform him.

Washington's legacy was passed down to us, not as written decrees.

Washington's legacy was passed down to us, not as written decrees but understood norms. How we ought to act, how we ought to conduct ourselves, term after term each occupant has observed those norms out of a recognition that our Constitution's articles are not the only preservative of our democracy. For more than two centuries, Madam Speaker, whenever those norms were tested and strained, good and virtuous citizens on both sides of the aisle found common purpose in reaffirming those norms. But memory fades, and from time to time, it must be refreshed. Madam Speaker, as the framers emerged from the Constitutional Convention, Benjamin Franklin was asked whether they had made America a monarchy or a republic. Probably all of us know this response. "A republic," he answered. "If you can keep it." That's the question today, if we can keep it. And the way we keep it is to say no to actions and words that do not promote the keeping of that republic.

For millennia, people have understood that a republic is only as stable as and lasting as the citizens and leaders who commit themselves to its upkeep. This president has shown us he's not committed to that project. His tweets every day have shown he is not committed to that project. Indeed, he openly disdains it and appears to prefer the alternative. But what of the rest of us? Those of us who have the honor and the great privilege and the weighty responsibility to represent the views of 750,000 of our fellow citizens. We in this Congress have an opportunity, no, a duty, to demonstrate our commitment, both as leaders and as citizens to keeping America a republic, a republic that resolves its differences, not through being ordered to come to the Capitol to prevent them from stealing the election, which was an absurd assertion from the very first day it was made.

We cannot erase the last four years, Madam Speaker. We cannot turn back the clock, but we can look to the ideals and principles inherited from great presidents like Washington, like Jefferson. And yes, certainly like Abraham Lincoln and Franklin Roosevelt. And from outstanding Americans like Frederick Douglass, Harriet Tubman, Susan Anthony, Cesar Chavez, Martin Luther King, Thurgood Marshall, our beloved John Lewis, and yes, RBG, Ruth Bader Ginsburg, who taught us a lot about equality and inclusion. It's up to us to restore the vibrancy, Madam Speaker, of our democracy by reaffirming our commitment to the norms they passed on to us and entrusted to our care. But to make that possible, Madam Speaker, we must rise to this moment and not only affirm the virtues we cherish, but reject the vices we abhor. That's what I'm asking my fellow representatives on both sides of the aisle to do today.

We all stood and we abhorred the violence that occurred and the threat to the very democracy that we hold so dear and swore an oath to protect and uphold. Reject deceit; reject fear-mongering; reject sedition, tyranny, and insurrection. Reject the demand for fealty to one man over fidelity to one's country. When I addressed the House during the debate over the articles of impeachment in December 2019, I said the following: "We need not ask who will be the first to show our courage by standing up to President Trump. The question we must ask, who will be the last to find it?" Senator McConnell, Representative Cheney, a number of other representatives who have spoken on this floor with great courage, Madam Speaker, because there is much fear of Donald Trump. There's much fear of Donald Trump's tweets. There's much fear of Donald Trump's retribution for opposition. In my view, Donald Trump demands absolute loyalty and gives none in return.

I hope others will join Liz Cheney, hope others will be honest with themselves and with their constituents. As Liz Cheney was saying, there has never been a greater betrayal by a President of the United States of his office and his oath to the Constitution. Don't dismiss that. She's the daughter of a Vice President of the United States, who was the whip when I came to Congress. As she has taken a stand, I hope others will as well, Madam Speaker. Soon, the clerk will call the roll and ask for our votes. Make no mistake, this will be no ordinary roll call.

This is about our country, our Constitution, and our democracy. These votes will be inscribed on the roll of history, a record of courage and of our commitment to country and Constitution, of our commitment to the rule of law and renewal of that which we inherited and hope to pass on, unbroken, unshattered. With just seven days left in the president's term, this vote is not about timing. It is about principle and fidelity to our constitution. It concerns the clear and present danger facing our country, not only in these final days of the Trump administration, but in the weeks, months, and years that will follow. It is about the necessity to demonstrate to this generation and to future generations the duty we share to protect our democracy every single day.

Do not pretend, my friends, that it was simply those who came into the Capitol, encouraged by our president to stop the steal at any cost. And by the way, if the vice president doesn't do my bidding and follows the Constitution, sweep him away. We know that this president would never emulate George Washington and give up his power for the good of our republic even after losing an election. Somebody talked about a peaceful transition. There has not been a peaceful transition. I don't know what you're talking about. You're not living in the same country I am.

It was just days ago that the president, after committing this terrible act, thought he had to admit that Joe Biden might, yes, be President of the United States. We know that this president neither recognizes norms nor reflects the rule of law. We know that this president is not a patriot. So I asked this House, who among us, Madam Speaker, will be recorded on the roll of history for their courage, their commitment, the Constitution, and their country.

We do this today, not for politics. We don't need this for politics. Georgia showed that there was no mistake in this election. We do this today to preserve and protect this great democracy. We do it for the America we love, our America the beautiful, whose founders' sacrifices we praise in song, "Oh, beautiful for heroes proved in liberating strife, who more than self their country loved and mercy more than life." Sadly, Madam Speaker, as our current president, the appropriate words would be who less than self his country loved and victory more than truth. Vote for this, for America, for our Constitution, for democracy, for history.

CHAPTER 7

Biden Inaugural Address on the US Capitol Riot, 6 January 2021

12 January 2021
The Pentagon
Washington, DC

Memorandum for the Joint Force

The American people have trusted the Armed Forces of the United States to protect them and our Constitution for almost 250 years. As we have done throughout our history, the US military will obey lawful orders from civilian leadership, support civil authorities to protect lives and property, ensure public safety in accordance with the law, and remain fully committed to protecting and defending the Constitution of the United States against all enemies, foreign and domestic.

The violent riot in Washington, DC, on January 6, 2021, was a direct assault on the US Congress, the Capitol building, and our constitutional process. We mourn the deaths of the two Capitol policemen and others connected to these unprecedented events.

We witnessed actions inside the Capitol building that were inconsistent with the rule of law. The rights of freedom of speech and assembly do not give anyone the right to resort to violence, sedition, and insurrection.

As service members, we must embody the values and ideals of the nation. We support and defend the Constitution. Any act to disrupt the constitutional process is not only against our traditions, values, and oath; it is against the law.

On January 20, 2021, in accordance with the Constitution, confirmed by the states and the courts and certified by Congress, President-elect Biden will be inaugurated and will become our forty-sixth Commander in Chief.

To our men and women deployed and at home, safeguarding our country: stay ready, keep your eyes on the horizon, and remain focused on the mission. We honor your continued service in defense of every American.

Mark A. Milley
General, US Army
Chairman of the Joint Chiefs of Staff

John E. Hyten
General, US Air Force
Vice Chairman of the Joint Chiefs of Staff
James C. McConville
General, US Army
Chief of Staff of the Army
David H. Berger
General, US Marine Corps
Commandant of the Marine Corps
Michael M. Gilday
Admiral, US Navy
Chief of Naval Operations
Charles Q. Brown, Jr.
General, US Air Force
Chief of Staff of the Air Force
John W. Raymond
General, US Space Force
Chief of Space Operations
Daniel R. Hokanson
General, US Army
Chief of the National Guard Bureau

CHAPTER 8

INAUGURAL ADDRESS OF THE FORTY-SIXTH PRESIDENT OF THE UNITED STATES

Joseph R. Biden Jr.
Forty-Sixth President of the United States of America
20 January 2021
The Capitol
Washington, DC

Chief Justice Roberts, Vice President Harris, Speaker Pelosi, Leader Schumer, Leader McConnell, Vice President Pence, and my distinguished guests, my fellow Americans: This is America's day. This is democracy's day. A day of history and hope of renewal and resolve through a crucible for the ages. America has been tested anew and America has risen to the challenge. Today we celebrate the triumph, not of a candidate, but of a cause, the cause of democracy. The people, the will of the people, has been heard and the will of the people has been heeded. We've learned again that democracy is precious. Democracy is fragile. And at this hour, my friends, democracy has prevailed.

So now on this hallowed ground where just a few days ago violence sought to shake the Capitol's very foundation, we come together as one nation, under God, indivisible, to carry out the peaceful transfer of power as we have for more than two centuries. As we look ahead in our uniquely American way—restless, bold, optimistic—and set our sights on the nation we know we can be, and we must be, I thank my predecessors of both parties for their presence here today. I thank them from the bottom of my heart, and I know the resilience of our Constitution and the strength, the strength of our nation, as does President Carter who I spoke with last night, who cannot be with us today, but whom we salute for his lifetime and service.

I've just taken a sacred oath each of those patriots have taken. The oath first sworn by George Washington. But the American story depends not in any one of us, not on some of us, but on all of us. On we the people who seek a more perfect union. This is a great nation. We are good people. And over the centuries through storm and strife, in peace and in war, we've come so far, but we still have far to go. We'll press forward with speed and urgency, for we have much to do in this winter of peril and significant possibilities. Much to repair, much to restore, much to heal, much to build, and much to gain.

Few people in our nation's history have been more challenged or found a time more challenging or difficult than the time we're in now. Once in a century, a virus that silently stalks the country has taken as many lives in one year as America lost in all of World War II. Millions of jobs have been lost. Hundreds of thousands of businesses closed. A cry for racial justice, some four hundred years in the making, moves us. The dream of justice for all will be deferred no longer. A cry for survival comes from [the] planet itself. A cry that can't be any more desperate or any more clear, and now arise a political extremism, White supremacy, domestic terrorism that we must confront and we will defeat.

To overcome these challenges, to restore the soul and secure the future of America requires so much more than words. It requires the most elusive of all things in a democracy: unity, unity. And another January on New Year's Day in 1863, Abraham Lincoln signed the Emancipation Proclamation. When he put pen to paper, the president said, and I quote, "If my name ever goes down into history, it will be for this act, and my whole soul is in it."

My whole soul was in it today on this January day, my whole soul is in this. Bringing America together, uniting our people, uniting our nation, and I ask every American to join me in this cause.

Uniting to fight the foes we face: anger, resentment and hatred, extremism, lawlessness, violence, disease, joblessness, and hopelessness. With unity we can do great things, important things. We can right wrongs. We can put people to work in good jobs. We can teach our children in safe schools. We can overcome the deadly virus. We can reward work and rebuild the middle class and make health care secure for all. We can deliver racial justice and we can make America, once again, the leading force for good in the world. I know speaking of unity can sound to some like a foolish fantasy these days. I know the forces that divide us are deep and they are real. But I also know they are not new. Our history has been a constant struggle between the American ideal that we all are created equal and the harsh ugly reality that racism, nativism, fear, demonization have long torn us apart.

The battle is perennial, and victory is never assured. Through Civil War, the Great Depression, world war, 9/11, through struggle, sacrifice, and setbacks our better angels have always prevailed. In each of these moments, enough of us, enough of us have come together to carry all of us forward, and we can do that now. History, faith, and reason show the way, the way of unity. We can see each other, not as adversaries, but as neighbors. We can treat each other with dignity and respect. We can join forces, stop the shouting, and lower the temperature, for without unity there is no peace, only bitterness and fury. No progress, only exhausting outrage. No nation, only a state of chaos.

This is our historic moment of crisis and challenge, and unity is the path forward. And we must meet this moment as the United States of America. If we do that, I guarantee you, we will not fail. We have never, ever, ever, ever failed in America when we've acted together. And so today, at this time in this place, let's start afresh all of us. Let's begin to listen to one another again, hear one another, see one another, show respect to one another. Politics doesn't have to be a raging fire, destroying everything in its path. Every disagreement doesn't have to be a cause for total war. And we must reject the culture in which facts themselves are manipulated and even manufactured.

My fellow Americans, we have to be different than this. America has to be better than this, and I believe America is so much better than this. Just look around. Here we stand in the shadow of the Capitol dome as it was mentioned earlier, completed amid the Civil War when the Union itself was literally hanging in the balance. Yet we endured, we prevailed. Here we stand looking out on the great mall where Dr. King spoke of his dream. Here we stand where 108 years ago at another inaugural thousands of protesters tried to block brave women marching for the right to vote. And today we mark the swearing in of the first woman in American history, elected to national office, Vice President Kamala Harris. Don't tell me things can't change.

Here we stand across the Potomac from Arlington Cemetery, where heroes who gave the last full measure of devotion rest in eternal peace. And here we stand just days after a riotous mob thought they could use violence to silence the will of the people, to stop the work of our democracy, to drive us from this sacred ground. It did not happen. It will never happen. Not today, not tomorrow, not ever, not ever.

For all of those who supported our campaign, I'm humbled by the faith you've placed in us. To all those who did not support us, let me say this. Hear me out as we move forward. Take a measure of me and my heart. If you still disagree, so be it. That's democracy. That's America. The right to dissent peaceably within the guardrails of our republic is perhaps this nation's greatest strength. Yet hear me clearly: disagreement must not lead to disunion. And I pledge this to you: I will be a president for all Americans, all Americans. And I promise you, I will fight as hard for those who did not support me as for those who did.

Many centuries ago, Saint Augustine, a saint in my church, wrote that a people was a multitude defined by the common objects of their love, defined by the common objects of their love. What are the common objects we as Americans love that define us as Americans? I think we know: opportunity, security, liberty, dignity, respect, honor, and yes, the truth. Recent weeks and months have taught us a painful lesson. There is truth, and there are lies. Lies toll for power and for profit, and each of us has a duty and a responsibility as citizens, as Americans, and especially as leaders, leaders who have pledged to honor our Constitution and protect our nation to defend the truth and defeat the lies.

I understand that many of my fellow Americans view the future with fear and trepidation. I understand they worry about their jobs. I understand, like my dad, they lay [sic] in bed at night, staring at the ceiling, wondering, "Can I keep my healthcare? Can I pay my mortgage?" Thinking about their families, about what comes next. I promise you I get it. But the answer is not to turn inward, to retreat into competing factions, distrusting those who don't look like you or worship the way you do, or don't get their news from the same sources you do. We must end this uncivil war that pits red against blue, rural versus urban, conservative versus liberal. We can do this, if we open our souls instead of hardening our hearts. If we show a little tolerance and humility, and if we're willing to stand in the other person's shoes, as my mom would say, just for a moment, stand in their shoes.

Because here's the thing about life. There's no accounting for what fate will deal you. Some days when you need a hand, there are other days when we're called to lend a hand. That's how it has to be; it's what we do for one another. And if we are this way, our country will be stronger, more prosperous, more ready for the future, and we can still disagree. My fellow Americans, in the work ahead of us we're going to need each other. We need all our strength to persevere through this dark winter. We're entering what may be the toughest and deadliest period of the virus. We must set aside politics and finally face this pandemic as one nation, one nation. And I promise you this, as the Bible says, "Weeping may endure for a night, but joy cometh in the morning," we will get through this together, together.

Look, folks, all my colleagues I serve with in the House and the Senate up here, we all understand the world is watching, watching all of us today. So here's my message to those beyond our borders: America has been tested and we've come out stronger for it. We will repair our alliances and engage with the rural once again, not to meet yesterday's challenges, but today's and tomorrow's challenges. And we'll lead not merely by the example of our power, but by the power of our example.

It will be a strong and trusted partner for peace, progress, and security. Look, you all know we've been through so much in this nation. And my first act as president, I'd like to ask you to join me in a moment of silent prayer to remember all those who we lost this past year to the pandemic, those 400,000 fellow Americans: moms, dads, husbands, wives, sons, daughters, friends, neighbors, and coworkers. We'll honor them by becoming the people and the nation we know we can and should be. So I ask you, let's say a silent prayer for those who've lost their lives and those left behind and for our country.

(silence)

Amen. Folks, this is a time of testing. We face an attack on our democracy and untruth—a raging virus, growing inequity, the sting of systemic racism, a climate in crisis, America's role in the world. Any one of these would be enough to challenge us in profound ways. But the fact is we face them all at once, presenting this nation with one of the gravest responsibilities we've had. Now, we're going to be tested. Are we going to step up, all of us? It's time for boldness, for there's so much to do. And this is certain, I promise you, we will be judged, you and I, by how we resolve these cascading crises of our era. We will rise to the occasion, is the question. Will we master this rare and difficult hour? When we meet our obligations and pass along a new and better world to our children, I believe we must. I'm sure you do as well. I believe we will.

And when we do, we'll write the next great chapter in the history of the United States of America, the American story. A story that might sound something like a song that means a lot to me. It's called "American Anthem." There's one verse that stands out, at least for me. And it goes like this, "The work and prayers of century have brought us to this day. What shall be our legacy? What will our children say? Let me know in my heart, when my days are through America, America, I gave my best to you." Let's add, let's us add our own work and prayers to the unfolding story of our great nation. If we do this, then when our days are through, our children and our children's children will say of us, "They gave their best. They did their duty. They healed a broken land."

My fellow Americans, I close today where I began, with the sacred oath. Before God and all of you, I give you my word: I will always level with you. I will defend the Constitution. I'll defend our democracy. I'll defend America and will give all. All of you keep everything I do in your service. Thinking not of power, but of possibilities. Not of personal interest, but the public good. And together we shall write an American story of hope, not fear; of unity, not division; of light, not darkness. A story of decency and dignity, love and healing, greatness and goodness. May this be the story that guides us, the story that inspires us, and the story that tells ages yet to come that we answer the call of history. We met the moment. Democracy and hope, truth and justice did not die on our watch, but thrived. That America secured liberty at home and stood once again as a beacon to the world. That is what we owe our forebearers, one another, and generation[s] to follow.

So with purpose and resolve, we turn to [the] task of our time, sustained by faith, driven by conviction, devoted to one another and the country we love with all our hearts. May God bless America and may God protect our troops. Thank you, America.

CHAPTER 9

US Senate Majority Leader Comments After Second Impeachment Trial

Charles E. Schumer
Senate Majority Leader
13 February 2021
The CapitolWashington, DC

The case of Donald Trump's second impeachment trial was open and shut. President Trump told a lie, a big lie, that the election was stolen and that he was the rightful winner. He laid the groundwork for this big lie in the months before the election, he told the big lie on election night, and he repeated the big lie more than a hundred times in the weeks afterward.

He summoned his supporters to Washington, assembled them on the Ellipse, whipped them into a frenzy, and directed them at the Capitol. And then he watched as the violence unfolded and the Capitol was breached, and his own vice president fled for his life, and President Trump did nothing.

None of these facts were up for debate. We saw it, we heard it, we lived it. This was the first presidential impeachment trial in history in which all senators were not only judges and jurors but witnesses to the constitutional crime that was committed.

The former president inspired, directed, and propelled a mob to violently prevent the peaceful transfer of power, subvert the will of the people, and illegally keep that president in power. There is nothing, nothing more un-American than that. There is nothing, nothing more antithetical to our democracy. There is nothing, nothing more insulting to the generations of American patriots who gave their lives to defend our form of government.

This was the most egregious violation of the presidential oath of office and a textbook example, a classic example of an impeachable offense worthy of the Constitution's most severe remedy. In response to the incontrovertible fact of Donald Trump's guilt, the Senate was subject to a feeble and sometimes incomprehensible defense of the former president. Unable to dispute the case on the merits, the former president's counsel treated us to partisan vitriol, false equivalence, and outright falsehoods.

We heard the roundly debunked jurisdictional argument that the Senate cannot try a former official, a position that would mean that any president could simply resign to avoid accountability for an impeachable offense, a position which in effect would render the Senate powerless to ever enforce the disqualification clause in the constitution.

Essentially, the president's counsel told the Senate that the Constitution was unconstitutional. Thankfully, the Senate took a firm stance, set a firm precedent with a bipartisan vote in favor of our power to try former officials for acts they committed while in office.

We heard the preposterous claim that the former president's incitement to violence was protected by the First Amendment. The First Amendment, right to free speech, protects Americans from jail, not presidents from impeachment. If the president had said during World War II that "Germany should attack the United States on Long Island, we've left it undefended," I suspect Congress would have considered that an impeachable offense.

Finally, the defense counsel said that President Trump was not directly responsible for the violence at the Capitol. "His words were merely a metaphor. His directions were merely suggestions, and the violent mob was just a spontaneous demonstration." But wind the clock back and ask yourself, if at any point Donald Trump did not do the things he did, would the attack on the Capitol have happened? There's only one answer to this question. Of course not.

If President Trump hadn't told his supporters to march to the Capitol, if he hadn't implored them to come to Washington on January 6th in the first place, if he hadn't repeatedly lied to them, that the election was stolen, their country was being taken from them, the attack would not have happened, could not have happened. January 6th would not have happened but for the actions of Donald Trump.

Here's what the Republican leader of the Senate said: "The mob that perpetrated the 'failed insurrection' was on January 6, was 'provoked' by President Trump." You want another word for provoke? How about incite? Yet still, still the vast majority of the Senate Republican caucus, including the Republican leader, voted to acquit former President Trump, signing their names in the columns of history alongside his name forever.

January 6th will live as a day of infamy in the history of the United States of America. The failure to convict Donald Trump will live as a vote of infamy in the history of the United States Senate. Five years ago, Republican senators lamented what might become of their party if Donald Trump became their presidential nominee and standard-bearer. Just look at what has happened. Look at what Republicans have been forced to defend. Look at what Republicans have chosen to forgive.

The former president tried to overturn the results of a legitimate election and provoked an assault on our own government. And well over half the Senate Republican conference decided to condone it. The most despicable act that any president has ever committed, and the majority of Republicans cannot summon the courage or the morality to condemn it.

This trial wasn't about choosing country over party, even not that. This was about choosing country over Donald Trump, and forty-three Republican members chose Trump. They chose Trump. It should be a weight on their conscience today, and it shall be a weight on their conscience in the future.

As sad as that fact is, as condemnable as the decision was, it is still true that the final vote on Donald Trump's conviction was the largest and most bipartisan vote of any presidential impeachment trial in American history. I salute those Republican patriots who did the right thing; it wasn't easy, we know that.

Let their votes be a message to the American people, because my fellow Americans, if this nation is going to long endure, we as a people cannot sanction the former president's Congress. Because if lying about the results of an election is acceptable, if instigating a mob against the government is considered permissible, if encouraging political violence becomes the norm, it will be open season, open season on our democracy. And everything will be up for grabs by whoever has the biggest clubs, the sharpest spears, the most powerful guns.

By not recognizing the heinous crime that Donald Trump committed against the Constitution, Republican senators have not only risked but potentially invited the same danger that was just visited upon us. So let me say this, despite the results of the vote on Donald Trump's conviction in the court of impeachment, he deserves to be convicted, and I believe he will be convicted in the court of public opinion.

He deserves to be permanently discredited, and I believe he has been discredited in the eyes of the American people and in the judgment of history. Even though Republican senators prevented the Senate from disqualifying Donald Trump for any office of honor, trust, or profit under these United States, there is no question Donald Trump has disqualified himself.

I hope, I pray, and I believe that the American people will make sure of that. And if Donald Trump ever stands for public office again, and after everything we have seen this week, I hope, I pray, and I believe that he will meet the unambiguous rejection by the American people.

Six hours after the attack on January 6th, after the carnage and mayhem was shown on every television screen in America, President Trump told his supporters to "remember this day forever." I ask the American people to heed his words, remember that day forever, but not for the reasons the former president intended. Remember the panic in the voices over the radio dispatch, the rhythmic pounding of fists and flags at the chamber doors.

Remember the crack of a solitary gunshot. Remember the hateful and racist Confederate flags flying through the halls of our union. Remember the screams of the bloody officer crushed between the onrushing mob and a doorway to the Capitol, his body trapped in the breach. Remember the three Capitol police officers who lost their lives.

Remember that those rioters actually succeeded in delaying Congress from certifying the election. Remember how close our democracy came to ruin. My fellow Americans, remember that day, January 6th, forever.

The final terrible legacy of the forty-fifth President of the United States, and undoubtedly our worst. Let it live on in infamy, a stain on Donald John Trump that can never, never be washed away.

Mr. President, on Monday we'll recognize President's Day. Part of the commemoration in the Senate will be the annual reading of Washington's Farewell Address. Aside from winning the Revolutionary War, I consider it his greatest contribution to American civil life. And it had nothing to do with the words he spoke, but the example it set. Washington's Farewell Address established for all time that no one had the right to the office of the presidency, that it belonged to the people.

What an amazing legacy, what an amazing gift to the future generations— the knowledge that this country will always be greater than any one person, even our most renowned. That's why members of both parties take turns reading Washington's address once a year in full into the record, to pledge common attachment to the selflessness at the core of our democratic system.

This trial was about the final acts of a president who represents the very antithesis of our first president and sought to place one man before the entire country— himself. Let the record show, let the record show, before God, history, and the solemn oath we swear to the Constitution that there was only one correct verdict in this trial: guilty.

And I pray that while justice was not done in this trial, it will be carried forward by the American people who above any of us in this chamber determine the destiny of our great nation. I yield the floor.

CHAPTER 10

U.S. Senate Minority Leader Comments After Second Impeachment Trial

A. Mitchell McConnell, Jr.
Senate Minority Leader
U.S. Capitol
13 February 2021

January 6th was a disgrace. American citizens attacked their own government. They use terrorism to try to stop a specific piece of domestic business they did not like. Fellow Americans beat and bloodied our own police. They stormed the center floor. They tried to hunt down the Speaker of the House. They built a gallows and chatted about murdering the vice president. They did this because they'd been fed wild, falsehoods by the most powerful man on earth because he was angry. He lost an election. Former President Trump's actions preceded the riot or a disgraceful dereliction of duty. The House accused the former president of quote "Incitement". That is a specific term from the criminal law. Let me just put that aside for a moment and reiterate something I said weeks ago. There's no question, none, that President Trump is practically and morally responsible for provoking the events of the day. No question about it.

The people who stormed this building believed they were acting on the wishes and instructions of their president and having that belief was a foreseeable consequence of the growing crescendo of false statements, conspiracy theories, and reckless hyperbole, which the defeated president kept shouting into the largest megaphone on planet Earth. The issue is not only the president in temperate language on January 6th. It is not just his endorsement of remarks in which an associate urged quote "Trial by combat". It was also the entire manufactured atmosphere of looming catastrophe. The increasingly wild myths about a reverse landslide election that was somehow being stolen. Some secret coup by our now president.

Now I defended the President's right to bring any complaints to our legal system. The legal system spoke, the electoral college spoke. As I stood up and said, clearly at that time, the election was settled. It was over, but that just really opened a new chapter of even wilder and more unfounded claims. The leader of the free world cannot spend weeks thundering that shadowy forces are stealing our country and then feign surprise when people believe him and do reckless things. I sadly many politicians sometimes make overheated comments or use metaphors. We saw that. That unhinged listeners might take literally, but that was different. That's different from what we saw. This was an intensifying crescendo of conspiracy theories orchestrated by an outgoing president who seemed determined to either overturn the voter's decision or else torch our institutions on the way out. The unconscionable behavior did not end when the violence actually began.

Whatever our ex-president claims he thought might happen a day, whatever right reaction he's says he meant to produce by that afternoon we know he was watching the same live television as the rest of us. A mob was assaulting the Capitol in his name, these criminals who are carrying his banners, hanging his flags and screaming their loyalty to him. It was obvious that only President Trump could end this. He was the only one who could. Former aides publicly begged him to do so. Loyal allies frantically called the administration. The president did not act swiftly. He did not do his job. He didn't take steps so federal law could be faithfully executed and order restored. No, instead, according to public reports, he watched television happily as the chaos unfolded. He kept pressing his scheme to overturn the election. Now, even after it was clear to any reasonable observer that Vice President Pence was in serious danger. Even as the mob carrying Trump banners was beating cops and breaching perimeters their president sent a further tweet, attacking his own vice president.

Now predictably and foreseeably under the circumstances, members of the mob seemed to interpret this as a further inspiration to lawlessness and violence not surprisingly. Later, even when the president did halfheartedly began calling for peace he didn't call right away for the riot to end. He did not tell the mob to depart until even later. And even then with police officers bleeding and broken glass covering Capitol floors, he kept repeating election laws and praising the criminals. In recent weeks, our ex-president's associates have tried to use the 74 million Americans who voted to reelect him as a kind of human shield against criticism. Using the 74 million who voted for him as kind of a human seal shield against criticism. Anyone who decries his awful behavior is accused of insulting millions of voters. That's an absurd deflection. Seventy-four million Americans did not invade the Capitol, hundreds of rioters did. Seventy-four million Americans did not engineer the campaign of disinformation and rage that provoked it. One person did, just one.

I've made my view of this episode very plain, but our system of government gave the Senate a specific task. The Constitution gives us a particular role. This body is not invited to act as the nation's overarching moral tribunal. We're not free to work backward from whether the accused party might personally deserve some kind of punishment. Justice Joseph Story, our nation's first great constitutional scholar, as he explained nearly 200 years ago, the process of impeachment and conviction is a narrow tool. A narrow tool for a narrow purpose. Story explained

this limited tool exists to quote, "Secure the state against gross official misdemeanors," end quote. That is to protect the country from government officers. If
President Trump were still in office, I would have carefully considered whether
the House managers proved their specific charge. By the strict criminal standard
the president's speech probably was not incitement.

However, in the context of impeachment, the Senate might have decided this
was acceptable shorthand for the reckless actions that preceded the riot. But in
this case, the question is moot because former President Trump is constitutionally
not eligible for conviction. Now this is a close question. No doubt. Donald Trump
was the president when the House voted. Though, not when the House chose to
deliver the paper. Brilliant scholars argue both sides of this jurisdictional question.
The text is legitimately ambiguous. I respect my colleagues who've reached either
conclusion. But after intense reflection, I believe the best constitutional reading
shows that article two, section four, exhausts the set of persons who can legitimately be impeached, tried, or convicted. It's the president, it's the vice-president
and civil officers. We have no power to convict and disqualify a former office
holder who is now a private citizen.

Here is Article Two, Section Four, quote, "The President, the Vice-President and all civil officers of the United States shall be removed from office on
impeachment for and conviction of treason, bribery, or other high crimes and
misdemeanors," end quote. Now, everyone basically agrees that the second half of
that sentence exhausts the legitimate grounds for conviction. The debates around
the Constitution's framing make that abundantly clear. Congress cannot convict
for reasons besides those. It therefore follows that the list of persons in that same
sentence is also exhausted. There's no reason why one list would be exhaustive, but
the other would not. Article two, section four must limit both why impeachment
and conviction can occur and to whom if this revision does not limit impeachment and conviction powers then it has no limits at all. The House has sole power
of impeachment and the Senate's sole power to try all impeachments, would create an unlimited circular logic empowering Congress to ban any private citizen
from federal office.

Now, that's an incredible claim, but it's the argument of the House managers seem to be making. One manager said the House and Senate have quote,
"Absolute unqualified, jurisdictional power", end quote. Well, that was very honest because there is no limiting principle in the constitutional text that would
empower the Senate to convict former officers that would not also let them
convict and disqualify any private citizen, an absurd end result to which no one
subscribes. Article two section four must have force. It tells us the president,
the vice president, and civil officers may be impeached and convicted. Donald
Trump's no longer the president. Likewise, the provision states that officers
subject to impeachment and conviction shall be removed from office if convicted.
Shall be removed from office, if convicted. As Justice Story explained, the Senate
upon conviction is bound, in all cases, to enter a judgment of removal from office.
Removal is mandatory upon conviction.

Clearly he explained that mandatory sentence cannot be applied to someone who's left office. The entire process revolves around removal. If removal becomes impossible, conviction becomes insensible. In one light it certainly does seem counterintuitive that an office holder can elude Senate conviction by resignation or exploration of term, an argument we heard made by the managers. But this underscores that impeachment was never meant to be the final forum for American justice. Never meant to be the final forum for American justice. Impeachment conviction and removal are a specific intra-governmental safety valve. It is not the criminal justice system where individual accountability is the paramount goal. Indeed Justice Story specifically reminded that while former officials were not eligible for impeachment or conviction, they were, and this was extremely important, still labile to be tried and punished in the ordinary tribunals of justice. Put another way in the language of today, President Trump is still liable for everything he did while he was in office as an ordinary citizen. Unless the statute of limitations is run, still liable for everything he did while he was in office.

He didn't get away with anything, yet. Yet. We have a criminal justice system in this country. We have civil litigation and former presidents are not immune from being accountable by either one. I believe the Senate was right not to grab power the Constitution doesn't give us. And the Senate was right not to entertain some light speed sham process to try to outrun the loss of jurisdiction. It took both sides more than a week just to produce their pre-trial briefs. Speaker Pelosi's own scheduling decisions conceded what President Biden publicly confirmed, a Senate verdict before inauguration day was never possible. Now, Mr. President this has been a dispiriting time, but the Senate had done our duty. The framers' firewall helped held up again. Oh, in January the sixth, we returned to our posts and certified the election. We were uncowed. We were not intimidated. We finished the job. And since then we resisted the climber to defy our own constitutional guardrails in hot pursuit of a particular outcome.

We refused to continue a cycle of recklessness by straining our own constitutional boundaries in response. The Senate's decision today does not condone anything that happened on or before that terrible day. It simply shows that senators did what the former President failed to do. We put our Constitutional duty first.

CHAPTER 11

A CALL TO ACTION

Joseph R. Biden Jr.
Forty-Sixth President of the United States of America
1 September 2022
The White House Washington, DC

My fellow Americans, I speak to you tonight from sacred ground in America, Independence Hall in Philadelphia, Pennsylvania. This is where America made its Declaration of Independence to the world more than two centuries ago, with an idea unique among nations, that in America, we're all created equal. This is where the United States Constitution was written and debated. This is where we set in motion the most extraordinary experiment of self-government the world has ever known with three simple words: We the People.

We the People.

These two documents and the ideas they embody—equality and democracy—are the rock upon which this nation is built. They are how we became the greatest nation on earth. They are why, for more than two centuries, America has been a beacon to the world. But as I stand here tonight, equality and democracy are under assault. We do ourselves no favor to pretend otherwise, so tonight I've come to this place where it all began to speak as plainly as I can to the nation about the threats we face, about the power we have in our own hands to meet these threats, and about the incredible future that lies in front of us, if only we choose it.

We must never forget: We the People are the true heirs of the American experiment that began more than two centuries ago. We the People have burning inside of each of us the flame of liberty that was lit here at Independence Hall, a flame that lit our way through abolition, the Civil War, suffrage, the Great Depression, world wars, civil rights. That sacred flame still burns now, in our time, as we build an America that is more prosperous, free, and just.

That is the work of my presidency, a mission I believe in with my whole soul, but first, we must be honest with each other and with ourselves. Too much of what's happening in our country today is not normal. Donald Trump and the MAGA [Make America Great Again] Republicans represent an extremism that threatens the very foundations of our republic.

Now, I want to be very clear, very clear up front. Not every Republican, not even the majority of Republicans are MAGA Republicans. Not every Republican embraces their extreme ideology. I know because I've been able to work with these mainstream Republicans, but there's no question that the Republican party today is dominated, driven, and intimidated by Donald Trump and the MAGA Republicans, and that is a threat to this country.

These are hard things, but I'm an American president, not a president of red America or blue America, but of all America. And I believe it's my duty, my duty to level with you, to tell the truth, no matter how difficult, no matter how painful, and here, in my view, is what is true.

MAGA Republicans do not respect the Constitution. They do not believe in the rule of law. They do not recognize the will of the people. They refuse to accept the results of a free election, and they're working right now as I speak, in state after state, to give power to decide elections in America to partisans and cronies, empowering election deniers to undermine democracy itself. MAGA forces are determined to take this country backwards, backwards to an America where there is no right to choose no right to privacy, no right to contraception, no right to marry who you love. They promote authoritarian leaders and they fan the flames of political violence that are a threat to our personal rights, to the pursuit of justice, to the rule of law, to the very soul of this country.

They look at the mob that stormed the United States Capitol on January 6th, brutally attacking law enforcement, not as insurrectionists who placed a dagger at the throat of our democracy, but they're looking at them as patriots, and they see their MAGA failure to stop a peaceful transfer of power after the 2020 election as preparation for the 2022 and 2024 elections. They tried everything last time to nullify the votes of 81 million people. This time, they're determined to succeed in thwarting the will of the people. That's why respected conservatives like Federal Circuit Court Judge Michael Luttig has called Trump and the extreme MAGA Republicans "a clear and present danger to our democracy." But while the threat to American democracy is real, I want to say as clearly as we can, we are not powerless in the face of these threats. We are not bystanders in this ongoing attack on democracy. There are far more Americans, far more Americans, from every background and belief who reject the extreme MAGA ideology than those that accept it.

Folks, it is within our power. It's in our hands—yours and mine—to stop the assault on American democracy. I believe America's at an inflection point, one of those moments that determine the shape of everything that's to come after, and now America must choose to move forward or to move backwards, to build a future or obsess about the past, to be a nation of hope and unity and optimism or a nation of fear, division, and of darkness.

MAGA Republicans have made their choice. They embrace anger. They thrive on chaos. They live not in the light of truth, but in the shadow of lies. But together, together we can choose a different path. We can choose a better path forward to the future, a future of possibility, a future to build and dream and hope. And we're on that path, moving ahead.

I know this nation. I know you, the American people. I know your courage. I know your hearts, and I know our history. This is a nation that honors our Constitution. We do not reject it. This is a nation that believes in the rule of law. We do not repudiate it. This is a nation that respects free and fair elections. We honor the will of the people. We do not deny it. And this is a nation that rejects violence as a political tool. We do not encourage violence.

We are still an America that believes in honesty and decency and respect for others, patriotism, liberty, justice for all, hope, possibilities. We are still, at our core, a democracy. And yet, history tells us the blind loyalty to a single leader and a willingness to engage in political violence is fatal in democracy. For a long time, we've told ourselves that American democracy is guaranteed, but it's not. We have to defend it, protect it, stand up for it, each and every one of us. That's why tonight, I'm asking our nation to come together, unite behind the single purpose of defending our democracy regardless of your ideology.

We're all called by duty and [conscience] to confront extremists who put their own pursuit of power above all else. Democrats, Independents, mainstream Republicans, we must be stronger, more determined, and more committed to saving American democracy than [MAGA] Republicans are to destroying American democracy. We the People will not let anyone or anything tear us apart. Today, there are dangers around us we cannot allow to prevail. We hear you've heard it—more and more talk about violence as an acceptable political tool in this country. It's not. It can never be an acceptable tool. So, I want to say this plain and simple: There is no place for political violence in America. Period. None ever.

You saw law enforcement brutally attacked on January 6th. We've seen election officials, poll workers—many of them volunteers of both parties—subject to intimidation and death threats. And can you believe it? FBI agents just doing their job as directed, facing threats to their own lives from their own fellow citizens. On top of that, there are public figures today, yesterday, and the day before predicting and all but calling for mass violence and riot in streets. This is inflammatory. It's dangerous. It's against the rule of law, and We the People must say, "This is not who we are."

Ladies and gentlemen, we can't be pro-ex pro-insurrectionist and pro-American. We're incompatible. We can't allow violence to be normalized in this country. It's wrong. We each have to reject political violence with all the moral clarity and conviction this nation can muster. Now, we can't let the integrity of our elections be undermined, for that is a path to chaos. Look, I know politics can be fierce, and mean, and nasty in America. I get it. I believe in the give-and-take of politics, in disagreement, and debate, and dissent. We're a big, complicated country, but democracy endures only if We the People respect the guardrails of the republic. Only if We the People accept the results of free and fair elections. Only if We the People see politics not as total war, but mediation of our differences. Democracy cannot survive when one side believes there are only two outcomes to an election. Either they win, or they were cheated. And that's where the MAGA Republicans are today.

They don't understand what every patriotic American knows: you can't love your country only when you win. It's fundamental. American democracy only works only if we choose to respect the rule of law and the institutions that were set up in this chamber behind me, only if we respect our legitimate political differences. I will not stand by and watch. I will not [let] the will of the American people be overturned by wild conspiracy theories and baseless evidence for claims of fraud. I will not stand by and watch elections in this country stolen by people who simply refused to accept that they lost.

I will not stand by and watch the most fundamental freedom in this country—the freedom to vote and have your vote counted—be taken from you and the American people. Look, as your president, I will defend our democracy with every fiber of my being, and I'm asking every American to join me.

Throughout our history, America's often made the greatest progress coming out of some of our darkest moments like you're hearing that bullhorn. I believe we can and must do that again, and we are. MAGA Republicans look at America and see carnage and darkness and despair. They spread fear and lies—lies told for profit and power. But I see a different America. An America with an unlimited future. An America that's about to take off. I hope you see it as well. Just look around.

I believe we could lift America from the depths of COVID, so we passed the largest economic stimulus package since Franklin Delano Roosevelt. And today, America's economy is faster, stronger than any other advanced nation in the world. We have more to go. I believe we could build a better America, so we passed the biggest infrastructure investments since President Dwight D. Eisenhower. And we've now embarked on a decade of rebuilding the nation's roads, bridges, highways, ports, water system, high-speed internet, railroad. I believe we could make America safer, so we passed the most significant gun safety law since President Clinton. I believe we could go from being the highest cost of prescriptions in the world to making prescription drugs and healthcare more affordable, so we passed the most significant healthcare reform since President Obama signed the Affordable Care Act. And I believe we could create a clean energy future and save the planet, so we passed the most important climate initiative ever, ever, ever.

The cynics and the critics tell us nothing can get done, but they're wrong. There is not a single thing America cannot do, not a single thing beyond our capacity if we do it together. It's never easy, but we're proving that America—no matter how long the road—progress does come. Look, I know the last year, a few years, have been tough, but today, COVID no longer controls our lives. More Americans are working than ever. Businesses are growing. Our schools are open. Millions of Americans have been lifted out of poverty. Millions of veterans once exposed to toxic burn pits will now get what they deserve for their families and their compensation. American manufacturers come alive across the heartland, and the future will be made in America. No matter what the white supremacists and the extremists say, I made a bet on you, the American people, and that bet is paying off, proving that from darkness, the darkness of Charlottesville, of COVID, of gun violence, of insurrection, we can see the light; light is now visible. Light that will guide us forward—not only in words, but in actions, actions for you, for your children, for your grandchildren, for America.

Even in this moment, with all the challenge[s] that we face, I give you my word as a Biden: I've never been more optimistic about America's future. We are going to end cancer as we know it, mark my words. We're going to create millions of new jobs in a clean energy economy. We're going to think big, we're going to make the twenty-first century another American century, because the world needs us to. That's where we need to focus our energy, not in the past, not on divisive culture wars, not on the politics of grievance, but on a future we can build together.

The MAGA Republicans believe that for them to succeed, everyone else has to fail. I believe America's big enough for all of us to succeed, and that is the nation we're building, a nation where no one is left behind. I ran for president because I believe we're in a battle for the soul of this nation. I still believe that to be true. I believe the soul is the breath, the life, and the essence of who we are; the soul is what makes us. The soul of America is defined by the sacred proposition that all are created equal in the image of God, that all are entitled to be treated with decency, dignity, and respect, that all deserve justice and a shot at lives of prosperity and consequence, and that democracy must be defended, for democracy makes all these things possible.

Folks, and it's up to us. Democracy begins and will be preserved in We the People's habits of the heart, in our character, optimism that is tested yet endures, courage that digs deep when we need it, empathy that fuels democracy, the willingness to see each other not as enemies but as fellow Americans. Look, our democracy is imperfect; it always has been. Notwithstanding those folks you hear on the other side there, they're entitled to be outrageous. We have never fully realized the aspirations of our founding fathers, but every generation has opened those doors a little bit wider to include more people that have been excluded before.

My fellow Americans, America is an idea—the most powerful idea in the history of the world, and it beats in the hearts of the people of this country. It beats in all our hearts. It unites America. It is the American creed, the idea that American guarantees that everyone be treated with dignity. It gives hate no safe harbor. It installs in everyone the belief that no matter where you start in life, there's nothing you can't achieve. That's who we are. That's what we stand for. That's what we believe, and that's precisely what we're doing: opening doors, creating possibilities, focusing on the future. And we're only just beginning.

Our task is to make our nation free and fair, just and strong, noble and whole—this work is the work of democracy. The work of this generation is the work of our time, for all time. We can't afford to leave anyone on the sidelines. We need everyone to do their part, so speak up, speak out, get engaged, vote, vote, vote. And if we do our duty in 2022 and beyond, then ages still to come will say we—all of us here—we kept the faith, we preserved democracy, we heeded not our worst instincts but our better angels. And we proved that, for all its imperfections, America is still the beacon to the world, an ideal to be realized, a promise to be kept. There's nothing more important, nothing more sacred, nothing more American. That's our soul, that's who we truly are, and that's who must, we must always be.

I have no doubt, none, that this is who we will be, and that we'll come together as a nation that will secure our democracy, that for the next two hundred years we'll have what we had the past two hundred years: the greatest nation on the face of the earth.

We just need to remember who we are: We are the United States of America.

⤸ SECTION II ⤷

AN INSTITUTIONAL DIALOGUE

Every system is perfectly designed to yield the behaviors observed.

While authoring this introduction, an email notification popped up on the computer screen with a subject line that read, "USAFA Extremism Stand-Down All-Call." Although a couple weeks had passed since the Capitol Insurrection of January 6, 2021, we could not help but wonder, Is this our new reality? Unconsciously, we reflected back to the morning of 9/11 when we found ourselves in a similar state of shock. No one expected a massive terrorist attack coming to US soil to kill innocent, unsuspecting Americans that day. After all, we had been trained to fight wars through an industrial-state warfare paradigm. We knew this model worked. We had the proof of concept from WWII. Of course, our Vietnam War experience was problematic for our preferred paradigm of war—a paradigm that allowed the US military to dominate an adversary through precise application of technology, firepower, and maneuver. Military strategists hoped that Vietnam merely provided an exception to our preferred paradigm of modern warfare, and not a context that could negate our entire way of thinking about how future wars should be fought. It was easier to rely on what we knew, and we hoped things would be different in the future.

We were correct. Wars would definitely be different in the decades to come. We just didn't fully understand until we were confronted with a new reality in 2001 that forced us to accept our failed assumptions on 9/11, which became a tremendously painful experience for the entire country.

Those service members who grew up in the 1980s and 1990s were fortunate in that the US had no major armed conflict that we had experienced in the earlier periods of the twentieth century (Operations Desert Shield/Storm being a minor exception). That was, until 9/11 and the aftermath that ensued with the Global War on Terror. At the time, we didn't see "terror" as it was, but instead, we saw it as we wanted it to be. We wanted to tie the actors of terror to a sovereign state, one with well-defined borders, industrial centers that we could attack, and a centralized command structure that could be "decapitated" to decisively win. That was a war we knew we could win. Once again, we found ourselves knowing that we didn't know what we didn't know. Our experiences in the years to follow with Operations Iraqi Freedom and Enduring Freedom eventually convinced our military leaders that we needed a new model of warfare—a new paradigm—as the paradigm that we had finally come to understand so well ceased to be relevant for the wars we were now facing. And just as we never imagined terrorists hijacking US airliners and flying them into buildings, we never imagined red-blooded Americans storming the epicenter of our democratic government to disrupt the peaceful transition of power. And yet, once again, nearly two decades following 9/11, we found ourselves back at the drawing board mentally unprepared to accept the facts that were unfolding on television before our eyes, in our own country, with our own citizens. And once again, we were asking ourselves, "How could we have missed this?" We found ourselves in an entirely different context but with equally familiar ambiguity.

Then it started to become more clear. Yes. We should have anticipated this. Of course, none of us could have predicted the act of storming the Capitol to disrupt the certification of the Electoral College votes, but we could have predicted that a new form of conflict was to be expected. We should have expected it because we literally talked about it all the time. It wasn't a foreign concept at all. In fact, most everyone reading this book likely took an oath of office and uttered the words that foreshadowed what we observed on January 6, 2021, when we "solemnly [swore] to support and defend the Constitution, against all enemies, foreign and domestic ..."

Domestic enemies. The enemies within. Right ...

Up until this moment, these were just words describing an ethereal concept that none of us believed would be possible. And yet, it still felt so strange that such was not only possible, it was happening. We were all bearing witness to it. Perhaps we missed it because, once again, we had been too preoccupied with thinking about the last war we fought, instead of preparing for the next. Cyberwar was innovative in the 1990s before we actually had to start engaging in a battlespace to confront enemies using it against us. *Why didn't we see the signs? How did we miss the signals and trends? Could we have reasonably predicted this new form of conflict coming?* The answer is "probably." But like with any aircraft accident investigation, it's usually never one thing that causes the crash. After a careful investigation of the warning signs and trends, most accident investigations identify a *chain of events* that led to an outcome that was inevitable. Only in hindsight does it become "obvious."

Every system is perfectly designed to yield the behaviors observed.

Like so many times before in our modern experience of warfare, here we are, once again having to address extremism in the ranks and within society as a whole. This is a new war that has come to us, and thus, it is again up to the military and its political leaders to accept the facts at hand. We must rethink our assumptions about the wars that we have to fight, and not just those that we would prefer, and begin the hard work of building a system within our military organizations to produce the outcomes we desire while eradicating the extremist behaviors we loathe. It is ultimately what society expects of our nation's armed forces who have all sworn to protect America against all enemies, and thus, the hard work of developing a new paradigm begins once more.

The following chapters in this section provide some context for some of the warning signs that may have contributed to where we now find ourselves. The events of January 6th remain too recent with too many investigations underway to know for sure, but what we do know is that we can start acting now to re-create the inclusive environments within every military organization to foster the most effective teams who are most capable of discharging their missions by the chain of command.

As we continued to gaze at the "USAFA Extremism Stand-Down All-Call" message on the computer screen, we questioned whether or not such stand-downs like this would have any impact at all. To the extent such a stand-down did have a positive outcome, what would that look like? How would we know if we succeeded or not? How would we measure our success? After all, much of extremist behavior is rooted in attitudes and beliefs, and all too often, we are surprised to find out "how normal" alleged extremists are, until, of course, we review their private social media and web browsing history and realize we should have seen it all along, but we missed it.

We came to the unfortunate conclusion that events such as the "USAFA Extremism Stand-Down All-Call" would likely have no effect. Organizations do what they know how to do, based on the assumptions they've made in the past, to do what they can to try to make a bad situation better. The problem is that organizations are inherently complex, because organizations are comprised of people, who individually are the most complex organisms of all. We believe that in order for the military to grapple with this complexity to create inclusive environments to overcome the nascent complexity, there needs to be a deeper understanding of what a "typical military environment" is like, and to identify in what ways the various organizational environments need to change, and finally, how to go about changing them.

Variety begets variety. As the complexity of our society, of war, of technology increase, we must develop more diverse strategies to combat the requisite variety of the threats we now face. We believe that in order for the US military to maintain control over the complexity of the newest threats, it is vital to embrace diversity and inclusion among the ranks. We must develop new thought patterns and rely on new perspectives, and it starts with an acute focus on creating a deep sense of belonging for all service members. This will not be easy. It will not involve speeches, sound bites, platitudes, training stand-downs, open-door policies, diversity offices, or programs. It will require the resolve and commitment to win that has defined the American military since the earliest moments of the Revolutionary War.

The new approach will require a fundamental change to how leadership is viewed and practiced, and a sincere commitment by leaders at all levels to support the new paradigm. Yes, we have to completely reenvision how we think of the leadership models that have brought us to this point but likely will not get us to where we desire to go. Military leadership has traditionally been viewed through an individualistic lens. The most basic model involves a leader and a group of underlings who need to be led—the classic "followers," if you will. The military has always promoted a separation, or as it is often characterized, "a professional distance" between the two groups. Leaders can choose to act as servants, they can value and reward their people, and they can possess the best of intentions, but through this perspective, divisions are necessarily created by the very nature of the model. These divisions cascade throughout the unit, as separations exist between every level of supervision and within the organizational chart. The organizational chart depicts where these divisions shall occur. Please don't misunderstand—we are not, for a moment, suggesting that we dispose of organizational charts. Quite the contrary. What we are trying to illustrate is a new model whereby we continue to take for granted something that matters quite significantly. With these inherent structural divisions come norms and expectations of (1) how military members should interact with one other; (2) whose voices get heard; and, (3) if such voices are heard, to whom do they belong; (4) when will they be heard; and, (5) who will hear them. Then ultimately the final question: (6) what actionable measure will emerge of such an inclusive dialogue?

If we are to create a deep sense of belonging among all military members, it is absolutely essential that all voices have an opportunity to be heard, that everyone feels engaged, and that this becomes as natural and unnoticed as the air we breathe. No exceptions. There isn't a speech, training program, or stand-down that is likely powerful enough to overcome the norms of division and individualistic power that currently exist as rooted so deeply into the very fabric of military culture as we know it today.

So how do we do this?

It starts with culture. Culture can change just as our perspectives on leadership can change. Systems-level tools that are both collaborative and inclusive can be employed both to model the type of inclusive behavior necessary to create a deep sense of belonging and to eliminate unnecessary divisions that currently exist. Simple tools such as those described in "The BAR Manifesto"1 offer a great start toward that end. The model grows from the academic field of Action Research as first described by Kurt Lewin from MIT in the 1940s. This particular model, the BAR Model, provides prescriptions for inclusion and collaborative engagement, and has voice built in. Describing how action research is conducted is not our aim here, and a quick Google search can give you the basics, but we do want to take a moment to demonstrate how this model relates to creating a sense of belonging while equipping leaders with a broader perspective on their roles as leaders. It is this type of thinking that will not only empower the entire organization to act, but it can also provide insights to the future problems we will inevitably face before we actually encounter them.

---

[1] D. DePorres, C. Ferrante, D. Levy, M. Orlowsky, E. Tucker, & J. Wilson, "The Bar Manifesto," OD Practitioner 50, no. 3 (2018), 40–46.

*The process starts with a leader becoming aware of
an issue that needs to be addressed in the organization.*

Rather than calling on a select group of subordinates for advice or simply addressing the issue themselves, leaders ask that a baseline understanding of the observed issue take place. This means that anyone who might have knowledge of the issue must be included in the process. This process can engage quickly and certainly doesn't, nor shouldn't, become the latest bureaucratic program. What is vital to understand here is that all these voices must be heard. This process not only unlocks a capability for leadership to develop a deep understanding of the issue, it also engages people, gives them voice, and breaks down power hierarchies that threaten a sense of inclusion and belonging within the organization.

The next step in the process is to figure out what actions to take.

This step involves the sharing of information gathered during the baseline assessment as well as brainstorming potential actions within the organization. This is another collaborative and inclusive process that fosters positive relationships, inclusion, and gives voice to all members. Importantly, once an action is selected, the team becomes well aware that the action may not have the desired effect. In fact, such an action could make the situation worse. It is understood that organizations are complex and leaders must follow a disciplined approach, applying rigorous scientific methods to ensure actions are data-driven and not based on bias or conjecture. And if the proposed action doesn't work, it is okay. It is not personal. The leader is not doing a bad job. Mistakes are a fundamental part of this process. In fact, full-speed mistakes are essential. Fail fast, then wash, rinse, and repeat. Success will manifest sooner or later with a proposed action, but success cannot be "wished" into the process. It must emerge from the process in an authentic manner.

*The final step of the process is to analyze the results.
That concludes one cycle.*

The process continues until a desired state is achieved, which could include a number of repeating cycles, but it can work, and it will. We have seen this process transform organizations in our own work over and over again. Note that in the explanation of this proposed leadership model, the leader isn't the primary focus. The leader ultimately owns it all, but ownership and power must be shared. Many leaders with whom we engaged this process initially have difficulty internalizing this perspective. We understand the difficulty in understanding it at first, because this is a new leadership paradigm, and it challenges so many assumptions that we have all come to hold as sacrosanct.

Leaders who struggle with this new approach often don't say much directly, but the expressions on their faces indicate to us that this process somehow feels threatening and that through using it, they fear they will look weak by seemingly asking for help or that they will be giving up power. This couldn't be further from the truth. This process creates power. Power isn't a zero sum game. Collaboration and inclusion become multiplies as commitment and belonging-ness increase. The group of leaders we worry about the most are those that read this and say, "Oh, I'm already doing this, but in my own way." The US military dropped more munitions on Vietnam than we did in WWII. Doing the wrong thing better never works, even if we are more comfortable in believing that it might. We've talked to many leaders like this and have yet to find one who is actually doing what we are suggesting, and yet, every one of them disagrees and believes that they are. It's not a debatable point. The truth lies in the data of the outcome. Again, as we've said before: Every system is perfectly designed to yield the behaviors observed. And thus, if you want to change the behaviors, you must change the structure of the system.

This is the message we ask you to consider as you now engage in the following chapters. Onward~

CHAPTER 12

A Paean to our Nation's Service Academies: The "Holy Sepulchers" of the Soul and Ideals of the United States of America

Fletcher H. "Flash" Wiley, BG-5
USAFA Class of 1965

The Rationale

The nation's five service academies were founded in 1802 (Army), 1845 (Navy), 1876 (Coast Guard), 1943 (Merchant Marine), and 1954 (Air Force) to serve as the crucibles in which to educate and formulate a professional class of warriors and leaders, officers and gentlemen. These "knights of the realm," steeped in the history, philosophy, science, technology, tactics, and strategies of their own specific brand of waging warfare existed to protect and preserve peace in the homeland. In the golden days of chivalry during the Middle Ages, knights were expected to embody and uphold the character and integrity of the realm and the freedoms and rights of the people. As with any rigorous, first-class education and training institution with lofty objectives for its student body, those primary student parameters were set long before the institutions commenced recruiting attendees.

Accordingly, each of the service academies expended a great deal of time and care on maximizing the selection quality of its outstanding students, i.e., focusing primarily on persons who had already demonstrated solid academic capabilities, leadership traits, qualities, and experiences showing love of country, care for others, and sturdy and reliable character traits, the principles of which are honor, integrity, and sacrifice for the nation. Endemic to their comprehensive training and educational regimes, the US service academies consequently became *the* principal institutions in the nation. Drilled into the hearts and minds of the students were the fundamental ideals and icons of knighthood, to forever carry the vision and values forward toward establishing this unique nation of self-governing people devoted to those democratic principles.

High on the list of desirable traits is "personal integrity," and even higher is the special training afforded to a person to become a citizen who is a strong, reliable, and incorruptible Knight of the Realm. Moreover, the foregoing mantra was not only embedded in the minds, veins, and souls of service academy preparatory schools' graduates but also in the service academies themselves, which taught cadets and midshipmen to freely, happily, devotedly, and gratefully **give one's "last full measure of love and devotion"** to maintaining and enhancing the safety and prospects of the realm.

The Critical Central Core of a Service Academy Curriculum: America's Essence

Central to the core curricula of a service academy leadership development program was to instill deep knowledge of and reverence for the American "holiest of holies": (1) The Declaration of Independence; (2) the Constitution of the United States, as amended; (3) the principal of the "suzerainty of the Federal Union's Rights"; and, (4) the valuable, contrasting, and contradictory principle of "states' rights," particularly as they appertained to the pernicious institution of human slavery. When a cadet or midshipman at a service academy graduates, s/he receives a commission to the service of his/her choice and makes a solemn oath of allegiance to strictly obey and abide to the "holies" and to *protect* and *defend* them against the enemies of the United States, *both foreign* and *domestic*. Other "holies" were derived from our Declaration of Independence, which included the notions of every person being equal with "unalienable rights." An additional "holy" is the guiding motto of each respective service academy such as "duty, honor, and country" and also the Honor Code, guaranteeing the integrity of the cadet or midshipman, in that "we will not lie, cheat, steal, nor tolerate in our midst those who do."

Taken from the very best of the raw human "ores" that could be found from all across the nation, service academy individual attendees eventually become steel ingots commonly forged and melded to amalgamate friendship, brotherhood, purpose, and devotion to the nation and the "holies" into the glistening, untarnished product of freshly minted knights of the realm.

The "Best of the Best" with Whom I Attended USAFA: Lance Peter Sijan

Lance and I were both recruited as football players after our 1960 high school graduations, him from Bay View High School in Milwaukee, Wisconsin, and me from Shortridge High School in Indianapolis, Indiana, to attend a nine-month USAFA preparatory school program at the US Naval Academy Prep School at Bainbridge, Maryland. On July 22, 1960, we joined 118 similar recruits from all over the country as USAFA "preppies" at basic training at Lackland AFB in San Antonio, Texas. I was *the only* black guy in the group and felt very uncomfortable being below the Mason–Dixon Line, whereas my prep school colleagues and the training instructors—the "TIs"—were all white.

This training was normally an eight-week program but was truncated into four to give us the basics to become an enlisted serviceman in the Air Force Reserves. The most efficient and effective training system used the buddy system, i.e. using roommates to train each other. The befuddled TIs began asking around, "Who wants to room with the black guy?" Without hesitation, Lance volunteered to room with me. He came over to introduce himself with warmth and a signature bright and friendly smile. He was a hulking figure with a broad chest and of uncommon strength. He affably shook my hand and said: "I'm Lance Sijan; call me 'Si.'" We were put together, and along the way, we became friends and mutual aids. By then, that morning, I had received the sobriquet "Flash."

With Lance's help, I was elected the barracks chief of one of the two barracks our prep school contingency occupied. We both learned a lot about the Air Force and each other at Lackland. He came from a strong Midwest family of Serbian Americans. Along the way, his father, mother, sister, and brother became familiar friends. To ensure our mutual best academic performances, we drilled each other night and day regarding Air Force customs, nomenclature, and practices; the phonetic alphabet; the Uniform Code of Military Justice; and the American Fighting Man's Code of Conduct. Lance internalized both the lessons and the principles.

In August of 1960, we finished the basic program and moved on to the Bainbridge Naval Base in Maryland to attend the US Naval Academy Preparatory School. We started playing football and methodically posted an undefeated season, except for one notable loss to the Air Force Academy Junior Varsity. We were conquered by weariness exacted by the enervating 7,250-foot altitude, and travel fatigue from a twenty-three-hour cross-country flight from Maryland to Colorado Springs aboard a plane known as a Gooney Bird—a slow, propeller-driven, drafty, and uncomfortably accommodated World War II transport.

When we finally saw the campus, we were all stunned and excited by the Air Force Academy's space-age architecture, utilitarian beauty, and layout along the southeast Front Range of the majestic Rocky Mountains. Mesmerized by the breathtaking surroundings and the cadets in their snappy uniforms, Lance and I vowed to work hard at Bainbridge, successfully finish our program, and enter the Academy in June 1961 with the class of '65. We took our final college boards in March 1961 and were released immediately thereafter for home to await the final word from USAFA. In our parting embrace, Si and I shared our confident thoughts that because of football and academic successes, we both would be admitted and would be sharing, yet again, the real thing in June.

Sure enough, as the celebrated members of the class of '65 (self-described "Best Alive") gathered to enter USAFA beneath the Academy's then-iconic "BRING ME MEN" sign, Lance and I were there together with others from Bainbridge. Like me, since successful matriculation meant so much to him and his family, our jaws were resolutely set to successfully meet the challenge, no matter what, and to help each other along. We were assigned to the same Basic Cadet Training squadron, and Lance was a model trainee. Those summer sessions included both physical and mental challenges: obstacle courses, cadet knowledge, competitive athletics, long-distance "motivational runs," military indoctrination courses, and Air Force knowledge. Lance distinguished himself by not only excelling individually, but also by lending his physical strength and indomitable will to the aid of his struggling classmates. It was "Big Si" to the rescue.

During the summer, we were also steeped in the Honor Code, the Code of Conduct, and American values, jurisprudence, and traditions. These were all topics that Lance internalized, in the way that he knew that someday he might personally have to draw upon these lessons. On Sundays, we all attended mandatory chapel to hear the philosophical and historical premises underpinning America's development and elevation among the world's community of nations. We were all being trained to become raging fighting machines for God and Country, and to be ready without a moment's hesitation on the notion of expending our lives on behalf of the nation. Lance was always prepared to stand up and make the sacrifice.

While at the Naval Prep School and USAFA , I never, ever felt that I was being treated like a *"nigger,"* nor did I ever experience the gross indignity of being called one. Lance and others in my class would have been the very first persons to defend my honor, dignity, and rights. In truth, I was treated by Lance and my fellow cadets as a friend, brother, classmate, and a fully-fledged member of the Cadet Wing. Racial strife was a topic that we privately lamented during hours of introspection and reflection but a topic that we joked about comfortably and informally in bipartisan teasing and revelry. We all learned about each other, and we respected each other as fellow members of the Long Blue Line.

For most of the time while we were at the Academy together, repressive Jim Crow laws and practices still plagued much of the land. I shared with Lance and others of my classmates my own deep personal shame and impatience for not being more vigorously involved like many of my admirable and courageous African American contemporaries challenging the systemic racism that many Blacks of my age confronted through direct amelioration action like sit-ins, boycotts, freedom rides, and marches. Lance fervently believed that the inherit good ingrained in Americans would turn around the putrid racial environment. "Don't worry, Flash," Lance optimistically encouraged me, "democracy will prevail, and this vile, volatile, and oppressive racial climate will disappear; and you'll be an important part of the solution." He felt that I would make a difference because of my presence, personality, and deeds. He reminded me to stay focused on achieving the cardinal goal: graduate from USAFA, and all else will come. "And when the time comes for your civil rights activities; I'll be there to help you."

After the class of '65 was accepted in August 1961 into the Cadet Wing, Lance and I launched into classwork and freshman football. We continued our usual association throughout football, being close families and rooming together on football road trips. Eventually, we both prematurely surrendered the fellowship and joy of playing football—me because I had a nasty knee injury during spring training of my sophomore year, and Lance because he needed to concentrate on the principal task at hand: bolstering his academic performance to graduate on time. He was in the same cadet squadron as Bart Holaday (CS-21, the "Black Jack" Squadron). I never saw two guys "cinch-up" academically so thoroughly with late-night studies, extra sessions, and additional courses. Bart became a Rhodes Scholar and our Cadet Wing Commander; and emulating our long-time football teammate Bart, Lance impressively raised his academic profile and graduated with the rest of our class.

Our four years as cadets breezed by quickly with activity-laden schedules including the academic semesters and summertime travel and training. Before we knew, it was our graduation day, June 9, 1965. As expected, the Sijans and Wileys convened at graduation to fete their boys. We shared congratulations and fare-wells, pledging to stay in touch as the rest of our lives unfolded. Ironically, given our respective professed lifelong intent, it was the very last time we ever saw each other. Lance, as he desperately wished, went off to pilot training, where a sizeable batch of '64 and '65 grads ended up flying fighters, the two-seat F-4 Phantom being the workhorse fighter of the Vietnam Era. Lance dutifully earned the back seat of the plane as a weapons systems officer ("WSO") and was on the way to becoming a front-seater pilot.

A Knight of the Realm Valiantly Confronted His Destiny

Lance bailed out from his incapacitated F-4 aircraft on November 9, 1967, over North Vietnam due to a cockpit fire created by faulty fuses on the government-sup-plied ordnance his plane was carrying. He was listed as MIA (missing in action), and his family and friends grimly contemplated the worst fate for him. Subsequent-ly, I got news that he had crashed and become MIA, and as a surrogate son of the family, I got in touch with his folks to offer the Wileys' love and condolences.

In February of 1972, I was already out of the Air Force and had begun the active civil rights phase of my life. My academic and business schedules required my pres-ence in the Chicago area, and I made plans to drive up to Milwaukee at the time to visit with the Sijans. One of Lance's girlfriends, Kim Dougherty, to whom I had introduced Lance in the early winter of 1965, asked to meet me in Chicago from her East Coast home to drive up together to Milwaukee to meet the Sijan Family. She was crazy about Lance and wanted to personally pay her respects. It was a hard meeting for all of us, especially for Syl and Jane; but I knew that the family appreciated seeing their "other" son and welcomed the opportunity to meet one of Lance's lady friends. (He had a romantically devastating effect on women, and I knew that when I made the introduction, the two would click.) As we departed Milwaukee, we exchanged hugs and vowed to stay in touch and keep each other informed on Lance's fate.

When the POWs came home from Vietnam in February 1973, Lance's fate was then related to the world by fellow prisoner Guy Gruters, USAFA '64, and the full story about Lance's POW experience and gallant death on January 22, 1968, was circulated. He was mentally intrepid, defiant, and maintained a non-cooperative attitude with the enemy throughout his harrowing and torturous experiences after he bailed out from his flame-engulfed airplane sabotaged by clumsy, ineffective, and self-destructive ordnance. Even in the face of grave injuries, personal danger, weakness, emaciation, and torture, he assiduously adhered to the American Fighting Man's Code of Conduct as he had learned and internalized at Bainbridge and USAFA. Throughout his harrowing and torturous ordeal, he derived strength and fortitude from his devout beliefs in the "holy principles" upon which America was founded.

Consequently, on March 4, 1976, he posthumously was awarded the Congres-sional Medal of Honor, and on Memorial Day of that year, the new Cadet Dor-mitory at the Academy was officially named Sijan Hall to forever keep alive in the minds and hearts of cadets, grads, and visitors of Lance's exploits, moral, spiritual, and patriotic underpinnings. Lance was not alone in his valorous performance as a USAFA graduate in the Vietnam War, but he was, up until that time and ever since then, the *only* USAFA grad to receive the Medal of Honor.

His life and death most certainly stood for something; and indeed, our entire class and many contemporaries were imbued with the same principles and values. Lance has been elevated and revered as a universal exemplar over time as to what type of magnificent performance one should expect from the actions and deeds of an Air Force Academy graduate. To further commemorate his valor and patriotic beliefs and performance, on the fiftieth anniversary of our graduation, we, his brethren in the class of '65, gifted to the Academy a million-dollar bronze statue extolling his heroism, ideals, and travails. Always, to maintain family ties to the class of '65, whenever they were able to travel, Sijan family members, particularly Lance's younger sister, Janine, have joined us in Colorado on celebratory occasions.

What Was My Destiny to Be; and Did I Have a Heroic, Knightly Quest to Which I Dedicate My Life?

As for me, upon USAFA graduation, I began graduate studies at Georgetown University in Washington, DC; at L'Institut des Etudes Politiques in Paris, France; and at Howard University in Washington, DC, where I audited several courses in Black studies. It was in those diverse academic and metropolitan milieus among races and nationalities from all over the world that I gained a broader perspective on (a) the true meaning of life; (b) geopolitics; (c) as well as a firm perspective on the essential and binding commonalities among the human family in the midst of its glorious diversity around the globe. It was during this awakening era that I began to understand the similarities of the quest of the downtrodden Vietnamese people and of all colonized and abused people all over the world, and how similar their fates resembled the mighty woes of the children of Africa who had been kidnaped from their homeland and subjected to miserable slavery in the United States. As I speculated intellectually on the Vietnam War with students from the United States, Vietnam, and France, I revisited the question of what I personally was going to do to advance the African American's struggle for freedom.

As a military man, I had studied the slave rebellions of Denmark Vesey and Nat Turner; and I concluded, like Gandhi and Martin Luther King Jr., that using violence to respond to violence did not seem to be exactly the optimal approach to resolve the dilemma. Yes, there was a certain visceral appeal to the belligerent notion of "standing up like a man" to physically assert one's rights, as voiced menacingly by Malcolm X. But the problem with that approach is that the residual memory of violence by one party makes the building of goodwill and forging a lasting peace a much more difficult task. Once bitter memories prevail, a substantive, just, mutually satisfactory, and lasting peace is very hard to achieve. Still, when confronted by immediate, overt, and deadly assault as practiced by the Ku Klux Klan, the cardinal principles of self-defense and self-preservation supersede all else. I also gave serious consideration to the "Back to Africa" solution proffered by Marcus Garvey. Living overseas and being away from American values, culture, and cherished and familiar places and people made me realize how much of an American I was, particularly after attending the Air Force Academy.

I realized that my birthright in the nation was established "before the Mayflower" in 1619, and that my people had endured, labored, and done much of the hard work of the development of this nation without recompense. Without my input, African Americans had already paid the dues for our people to become full-fledged and free citizens. What was beautiful, essential, and endearing to me and that which I loved about my American "home" were family gatherings, home cooking, apple pie, Black culture, the melting pot, and old and cherished relationships and memories. And finally, as anchors to my love, devotion, and loyalty were my deep admiration, belief in, and respect for the fundamental principles upon which the nation was founded and upon which it has stubbornly stood and was strenuously unreceptive to the notion of being toppled by external or internal enemies.

America's lofty principles were meticulously thought out and articulated, inspired by history's greatest thinkers. The brilliant and wise architects of our philosophical infrastructure realized that they might not perfectly lay, on first blush, the firm constitutional foundation to last the nation perpetually. Accordingly, at the outset, the framers immediately added ten amendments to preserve universal and fundamental rights in the Bill of Rights. Afterward, they structured two key processes: (1) a high court to interpret the written provisions of the document; and (2) a mechanism to allow citizens to add future amendments as the republic's needs evolved over time. Two "imperfections" and logical inconsistencies were embedded in the original for sake of the political viability of the document. One, denying America's inalienable rights and equality as discussed in the Declaration of Independence, was intentionally written into the original constitutional document: (1) the recognition of the iniquitous, economically advantageous, and social-stratification institution of slavery that treated Black human beings as chattel; and (2) the sexist and misogynous denial of general freedoms and voting rights to women. Those flaws have been addressed by amendments, a bloody America Civil War, a violent Reconstruction, and a post-Reconstruction era that led to grave social and political upheavals.

It became crystal clear to me that I must intently follow the noble and earnest quest that my mother, grandmother, relatives, and ancestors had set me and my generation on to gain full-fledged freedom and equality for African Americans. Like Lance and others, the educational, political, physical, and social grooming at the Air Force Academy gave me tools to pursue my quest. Not only was I further steeped in the nation's philosophical underpinnings, but was also regularly exposed to a rare class of American citizens who had graduated from all of the nation's service academies in addition to USAFA who had also become noble knights of the realm.

My approach was to ally myself with like-minded citizens of all races, colors, creeds, genders, sexual persuasions, professions, and economic classes who all had a deep belief in American democracy. My methodology was to build and strengthen bridges among all of these Americans who seek to "do the 'right thing' on behalf of the *nation* and *humankind*." The first question my would-be allies confronted me with was: "How do we know what is the 'right thing'?" My answer is "use your compass"—the moral compass that we as knights were all given as cadets. Along the way, there also comes a visceral feel for actions and ideas that veer astray from the "holies."

How is my quest going, one might ask? I have concluded over the years that it is an uphill struggle all the way to get *everyone* on board at the same time to the "Love Train." The daunting task is made that much easier by incorporating fellow knights and people of good intensions, goodwill, and good judgment into the effort.

What Would Lance Sijan's Views Be On Events in Today's World?

I recognize that, to some observers, my query may seem blasphemously presumptuous. Who am I to speculate on what Lance may have thought about contemporary issues? Conversely, I wonder how many people in America have ever intimately known a Medal of Honor recipient in the formative stages or after having developed an accurate sense as to what strengths it takes to be able to "rise to the occasion"? In Lance's case, one must consider his years and years as a good and dutiful Midwest boy with strong influences from family, church, teachers and schools, coaches and team sports, Academy and Air Force, and peer training. He was a boy of eighteen when we first met, and already he had acquired the fundamentals of knighthood: respect for the nation and its elders; patriotism; loyalty; being the quintessential team player; possessing a mature leader's sense of responsibility; dedication to and a robust belief in the "American 'holies"; and an uncommon belief in the nation's continuing democratic destiny. Many of my USAFA classmates had amassed similar backgrounds when they came to Colorado. When they graduated and became knights as well, they were also in full possession of the raw materials to become a Medal of Honor recipient. All they needed were the dire, demanding, and deadly circumstances.

What would Lance think about me and my generation's steadfast pursuit for Civil Rights for African Americans and other disenfranchised citizens? Indeed, he and other White classmates periodically frankly disclosed that amid the reported lynchings, billy-club beatings, wild-dog attacks, water-hosings, jailings, bombings, and other deterrents employed to enforce Jim Crow, that if they were Black, they would fight for their rights too. Accordingly, *every* civil rights pursuit in the nation over history, including most glaringly the effort by women for equality, has used the "peaceful resistance" and legal platform created by Blacks.

Lance would have congratulated me and the other traditionally disenfranchised citizens on the progress we've made thus far, and he would have joined me in resisting White supremacy recidivism. A proud Serbian American, he lauded the melting pot concept, saw its value to the nation in adding the talents, skills, genius, and seasoning of the diverse ingredients; and he extolled the American virtues immortalized by Abraham Lincoln: an everlasting land of the people, governed by the people, and for the people.

How, as a Vietnam War veteran, would he feel about the facts that our national leaders *misunderstood* the worldwide zest after World War II for national liberation after a centuries-long period of brutal colonial dominance, and then pushed the

United States into the Vietnam War and lied about the circumstances to secure support for ever-increasing involvement against a falsely described enemy in the north and a falsely described ally in the south? Now, today's Socialist Republic of Vietnam is a pillar of Asian political stability and a popular American tourist attraction. How would he feel about having given his life on the word of prevaricating leadership; and what difference to the world of geopolitics did his precious sacrifice make? We could really use in America today a man of his talents, character, and leadership capabilities.

In addition to the leadership faults of Presidents Kennedy and Johnson, other American presidents since then have exhibited character flaws in honor, truthfulness, transparency, and leadership: President Nixon, President Reagan, President Clinton, President George W. Bush, and President Donald Trump. President Jimmy Carter, a Naval Academy graduate, and President Barack Obama are the only exceptions. Clearly, fuller use of the many talents and capabilities of the entire melting pot could result in better choices.

When I think about some of the unimaginable things that have happened in the beloved nation that Lance and others died and suffered so willingly for, like the unconscionable murders of African Americans like Trevon Martin, George Floyd, and others in the name of law enforcement, and also the January 6, 2021, destructive, venous, murderous, and riotous assault on the US Capitol by many enraged and incited perpetrators brandishing and bludgeoning with American and Confederate flags as weapons—in watching these events on television in living color, with horrific disbelief, I kept wondering to myself, *What would Lance Sijan have thought about all of this demonic rebuff of the immaculate American ideals and principles he lived and died by?* Adding to Lance's consternation would be the fact that the January 6th riot was incited by a sitting President of the United States, and that the rioters included a graduate from the Air Force Academy. Were he alive today, I know that Lance and other Academy grads would stand up to bring America back in line with her laudable, elegantly, and explicitly stated principles.

A Call to Arms to All Knights of the Realm

Yes, we knights know intrinsically what is right and that it is now time for all of us similarly trained and indoctrinated knights for America *to collectively stand up, embrace, and collectively make a difference.* Let's step up to our knightly pledge to protect our democratic platform from enemies both foreign and domestic, as not only the "home of the brave" and also as the "land of the free." Finally, let's bind in togetherness and mutual respect and forever exorcize from our midst America's demons that would lead us astray from our laudable, basic values.

Renowned European observers of our prideful republic, French political observer and commentator Alexis de Tocqueville and Swedish sociologist Gunnar Myrdal, commented in the nineteenth and twentieth centuries, respectively, that American democracy could not endure unless the nation found a rational and concerted way to eliminate the systemic vestiges of African slavery. It is a worthy and worthwhile quest for *all* of us to confront together to produce the likely enormous dividends for the entire nation, including for our White brothers who may temporarily recoil from the judicious tempering of their historic unbalanced preferences.

CHAPTER 13

OPEN LETTER TO THE UNITED STATES AIR FORCE ACADEMY

Michael L. "Mikey" Weinstein, Esq.
Founder and President, Military Religious Freedom Foundation
12 January 2021

For over fifteen years, the Military Religious Freedom Foundation (MRFF) has fought the shockingly systemic and unconstitutional influence and spread of fundamentalist Christian power and supremacy within the US military. While defending over 71,000 MRFF clients in that period in all services and hundreds of armed forces units worldwide, no single institution has more consistently produced odious cases and complaints than my alma mater (and the alma mater of four of my kids), the United States Air Force Academy (USAFA).

Sadly and most tellingly, MRFF still has hundreds of faculty, cadet, staff, active duty, Air National Guard, Reserve, and graduate clients derivative from and with the Academy.

From some of the scandals that led to the founding of the MRFF, like the antisemitic flyers and associated promotion of The Passion of the Christ in the Academy's cavernous Mitchell Hall dining facility as far back as 2004 to basic cadets marching in "Heathen Flight" in the early 2000s, we've progressed to warnings about "Special Programs in Religious Education" (SPIRE) groups that coerced misogynistic behavior and encouragement of discrimination against female cadets ("Cadets for Christ") through role indoctrination, and sought to transform cadets into "government-paid missionaries." But there is much more: quasi-mandatory Bible studies; uneven off-base privileges to attend fundamentalist churches; off-base organizations led by retired colonels recruiting Christian cadets and forming closed-door clubs that self-select Cadet Wing leadership, causing some cadets to resort to pretending to be fundamentalist Christians to fit in and succeed; pressure to participate in fundamentalist Christian proselytizing projects; professorial coded messages in the classrooms; tacit encouragement of homophobia and gay conversion therapy; and nearly unanimous displays of exclusivist Christian public prayer in the Falcon Stadium end zone. The shameful list is both ignominious and almost endless.

We warned you that this radical, right-wing influence found not only at USAFA but tolerated or even endorsed by senior officers throughout the Air Force caused a toxic leadership environment and eroded unit cohesion, good order, morale, and discipline. We constantly worried and warned that these seemingly (to some) innocuous events would lead to embarrassment for our Air Force Academy or worse—and that's exactly what's happened.

Mr. Larry R. Brock, class of '89 and a retired USAF Lt. Col./pilot presumptively drawing full military retirement pay and benefits, has now been arrested for his well-publicized participation in one of the darkest chapters of our nation's history—identified as a USAFA graduate in virtually every major media outlet in America and around the world. The simplest search of his social media presence shows him to be an adherent of exactly the kind of religious/political extremism mentioned above. Indeed, the avatar for his now-deleted Twitter handle was a Christian Crusader warrior.

Moreover, we know of at least three other graduates, all members of one of the USAFA classes in the 1990s (one being a former Cadet Wing Commander), who attended the failed coup d'état, posing for smiling selfies in Air Force Academy garb. While we may not know the religious affiliation of all three at this time, we do know that one was widely known among his/her classmates as an overt, evangelizing Christian during his/her cadet days and after.

The MRFF now calls on the Air Force Academy to not only clearly and publicly condemn the actions of its graduate, Mr. Brock, in the harshest possible manner, but also to call on all other USAFA graduates who attended the insurrection to identify themselves and either turn themselves in to police if they broke the law or disavow the violence and storming of the Capitol—if they, themselves, behaved in an otherwise peaceful manner.

We know that one graduate, a newly elected Republican member of Congress from Texas, August Pfluger, embarrassed a multitude of fellow USAFA graduates by objecting to the results of the largest and most scandal-free election in American history—and for that he is complicit in encouraging this mob and should be held responsible for the physical and moral damage caused to our Capitol and the republic.

The USAFA must address its decades old, complicit role in developing fundamentalist Christian religious/political extremists who are now widely serving in our military. It must, as well, hold itself responsible for creating horrors like Mr. Brock in the same way it does USAFA graduate heroes whom we praise on the other end of the patriotic spectrum.

We told you this was happening.

We told you the consequences.

It happened.

Now condemn it on the public record and work with us to fix it.

CHAPTER 14

For God and Country: Circa 2013

James E. Parco, PhD
Lieutenant Colonel, USAF (ret.)

In December 2012, West Point Cadet First-Class Blake Page resigned from the United States Military Academy just months prior to his graduation. Page stated that he could no longer stay at West Point and endure the organizational climate that endorsed fundamentalist Christianity.[3] Page's story was another in a series of similar stories in an ongoing, decade-long saga of growing religious fundamentalism in the US military. In an interview with the author of this paper, Page described the cultural fabric at West Point—one of the nation's most pre-eminent military commissioning sources—as imbued with implicit expectations that cadets have particular religious beliefs. Page explained:

> *You know, it really hurt, and it shouldn't be this way at West Point, but it is, and it needs to change. I didn't want the public display that my story has been. I simply wanted the senior leadership of the Army to know what's going on in hopes that they can change things to match with what they say.* [4]

It is uncommon to hear stories from junior military members like Blake Page, and yet there are hundreds, if not thousands, of people who feel the same way and yet continue to serve in silence.[5] "Speaking out" is considered unprofessional behavior, even when such speech is an honest effort to inform leadership and the public of inappropriate behavior inside the military. The unspoken message is clear: if you know what's good for you, you'll keep quiet, and if you don't, you'll pay the price—the Blake Page price.

In the pages that follow, this paper will describe the current military environment (circa 2013) as it pertains to religious expression. After providing several prominent examples of overtly inappropriate behavior, three case studies will be discussed that showcase some of the most egregious examples of leaders putting their religious beliefs before their professional duties, and in most cases, getting away with it.

In the Beginning . . .

The argument over what constitutes permissible religious expression in regards to members of the military has ebbed and flowed since our nation's birth. It prominently reemerged during the 2000 presidential debates, with then Texas Governor George W. Bush remarking in Iowa that Jesus Christ was his "favorite philosopher." He explained, "When you turn your heart and your life over to Christ, when you accept Christ as the Savior, it changes your heart and changes your life, and that's what happened to me."[6] This raised the eyebrows of both secularists concerned with keeping religion and government separate and Christian leaders seeking to combine the two.

In January 2001, Bush became the forty-third President of the United States, thus also Commander in Chief of the US Armed Forces.[7] Nine months later, the US would suffer its greatest domestic attack since World War II.[8] The result was the country involved in two wars and the United States again relying on its military to pursue its interests. Given Bush's proclivity for mixing politics with religion,[9] few were surprised when he framed America's reaction to the 9/11 attacks as "this crusade, this war on terrorism."[10] Cloaking political rhetoric in religious language, the Commander in Chief insinuated that religion *did matter* in the military operations to come. This sentiment was made even clearer by Air Force Major General Glen Shaffer, the Director of Intelligence. General Shaffer had been responsible for producing the daily worldwide intelligence update circulated within the Pentagon and briefed to the president during the early days of the Operation Iraqi Freedom. Normally, cover sheets had featured significant images from the previous day's war effort, but in the days following the initial US attack on Baghdad, biblical verses and selectively chosen photos began to appear on these highly classified official government documents.

As an example, the March 31, 2002, cover page included a photo of a tank racing through the Iraqi desert with a caption that read, "Therefore put on the full armor of God, so that when the day of evil comes, you may be able to stand your ground, and after you have done everything, to stand."[11] The following week, under a dictatorial pose of Saddam Hussein, read the phrase "It is God's will that by doing good you should silence the ignorant talk of foolish men."[12] And, when the Americans had taken Baghdad three days later, the caption below the picture of a fallen Saddam Hussein statue read, "Behold, the eye of the Lord is on those who fear Him . . . to deliver their soul from death."[13] Not everyone who saw these reports was comfortable with this sort of religious framing. Yet, when questioned about the appropriateness of this behavior, General Schaffer "politely informed them [dissenters] that the practice would continue because my seniors [JSC Chairman Richard Myers and Defense Secretary Donald Rumsfeld] appreciated the cover pages."[14]

Outside the walls of the Pentagon, a "third front" was emerging in the Global War on Terror. This front has since raged quietly beneath the veneer of military professionalism, between soldiers who believe the United States is primarily a

Christian nation with her military a force for Christianity, and soldiers who seek to keep their religious beliefs and military duties completely separate and maintain the military as a force for American ideals. For many fundamentalist Christians who serve in uniform, they aren't merely serving their country: in their hearts and minds they are serving both God and country—in that order of priority.[15]

My God Is Bigger Than Your God

General Shaffer wasn't alone in his zeal to promote Christian fundamentalism in an official capacity, nor was he the first. One year earlier, US Deputy Under-secretary of Defense for Intelligence and Army Lieutenant General Jerry Boykin took to the microphone to outline his strategy for defeating the enemy in the wake of the 9/11 attacks. Appearing in his military uniform, he told attendees of the Southern Baptist Convention's National Faith Institute in January 2002, "Bin Laden is not the enemy. No mortal is the enemy. It's the enemy you can't see. It's a war against the forces of darkness. The battle won't be won with guns. It will be won on our knees."[16]

Later that year, in June, speaking from the pulpit at a Baptist church in Broken Arrow, Oklahoma, Boykin showed photos he had taken in Mogadishu, Somalia, in 1993. He had noticed a dark mark in a photo and had his intelligence imagery specialists examine it to determine its origin. Boykin revealed to the congregation, "Ladies and gentlemen, this is your enemy," pointing to the dark image over the photo. "It is a demonic presence in that city that God revealed to me as the enemy."[17]

Continuing his religious tour in uniform, at a sermon at the First Baptist Church in

Daytona Beach the following January, Boykin told the story of Osman Atto, a Somali warlord who taunted US allies that they would never capture him because he knew Allah would protect him. Boykin concluded, "Well, you know what I knew, that my God was bigger than his. I knew that my God was a real God, and his was an idol. But I prayed, Lord let us get that man." As it turned out, Osman Atto was captured, and when Boykin finally had the opportunity to confront him, he recounted saying, "Mr. Atto, you underestimated our God."[18]

Boykin's comments generated a firestorm of criticism and prompted an investigation by the Department of Defense's Inspector General. A year later, investigators concluded, "as described throughout this report, LTG Boykin's speeches to religious-oriented groups were a personal activity . . . and the circumstances of their presentation [in military uniform, introduction by rank/position] created a perceived association with his official duties."[19] In addition to failing to properly disclose a $520 travel expense, Boykin was found to have violated Defense Department regulations pertaining to the release of official information by failing to clear his speeches with proper Defense Department authority, and failing to preface his remarks with a disclaimer, for which the Secretary of the Army was ordered to take appropriate corrective action against him. Congress reacted by calling on President Bush to censure Boykin for his actions and words, including his claim that the United States' "spiritual enemies will only be defeated if we come against them in the name of Jesus."[20] Yet nothing came of the call, and the lack of consequences for Boykin's actions sent a very clear message to thousands of uniformed American religious fundamentalists that such behavior would be condoned.[21]

Despite Boykin's desire for a crusade, he had overlooked the lessons learned from his centuries-old brethren crusaders. In a sharp departure from Christian doctrine, Pope Urban II called on his followers in 1096 to join the military ranks and march to the aid of fellow Christians in the East. Promoted as the culmination of a peace movement, Urban declared a cessation of all Christian vs. Christian hostilities. The Pope understood the power of incentives, and thus offered an automatic "indulgence," or remission of temporal punishment, for anyone who joined his crusade to fight the "real" (non-Christian) enemies. Historians attribute many proximate causes for the Crusades, but there is a general consensus that religious hysteria combined with a sense of nationalism fueled the fires of war for the ensuing century. Despite the complexity and devastation of these holy wars more than nine hundred years ago, one lesson is certain: when military power is combined with a nationalistic fervor, *especially* religiously tinged, crisis looms large.

The Great Debate Over Separation of Church and State

Fortunately, the lessons learned from the holy wars, so common throughout Europe's past centuries, were not lost on America's Founding Fathers. When it came to the proper interplay between religion and government, Thomas Jefferson and James Madison collectively forged the philosophical underpinnings that eventually became manifest in the First Amendment to the US Constitution. In just sixteen words, the proper place for religious behavior in a governmental context was defined: "Congress shall make no law respecting an establishment of religion or prohibiting the free exercise thereof." The founders recognized what would happen if and when religious fervor met state power, including military force, within a nationalistic society. After exhaustive deliberations, they concluded the best position for a free society would be to keep government and religious authorities out of each other's business. Both would be allowed to flourish without either entangling with one another.

However, the First Amendment could not be expected to resolve all possible church-state questions. In 1971, the US Supreme Court issued its seminal decision in *Lemon v. Kurtzman*, which clarified the relations between religion and government. In their ruling, the Court held that for any statute to be constitutional in respect to the Establishment Clause, it must pass a three-part test:

1. It must have a clear secular purpose;
2. It must not have a primary effect of either advancing or inhibiting religion;
3. It must not foster excessive entanglement with religion.

Although this so-called "lemon test" focused on the constitutionality of statutes, it also informs behavior of any government official who is in a position to create or enforce policy. Simply put, when dealing with matters of religion and religious expression, neutrality is the only viable policy.

The great debate regarding church-state relations remains far from settled. Two of the most prominent contemporary voices on the proper role of religious expression in the military have been Jay Alan Sekulow, chief counsel for the Christian legal advocacy group American Center for Law and Justice,[22] and Barry Lynn, executive director of the church-state watchdog group Americans United for Separation of Church and State.[23] In 2010, both Sekulow and Lynn authored chapters in the first volume of *Attitudes Aren't Free: Thinking Deeply About Diversity in the US Armed Forces*, outlining the basis of their respective positions.[24] Whereas Sekulow was chiefly concerned with promoting unregulated religious speech of chaplains and military members, Lynn saw the entanglement of government and religion as the most vexing threat.

Sekulow argued that one's religious beliefs are often inextricably tied to the person's desire and willingness to serve, and thus, it is unthinkable to make a distinction between religion and military service. Although he offered a series of examples that demonstrated patently inappropriate behavior, he also had no issue with commanders speaking openly and freely about their religious values and beliefs in a public setting or in official capacity.[25]

Lynn, on the other hand, was far more concerned about the persistent trends in the military that abused the Establishment Clause. Through the lens of an extensive body of case law, he contends there should be a strong line separating issues of religious expression and one's professional duties and speech—a line that Sekulow outright rejected. Lynn argued that Sekulow's position on the right to free speech could be considered in isolation of the Establishment Clause.[26]

Although there is considerable common ground between Sekulow and Lynn's perspectives, they diverge rather dramatically on two specific issues. First, they differ in their opinions on the permissibility of chaplains to proclaim their personal religious beliefs in their professional capacity as a military chaplain. While Sekulow advocated for chaplains to have near unrestricted speech, context matters to Lynn. Lynn acknowledged the importance of an individual's right to freedom of conscience—whether that meant to express one's religious beliefs or no beliefs at all—but this freedom is rightfully restricted during official duties, especially when coercion may exist or when an individual cannot opt out of the discussion. Sekulow and Lynn also differ on the permissibility of external religious organizations' affiliation with military organizations. While Lynn was a longtime advocate on strict neutrality,[27] Sekulow argued that in the then-current environment, such a distinction is impractical.[28]

Through the lens of the Sekulow-Lynn debate, the most prominent issues that received national attention are presented in the following section as three separate case studies. These case studies illustrate clear patterns of religiously expressive behavior in the professional military realm in the areas of (1) training and education; (2) deployed presence overseas; and (3) leadership. Collectively, these case studies provide some of the most compelling evidence by which to analyze the merits of the competing philosophical perspectives on the proper role of religious expression by men and women in uniform.

CASE STUDY #1:
The United States Air Force Academy

Over the past two decades, United States Air Force Academy (USAFA) has had a disproportionate number of allegations of religious endorsement as compared to its sister-service academies at West Point and Annapolis for two primary reasons. First, the sheer density of ultraconservative religious organizations surrounding the Colorado Springs institution provides a religiously aggressive environment. These organizations, many of which are headquartered in Colorado Springs, include the National Association of Evangelicals, Focus on the Family, the Navigators, and the renowned megachurch founded by fallen-from-grace pastor Ted Haggard.[29] Watchdog groups such as the Military Religious Freedom Foundation and the Military Association of Atheists and Freethinkers[30] levy persistent allegations, based upon complaints received from students, that fundamentalist Christian organizations are tacitly given inside access to interface with cadets on campus grounds. Moreover, senior leaders, who themselves are fundamentalist Christians, have systemically sanctioned efforts to evangelize to others when their official positions yielded them an opportunity and ability to do so, while others failed to stop efforts when opportunities arose.

Before serious charges of religious intolerance began to emerge in 2004, the Air Force Academy was already mired in troubling allegations of sexual harassment and assault. On January 2, 2003, an anonymous email using the pseudonym Renee Trindle was sent to the Secretary of the Air Force, his chief of staff, both US senators from Colorado, and the House member in whose district the Academy is located, alleging that there was a significant sexual harassment and assault problem at the Air Force Academy, and that senior leaders were ignoring it. Twelve percent of the women who graduated from the institution had reported they were the victims of rape, and of all the female students, 70 percent claimed they had been the victims of sexual harassment.[31]

The Air Force's reaction was deliberate and swift. Integral to its efforts was the immediate replacement of all Air Force Academy senior leaders. As part of this sweeping change, Brigadier General Johnny Weida arrived at the Air Force Academy in April 2003 as the commandant of cadets, taking charge of all aspects of cadet training. However, because a three-star superintendent had not yet been named, Weida temporarily assumed command as the acting superintendent, a job he would hold for four months until the permanent three-star general would assume command of the school.

Weida understood the gravity of the problem and recognized the need for strong, principled leadership to return to the institution to its core values to regain the public trust. However, like all senior leaders, Weida was left to his own judgment as to how best to move the organization forward. Two specific examples shed insight on the path he would choose. What would later become apparent is that, in the Air Force's desire to regain the public trust over the sexual harassment and assault scandal, the institution fixed one problem while inadvertently creating another.[32]

In his first month on the job, Weida issued his superintendent's guidance, reminding cadets they were "accountable first to your God" and that "he [God] has a plan for each of us."[33] Later that summer, speaking at a Protestant religious service during basic training, he told the cadets in attendance the New Testament parable about the two men who built their houses: one on the sand, and the other on the rock.[34] He then instructed them that whenever he appeared in front of the student body and yelled "Air power!" they were to reply "Rock, sir!" This would cause others to ask what this chant meant, providing cadets with an opportunity to help them "find salvation in our Lord and Savior Jesus Christ."[35]

Weida never shied away from an opportunity to instill Christianity into cadets as a proxy for morality. During National Prayer Week he sent a note to all cadets instructing them to "ask the Lord to give us the wisdom to discover the right, the courage to choose it, and the strength to make it endure."[36]

In the fall of 2003, Lieutenant General John Rosa arrived as the institution's newest superintendent, and by the following summer, he had become completely established as the Air Force Academy's senior leader.[37] As a college president equivalent, Rosa regularly fought internal fires, but until in particular a meeting with two prominent alumni in July 2004, he had been completely unaware that his institution was on a collision course with Christian fundamentalism. He also could not have imagined that one of his very own subordinate generals would lead the charge for the opposition he would eventually face.

Knowing that the topic of the meeting would involve alumni complaints of religious intolerance, Rosa asked his newly assigned head chaplain to attend. During the course of the discussion, the two alumni who had requested the meeting produced documents that substantiated an undeniable embedding of Christianity in many facets of the organization. After a two-hour meeting, Rosa looked to his head chaplain and said, "Well, this certainly seems to have become a problem and we need to fix it." Then, turning to the two alums, he continued, "But it's obviously going to take us some time, and I ask for your patience."[38]

Over the next five months, Lieutenant General Rosa and his head chaplain made the development of a comprehensive religious tolerance training program their top priority. Recognizing the importance of good marketing, they gave it a bumper sticker–style slogan, RSVP: Respecting the Spiritual Values of Persons. More than two-dozen personnel were assigned to the development, including members of both the commandant's training staff and the dean's faculty.

Shot Heard 'Round the World

After months of development, the Air Force Academy's staff chaplains unveiled the abridged version of the RSVP program in November 2004 to a special group of three hundred of the institution's most senior leaders.[39] Seated at the front of the audience were the Academy's three general officers: the superintendent (Rosa), the commandant (Weida), and the dean (Born). Throughout the rest of the room sat all cadet commanders, officers, and senior non-commissioned officers (NCOs). After a fifty-minute presentation by two staff chaplains, the vice commandant took the microphone to field questions from the crowd. After several minutes of questions, a cadet commander stood up and asked the vice commandant, "Ma'am, in light of this training, I'm curious, can we have Bible studies in a cadet TV room?"

The colonel froze for several seconds, not knowing how to answer. The point of the training had been to create an awareness of religious tolerance. Behavior had not been addressed. Sensing her unease, the head chaplain rescued his colleague. He stood up, took the microphone from her hand, turned to the student, smiled, and replied:

> It's a very good question. You see, here at the Air Force Academy, we are blessed to have a great deal of resources available for religious expression. For instance, we have the Oasis Club in Sijan Hall with many rooms for gatherings. We have the Cadet Chapel with the Protestant, Catholic, Jewish, and all-faith areas. In each cadet group, we have a dedicated chaplain with a conference room. Thus, given the availability of all these resources for worship or spiritual gathering, it would probably be inappropriate to use a common-use room for religious purposes if it disenfranchised the use to other cadets who didn't want to participate.[40]

As the cadet said, "Thank you, sir" to the head chaplain for what most everyone in attendance later regarded as a superb answer, General Weida suddenly rose from his chair, took the microphone from the head chaplain's hand, turned to face the crowd, and said, "I'll give some guidance here. You wanna have a Bible study in a cadet TV room? No problem." He handed back the microphone to the head chaplain, who stood there speechless and sat back down—directly next to his boss, General John Rosa, the three-star superintendent. For several seconds, no one moved or knew what to say, until finally one of the junior chaplains who had moderated the training leaned forward into the podium and said, "Thank you all for coming. This concludes our training." Within a week, the story became public, placing USAFA back in the eye of public scrutiny for not only religious fundamentalism prevalent in its culture, but for the complacency of the institution's senior leaders who allowed it to happen on their watch.[41]

Reflecting back on the Academy's initial response to allegations of religious promotion and intolerance, RSVP was a monumental failure. What the Air Force failed to learn from the sexual harassment scandal was that a permanent solution could only be grounded in immediate practical boundaries with accountability through reprimands for bad behavior. The "increase awareness" and "spiritual tolerance" nonsense was doomed from the start. When organizations face problem of an abuse of freedoms, leaders cannot fix them by merely promoting more freedoms.

The Mothership Responds

Months later, in January 2005, following a steady flow of complaints of religious bias and intolerance emanating from the emerging culture of proselytization by faculty, staff, and students at the USAFA, the Pentagon dispatched a task force led by another Air Force three-star general to investigate.[42] The resulting ninety-one-page report effectively concluded that the allegations were not sufficient to recommend any substantive changes. Once again, bad behavior was sanctioned, further emboldening religious fundamentalists throughout the ranks. All senior leaders kept their positions, no additional policies were issued, and business continued as usual. Not surprisingly, the number of allegations of pressuring cadets by fundamentalist Christians has only increased over the past eight years.

Apologists argued that the situation, alleged by anonymous sources, was overblown. However, substantiation of the allegations from anyone personally affected was unlikely; anonymity was the only option for victims who wanted to avoid reprisal. The case of Air Force Captain MeLinda Morton is illustrative of how the organization can end the career of anyone who dares to come forward openly.

In May 2005, as one of the principal architects of the RSVP training, Captain Morton, a Lutheran chaplain, went public. For years she had worked as a staff chaplain for the Air Force Academy and recognized the blatantly corrupt practices endorsed by both the chaplaincy and senior leadership. Morton was one of the most knowledgeable staff members at USAFA, having been assigned there for several years. At the height of the crisis, when senior leaders began to embrace the excuse that there were really nothing more than a few disgruntled individuals seeking their fifteen minutes of fame, Captain Morton made the ultimate career sacrifice. To counter the arguments and preserve her own integrity, she agreed to an interview with the *New York Times* in May 2005. In it she described how the highest levels of senior leadership not only failed to create a climate of religious pluralism and inclusion, but also acted to make matters worse.

For example, Morton described how one month before the debut of RSVP, the Air Force chief of chaplains visited the Academy to preview the training program. At the conclusion, he asked, "Why is it that the Christians never win?" The end result was to cut the program from ninety minutes to fifty minutes and remove segments on Buddhism, Judaism, and Native American spirituality.[43]

Within one week of the interview being published, Chaplain Morton was fired.[44] Facing national scrutiny, General Rosa went public and spoke openly and honestly about the religious intolerance crisis he faced. In a speech to the Anti-Defamation League, he told the audience, "I have issues with my students, I have issues in my staff, and I have issues in my faculty—and that's my whole organization."[45] He also noted the problem would take at least six years to fix. However, he knew he would not be the one to fix them, for he had accepted a post-retirement position to become the nineteenth President of The Citadel. Chaplain Morton was reassigned to a remote overseas station, but instead elected to resign her commission in protest of the retributive action.[46] Soon after Morton's revelations, the Air Force's Headquarters Task Force[47] published the final report airbrushing the entire scandal.[48] By June 2005, the institution saw to it that the case was effectively closed, with the exception of the senior officer who had started it all. In August 2005, the press reported that Brigadier General Weida's name had been pulled from the promotion list to receive his second star.[49] After a sufficient cooling-off period, when the events were finally below the public radar, Weida was quietly promoted to major general in May of 2006.[50] The message communicated by Air Force leaders was clear: be whatever you want, but it is best if you are Christian. Despite the allegations and ongoing public pressure, the organization continued to quietly sanction command-directed Christianity and reward its chief architects and practitioners.

When General Rosa retired in October of 2005, he passed command of the Air Force Academy to Lieutenant General John Regni. Shortly thereafter, investigative journalist Jeff Sharlet interviewed Regni about the religious crisis that had embroiled the institution for the previous eighteen months. Sharlet wrote:

> I began our phone conversation with what I thought was a softball, an opportunity for the general to wax constitutional about First Amendment freedoms.
>
> "How do you see the balance between the Free Exercise Clause and the Establishment Clause?" I asked. There was a long pause. Civilians might reasonably plead ignorance, but not a general who has sworn on his life to defend these words: "Congress shall make no law respecting an establishment of religion or prohibiting the free exercise thereof."
>
> "I have to write those things down,"
>
> Regni finally answered. "What did you say those constitutional things were again?"[51]

Eight years and two superintendents later, the situation at the Air Force Academy remained largely unchanged. In June 2009, Lieutenant General Michael Gould, yet another self-acknowledged fundamentalist Christian, was appointed as General Regni's successor.[52] As far as the Air Force was concerned, the problems were solved when 100 percent turnover had been achieved. To this day, they still do not recognize it as a subsisting cultural problem. In November 2012, local media reported on a summit of twenty religious leaders who met at the Air Force Academy to review the religious respect training program for cadets.[53] Despite the institutional review stating, "We have a great story to tell here," the truth is that overtly religious training continued to effectively impart the corrosive understanding that to be a "good officer," one needed to ascribe to a religious code.

CASE STUDY #2:
Military Missionaries

Embedded journalists have become a staple of American media serving a nation at war. Although the practice emerged with the major news networks, over the years covering the wars in Iraq and Afghanistan, the method spread to a variety of media venues. In September 2008, the Discovery Channel aired a two-hour program entitled *God's Soldier*.[54] Filmed on-site at a forward operating base in Iraq, the film had been produced "with the full cooperation of the 2-27 Infantry Battalion" according to the program's credits. *Travel the Road*, another popular Christian reality television show, ended their second season with several episodes filmed on location in Afghanistan. When *ABC News Nightline* did an investigative report on the connection between the program, which was owned by the Trinity Broadcasting Network (TBN), and the US military, one of the missionaries acknowledged: "They [military commanders] knew what we were doing. We told them we were born again Christians, we're here doing ministry, we shoot for this TV station and we want to embed and see what it was like."[55]

As the military faced criticism for its complicity in giving preferential access to fundamentalist Christian organizations, in May 2009 the public affairs arm of the Army announced that it would be destroying thousands of Christian Bibles sent by a private American religious organization to a chapel at Bagram Air Base in Afghanistan.[56] These particular Bibles had been printed in the local Pashto and Dari languages, and critics argued the intent behind them was clear—private religious organizations in the United States were using the US military as taxpayer-funded international missionaries.

Yet others argued that these Bibles given out by American chaplains to American service members were protected speech under the First Amendment, and the confiscation and

destruction of the books amounted to government censorship and deprivation of private property.[57] The leading voice of opposition was former US Navy Chaplain Gordon James Klingenschmitt. Klingenschmitt gained national notoriety in 2006 when he was found guilty at a general court martial of disobeying a lawful order.[58] Klingenschmitt had reasoned that General Order No. 1B, which "prohibits proselytizing of any religion, faith or practice,"[59] does not include evangelism, which according to Klingenschmitt, unlike proselytization, is not forcible.[60]

Although this distinction has never been codified in law, the US government continued to distribute Bibles, printed in English with camouflage covers brandishing official military insignias on their covers, to American troops overseas.[61] One only needs to read through the volumes of Christian soldier blogs to see first-person testimonials, such as from a chief warrant officer from the 101st Airborne Division:

> "The soldiers who are patrolling and walking the streets are taking along this copy [official Bibles] and they are using it to minister to local residents," and he continues, "The soldiers are being placed in strategic places with a purpose. They're continuing to spread the word."

Such evidence demonstrated how little regard fundamentalist Christians had for government regulations when those regulations were seen to conflict with the belief that he or she answers to a higher authority beyond his or her chain of command.[62]

Jesus Rifles

Despite the prohibitions of General Order 1B, these examples are only a small sampling of a much larger collection that has emerged illustrating the growing influence of fundamentalist Christianity in the military. *Harper's* published a stunning article in May of 2009 entitled "Jesus Killed Mohammed," in which the author (again, Jeff Sharlet) described how the title comes from actual words, in red Arabic lettering, painted on the side of a Bradley Fighting Vehicle in Iraq.[63] The article revealed that this inscription was only one of many inflammatory crusader-tinged messages that had been openly displayed on military equipment.

Later that year, *ABC News* broke a story about the Michigan-based rifle-sight manufacturer Trijicon, which had been inscribing Bible verse numbers on rifle sights sold to the US military under a $660 million contract.[64] At the time of the report, these rifle sights were already widely used in Iraq and Afghanistan by US Marines, Soldiers, and members of allied militaries. Facing scrutiny, the company announced plans to provide kits to remove the inscriptions from the 800,000 sights already sold.

Spiritual Fitness

General David Petraeus, then commander of the military's Central Command (CENTCOM, responsible for Iraq and Afghanistan operations) commented that the spiritual fitness issue was "disturbing . . . and a serious concern for me." However, it's not clear why Petraeus found the story so concerning. Unaware observers were likely to have taken the commanding general's comments on face value, but Petraeus himself was known by insiders to be part of the problem, due to his strong commitment to "spiritual fitness."

The Department of the Army's spiritual fitness program provides commanders "with a definition of spiritual fitness and suggest[s] alternatives to enhance the soldier's total well-being increasing spiritual fitness."[65] Spiritual fitness came to the forefront in 2009 when the US Army unveiled a $125 million "holistic fitness" program intended to address the growing issue with post-traumatic stress disorder cases. The program aimed at teaching soldiers how to become "psychologically resilient" emotionally, physically, family-oriented, socially, and spiritually in dealing with traumatic events. However, the online assessment tool included in the program assessed a soldier's spiritual fitness by using "questions written predominantly for soldiers who believe in God or another deity, meaning nonbelievers are guaranteed to score poorly and will be forced to participate in exercises that use religious imagery to 'train' soldiers up to a satisfactory level of spirituality."[66]

Spiritual fitness wasn't a new concept. Dating back to the 1980s, Army regulations have described and encouraged spiritual fitness as:

> All aspects of total wellness addressed by the Army Health Promotion
> Program come under the physical, emotional, and spiritual dimensions
> of human beings. A great amount of training time is devoted to physical

health and conditioning. This is a positive effort and appropriate for our mission accomplishment, however, TOTAL fitness also involves emotional and spiritual aspects![67]

Moreover, specific religious devotionals and prayers were listed in the military regulation itself, in an appendix. As an example:

C–1. By the grace given me, I laid a foundation as an expert builder, and someone else is building on it. But each one should be careful how he builds. For no one can lay any foundation other than the one already laid, . . . Don't you know that you are God's temple and that God's Spirit lives in you? If anyone destroys God's temple, God will destroy him; for God's temple is sacred, and you are that temple. (1 Corinthians 10:11, 16–17)

C–2. Our society's emphasis on physical fitness and other ways to benefit ourselves leads one to conclude that "do your own thing" is the best way to go. Our scripture lesson provides an important reminder that our "own thing" must be built on the foundation which God provides—physically, emotionally, and spiritually.

On multiple occasions, General Petraeus had expressed support—as an active-duty four-star general—for such "spiritual fitness" evaluation programs and social events. He had first been implicated in endorsing fundamentalist Christian events that targeted soldiers in 2007, when his photo and endorsement appeared on the Eric Horner Ministries website, praising Horner's Christian rock concerts on military bases.[68] Then, in the August 7, 2008, edition of *Air Force Times*, Army Chaplain Lieutenant Colonel William McCoy took out a half-page ad promoting his book *Under Orders: A Spiritual Handbook for Military Personnel*, which promoted Christianity and asserted that non-religious service members had no defense against sin and could therefore cause the failure of their units.[69] As reported by religious watchdog author Chris Rodda, the book was endorsed by none other than Gen. Petraeus, whose blurb on the book's cover read: "*Under Orders* should be in every rucksack for those moments when Soldiers need spiritual energy."

In the November 2011 issue of *Baptist Press*, Colonel Brent Causey, who had been the top chaplain to Petraeus in Afghanistan, exclaimed, "Gen. Petraeus played a leadership role in stressing the importance of spirituality." Specifically:

It was incredible to see the growth of Bible studies and the growth of conversions among our own service people—not just battlefield conversions but the maturity of faith and development of mentorship at all levels. We started out with four of us in Bible study and when I left, 85 percent of our leadership were active in dynamic Bible study—18 out of 22 of Petraeus' directorates (direct reports). It's always an impact when anyone comes to Jesus Christ as Savior, but I saw guys aged 45 and above making first-time commitments to Christ, and at least 40 percent of service people were attending chapel.[70]

As the senior military commander in the Middle East, for years Petraeus had turned a blind eye to evangelical Christian fervor under his command, while ironically leading others in battle against a different type of religious zealotry.

Nuclear Ethics

Ethics and nuclear weapons are two areas that any military commander takes very seriously. So it came as a surprise to Air Force Chief of Staff General Norton Schwartz when, after a journalistic investigation in July 2011, he had to suddenly account for the odd details of the "nuclear ethics program" used in the nuclear weapons training school at Vandenberg Air Force Base.[71] The training, which had been in place for more than two decades, included an Air Force chaplain instructing future missile launch officers on the moral justification for the use of nuclear weapons. The program materials, which included more than a dozen biblical references, also included a statement by former Nazi scientist Wernher von Braun—cited as a moral expert—claiming, "We wanted to see the world spared another conflict such as Germany had just been through and we felt that only by surrendering such a weapon to people who are guided by the Bible could such an assurance to the world be best secured."[72] General Schwartz immediately put an end to the religious-based nuclear ethics training program[73] and soon thereafter issued an unprecedented warning to all Air Force commanders to refrain from endorsing any specific religion, or religion in general.[74,75] Not surprisingly, the one Air Force installation where the letter was not widely distributed was none other than the US Air Force Academy. After four weeks of zero effort on the part of the then-current superintendent[76] to disseminate the memo throughout the service academy, the Military Religious Freedom Foundation rented a billboard outside the school's gates prominently displaying it.[77] Bowing to local pressure, General Gould finally distributed the memo three days later.[78]

Military commanders have to make ethical and moral judgments every day, but with the growing religious fundamentalism in the officer corps, the criteria by which these judgments are made are of increasing concern. When commanders make it clear to their subordinates that "spiritual fitness" is on par with physical fitness, neutrality between religions—and more specifically, between religion and non-religion—is put at risk. More and more, military leaders are confusing their own personal religious beliefs with their moral duties as commanders. To them, it is very difficult to separate religious belief from ethical action, blurring the lines between their duty to their God, their duty to their subordinates, and their duty to their superiors and country.

CASE STUDY #3:
Faith-Based Leadership Development

Glen Shaffer, Robert Boykin, and Johnny Weida may have been among the first prominent generals to capture public attention for promoting their own personal religious beliefs in the course of their official duties, but they certainly aren't isolated cases. Air Force Major Generals Jack Catton and Cecil Richardson provide two additional examples of unapologetic zeal by senior leaders in promoting their fundamentalist religious beliefs to those serving under them. Appearing in uniform and sitting behind his desk in 2006, Catton invited in the *Christian Embassy*, an unofficial but government-sounding organization that is a part of Campus Crusade for Christ,[79] to film his testimony on the need to "build disciples of Christ."[80] Also appearing in the video with Catton were another Air Force major general and two Army brigadier generals, along with Peter Geren, then acting Secretary of the Army.[81] Unlike the findings at the Air Force Academy a year earlier, the Department of Defense's Inspector General deemed that these senior officers endorsing a private organization in uniform was a breach of ethics, and recommended "corrective actions" be taken.[82] Although Catton's career ended when he retired in 2008,[83] Geren was named to a permanent post before the investigation was completed, and Robert L. Caslen Jr. was named as the next commandant of cadets at the West Point. Unsurprisingly, Caslen was eventually promoted to lieutenant general in March 2010, following his tenure as the commandant of the US Army's Command and General Staff College.[84] After seven months as Chief of the Office of Security Cooperation—Iraq, in January 2013 it was announced that Caslen was being promoted to the prestigious post of superintendent (commanding officer) of the United States Military Academy at West Point,[85] an institution that has itself recently suffered complaints of Christian bias.[86]

With so much ado about religious expression in the military, many might wonder where the chaplains were in all of this. Not to be left out, and staying in lock step with his boss, Major General Charles Baldwin (who quietly ordered the RSVP training at the Air Force Academy to be "more Christian,"), then Brigadier General Cecil Richardson (the second highest ranking chaplain for the Air Force) told the *New York Times* in a 2005 interview following the Air Force Academy scandal, "We will not proselytize, but we reserve the right to evangelize the unchurched." In Richardson's defense, he wasn't speaking off the cuff, but rather reading from leadership guidance.[87] Reacting to a firestorm of criticism, the Air Force pulled the guiding document, which had been an official part of its "code of ethics" for chaplains. Although never sanctioned by the Air Force or the Department of Defense, the document, written by an outside private organization, had been routinely given to chaplains at their initial training under the auspices of official policy. Once again, few critics were surprised.[88]

But the story with Richardson did not end there. Three years later, after having been promoted to the highest position in the chaplain corps, the *Air Force Times* interviewed Major General Richardson and asked him about his philosophy on pastoral care of junior military members. The reporter inquired, "Say a Christian chaplain is visited by a troubled airman who isn't interested in hearing about religion. Do you trust your chaplains to advise that airman without steering him toward Jesus?" Without pause, the general smiled and replied, "Well, you know, sometimes Jesus is what they need."[89]

Such a view—as articulated by the highest-ranking chaplain in the Air Force—is not merely his own opinion, but rather an articulation of policy. Part of the reason that unofficial documents and statements such as Cecil Richardson's take on the role of policy is partly a function of the disproportionate overrepresentation of fundamentalist Christian chaplains currently serving on active duty. According to a 2011 report from *The Christian Century*:

> Government statistics show that the nation's corps of chaplains leans heavily toward Christianity, failing to mirror the military it serves. Even though just 3 percent of the military's enlisted personnel and officers call themselves Southern Baptist, Pentecostal or some form of evangelical, 33 percent of military chaplains are members of one of those groups, according to the Pentagon. The disparity could soon widen: data from the Air Force indicate that 87 percent of those seeking to become chaplains are enrolled at evangelical divinity schools.[90]

The overrepresentation of evangelical Christian chaplains took root during the Vietnam War. According to historical scholar Anne Loveland, while many mainline Protestant churches opposed the Vietnam War, many evangelical churches supported it to show their patriotism and oppose communism.[91] While applauding the war effort at home, they commissioned chaplains to minister to the American soldiers abroad. Having gained a foothold in the military arena, their political influence increased throughout the 1970s and flourished in the 1980s.[92] Under the Reagan Administration, regulations for the endorsement of chaplains were modified to make it easier for evangelicals to increase their numbers, and increase their numbers they did. Today Christians fill 98 percent of chaplain billets, even though the general military population is only 68.6 percent Christian.[93] Likewise, of that group, fundamentalist Christian chaplains are disproportionally represented.[94]

More contemporary research also indicates that religious messages are beginning to migrate not only into commanders' offices, but also into the military schoolhouses as well. A 2011 Harvard study found significant evidence of Christian themes present across the professional publications of the Air Force. In a 138-page report, the author summarized his findings:

> The evidence found in the professional journals of the USAF included unique Christian terminology and general themes used in the evangelical Christian subculture. While the majority of the articles in the professional journal of the USAF contained material on air, space, and cyber issues, there was enough evidence to determine that the proselytizing of Christian messages helped contribute to the current environment of evangelical Christian influence in the USAF.[95]

Although the author of the study found no direct evidence of systemic proselytization within professional military educational organizations, the body of evidence clearly illustrates the pervasiveness of Christian fundamentalism in course materials.

Evidence also suggests that senior military leaders have taken action to withhold from public view some of the most egregious instances of religious promotion within the education and training realm. A prime example comes from a 2006 paper entitled "Don't Ask, Don't Tell: A Strategic Consideration." The research was conducted by a senior Coast Guard officer who authored a paper as a student thesis at the US Army War College, which argued against the repeal of the military's gay ban. It cited evidence that "anal sex leads to leakage of fecal material that can easily become chronic."[96] Furthermore, the author cited the Bible and numerous fundamentalist Christian sources to condemn homosexual behavior as immoral.[97] Although the document had not been officially classified, it was categorized in such a manner that it was neither searchable nor accessible to anyone outside of official military channels. It remains available to faculty and students who wish to access it for their own "research" needs but is held in a secure area with all other classified material.

These examples illustrate the extent to which religious dogma is creeping into the military educational realm with such "research" going unchallenged. Calls for Congress to close the military's war college system in 2012 were due partly to the military's inability to self-correct.[98] As a former war college faculty member put it, "Military culture has become far out of sync with the culture of the society that pays its way."[99]

ANALYSIS

The case studies presented in this paper are neither isolated nor happenstance aberrations. Although these case studies are now nearly a decade old, they still illustrate how effectively the fundamentalist Christian movement has been integrated into the culture and structure of the US military over the decades. To test a hypothesis of pluralism, an informal study was conducted in 2010 with groups of officers from across the military services using "The Oath of Equal Character."[100] Although the oath was originally authored from a Christian's perspective, one could substitute their own belief set, as applicable. Simply put, the oath is as follows:

> I am a <Christian>. I will not use my position to influence individuals or the chain of command to adopt <Christianity>, because I believe that soldiers who are not
>
> <Christians> are just as trustworthy, honorable and good as those who are. Their standards are as high as mine. Their integrity is beyond reproach. They will not lie, cheat or steal, and they will not fail when called upon to serve. I trust them completely and without reservation. They can trust me in exactly the same way.

When informally responding in a military academic setting, 35 percent of mid-grade military officers admitted that they could never affirm the oath because "it isn't true." In other words, they believe that someone who doesn't share their own faith cannot be as trustworthy as someone else who does.[101] This was a remarkable finding given that trust underpins nearly every aspect of military command. There are officers in command at all levels who believe, in stark contrast to the constitutional prohibition against religious tests for any and all public offices, that religious belief congruence among group members is necessary to attain mutual trust in an organization.102 For this group of officers, the guiding leadership principle is not one based on professional ethics, but rather a variant based on a narrow, sectarian, religious-moral view.

One of the more clever arguments supporting the religious-moral view is rooted in Sekulow's "warrior ethos." To those who ascribe to this view, one's moral character is synonymous with his or her religious devotion. The religious-moral view contends that: (1) one must be moral to be a military professional; (2) those who are not religious are of a lesser moral fitness; therefore, (3) those with the strongest religious convictions are "best fit" to serve in the military, particularly in a position of authority or command. This religious-moral view underlies the "warrior ethos" characterized into "three disciplines: physical, mental and moral."[103] To preserve the moral standing of the warrior ethos, it becomes necessary to prevent all external influences from meddling with the existing organizational—culture[104]—the same culture in which the fundamentalist Christian movement has been so effective in infiltrating.[105] This is one reason why there was such animosity within the senior ranks of the military toward the repeal of "Don't Ask, Don't Tell" policy in 2011, allowing homosexuals to serve openly. Because many adherents to the religious-moral view see homosexuality as "an abomination unto their particular God," homosexuals are thus felt to be immoral and, therefore, unfit to serve *or* lead.[106] Among the many problems with relying on a religious-moral view,[107] two of the most critical are (1) the role of organizational exemplars in the socialization process; and, (2) the structural exclusivity created by fostering a strong internal culture with deeply embedded sectarian religious values.

Theoretical Considerations

The military socializes its members as well as any institution or organization could. As part of the socialization process during basic military training, individuals are stripped of their identities and intensely subjugated to those senior to them in the chain of command. Once an individual is appropriately "broken down" and has relinquished his or her personal identity in the basic training environment, the military trainers begin the process of building the trainee back up into a collective identity.[108] During this stage, individuals engage in a sense-making process to better understand how to deal with the nascent complexity of adopting the new attitudes, beliefs, and behaviors.[109] Organizational exemplars become a profound influence, particularly in military training. As part of the sense-making process, individuals identify those around them who best epitomize success in the organization. With such a limited scope, the exemplars chosen are often the military training instructors and training commanders themselves. The resilience of the development that occurs during initial organizational socialization[110] cannot be overstated. Thus, when military training leaders, such as many of those identified in this paper, contaminate the socialization process with their own personal beliefs, individuals cannot effectively make a distinction between the exemplar's personal and professional attitudes, beliefs, and behaviors. As the individuals internalize and emulate the behaviors of the organizational exemplars, a fractal, self-replicating effect takes hold. The fundamentalist Christian movement, understanding of the power of exemplars in the socialization process, is clearly on par with the military. Not only do they accommodate the system-socialization process as well as any military training organization, they have also been able to infiltrate and co-opt certain facets of military training itself at all levels, and thus perpetuate the religious-moral view within the military.

The second major concern with a religious-moral view is rooted in its desire for exclusivity, a characteristic embraced by both military and religious organizations alike. The very nature of the evangelical Christian tradition is to save the souls of everyone outside the set of already professed Christians.[111] One is either in the group or not in the group. Examining the religious conflicts between Protestants and Catholics, Sunnis and Shiites, or the recent division in the American Episcopal Church, exclusivity defines the boundaries of religious groups.

Likewise, the culture of the military has become increasingly exclusive. Conservative activist Elaine Donnelly, like Sekulow, argues for the necessity to maintain the status quo within military culture to preserve the military's effectiveness. Regardless of the veracity of the argument, they contend that military commanders should be trusted to train their troops as they see fit without any unwanted outside influence of any kind.

One critic of this argument, international relations scholar Andrew Bacevich, warned of the danger of "praetorianism, warriors becoming enamored with their moral superiority and impatient with the failings of those they are charged to defend."[112] Reflecting on the civilian-military relations crisis instigated by General Stanley McChrystal that led to his firing in 2010 (after a *Rolling Stone* magazine exposé), Bacevich explains:

> The smug disdain for high-ranking civilians casually expressed by McChrystal and his chief lieutenants—along with the conviction that "Team America," as these officers style themselves, was bravely holding out against a sea of stupidity and corruption—suggests that the officer corps of the United States is not immune to this affliction. [113]

Just as with fundamentalist Christian organizations that view themselves as possessing a superior belief system, even absolute truth, the parallel belief within the military holds that only members of that culture represent the true America—"Team America."[114] Although McChrystal's words and deeds had nothing to do with religious fundamentalism, they are indicative of the widening gap between military culture and American culture in general. Any added layer of religious fundamentalism only promises to increase civil-military tension, especially when espoused by those who view God as a higher authority than the chain of command. Soldiers are taught to "obey any lawful and moral order."[115] However, allowing the word "moral" to take on a dogmatic religious connotation opens a Pandora's box of sectarian rivalry and institutional fracture.

Thus, civilian leaders must proactively and preemptively draw a clear line for senior officers who believe that they must, in their official capacity, win hearts and minds for their particular god. Such a challenge to a democratic body becomes especially difficult to meet when many of those elected leaders have the same sectarian religious convictions as the military leaders under their charge. The evidence has shown that too often problems with commanders who endorse fundamentalist Christianity in their professional roles are not only overlooked, but in some cases, defended or endorsed.[116] The following section proposes several ways in which this might be corrected.

RECOMMENDATIONS

Although this paper was originally written for and published by the Center for Inquiry in 2013, its relevance has not diminished based on the continued string of examples conflating military leadership and religious beliefs. Thus, adopting any of the following recommendations today would be an important contribution to restore behavior that avoids the improprieties of official endorsement of religious beliefs. Whether it comes from the Executive or Legislative branches (preferably both), positive action is needed to establish clear behavioral limits and proscriptions for military members at all levels.[117] None of the recommendations offered here would prevent anyone from expressing his or her own beliefs just because they don a military uniform. However, because religious beliefs are a deeply personal and unavoidably divisive and sectarian matter, they must remain personal and completely out of the professional realm, where neutrality must be the primary goal.

1. **Beware claims of false progress.** As noted by Blake Page at West Point, the nonreligious still have little voice, little support, and little respect. Likewise, the Air Force Academy's declaration of "Mission Accomplished" with respect to religious diversity misses the point. We need to call a charade a charade and hold military leaders accountable for real change that eliminates all religious tests for military service, most critically the implicit tests that so many aspiring young service members face on a daily basis. The point is *beyond just* tolerance of religious beliefs or lack of religious beliefs, but rather *strict and clear institutional neutrality* on the matter of religious belief overall. To this day, the Air Force Academy specifically, and the military services generally, have failed to adequately understand this most basic premise.

2. **Stop treating command-sponsored functions like sporting events.**[118] Everyone has the right to bow their head and silently pray in any way they see fit. A moment of silence allows for all to observe it without any undue

influence or seeming endorsement of a specific sect or religious belief in general. When it comes to religious rights, majority rule is irrelevant. At private events, where there really is a way for individuals to freely opt in or out—and without professional repercussions—judgment should be left to those organizing the event.

3. **Hold commanders accountable to a "Grade School Standard" for inappropriate speech.**[119] No longer should coercive evangelizing or proselytizing result in a promotion or pay increase. A junior military member can be court-martialed for inappropriate speech to a senior leader. The same standard should be held in the other direction. In fact, senior enlisted and officers should be held to a higher standard. Whether insubordination or abuse of rank and authority through coercive evangelizing, inappropriate speech that undermines good order and discipline should never be tolerated, and always be punished. We don't let privates speak out of line without firm consequences. We should hold colonels and generals to an equal, if not more exacting standard.

4. **"Reprise: Don't Ask, Don't Tell."** As a commander, this is the best advice to guide discussions of your own spiritual beliefs or those of your subordinates—stop assuming others think like you, and don't ask if you suspect they don't. What religious beliefs they may or may not hold do not matter, precisely because the Constitution and human decency says they do not.

5. **If someone suggests it would be a good idea to rename your unit "The Crusaders" as you deploy to the Middle East, don't.** Commanders continue to find creative ways to promote their religious beliefs and make the act seem official. It is not, and they must stop pretending it is. "Tradition" is often nothing more than a thinly veiled excuse to keep doing what you want to do without having to appropriately justify it. Past violations of the Constitution do not excuse continued violations of the Constitution.

6. **The Golden Rule applies to you too.** Violations are violations, even if the majority of people do not express concern. You tolerate a certain behavior likely because you just happen to agree. If you did not, you would be the loudest voice in the opposition.

7. **Not everything looks better in camouflage.** Stop printing official military logos on Bibles and other religious paraphernalia to give them the appearance of "military issue" literature. If you think this is not a problem, consider doing the same thing with the Holy Qur'an and distributing it. If you find this idea offensive, you get the point.

8. **The show must not go on.** It almost defied understanding how, in 2010, Army leaders engendered controversy by sponsoring the "Rock the Fort" evangelical concert at Fort Bragg in North Carolina. When challenged, they responded that any group who wanted to put on a concert to promote their beliefs would receive equal support. That was until Sergeant Justin Griffith planned a pro-atheism event called "Rock Beyond Belief." The

event was nearly cancelled when Army leadership refused for months to provide support.[120] These controversies illustrate the wisdom of neutrality. It is time to put an end to all command-endorsed religious activities, evangelistic rallies, prayer breakfasts, and command-advertised religious retreats. There are few clearer examples of government entanglement with religion and religious organizations—a clear and present affront to the very First Amendment the military is tasked with defending.

9. **Consider reforms to the chaplaincy.** The military should explore options on how to best provide secular members of the armed forces with the same rights and benefits that religious members receive, including the possibility of instituting a secular program similar to the religious chaplaincy program. One of the more prominent recommendations by Jason Torpy of the Military Association of Atheists and Freethinkers is to include a population of humanist chaplains in the chaplain corps of all services, to serve the needs of *all* service members, not just the religious ones. Having metastasized with fundamentalist Christianity, measures are necessary for military organizations to bring the proportions of spiritual leaders into better alignment with the population being served. Relying on lessons learned from a recent debacle involving the Department of the Army, Arlington National Cemetery, and the funeral of a nonreligious WWII veteran, the military must afford respect to all who serve in uniform, regardless of one's religious or irreligious beliefs.[121]

10. **End the quasi-official status of evangelical groups.** The best way to adhere to guiding legal prescriptions is to let religious organizations do as they wish, but do not help or hinder them. As a commander, what you do for one, you must do for all, and if you cannot do for all, do not do for any.[122]

11. **Before you can take command, publicly affirm the Oath of Equal Character.** When they take command, officers and senior enlisted individuals should acknowledge that those under them have no obligation to change their belief systems. A good Soldier, Sailor, Airman, Marine, or Coastguardsman can hold a variety of beliefs or a variety of doubts, and commanders and leaders should publicly acknowledge this before being entrusted with responsibility over them.[123, 124]

12. **Stop the next Crusade before it begins.** Change the wording of General Order 1B to "evangelizing or proselytizing of any religion." [125] Although a very simple change, banning any sort of aggressive recruitment of military members in another country, for reasons of national security, just makes sense.

CONCLUSION

Let me give you a word on the philosophy of reform. The whole history of the progress of human liberty shows that all concessions yet made to her august claims, have been born of earnest struggle. If there is no struggle, there is no progress. This struggle may be a moral one, or it may be a physical one, and it may be both moral and physical, but it must be a struggle. Find out just what any people will quietly submit to—and you have found out the exact measure of injustice and wrong, which will be imposed upon them. The limits of tyrants are prescribed by the endurance of those whom they oppress. Power concedes nothing without a demand. It never did and it never will.

—Frederick Douglass, August 3, 1857

The inappropriate behavior of fundamentalist Christian military leaders has not changed over the past decade when this paper was first written and published, and given the plethora of similar examples that we are witnessing in 2021, it is clear the behaviors are not likely to change on their own. Ample rules and regulations remain in place to appropriately separate the religious beliefs of military leaders from their official duties and responsibilities. Most lacking, however, remains the social and political will to enforce the existing rules and hold military commanders accountable for breaches of conduct.

The cases outlined in this paper raise the fundamental question captured by the classic Latin dictum, *quis custodiet ipsos custodes*—who will guard the guards themselves? Based on the evidence presented herein, the status quo remains resilient. Military institutions have shown significant reticence to discipline any of their own who use the power of their official positions to promote their own fundamentalist religious beliefs. Fundamentalist Christianity continues to run rampant through the senior ranks of the military simply because it is allowed to do so. After all, every system is perfectly designed to yield the behaviors observed.

The answer to this dictum is that the American people, both elected officials and ordinary citizens, are tasked with guarding the guards. As the previous pages make clear, there continues to be a serious problem with religious endorsement in the US Armed Forces which needs to be addressed and changed. It is up to those with social and political power to demand this action. If this problem persists, members of the military will continue to face hostility and indoctrination, and the US government will continue to experience public relations problems in future military missions. If it is addressed, the US military could become a neutral and safe space for members of all religious backgrounds, and none at all, and the image of the America, as seen through its military forces abroad, could change from one of Christianity to one of a diverse people united for liberty and justice for all.

REFERENCES

Allen, Bob. "Boykin Broke Rules in Speeches to Churches, Probe Determines." *Ethics Daily.* August 20, 2004.

Americans United for Separation of Church and State. "AU, ACLU Investigate Possible Bias Over Concerts At Fort Bragg." May 2011. https://www.au.org/church-state/may-2011-church-state/people-events/au-aclu-investigate-possible-bias-over-concerts-at. Last accessed December 26, 2012.

Bacevich, Andrew. "Endless War, a Recipe for Four-Star Arrogance." *The Washington Post.* June 27, 2010.

Brandies, Louis. "What Publicity Can Do." *Harper's Weekly.* December 20, 1913.

Bruni, Frank. "Bush Tangles with McCain over Campaign Finance Reform." *New York Times.* December 14, 1999.

Bush, George W. "Jesus Day." State of Texas, Official Memorandum. Office of the Governor. June 10, 2000. Archived at http://www.pbs.org/wgbh/pages/frontline/shows/jesus/art/pop_jesusday.jpg. Last accessed December 26, 2012.

Cooperman, Alan. "Air Force Withdraws Paper for Chaplains." *Washington Post.* October 11, 2005.

Cooperman, Alan. "Inquiry Sought Over Evangelical Video." *Washington Post.* December 11, 2006.

Chicago Tribune. "Academy Sees Religious Bias." June 5, 2005.

Congressional Record (House), v.149, pt.19, October 28, 2003, 26006.

Department of the Army. Pamphlet 600-63-12. Sept 1,1987.

Department of the Army. Regulation 600-63. Sept 7, 2010.

Department of Defense Office of the Inspector General. "Alleged Misconduct by DoD Officials Concerning Christian Embassy." July 2007.

Department of Defense Office of the Inspector General, "Allegations of Improprieties Related to Public Speaking: Lieutenant General William Boykin, US Army, Deputy Undersecretary of Defense for Intelligence.' August 5, 2004. Case Number: H03L89967206.

Goodstein, Laurie. "Air Force Chaplain Tells of Academy Proselytizing." *New York Times.* May 12, 2005.

Goodstein, Laurie. "Air Force Chaplain Says She Was Removed for Being Critical." *New York Times.* May 15, 2005.

Goodstein, Laurie. "Evangelicals Are a Growing Force in the Military Chaplain Corps." *New York Times.* July 12, 2005.

Grant, Paula M. "The Need for (More) New Guidance Regarding Religions Expression in the Air Force." *Attitudes Aren't Free.* Montgomery: Air University Press. 2010.

Hill, Michael. "Blake Page, West Point Cadet, Quits Military Academy Over Religion." *Huffington Post.* December 5, 2012.

Holy Bible. King James Version. Matthew 7:24–29; Luke 6:46–49.

Klingenschmitt, Gordon J. "Burning Bibles and Censoring Prayers: Is That Defending our Constitution?" *Attitudes Aren't Free.* Montgomery: Air University Press. 2010

Leopold, Jason. Army's "Spiritual Fitness" Test Comes Under Fire. *Truthout.* January 5, 2011.

Levy, D.A., Blass, F.R. (2006). "Can we Over-socialize? Applying the Systems Socialization Model to US Military Accession Programs." *Global Education Journal.*1, 3–17.

Liscombe, Jonathan. "Evangelism in the Profession of Arms: An Evaluation of Evangelical Christian Proselytizing in the Professional Journal of the United States Air Force." Unpublished thesis, Harvard University, March 2011.

Loveland, Anne. American Evangelicals and the US Military, 1942–1993. Louisiana State University Press. 1997.

Lynn, Barry W. "Religion in the Military: Finding the Proper Balance." *Attitudes Aren't Free*. Montgomery: Air University Press. 2010.

Parco, James E. and Fagin, Barry S. "The One True Religion in the Military." *Attitudes Aren't Free*. Montgomery: Air University Press. 2007.

Parco, J.E. and Levy, D.A. Eds. *Attitudes Aren't Free: Thinking Deeply About Diversity in the US Armed Forces*. Montgomery, AL: Air University Press, 2010.

Rhee, Joseph. "US Military Weapons Inscribed With Secret 'Jesus' Bible Codes." *ABC Nightline News*. January 18, 2010.

Ricks, Markeshia. "*READ THIS!* MRFF Plants Billboard in Academy Backyard." *Air Force Times*. September 28, 2011.

Rodda, Chris. *Liars For Jesus: The Religious Right's Alternate Version of American History Vol. 1*. BookSurge Publishing. 2006.

Rodda, Chris. "Against All Enemies, Foreign and Domestic." *Attitudes Aren't Free*. Montgomery: Air University Press. 2010.

Rodda, Chris. "Petraeus Endorses 'Spiritual Handbook,' Betrays 21% of Our Troops." *Huffington Post*. August, 17, 2008.

Russ, Lee. "What First Amendment? Proselytizing and Christians in the US Military." *Watching the Watchers*, Sep. 12, 2007.

Sekulow, Jay and Ash, Robert. "Religious Rights and Military Service." *Attitudes Aren't Free*. Montgomery: Air University Press. 2010.

Shanker, Tom and Goodstein, Laurie. "Air Force Chaplain Submits Resignation." *New York Times*. June 22, 2005.

Sharlet, Jeff. "Jesus Killed Mohammed." *Harper's Magazine*. May 2009. 31–43.

Torpy, Jason. "Arlington Cemetery Confirms Secular Policy." *Secular Coalition for America*. September 15, 2011.

United States Air Force. Report to the Secretary of the Air Force: Air Force Inspector General Summary Report Concerning the Handling of Sexual Assault Cases at the United States Air Force Academy. September 14, 2004.

United States Air Force. "The Report of the Headquarters Review Group Concerning the Religious Climate at the U. S. Air Force Academy." June 22, 2005.

Weinstein, Michael L. and Seay, Davin. *With God on Our Side: One Man's War Against an Evangelical Coup in America's Military*. New York: Thomas Dunne Books, 2006.

Weinstein, Mikey. "Petraeus, Supporter of Military's 'Spiritual Fitness' Program, Should Have Been Fired Years Ago." *Truthout*. November 20, 2012.

Weller, Robert. "Air Force General Cut From Promotion List: Was Involved in Religious Furor." Associated Press. August 3, 2005.

White, Josh. "Officers' Roles in Christian Video Are Called Ethics Breach." *Washington Post*. August 4, 2007.

Winn, Patrick. "Chief of Chaplain Speaks Out." *Air Force Times*, August 7, 2008.

Zubeck, Pam. "AFA Finds Faith Bias Roots Deep," *Gazette*, November 20, 2004, A14.

ENDNOTES

[1] Lynn, Barry. "Religion in the Military." *Attitudes Aren't Free*. 2010. Section I.

[2] Cooperman, Alan. "Air Force Withdraws Paper for Chaplains." *Washington Post*. October 11, 2005. A03. See http://www.washingtonpost.com/wp-dyn/content/article/2005/10/10/AR2005101001582_pf.html Last accessed December 26, 2012.

[3] Hill, Michael. "Blake Page, West Point Cadet, Quits Military Academy Over Religion." *Huffington Post*. December 5, 2012. http://www.huffingtonpost.com/2012/12/05/blake-page-west-point-cadet-quits-over-religion_n_2247067.html Last accessed December 26, 2012.

[4] Telephone interview, December 7, 2012.

[5] According to the Military Religious Freedom Foundation, "Over 30,000 active duty members of the United States Armed Forces have come to our foundation as spiritual rape victims/tormentees, with hundreds more contacting MRFF each day. 96 percent of them are Christians themselves." http://www.militaryreligiousfreedom.org/about/. Last accessed December 26, 2012.

[6] Bruni, Frank. "Bush tangles with McCain over Campaign Finance Reform." *New York Times*. December 14, 1999. See http://www.nytimes.com/1999/12/14/us/bush-tangles-with-mccain-over-campaign-financing.html?pagewanted=all&src=pm.

[7] See bio at http://www.whitehouse.gov/about/presidents/georgewbush. Last accessed December 26, 2012.

[8] September 11th Digital Archives. See http://911digitalarchive.org/ Last accessed December 26, 2012.

[9] As an example, on June 10, 2000, then Governor George W. Bush proclaimed June 10th as "Jesus Day" as an example to all Texans for "moral leadership." By virtue of such actions, he saw no line separating church and state, and many of his soon-to-be military subordinates were quick to take note. http://www.pbs.org/wgbh/pages/frontline/shows/jesus/art/pop_jesusday.jpg. Last accessed December 26, 2012.

[10] Bush, George W. "Remarks on Arrival at the White House and an Exchange with Reporters." The American Presidency Project. September 16, 2001. See http://www.presidency.ucsb.edu/mediaplay.php?id=63346&admin=43. Last accessed December 26, 2012.

[11] The Holy Bible (1984). Ephesians 6:10–18. New International Version.

[12] The Holy Bible, 1 Peter 2:15.

[13] The Holy Bible, Psalm 33:18–22.

[14] Draper, Robert. And He Shall Be Judged. *GQ*, June 2009 available at http://www.gq.com/news-politics/newsmakers/200905/donald-rumsfeld-administration-peers-detractors. Last accessed December 26, 2012.

[15] As reported by noted by Chris Rodda in her May 3, 2011 article entitled "We're Not at War With Islam, But Let's Do Everything We Can to Make it Look Like We Are" available at http://www.huffingtonpost.com/chris-rodda/were-not-at-war-with- isla_b_857018.html, the commander of the SEAL unit, who had the respon-

sibility to signal up the chain of command that the mission to kill Osama bin Laden had been successfully accomplished, he took it upon himself to embellish his communication by prefacing the code word with "For God and Country." Last accessed December 26, 2012.

[16] Allen, Bob. "Boykin Broke Rules in Speeches to Churches, Probe Determines." *Ethics Daily.* August 20, 2004, http://www.ethicsdaily.com/boykin-broke-rules-in-speeches-to-churches-probe-determines-cms-4612. Last accessed December 26, 2012.

[17] Congressional Record (House), v.149, pt.19, October 28, 2003, 26006.

[18] Congressional Record.

[19] Department of Defense Office of the Inspector General, "Allegations of Improprieties Related to Public Speaking: Lieutenant General William Boykin, US Army, Deputy Undersecretary of Defense for Intelligence. August 5, 2004. Case Number: H03L89967206. www.dodig.mil/fo/foia/ERR/h03l89967206.pdf. Last accessed December 26, 2012.

[20] Congressional Record (House), pg. 26007.

[21] On July 16, 2012, Boykin was named executive vice president at the far-right Family Research Council. http://www.frc.org/newsroom/lt-gen-jerry-boykin-joins-family-research-council-as-executive-vice-president. Last accessed December 26, 2012.

[22] See bio at http://aclj.org/jay-sekulow. Last accessed December 26, 2012.

[23] See bio at http://www.au.org/about/people/lynn. Last accessed December 26, 2012.

[24] Parco, J.E. and Levy, D.A. Eds. *Attitudes Aren't Free: Thinking Deeply About Diversity in the US Armed Forces.* Montgomery, AL: Air University Press, 2010.

[25] Sekulow, Jay A., and Ash, Robert. "Religious Rights and Military Service" *Attitudes Aren't Free.* Montgomery: Air University Press. 2010.

[26] Lynn, Barry W. "Religion in the Military: Finding the Proper Balance." *Attitudes Aren't Free.* Montgomery: Air University Press. 2010.

[27] Lynn, "Religion in the Military."[28] Sekulow and Ash, "Religious Rights."[29] New Life Church in Colorado Springs, Colorado, was identified by *Outreach Magazine* in 2007 as one of the fifty most influential churches in America. See http://churchrelevance.com/resources/top-churches-in-america/. Last accessed December 26, 2012.

[30] See http://www.militaryreligiousfreedom.org. Last accessed December 26, 2012.

[31] Report to the Secretary of the Air Force: Air Force Inspector General Summary Report Concerning the Handling of Sexual Assault Cases at the United States Air Force Academy. September 14, 2004. http://www.af.mil/shared/media/document/AFD-060726-033.pdf. Last accessed December 26, 2012.

[32] For a complete documented narrative of the religious establishment problems leading up to the USAFA scandal, see Americans United report included as Attachment H (page 52–65) of "The Report of the Headquarters Review Group Concerning the Religious Climate at the U. S. Air Force Academy."[33] "The Report of the Headquarters Review Group Concerning the Religious Climate at the US. Air Force Academy." June 22, 2005. http://www.af.mil/pdf/HQ_Review_Group_Report.pdf. Attachment H, page 8 of 16. Last accessed December 26, 2012.

[34] The Holy Bible. See Matthew 7:24–29 and Luke 6:46–49.

[35] "The Report of the Headquarters Review Group Concerning the Religious Climate at the U. S. Air Force Academy." June 22, 2005.

[36] "Report of the Headquarters Review Group," 57.

[37] See military bio at http://www.af.mil/information/bios/bio.asp?bioID=6967. Last accessed December 26, 2012.

[38] Attendee interview, July 7, 2004.

[39] Goodstein, Laurie. "Air Force Chaplain Tells of Academy Proselytizing." *New York Times*. May 12, 2005. http://www.nytimes.com/2005/05/12/education/12academy.html?pagewanted=all. Last accessed December 26, 2012.

[40] Author's personal meeting notes, November 17, 2004.

[41] Zubeck, Pam. "AFA Finds Faith Bias Roots Deep," *Gazette*, November 20, 2004, A14.

[42] A self-described fundamentalist Christian, acknowledged in a telephone phone interview on April 18, 2012.

[43] Goodstein, "Air Force Chaplain Tells."[44] Goodstein, Laurie. "Air Force Chaplain Says She Was Removed for Being Critical." *New York Times*. May 15, 2005. http://www.nytimes.com/2005/05/15/national/15chaplain.html. Last accessed December 26, 2012.

[45] "Academy Sees Religious Bias." *Chicago Tribune*. June 5, 2005. http://articles.chicagotribune.com/keyword/religious- intolerance/featured/3. Last accessed December 26, 2012.

[46] Shanker, Tom and Goodstein, Laurie. "Air Force Chaplain Submits Resignation." *New York Times*. June 22, 2005. http://www.nytimes.com/2005/06/22/politics/22chaplain.html. Last accessed December 26, 2012.

[47] Headed by a self-proclaimed fundamentalist Christian.

[48] See "The Report of the Headquarters Review Group Concerning the Religious Climate at the U. S. Air Force Academy." www.foxnews.com/projects/pdf/HQ_Review_Group_Report.pdf. (22 June 2005).

[49] Zubeck, Pam. "Commandant at AFA won't be promoted." *Gazette*. August 2, 2005. http://www.gazette.com/news/weida-17377-force-air.html. Last accessed December 26, 2012.

[50] Receiving all the backpay for a promotion that had been on hold during the controversy.

[51] Sharlet, Jeff. "Jesus Killed Mohammed." *Harper's Magazine*. May 2009. http://harpers.org/archive/2009/05/0082488. Last accessed December 26, 2012.

[52] See military bio at http://www.af.mil/information/bios/bio.asp?bioID=5596. Last accessed December 26, 2012.

[53] Koen, Andy. "Religious Reforms Celebrated at the Academy." November 1, 2012. http://www.koaa.com/news/religious- reforms-celebrated-at-academy/. Last accessed December 26, 2012.

[54] As reported by "Violation on Video" by the Military Religious Freedom Foundation. See http://www.militaryreligiousfreedom.org/weekly-watch/12-12-08/gods_soldier.html. Last accessed December 26, 2012.

[55] Rodda, Chris. "Against All Enemies, Foreign and Domestic." *Attitudes Aren't Free*. Montgomery: Air University Press. 2010. http://books.google.com/books?id=-5FnvJEclewC&lpg=PP1&pg=PA69#v=onepage&q&f=false. Last accessed December 26, 2012.

[56] CNN, May 20, 2009. "Military burns unsolicited Bibles sent to Afghanistan." http://articles.cnn.com/2009-05-20/world/us.military.bibles.burned_1_bibles-al-jazeera-english-military- personnel?_s=PM:WORLD. Last accessed December 26, 2012.

[57] Klingenschmitt, G.L. "Burning Bibles and Censoring Prayers." *Attitudes Aren't Free.* Montgomery: Air University Press. 2010, 26.

[58] Cooperman, Alan. "Navy Chaplain Guilty of Disobeying Order." *Washington Post.* September 15, 2006. http://www.washingtonpost.com/wp-dyn/content/article/2006/09/14/AR2006091401544.html. Last accessed December 26, 2012.

[59] Dated March 13, 2006. See paragraph 2(k). See http://www.tac.usace.army.mil/deploymentcenter/tac_docs/GO-1B Policy.pdf Last accessed December 26, 2012.

[60] Technically speaking, proselytization and evangelizing are different terms with different meanings. Webster's defines "proselytize" as "the conversion or attempted conversion of a person from one opinion, belief or religion to another." Likewise, "evangelize" is defined as "to convert or seek to convert someone to Christianity." Christian advocates often identify the distinction between the words in terms of the method of conversion: forcible conversion (proselytization) versus voluntary conversion (evangelizing). However, in a military context where a commander or any person in a position of authority or higher rank is promoting their own beliefs, the difference is nil. Unlike civilian contexts where individuals have the freedom to walk away or ignore unwanted solicitations, telling a military superior "Go away and please stop evangelizing me!" is not an option. Any act of evangelizing in an organizational structure where there is a profound power differential between individuals (as in military rank) is tantamount to proselytization.

[61] Rodda, "Against All Enemies."

[62] Rodda, "Against All Enemies."

[63] Sharlet, "Jesus Killed Mohammed."

[64] Rhee, Joseph. "US Military Weapons Inscribed with Secret 'Jesus' Bible Codes." January 18, 2010. See http://abcnews.go.com/Blotter/us-military-weapons-inscribed-secret-jesus-bible-codes/story?id=9575794#Tt0d40rwNh4. Last accessed December 26, 2012.

[65] Link to a downloadable copy of the pamphlet is at http://militaryatheists.org/advocacy/spirituality/. Last accessed December 26, 2012.

[66] Leopold, Jason. Army's "Spiritual Fitness" Test Comes Under Fire. *Truthout.* January 5, 2011. http://truth- out.org/news/item/268:army percentE2 percent80 percent99s- percentE2 percent80 percent9Cspiritual-fitness percentE2 percent80 percent9D-test-comes-under-fire. Last accessed December 26, 2012.

[67] Department of the Army Pamphlet 600-63-12, Section 3, para (a). Sept 1,1987, page 1. Although later revisions of the Army

Regulation 600-63, chapter 6-2 (Sept 7, 2010) have been revised to state "Army leaders should develop an awareness of the lifestyles, cultural backgrounds, stages of development, possible relationships to religious beliefs, and the needs of their Soldiers, Army civilians, and Family members," commanders have routinely taken "spiritual fitness" as license to push their own religious beliefs.

[68] Weinstein, Mikey. "Petraeus, Supporter of Military's 'Spiritual Fitness' Program, Should Have Been Fired Years Ago." *Truthout.* November 20, 2012. http://truth-out.org/opinion/item/12869-petraeus-should-have-been-fired-years-ago. Last accessed December 26, 2012.

[69] Rodda, Chris. "Petraeus Endorses 'Spiritual Handbook,' Betrays 21% of Our Troops." *Huffington Post.* August 17, 2008. http://www.huffingtonpost.com/chris-rodda/petraeus-endorses-spiritu_b_119242.html. Last accessed December 26, 2012.

[70] Mickey. "Army chaplain Brent Causey: His hero is wife." *Baptist Press*. November 11, 2011. http://www.bpnews.net/bpnews.asp?id=36548. Last accessed February 16, 2013.

[71] Leopold, Jason. "Air Force Cites New Testament, Ex-Nazi, to Train Officers on Ethics of Launching Nuclear Weapons." Truthout. July 27, 2011. See http://www.truth-out.org/air-force-cites-new-testament-ex-nazi-train-officers-ethics-launching-nuclear-weapons/1311776738. Last accessed December 26, 2012.

[72] Leopold, "Air Force Cites New Testament."

[73] Ricks, Markeshia. "Air Force Yanks Nuclear Ethics Course." *Air Force Times*. August 4, 2011. See http://www.airforcetimes.com/news/2011/08/air-force-nuclear-ethics-course-yanked-080411/. Last accessed December 26, 2012.

[74] Ricks, Markeshia. "Schwartz: Don't Endorse Religious Programs." *Air Force Times*. September 16, 2011. See http://www.airforcetimes.com/news/2011/09/air-force-schwartz-warns-commanders-on-religious-programs-091611/. Last accessed December 26, 2012.

[75] See original letter at the Military Religious Freedom Foundation archive at http://www.google.com/url?sa=t&rct=j&q=&esrc=s&source=web&cd=1&sqi=2&ved=0C-CgQFjAA&url=http percent3A percent2F percent2Fww w.militaryreligiousfreedom.org percent2Fdocs percent2Fgen_schwartz_letter_religion_neutralilty.pdf&ei=zlLdTv_5A8ewiQK0wLHqAw&u   sg=AFQjCNFpw47vY-mCKb-u3ojWA-PUGveQnRA&sig2=vdRMBfkzVhuG7wEa2GUbMw. Last accessed December 26, 2012.

[76] Lieutenant General Michael Gould, a self-proclaimed evangelical Christian.

[77] Zubeck, Pam. "It's a Sign!" *Colorado Springs Independent*. September 27, 2011. See http://www.csindy.com/IndyBlog/archives/2011/09/28/its-a-sign. Last accessed December 26, 2012.

[78] Email dated September 30, 2011, on file with the author.

[79] Christian Embassy official website at http://www.christianembassy.com/content.asp?contentid=447. Last accessed December 26, 2012.

[80] Cooperman, Alan. "Inquiry Sought Over Evangelical Video." *Washington Post*. December 11, 2006. http://www.washingtonpost.com/wp-dyn/content/article/2006/12/10/AR2006121000883.html. Last accessed December 26, 2012.

[81] Although the Christian Embassy immediately removed the video from their website, it remains accessible at https://www.youtube.com/watch?v=BLhpoRP8VkE. Last accessed December 26, 2012.

[82] White, Josh. "Officers' Roles in Christian Video Are Called Ethics Breach." *Washington Post*. August 4, 2007. http://www.washingtonpost.com/wp-dyn/content/article/2007/08/03/AR2007080301907.html. Last accessed December 26, 2012.

[83] See official bio at http://www.af.mil/information/bios/bio.asp?bioID=4960. Last accessed December 26, 2012.

[84] See official US Army website at http://carl.army.mil/resources/ftlvn/command.asp. Last accessed December 26, 2012.

[85] See report: ttp://militaryatheists.org/news/2013/01/christian-embassy-video-culprit-given-top-post-at-west-point/.

[86] See report: http://www.csmonitor.com/USA/Military/2012/1207/Too-much-religion-at-military-academies-West-Point-cadet- revives-charge.

[87] Cooperman, Alan. "Air Force Withdraws Paper for Chaplains." *Washington Post*. October 11, 2005. http://www.washingtonpost.com/wp-dyn/content/article/2005/10/10/AR2005101001582.html. Last accessed December 26, 2012.

[88] Goodstein, Laurie. "Evangelicals Are a Growing Force in the Military Chaplain Corps." *New York Times.* July 12, 2005. http://www.nytimes.com/2005/07/12/national/12chaplains.html?pagewanted=all. Last accessed December 26, 2012.

[89] Winn, Patrick. "Chief of Chaplain Speaks Out." *Air Force Times*, August 7, 2008 http://www.airforcetimes.com/news/2008/08/airforce_chaplain_080708/. Last accessed December 26, 2012.

[90] See report: ttp://militaryatheists.org/news/2013/01/christian-embassy-video-culprit-given-top-post-at-west-point/.

[91] Loveland, Anne. *American Evangelicals and the US Military, 1942–1993.* Louisiana State University Press. 1997. See www.amazon.com/dp/080712091X/. Last accessed December 26, 2012.

[92] Loveland, *American Evangelicals and the US Military.*

[93] Military Association of Atheists and Freethinkers. Military Religious Demographics. See http://www.militaryatheists.org/demographics.html. Last accessed December 26, 2012.

[94] For an excellent treatment of the early history of the chaplaincy, see Chris Rodda's 2006 book *Liars For Jesus: The Religious Right's Alternate Version of American History Vol. 1* at www.amazon.com/dp/1419644386. Last accessed December 26, 2012.

[95] See report: ttp://militaryatheists.org/news/2013/01/christian-embassy-video-culprit-given-top-post-at-west-point/.

[96] Although the topic of gays openly serving in the military is a topic beyond the scope of this paper, the connection to the growing Christian fundamentalism in the US military is clearly connected. To read further on this topic, see "An Elephant Named Morality" in *Armed Forces Journal*, September 2010. http://www.armedforcesjournal.com/2010/09/4679369/. Last accessed December 26, 2012.

[97] Baker, Joseph T. "Don't Ask, Don't Tell: A Strategic Consideration." US Army War College. March 15, 2006. Unclassified but stamped "*DISTRIBUTION AUTHORIZED US GOVERNMENT AGENCIES ONLY: ADMINISTRATIVE/OPERATIONAL USE. Other requests shall be referred to US Army War College, Carlisle Barracks, Carlisle, PA 17013-5050.*"

[98] Ricks, Thomas E. "Need budget cuts? We probably can start by shutting Air War College." April 11, 2011. See http://ricks.foreignpolicy.com/posts/2011/04/11/need_budget_cuts_we_probably_can_start_by_shutting_the_air_war_college. Last accessed December 26, 2012.

[99] Hughes, Daniel J. "Professors in the Colonels' World" in *Military Culture and Education.* 2010. 149–166.

[100] Parco, James E. and Fagin, Barry S. "The One True Religion in the Military." *Attitudes Aren't Free.* Montgomery: Air University Press. 2007.

[101] Data came from more than 100 company and field grade officers in academic settings within the professional military education realm during the period 2007–2011.

[102] One must hold some form of religious belief generally, and Protestant Christianity specifically.

[103] Sekulow and Ash, "Religious Rights," 104.

[104] Sekulow and Ash, "Religious Rights," 104.

[105] For the sake of space, the religious connection is not explicated here but is very well articulated by the authors themselves as evidenced by their chapter's title "Religious Rights and Military Service."

[106] The Holy Bible. Leviticus 18:22.

[107] Notwithstanding the US Constitutional prohibition in Article VI, paragraph 3.

[108] See Levy, D.A., Blass, F.R. (2006). Can We Over-socialize? Applying the Systems Socialization Model to US Military Accession Programs. *Global Education Journal* 1, 3–17, for a complete theoretical articulation.

[109] See Weick's seminal work *Sensemaking in Organizations*, 1995.

[110] In this case, basic military training.

[111] For many fundamentalists, it is also necessary to be "born again," which relegates all mainstream Christians as "not saved" and outside the set. This is a literal translation of John 3:3 of the New Testament.

[112] Bacevich, Andrew. "Endless War, a Recipe for Four-Star Arrogance." *The Washington Post.* June 27, 2010. http://www.washingtonpost.com/wp-dyn/content/article/2010/06/25/AR2010062502160.html.

[113] Bacevich, "Endless War."

[114] Allsep, L. Michael, Parco, James E. and Levy, David A. "The culture war within." *Armed Forces Journal*, February 2011. http://www.armedforcesjournal.com/2011/02/5363912/. Last accessed December 26, 2012.

[115] As required by Article 90 of the Uniform Code of Military Justice.

[116] The best example being the promotion of Johnny Weida to major general on May 26, 2006, after his May 9, 2005, promotion was originally pulled from consideration on July 29, 2005. See http://www.boston.com/news/nation/washington/articles/2005/08/03/air_force_general_cut_from_promotion_list/. Despite the affirmation of allegations, his promotion was approved in 2007 but backdated to 2006. Last accessed December 26, 2012.

[117] All recommendations come from chapters in the "Religious Expression" section of *Attitudes Aren't Free*. For specific examples, please see individually footnoted chapters below.

[118] Grant, Paula M. "The Need for (More) New Guidance Regarding Religions Expression in the Air Force." *Attitudes Aren't Free.* Montgomery: Air University Press. 2010. http://books.google.com/books?id=-5FnvJEclewC&dpg=PP1&pg=PA39#v=onepage&q&f=false Last accessed December 26, 2012.

[119] Grant, "New Guidance Regarding Religious Expression."

[120] See the May 2011 Americans United summary of events at https://www.au.org/church-state/may-2011-church-state/people-events/au-aclu-investigate-possible-bias-over-concerts-at. Last accessed December 26, 2012.

[121] Torpy, Jason. "Arlington Cemetery Confirms Secular Policy." *Secular Coalition for America.* September 15, 2011. http://secular.org/blogs/Jason percent20Torpy. Last accessed December 26, 2012.

[122] Grant, "New Guidance Regarding Religious Expression."

[123] Grant, "New Guidance Regarding Religious Expression."

[124] Lynn, "Religion in the Military."

[125] Rodda, Chris. "Against All Enemies."

CHAPTER 15

Balancing Religious Freedoms in the Military During Extraordinary Times

Chris Rodda
Senior Research Director, Military Religious
Freedom Foundation (MRFF)

I t's a Sunday morning in March 2020. You're stationed at an installation in Germany, where you and your family live in a military housing apartment complex. Like the rest of Europe, you're under a stay-at-home order due to the coronavirus pandemic. Suddenly your peaceful Sunday morning is interrupted by the strains of evangelical Christian worship songs coming through your windows. The singing goes on for fifteen minutes, immediately followed by someone loudly shouting scripture verses, which goes on for another fifteen minutes. The same thing happens the next Sunday, and the Sunday after that, and the Sunday after that. You've identified the source of these intrusive Sunday worship services—an Air Force officer, known to be a fundamentalist Christian, is leading them from his apartment balcony. In between the weekly services, flyers with the song lyrics, guitar chords, and scripture verses for the next Sunday's worship are left on your and all your neighbors' doorsteps, indicating that you are expected to participate.

In effect, you and your family, being unable to escape this Sunday "porch preaching" because of the stay-at-home order, are being forced to attend mandatory religious services. And you are not alone. Your family is just one of twenty-eight families, twenty-two of them Christian families, who object to the officer's inescapable Sunday services.

After eight weeks of this forced religious worship, you've had enough, but you're not sure what to do about it. You and the others who object fear retribution or being ostracized by your neighbors if you complain, but you feel that your right to be free from unwanted proselytizing is being severely violated. In the end, you decide to contact the Military Religious Freedom Foundation (MRFF), an organization dedicated to ensuring the religious freedom of all service members, including their right to be free from unwanted religion, and send MRFF the following email explaining your situation:

> Hi - I am reaching out because of a situation going on in military housing that I am not sure how to approach. We live in stairwell housing in an overseas location. You aren't given a choice where you are allowed to live if housing is available when you arrive. On the particular base that I live on, it is all 5 bedroom apartments for families of 4 children or more. This typically has religious connotations.
>
> Since the forced stay at home orders of COVID-19, we have an Air Force Officer that leads a Sunday evangelical service from their balcony every Sunday. It is 15 minutes of religious singing followed by another 15 minutes of shouting of scriptures. Their children run around passing out flyers. This is the same family that hands out damnation dollars during the annual Halloween trick or treating on post every year. The buildings are not air-conditioned and for temperature regulation, you need to have windows open/cracked. There is no way to avoid this Sunday service if your building is co-located.
>
> Because the small housing area is so heavily religiously affiliated, it is a touchy subject. It is also a noise ordinance that the Military Police will not touch as it is not an emergency situation during COVID-19 conditions. Are you able to offer any direction in the best way to handle this?

After getting some more specific information, MRFF contacted the installation's commander, and the issue was quickly resolved. The officer who was leading the worship services sent a letter to his neighbors apologizing for disturbing them and moved his services to a nearby area out of earshot of the housing complex.

In this case, the rights of both the preaching officer and all the other residents of the housing complex were protected. The officer was able to continue to exercise his religion by holding his services in a nearby alternate location, residents who wanted to participate in the services were able to attend them, and those who did not want to participate were free from being forced to listen to half an hour of unwanted religious worship every Sunday morning. This was a balancing of the First Amendment's two religion clauses, the Free Exercise clause and the Establishment clause.

One of the most common complaints reported to MRFF throughout the coronavirus pandemic has been the posting of religious COVID-19 chaplain videos on official command Facebook pages.

Most commands have both a main command page and a separate chapel page. But while chapel pages typically have only a few hundred followers, command pages have thousands or even tens of thousands. If you were a chaplain bent on evangelizing or proselytizing, which page would you want your videos to be posted on—a chapel page where you'd only be reaching a few hundred people who have already chosen to engage with religious content, or your command's page where your religious message would not only reach thousands of potential converts, but reach them at a time when they might be feeling depressed and anxious over the pandemic and be more vulnerable than usual? Unfortunately, some chaplains took advantage of the pandemic to capitalize on the large audiences on command Facebook pages to proselytize either their particular religious beliefs or religion over non-religion.

It should be noted that there have also been many chaplains who have done a good job during the pandemic, creating morale-boosting and informational videos that did not push religion and could be beneficial to all members of their commands, religious or not, reserving their religious messages for their chapel pages. These chaplains should be commended. But those who chose to go the other route and use the pandemic's increased social media usage to proselytize on their commands' pages were the deserved subjects of many complaints.

In a number of instances, service members came to MRFF with their complaints, and in all cases, when MRFF reached out to the command responsible for the Facebook page on which the religion-promoting videos appeared, the videos were promptly removed.

The religious video issue even led the Army's Office of the Chief of Chaplains to issue new social media guidelines for chaplains. Issued in May 2020, the new guidelines, titled "Additional guidelines for displaying UMT internet content," began:

> Using Technology and Social Media Platforms is vital to providing religious support, especially during this COVID-19 pandemic. As a Corps, we have been connecting with and supporting our Soldiers, their Families, and our Army Civilians in amazing new ways these past several months. Unfortunately, our Corps' increased exposure has brought with it an increased level of scrutiny—but it's important that we learn from that scrutiny and continue to hone our craft.

Sections 3 and 4 of the new guidelines were completely in agreement with MRFF's stance that the only proper place for religious videos is chapel pages, not command pages (emphasis added):

3. General encouragement can be placed on a unit webpage, but **specific religious support content should be on a dedicated UMT, RSO, or Chapel webpage.**

4. UMT, RSO, and Chapel home pages should be "one click away" from the associated unit page—and **religious support content other than those hyperlinks should never be displayed on any unit page.**

Sections 5 and 6 went even further than MRFF's stance, saying that content promoting a "specific religion" shouldn't even be directly posted on chapel pages, but should only be linked to or provided via private platforms for those who make a *choice* to engage (emphasis added):

5. Any content in support of a specific religion should be "one click away" from the associated UMT, RSO, or Chapel home page—and content in

support of a specific religion should never be displayed on a UMT, RSO, or Chapel home page.

6. When providing content with a limited audience, as you often should, use a more secure platform than a simple webpage—such as a Facebook Group, Microsoft Teams, or Zoom—so that **individuals must make a choice to engage the material.**

Here again we have a balance of the First Amendment's Free Exercise and Establishment clauses. The chaplain's right to exercise his or her religion by putting out religious videos for those who wish to watch them is not infringed, those who choose to engage with religious content have access to it, and those who choose to be free from religious material are not confronted by it on their commands' pages. Under these guidelines, the rights to both freedom of and freedom from religion are protected.

The outcomes of these cases of the porch-preaching officer and the COVID-19 chaplains' videos did not sit well with some, however. A fundamentalist Christian legal organization, along with its like-minded allies in Congress, wrote letters to the Secretary of Defense, condemning the decisions of the commanders who struck this balance between freedom of and freedom from religion, and particularly attacked MRFF.

Pressured by twenty members of the House of Representatives and one senator, the Under Secretary of Defense for Personnel and Readiness took an action that has grave implications for that delicate balance between free exercise and non-establishment of religion in the military. He rewrote a core DoD regulation on religion, DoD Instruction 1300.17. In fact, the under secretary changed this DoD instruction so drastically that even its title needed to be changed.

DoD Instruction 1300.17 was titled "Accommodation of Religious Practices Within the Military Services." It was an instruction that, as the word *accommodation* implies, made exceptions to the usual regulations to accommodate religious practices. Under this instruction, a service member could submit a request to their commander for a religious accommodation, also called an exception to policy. It was intended to allow for special religious accommodations such as religious dietary requirements, the wearing of religious apparel with the uniform, the wearing of a beard, etc.

The new DoDI 1300.17, issued by the Under Secretary of Defense for Personnel and Readiness on September 1, 2020, completely deviates from the intent of the original instruction, allowing all manner of otherwise prohibited religious behavior as the *rule* rather than the *exception*. It no longer covers only what would be considered a special accommodation, but allows any religious "behavior" or "conduct," and the burden of proof is now on the commander to show why a conduct or behavior *shouldn't* be allowed, rather than the burden being on the service member, by their exception to policy request, showing why it *should* be allowed.

With the instruction no longer being about religious *accommodations* as they were understood in the prior instruction, but now being about religious practices, which are newly defined, as explained below, as *behaviors* or *conduct*, the instruction's title was changed from "Accommodation of Religious Practices Within the Military Services," to "Religious Liberty in the Military Services."

At the core of the drastic changes in the revamped and renamed DoDI 1300.17 is the greatly increased prominence of the "Religious Freedom Restoration Act" (RFRA), a 1993 act that has become the go-to law for fundamentalist Christian legal organizations, which stretch it to its limits in their defense of completely unconstitutional promotions of religion.

This law is the epitome of the right-wing fundamentalist Christians' view of the First Amendment's religion clauses as creating only a one-way wall—that the Free Exercise clause is the only religion clause that matters, and that the other direction of the wall, the Establishment clause, doesn't exist.

This preeminence of the Free Exercise clause to the exclusion of the Establishment clause comes through loud and clear throughout the new DoDI 1300.17, starting with the instruction's "Purpose" statement. The purpose as it appeared in the previous version was:

> Prescribes policy, procedures, and responsibilities for the accommodation of religious practices in the Military Services.

In the new version, the "Purpose" statement begins (emphasis added):

> Establishes DoD policy in ***furtherance of the Free Exercise Clause*** of the First Amendment to the Constitution of the United States . . .

The new purpose also says:

> Implements requirements in Section 2000bb-1 of Title 42, United States Code (U.S.C), also known as "The Religious Freedom Restoration Act" (RFRA), and other laws applicable to the accommodation of religious practices for DoD to provide, in accordance with the RFRA, that DoD Components will normally accommodate practices of a Service member based on a sincerely held religious belief.

This is what the Religious Freedom Restoration Act says:

(a) IN GENERAL
Government shall not substantially burden a person's exercise of religion even if the burden results from a rule of general applicability, except as provided in subsection (b).

(b) EXCEPTION
Government may substantially burden a person's exercise of religion only if it demonstrates that application of the burden to the person—
(1) is in furtherance of a compelling governmental interest; and
(2) is the least restrictive means of furthering that compelling governmental interest.

To fundamentalist Christians, like the Congress members and senator who wrote to the Secretary of Defense, any limit whatsoever on a chaplain's or service member's ability to shove their religion down the throats of others is a *"substantial burden"* on their free exercise of religion. There is no consideration of the *"substantial burden"* that unfettered proselytizing and promotions of religion by service members whose "conduct motivated by a sincerely held religious belief" puts on the right of other service members to be free from unwanted proselytizing and promotions of religion.

The most deleterious changes in new DoDI1300.17 are the definitions of what a "religious practice" is and what a "substantial burden" is.

A "religious practice," which under the previous DoDI 1300.17 meant what a reasonable person would consider a religious practice (e.g., a special dietary requirement, or the wearing of religious apparel or a beard)—accommodations that, it is important to note, would not infringe on anybody else's rights—has been redefined in the new DoDI 1300.17 as (emphasis added):

> An action, *behavior, or* course of *conduct* constituting individual expressions of religious beliefs, whether or not compelled by, or central to, the religion concerned.

The definition by which a "governmental act is a 'substantial burden' to a service member's exercise of religion" now includes anything that (emphasis added):

> Prevents participation in *conduct motivated* by a sincerely held religious belief

Behavior and conduct? This could include just about anything. Is God *motivating* you to proselytize to your fellow service members? Go ahead! That's "*conduct motivated* by a sincerely held religious belief." Want to pray loudly at your desk to show your coworkers how religious you are? No problem! That's just *behavior* "constituting individual expressions" of your religious beliefs!

With burden of proof now on a commander to show why a conduct or behavior of a subordinate *shouldn't* be allowed, the commander can no longer turn to DoD Instruction 1300.17 because the new proselytizing-friendly version of this instruction is the very thing that's allowing what was hitherto prohibited conduct or behavior!

Think of the two scenarios presented at the beginning of this chapter in light of the new DoDI 1300.17. In both of those cases a balance was struck between the free exercise of religion and the right to be free from unwanted religion—between the coequal Free Exercise and the Establishment clauses of the First Amendment. Under the new DoDI 1300.17, so heavily weighted toward the Free Exercise clause, almost to the complete exclusion of the Establishment clause, the balance is all but completely obliterated. The negative effects of these changes will be felt throughout the military, not only during these extraordinary times of a global pandemic when striking an equitable balance between freedom of and freedom from religion is trickier than usual, but long into the future when ordinary times return.

ENDNOTES

[i]https://militaryreligiousfreedom.org/press-releases/2020/Additional-guidelines-for-displaying-UMT-internet-content.pdf

[ii]Unit Ministry Team.

[iii]Religious Services Office.

[iv]First Liberty Institute.

[v]Rep. Doug Collins and nineteen other members of Congress May 14, 2020 letter to Secretary of Defense Mark Esper, https://dougcollins.house.gov/sites/dougcollins.house.gov/files/05.14.20%20Member%20Letter%20to%20Sec.%20Esper%20%28Military%20Chaplains%29.pdf ; Senator Ted Cruz June 9, 2020 letter to Secretary Esper, https://www.militaryreligiousfreedom.org/wp-content/uploads/2020/06/Cruz-2020.06.09-Religious-Freedom-for-Chaplains-Letter.pdf ; Reps. Doug Collins and Doug Lamborn July 1, 2020 letter to Secretary Esper, https://dougcollins.house.gov/media-center/press-releases/collins-lamborn-blast-esper-failing-protect-religious-liberty ; also see "20 Members of Congress Recognize the Impact of MRFF's Work," https://www.dailykos.com/stories/2020/5/14/1945083/-20-Members-of-Congress-Recognize-the-Impact-of-MRFF-s-Work ; "GOP Congress Members Incensed Over the Army Standing Behind Decisions in Favor of MRFF," https://www.dailykos.com/stories/2020/7/2/1957807/-GOP-Congress-Members-Incensed-Over-the-Army-Standing-Behind-Decisions-in-Favor-of-MRFF ; "Factually-Challenged Ted Cruz Attacks the Military Religious Freedom Foundation," https://www.dailykos.com/stories/2020/6/10/1952067/-Factually-Challenged-Ted-Cruz-Attacks-the-Military-Religious-Freedom-Foundation

[vi]Archived 2014 version of DoDI 1300.17, https://web.archive.org/web/20150416165641/http://www.dtic.mil/whs/directives/corres/pdf/130017p.pdf

[vii]September 1, 2020 version of DoDI 1300.17, https://www.esd.whs.mil/Portals/54/Documents/DD/issuances/dodi/130017p.pdf?ver=2020-09-01-151756-730

CHAPTER 16

FROM SEGREGATION TO THE EXECUTIVE SUITE: LESSONS LEARNED FORGOTTEN

John D. Hopper Jr.
Lieutenant General, USAF (ret.)
Former Vice Commander, Air Education and Training Command

A lingering sentiment in the African American community is that being in the Army is not considered a career, but a chance to jump-start life then move on. Not the last time I would hear this said. I attended segregated schools in Clarksville right up to 1956 when my father was deployed and we moved to Germany for three years. When we returned to Clarksville in 1959, two significant events validated my naivete. First, I couldn't explain to my little brother why there were still signs directing "colored" to the back of the bus, and my school was still segregated, five years after the Supreme Court ruled in *Brown vs. Board of Education.*

In 1962, I was a high school junior; my Clarksville, Tennessee, school was still all Black, and the civil rights movement was about to go from brush fire to inferno. However, my life plan was starting to come into focus. I was part of the movement, a foot soldier boycotting and picketing for freedom. My best friend and I had our sights set on attending Fisk University, a well-known Historically Black College (HBCU) in Nashville, Tennessee. It even looked like I might get one of their early admittance scholarships and skip my senior year in high school, but that plan was about to hit reality. I was informed by my dad there would be no Fisk University and I would be accompanying the rest of the family to his post in Columbus, Ohio, and I should start thinking about Ohio State University.

At first, I was pretty sure my grandmother, the matriarch of the family, would not allow this to stand. Imagine my surprise when she came down squarely with my dad and I was off to Columbus. I never had a serious conversation with my family about the why, but hindsight makes it quite clear something I was doing had them fearing for my safety. Perhaps it was participating in marches/demonstrations, but I couldn't imagine why anyone would single me out. There were also some anonymous calls from a young woman for me, some answered by family members that raised the stakes. The consensus of the family was the caller was a White woman and someone was trying to "set me up." I continued with the "why me?" accompanied by the "poor me" attitude all the way to Columbus. What I should have done is learn more about the lives of my grandparents and parents, and what experiences they had lived through that prompted (to me) their swift and decisive action. Timing is everything, and so it was in Columbus.

Shortly after we settled in Columbus, Ohio, my dad got orders for Korea (sent me into another poor-me funk) that left me (now the "man of the house") in a new town with two cars, a mother that didn't drive, and a ten-year-old little brother. Actually, it could have made for a "wild and crazy" senior year, but I finally stopped sulking long enough to realize I had some responsibilities I had better step up to. I got comfortable with looking at the fabled senior year as a write-off and got down to the business of preparing myself for a college with a student body larger than the entire population of Clarksville, Tennessee. The one thing I didn't count on was a friendly guidance counselor and an Air Force Academy Liaison Officer (ALO), who were about to offer me a firsthand look at something later known as "Affirmative Action."

Let me take a half-step back. We say everyone knows where they were when they learned President Kennedy had been shot. I don't know if that is true for everyone, but I was anchored to my normal spot in study hall, completely devastated and disoriented by the news. Three months later, I was in the guidance counselor's office sitting across from a USAFA/ALO explaining how this affirmative approach pushed forward by President Kennedy was prepared to offer me an appointment to the Academy's Preparatory School. There was no guarantee I would earn an appointment to the Academy the following year and I would have to join the AF Reserve and go to Basic Military Training at Lackland AFB, but they had a good record of success.

I thought my dad would be pleased; he was not. For my part, they had killed my opportunity for Fisk University, and he didn't want me to follow a military path, so that's exactly what I would do. I should have had a deeper discussion with Dad. My amateur research said the military (and particularly the Air Force) was the first/best option for equal treatment and equal opportunity. My dad seemed less inclined to buy the equal treatment argument. Another lost opportunity. I should have asked Dad why, after eighteen years of service, he was not buying into the equal opportunity argument. In fact, his only concession was at least it wasn't the Navy.

It's not easy to get an eighteen-year-old to take the long view and agree to spend extra time after high school to compete for an appointment to a service academy. I have had the opportunity to discuss/convince groups large and small, but it is a tough sell. Even when I remind them of some of those that took extra time to "prepare," names like Gen. Omar Bradley, Gen. Douglas MacArthur, and President Dwight Eisenhower. Even when I encourage them to look at the list of previous Air Force Chiefs of Staff and see how many took extra time, for many young men and women, that additional year seems an eternity. For me, the USAFA Preparatory School was a year well spent. Although I'm not convinced anything can completely prepare one for that grueling first year as a cadet, the Prep School curriculum, getting used to the military environment, and another year of maturity were a bonus.

In 1965, when the class of 1969 entered USAFA, I was one of seven African American cadets in the class. Finding someone that looked like us was difficult since there were no African Americans in the senior class, only one in the junior class and five in the sophomore class. Said another way, the seven of us doubled African American representation in the 2400-man (no women yet) cadet wing. Six of us would make it through to graduation, bringing the total number of African American USAFA graduates in 1969 to fifteen. African American representation on the staff was no better. As a cadet, your view of USAFA is shaped by those you see and interact with the most. That puts the dean's academic instructors, the Commandant's Air Officers Commanding (the "AOC," a commissioned officer to lead each of the twenty-four cadet squadrons and four cadet groups), and the director of athletic coaches (a mix of military and civilian) center stage.

My memory (as validated by perusing my class yearbook and others) tallies one African American commissioned officer on the faculty and none working for the commandant or director of athletics. It is not as if the AF did not recognize the impact these officers had on cadets. Working at USAFA was a "special duty" assignment—officers were handpicked to lead, teach, and mentor the next generations of AF leaders, and all save one were White men. To be fair, I would characterize them as "good men," and more than a few were the future of the Air Force. Among that early staff are names like former CSAF Gen. Charles Gabriel; Lt Col (BG) Wesley Posvar; first AF Rhodes Scholar and later chancellor of the University of Pittsburgh; his West Point classmate and my former boss Maj (Lt Gen) Ken Tallman, the 4th Group AOC; and Col (Gen) George Simler, the director of athletics. I plucked these names from the yearbook of the class of '59, the first graduating class. It seemed clear the AF was determined to populate this newest service academy, our service academy, with the best and the brightest. We would have a similar staffing adjustment in preparation for the first class of women, a new cadre of "best and brightest" women officers to be role models and mentors.

Think back now to 1959—the graduating seniors are commissioned and on their way. You have about thirty-five days to prepare for the arrival of the class of '63, the first class to include men of color among their ranks (with hopefully more to follow), and you have no AF officers of color assigned to any of the primary mission elements. My point is not intended to denigrate the staff—they were great choices—but they were not the only choices. There were AF officers of color available then and still available in 1969 to serve at the AF Academy. Many of us know some of them but not all; but, all of us recognize them as veterans whose service we celebrate. We know them collectively as the Tuskegee Airmen. Can you imagine having Col (now Brigadier) Charles McGhee as, say, deputy commandant of cadets? What an inspiration that would have been for all cadets as well as a source of pride for African American cadets.

Our four years at USAFA seemed to occur in a place separate from what our countrymen and peers were dealing with. The Civil Rights Movement was front and center, sometimes quiet and other times bursting with attack dogs and burning neighborhoods. I will dare to speak for my African American classmates to say that we felt disconnected, unable to lend our voices and support. The assassination of Dr. Martin Luther King Jr. led to the most racist comment I heard during my four years. While passing through a crowd of cadets, I overheard a conversation opining that "Martin Luther 'Coon' finally got what he deserved." Finding the speaker was impossible, and at the time, it was a singular event, but I knew there were more such comments; I just hadn't heard them. The reality was that some portion of the cadet wing had not grown beyond the communities that sent us to this place. Young men often make promises to each other only to see them float away. My African American classmates and I, as well as other cadets of color, made such a promise, that we would take on the fight for equal rights, to do our part. Perhaps this is the right place to talk about how cadets of color communicated the USAFA lessons from class to class.

To remind, for USAFA in the mid-1960s, cadets of color represented less than 1 percent of the cadet wing. And, as best I can determine, there were no (nor had there been) officers of color on the USAFA staff. Beginning with those first few Black cadets, it became clear there was a need to communicate, especially to provide a conduit for new freshmen who were literally at the bottom of the totem pole. These informal discussions grew as representation increased and the organization took on a name, the Way of Life Committee (WOL). WOL still exists and is an integral part of the USAFA community. It now includes a vigorous alumni group as well that extends its outreach to prospective cadets and their families. It is not reasonable to expect WOL/AFCOMAA to be the only mentors that new cadets/officers of color should expect. First, there are not enough mentors (particularly mentors of color) to go around. Second, if you're only mentoring people that look like you, you are doing them and the AF a disservice. Finally, it is the responsibility of every serving officer to be an active participant in growing the next generation of AF leaders and ensuring they respect and value the diversity of all with whom they serve.

Reflection Questions:

1. What are the main lessons from Gen. Hopper's story?
2. To what extent do you agree that "there are not enough mentors (particularly mentors of color) to go around"?

Group Discussion:

What is the "mold" that certain people fit to become officers? Develop an exhaustive list that includes attributes and characteristics that a person controls and those that they don't control.

What elements of the mold are critical to the mission?

What elements of the mold prevent the organization from developing and valuing those that don't seem to fit it (especially along dimensions the person does not control)?

What realizations have emerged as a result of thinking about this?

CHAPTER 17

THOSE LAST FOUR WORDS . . .

Martin E. France, PhD, Brigadier General, USAF (ret.)
Professor Emeritus, US Air Force Academy (2005–2018)

I think I must have been born this way. I sensed that I was different very early in my life, as I often asked questions that embarrassed some adults. Others just chuckled and said something about how curious I was. As I approached my teens, the contrast became more apparent to me, my mother, and a few close friends in whom I could confide. I think my dad just tried to deny it, and he didn't want to talk about it. Sure, I tried to fit in with the group. I participated in organized outings, spent time with my contemporaries, and discussed things we read and studied. Every time, though, I would ask some uncomfortable question and end up feeling isolated. "Wow, is he weird or just trying to make trouble?" they'd ask. I soon found other friends and outlets where the topic wasn't so provocative and I could be myself.

I am an atheist. I learned through my early life experiences that having divergent religious beliefs from the majority had an impact on my feelings about myself, my behaviors, my path in the world. My differentness continued to distinguish me during my Air Force career as well, giving rise to a passion and commitment to champion the autonomy for each person to be able to pursue their career regardless of their chosen religious beliefs. Below, I will share some of my experiences in the hope that others will appreciate the challenges faced by atheists in a military dominated by Christians—many of whom are evangelical and internally consider their religious perspective a necessary condition for honorable service.

As a boy, sports were a great outlet for my energy. I learned how to hide inside myself, to stay quiet when the occasion warranted, and to let most others think that I was "normal" like them, with the same beliefs, needs, habits, and speech patterns. I repeated the correct phrases and displayed all the right mannerisms. I became well-practiced at giving the impression that I was an All-American (Christian) boy.

Following high school, the only university for which I completed the application process was the US Air Force Academy—an honorable and admirable path consistent with the expectations many had for me. It seemed romantic and challenging. I wanted to go somewhere where I'd be different from all of my high school friends. During Basic Cadet Training and my first year, I donned my "mainstream" appearance when the situation required it. It seemed easier to just go with the flow, sequester my real feelings, and adopt accepted practices— though I usually used any downtime to sleep or daydream rather than conform with some who chose to attend optional religious services.

I also finally had some deep conversations regarding my feelings about religion with my open and friendly Mormon roommate. While I knew he thought I was wrong and sinful, he addressed the issue with grace and understanding, and he was willing to engage in rational debate. By this time, I had read the entire Bible but considered it a work of epic fiction (more like the Iliad) and philosophy rather than the inerrant word of a grand, singular deity. He, though, seemed to deeply believe in not only the details of New Testament miracles, but also in the Latter-Day Saints' interpretation of what followed. I knew that many fellow cadets were extremely devout Christians, including several who were senior to me, and it was not uncommon for my active-duty professors to declare and profess their faith in the classroom as part of a Lesson 1 introduction.

Eventually, these open discussions left me questioning myself: Was I really born this way? Was I truly created in the image of God, or not? If so, then why did I feel like such an outlier, that at some level my beliefs might be wrong or at least well out of the mainstream to the extent that I would need to hide them if I wanted to be successful during my cadet time and subsequent Air Force career? My four years as a cadet at the Academy went by in a flash. It was a time (late '70s and early '80s) of accepted practice but limited inquiry. While some were more insistent and overt about their beliefs than others, one could go about their private affairs without too much investigation, so long as they remained discreet. The majority might express their views, but they did not force them on others. Identity was more personal and guarded, I think. This was a relief.

Yet, public displays of at least surface-level conventional religious belief were expected. I married my wife right after graduation, as so many others do, in the magnificent beauty of the Air Force Academy Chapel. Our parents all thought it was grand and that we were both exactly what they wanted us to be. The sabers, guidons, and formal black-tie mess dress of our Cadet Chapel June Week wedding were the perfect backdrop of a faithful couple as we pretended to pray along with the congregation.

The situation changed quickly at my first assignment. No sooner than we had moved to our first on-base abode, a senior ranking officer verbally confronted me in a private off-duty situation. He was actually going door-to-door in on-base military housing, introducing himself by rank and recruiting attendees for his church off-base. I politely declined, but he persisted with questions. He asked for my views on several issues that I considered private, including religion. I explained—in general terms—my perspective. He said that he was curious and that he wanted to be helpful with the new crop of lieutenants who had just arrived. He was also shocked by my response to his inquiry. I was told that I was destined for eternal damnation, as was my spouse for living and agreeing with me.

I told myself it was time to climb back under my rock, if I was going to succeed at this base, and not voice any opinions on religion, trying to avoid the subject whenever possible. I would ignore Christian symbology and pretend to play along with the invocations and benedictions at required-attendance official events and not disturb the status quo.

During our two years at this first base, my spouse and I found some like-minded friends in uniform. We hung out on the weekends, went camping, traveled to USAFA for football games or to see old friends, and exchanged furtive glances during official events or dinners. We shared a secret we thought would certainly kill our careers if it were to be made public. We heard whispers that some of our senior officers might be in our camp, and we'd occasionally catch their eyes at dinings-out or promotion parties. This provided some solace that we weren't entirely alone.

Civilian graduate school, my next assignment, was liberating. There was certainly no pressure to conform to specific religious or spiritual mores in the Bay Area, and that's why I chose to attend Stanford University. My return to USAFA that followed was a bit of a culture shock, though. New housing developments and booming growth in the city had brought in organizations with agendas that many thought meshed well with the conservative, largely military population of Colorado Springs. Large churches sprang up, and pastors were driving around in their cars "anointing" the city from a bucket of holy vegetable oil. We had returned to both work and personal environments that demanded we not be completely authentic, hiding what we knew could derail our professional and personal lives.

While my department head was "cool" and considered private matters private, I distinctly remember a senior faculty member advocating that it was fully acceptable—and even desirable—for us to question a potential new hire during an interview about his or her religious preferences (e.g., "Where do you go to church on Sunday?") to make sure we knew what we were getting. He said he was certain that *how* a potential faculty member answered these questions reflected an important part of that person's ability to serve as a proper role model for our malleable cadets who were striving to be patriotic American Airmen, patriotism that included believing in God and practicing that belief in a specific manner. Happily for me, the department head pushed back on this and said that no such questions would be allowed. I still saw, however, where code was often used to dig out this info, as the candidates were (inappropriately, in my mind) asked about their family, hobbies, and general outside-of-work activities. Many used this opening to talk fervently about their church ties and Sunday school support, for example, to the approving nods of the blue-suit believers.

I was also invited to lunchtime Bible studies in the department's main conference room—something that was common throughout the faculty—but was able to successfully decline attendance, preferring to run or work out with others during this time. My wife was invited to be part of the spouses' (really, wives only) MOPS (Mothers of Pre-Schoolers) social group, but declined later with invented excuses when she discovered that it was really just a women's Bible study and church recruitment tool.

The years went by, and I dodged a few career-ending bullets by keeping my comments and discussions on religion and spirituality to the hypothetical and the rhetorical. I know that many sensed I didn't subscribe to the same beliefs they did and that they thought they could help me find the right path; I managed to politely put them off and change the subject to avoid any terminal statement or action. Looking back, I can't believe how lucky I was to have not experienced the career decimation other Airmen experienced once their beliefs were revealed. Still, meeting your new boss in his office and seeing a Bible on the desk and a plaque that specifically cited priorities as Faith, Country, Family in numbered descending order meant that I needed to be careful.

Things changed in 2002 when a note arrived from our eldest son who had just begun his own journey as a cadet at USAFA. Despite guidance from me to find his own path, he'd decided that the Academy was also his path—in part, I'm sure, because it was the only life he'd known. Unlike me, he had applied and been accepted to other schools; but I think he, too, saw refuge for his unique identity in the Long Blue Line of outward conformity.

He wrote in his first letter home that he'd been "outed" by his cadre during Basic Cadet Training. He was punished by being forced to stand at attention in his room for the hour during which his mainstream classmates were casually chatting with civilians (male and female), eating cookies, making cell phone calls to parents, and drinking soda. This hour was the institutionally encouraged Bible study program our cadets called SPIRE (Special Programs in Religion and Ethics). The cadre soon discovered that my son was not alone—his squadron had several like him who chose not to participate. Without knowing exactly what to do with multiple basic cadets standing at attention in their rooms, the cadre called them "Heathen Flight" and decided to march them around the Terrazzo on public display.

Two years after we received our son's note, during a summer USAFA Graduate Leadership Conference, the results of a survey of cadets, faculty, and staff (originally intended to illuminate potential issues with sexual assault and harassment as well as acceptance of women within the institution) indicated a level of institutional intolerance and bias based on their religious perspectives. Non-Protestant Christian cadets and staff noted that they had either experienced discrimination or they perceived that bias existed against non-Christians in general. The topic was now on the table in a more public way. Ideally, I thought this might bring us to the brink of exploring, if not embracing, culture change that would address the full acceptance of non-Christians within the Air Force Academy and throughout the Air Force.

As a result of the informal conversations that occurred in the shadows, I met a fellow officer and Academy grad who not only shared my concerns, but who was also the parent of cadets who had experienced similar issues to my son. We bonded through our offsprings' shared struggles in facing the clear Evangelical Christian bias coursing throughout USAFA. My new friend channeled those painful experiences into forming the Military Religious Freedom Foundation

(MRFF). I became an unofficial confidential advisor to the MRFF in my quest to protect the rights and future of all non-Christians serving within the military.

One year later, I applied for the position of permanent professor and head of one of the Academy's premier STEM Departments, astronautics. I was concerned about the selection process and whether my religious identity would be called into question. I prepared to respond to any questions along those lines with praise for the incumbent and his integrity (an overt Fundamentalist whom I had known since my cadet days), while also staying noncommittal on any specific declarations of my own faith and keeping my views private. In the end, I was relieved not to have noticed any questions centered on religion.

During the hiring period—which included approval at the Secretary of the Air Force level, a presidential nomination, and Senate confirmation—some forces were acting against my selection, though. The then dean of faculty was aware of my support for the newly formed MRFF and called a special meeting of all the sitting permanent professors to discuss whether my selection should continue to move forward or if it should be reopened to consider one or more of the other finalists. In the end, either I had enough supporters to keep my nomination or the permanent professors were wary enough of the growing influence of the MRFF and the potential for unwanted media attention that such a move might bring. I was honored to have been chosen and confirmed for the job. Maybe things were changing. Or not.

It's an Air Force tradition that whenever one is promoted to a higher rank, you retake the Oath of Office, publicly reaffirming your commitment to the Constitution. In every other instance throughout my career I'd played along and said the last four words—trying, as I've said earlier, to just "get along." That changed on 1 November 2003, when I was promoted to full colonel. At that ceremony, I told the officiating officer (who was a career mentor that was also quietly atheist) that I did not want to say the last four words. He agreed without comment, and the ceremony went off without a hitch. My rationale for this decision was that, at the time, I saw little reason to think that I'd be promoted beyond O-6, and I concluded that it was time to stop lying to myself and others about my beliefs. My wife and my family supported that decision. I didn't realize it at the time, but this decision would set the stage for another event that would profoundly impact how senior leaders viewed me in a subsequent position.

My investiture as a permanent professor was set for early December of 2005. The dean of faculty's staff sent me an advance event script to review. The investiture ceremony contained a re-administration of the Oath of Office, similar to common practice described above for promotions, and the script included the full oath word for word. I made a few cosmetic edits to the script to make sure that the dean understood my family history, names, etc. for her personal comments, and then I lined out *in red ink* the last four words of the oath: "so help me God."

The dean's executive officer contacted me the next day to tell me that the dean had asked him to pass along that I couldn't line out those last four words. I replied in no uncertain terms that I could, that the words were my right to keep optional, and that I didn't want to embarrass the dean by *not* responding to her recitation of those four words, as it would have left an awkward pause at the end of the ceremony. He responded by notifying me that the dean would "check with the JAG [judge advocate general] to see if we could do that." A few days later, I received word that it was okay, and the script went forward as edited.

On the day of my investiture, the dean and I were standing at the back of the room in which the ceremony was being conducted, and we were waiting to enter as part of the official party. Moments before we walked in, she gave me a serious look and said, "Are you sure you want to do this? Not say the last four words?" I said, "Yes, I'm sure. I have to be true to myself and my family." She said, "Okay then," and we marched in. A few minutes later, during the investiture ceremony, there was a bit of an odd silence during the moment that most in the audience expected to hear, "so help me God," but nothing else happened—at first.

However, a week after the event, the dean summoned me into her office and handed over a letter that a local retired colonel had sent to the superintendent. This retired colonel, who had full access to the cadet area as a volunteer mentor in the aforementioned SPIRE program and was also a volunteer in the laboratory of the department I now led, had written a full-page screed on how he thought I should be fired and disciplined immediately for taking an invalid version of the Oath of Office that omitted the last four words.

My commander told me that it was up to me to respond to the letter, voicing no support for me or my rights—just disappointment that my decision to omit the last four words had brought an unwanted negative letter to senior leadership. I sent a courteous letter to the retired colonel, thanked him for his past service to the department, omitted any mention of his letter to the superintendent or the ceremony, and I told him that his services were no longer necessary. I sent a copy to the dean and heard no more about the situation.

During the next thirteen years that I was privileged to serve as the department head and permanent professor of my department, I led a staff of about thirty military and civilian members. I had finally achieved the positional power to affect the culture of the department I led and could have some impact on the larger USAFA culture. For example, at the beginning of every semester during a regular event that was meant to establish culture and standards, I made known that religious issues were private and were not to be discussed in the office area or in the classroom with cadets (and the same held for political and private, romantic issues and preferences). I also ceased our departmental practice of event invocations and replaced them with "a moment of silence for private reflection." Private religious study in one's own office space was certainly permissible. However, I discontinued group Bible study meetings that took place during the duty day in our department conference room—a tradition still common in other USAFA departments at the time. I worked to help the Academy avoid missteps by channeling (to senior leaders like the dean) complaints that USAFA cadets, family members, and staff filed with the MRFF. Some of those efforts were successful, and others not so much, additional evidence that culture change is laborious and longitudinal.

In some cases, parents of cadets applying to USAFA who were concerned about the overtly evangelical environment at USAFA contacted me through the MRFF. I did all I could to convince them that USAFA was a great institution and that their children would be safe there—though challenges would continue. In many cases, my wife and I agreed to be the "sponsor parents" for these cadets and helped them navigate their four years there. We also served as sponsor parents for a large number of international cadets—almost all non-Christian—in part to help them deal with similar issues. Muslim cadets felt particularly isolated for many years, and our home served for many as a "safe space" in which all were welcome to discuss political, religious, and other issues free of the muzzling bias many experienced in the cadet area.

Cadets also established a non-religious club during this period, in part to counter the proliferation and penetration of the many religious programs provided by the USAFA chaplains, volunteers, and off-base church and organizations. The name changed many times from Cadet Free-Thinkers to Cadet Humanist Club to the Cadet Secular Alliance, but in each case I provided quiet, unofficial support, making sure that the cadets involved knew that they had access to at least one member of the USAFA senior leadership where they could come with their concerns. I also promoted the organizations' visibility by inviting them to take the lead in several public service projects in Colorado Springs that I had organized.

In spite of small advances, some events continued to highlight the issue of religious bias. One of our NCOs who worked in our laboratory was chosen as the dean of faculty's NCO of the Year, and because of this honor, he was also a nominee for the USAFA NCO of the Year award. He was invited to the regularly scheduled "Academy Annual Awards" banquet, during which the base-level winners would be announced. As his boss, I was invited to attend with him. It was a formal affair in mess dress.

After we stood for the national anthem, we were instructed to "please remain standing as Chaplain X [I do not recall the name] delivers the invocation." I remained standing, as did my NCO. The event went as planned, but my NCO did not win the base-level award. The following day, my NCO came forward to make a complaint with me. He explained that he was not Christian. He said that he thought it was completely against Air Force policy to hold a distinctly Christian prayer at a mandatory military event and then direct that everyone participate. This placed any who publicly disobeyed at considerable professional risk. I agreed with him, and I told him that I would raise his (and my) concerns to the dean and the superintendent. I did so over the next two weeks.

The dean dismissed my position out of hand, stating that the event was voluntary and we weren't forced to attend. I sent a note to the superintendent, and he scheduled a meeting in the office of the head chaplain to discuss my concerns. I expected the superintendent to attend, but he did not. Instead, I was greeted by three chaplains who all told me that I was wrong—for the same reason the dean had cited. I emailed the superintendent again, and he finally agreed to meet me three weeks later for a private lunch.

At the lunch, the superintendent repeated the position—the event was not mandatory, and my NCO and I were free to choose not to attend. I told him that I didn't know there would be an invocation, nor did my NCO, but that didn't seem to matter to the superintendent. I also told him that had my NCO and I *not* attended the event, we would have been judged harshly for failing to support an important Academy awards program. He dismissed this argument as well.

Still, I continued to serve as the unofficial eyes and ears of the MRFF, and I think my willingness to serve as an avenue to express general concerns about religious bias became more well known throughout the USAFA community. I openly admitted to my supervisors that I supported the MRFF, but I also pledged to work within the system and the chain of command to the maximum extent possible to save the Academy from embarrassment.

The problem was quite complex, though, and few cadets (with such limited power and even less knowledge of or confidence in how the "system" should work) were willing to report cases of bias. One cadet reported to me that an instructor—after reviewing a particularly difficult test—told the class that, in the future all they needed to do was "pray to the Lord" and realize that the only math they needed to know was "one cross plus three nails equals fo[u]r-given." The instructor even diagrammed the equation on the white board. The cadet sent a cell phone photo of the diagram to the MRFF, but the cadet was afraid to tell me or anyone else the name of the instructor or even the department in which the incident occurred.

In this same time frame, one of my students came to me and asked if I knew of a specific person who led an off-base Bible study. I told him that I did, and I inquired why he asked. This cadet then told me about an invitation he'd received to attend weekly sessions with this retired colonel and his protégés. The invitation made it clear that only the very best cadets were asked to join this group and that, once in, they could depend upon the loyalty and the recommendations of the group to assure them of selection of top leadership positions within the Cadet Wing hierarchy. He told me that he didn't feel comfortable with what he thought seemed like a cult. I encouraged him to stop attending, and he did so. The retired colonel was the same person who had, several years before, written the letter to the superintendent calling for my removal for the "so help me God" omission.

Many cadets continued to experience religious bigotry. Some found refuge in the aforementioned Cadet Secular Alliance. However, open participation in this group was low. I attended several of their evening meetings, during which they told me that most non-theist cadets were afraid of revealing their religious identities and they didn't need the added pressure or hassle on their already full plates that came with simply trying to graduate from the Air Force Academy. During these meetings, I assured the cadets that they needed to exercise the system with their complaints of bias when they occurred, or nothing would change. I continued to make complaints myself when base-wide messages were sent that encouraged attendance at prayer lunches and breakfasts held in uniform, during the duty day, attended by senior officers and commanders. These attempts typically gained no traction. Event attendance was robust, and I was again labeled as a troublemaker.

Some cadets chose other ways to deal with the bias at USAFA. One group of more than one hundred cadets came to be known as "Spartacus" or "the Spartaci." They confided to MRFF leadership that the only way one could survive without religious harassment from evangelical Christians was to put a Bible on his or her bookshelf, go to the Bible study meetings, say the "right things," and pretend to be Christian to just get by. When "Don't Ask, Don't Tell" was repealed, one of these cadets told me, "Well, sir, it's now officially tougher to be atheist at USAFA than to be gay."

At one point, the Chief of Staff of the Air Force (CSAF) wanted to know more about the situation, and he arranged through the MRFF to meet with me in 2011. He couldn't and wouldn't meet openly with me for fear of damaging both of our careers. During one of his visits for a fall football game and the annual Corona Conference, I was told to arrive unaccompanied and to meet a limousine at the Academy's North Overlook at a specific time. I did as ordered, walked over to the limo, and was invited into the back seat with the CSAF. We spoke for about twenty minutes, and I outlined all of the above concerns. I told him that nothing had really changed—much of the religious intolerance still went on, albeit underground and behind the closed doors of the Academy's top leadership, manifested in hiring, promotion, programmatic, and other decisions.

In August 2012, *Air Force Instruction 1-1* was first published. It contained several key provisions that, while not always enforced, were clearly the result of CSAF's guidance. In particular, sections 2.11 and 2.12 not only guaranteed religious freedom for Air Force personnel, they also put restrictions on proselytization and religious coercion in the Air Force. The key phrases from these two sections are:

> Every Airman is free to practice the religion of their choice or subscribe to no religious belief at all. You should confidently practice your own beliefs while respecting others whose viewpoints differ from your own.
>
> Leaders at all levels must balance constitutional protections for their own free exercise of religion, including individual expressions of religious beliefs, and the constitutional prohibition against governmental establishment of religion. They must ensure their words and actions cannot reasonably be construed to be officially endorsing or disapproving of, or extending preferential treatment for any faith, belief, or absence of belief.

While an outward sign of culture change, I am unaware of any case in which an active-duty Air Force officer has been disciplined for violating this instruction, despite many complaints lodged through the MRFF.

Issues existed not only at USAFA, but throughout the greater Air Force. Starting in late 2004, I was one of about a dozen colonels within the acquisition/research and development career field who served on what the Air Force Personnel Center calls a "developmental team." Our job was to meet two to four times per year to review the records of junior officers in our career field, recommend them for assignments, select those who would attend developmental education programs, and otherwise rank them among their peers. It was serious business. As we scored the records from a low of six to a high of ten (with half steps), it was clear that the tiniest of scoring differences could mean the difference between a job that would lead these officers to full colonel and beyond or to be passed over for promotion at some point in their career before earning their "birds."

In each board scoring example, we were given a career summary that included assignments, awards, education, etc. I was immediately struck by the fact that the record also included the member's marital status, number of dependents, race/ethnic identity, gender, and declared religious preference. I told the board chairperson that I thought this was a potential source of conscious and unconscious bias. I fought this battle for over ten years, complaining at every single developmental team meeting and, on at least two occasions, to the commander of the Air Force Personnel Center. Sometimes I was told that it couldn't be done without a major software rewrite. "Well then," I said, "rewrite the software." Finally, in 2016, the policy changed and religious preference was removed.

The last five years of my tenure at USAFA were trying. My commander, the new dean of faculty, hand-picked by the outgoing evangelical Christian superintendent, attempted to serve me with paperwork three times (a letter of counseling, a letter of admonishment, and a commander directed investigation)—all of which were withdrawn upon rebuttal and JAG review or completed with "no finding." Worn down by the constant harassment that I felt was linked to my advocacy for elimination of religious bias throughout the Air Force, I submitted my request for retirement in October of 2017, an act that became official in August of 2018 after more than thirty-seven years of active-duty service.

At our last graduation ceremony in May 2018, prior to my retirement a few months later, my wife demonstrated the kind of bravery that I wish I (and others) had shown over the years. We were seated in the front row of permanent professors on the Falcon Stadium floor. Apart from the main platform and dais, there is hardly a more visible location from the vantage of the stadium's general seating. After the national anthem, the head chaplain stepped to the microphone and began the typical long, speech-like, monotheistic, Christian-terminology-laden invocation we'd come to dread over the years. My wife, though, had finally had enough. She sat down seconds into the speech. I did the same seconds later. We were done with quasi-mandatory Christianity.

In the years since my retirement, strong evidence still exists that pressure and bias against non-theists still exists within the institution and throughout the Air Force and Department of Defense. After years of complaint, the SPIRE program has been renamed "developmental time," "personnel excellence time," or something similar during various iterations of Basic Cadet Training. During these periods, signs steered basic cadets to regular meetings for church or religious groups once or twice per week. One such group was for secular cadets, and the sign clearly pointed them toward the direction in which they could meet with upper class cadets and staff who held similar views.

I attended a few of these meetings in the last two years, and I attempted to reassure the basic cadets that they could succeed at USAFA without overtly embracing evangelical Protestant views. However, attendance at the meetings was light—with never more than about a dozen (of over 1,100 basic cadets) who chose to join the secular group. When COVID-19 struck, things changed. Now, basic cadets did not have to physically display their beliefs by following signs and taking the public "atheist walk" in the direction of the Secular Cadet Alliance. They could simply join the Microsoft Teams meeting of the Alliance in the privacy of their own rooms and without their cadre or peers knowing of their decision. Attendance increased by over an order of magnitude, with (in some cases) more than 150 basic cadets participating. To me, this clearly demonstrated the inherent and perceived religious bias that continues to exist. Given a level playing field, a sense of the privacy and autonomy that (I'd hope) we all should have regarding our religious beliefs, we can truly choose our own path.

Where to go now and in the future?

The answer is simple, but the implementation and enforcement will continue to be troublesome. The guidance for the acceptance of religious diversity at USAFA already exists in the US Constitution and in *Air Force Instruction 1-1*. These documents, though, represent our espoused cultural values as opposed to our value-in-use. Yet, with a greater awareness of inequities related to religious freedom, active-duty leaders continue to have legal obligations to ensure we constantly strive to craft a culture that is free of religious bias and proselytization throughout the military.

CHAPTER 18

SACRIFICING SELF TO SERVE: SURVIVING THE MILITARY'S TWENTIETH-CENTURY BAN ON GAYS

Edith A. Disler, PhD
Lieutenant Colonel, USAF (ret.)

A dewy evening with a chill in the air closed out the California summer day during this TDY to Northern California in July of 1985. I was a second lieutenant, having been on active duty in the Air Force for a little over a year. After roaming around the base a bit and drinking a couple of beers, Carol and I sat on a set of slowly chilling metal bleachers. We had only known one another for a couple of days, so we were chatting about this and that. There had been a playful chemistry between us during the softball tournament, but pretty much everyone was happy to be on a sports TDY, playing ball, and having a good time. As we were chatting, her next question, she later informed me, was going to be how I felt about gays. But before she even got to the question, she brought her lips to mine.

It was hardly my first kiss, but it was certainly my first magical kiss—one which opened a well of emotions. With that kiss, I experienced a singular moment in which an existential question had been answered, the curtains were thrown open, and daylight was shed upon such an important aspect of my very being. Whether I simply had yet to discover that I was gay, or whether I had been actively resisting that realization, here I was, at age twenty-three, finally in my own skin. For a moment, I could be joyful that the pieces finally fell into place. This was me. This was mine. I felt no guilt or regret. This was beautiful . . . until it was terrifying. Now I had a secret to keep.

When the TDY came to a close and our group from Little Rock AFB boarded the bus to head for our C-130 flight back to Arkansas, Trudy sat down beside me. She was a Captain, prior enlisted, a mentor and friend. Apparently she could read the dynamic that had played out for me that week. She said, simply, "It's hard, isn't it? I understand." With that, she became my safe harbor and taught me how to negotiate the choppy seas that lay ahead.

Even to this day, some thirty-five years later, I never again experienced that same wholeness nor that joy of self-understanding—that internal swell of delight.

One year into what would be a career of twenty-five years, I came out to myself. But I knew the policy. While in Air Force ROTC at the University of Michigan, I was required to sign a statement attesting that I was "not a homosexual" and that I had not "engaged in homosexual activity." At the time, it was the truth. Never again would I be required to sign such a statement, even though I now knew differently.

As soon as my sexuality became my truth, the walls of secrecy and deception laid their foundations, and the walls slowly heightened and thickened. It takes a long time to realize that the walls that keep out the threats also trap you inside. The walls, though necessary, block the sunlight, and over the long haul, a bright soul can melt into a shadow. The ultimate irony was that the gay ban in the military existed ostensibly because gay service members could be coerced to give up secrets if they feared being outed. Yet, without the ban, there is no fulcrum for the coercion. A Catch-22 if ever there was one.

Secrecy, back then, was a bit easier, if you will—before cell phones and their ever-present cameras, and before social media—though we still worried about phone taps, our mail being read, and being followed by the Office of Special Investigations, or OSI. Those of us who held security clearances had been trained to handle classified information and, certainly, to keep the nation's secrets. Those secret-keeping skills came in handy.

Despite the obstacle of my sexual orientation, I had held several top secret clearances, including an SCI. I had been a missile crew member—part of a team operating the most powerful single weapon system the US has ever had in its inventory: the Titan II Intercontinental Ballistic Missile. I had provided executive support to the Secretary and Deputy Secretary of Defense—privy to much regarding their personal lives, as well as their professional obligations, while exercising the utmost discretion in their interactions with international leaders, Congress members, and other Cabinet-level leadership. I had been a Pentagon speechwriter and member of the Air Staff, twice—writing for and advising the Secretary of the Air Force and the Chief of Staff of the Air Force. As an arms control inspector, I had represented the United States and NATO in places as far-flung as Kazakhstan, Romania, and Russia.

Even though I suddenly knew this fact about myself, I felt no less professional as an Air Force officer, no less qualified to do my job, no less able to protect classified information, and no less competent to wear my uniform perfectly and with pride. On the contrary, I felt more whole, and found no reason to leave the Air Force. I had a top secret clearance. I would keep my truth top secret. If I needed to lie to protect classified information, it wouldn't have been frowned upon. If I needed to lie to live a secret existence while serving, so be it.

Eventually I would regard the policy of discrimination against gays as an "unjust order"—akin to the military excluding Jews, or Muslims, or people of Asian or African descent. Members of the military are not required to obey an unjust order. Whether legitimate reasoning or rationalization, I would spend the next twenty-four years juggling my many selves: my professional self, my public self, myself with my gay friends, myself with my straight friends, myself as a partner, and myself as a daughter and sister. It would take decades, but in the end, the orders discriminating against LGBT members of the military were, indeed, determined to be unjust.

I learned several survival lessons the first time I was invited to join a group to go to a local women's bar. I was warned that we might run into other members of the missile wing at the bar. I was okay with that, as I assumed we were under the same veil of secrecy. I wasn't told who I might see—that would have been a violation of the code.

Heading to any gay bar in Little Rock in the 1980s took some preparation. "Don't take your military ID; leave it at home. If there is a raid, you don't want them to know you're military. That's also why we take a civilian's car, in case the OSI is looking for cars with Department of Defense registration stickers on them in the parking lot."If you are approached, you should ask if the person approaching you is a police officer or OSI agent. If they are, they have to tell you so." I assumed at the time that this was accurate. Now, I'm not so sure it was.

Gay bars are their own cultural zones. Sure enough, when we got to the women's bar, other members of the wing were there. We were excited to see each other, and as the circle of gay friends grew larger, the secret seemed less lonely. We all want to be able to see people like ourselves—whatever that means to us individually—in our professional surroundings. Here were other gays, men and women, in community. The fact of our mutual secret, and the biases against us, made our friendships very tight and protective.

Coming out to anyone, especially straight people, was immensely dangerous for gays in the military during both the gay ban and the Don't Ask, Don't Tell era. Though there were plenty of reasons one could get kicked out of the military— divulging classified information, adultery, fraternization—one of the infractions that could get you kicked out pretty much overnight was homosexuality. And the threat didn't even end there. Once a straight person knows you're gay, your other friends—particularly the "single" ones—are "guilty by association." Or at least suspect. The OSI loved those leads. If your job specialty required a security clearance, family members, friends, and work associates would inevitably be questioned by investigative personnel. So, before you came out to anyone outside of your circle of gay friends, they had to be people who could keep your secret, and even lie for you. This was a key reason gay service members didn't even come out to members of their own family; family dynamics were another reason.

I was one of those 70s-era kids: the child of 50s- and 60s-era conservative Midwestern parents. In this era, we grew up saying, "My parents are going to kill me when they find out," and that was only for little stuff, like scratching the car or breaking a plate. Imagine the consequences of coming out to them. Nearly every phone call with my parents came with a question from my father: "Have you met any interesting men lately?" I met interesting men all the time, but that's not where he was going with that question. I finally had Mom on the phone by herself one call, and I asked, "Why does Dad ask if I have met any interesting men? Why doesn't he just ask whether or not I'm happy?" These kinds of signals are sometimes the hardest for people who fear coming out to their families. Even the slightest disparaging remark at home could make a gay service member even more defensive and secretive. One friend, for example, had an older brother who joked about "fudge packers" and asked that her friend—her partner at the time—not join them for family gatherings. These comments, which anyone else would consider to be off the cuff, sent her a message, loud and clear. She felt she would need to keep her secret indefinitely.

One of the more annoying upshots of having to keep secret about sexual identity was the need to role-play being heterosexual. The first place I realized this would be highly inconvenient was during my physical. The provider went through a raft of questions, including, "What do you use for birth control?" Options: abstinence (read "prude"), sponge (they were around for a while), condoms (I'll never need one, but it's a good answer to the question). Military personnel were given no immunity. If you outed yourself to get appropriate medical care, the medical staff could report your sexuality through the chain of command and you'd be discharged practically before you could blink. The same was true of talking to anyone in the chaplain corps.

The health implications were much more severe for those with HIV—mostly gay men. One of my dear friends, Barry, tested positive for HIV while on active duty—a situation that became a nightmare for him. He counted back to when it could have happened, and told the health professionals he had been with a prostitute at about that time and probably got it from her. This was an indignity of lies for a gay man, but more socially acceptable than the truth. Testing positive for HIV and/or AIDS set into motion a protocol which required that the unit commander, the base commander, the dental staff, and the hospital commander be informed of his status. Naturally, his sexual orientation became suspect. At one point, the OSI called to question him, asking when he would be available to meet them at his apartment. Barry realized they wanted to search his apartment for incriminating evidence: letters, photos, or videos. Figuring that the entrance to his apartment was being watched, he broke into his own apartment from a rear window in order to clear out anything incriminating before the meeting he had arranged with the OSI. Had the institution of the Air Force been as loyal to its members as Barry had been to it, it should have been more concerned with giving him proper medical care than with reading his mail or screening his photos under duress.

Barry left the Air Force. After a four-year decline, he was sent to Walter Reed under the assumption that Walter Reed would have state-of-the-art treatment and be able to prolong his life. Instead, he was sent there to die. He was not alone. His sisters and I were there with him.

AIDS was still severely stigmatized and misunderstood. Even being there with a dying friend was fraught with precarious details. I needed to take leave to go see him when I got the call. I was teaching at the Air Force Academy and had a full class load. My colleagues would need to substitute for me while I was away.

Taking leave during the teaching schedule just wasn't done. I feared letting my supervisor know why I needed to take this short-notice leave, and I would need to withhold the full truth, lest I be suspected. I kept it simple: a friend was dying—I needed to go.

For gay men and women, role-playing as heterosexual also meant coming up with ways to fend off all those well-meaning people trying to play matchmaker. Obviously, we didn't need that kind of matchmaking. If a gay man needed a date, there were gay women to step in, and vice versa. Luckily, I had the added bonus that, as a single woman, social norms meant that I could attend functions singly, or innocently take a woman friend with me. It wasn't easy for gay men to pull off bringing a male friend with them to functions.

Regretfully, role-playing as a heterosexual woman out of necessity also meant sending confusing signals to men who were genuinely attracted to me, though I had a hard time seeing myself as being attractive to men at all. And, whereas I really enjoyed my friendships with gay men because we could just be ourselves with no tension, I erringly projected that capacity onto straight men. I went out with straight men that I just wanted to be friends with, not fully understanding the dynamic straight men are operating from when going out for drinks or dinner.

The ultimate way to play the role of a heterosexual was for a gay man and a gay woman to engage in a "marriage of convenience." These were rare. I had heard of them, and only knew of one. Such marriages, for any reason, could go before a court martial and were punishable. I suppose marriages of convenience would be considered by some, because the stakes for gay men were different than the stakes for lesbians.

On the officer side, when I was a lieutenant, the military was still old school. As a second lieutenant I was advised by a female lieutenant colonel mentor that if a woman wanted a career, she needed to stay single. On the flip side, men were cautioned that they were lucky to make the rank of major if they weren't yet married, and if they expected to make lieutenant colonel, they'd better get married. I will spare you, dear reader, the full measure of advice from the "Officer's Wife Handbook," which coached women on what they should look like when their patriotic husband comes home from work, what kind of "oasis" his home should be for him, and the wife's job in making it an oasis, even if it requires that she sew some seat covers and tablecloths in order to spruce up base housing. It is this iconic 1950s notion of man as officer, with officer's wife and kids in tow, which has contributed to the quandaries faced by gays in the military, as well as the discrimination faced by women. The image of the heroic male officer flanked by adoring wife and disciplined "military brats" etched military heterosexuality—and 1950s gender norms—into the stone-hard military subculture.

While I was in my late twenties and early thirties, at the age when most are making a lifelong commitment to another, the need for secrecy destroyed the most important relationship in my life. I wanted us to be that couple that had been together for thirty or forty years, but the stresses of distance and fear of our families' reactions, while trying to hold onto our professional aspirations, were just too great. Had we been a straight couple, we would have had support through the joint spouse program, consideration for leave, and support for our military careers while balancing family obligations. But we had only obstacles. Managing a relationship, careers, and family can be a challenge in a heterosexual world, where your commitment is acknowledged and supported. Managing a relationship, careers, and family in secrecy is a challenge of mighty proportions. It is a challenge with which I have been less than successful, and I readily acknowledge my agency in that. Still, I do not know the degree to which my relationship struggles have been a result of the cultural and institutional biases I and my significant others have endured, while trying to do our best under a veil of secrecy.

Because of the secrecy involved, there are no truly accurate statistics as to how many LGBT people served during the military's various gay bans, despite the fact that the Rand Corporation and other sociologists have generated some percentages based on survey and interview data. Even in surveys by outside agencies, academics, or think tanks, there would still be plenty of reason to withhold sexual orientation from anyone who asked about it. If someone found out, would I lose my retirement? Would I lose my VA services? Would I lose my GI Bill? These were, and continue to be, very real concerns. I can say that nowadays, however, the VA is sensitive to its LGBT clients, providing couples counseling for same-sex couples, offering transgender support groups, and fast-tracking LGBT claims which are tied to depression or military sexual trauma.

I served under a gay ban which had been formally instituted in 1981, but other versions of gay bans had existed, going back to World War II. In 1992, when then Governor Clinton was running for office, I was stationed at the Air Force Academy. In the car with my partner at the time, we heard the news that if elected president, he wanted to end the gay ban. For a moment—just a moment—I felt a deep, internal sense of relief to think that the threat of discharge would no longer be hanging, like the sword of Damocles, over our heads. That moment was fleeting. What would follow was the Don't Ask, Don't Tell policy, which was almost as bad as the gay ban. It presented yet another Catch-22. If you ask me if I'm gay, which you aren't supposed to do, you put me in a position to either lie and say "no"; to say "yes" and be summarily discharged; to say "you can't ask that," which immediately generates suspicion; or to just remain silent, which would also immediately generate suspicion.

There is an old adage that "if the military wanted you to have a wife, they would have issued you one!" Apparently, they started issuing them, because only service members with at least one "dependent" (spouse and/or child or children) were authorized on-base housing. After two or three military assignments, the circle of gay friends widened enough that gay service members could generally connect with the gay community nearly anywhere we were assigned. Ironically, the military's housing policies actually helped us protect our home life identities, with the downside of keeping us from feeling like we were otherwise a full part of the military community. As far as the military was concerned, gays were single or "bachelor" officers or personnel; as such, we weren't authorized on-base housing, requiring us to live "on the economy." While this was better for helping us keep our private lives private, the reimbursement for off-base housing and utilities was only geared to cover 65 percent of those costs, meaning that it generally cost more to live off-base than on-base. In addition, it isolated us from the unique feeling of community experienced by those who live on-base. Though I spent twenty-five years in the military, I don't know what it was like to live on a military base.

Another "port in the storm" of gay military life was a large metropolitan area. Most of my gay military friends and I served intermittent tours in the Washington, DC, area. Between the Pentagon, Fort Belvoir, the Washington Navy Yard, the Marine Barracks, Fort McNair, Fort Myer, Bolling AFB, Andrews AFB, the Marine Base Quantico, and the various off-post military assignments throughout DC, it was easy to keep a fairly anonymous personal life there. One needed worry less about who might see you walking about with your significant other. Best of all, the number of military personnel in the area meant that our circle of "family" was large. As a community unto ourselves, we helped one another in a variety of ways. If someone needed a shed built, we all showed up. If someone needed some major yard work done, we were there. And if a group needed a place to crash for the Navy–Air Force game, someone's house suddenly became "lesbian central." Even mixing with civilian members of the gay community who might not understand the discretion required for gay military members was dicey, so we made our own fun and had our own meetups. One group consisted of a monthly "brunch-bunch." The circle of friends was scattered from the far reaches of northern Virginia to as far as southern and eastern Maryland. Gathering for brunch might require a two- to three-hour round-trip drive, but to have the opportunity to simply be ourselves for a couple of hours, crack jokes only we would understand, and share in one another's successes and challenges, it was worth it.

In 2002, and while stationed within the anonymity of the metro DC area— and academia—my partner and I pursued getting pregnant. After nine months of inseminations at the civilian fertility clinic, I was going to need IVF. Luckily, Walter Reed had an IVF program right there in Washington, DC. But, because I was a "single soldier," I could only get IVF services after I submitted a letter, signed by my commander, indicating that he was aware that I was being treated by the IVF program at Walter Reed. Because I was a doctoral student at Georgetown University, my boss was the ROTC commander at Howard University. His administrative assistant put the single required sentence on the commander's letterhead. He was almost embarrassed to sign it, as it seemed such a ridiculous requirement. Needless to say, this "permission slip" requirement chapped my hide.

Finally, pregnant with twins in June of 2003, we were delighted. Being of advanced maternal age, and having an IVF pregnancy, the military watched me closely. I ended up on bed rest at the National Naval Medical Center at Bethesda at twenty-eight weeks. I would only manage to keep the babies in utero for two more weeks. My daughter was in distress at thirty weeks, so both my babies came into the world by C-section, though ten weeks premature. I asked my partner to be in the delivery room. She was worried about the "guilt by association." I was less worried about it by that time. The medical staff was a mix of civilian and military. And, with the wars in Iraq and Afghanistan, husbands were deployed, so friends, sisters, and mothers were helping women through their IVF and pregnancies.

Pregnancy while gay in the military was new territory, as was having children. There was no one to teach us the ropes on this one. We needed to figure it out day by day. First up, after the babies were born, I was headed to my final duty assignment, where I was known fairly well, with infant twins. Would we declare my partner to be their nanny? Next up, what would the children call my partner? I had five years of military service to go, and if we were out and about being called "mama" and "mommy" while still under DADT, we would be outed. She chose for them to call her "Nana," as it was socially acceptable—anyone nearby would assume the kids were her grandchildren. It would draw less attention. The DADT policy and the ban on gays had played a role in determining what my children would call their second parent for the rest of their lives.

When my partner went back to work, on-base childcare was out of the question. We couldn't afford to both be considered parents—again, the exposure would be too risky. So, off the kids went to private day care—very expensive private day care. One of the day care providers there quietly approached my partner one day, saying, "It's military spouse appreciation day" and gave her a small bundle of treats, as they were doing with all the military spouses who used the day care. What a kind gesture that was, but regrettably secretive.

Though my active duty service commitment ran until June of 2009, I asked the Air Force to curtail it by a few months. I was just done—used up. The Air Force agreed to the curtailment, and I was given my retirement orders. I was retired under a cloud of suspicion tied to the issue of gays in the military. My crime: late in 2008 I invited the leadership of the Blue Alliance, a formal organization of LGBT Air Force Academy graduates, to speak with my students at the Air Force Academy.

The members of the Blue Alliance loved their alma mater. They wanted to understand how the cadets felt about the likely fall of the DADT policy, and how they might be of assistance when the time came for the Air Force Academy to transition to a policy of non-discrimination. My students, all seniors (nicknamed "firsties"), were literally months away from being commissioned as Air Force officers. They would certainly, during their career, see the end of the ban on gays in the military, so this discussion would hopefully add to the skills in their leadership kit bag. But bigotry dies hard.

The Blue Alliance leadership was comprised of three Air Force Academy graduates—a C-130 pilot, a C-130 navigator, and an A-10 pilot—all with wartime flying in their past, including combat missions. None were still active duty; two were successful in business, and the third was successful in academics, earning a PhD and working with a nonprofit organization. Had I invited them to talk to my students about bombing targets, surviving tactical landings and takeoffs in a C-130, or pumping 30-millimeter rounds into enemy artillery, that would have been fine. But one of my students—a home-schooled conservative Christian—was offended by my guests and complained to the military training chain of command. My academic leadership buckled to criticism from the military training side. A better response would have been for my supervisor and my dean to point out that it is the intent, at the Air Force Academy, for future officers to hash out topics in their college classroom—even the touchy subjects. This was a leadership training issue and a human issue, not to mention a matter of academic freedom. But I had no support and no allies within my chain of command; they answered to a lieutenant general and would do what they needed to do to serve that master. Throwing one field grade officer under the bus, especially when she was about to retire anyway, was no problem. I was pulled from the classroom and investigated for violation of policies and procedure.

Other department members, already teaching their own full loads, were forced to pick up my teaching load. I was forbidden from communicating with my students regarding why I was pulled from class for the rest of the semester. One of my friends noticed that people went out of their way to avoid walking past my office. Many of my civilian colleagues were stunned by the way I was treated, sending me notes of support. Other colleagues, military and civilian, avoided me altogether, and some were critical, if not hostile, toward me. I had taught at the Air Force Academy for a total of nineteen semesters—almost ten years of my life—but after this incident, I would only venture into the classroom one more time, to substitute teach for a colleague.

In the end, the investigator, an active duty colonel, found no infractions—no violation of policy or procedure. So, I was given the default punishment: a letter of counseling for poor judgment.

Poor Judgment.

The serendipitous visit to the Air Force Academy of the Blue Alliance leadership gave me the opportunity to hope for one more accomplishment: to bring an open discussion regarding LGBT individuals and military service to the Air Force's future leaders in my English classroom at the United States Air Force Academy. It was 2009. I thought my students would benefit from the discussion. I judged that open discussion in a classroom environment would be a good thing for these future leaders. I was wrong. It was "poor judgment" on my part to think

I could score a victory for decency and against bigotry. It was "poor judgment" to even discuss this unjust order.

That accomplishment was too much to hope for. But I did score a small victory.

In my students' final assignment, one of them wrote that she found the visit by the Blue Alliance to be very valuable. She wrote that she would be attending nursing school following graduation and that the visitors from the Blue Alliance had given her a new way of seeing her future patients as complex human beings— remembering that their lived experience may be very different from her own, and require sympathy in ways broader than she imagined.

I took heart from that.

She is a leader.

The cadet who was offended by the mere presence of LGBT persons who, themselves, attended the Air Force Academy and who, themselves, served in wartime will be a problem. He is likely the kind of officer whose bias runs so deep that he is a threat to the careers of the LGBT officers and enlisted who would serve under his supervision. While that young man was in training to be an officer, the institution rewarded and validated his bigotry with my investigation and punishment. Now an officer, whether his bias manifests overtly, by giving LGBT troops poor reviews or denying them opportunities to advance, or whether his bias manifests more covertly, he will not give LGBT troops a fair shot. He will not support them the way he supports others, and it is not unfair to say that if his bigotry reaches into the LGBT community, then he may also have an aversion to those of a different race, ethnicity, or religion. These are not the qualities of a good leader.

I have yet to fully recover from this final episode of my long Air Force career even though it happened shortly before I was due to retire. Though I would like to pull the feelings of resentment up by their roots, those roots are deep and hard to reach. They keep growing back, like a tenacious dandelion. After serving in the English Department at the Air Force Academy from 1988 to 1993, the place was like a home away from home for me. The department head at the time had nurtured my academic interests and teaching skills, and some of my deepest friendships started while I was stationed there. Between 1993 and 2004 I would see my students and colleagues from the Air Force Academy out and about in the Air Force, worldwide. So, when I went back to my "home away from home," where I was eventually summarily thrown out of the tribe, the emotional pain ran deep. I was cast aside for merely discussing the issue of gays in the military with students who would one day be expected to lead all with compassion: gay, straight, black, brown, white, Christian, Muslim, Jew, and atheist. It was a resounding commentary on the gay community and especially on LGBT members who want to serve: we don't care how hard you work or what you contribute, we don't want you around, you aren't "one of us," and we will cast you out.

Now, in 2020, at the age of fifty-eight, I am thankful for what I have, and I can say that, on the whole, my Air Force experience was fulfilling, fun, and rewarding. I served an operational tour when few operations positions were open to women, and I am proud to call myself a missileer. I served overseas, traveling much of Europe and the former Soviet Union. I availed myself of the military's generous education benefits. Most importantly, I gave birth to two amazing children and collected many wonderful friends from my years of service, some of whom I have been able to reconnect with through social media. I will always wonder, though, what could have been. However, the emotional damage was deep and intractable by the time I left the military after decades of service. Before the end of my twenty-five-year career I was hoping to serve one day—a single day—as a free, open person. I retired as of May 31, 2009.

I did not get my day.

Though the ban on gays and lesbians in the military is gone, bias will never die. My girlfriend—a combat Army veteran and herself a mother—and I have agreed that we would rather accept the possibility of being shot dead for holding hands in public than bow to other's bigotry. We would rather our three children see what it looks like for a couple to express affection and devotion than hide our partnership because of outdated societal prejudices. After serving to keep our children's country safe, what we want for our children are healthy and rewarding relationships, and stimulating careers, where their leadership and colleagues support their best efforts by accepting them for who they are. In other words, we want them to have what we did not.

CHAPTER 19

Reflections of a Cadet Wing Commander

Aryemis Brown, Cadet First Class
US Air Force Academy Cadet Wing Commander (Fall 2020)

"Sir, I assume command."

I relinquished my blue beret, the uniform of a cadet instructor, on the same day I accepted the golden saber, the symbol of the cadet wing commander. My mission had changed dramatically from the training of thirty basic cadets to the leadership development of 4,400+ officer candidates for the US Air and Space Forces.

Following my acceptance address, an African American freshman fourth-class cadet remained in the auditorium and asked to speak with me privately. He told me about how he felt that his chain of command mistook him to be an "arrogant, undisciplined, and problematic basic cadet." According to him, this assessment was, in part, due to race. It would be naive to fully discount the role of implicit bias in our interactions with other people, as I listened to him recount multiple examples of varying degrees of (often lesser) punishment for different members of his unit for the same infraction. After he finished speaking, he asked me, "How have you, as a Black man who inspires people like me, succeeded in your life?"

It is people like this cadet, who share their experiences of challenges and difficulties experienced and overcome, which have taught me to persevere in pursuit of decency and respect of the dignity of all people. It is on behalf of people like him that I was proud to support our institutional diversity review. When we looked deeper, we found a harsh truth (one that could only be solved by first acknowledging the issue) of disparities in how we treated minority Airmen in areas of command discretion. To say this another way, we found immutable characteristics, like race, affected our decisions—often to the detriment of minority people—where human autonomy was involved. For many, including me, this finding was difficult to absorb, but it created an objective foundation for reflection and improvement.

The first order of business as cadet wing commander was to assemble my team. My aspiration to convene the most optimal team informed my choice of a command chief. The applicant we selected was a thoughtful and optimistic second-class cadet (in her third year at the Academy). Though her kindness and compassion were assets, it was her cognitive diversity that gained her the position. She was the only candidate to considerately question my position on our training program and present a counterview. I knew that our command team would benefit from her varied perspective, and I was committed to supporting incorporation and consideration of her unique ideas.

Inclusion is an important piece of my command style. To me, it is a strategic and national imperative that we appreciate all voices, stories, and ideas; only then can we have a reasonable assurance that we have reached the best solution to hard problems for all people.

At the end of a one-month hiring process, we assembled a wing staff team of fifty-six cadets that reflected the multiplicity of our Cadet Wing. Our team was diversified by race, gender, ideology, affiliation, interests, and participation in extracurricular activities, to name a few. I attribute the many successes and accomplishments, during our command tour, to our different perspectives. Together, we formulated our commander's intent—the anchoring direction for our entire unit. A simplified version of this ten-page articulation follows:

The Air Force Cadet Wing will demonstrate excellence and professionalism in military conduct and decorum; practice good order and discipline; and bond as a cohesive, team-oriented community—motivated by pride, dignity and respect, and a common purpose to join the world's greatest Air Force and Space Force.

This objective underpinned our effort in four ways: (1) completing academic, military, aviation, and athletic requirements for the semester; (2) maintaining the health and safety of the Cadet Wing; (3) building a courageous culture of care and belongingness grounded in dignity and respect; and (4) developing training, discipline, accountability, and ownership. More importantly, I shared five focus areas meriting special attention: (1) diversity, equity, and inclusion; (2) sexual assault prevention; (3) comprehensive cadet fitness; (4) citizen-Airmen and political activities; and (5) mental well-being. To accomplish these command responsibilities, I relied principally on my command team: the vice commander, the director of operations, and the command chief. As such, the "command team," not the "commander," became our moniker. In this essay, I would like to share three short reflections with you.

In the time leading up to our assumption of command, we faced an early leadership challenge—the global pandemic forced the cadet population to depart the installation and complete the previous academic semester online, which compelled significant academic hardship for many. A large portion of cadets, regrettably, engaged in dishonest practices and use of unauthorized resources to cope with the adversity, resulting in the largest cheating scandal in the history of our institution. Two of the incoming wing staff members, including the director of operations (the third in command), took part in this honor violation. While it was difficult to accept the resignation of people I knew to be good at heart who made mistakes, it was important for them to accept responsibility for their actions and focus on personal remediation before commissioning as military officers.

Our new director of operations immediately went to work implementing our capstone project—a new unit manning document. It is an accepted maxim that people are our most precious resource; therefore, making sound personnel decisions is central to effective management and retention. Notably, every cadet—no matter current experience, skill, or aptitude—had the opportunity to explore and develop their leadership style through practical supervisorial responsibilities. As I reflect on this pivotal project, I am proud that its momentum originated from a desire of many cadets to be heard and contribute to the advancement of their squadrons. This moment, in part, started with the deep need for steady leadership in response to the global health crisis, but ultimately compelled our senior leaders to advance mission critical changes that have the ability to provide lasting benefits.

Responding to a sudden global health emergency required immediate and deliberate action. And then, the shooting of an unarmed Black man ushered in an unimaginable and timely demand for change of a system entrenched in systematic bias and racism. There are no words to describe the pain I felt about the death of George Floyd, indirectly experienced through graphic videos taken by helpless bystanders. It hurts to think about the implications of the skin color shared with a man who died as a result of his hue. My family and friends helped me make sense of this national tragedy. The heartbreak for my country increased my resolve to command equitably and inclusively. I immediately penned a letter to our staff to define a collective purpose to be achieved through individual contribution on the topic of diversity and inclusion:

> It has been a difficult and troubling week for our nation, as we confront ugly truths about race, injustice, and inequality. As protests span the country, I guarantee that the death of George Floyd, and the ensuing aftermath, is on the minds of our cadets and Airmen. Unfortunately, I do not have a magic answer, but I do understand we're in an Air Force that values diversity, inclusion, and equity. Our unique stories are a force multiplier; every Airmen is a valuable member of our team. My words are not nearly enough to address the extraordinary circumstances hurting our communities. However, I trust our leadership team—you—with the compassion, emotional intelligence, and leadership to build a culture of belonging in our shared community, the Air Force Cadet Wing. There will be a presidential election this semester, so in addition to the global pandemic, many social issues will be on the minds of our cadet population. It is our responsibility, as a cadet leadership team, to respect and appreciate the diverse attitudes that inform our collective ethic.

In a virtual call with the team a few days later, it was important to distinguish the terms diversity, inclusion, and belonging. I used the example of a gathering around a dinner table to depict the meaning of these three terms. Diversity is bringing different people to sit at the dinner table. Inclusion is appreciating the different food, dessert, and conversation brought by those people sitting around the table. Belonging is the connective affection formed while at the dinner table, that unspoken invitation to return any time and never be afraid to bring your new dish for others to try or for you to sample the different dishes they have brought with them. Translate this analogy to our daily interactions in the classroom, on the athletic fields, and in the dormitory, and there you will find our diversity goal for the cadets: to simply be good people respectful of the distinctive contributions that we each have to offer.

This was the catalyst for development of a diversity training provided to the Cadet Wing. While training is not the solution to every problem, it certainly increased our exposure to this area of focus. The diversity training received mixed reviews. There was a virtual debate, in the chat box, about whether racism was an actual problem in the military and if this training actually heightened tension and divergence by bringing attention to racial differences. While those questions were not resolved, I was satisfied that we provided a forum for people with different opinions to actively engage with each other, as the only sentiment worse than hatred is indifference, and we cannot be indifferent to our neighbor's plight.

This first attempt at a conversation served as a guidepost to many tangible approaches to culture and climate in the future. We stood up a Critical Conversation Working Group to help cadets intelligently and honestly engage in tough conversations. We created Roundtable, a cadet advisory panel featuring cadets from diverse backgrounds (such as intercollegiate athletes, wing staff, and affinity groups) to propose recommendations to difficult problems. And, we incorporated equal opportunity and personal development themes into our training pedagogy. At the strategic level of command, it is difficult to win the individual hearts and minds of thousands of people; but our hope is that these actions established a framework or tool kit for tactical commanders to meaningfully pursue enduring cultural responsiveness and change.

I had one such opportunity to step away from my strategic mindset to address a tactical situation with larger implications. During the question-and-answer portion of a future warfare immersion briefing, an African American cadet grabbed the microphone and shouted, "Another Black man was shot and killed today, so why is this briefing important right now?" This event brought a spectrum of reactions from our wing staff team. The interaction, during which one member demanded speedy discipline of this cadet for making political statements, is broadly recaptured below.

Member: That cadet commandeered my briefing to make a political statement.

Me: Why do you consider that a political statement?

Member: Because it was in reference to Black Lives Matter (BLM), which is a political movement.

Me: Are you aware that the Department of Defense determined that BLM was a social justice movement, not a political one?

Member: Even if that were the case, that wasn't the time or the place.

While many might debate that potentially racially motivated killing is not materially relevant to future warfare immersion, this exchange made me consider, "When is the time and place for these important conversations?" My team member unknowingly exposed a root cause of this hesitance, to provide the necessary outlet to have this dialogue, in our apolitical military. Rather, we most often avoid divisive topic areas for fear that we advance an inappropriate partisan position. Beyond an informal counseling session, we used this event to empathize with this cadet's experiences and speak to his concerns in lieu of penalizing him. We invited him to take part in our institutional diversity response efforts to share his important perspective. As I write this reflection, I can happily report that this cadet has spearheaded some of the most important diversity efforts at the USAFA subsequent to these events.

As November 2020 approached, it became increasingly evident that the federal presidential and congressional election cycle posed another threat to maintaining our apolitical environment. We found ourselves struggling with yet another question: "How do we appreciate our civic rights and attitudes while maintaining the impartial appearance of the military?" The Air Force authored well-defined, performative guidance on political activities and free expression, yet this direction does not fully express the rationale reinforcing its mandate. In our monthly letter to the Cadet Wing, we addressed the topic:

> Our November focus area is citizen-Airmen and political activities! Civilian control of the military is an essential component of our profession. We fully expect you to critically engage, participate, discuss, and think about the political process; that is your duty as members of the
> American public. In the process of this dialogue, and in service to our sworn oath to a larger society, we must maintain the apolitical nature of the military. Regardless of the outcome of the election, we expect you to refrain from overt demonstrations of partisan loyalty. Let us commonly facilitate civil discourse over bigotry and celebrate unity over divide.

It is appropriate to note our similarities—how we are connected in common purpose: military service. The expression of political rights is one location where the demands of good order and discipline and a special military society surpass our individual wishes; however, it was far from our purpose to silence the personal political opinions of any person. Our strategic messaging campaign highlighted methods to express personal opinions through social media, political rallies, and most importantly, voting. We underscored ways to celebrate our similarities and differences and illuminate the desires of both agendas in proper ways and where appropriate.

I'd be remiss not to circle back and touch on the impact of the coronavirus to our command tour. The interruption to our normal operations tempo extended the need to enhance our squadron culture. Many cadets were now spending the bulk of their duty day in the squadron behind a computer screen. It was imperative to promote mental and psychological well-being within the right culture. Culture speaks to the personality of the unit. It reflects our artifacts, values, and assumptions. It reveals what we see, what we talk about, and what we believe, the murals on the wall, squadron events, the hallway talk, the commander's calls. In this challenging time, we needed to empower our people to own their self-care . . . and this started with the right culture.

We took a moment to observe our unit. As leaders, how could we create a culture of care and connectedness? What was hanging in our hallways? How did we communicate with our squadron? What stories did we share about our people and our unit? How did we own what was *within our control?* Squadron events, personnel recognition, community, gratitude, generosity, positive messaging. How did we respond to what was *out of our control?* COVID-19. Unpredictable scheduling. Disagreement. Cynicism, which means a mistrust in humanity, is a popular word in our unit. The Cadet Wing is not cynical; rather, they believe in each other.

If the squadron is the heartbeat of the Air Force, then the people are the blood pumping through our Air Force. What messages, values, and beliefs were we pumping into our most vulnerable Airmen? Our words and actions influenced their basic underlying assumptions. Even on those difficult days when the world seems full of bad news, we needed to find (or create) that bright spot for our people. We did not need to contribute to the misconstruction of the truth, but that did not limit our control of our attitudes and our responses. It was a challenging time, but our success depended on our people. We challenged them to: Continue to competitively collaborate with our fellow squadron leaders on community engagement. Own our culture. Empower our Cadet Wing to own their happiness.

That unchanging focus on the people and the mission carried us to the finish line of our command tour. It was time to select our replacements. Unfortunately, there is an ill-informed rumor that the cadet leadership roles follow a patterned quota, i.e., there is a schedule for people of different races and gender to take the mantel. Having chaired a selection board, I am saddened to think that anyone would believe that our cadet leaders lack the requisite qualifications and command potential to succeed in their role. *This is simply not true.* The guidance does identify the importance of diversity in an auspicious leadership command team, further recognizing that a homogeneous command team cannot adequately and appropriately represent a varied and wide-ranging cadet population. It was a credit to my team to have an intercollegiate athlete to understand the perspective of our cadet athletes and an accomplished history academician to understand the pressures of our cadet scholars. Our multifaceted team enhanced the quality of our critical conversations through honest commentary of lived experiences. We were able to account for the second- and third-order effects of decision processes because we had representative identities in our ranks.

I have witnessed the fabric of our nation, in all of its many shades, during my time at the Academy. Our classrooms, squadrons, and people come from all walks of life: faith groups, political ideology, gender, race, sexual orientation, perspectives, and most importantly, lived experiences. Our community makes me a better person, enabling me to figuratively step into their shoes and see the world through their eyes. My view of the assorted lives, represented within the American dream, has been illuminated. Equipped with the lessons learned, I look forward to deepening my respect for the collective diversity that makes our "ordinary extraordinary." I am conscious of the important role this diverse community has played in my life.

I closed my command tour by celebrating these consequential ideas. With sincere gratitude for an incredible learning experience, it was time to relinquish command to my successor. This time-honored tradition is important, for it begets a refreshing flow of energy and ideas into our organization every few months. I left my position confident in our people and our mission. It was only fitting to title my address: "Onward." The march for progress is not a straight line, though I am confident in its forward motion. As I departed my command, I took comfort in the many inspiring leaders stepping onto the scene. I am proud of the podium and microphone we left for them to employ their brilliance.

I envision the many champions who came before me and left a blueprint for which I might follow. They strengthen my resolve to become a leader of character and a decent person. They remind me of the inherent value of all people, and that every person deserves a standing ovation for something good in their life. As I close my amazing journey at this institution, I am certain of this: our greatest strength is our people. This awesome and noble privilege of service starts with appreciating our differences and celebrating the many similarities that connect us. Of this, I am sure, every cadet to my left and right, young and old, shares my sense of service and patriotism.

Today, I am a Rhodes scholar-elect—a scholarship once unavailable to people of color. Completing my tenure as cadet wing commander during a global pandemic, my successes were aided by the compendium of cadets on my team and the genuine care and compassion shared by every member of our Academy community.

CHAPTER 20

COMBATING RACE AND SEX STEREOTYPING

22 September 2020
Executive Order 13950
The White House

By the authority vested in me as President by the Constitution and the laws of the United States of America, including the Federal Property and Administrative Services Act, 40 U.S.C. 101 *et seq.*, and in order to promote economy and efficiency in Federal contracting, to promote unity in the Federal workforce, and to combat offensive and anti-American race and sex stereotyping and scapegoating, it is hereby ordered as follows:

Section 1. Purpose.

From the battlefield of Gettysburg to the bus boycott in Montgomery and the Selma-to-Montgomery marches, heroic Americans have valiantly risked their lives to ensure that their children would grow up in a Nation living out its creed, expressed in the Declaration of Independence: "We hold these truths to be self-evident, that all men are created equal." It was this belief in the inherent equality of every individual that inspired the Founding generation to risk their lives, their fortunes, and their sacred honor to establish a new Nation, unique among the countries of the world. President Abraham Lincoln understood that this belief is "the electric cord" that "links the hearts of patriotic and liberty-loving" people, no matter their race or country of origin. It is the belief that inspired the heroic black soldiers of the 54th Massachusetts Infantry Regiment to defend that same Union at great cost in the Civil War. And it is what inspired Dr. Martin Luther King Jr., to dream that his children would one day "not be judged by the color of their skin but by the content of their character."

Thanks to the courage and sacrifice of our forebears, America has made significant progress toward realization of our national creed, particularly in the 57 years since Dr. King shared his dream with the country.

Today, however, many people are pushing a different vision of America that is grounded in hierarchies based on collective social and political identities rather than in the inherent and equal dignity of every person as an individual. This ideology is rooted in the pernicious and false belief that America is an irredeemably racist and sexist country; that some people, simply on account of their race or sex, are oppressors; and that racial and sexual identities are more important than our common status as human beings and Americans.

This destructive ideology is grounded in misrepresentations of our country's history and its role in the world. Although presented as new and revolutionary, they resurrect the discredited notions of the nineteenth century's apologists for slavery who, like President Lincoln's rival Stephen A. Douglas, maintained that our government "was made on the white basis" "by white men, for the benefit of white men." Our Founding documents rejected these racialized views of America, which were soundly defeated on the blood-stained battlefields of the Civil War. Yet they are now being repackaged and sold as cutting-edge insights. They are designed to divide us and to prevent us from uniting as one people in pursuit of one common destiny for our great country.

Unfortunately, this malign ideology is now migrating from the fringes of American society and threatens to infect core institutions of our country. Instructors and materials teaching that men and members of certain races, as well as our most venerable institutions, are inherently sexist and racist are appearing in workplace diversity trainings across the country, even in components of the Federal Government and among Federal contractors. For example, the Department of the Treasury recently held a seminar that promoted arguments that "virtually all White people, regardless of how 'woke' they are, contribute to racism," and that instructed small group leaders to encourage employees to avoid "narratives" that Americans should "be more color-blind" or "let people's skills and personalities be what differentiates them."

Training materials from Argonne National Laboratories, a Federal entity, stated that racism "is interwoven into every fabric of America" and described statements like "color blindness" and the "meritocracy" as "actions of bias."

Materials from Sandia National Laboratories, also a Federal entity, for non-minority males stated that an emphasis on "rationality over emotionality" was a characteristic of "white male[s]," and asked those present to "acknowledge" their "privilege" to each other.

A Smithsonian Institution museum graphic recently claimed that concepts like "[o]bjective, rational linear thinking," "[h]ard work" being "the key to success," the "nuclear family," and belief in a single god are not values that unite Americans of all races but are instead "aspects and assumptions of whiteness." The museum also stated that "[f]acing your whiteness is hard and can result in feelings of guilt, sadness, confusion, defensiveness, or fear."

All of this is contrary to the fundamental premises underpinning our Republic: that all individuals are created equal and should be allowed an equal opportunity under the law to pursue happiness and prosper based on individual merit.

Executive departments and agencies (agencies), our Uniformed Services, Federal contractors, and Federal grant recipients should, of course, continue to foster environments devoid of hostility grounded in race, sex, and other federally protected characteristics. Training employees to create an inclusive workplace is appropriate and beneficial. The Federal Government is, and must always be, committed to the fair and equal treatment of all individuals before the law.

But training like that discussed above perpetuates racial stereotypes and division and can use subtle coercive pressure to ensure conformity of viewpoint. Such ideas may be fashionable in the academy, but they have no place in programs and activities supported by Federal taxpayer dollars. Research also suggests that blame-focused diversity training reinforces biases and decreases opportunities for minorities.

Our Federal civil service system is based on merit principles. These principles, codified at 5 U.S.C. 2301, call for all employees to "receive fair and equitable treatment in all aspects of personnel management without regard to" race or sex "and with proper regard for their . . . constitutional rights." Instructing Federal employees that treating individuals on the basis of individual merit is racist or sexist directly undermines our Merit System Principles and impairs the efficiency of the Federal service. Similarly, our Uniformed Services should not teach our heroic men and women in uniform the lie that the country for which they are willing to die is fundamentally racist. Such teachings could directly threaten the cohesion and effectiveness of our Uniformed Services.

Such activities also promote division and inefficiency when carried out by Federal contractors. The Federal Government has long prohibited Federal contractors from engaging in race or sex discrimination and required contractors to take affirmative action to ensure that such discrimination does not occur. The participation of contractors' employees in training that promotes race or sex stereotyping or scapegoating similarly undermines efficiency in Federal contracting. Such requirements promote divisiveness in the workplace and distract from the pursuit of excellence and collaborative achievements in public administration. Therefore, it shall be the policy of the United States not to promote race or sex stereotyping or scapegoating in the Federal workforce or in the Uniformed Services, and not to allow grant funds to be used for these purposes. In addition, Federal contractors will not be permitted to inculcate such views in their employees.

Sec. 2. Definitions.

For the purposes of this order, the phrase:

(a) "Divisive concepts" means the concepts that (1) one race or sex is inherently superior to another race or sex; (2) the United States is fundamentally racist or sexist; (3) an individual, by virtue of his or her race or sex, is inherently racist, sexist, or oppressive, whether consciously or unconsciously; (4) an individual should be discriminated against or receive adverse treatment solely or partly because of his or her race or sex; (5) members of one race or sex cannot and should not attempt to treat others without respect to race or sex; (6) an individual's moral character is necessarily determined by his or her race or sex; (7) an individual, by virtue of his or her race or sex, bears responsibility for actions committed in the past by other members of the same race or sex; (8) any individual should feel discomfort, guilt, anguish, or any other form of psychological distress on account of his or her race or sex; or (9) meritocracy or traits such as a hard work ethic are racist or sexist, or were created by a particular race to oppress another race. The term "divisive concepts" also includes any other form of race or sex stereotyping or any other form of race or sex scapegoating.

(b) "Race or sex stereotyping" means ascribing character traits, values, moral and ethical codes, privileges, status, or beliefs to a race or sex, or to an individual because of his or her race or sex.

(c) "Race or sex scapegoating" means assigning fault, blame, or bias to a race or sex, or to members of a race or sex because of their race or sex. It similarly encompasses any claim that, consciously or unconsciously, and by virtue of his or her race or sex, members of any race are inherently racist or are inherently inclined to oppress others, or that members of a sex are inherently sexist or inclined to oppress others.

(d) "Senior political appointee" means an individual appointed by the President, or a non-career member of the Senior Executive Service (or agency-equivalent system).

Sec. 3. Requirements for the United States Uniformed Services.

The United States Uniformed Services, including the United States Armed Forces, shall not teach, instruct, or train any member of the United States Uniformed Services, whether serving on active duty, serving on reserve duty, attending a military service academy, or attending courses conducted by a military department pursuant to a Reserve Officer Corps Training program, to believe any of the divisive concepts set forth in section 2(a) of this order. No member of the United States Uniformed Services shall face any penalty or discrimination on account of his or her refusal to support, believe, endorse, embrace, confess, act upon, or otherwise assent to these concepts.

Sec. 4. Requirements for Government Contractors.

(a) Except in contracts exempted in the manner provided by section 204 of Executive Order 11246 of September 24, 1965 (Equal Employment Opportunity), as amended, all Government contracting agencies shall include in every Government contract hereafter entered into the following provisions: "During the performance of this contract, the contractor agrees as follows:

  1. The contractor shall not use any workplace training that inculcates in its employees any form of race or sex stereotyping or any form of race or sex scapegoating, including the concepts that (a) one race or sex is inherently superior to another race or sex; (b) an individual, by virtue of his or her race or sex, is inherently racist, sexist, or oppressive, whether consciously or unconsciously; (c) an individual should be discriminated against or receive adverse treatment solely or partly because of his or her race or sex; (d) members of one race or sex cannot and should not attempt to treat others without respect to race or sex; (e) an individual's moral character is necessarily determined by his or her race or sex; (f) an individual, by virtue of his or her race or sex, bears responsibility for actions committed in the past by other members of the same race or sex; (g) any individual should feel discomfort, guilt, anguish, or any other form of psychological distress on account of his or her race or sex; or (h) meritocracy or traits such as a hard work ethic are racist or sexist, or were created by a particular race to oppress another race. The term 'race or sex stereotyping' means ascribing character traits, values, moral and ethical codes, privileges, status, or beliefs to a race or sex, or to an individual because of his or her race or sex, and the term 'race or sex scapegoating' means assigning fault, blame, or bias to a race or sex, or to members of a race or sex because of their race or sex.

2. The contractor will send to each labor union or representative of workers with which he has a collective bargaining agreement or other contract or understanding, a notice, to be provided by the agency contracting officer, advising the labor union or workers' representative of the contractor's commitments under the Executive Order of September 22, 2020, entitled Combating Race and Sex Stereotyping, and shall post copies of the notice in conspicuous places available to employees and applicants for employment.

3. In the event of the contractor's noncompliance with the requirements of paragraphs (1), (2), and (4), or with any rules, regulations, or orders that may be promulgated in accordance with the Executive Order of September 22, 2020, this contract may be canceled, terminated, or suspended in whole or in part and the contractor may be declared ineligible for further Government contracts in accordance with procedures authorized in Executive Order 11246, and such other sanctions may be imposed and remedies invoked as provided by any rules, regulations, or orders the Secretary of Labor has issued or adopted pursuant to Executive Order 11246, including subpart D of that order.

4. The contractor will include the provisions of paragraphs (1) through (4) in every subcontract or purchase order unless exempted by rules, regulations, or orders of the Secretary of Labor, so that such provisions will be binding upon each subcontractor or vendor. The contractor will take such action with respect to any subcontract or purchase order as may be directed by the Secretary of Labor as a means of enforcing such provisions including sanctions for noncompliance: Provided, however, that in the event the contractor becomes involved in, or is threatened with, litigation with a subcontractor or vendor as a result of such direction, the contractor may request the United States to enter into such litigation to protect the interests of the United States."

(b) The Department of Labor is directed, through the Office of Federal Contract Compliance Programs (OFCCP), to establish a hotline and investigate complaints received under both this order as well as Executive Order 11246 alleging that a Federal contractor is utilizing such training programs in violation of the contractor's obligations under those orders. The Department shall take appropriate enforcement action and provide remedial relief, as appropriate.

(c) Within 30 days of the date of this order, the Director of OFCCP shall publish in the *Federal Register* a request for information seeking information from Federal contractors, Federal subcontractors, and employees of Federal contractors and subcontractors regarding the training, workshops, or similar programming provided to employees. The request for information should request copies of any training, workshop, or similar programing having to do with diversity and inclusion as well as information about the duration, frequency, and expense of such activities.

Sec. 5. Requirements for Federal Grants.

The heads of all agencies shall review their respective grant programs and identify programs for which the agency may, as a condition of receiving such a grant, require the recipient to certify that it will not use Federal funds to promote the concepts that (a) one race or sex is inherently superior to another race or sex; (b) an individual, by virtue of his or her race or sex, is inherently racist, sexist, or oppressive, whether consciously or unconsciously; (c) an individual should be discriminated against or receive adverse treatment solely or partly because of his or her race or sex; (d) members of one race or sex cannot and should not attempt to treat others without respect to race or sex; € an individual's moral character is necessarily determined by his or her race or sex; (f) an individual, by virtue of his or her race or sex, bears responsibility for actions committed in the past by other members of the same race or sex; (g) any individual should feel discomfort, guilt, anguish, or any other form of psychological distress on account of his or her race or sex; or (h) meritocracy or traits such as a hard work ethic are racist or sexist, or were created by a particular race to oppress another race. Within 60 days of the date of this order, the heads of agencies shall each submit a report to the Director of the Office of Management and Budget (OMB) that lists all grant programs so identified.

Sec. 6. Requirements for Agencies.

(a) The fair and equal treatment of individuals is an inviolable principle that must be maintained in the Federal workplace. Agencies should continue all training that will foster a workplace that is respectful of all employees. Accordingly:

(i) The head of each agency shall use his or her authority under 5 U.S.C. 301, 302, and 4103 to ensure that the agency, agency employees while on duty status, and any contractors hired by the agency to provide training, workshops, forums, or similar programming (for purposes of this section, "training") to agency employees do not teach, advocate, act upon, or promote in any training to agency employees any of the divisive concepts listed in section 2(a) of this order. Agencies may consult with the Office of Personnel Management (OPM), pursuant to 5 U.S.C. 4116, in carrying out this provision; and

(ii) Agency diversity and inclusion efforts shall, first and foremost, encourage agency employees not to judge each other by their color, race, ethnicity, sex, or any other characteristic protected by Federal law.

(b) The Director of OPM shall propose regulations providing that agency officials with supervisory authority over a supervisor or an employee with responsibility for promoting diversity and inclusion, if such supervisor or employee either authorizes or approves training that promotes the divisive concepts set forth in section 2(a) of this order, shall take appropriate steps to pursue a performance-based adverse action proceeding against such supervisor or employee under chapter 43 or 75 of title 5, United States Code.

(c) Each agency head shall:

(i) issue an order incorporating the requirements of this order into agency operations, including by making compliance with this order a provision in all agency contracts for diversity training;

(ii) request that the agency inspector general thoroughly review and assess by the end of the calendar year, and not less than annually thereafter, agency compliance with the requirements of this order in the form of a report submitted to OMB; and

(iii) assign at least one senior political appointee responsibility for ensuring compliance with the requirements of this order.

Sec. 7. OMB and OPM Review of Agency Training.

(a) Consistent with OPM's authority under 5 U.S.C. 4115-4118, all training programs for agency employees relating to diversity or inclusion shall, before being used, be reviewed by OPM for compliance with the requirements of section 6 of this order.

(b) If a contractor provides a training for agency employees relating to diversity or inclusion that teaches, advocates, or promotes the divisive concepts set forth in section 2(a) of this order, and such action is in violation of the applicable contract, the agency that contracted for such training shall evaluate whether to pursue debarment of that contractor, consistent with applicable law and regulations, and in consultation with the Interagency Suspension and Debarment Committee.

(c) Within 90 days of the date of this order, each agency shall report to OMB all spending in Fiscal Year 2020 on Federal employee training programs relating to diversity or inclusion, whether conducted internally or by contractors. Such report shall, in addition to providing aggregate totals, delineate awards to each individual contractor.

(d) The Directors of OMB and OPM may jointly issue guidance and directives pertaining to agency obligations under, and ensuring compliance with, this order.

Sec. 8. Title VII Guidance.

The Attorney General should continue to assess the extent to which workplace training that teaches the divisive concepts set forth in section 2(a) of this order may contribute to a hostile work environment and give rise to potential liability under Title VII of the Civil Rights Act of 1964, 42 U.S.C. 2000e *et seq.* If appropriate, the Attorney General and the Equal Employment Opportunity Commission shall issue publicly available guidance to assist employers in better promoting diversity and inclusive workplaces consistent with Title VII.

Sec. 9. Effective Date.

This order is effective immediately, except that the requirements of section 4 of this order shall apply to contracts entered into 60 days after the date of this order.

Sec. 10. General Provisions.

(a) This order does not prevent agencies, the United States Uniformed Services, or contractors from promoting racial, cultural, or ethnic diversity or inclusiveness, provided such efforts are consistent with the requirements of this order.

(b) Nothing in this order shall be construed to prohibit discussing, as part of a larger course of academic instruction, the divisive concepts listed in section 2(a) of this order in an objective manner and without endorsement.

(c) If any provision of this order, or the application of any provision to any person or circumstance, is held to be invalid, the remainder of this order and the application of its provisions to any other persons or circumstances shall not be affected thereby.

(d) Nothing in this order shall be construed to impair or otherwise affect:

    (i) the authority granted by law to an executive department, agency, or the head thereof; or

    (ii) the functions of the Director of the Office of Management and Budget relating to budgetary, administrative, or legislative proposals.

(e) This order shall be implemented consistent with applicable law and subject to the availability of appropriations.

(f) This order is not intended to, and does not, create any right or benefit, substantive or procedural, enforceable at law or in equity by any party against the United States, its departments, agencies, or entities, its officers, employees, or agents, or any other person.

Signed:
Donald J. Trump
President of the United States of America

Filed 9-25-20; 8:45 am
Federal Register Document 2020-21534

CHAPTER 21

LETTER FROM THE UNITES STATES OFFICE OF PERSONNEL MANAGEMENT

Friday, October 2, 2020

MEMORANDUM FOR HEADS OF EXEC DEPTS AND AGENCIES CHCOs AND HR DIRECTORS

From: DENNIS DEAN KIRK, ESQ., EMPLOYEE SERVICES, ASSOCIATE DIRECTOR

Subject: Mandatory Review of Employee Training under E.O. 13950 September 22, 2020

On September 22, 2020, the President signed Executive Order 13950, titled "Executive Order on Combating Race and Sex Stereotyping." https://www. whitehouse.gov/presidential-actions/executive-order-combating-race-sex-stereotyping/. Section 7(a) of the Executive Order provides: "Consistent with OPM's authority under 5 U.S.C. 4115-4118, all training programs for agency employees relating to diversity and inclusion shall, before being used, be reviewed by OPM for compliance with the requirements of section 6 of this order." (Emphasis supplied.)

The purpose of this memorandum is to provide general guidance on the implementation of Executive Order 13950 and to inform recipients that specific instructions for implementation are forthcoming. All Departments, Agencies, Boards, and Commissions in the Executive Branch of the Federal Government are affected by and subject to this Executive Order.

The Executive Order applies to all diversity and inclusion training programs, including programs developed prior to the issuance of this Executive Order, as well as new programs that may be proposed or established after September 22, 2020. Coverage includes, but is not limited to, all training that is paid for with Federal funds or that Federal employees are required or permitted to view, listen to, or participate in while on Government-paid time. Included is training that is conducted or led by Government employees; training that is conducted or led by contractors or others; live training sessions conducted in person or by any electronic means, whether telephonic or video; materials posted on any Federal agency's public-facing or internal Internet or Intranet sites; and, written or video materials or other content that have been produced or procured with Federal funds and that are available to the general public or that Federal employees are required or permitted to read or view.

The U.S. Office of Personnel Management (OPM) must review and approve training materials before they are used, even if those materials have been utilized in the past.

Please note that OPM will insist upon one complete and all-inclusive submission from each Department, Agency, Board, or Commission. OPM will not accept requests for approval of individual training sessions. OPM will review materials in the order that they are submitted, under the First In First Out (FIFO) business rule and will provide analysis and feedback as quickly as possible.

Agency submissions should be uploaded to the agency-specific section of the Diversity and Inclusion Training Collection Page linked here: https://community.max.gov/display/HumanCapital/Diversity+and+Inclusion+Training+Collection+Page. Submissions will be reviewed in the order they are received.

Agencies are encouraged to review and improve agency materials before submitting them to OPM. OPM must review and approve all diversity and inclusion materials before they are utilized, but if agencies can improve their materials before submitting them, that will expedite completion of the review process.

Please report training that is not done in compliance with the Executive Order 13950, to FEDalerts@omb.eop.gov.

cc: Deputy Chief Human Capital Officers

CHAPTER 22

ADVANCING RACIAL EQUITY AND SUPPORT FOR THE UNDERSERVED COMMUNITIES THROUGH THE FEDERAL GOVERNMENT

20 January 2021
Executive Order 13985
The White House

By the authority vested in me as President by the Constitution and the laws of the United States of America, it is hereby ordered:

Section 1. Policy.

Equal opportunity is the bedrock of American democracy, and our diversity is one of our country's greatest strengths. But for too many, the American Dream remains out of reach. Entrenched disparities in our laws and public policies, and in our public and private institutions, have often denied that equal opportunity to individuals and communities. Our country faces converging economic, health, and climate crises that have exposed and exacerbated inequities, while a historic movement for justice has highlighted the unbearable human costs of systemic racism. Our Nation deserves an ambitious whole-of-government equity agenda that matches the scale of the opportunities and challenges that we face.

It is therefore the policy of my Administration that the Federal Government should pursue a comprehensive approach to advancing equity for all, including people of color and others who have been historically underserved, marginalized, and adversely affected by persistent poverty and inequality. Affirmatively advancing equity, civil rights, racial justice, and equal opportunity is the responsibility of the whole of our Government. Because advancing equity requires a systematic approach to embedding fairness in decision-making processes, executive departments and agencies (agencies) must recognize and work to redress inequities in their policies and programs that serve as barriers to equal opportunity.

By advancing equity across the Federal Government, we can create opportunities for the improvement of communities that have been historically underserved, which benefits everyone. For example, an analysis shows that closing racial gaps in wages, housing credit, lending opportunities, and access to higher education would amount to an additional $5 trillion in gross domestic product in the American economy over the next 5 years. The Federal Government's goal in advancing equity is to provide everyone with the opportunity to reach their full potential. Consistent with these aims, each agency must assess whether, and to what extent, its programs and policies perpetuate systemic barriers to opportunities and benefits for people of color and other underserved groups. Such assessments will better equip agencies to develop policies and programs that deliver resources and benefits equitably to all.

Sec. 2. Definitions.

For purposes of this order: (a) The term "equity" means the consistent and systematic fair, just, and impartial treatment of all individuals, including individuals who belong to underserved communities that have been denied such treatment, such as Black, Latino, and Indigenous and Native American persons, Asian Americans and Pacific Islanders and other persons of color; members of religious minorities; lesbian, gay, bisexual, transgender, and queer (LGBTQ+) persons; persons with disabilities; persons who live in rural areas; and persons otherwise adversely affected by persistent poverty or inequality.

(b) The term "underserved communities" refers to populations sharing a particular characteristic, as well as geographic communities, that have been systematically denied a full opportunity to participate in aspects of economic, social, and civic life, as exemplified by the list in the preceding definition of "equity."

Sec. 3. Role of the Domestic Policy Council.

The role of the White House Domestic Policy Council (DPC) is to coordinate the formulation and implementation of my Administration's domestic policy objectives. Consistent with this role, the DPC will coordinate efforts to embed equity principles, policies, and approaches across the Federal Government. This will include efforts to remove systemic barriers to and provide equal access to opportunities and benefits, identify communities the Federal Government has underserved, and develop policies designed to advance equity for those communities. The DPC-led interagency process will ensure that these efforts are made in coordination with the directors of the National Security Council and the National Economic Council.

Sec. 4. Identifying Methods to Assess Equity.

(a) The Director of the Office of Management and Budget (OMB) shall, in partnership with the heads of agencies, study methods for assessing whether agency policies and actions create or exacerbate barriers to full and equal participation by all eligible individuals. The study should aim to identify the best methods, consistent with applicable law, to assist agencies in assessing equity with respect to race, ethnicity, religion, income, geography, gender identity, sexual orientation, and disability.

(b) As part of this study, the Director of OMB shall consider whether to recommend that agencies employ pilot programs to test model assessment tools and assist agencies in doing so.

(c) Within 6 months of the date of this order, the Director of OMB shall deliver a report to the President describing the best practices identified by the study and, as appropriate, recommending approaches to expand use of those methods across the Federal Government.

Sec. 5. Conducting an Equity Assessment in Federal Agencies.

The head of each agency, or designee, shall, in consultation with the Director of OMB, select certain of the agency's programs and policies for a review that will assess whether underserved communities and their members face systemic barriers in accessing benefits and opportunities available pursuant to those policies and programs. The head of each agency, or designee, shall conduct such review and within 200 days of the date of this order provide a report to the Assistant to the President for Domestic Policy (APDP) reflecting findings on the following:

(a) Potential barriers that underserved communities and individuals may face to enrollment in and access to benefits and services in Federal programs;

(b) Potential barriers that underserved communities and individuals may face in taking advantage of agency procurement and contracting opportunities;

(c) Whether new policies, regulations, or guidance documents may be necessary to advance equity in agency actions and programs; and

(d) The operational status and level of institutional resources available to offices or divisions within the agency that are responsible for advancing civil rights or whose mandates specifically include serving underrepresented or disadvantaged communities.

Sec. 6. Allocating Federal Resources to Advance Fairness and Opportunity.

The Federal Government should, consistent with applicable law, allocate resources to address the historic failure to invest sufficiently, justly, and equally in underserved communities, as well as individuals from those communities. To this end:

(a) The Director of OMB shall identify opportunities to promote equity in the budget that the President submits to the Congress.

(b) The Director of OMB shall, in coordination with the heads of agencies, study strategies, consistent with applicable law, for allocating Federal resources in a manner that increases investment in underserved communities, as well as individuals from those communities. The Director of OMB shall report the findings of this study to the President.

Sec. 7. Promoting Equitable Delivery of Government Benefits and Equitable Opportunities.

Government programs are designed to serve all eligible individuals. And Government contracting and procurement opportunities should be available on an equal basis to all eligible providers of goods and services. To meet these objectives and to enhance compliance with existing civil rights laws:

(a) Within 1 year of the date of this order, the head of each agency shall consult with the APDP and the Director of OMB to produce a plan for addressing:

   (i) any barriers to full and equal participation in programs identified pursuant to section 5(a) of this order; and

   (ii) any barriers to full and equal participation in agency procurement and contracting opportunities identified pursuant to section 5(b) of this order.

(b) The Administrator of the U.S. Digital Service, the United States Chief Technology Officer, the Chief Information Officer of the United States, and the heads of other agencies, or their designees, shall take necessary actions, consistent with applicable law, to support agencies in developing such plans.

Sec. 8. Engagement with Members of Underserved Communities.

In carrying out this order, agencies shall consult with members of communities that have been historically underrepresented in the Federal Government and underserved by, or subject to discrimination in, Federal policies and programs. The head of each agency shall evaluate opportunities, consistent with applicable law, to increase coordination, communication, and engagement with community-based organizations and civil rights organizations.

Sec. 9. Establishing an Equitable Data Working Group.

Many Federal datasets are not disaggregated by race, ethnicity, gender, disability, income, veteran status, or other key demographic variables. This lack of data has cascading effects and impedes efforts to measure and advance equity. A first step to promoting equity in Government action is to gather the data necessary to inform that effort.

(a) Establishment. There is hereby established an Interagency Working Group on Equitable Data (Data Working Group).

(b) Membership.

   (i) The Chief Statistician of the United States and the United States Chief Technology Officer shall serve as Co-Chairs of the Data Working Group and coordinate its work. The Data Working Group shall include representatives of agencies as determined by the Co-Chairs to be necessary to complete the work of the Data Working Group, but at a minimum shall include the following officials, or their designees:

(A) the Director of OMB;

(B) the Secretary of Commerce, through the Director of the U.S. Census Bureau;

(C) the Chair of the Council of Economic Advisers;

(D) the Chief Information Officer of the United States;

(E) the Secretary of the Treasury, through the Assistant Secretary of the Treasury for Tax Policy;

(F) the Chief Data Scientist of the United States; and

(G) the Administrator of the U.S. Digital Service.

(ii) The DPC shall work closely with the Co-Chairs of the Data Working Group and assist in the Data Working Group's interagency coordination functions.

(ii) The Data Working Group shall consult with agencies to facilitate the sharing of information and best practices, consistent with applicable law.

(c) Functions. The Data Working Group shall:

(i) through consultation with agencies, study and provide recommendations to the APDP identifying inadequacies in existing Federal data collection programs, policies, and infrastructure across agencies, and strategies for addressing any deficiencies identified; and

(ii) support agencies in implementing actions, consistent with applicable law and privacy interests, that expand and refine the data available to the Federal Government to measure equity and capture the diversity of the American people.

(d) OMB shall provide administrative support for the Data Working Group, consistent with applicable law.

Sec. 10. Revocation.

(a) Executive Order 13950 of September 22, 2020 (Combating Race and Sex Stereotyping), is hereby revoked.

(b) The heads of agencies covered by Executive Order 13950 shall review and identify proposed and existing agency actions related to or arising from Executive Order 13950. The head of each agency shall, within 60 days of the date of this order, consider suspending, revising, or rescinding any such actions, including all agency actions to terminate or restrict contracts or grants pursuant to Executive Order 13950, as appropriate and consistent with applicable law.

(c) Executive Order 13958 of November 2, 2020 (Establishing the President's Advisory 1776 Commission), is hereby revoked.

Sec. 11. General Provisions.

(a) Nothing in this order shall be construed to impair or otherwise affect:

    (i) the authority granted by law to an executive department or agency, or the head thereof; or

    (ii) the functions of the Director of the Office of Management and Budget relating to budgetary, administrative, or legislative proposals.

(b) This order shall be implemented consistent with applicable law and subject to the availability of appropriations.

(c) Independent agencies are strongly encouraged to comply with the provisions of this order.

(d) This order is not intended to, and does not, create any right or benefit, substantive or procedural, enforceable at law or in equity by any party against the United States, its departments, agencies, or entities, its officers, employees, or agents, or any other person.

Signed:
JOSEPH R. BIDEN JR.
President of the United States of America
Filed 1-22-21; 11:15 am
Federal Register Document 2021-01753 2021-01753

ᔇ SECTION III ᔇ

INDIVIDUAL PERSPECTIVES—
BEARING WITNESS

Take care of your people. Take care of your people.
Take care of your people.

Anyone affiliated with a US military organization is likely to be very familiar with the mantra above. Military leaders understand that the failure or success of any military operation inherently rests on the ability of its organizational members to execute their mission as an effective team. It's hard to imagine a more important phrase for any military leader to internalize than the importance of taking care of those in the unit to enable them to accomplish their missions.

In fact, "take care of your people" is so simple that it is easy to take for granted. After all, what does the phrase even mean? And more importantly, how does a leader go about taking care of his/her/their people? There is no checklist for this leadership task, and it is among the most important task of all.

We believe that "taking care of people" depends on a leader's deep understanding of organizational life, a recognition of his/her/their role within it, and a sincere commitment to internalizing it within one's own leadership philosophy. What we've learned over the years, working with thousands of cadets and military leaders of all ranks, is that the inherent truth lies within the following leadership tenets:

- Organizations are complex.
- Effective leaders must continually adapt to the complexity.
- Reflection is the tool that can effectively empower a leader to understand and adapt to the nascent complexity.
- You, as the leader, own it all.

Collectively, these tenets bring forth some of the most powerful aspects of an organizational system that is dynamic and complex—a system that requires an intentionality of design to allow leaders to form a vision, communicate that vision, and finally execute on that vision in a manner that controls behavior with precision toward mission accomplishment. Commanders, irrespective of the unit, have a singular charge: achieve the organization's mission. Period. And yet, no commander can effectively accomplish a unit's mission without building a trust within a team to motivate that team toward the espoused vision. This can sound trite and easy to do, but yet, we must wonder why we constantly bear witness to the persistent issues that exist in every organization. We believe the fundamental reason that the undesirable issues continue to dominate the headlines is because we inadvertently try to do the wrong things better. Instead, we must rethink the entire approach. If leaders don't like the game they are playing, they must change the game.

In the following section, the contributors are all military members, past and present, who each possess a deep expertise of their own perspectives, as they have been forced to bear witness to issues that most of us have not even recognized, let alone understood. And once these issues are brought forth by minority voices, we quietly would prefer not to address them and hope they will just go away. Why? Because the issues often make us uncomfortable. Attitudes and behaviors that give rise to these challenges are extremely difficult to change. And yet, as leaders, we must. If you accept the charge that leaders have no choice but to take care of the people who look to them for leadership as we work within our units to accomplish our missions, we can only do so by building world-class teams; and to do so, we, as leaders, must constantly put ourselves in the skin of others and try to see the world as they do. We would all be better off if we would spend more time seeking to understand rather than putting our energies in seeking to be understood.

Section 3: Bearing Witness provides strong anecdotal evidence that our organization's systems require continual improvement. The unfortunate truth is that we can never really "fix" the "problems" we recognize because of the inherent turnover that is part of military life. Moreover, a "problem" requires a perspective. What one sees as a problem, others may not. This is one of the key takeaways from the chapters in *Section I* regarding the national dialogue in 2021. Complexity is inherent in any organization, but military organizations are often more complex than other sectors because of the necessary turnover of unit members. Deployments, TDYs, deployments, new recruits, and retirements are all necessary forms of turnover. As soon as a person leaves the unit, another joins, and the system is changed. Expertise is lost from a member who departs, and new expertise is gained from the individual assessing in. Leadership is a continual and ongoing effort that requires constant tweaking of the thousands of proverbial knobs to keep the organization in tune. Regarding the tuning required of "taking care of your people," we must pause, listen, reflect, and try our best to understand the social realities as viewed from every single person within our unit. Everyone matters and everyone is different. It is a difficult, recurrent cycle that will never finish or resolve, but perhaps the leadership challenge posed is not as difficult as one might imagine. Let's consider this challenge through the lens of the four themes above.

Organizations are complex.

A leader cannot "take care of her people" if she doesn't know what they need. In general, military leaders do an excellent job of simplifying the complexity that exists in organizational life by making assumptions, creating heuristics, and applying generalizations that allow a manageable picture of organizational life to emerge. With that picture in place, decisions are made and military units carry out their missions. The picture is never perfect, however, as many of the contributors in the following section point out; some people are being prevented from maximizing the good they can do in the roles they are in. The experiences shared in this section collectively paint a picture illustrating the complexity that isn't always seen by organizational leaders. For that reason alone, we owe them a great deal of gratitude. Their experiences also show us that "taking care of your people" requires more than the repeating of an empty platitude. Organizations are complex. People are complex and have complex needs. It is difficult to take care of people without understanding this at a deep level.

Effective leaders must continually adapt to the complexity.

The main idea here is the "leaders adapt." It's not the other way around. We've been told many stories about generals arriving to their new assignments, gathering all of their officers together, and telling the group how best to adapt to the general. This demonstrates a level of self-awareness while lacking a deep understanding of organizational culture or the nature of organizational systems. The underlying message is, "I'm a general. I'm great. I will share with you my approach that makes me great. Now go figure out how best to adapt to me." This perspective is completely backward. Effective leaders must listen to the voices of all members, then figure out what adaptations are necessary. Every voice matters, and more often than not, it's the most quiet and least shrill that have the deepest insights. This section offers an opportunity for leaders to hear some voices we may not have fully grasped prior to now because we never paid close enough attention. Nevertheless, these voices will, hopefully, help every leader reading the following chapters to better adapt his/her/their understanding so each of us may more effectively take care of our people.

Reflection is the tool that can effectively empower a leader to understand and adapt to the nascent complexity.

At the end of each chapter in this section you will find reflection and group discussion questions. Our hope is that leaders will spend more time on those questions than any other part of this book. *In other words, we feel strongly that these questions are the most important part of the book, as questions are, in and of themselves, a reflective tool that helps us understand the nature of complexity within our organizations.* Please grapple with the questions. Do not assume your initial answers to the questions are correct or someone else's answer is wrong. Watch your reaction to the questions as you encounter them. Watch your reaction to the answers of others. Good reflection is both a skill and an art. We hope that you will seek to become an artisan of reflection, as it can become an incredibly valuable leadership tool—a tool we use to understand the dynamic complexity that exists in organizations today. Reflect on what the contributors in this section are saying about their experiences with diversity and inclusion.

You, as the leader, own it all.

You, as a leader, own it all. It's rare to find a leader who doesn't feel they understand this when things go well. It's equally difficult to find a leader who understands this when things are going poorly. Leaders own it all. In the world of information technology, a system architect is one who designs how technology is laid out and utilized within an organization to make it maximally efficient and improve effectiveness. It's a term we feel leaders should internalize as well, becoming system architects within their respective units, at all levels. Leaders can benefit greatly from seeing themselves as a system architect. Taking care of your people has little meaning in and of itself. However, through the lens of being a system architect—the person who owns and controls the entire system—the term has profound meaning. If a person doesn't feel included or valued, it is, at least partly, because the leader failed to design and control the systems within their unit that excluded someone on the team. Why would any leader take any action that would divide his/her/their command? And yet, as the chapters below illustrate, it happens more often than we would care to admit.

One final thought before you move to the important chapters in this section . . .

We usually associate diversity with inclusion. This is important, but we think there are other aspects beyond inclusion when it comes to both diversity and people, in general. We feel strongly that a major task and competitive advantage for future leaders will be to create environments where all members can thrive. The final chapter in this book articulates the call to action we believe is a viable path, and a call to action for all leaders to improve their organizational effectiveness and performance. It has become known as The Thrive Project, developed by a cross-functional, cross-disciplinary team at the US Air Force Academy. We ask that you do not read it until you have fully engaged and digested the complexity of the remaining chapters in this book.

For it is the Call to Action whose time has come.
Onward~

CHAPTER 23

Defining Moment & Discovery

William D. Rodriguez, Rear Admiral, USN (ret.)
Board Member, Hispanic Veterans Leadership Alliance

Throughout my career, I never experienced any personal discrimination or otherwise diversity-related situation. I treated my fellow officers, my Sailors, and my civilians of all races, ethnicities, and genders with respect and dignity, and I expected the same from them. Throughout my career, I expected the best from my officers, Sailors, and civilians—juniors and seniors alike regardless of their backgrounds. I held myself to similar standards, all the while working hard and performing well.

There are times when you need to evaluate your biases and "check them at the door." Further, there are times when you need to remember the oath you took and swore: to uphold the constitution against all enemies, foreign and domestic. Moreover, there are times in your career when you have one or more "defining moments of leadership." In the fall of 1994, as a mid-grade commander (O-5), I was selected and assigned to my first command—Officer-in-Charge (OIC) of the Naval Command, Control and Ocean Surveillance In-Service Engineering Center East Coast Division, Norfolk Detachment (NISE East Det Norfolk—formerly Naval Electronics Systems Engineering Station Portsmouth, VA). To set the stage, this was a detachment of approximately 350 civilian personnel, a dozen military, and about 400 contractors. I also became the "owner" of approximately fifty separate buildings, ranging in size from 5,000 to 10,000 square feet, that were used as offices, laboratories, and storage, where most of my personnel worked. Furthermore, I assumed command of an organization that was on the Base Realignment and Closure (BRAC) list from FY93, to be closed by 1998. I have always believed in the philosophy of "management (leadership) by walking around (MBWA or LBWA)"—being seen and getting to know your people. I took pride in meeting everyone under my charge and taking interest in their professional and personal lives.

Two months after assuming the position as OIC, NISE East Det Norfolk, I received a very important and private letter from a lawyer representing one of my employees. The letter stated that one of my civilian employees was on a regimen of hormone treatment pills for the past six months in preparation of physically changing his sex to that of a female. Even though my employee had not endured the full sex-change operation, the letter further stated that as of the date of the letter, my employee's name had been changed to a female name and that he was now to be considered, for all intents and purposes, a woman, including using the female facilities/head. (For obvious reasons, I have purposely left out the names of the person(s) involved.) Now, having been in the OIC position for only two months, I had not met all of my employees yet. I also realized that I had a personal dilemma with regard to sex change, and I needed to meet this person in order to understand his or her personal and professional issues with regard to this life-altering change. At the time of this bit of news, I was thirty-nine years of age; I had been in the Navy for seventeen years, and I had never been presented with a personal and professional challenge before, as I saw it. The thought of someone changing sexes and challenging what God had done was personally appalling to me. Nonetheless, I "checked my bias at the door" and in my effort to meet all of my employees, I mustered the courage to go meet this person in hopes that I would try to understand what was occurring in his/her life, and to offer my assistance and support. As you would imagine, NISE East Det Norfolk being a relatively small command, the word had slipped out and spread like wildfire that this person was changing sexes. Rumors abound the command. I was told prior to meeting this person that as a man, he was a former Sailor who was a Submariner, a "biker" who generally had a bad, caustic attitude about people and life in general. When I met this person, I was pleasantly surprised. She had started to take on the features of a woman, and our first meeting was very cordial and informative. For example, she was a very detailed and outstanding computer graphic technician (remember, this was 1994). She was an amateur radio operator, and of all things, she was a practicing Wiccan witch. Moreover, she was working with a local rock and roll radio station to raise the $25,000 for the sex-change operation that was to be done in Sweden. There was not much for me to do for her other than offer my understanding, my support, and to quell the rumors.

About two weeks after meeting this particular employee, an incident occurred between this employee and one of my female employees that became one of my "defining moments of leadership." One Friday afternoon as I was preparing to go home for the weekend (I was a geographic bachelor, and my family lived in Northern Virginia; as a side note, being a geographic bachelor is something I would not recommend doing), my able-bodied administrative assistant busted into my office declaring that my particular employee had walked into the female head in her building, and "she" accidently interrupted a female employee, who was a nursing mother, pumping her breasts. I understood that it was quite an embarrassing moment. My administrative assistant also told me that the female employee had already gone over my head and reported the incident to my commanding officer's inspector general (IG). Well, telling me that particular bit of information concerned me, to say the least, as my female employee had jumped the chain of command.

I immediately called the IG and told her that I would resolve the issue and report my findings and actions taken the following Monday. I then drove over to the building in question and spoke with both parties. I was able to bring some calm to the situation, reassuring them both that this was purely an accidental meeting and that I would spend the weekend procuring the necessary signs and latches for the female head in that building in order to reduce this kind of event from happening again. Both parties agreed to my solution, and the situation was resolved. Afterward, I privately spoke to the female employee who had reported the incident to the IG about the importance of the chain of command, and that I was not happy with the fact that she had jumped the chain of command, regardless of the situation. The following Monday, I called the IG and explained what I had done and that the parties in question were satisfied. The IG was also satisfied . . . case closed.

Needless to say, the happenings of that particular Friday, along with a number of rumors, spread through the command like wildfire. I gave the incident plenty of thought, and regardless of my personal feelings on the matter, my particular employee was under my charge, and the legal system declared that legally he was a she . . . the physical change notwithstanding. It just so happened that I had a number of contractors working in my facilities as well. The following week, I received a call from the president of one of my contractors. He immediately put me on the defensive, declaring that some of his female employees who worked in the particular building where the incident from the Friday past had occurred were afraid and "feared for their lives," thinking that they may be assaulted by my particular employee. Then the president immediately said, "So, what are you going to do about it, Commander?" Well, keeping a calm head, I asked the president if he had ever met my particular employee, and he said that he had not. So, I talked about my particular employee; I explained what really happened and how I had remedied the situation. I further told the president that if he was that concerned about his female employees, he could remove them from my government facilities and take them back to his facilities. I finally told him that my particular employee was not a threat to anyone, that the legal system had declared that he was a she, and that I had sworn an oath to uphold the "law of the land"—the Constitution of the United States of America—and that was that. After that call, a positive word spread through the command about my phone call with the president of one of our contractors and how I had resolved the entire situation. It was quite a "defining moment of leadership" in my career, as well as an enlightening personal experience.

As I mentioned in the beginning of this essay, throughout my career, I never experienced any personal discrimination or otherwise diversity related situation. Toward the end of my career when I became engaged with ANSO, the Hispanic American affinity group that directly supports the sea services, I started looking at what was happening to our Sea Service Hispanic Americans and examining why their numbers in the senior ranks had dwindled and stagnated.

The Hispanic American population has grown to be the largest minority group in this country, and yet, comparatively speaking, our Armed Forces still do not reflect "the face of the nation" with regard to the Hispanic American population. This is particularly true in the flag and general officer, senior officer, and senior enlisted ranks. This is NOT diversity and inclusion! If we look toward the leadership within the Armed Forces for closer mentoring of Hispanic Americans, strive for the highest meritocracy, and push for positions of the highest visibility for Hispanic Americans, then we might make some well-founded headway. We need to examine who is coming up in the ranks; we need to examine who is in zone for O-6, O-7, and O-8, and we need to strongly advocate for them. DoD and the respective services should analyze the reasons why highly qualified Hispanic Americans were not promoted, understand why others were promoted, including possible bias, prejudice, and discrimination, and then present those facts to the powers that be. I am sure that this can be done, given the confidentiality of the deliberations of the promotion boards.

I find it difficult to believe that of all the highly qualified Hispanic Americans who are serving at the O-6 level in our Armed Forces, that very few, if any, "meet the requirements" of the precepts for the flag and general officer promotion boards and are not promoted to flag or general officer. There are a number of O-6s whose records and performance in tough leadership positions show that they are "head and shoulders" above their peers, that they meet the requirements of the promotion board precepts, and yet, they are not selected for flag or general officer. There is no question that the importance of meritocracy, i.e. becoming the best qualified candidate for promotion and for selection to higher positions of leadership, rather than the importance of any racial, ethnic, or diversity label, is understood in most organizations. However, when it is time to be looked at for promotion, they are not promoted. Is it an issue of subjectivity or objectivity on the particular promotion board? Are we seeing unconscious discrimination and bias at the more senior promotion boards?

Until 2007, an unconscious bias somewhat existed in our Navy toward those who were not serving aboard cruisers and destroyers, flying strike fighter jets, serving in special warfare teams, or serving aboard nuclear-powered submarines—"primary warfare platforms." If you were not assigned to one of those "primary warfare platforms," you were otherwise considered a "second-class citizen," and your chances for promotion to the senior ranks was minimized. (I suspect the same is true in the other services.) When I was assigned to the CNO's Diversity Council in 2007, I discovered that there still existed some unconscious bias toward Hispanic Americans and African Americans with regard to those "primary warfare platforms." The council members were told in one of our initial meetings that Hispanic Americans and African Americans "were not smart enough" to go through the training and education required in order to be assigned to one of the "primary warfare platforms." Needless to say, those of us in the meeting were shocked to hear this bit of information, and we immediately went to work to dispel this bias. I am afraid that that unconscious bias still exists today and will require a generation or two to make this change.

Another glaring issue that came to my attention was continuing discrimination and bias, be it conscious or unconscious, toward those Hispanic Americans who spoke with an accent and whose backgrounds originated from particular Latin American countries or islands. We are a "land of immigrants," and speaking with accents is common in country. Accents tend to identify where you are from and your background. There is no reason for any negative bias or discrimination toward those who speak with any kind of an accent.

Family ties within Hispanic American families are very close, especially in those countries and islands, e.g. Puerto Rico. Further, as we try to balance our professional career with our families and vice versa, it becomes increasingly important for those in leadership positions to understand the position that our Hispanic American officers and enlisted deal with on a daily basis relative to their families. There are some officers in the Coast Guard who take assignments in Puerto Rico, sometimes several assignments in a row, in order to care for their aging parents. This is sometimes seen as a detriment to the officer's career, when in fact, other officers who choose to take several assignments in a row in other places are not looked upon as detrimental to the officer's career.

During my tenure as the National President of ANSO (2011–2019), I discovered that the retention concerns of senior Hispanic American officers and enlisted, and why the promotion zone pools contain a small number, if any, of Hispanic Americans, should be analyzed and brought to the forefront. Within the sea services, we have seen more and more Hispanic American officers and enlisted taking advantage of retirement at their first opportunity. I saw many Hispanic American officers within the sea services at the O-4 and O-5 ranks and many enlisted at the E-6 and above ranks, retire at the twenty-year point in their career (by the way, these officers were clearly on a path toward promotion to O-6 and beyond). I further discovered that this was the time, at their twenty-year point, when their children were graduating from high school; that they were tired of longer deployments that were straining the family nucleus; that they did not want to contend with the stress of budget issues that they saw those in higher ranks having to deal with on a daily basis; and that they were being offered lucrative opportunities in the private sector. This dilemma is reducing the pool of qualified Hispanic American officers and enlisted who could possibly be promoted into the higher ranks and therefore help the sea services in particular reflect the "leadership face of the nation" in the senior officer and enlisted ranks. I am sure that this dilemma exists in the other services as well. It is obvious that we must work on retaining our best qualified Hispanic Americans past their twenty-year point. Most importantly, we must work to help them balance their family life with their service to our country.

Finally, I have discovered the importance of mentoring. As I climbed my career ladder to flag rank, I began to realize the importance of mentoring and how mentoring helped me climb that ladder. A mentor is someone who is not necessarily older, and perhaps a mentor is someone who doesn't "look like you," but a mentor is someone who is wiser and more experienced in your field of endeavor. Once you have established a professional and perhaps a personal relationship with your mentor, he or she will become your advocate and professional confidant. Your mentor will advise you along your career path, and he or she may even open "doors of opportunities" for you. Your mentor may have a broader vision for you, and your mentor's sage advice may take you out of your "comfort zone" in order to broaden your career. (As we all know, there are good jobs, and there are "good jobs"!) This advice is always subject to conversation between the two of you.

You may consider having more than one mentor in order to give you different perspectives on your career. But the entire point of having a mentor, or more, is to have a "different set of eyes," someone to help navigate you through the "minefield" called a career, and to help you become the best qualified candidate for promotion and selection to command.

I believe that the Armed Forces recognize that the recruitment of Hispanic American men and women is no longer a matter of equity, but rather a significant necessity given the rapid growth of this segment of the population. I firmly believe, as do many of our senior officer and enlisted leaders, that we will be better served by continuing to eliminate the racial, ethnic, and diversity labels. With that said, diversity and inclusion has been proven to be important and a factor in the strength of any organization. Nevertheless, we must continue to exhibit the inherent leadership qualities in continuing to promote the importance of diversity and inclusion; eliminating prejudice; focusing on eliminating the ethnic, racial, and gender gaps; promoting mentoring, career management, and advocacy in order to be the best qualified candidate for selection to command and promotion to the next higher grade; advocating those qualified Hispanic American officers for the "right" jobs; promoting Hispanic Americans to flag and general officer without prejudice; supporting recruiting the best qualified candidate for the Armed Forces; and supporting increased education of our local youth. Further, HVLA and other Hispanic-oriented professional groups must continue to be leadership role models for their subordinates, their peers, and their seniors alike, promoting recruitment, meritocracy, and retention of our Hispanic Americans.

Reflection Questions:

1. The author suggests that leaders should evaluate their biases and "check them at the door." What does that mean to you, and to what extent do you do it?

2. To what extent do your biases impact your behavior when it comes to treating others with dignity and respect?

Group Discussion:

The author discussed the importance of mentoring. What formal and informal mentoring programs does your organization have? What changes should be made to your organization's mentoring programs to ensure that all members of your organization get the mentoring they deserve?

The author suggests that leaders should evaluate their biases and "check them at the door." What can your organization do to create a system or culture where this becomes the norm for all organizational members?

CHAPTER 24

NOT SO INSULAR: CONTINUING A LEGACY OF PUERTO RICAN SERVICE

Hila Levy, DPhil
Major, USAFR

When I boarded a plane in San Juan, Puerto Rico, to depart for the US Air Force Academy in Colorado Springs, a bright-eyed seventeen year old, I was excited, nervous, scared, and anxious—all the things anyone headed to college, especially a university with basic training, might feel about the unknown. In my mind, I had a vision of a student body that would be a perfect representation of every corner of the country. Isn't that what the limited number of appointments from each congressional district, state, and territory would ensure? I would meet people from all over. I would see the American melting pot in action. We would become brothers and sisters. We would all have the same goal: a lifetime of service in the Air Force.

These "best and brightest" would come from the tops of their classes, where they were athletes and leaders of their communities, steeped in a deep sense of America's history and legacy in choosing to pursue a civic duty of military service. To me, at that tender age, the military held the promise of ultimate meritocracy—a place where no matter where you came from, the color of your skin, your ethnicity, how much money was in your bank account, or who your parents were, we would all start as equals. The military would be not just an apolitical public institution, but also one free of internal politics. Through hard work and performance, the best performers would move up the ranks and lead the nation. My brothers and sisters would be the ultimate team of Ameri-*CANs*: "Nothing can stop the US Air Force!"

I was quickly set straight. I would soon experience sexism, which I expected. I would experience hurtful religious discrimination, which I knew was sadly still commonplace. But what I was completely unprepared for in my earliest days in the US Air Force was hearing that Puerto Ricans were not Americans.

Thinking back, I can't quite pinpoint the first few times it struck me, but it was fairly early on that I was being asked if I was an international cadet. Innocent enough. They must not have heard me correctly. Maybe they heard Costa Rica, the longstanding Central American democracy, and not the US island territory I came from.

Me: No, I'm from Puerto Rico.

Cadre: So how can you be here?

Me: Umm, the same way you can be. I applied? (replying with a confused look)

Cadre: Did you have to get a green card?

Me: Why would I need that? I'm a US citizen.

I started putting two and two together. I was being asked about my citizenship. My *provenance*. My papers. Like a sparkling wine having to prove I came from Champagne or an artwork hanging on the wall that no one is sure is really a Picasso.

The implication was I had taken a *deserving American's* place, a twist on an accusation often leveled at women and minorities. The late Justice Ruth Bader Ginsburg often recounted being asked to justify taking a "man's place" as a female law student by the dean of Harvard Law in 1956. Was this how that felt almost fifty years later?

Puerto Rico has been a US territory since 1898. The island's US military history began with its invasion on July 25, 1898, in the Spanish-American War. Lieutenant General Nelson Miles, the Commanding General of the US Army who led the landing, publicly proclaimed on July 28, 1898, that the purpose of the American invasion was to bring Puerto Rico a "banner of freedom." The war progressed, and on December 10, 1898, the Treaty of Paris ceded the United States the Spanish territories of Puerto Rico and Guam, amid other concessions.

Puerto Ricans have been US citizens by birth since the Jones–Shafroth Act was signed into law by President Woodrow Wilson on March 2, 1917. For more than a century, persons born in the Puerto Rico have the same "papers" and passports as those born in Missouri, Pennsylvania, or any other state of the Union.

It was surprising then to get questions tinged with disdain, a dark laugh, and suspicion of some kind of crime. "How long was the raft ride?" "Did you have to cross the big, bad river?" These questions were less innocent, and when coming from upperclassmen, skirted into the realm of harassment. "How big is your treehouse?" "Is this your first time wearing shoes?" "How you learn to eh-speeek Eng-uh-lish?"

Maybe this is just part of the game, I would think. It is just the price we all pay to get through basic training. If this wasn't the land of equal opportunity, surely it would be just a few weeks away. Not so much. When Puerto Rico's Olympic basketball team defeated the US Dream Team in Athens that summer on 15 August, the pride I felt for my island was soon dimmed by the nasty commentary and tirades I was subjected to at the cadet dining facility. It would surely pass, right?

The finish line hasn't come yet. It's been over sixteen years, and I've now spent nearly half of my life explaining my "provenance" and defending my ability to serve in the American military whenever my hometown comes up.

I say "whenever my hometown comes up," because I live on a paradoxical edge whereby my answer is a can of worms. Both my "American-ness" and my "Puerto Rican-ness" can be questioned at the same time. For those who *otherize* people unlike them, I'm not American enough and I need to "bring the receipts." For those who think they know "what a Puerto Rican looks like" or "sounds like," that can't be me. My skin isn't dark enough [for them]. My accent isn't strong enough [for them]. This paradox is a personal and societal tragedy in so many ways, and it makes putting this into words painfully difficult.

For one, I understand that this duality privileges me. I can "pass" and not suffer much of the unconscious bias in place against Hispanic and Latinx military personnel (if you can get past my uncommon name and my gender, of course). Unless I'm speaking Spanish and being told to "go back to my country" at a grocery store, I generally do not experience random acts of hatred to which I know many friends have been subjected based on accents, skin colors, and appearances. I sit in rooms representing a "hidden" layer of diversity. Sadly, that has also meant that I have heard unfiltered comments that probably would not have been shared had I been wearing a name tag with "Martínez," "Rivera," or "Hernández," for example. Prejudices tend to come out when people think they are in shared company— until I come out of hiding, of course.

My response to this charged difference has long been to go it alone, to put my head down and work hard, and to not make myself a target. To be clear, I have never wanted to be a poster child for anything. I felt resilient enough to continue in my daily life pursuing my long-term goals and avoiding being either a victim or a vocal advocate.

On a weekend in November during my senior year, I was awarded a scholarship to attend graduate school in the United Kingdom. I was shocked and overjoyed. I never thought I had a chance and had applied mainly thanks to the encouragement of faculty who believed in me more than I ever did in myself. It was not until I read the press release the next day that I found out I was the first Puerto Rican resident to win a Rhodes Scholarship. Thrust into an uncomfortable spotlight, I no longer had the option to dissociate my public persona from my private identity. But on most days, I really wished I could.

> *Would I be accepted now?*
> *Would I be good enough for the unstoppable US Air Force?*
> *Would I be a good steward of the pressure of being inextricably linked as a representative of my island?*

Worse still in my mind was the idea that I had succeeded *because* of the Air Force instead of in spite of it, swimming upstream to *overcome* the barriers and attitudes in place. My internal debate was problematic. I felt so many burdens, and I didn't have a thick enough skin yet to shoulder it.

The duality of my experience only became starker. In Puerto Rico, and on paper, I was a role model, an inspiration, I was told. My achievements, limited in my view, were splashed across military public affairs releases. In person, the impostor syndrome was real. What could I ever hope to achieve? How could I make the world a better place when I felt so insecure? Keep studying, try harder, keep working?

I hid for a long time, yet had a target on my back for being a "first" that I could never fully ignore. My early assignments on active duty were exceedingly uncomfortable in the workplace. I remember being brought into a conference room the day I got my entry badge at my lieutenant-era duty station and being told, "Everybody hates you. You will not succeed here." My long days at work had to become performance art: confident enough to give brilliant briefings to commanders, but otherwise unassuming, hidden, and vastly apologetic at all other times to my bosses for my mere existence.

Thankfully, Air Force culture has since started an upward crawl away from some of its antiquated expectations of women and other minority groups. Restrictions on Don't Ask, Don't Tell were lifted, and it felt, to me, like incremental gains were being made. Nonetheless, the year 2020 has shown how little we have moved the needle in many ways—how far we still have to go. I am humbled by the numerous personnel who are voicing their experiences with discrimination and inequity and continue to learn from everyone around me.

I no longer feel I have to wait to be asked where I'm from anymore to show the real me. My Puerto Rican identity is a part of me. It is just *one* part, a label, and not the only one I bear. I don't need to box myself in with the things that make me unique as a Jewish, Puerto Rican, woman, wife, mother, scientist, scholar, friend, and officer. I joined the Air Force to serve a greater purpose, so if I am going to lead change, I want to do so in partnership with everyone around me who took an oath to defend our Constitution.

Reflection Questions:

1. To what extent have you had a similar experience to the author?
2. When interacting with others, are you more likely to feel excluded or make others feel excluded and why?
3. What can you do to help make those you associate with feel included?
4. How do you know if the environment you work in fosters inclusion?
5. To what extent do you feel the author was experiencing a sufficient sense of belonging in order to thrive?

Group Discussion:

What are the demographics of this country?
How did these demographics evolve? How does this evolution impact current society?
How does this evolution impact the US military?

What was the original concept of the American melting pot?
What gave rise to the idea that America is/could be a melting pot?
Why was this notion popular?
Where does the notion of a "melting pot" stand now?

If the people who have the same goal—a lifetime of service in the Air Force—are divided within the group due to different group memberships and different beliefs about others' groups, how does this impact the common goal? How does the division play out day-to-day?

If the "best and brightest" are gathered to form a group who will work and learn together, and this group is diverse across multiple categories, what must be in place within the organization to support the continued growth, development, and ultimately the contributions of those who were selected because they are the "best and brightest"?

To what extent should "starting as equals" mean treating everyone the same? To what extent should "starting as equals" mean treating each person according to his/her/their unique needs? If the answer is "it depends," what does it depend on?

Quick, name all of the US territories. Could you name them all?
What is the citizenship of people who live in one of the US territories?
What does your knowledge about the US territories indicate?
If you interact with a fellow military member who is from a US territory, how might the "filter" of your knowledge impact how you treat them?

As we recognize and seek to embrace diversity through our increased understanding of it, some groups have perceived that they are being displaced. Why do you think this might be?
Does this indicate that diversity is a zero sum game? Why? Why not?

When you think about your key group memberships and identities* which ones, in your perception, are currently being increasingly valued, and which ones seem to be increasingly displaced? What does this tell you about the complexity of our society, the treatment of individuals, and the challenges of managers to create workplaces where everyone can thrive?

*gender, race, geographic origin, religion, sexual orientation, socioeconomic group, family structure, political orientation, age, generation (e.g. baby boomer, millennial, Gen X, Y, Z), and more!

What is the problem with making comments to a person such as, "How long was the raft ride?" "Did you have to cross the big, bad river?" "How big is your treehouse?" "Is this your first time wearing shoes?" "How you learn to eh-speeek Eng-uh-lish?" What do you think is the impact of these questions a) on the individual whose group is targeted, and b) on the group witnessing the question?

Basic, and other military trainings, have goals. What are these goals? _____
(Think of a specific training you have most recently experienced or have a role in

executing.) Traditions and rituals are often part of training. What are the traditions and rituals in trainings you lead that are inclusive of all participants? What traditions and rituals serve to exclude one or more groups? What can you do with this information?

Select one of your own group memberships. What general expectations/norms does this group have about diversity or sameness within the group? What impact do these expectations/norms have on the group? What impact do these expectations/norms have on you? What do your answers tell you about diversity and how people are perceived and treated on a broader scale?

When you are (or think you are) in the company of people who are members of one of your groups, what comments or attitudes are sometimes voiced about other groups when your group thinks they are "behind closed doors"? What impact do these comments on you? What impact do these comments have on the group? What impact do these comments have on the behavior of group members when you/they are "in public"?

What parts of your own constellation of identities are "in hiding" (you don't openly identify with one or more identities when in the company of people of other identities). What impact does this have on you personally to have parts of yourself in hiding? What impact does being "in hiding" have on your contribution to the whole? How might you be different, your contributions be different, if you weren't in hiding?

If, in the previous question you responded, "I'm NOT in hiding in any way. I bring my full self to my work and life!" What benefits does this bring you? What benefits does this, by extrapolation, bring to the world? What do you think your life and your contributions would be if you could not be yourself because some part of you was not accepted? What do your answers tell you about the environments we collectively must create for all? What do your answers tell you about the environment you must create for the people in your life and work?

When in your life have you been a role model or inspiration for others? If becoming a role model involved multiple variables, not just your hard work, what are these elements? (For example, Hila Levy was thrust into the position of role model as a function of her geographic origin, her intelligence, her hard work, her gender, and more.) How does it impact you (positively and negatively) to know that you may be a role model or inspiration in part because of something you have little or no control over? How do your answers reflect on your own thriving? How do your answers reflect on your perceptions of the health of the institutions or organizations you belong to?

Maj Hila Levy has previously served in a variety of roles as an active duty and reserve Air Force intelligence officer at tactical, operational, and head-quarters-level assignments in the Republic of Korea, Japan, and the United Kingdom. She is a top graduate of the US Air Force Academy, where she became the first Puerto Rican resident to be awarded a Rhodes Scholarship. She earned a master's in historical research and a master's in biology from the University of Oxford, a master's in environmental planning and management from Johns Hopkins University, and a doctorate in zoology from the University of Oxford. Alongside her military career, she has published research in several peer-reviewed scientific journals, worked as a translator, and advised government agencies on data-driven policy-making. She is currently pursuing a master's in military strategy at the School of Advanced Air and Space Studies at Maxwell Air Force Base in Alabama.

The opinions expressed in this article are the author's own and do not represent the views of the United States Air Force, Department of Defense, and/or the United States government.

CHAPTER 25

BG1

Bettina Nicole Bush
Daughter of Charles V. Bush, USAFA Class of 1963

*T*his chapter celebrates the life and achievements of Charles V. Bush, the first Black cadet to graduate from the US Air Force Academy in the class of 1963. Chuck was an enduring champion for diversity in the Air Force. He passed away in 2012 and is buried at the Air Force Academy Cemetery.

Charles V. Bush, known as BG-1, was "the first" many times in his life. As he prepared to address the 2011 USAFA graduates, he knew this simple truth defined him. He was the first Black graduate—hence, the moniker—of the United States Air Force Academy. There was a lot to unpack in his short time on the commencement ceremony stage that afternoon in Colorado Springs.

At age fourteen, Chuck was the first Black page recruited to the United States Supreme Court panel. He was the first to speak out about the need for diversity in the Air Force, and he was the first to present factual evidence supporting the need for change to those who could make it happen. He used a lifetime of observations, a calm demeanor, and a realization that everyone is an individual to make the most of his time in government, from his page assignment, to his time in Vietnam, to his retirement, where he worked to increase Air Force diversity. And, he was one of the first people to encourage individuals who doubted their ability to succeed, saying, "Yes, you can." He would spend his retirement fighting for true equality and true opportunity in the United States military, propelling his ideas to the top of the Air Force chain of command.

Understanding Chuck, as his friends and family called him, means understanding his history. Charles V. Bush was a force in government facilities from the age of fourteen. At times, he broke ground unassumingly; other times, he did it with determination. His legacy, which benefits all future Air Force cadets of color, and all people of color, reaches beyond experience in the military. It extends beyond his death. His dedication to making the world a better place will continue to serve us for decades to come. In the weeks leading up to this return to his beloved USAFA, he painstakingly reworked the words he would deliver to the impressionable cadets. Had he captured it? He believed he had.

"Diversity is a leadership issue."

The statement had become his mantra, his mission, his legacy. This was the main point Chuck brought back from the war, and in fact from his collective experiences before and after the war. As he reflected upon his life, he wrote:

> It is a story of a boy who was given the opportunity to become a pioneer, pathfinder, and trailblazer and assumed the responsibility of providing the broadest and strongest possible shoulders upon which the, roughly 2,200 fellow Air Force Academy African American and other minority cadets and graduates can stand.

~ Bush, USAFA National Character and Leadership Symposium
Speech, 25 Feb 2011

As a child, Chuck was expected to succeed. This was fine with him. His love of reading landed him in the library most of the time, consuming books as voraciously as most kids consumed candy. His teachers told him he could either embrace and utilize the academic advantage presented to him or become a ditch digger. He chose to embrace his studies.

In 1954, at the end of Chuck's ninth-grade year, the United States Supreme Court, led by Chief Justice Earl Warren, in its groundbreaking decision *Brown v. the Board of Education*, ended school segregation. Chief Justice Warren then asked the board to find a short, Black page to be part of the Supreme Court system. Chuck was picked to be the first Black page in the United States Supreme Court because, according to him, he was short and wouldn't tower over the judges, and he was Black. He has been quoted as saying that there was no separating being a page from being Black at that time; the two could not be exclusive. The Supreme Court needed to show the American people that the Court was serious about its decision. Chuck learned early that showing people how to behave, rather than telling them, worked. This was modeled in Chief Justice Warren's leadership.

Chuck was ushered from a colored junior high school in the Washington, DC, metro area into an all-White environment, where only the Jewish page would sit with him at lunchtime. He completed his high school education at the page school, which was a private-public school: a private school funded by federal money. He was suddenly living in a world of fame, akin to an overnight celebrity, because he was the first. He recalls a conversation he had with his dad after he was selected, and how his father urged him to maintain a balance in his life. His parents wanted to emphasize that he was still a child, even though the world would begin treating him as an adult. He had a sudden responsibility to the future of his race, yet he remained a boy. That's a lot of pressure for a fourteen-year-old! Still, he took it all in stride, quietly observing the attitudes of those around him.

He'd need this determination and positive attitude to do well as the only Black page to the Supreme Court. At the time, Congress was controlled by Southern Democrats. Chuck was not well received overall, but no one wanted to cross the chief justice. Chuck was accepted by some, simply tolerated by others, but was never directly, or purposely, disrespected while serving his civic duty as page. There may have been some underhanded negative reactions to him, but he more readily focused on the positive experiences.

In the Supreme Court, all management and administrative positions were held by Whites, while all manual positions were held by people of color. This cultural difference was a reminder that Washington was still a Southern city. Chuck recognized the protection and admiration he received from the manual laborers, weighed against an uncertainty among some of the administrative professionals, as to how to treat him. This helped him realize relationships mattered. His relationships with not only the adults, but his fellow pages, helped him learn an essential lesson about people in general.

Everyone, no matter the color, had to adjust to his position with the Supreme Court. He was treated as if he were White by nearly everyone, as they weren't sure how else to treat him. They were very careful in dealing with him because they knew that if they differentiated between him and the other pages, it would be noted very quickly. The chief justice was not somebody to screw with. Chuck was Warren's idea, and Warren's appointment. No one wanted to step on the chief justice's toes.

Still, this caused resentment, confusion, and accidental slips by otherwise well-intentioned people. Observing the general reactions of those around him, and how each reaction changed between each individual, helped him realize that dealing with racism meant dealing with an individual person's flaws. In the future, when he would have issues with subordinates, he would try to find the individual's flaw, rather than assuming racism. He knew when racism was behind someone's actions; he simply chose to handle each instance as a flaw that could be improved.

His time as a page was also where he began to learn that diversity is a leadership issue. One ordinary day in biology class, his teacher unintentionally equated his hand to a bottom-feeding fish. She pointed out that the fish had a light underbelly and a dark back, similar to his hand. She was normally sensitive, yet in this instance, she mistakenly succumbed to an insensitive parallel. She never noticed his astonishment in not only being called out but also in being compared to a fish. Again, in this instance, it was clear that leading by example is far more important than telling someone what to do.

The teacher missed an opportunity to lead by example and as a leader, demonstrate moral diversity. Chuck encountered these accidental slips so often that he concurred, before he entered the Air Force, that diversity is something that must begin in our leaders, and therefore, it is the full responsibility of leaders to encourage diversity. His mantra, even if he didn't yet realize it, was taking shape.

Graduation day from page school soon arrived, and much to his disappointment, Chuck was denied awards at the ceremony. He had studied hard and become a class leader. He was expecting some of the prestigious awards that were instead given to his classmates. Ultimately, he learned that the school had allowed organizations, such as the Kiwanis Club, to disqualify him based on race. Again, diversity became a leadership issue, and his leaders had failed. They had an opportunity to openly promote diversity, but due to reasons unknown to Chuck at the time, chose instead to overlook him. Again, he took the slight in stride.

Chuck enrolled in Howard University after being a page because he was denied entrance into the USAFA the first time he applied. However, he would soon be recruited to the USAFA by Major General Benjamin L. Hunton (USAR) and the Honorable James C. Evans. They had been working toward integration of the US Armed Forces for years. Chuck's recruitment was, in part, used to further their recruitment efforts. Again, Chuck realized, diversity is a leadership issue. For the second time in his life, he had encountered leaders who wanted to incite change and who had chosen him to help them in their plans for change. He was meeting all types of leaders: those who used their leadership to promote diversity, such as Hunton; those who used it to reject diversity; and those somewhere in the middle, such as the insensitive biology teacher, who sometimes accidentally worked against themselves.

Sometimes, you have to see things done wrong in order to see to it that they're done right. When Chuck was a cadet—they called him Charlie in those days—they took a trip to a neighboring school. There was a class dance offered by the host school, at a local country club. The three Black cadets, including himself, were asked to find something else to do while their White classmates attended the event. Their leaders had failed them. Later, in an unrelated event, his classmate was reprimanded by a teacher for interracial dating. The teacher lowered the student's grade by two letters. When the head of the department found out, he said he would reinstate the grade, but the teacher would receive no punishment for the racism. The department head was worried about harming the career and family of the teacher more than offering justice to the student who was wronged. Chuck noted that this was protection of one's own kind and that this was how it felt to be a person of color in the military at that time. Already, he and his classmates were getting a feel for what their futures looked like with this type of leadership if they chose to stay on the military career path.

Often, he was seen as "just the Black guy in the room" instead of as an equal or even as ranking above someone else. Due to stark differences in how he was treated by different people, he in turn sought to regard everyone on an individual basis, no matter their outer appearances or biases. He realized he needed to learn the culture and customs of others in order to understand them. He had to learn to adapt at a young age, while retaining his culture and self-respect.

Chuck wanted a military career, but not if it meant fighting harder than everyone else for his earned advancements. He shared his questions with his wife, Tina, after he returned from Vietnam. Should I stay even if I have to do more than anybody else in order to make sure that I get promoted? Am I going to have to be on the path that they want me to be on or on the path that I feel I should be on? His deep love for his country and his insistence on serving one's country to the best of one's abilities made this a tough decision for him. Together, he and Tina struggled with it. This man, who had served the Supreme Court and broken color barriers, was still being denied privilege. He knew it was an unfair part of the cultural narrative, but he also remembered that people give advantages to those who are similar to themselves. In the end, Chuck and Tina correctly assumed that he could better support his family in the private sector, where he would have a better chance at getting merit-based promotions.

He loved America. He loved the American dream. He loved everything the military had to offer. However, he was torn between his love for his country and the inequality he saw in the Air Force, and later, in the Air Force Academy. He realized that people tend to give opportunities to people in which they see themselves. If everyone at the top is a White male, they are promoting all the White males. This gave him pause.

Chuck left the military and enrolled in Harvard Business School, because there weren't many businesspeople of color, and he wanted to change that.

He believed in a person's unique gifts, which is why he stayed involved in the minority youth of the USAFA. He helped many youngsters realize that their gifts were meant for service to self and service to country. He knew everyone wasn't meant for the military; he believed everyone could use their gifts to serve the country he loved. He continued to love this country, even after recognizing the military's lack of attention to diversity. It was this heart and this passion to make changes that would later bring him in front of top government military officials to fuel diversity in the military.

Chuck and a determined team of researchers had faced bureaucratic resistance to disclose public information regarding racial and ethnic Air Force officer corps profiles. They needed this information for a study they were conducting on actual USAFA diversity parameters. His team found a way around this, eventually building the "DOD Executive Diversity Study" in 2008. This document would be the base to support the debate Bush faced in the higher ranks of the United States military. The findings were that Caucasians received higher promotional rates to the executive corps as compared to minorities.

The study was presented to the two presidential candidates, their transition teams, and selected congressional leaders. The DOD civilian and military senior leadership were briefed on the study. The general response was a request for leadership on necessary change within the military ranks.

Chuck's team communicated that the issue must be made an operational mission element instead of a personnel program. Their study had been a success; now there needed to be a plan in place for moving forward. The result of his actions was attention from a range of different politicians, and the establishment of the Military Leadership Diversity Commission, which conducted a comprehensive evaluation and assessment of policies that provide opportunities for the promotion and advancement of minority members of the Armed Forces, including minority members who are senior officers.

The plan was pushed forward by General Norton A. Schwartz, with the support of Bush and his team. The diversity construct, proposed and approved, consists of an Air Force Diversity Committee and an Air Force Diversity Operations Office. The Diversity Office produced an Air Force Diversity Road Map, communication plan, and campaign plan. Finally, on October 13, 2010, Secretary of the Air Force Michael Donley promulgated Air Force Policy Directive 36-70, Personnel: Diversity, which commences with the statement: "Diversity is a military necessity." Diversity is a leadership issue.

This was among Chuck's proudest moments.

The Air Force Academy cadets listened intently as he stood before them that day in 2011, riveted by the words of one of their own. The first. He shared his journey from start to finish. This particular speech carried a deeper gravitas for him than could be understood by those who were unaware of his recent cancer diagnosis. He descended from the podium with a fierce sense of duty fulfilled, invigorated with hope for his country. He returned home to Montana, where he and Tina had retired and where he would hold on just long enough to see the 2012 reelection of President Barack Obama. The first.

Though he had left the Air Force officially, he never left the military completely, especially after retirement from the private sector. He continued to encourage minority Air Force cadets to keep going. He worked tirelessly to ensure young minorities made more of their lives than society expected. This is why, to this day, all USAFA Black graduates number themselves. Bush was the first. They're in the thousands now.

Chuck knew, after leaving the military, that promotion is influenced by favoritism, nepotism, and sexual and/or racial discrimination. He often spoke less about race, however, and more about individual flaws in people's perceptions. His time in the military, the Supreme Court, and the USAFA may have shown him racism, but it also showed him the individuality in all people. It showed him that embracing diversity must begin at the top, with the leaders.

Reflection Questions:

1. What does Chuck Bush's statement, "Diversity is a leadership issue" mean to you?

2. To what extent do you agree with the statement, "Diversity is a leadership issue"?

3. What can you do as a leader to "own" the diversity issue?

4. Do leaders have a responsibility to create environments where their members can thrive?

Group Discussion:

When have you been "the first"? What was your experience? What did your being "the first" contribute to the larger group or system. What were the gifts you received as a consequence of being "the first"? Specifically, what was the price you paid for being the first?

What do you think are the attitudes and behaviors required to persevere when you are "the first"? Why are these attitudes and behaviors important for yourself preservation? Why are these attitudes and behaviors important in the service of your personal mission?

What beliefs, values, and behaviors are required of an ally and of a champion of a) the inclusion of diverse individuals and b) creation and implementation of environments where all members can thrive?

Talk about the last time you said, "Yes, you can," to someone who was not a family member or friend? What happened? What were the effects of your words? If you cannot recall a time, who in your environment might you authentically say these words to? As a thought experiment, what do you think might happen if you said, "Yes, you can," and your actions supported these words?

What is the legacy you'd like to leave as it concerns creating and sustaining an environment where everyone can thrive? From where you stand right now, what is the first small step you can take this week toward building that legacy?

If diversity is a leadership issue, as Chuck Bush believed, what must leaders think and do to own the issue? In your own leadership role(s), what must you think and do to demonstrate your ownership of the issue?

How did your upbringing influence how you make your way in the world as it pertains to relating to people who are not like you? What do you think is most important to keep, related to how your upbringing influenced you? What might you want to rethink or change related to the influence of your upbringing on how you relate to people who are not like you?

We're not close to everyone we know. We're not friends with everyone we know. When was a time when you recognized you were simply tolerated (not just for a brief interaction, but over time)? How did being tolerated impact how you felt, what you thought, how you reacted? How did being tolerated impact how you saw yourself? How did being tolerated impact the way you saw the people around you? How do you wish "the tolerator(s)" had behaved differently? How might this have changed the interactions and the outcomes?

Chuck Bush's daughter recounted that at the Supreme Court, Bush was treated as if he were White because they didn't know how else to treat him. Thought experiment: Imagine that you are treated as a person from a race you know has a very different life experience than yours. Which race did you identify? What was the treatment? How is the treatment different from how your group is treated? What does this tell us about how we might want to consider how we treat our team members, subordinates, and superiors who are different from us?

Why is leading by example important, or is it? When it comes to valuing others, no matter their group identity, what are at least three things you must do to lead by example?

Where have you seen people in leadership positions granting advantages to people who are like themselves? What impact does this have on the group or organization? When have you unconsciously given an advantage to someone who was like you in some critical way? Were you aware of it at the time? When and how did you realize that you'd done this?

What is the American dream? *In addition to* smarts, action, and tenacity, a) what personal characteristics must be in place to achieve the American dream? B) What factors must be in place at the systems or organizational level for you to achieve the American dream? What systems or organizational factors are often missing when considering people who say there are barriers to their achieving the American dream?

What makes diversity a military necessity, as dictated on October 13, 2010, by the Secretary of the Air Force Michael Donley, Air Force Policy Directive 36-70, Personnel: Diversity?

Bettina Bush is an established and respected voice in parenting, multiculturalism, and gender equality. She began her lifelong career in entertainment and media at the age of seven, as an actress/singer voicing several pop culture icons such as Rainbow Brite.

She became the editor-at-large for *Working Mother* magazine after serving to bridge the digital divide in underserved communities as CEO of a telecommunications company. Bettina has spent the past decade hosting national radio shows and podcasts, appearing on daytime shows such as *TODAY* and Hallmark's *Home & Family*, and advocating at women's conferences and universities.

Following in the footsteps of her trailblazing father (the first African American to serve as page to the US Supreme Court, and the first African American to graduate from the US Air Force Academy) and schoolteacher mother of multicultural descent, Bettina has devoted much of her career to educating people on issues of diversity. Like Bettina, her two kids also are multicultural, which allows Bettina to bring a unique point of view to every conversation.

CHAPTER 26

A GENERAL'S SHORT STORY

Abel Barrientes, Maj Gen, USAF (ret.)
Class of 1982, US Air Force Academy

There I was, a twenty-eight-year-old USAF Captain, a C-5 aircraft commander at an airshow at Castle AFB in Merced, CA. The crew was having a great time at the airshow and the crowd was massive. As the day went by, I was approached by many people who wanted to take a picture with me or of me, and many more just came by to meet and greet me and walk away with a smile. After awhile I thought it was curious, and so I asked a fellow what made me so special that these folks were coming by. He said, "We have never seen a Mexican American pilot, and that makes us all very proud." WOW! Shoot, I thought it was my good looks and charm! But this incident was huge in my life, and it had a profound impact on my attitude and outlook going forward about who I was as an individual.

But first I have to go back to the beginning. I was born at Fort Belvoir, Virginia, in 1960 while my dad was assigned there in the US Army for his two-year stint. I was raised in San Antonio, Texas, where my parents were from, and I was the oldest of four kids. I think it is extremely important to tell you about my childhood because it shaped who I am, and more specifically, my parents shaped the man I would become.

My father, Guadalupe Barrientes, was a very strict disciplinarian. He was a hardworking, hard drinking, and passionate man. His experiences growing up in South Central Texas shaped his thinking for the rest of his life. From his challenging family life—he was adopted as an infant—to his life as a young man experiencing racism in its rawest forms, to life with my mother and our family, he led the family with passion, love, and an intense pride.

He also expected nothing but the best from me, especially when it came to my studies. You see, my father graduated from high school at twenty years old because he was told he should be in the fields rather than the classroom. But from my earliest memories I remember him telling me about *ganas* and that without that you could never be successful. He'd say, "Don't ever do anything half ass" and, "If someone has a problem with your heritage, that's their problem; never make it yours." True words to live by!

Frankly, Dad made these tiger moms we have read about look like furry little newborn kittens. It was tough, and the stress was ever present to be the best, and for the most part I did well because there wasn't any room for second best. He told me I would have to work twice as hard to be just as good. The *ganas* talk occurred daily, and he also told me I would go to the best university in the land. He spoke of Harvard and Stanford and the Ivies as goals that were well within my reach long before I knew what these schools were.

So, eventually all those talks took hold in my own thoughts and I set my goals for West Point because I knew I wanted to serve my country. I did well enough to get appointments to the three academies, and that's when I decided that the USAF Academy was best for me because the idea of flying intrigued me. So, in June of 1978, I boarded a plane for my first airplane ride to Colorado Springs and the USAFA.

The four years I spent at the USAFA were the most formative years of my life, bar none. Why, I was out from under my father's iron fist and was able to truly find out what I was capable of. I knew when I graduated I could do anything I set my mind to. The challenges academically, physically, and mentally were great but manageable. I will note most of the major challenges I faced while in school were self-imposed stresses (i.e., not studying enough and not always applying myself in my studies; Dad wasn't there to hammer me!). I will say that after I left home, Dad had done his job and never again asked me how my grades were. I knew there was no going back home if I was unsuccessful, and that was a huge incentive to succeed! Graduation day, 2 June 1982, was one of the proudest moments of my life, and my family's too.

Pilot training was next, and I was at Columbus, Mississippi, within three weeks after graduation. I experienced another challenging year with a class composed of mostly USAFA classmates, including three African Americans and two Latinos. I will note that we heard stories about people of color having a dismal pilot training graduation rate, and while those numbers were indeed true, I will also note that every one of us graduated!

I was assigned to Peterson AFB, Colorado, to fly the T-39 Sabreliner and had a great time in that detachment. Eighteen months later we all transitioned to the brand-new C-21A (Learjet 35). In 1986 I was assigned to fly the C-5 at Travis and traveled the world in service to the country. In 1989 I was hired by Delta Airlines and transitioned to the USAF Reserve. I stayed in the Air Force Reserve for twenty nine years and eventually retired as a major general in 2018, one of only four Hispanic general officers in the US Air Force, out of five hundred.

What did I learn during my forty years in the USAF? I learned a ton but want to emphasize a few key points.

- Attitude is everything. Throughout those years my attitude was positive. I was eager to learn, and if someone took the time to critique, mentor, or scold, I learned from it and moved on. But I tried to shape those others' thoughts into positives whether or not they were meant to be.

- Set goals. It is no accident that successful people set goals. Whether it is the next rank, evaluation, or class, do your due diligence and find out what it will take to be successful in achieving that goal. If it is the next rank, don't ever give them a chance not to promote you. Check every box that is required of that promotion.

- Do your best to learn everything about your current position, and strive to be the best and most informed about that position.

- Get out of your comfort zone. Learn to be comfortable being uncomfortable. What does that really mean? It means take on tasks that no one else wants to do. If you are apprehensive about speaking to groups, put yourself in a situation where you will have to brief. There are a lot of opportunities every day for you to step up and learn something new and make the unit a better place.

- Never stop learning. You don't and never will know it all. Successful leaders know this and will always strive to learn as much as they can about the world around them. A good leader will also learn from his peers and subordinates.

- Be a servant leader. Your people are your best asset; treat them well and you will be rewarded. Know your people, talk to them. Don't stay cooped up in the office. This will help you keep your hand on the pulse of the unit and how things are really going.

Now back to that story at the beginning of this chapter. Up to that point, I considered myself a great USAF pilot and officer. Now that was true, but there occurred an epiphany, if you will, that made me think harder about my role in this world. I had never really thought of myself as a role model, and although I was proud of my Mexican heritage, that fact wasn't on top of the things that identified who I was. I realized at this point that indeed I was a role model to the millions of Latinos in this country who are and have been unrepresented in our society.

It was at this point that I started to seek out others to mentor and guide in their careers, if I could. I also started to take on some more leadership roles in my USAF Reserve unit. As time went by and I came up the ladder, I became involved in an organization in the USAF Reserve named the Human Resources Development Council (HRDC), the purpose of which was to teach and preach the value of diversity and inclusion. It was fascinating to learn about unconscious bias—which I was guilty of—and the value of a diverse organization and the benefits of that diversity to that organization. We had annual conferences attended by hundreds with some real strategic goals to improve in the future. In the end I was the deputy of the program and was very proud of the work we did to inform and strive for a change in culture in our units. Unfortunately, the funds dried up after one of the government shutdowns, and the organization fell by the wayside.

At this point, a fellow USAFA classmate, Alfredo Sandoval, and I started to make some headway in starting another organization to improve the number of senior officers in the USAF. Through the last thirty-plus years, the USAF and DoD have had numerous studies about the lack of minority leadership in the armed services. Nothing had changed. In fact, in the last thirty years in the USAF, the number of Latino officers has tripled, but the number of Latino general officers has stayed the same. It was and is time for action and not the same old talk.

Alfredo and I expanded our team to include a third classmate, Col. Eddie Cabrera, USAF (ret.), and he has been the engine that has grown the organization into what is now the Hispanic Veterans Leadership Alliance (hvlanet. org). Some interesting statistics have come out of the research that the HVLA has done. For instance, in the first three classes that the USAFA had women, the classes of 1980–1982, 206 women graduated. Those 206 women have earned more stars than all of the Latino officers who have served in the USAF, about seven thousand since its inception in 1947. Women were authorized to fly fighters in 1993, and since that time six women have become Thunderbird pilots; we are still waiting for the first Latino Thunderbird. And last, the USAF has still not had a Latino four-star general.

What do these statistics tell us? In terms of the women, it tells us that what gets emphasized by leadership gets results. We need to apply that same level of emphasis to Latinos in our USAF and stop this embarrassing lack of Latino senior leaders. The Defense Advisory Committee on Women in the Services (DACOWTS) was established in 1951 and has been a powerful tool for women in the services. Something similar needs to be established for Latinos.

But change needs to come from the top. Diversity is a strategic imperative in our armed services. Unfortunately, leadership has fallen down on the job in this regard. This change needs to be directed and focused to get the real results they need. There needs to be accountability and consequences to make that change.

Hispanics in the USA account for 18 percent of the population, and in the next twenty-five to thirty years that number will be 30 percent. The USAF doesn't recruit general officers; they recruit second lieutenants. If they don't start now, change will never happen.

Reflection Questions:

1. The author notes that "what gets emphasized, gets results." When it comes to diversity, what gets emphasized in your organization?

2. What is the impact of not having senior leaders reflect those they serve?

3. If we wanted to increase the amount of diversity in our senior ranks in order to reflect those that serve, what should be done?

Group Discussion:

Identify one of your closest and most influential caregivers while growing up (mother, father, aunt, uncle, grandparent, foster parent, other). When you think about them, what examples, edicts, role modeling, and/or advice have they demonstrated or shared with you that you are proud of remembering and utilizing today?

How does this bear on how you treat and interact with others?

For the same caregiver above, when you think about them, what examples, edicts, role modeling, and/or advice they demonstrated or shared with you do you reject and not utilize today? (Your answer does not need to be connected to how much you love them.)

How does this bear on how you treat and interact with others?

For the same caregiver above, when you think about them, what examples, edicts, role modeling, and/or advice they demonstrated or shared with you might you have unconsciously absorbed? How does this bear on how you treat and interact with others in your life today?

Barrientes wrote that "if someone took the time to critique, mentor, or scold, I learned from it and moved on." What mode of feedback best motivates you to learn and grow?

How might you seek the feedback that supports your growth and development in how you treat, lead, and manage others?

On the job, what percentage of the time are you "in the comfort zone" because of who you are as opposed to what you do or what's going on around you?

On the job, what percentage of the time are you "out of the comfort zone" because of your group membership?

How do you explain both scenarios?

What are the benefits of being designated a role model when that designation is connected, in whole or in part to your group membership (e.g. race, gender, ethnicity, sexual orientation, etc.)?

What are the drawbacks of being designated a role model when that designation is connected in whole or in part to your group membership (e.g. race, gender, ethnicity, sexual orientation, etc.)?

What does underrepresentation mean? What groups are underrepresented, especially in leadership positions, in your branch of the service?

Can you list ten factors that represent or indicate barriers to representation?

CHAPTER 27

INVISIBLE NO MORE

Eddie Cabrera
Colonel, USAF (retired)

There I was . . . as the altimeter indicated 29,000 feet, I lowered the nose about four degrees to reduce the climb rate. The absolute maximum altitude for this one-of-a-kind experimental "X" aircraft was 30,000 feet, so I was carefully trying to level off at 29,900 feet to give myself a little margin and not overshoot the maximum altitude.

The date was December 21, 2000. It was a crisp winter morning with clear skies and unlimited visibility. I had just entered the supersonic corridor north of Edwards Air Force Base, flying the single-seat experimental X-32A Joint Strike Fighter (JSF), the Boeing entrant in the history-making Battle of the X-Planes "flyoff" between the Boeing X-32 and the Lockheed Martin X-35 concept demonstrators. The primary objective of this sortie was to achieve supersonic flight for the very first time in the X-32A conventional variant, a critical test and programmatic milestone.

I had two trusted wingmen that day, both flying F/A-18s—a safety chase in the event of any anomalies, and a photo chase to capture videos and photos of the historic flight. As I leveled off at 29,900 feet and reduced the throttle, the Machmeter indicated about 0.86 Mach. I verified that I had been cleared into the airspace. "Phantom 3, cleared into the Black Mountain supersonic corridor" the radio crackled. I queried, *Safety chase—in position?* "Ready." *Photo chase, in position?* "Ready." *Mission control?* "Ready." I slowly increased the throttle setting to establish a gradual but steady acceleration and began calling out the Mach. "On conditions." ".95" . . . ".96" . . . ".98" . . . "1.0" . . . "1.02."

The stealthy, one-of-a-kind X-32A had effortlessly joined the exclusive club of experimental aircraft to exceed the sound barrier in level flight. This was the first and only supersonic flight for the X-32A at Edwards AFB, and was an early Christmas present of sorts for the government and contractor teams.

At an estimated $200B life cycle cost, the winner-take-all JSF program represented the most lucrative fighter aircraft prize in history. I was fortunate to serve as one of the two Air Force pilots selected to fly the concept demonstrators and to lead the joint/international test team as Operations Officer. The X-32 and X-35 concept demonstration test program was a resounding success and set world records for most X-aircraft test sorties in a day and for transcontinental flight, among other records. Soon after the concept demonstration phase ended, contractor and government test team members were awarded the national Collier Trophy for the innovative X-35 propulsion system. To give you some sense of what this meant, previous Collier Trophy winners included aerospace legends such as Orville Wright, Chuck Yeager, and Apollo 11. I was also honored to win the Lieutenant General Bobby Bond Memorial Aviator Award—the annual Air Force award for the top test pilot in the entire command. Fewer than 1 percent of all pilots ever qualify to become an experimental test pilot, so to win this award in such a competitive cohort was surreal.

After closing out the JSF test program, I became the commander of the F-22A Raptor test squadron, the Air Force's number one priority acquisition program. The F-22A weapon system was still early in its development, and at that time, it was the only F-22 squadron in the Air Force. Of the seventy different aircraft types I've flown, the air superiority Raptor was easily the most impressive, highest performing, most capable fighter of all. Flying at 60,000 feet at more than twice the speed of sound with an advanced sensor fusion suite providing unparalleled situation awareness cannot be adequately described—only experienced.

As we left the Pentagon and headed to our new group command assignment, it seemed things were really falling into place. In just the past five years, I had been privileged to help lead a world-record-setting, history-making Collier Trophy–winning team; commanded the sole test squadron developing the Air Force's #1 priority fighter; promoted two years below-the-zone; earned two (additional) national awards; was featured on History Channel and Discovery Channel videos which aired nationwide; and deployed to Baghdad in support of Operation Iraqi Freedom. My selection by the Command Selection Board (led by eighteen three-star generals and one four-star) to become the group commander of a renowned, world-class developmental flight test group validated my entire career to that point. Taking command at this level meant anything was possible in terms of future command assignments and promotions.

Soon after we arrived at our new base, the wing commander took me around and introduced me to everyone as the incoming group commander. We finalized the date for the change of command ceremony, and began to send out invitations for an epic celebration immediately after the ceremony. This was going to be a particularly special event for my parents—they were beaming when I took command of the F-22 squadron as a lieutenant colonel, and were looking forward to celebrating my first command as a full colonel.

Then, one evening about one week prior to the change of command, we were relaxing at home when the phone rang. It was the wing commander. He went on to explain that my change of command had been *cancelled*. Naturally, I was shocked and in disbelief. The wing commander explained that a senior Air Force leader had intervened and directed the cancellation, stating that the incumbent group commander needed to serve a full two years in the position before relinquishing command. This didn't make any sense to me for multiple reasons, and just sounded wrong. The wing commander went on to say the local two-star general had appealed the cancellation decision, as did the four-star general at headquarters responsible for the entire base. However, the senior leader had rejected both appeals. All change of command preparations were cancelled. I had never heard of anything like this happening, nor did anyone else I knew. For a few weeks, I struggled with how to cope with this unsettling turn of events. I finally realized that I had no control over the decision, but I did have full control over how I would react. So, I treated my new non-command position as if it was the best job I ever had, and performed accordingly. A year later, the wing commander rated me as "top 1 percent of all officers I've ever worked with in my career" and wrote, "Make him a Wing Commander now!"

As the months went by, I was struck by the fact that none of the senior leaders in my chain of command wanted to talk about the elephant in the room. I thought that at some point a senior leader would sit down with me privately and say, here's what happened and why, and here's what we should do about it (some might call this mentoring). Unfortunately, that never happened. As the one-year mark approached, I thought perhaps I would take over the flight test group then, one year later than originally planned. However, another officer was announced as the incoming group commander, and as other command selections were announced over the ensuing months, *I realized my window had closed.* I was never again selected to command this or any other flying unit. Game (and military career) over. I felt—invisible.

Months later, as we began the next chapter after retirement, I tried to make sense of what had happened. Why would a senior leader intervene at the very last moment in just one change of command out of hundreds of group command change-overs that occurred every year? Why would a senior leader override the appeals of the two general officers that were directly in the chain of command? An even more pertinent question was, why would the rest of the leadership look the other way, pretending nothing had happened?

Diversity, Equity, and . . . Exclusion

After retirement, I periodically checked DoD progress regarding diversity and inclusion. I discovered that the needle was indeed moving—*but in the wrong direction*! Hispanic officer retention continued to be a problem, and representation at the higher ranks and in key command positions was worsening. Fortuitously, I reconnected with several Air Force Academy classmates, and as we compared notes from our time in uniform, it turned out we had similar experiences. We had all pushed for improved inclusion but encountered the same Machiavellian wall of resistance to changing the status quo. As we collaborated, we made some eye-opening discoveries. Consider a few factoids we uncovered:

- Women were not allowed to attend US service academies until legislation was passed in 1975. The first three classes of women at the Air Force Academy (classes of 1980, 1981, and 1982) graduated a total of 260 female officers. By 2012, this tiny cohort of 260 had produced more generals than 10,000+ Hispanic officers had ever produced since the Air Force became a service in 1947. This is a remarkable success story and a compelling lesson on the power of mentorship, sponsorship, and national will. It also demonstrates the consequences of singling out certain groups and ignoring others.

- From 1990 to 2020, the percentage of active-duty Hispanic officers across all branches of the military quadrupled. However, there has not been a corresponding increase in general and flag officers, and per capita representation in this executive group has actually declined over thirty years. Hispanics comprise only about 2 percent of all active-duty generals and admirals today even though we make up 8 percent (and growing) of all officers.

- In 1991, there were only three Hispanic brigadier generals (one-star) out of 315 or so total Air Force generals serving on active duty. There were zero Hispanics at the higher two-, three-, and four-star ranks. Thirty years later, out of 280 or so active-duty generals, there are only three Hispanic brigadier generals in the Air Force, and zero Hispanics at the higher levels—the same exact situation as 1991. *Furthermore, there has never been a 4-star Hispanic general in the Air Force's seventy-three-year history.*

We all quickly came to the same conclusion—if we were serious about driving change, we had to join forces. Thus, the Hispanic Veterans Leadership Alliance (HVLA) nonprofit organization was born. Our mission statement was short and simple: to advance the inclusion of Hispanics across every level of the DoD. One of our first actions was to compile the data (after all, it's all about the data) and take our story to Congress and the Pentagon. We hit the briefing trail in early 2016 and quickly garnered support from several members of Congress and their staffs. In fact, within about four months we sent a congressional letter to President Barack Obama highlighting the undeniable disparities and requesting immediate action. The letter highlighted the many reasons why military demographics should mirror the nation it protects, especially in a democracy defended by an all-volunteer military. We cited the example of how during the Vietnam War a virtually all-white officer corps commanded an enlisted force heavily comprised of minorities and how the underrepresentation of minorities in the officer corps, with perceived discrimination as its cause, led to some three hundred race-related incidents and seventy-one tragic deaths of American troops.

Given the letter was signed by twenty-six members of Congress, we had high hopes. Additionally, we also met in person with the highest levels of leadership in the Air Force, both civilian and uniformed. We briefed them on the data and our lived experiences and showed them the letter to President Obama. We were encouraged when Air Force leaders reiterated that diversity and inclusion was a mission critical issue, and they seemed keenly interested in what we had to say. Our optimism was ill-founded. We waited months for a reply from the White House to the congressional letter, yet never received a response. Similarly, even though we had met multiple times with key Air Force leaders, they never followed up, and as far as we could tell, took no action to address our concerns. We were dumbfounded—HVLA was a group of presidential appointees, generals, admirals, and other distinguished veterans who were reaching out to help our leaders navigate through turbulent times in the diversity and inclusion arena—yet the White House, Air Force, and DoD willfully chose to ignore us and more significantly, chose to ignore the critical diversity and inclusion problems we highlighted. However, what followed was even more alarming.

Given the underwhelming response, we revised our strategy and came up with a new three-pronged plan. Elevate the conversation directly to the Secretary of Defense; build a bicameral, bipartisan congressional coalition; and engage national Latino community leaders. From August 2018 through March 2019, we sent four letters to the Office of the Secretary of Defense (OSD). After the first two letters went unanswered, we had the League of United Latin American Citizens (LULAC) send the next letter, which triggered a brief back-and-forth discussion with various senior leaders acting on behalf of the Secretary of Defense. One of these letters from OSD included certain statistics along with a rosy assessment that Hispanics were doing great at all levels. The data OSD cited were incomplete and misleading, confirming one of our worst fears—military leaders were oblivious to Hispanic disparities, and were clearly not measuring the right data.

In April 2019 we sent yet another petition to the Secretary of Defense and to all service secretaries. For this HVLA petition, we obtained the signatures of twenty-four senior military members including over twenty retired generals, admirals, and senior executive service personnel representing the Army, Navy, Marine Corps, Air Force, and Coast Guard. The signatories collectively represented well over seven centuries of distinguished military service spanning every branch of service. To our knowledge, this was the first time in history such a group of Hispanic senior leaders had written to the Secretary of Defense calling out longstanding diversity and inclusion shortfalls. Again, we offered our experience and insights to help address this national imperative. The months ticked by without a formal response to our letter. Thanks to a member of Congress who engaged with the secretary on our behalf, we did start discussions with OSD, but the "dialogue" turned out to be a two-year slow roll characterized by zero progress. When you consider the pattern from the 1990s through the present day, the conclusion is indisputable—*the Defense Department has effectively ignored calls to action by the Hispanic community for decades*. Despite a legacy of patriotic and courageous service dating back to the Civil War and every conflict since then, capped by sixty Hispanic Medal of Honor winners, the nation's largest, second-fastest growing, and youngest (by far) minority demographic in America remains invisible.

Path to Parity: Congress and the National Latino Community

Since 2016, we've forged a strong relationship with many members of Congress, including the Congressional Hispanic Caucus as well as various national Latino community civil rights and veterans organizations. This strategy turned out to be the proverbial tipping point, as the partnerships we had established with LULAC, Association of Naval Services Officers, etc. began to pay dividends. After the Army Private Vanessa Guillén story went viral, LULAC spoke out on behalf of the Hispanic community. Vanessa had been brutally murdered at an armory *on base* at Fort Hood, Texas, by a fellow soldier—inexplicably, the initial investigation into her disappearance was delayed for months. LULAC took the unprecedented step of ***calling for all Latinas to stop enlisting in the Army*** until the Army addressed Hispanic community concerns and showed they could protect our most vulnerable members. This led to a face-to-face meeting with Army leadership, including the Secretary of the Army and Army Chief of Staff. LULAC and HVLA spoke truth to power on numerous issues that day, including justice for Vanessa and her family as well as the need for improved inclusion of Hispanics at all levels. A subsequent independent report into the Vanessa Guillén case identified multiple leadership failures and other breakdowns within the Army, which led to the firing of more than a dozen mid-level and senior leaders. Not surprisingly, the Guillén case has galvanized the Hispanic community and key members of Congress, and will serve as a catalyst for the foreseeable future. Vanessa's voice may have been silenced, but we are her voice now.

WAY AHEAD

Let me try and put all of this in perspective using a simple construct—pre–George Floyd, and post–George Floyd.

Pre–George Floyd

It's difficult to understand why DoD leaders chose not to respond to the many petitions presented by Hispanic senior leaders during past decades. Dozens of accomplished veterans advised the Defense Department they had a diversity and inclusion problem and offered to help develop more effective strategies. Yet, the DoD repeatedly declined to even have a conversation and chose to ignore the subject matter experts. This was unconscionable and antithetical to the most basic principles of inclusion. Imagine the progress that could have been made in the four years leading up to the George Floyd incident had defense leaders listened and, more importantly, acted. This was an epic missed opportunity. When you consider the steady drumbeat of reports, studies, task forces, and other events calling out the lack of Hispanic inclusion dating back to the 1990s, the DoD's failure to engage over the past quarter century is inexplicable.

Another disconnect is the approach to strategic planning and resource management. The Defense Department commits significant resources to analyze and predict the future threat environment, then develops required capabilities to cope with those threats. Yet, when it comes to analyzing and predicting how changing demographics will impact the armed forces, the DoD falls well short in developing effective strategies. If you listen to any senior military leader talk about military capabilities, they always proclaim the military's greatest resource is its people. So why not commit the necessary energy and focus to manage this "great" resource and prepare for a very predictable future regarding demographic change? We knew decades ago how the face of America was going to change, and we know how America will continue to evolve in the coming decades. Yet today our military leadership utterly fails to reflect the face of America (especially when it comes to Hispanics), and future projections look no better. Given the length of time it takes to "grow" a senior leader, this is extremely concerning since there is no quick fix.

My firsthand experience with the Air Force Board of Corrections for Military Records (AFBCMR) further reinforced this same longstanding pattern of exclusion. Several years after retirement, as I learned more about what was happening (or not happening) in the military, it became obvious I needed to document my story. Subsequently, a law firm filed a formal petition on my behalf with the AFBCMR, the Air Force's highest level of administrative appeal for correcting injustices. It took the Air Force board *nearly three years* just to answer the petition, and when I read their dismissive response, I was shocked at the lack of diligence and equivocation. The petition represented a golden opportunity for the Air Force to conduct an introspective review and come to grips with the well-documented realities. Instead, they ignored the data and looked the other way—again.

If you want to gain a better understanding into the how and why of this decades-long leadership breakdown, I suggest reading two books: *Right Before Our Eyes: Latinos Past, Present and Future* by Robert Montemayor, and *White Fragility* by Robin DiAngelo. The first book describes the chronic exclusion of Hispanics from the upper echelons of institutional power structures across America, while DiAngelo's book offers important insights regarding why it is so difficult for many of our leaders to have productive and meaningful conversations on the topic of diversity and inclusion.

Post–George Floyd

An unfortunate but obvious reality for any member of the Black or Brown community is that racism and bias still exist and persist in American society. Since the military is a reflection of society, by definition some degree of discrimination and bias also persists in the armed forces. We have argued this basic premise for many years, and tried to engage military leadership to address these realities and better harness the talents of all Americans for a more capable military and improved readiness. Yet, defense leaders consistently rejected the notion of racism and bias in the military—until George Floyd, months of civil unrest across America, and a certain criminal justice report concerning Air Force Airmen. Let's be clear—the culture didn't suddenly change overnight nor did discrimination and bias spontaneously erupt in the military. What did change overnight was that defense leaders finally acknowledged the same reality many of us have been coping with our entire lives.

Sadly, the same disparities described in *Right Before Our Eyes* continue to persist in the US and in some cases have worsened. Hispanics are still severely underrepresented within the upper tiers of America's C-suites, corporate boards, entertainment, government civilian executive positions, military flag and general officer, and many other areas. According to a CBS News report in 2020, Latinas in the US earn some 54 cents on the dollar compared to White, non-Hispanic males. This is incomprehensible, considering that for many years Latinas have topped the list of all groups for entrepreneurship and new business starts.

In December 2020, the Air Force released the Independent Racial Disparity Review, which acknowledged racial disparities for Black service members in eight different areas including criminal justice, promotion rates, and leadership opportunities. These disparities obviously date back decades. In fact, the IRDR looked at twenty-three past studies and reports dating back to 1973 and concluded past efforts "often did not identify root causes, often did not compel follow-through, often lacked mechanisms to measure effectiveness over time, and broadly lacked accountability for progress." In other words, a failure of leadership. Prompted by an HVLA complaint, the Air Force then conducted another Disparity Review for other minority groups. The Disparity Review subsequently identified many different disparities impacting the Hispanic cohort (enlisted, officer, and civilian), thus corroborating claims HVLA has made for many years.

There is yet another sobering fact to consider. The senior leader I referred to earlier that intervened in my command opportunity was not just any senior leader. You see, the senior leader was the Chief of Staff of the Air Force, a four-star general, and the highest-ranking person in the service. When it comes to bias, unconscious or conscious, *no one* is immune or exempt. The Hispanic community needs to be clear-eyed about the challenge ahead and must hold ourselves and our defense leaders accountable by continuously assessing progress through meaningful metrics and measurable outcomes. Deeds matter, not words.

George Floyd inspired a national awakening along with other seismic changes in America and the DoD. The national conversation is now much more encompassing than just police brutality against Black and Brown. Why is this important? Because now is the time to reset our understanding of American Hispanic contributions to our country's prosperity, now is the time for American Hispanics to take a seat and have an equal voice at the table, and now is the time to discard the stereotypes. According to a recent 2020 report by researchers from UCLA and California Lutheran University, the total economic contribution of Latinos in the United States, the Latino GDP, was $2.6 trillion in 2018. If it were an independent country, the US Latino economy would be the eighth largest in the world, larger than Italy, Brazil, or South Korea. Similar research also shows Latinos account for **85 percent** of all farmworkers, **59 percent** of the country's construction crews, **53 percent** of all employees in food services, and **39 percent** of the nation's total workforce. There are over 60 million Hispanics in the US today, and within the next few decades, one in four Americans will be of Hispanic heritage. The Latino demographic is America's fountain of youth—one million Latinos will turn eighteen this year and every year for the next two decades, 20 percent are millennials, and 33 percent are alpha generation (think about the implications of this for military recruiting and national security!). As Steve Forbes of *Forbes* magazine said, "Latinos are the cavalry coming to the economic rescue of our country." When the Hispanic community succeeds, America succeeds.

One Last Thing

Between 2021 and 2022, the DoD and Air Force announced several important diversity and inclusion initiatives, including a partnership with Tuskegee University and a $60M, five-year program supporting Historically Black Colleges & Universities. Unfortunately, none of these initiatives benefit the Hispanic community. *Not a single dollar of the sixty-million dollar* commitment was directed to Hispanic Serving Institutions. In fact, this continued exclusion of Hispanics and Latinos prompted a retired Air Force brigadier general and HVLA leader to pen an op-ed during the summer of 2022 titled, "The Forgotten Minority: Hispanics Still Being Ignored!" The good news is, the continued exclusion of Hispanics has driven HVLA to redouble its efforts and is helping to fuel a surge in HVLA membership, partnerships, and congressional engagement. Fight's on!

Reflection Questions:

1. What was the primary issue the author discussed, and to what extent do you feel that it is still an issue in the US military?
2. Do you agree with the distinction the author made between pre–George Floyd and post–George Floyd and why?

Group Discussion:

How can leaders in your organization know rewards and opportunities are given based on merit and are not subject to bias or favoritism?

To what extent does systemic racism exist in the US Armed Forces, and what should be done about it?

CHAPTER 28

THE BEST MISTAKE OF MY LIFE

Kathryn L. Smith, Esq.
Social Justice Advocate

I left Atchison, Kansas, a small town on the Missouri River, three days after my eighteenth birthday to attend the United States Air Force Academy. I excelled at Atchison High and was awarded the All-Around Girl Student Award. I was a two-sport athlete, active in speech, theatre, and debate, and active in my church. Several students from Atchison had attended military service academies, but I was the first woman from Atchison to go to the Air Force Academy. I knew cadets in the classes of 1979 and 1980, so I thought I was prepared for the academic, mental, and physical demands.

I was wrong.

My cousin drove me from Denver to the base of the "Bring Me Men" ramp, hugged me, and told me goodbye. I was ready. I had gotten my big "Angela Davis-esque" afro cut short before I left. I was confident. I in-processed with the rest of my classmates and was pleasantly surprised, and very lucky, that my basic cadet roommate was another Black woman. We bonded immediately, and I maintain a friendship with her, her twin sister, and the other six Black women in our class who survived and graduated. I also know the three Black women who graduated in 1980 who made a way for us. By my count, I am the tenth Black woman to graduate from USAFA. I barely made it.

Much of Basic Cadet Training ("BCT") is lost in my memory. My brain protects me from most of it. But three incidences are stuck in my memory as if they happened yesterday.

My BCT roommate [Martha Stevenson] and I were in different flights, and we had different upper-class cadre who were responsible for us. It didn't stop my cadre from yelling at her or her cadre from yelling at me, but it should have kept her cadre from coming into our room in the middle of the night and taking me on a spirit mission. Not all Black women basics look alike. Nothing I could say convinced Cadet First Class whoever he was that I was not Basic Cadet Stevenson and I wasn't in his flight. He wouldn't let me make a statement to explain.

The next incident led to the biggest challenge. During BCT, they tested us for class placement. I tested out of foreign language and tested into remedial swimming. I remember the day we went to the gym for swimming. The officer in charge told me to get in the pool and swim as far as I could in five minutes. It was the second or third time I had been in a swimming pool. In Kansas, in the 1960s and 1970s, Black and White kids didn't swim in the same pool—not unlawful, but not by customs or practice. There were no certified lifeguards and regular swim lessons on my side of Division Street. I told him, "Sir, I do not know how to swim." I got in the pool. I received a score of fifteen feet because it was the minimum number on the form. No one had told me swimming was a graduation requirement at the Air Force Academy. No one told me that I would almost drown three times.

Lieutenant Mike Evers was the first instructor to try to drown me. He thought that if I could execute a dive, I could gain more distance to start. He showed me how to dive off the side into what was seven feet of water. I'm five foot nine inches tall—too deep for me to stand up. I didn't know him at the time, but forty years later I can remember his face when he had to pull me out of the pool. The second drowning attempt came the following quarter. My volleyball coach, Major Ed Halik, who I thought liked me, decided that if I had more walls to push off from and glide, I could improve my distance by giving me a little rest at the end of each lap. He took me to the water polo pool, which was fifteen feet shorter and would give me two more turns.

At the end of my allotted time, he ordered me to stop. Obeying orders, I stopped swimming and sunk. He had to use the rescue hook to tow me out from the middle. During the last quarter, my other volleyball coach, who was a Naval Officer, Lieutenant Junior Grade Carol West, who I knew liked me, decided I should learn to save myself in the water. I had confidence in her teaching skills— she was in the Navy, after all. She taught me how to do the "dead man's float." It's a technique where you relax in the water, dangling your legs, arms, and head, and just surface to take a breath before floating again. Because I had almost mastered the technique but would grab onto the side when I panicked a little, she decided to tie a rope around me and drag me to the center of the diving pool, which was at least fifteen feet deep. At some point, she let go of the rope and I sank. I'm not sure how I got out of the pool that day. They should call it the dead cadet's float in my honor. I took freshman swimming three quarters as a freshman. Ten lessons each time. I also took swimming as a sophomore, again as a junior, and finally passed midway in my senior year. It took fifty-six lessons. I didn't conquer my fear of deep water, but I gained respect for it. I also gained a certain confidence in myself. With a good life vest, I'm willing to get on a boat or go snorkeling. Nothing before or since has been as hard over a long time.

Swimming wasn't the only incident that sticks out in my mind from BCT. After a few weeks of training, and time in Jack's Valley field encampment, my small afro did not conform to Air Force standards. There were no ethnic hair products in the gear we were issued, and I could not properly care for my hair.

There were only a few women in the cadre, but one had the mission to take me to the cadet beauty shop for a regulation haircut. I sat in the chair, as ordered, and the beautician began to cut my hair. She was hesitant. Halfway through, she confessed she had never cut a Black person's hair before. She sought assistance from a Black barber next door. He came over, looked at what she had done, and whispered in my ear, "I'm sorry, sister. I will try to do the best I can to fix this." It was Christmas before my hair looked respectable again. The haircut was the worst one ever in my life, but the incompetence of the beautician pales in comparison to the hazing I received from the C2C who escorted me back to my room. She teased me about the haircut, she dared me to cry, and she called me ugly. I kept my chin in and gave her the appropriate "yes, ma'am" or "no, ma'am" responses. I kept it together until she left and I could go to the converted latrine to cry. I was prepared for discipline and military rigor, but I wasn't prepared for cruelty.

I survived swimming. I made the varsity volleyball team and played club rugby. I was on the dean's list one semester and the dean's "other list" at least twice. I kept clear of the commandant and seldom received demerits and I never marched a tour. Like all of the women cadets during my time, I was sexually harassed personally or as a member of a group. I sang along to bawdy marching songs, and I heard tourists shout, "Hey, honey, there's a girl cadet" from the Cadet Chapel Wall. I never knew, when I was getting yelled at, whether the cadet was racist or sexist or if he was having a bad day. Something changed my first year. My squadron was led by a former Army warrant officer who later had been commissioned in the Air Force. He had a reputation for being a no-nonsense Air Officer Commanding, and he really changed the squadron culture. I was written up repeatedly and served hours of restrictions for offenses my classmates openly did. He wrote me up for uniform infractions, including my hair, yet he would whisper in my ear during formation about how nice it looked if I had managed to find someone to style it. He made inappropriate comments about my body. At the time, I was offended, but I didn't know it was sexual harassment, and I certainly didn't know that I could have reported it or to whom.

I have positive memories as well. The best one was meeting an upper-class woman who played volleyball. Mo Ma'am became one of my teammates, and I doubt I would have survived my freshman year without her. She left M&M candies in my mailbox for me to find, and our friendship was technically fraternization, but it was so worth the risk. During the academic year, her squadron was directly below mine, and I would spend more than one evening hiding in her room in order to escape. We spent a lot of time sitting on the bench together.

There had been a common (sexist) saying when I was a doolie, "They can make it harder, but they can't make it longer." For me, my AOC did both. I was just trying to cooperate and graduate, and I counted the days until graduation. One week before graduation, I was notified that he recommended that I not be commissioned because of my aptitude. I faced an Academy board, and the panel agreed to delay my commissioning so that I could prove myself and be retrained. I served as the cadet in charge of quarters on the day the rest of my classmates tossed their hats into the air. The summer of 1982, when I should have been enjoying being a second lieutenant and celebrating my freedom, I had to accomplish in nine weeks what I supposedly hadn't been able to achieve in the previous four years: to make myself into an officer.

The commandant's staff assigned me to give tours to VIP guests of the superintendent from Harmon Hall for three weeks. I had little guidance and no supervision or aptitude retraining. Next, I worked as an element leader for BCT. Again, no real review of my performance. My Basics did what they were tasked to do, and I showed up to formation. The last assignment was as a SERE instructor. Again, no one evaluated my aptitude for commissioning. I graduated in August, with my BCT roommate and other athletes who had a few academic courses to finish. Then, and now, I felt I was being punished because of my race and gender by my AOC, and the command system that allowed him to ruin my career. I served my commitment and went to work in private industry.

It took me almost twenty years to make peace with my Academy experience. I didn't have a June Week wedding, but I did have a ceremony in the chapel. In August 2001, my daughter was baptized there. The priest said it was the first one he had performed there. I have returned to attend class reunions and football games. For a few years I was a squadron ethics advisor, and served on congressional selection panels. I'm the advocacy director for the affinity group Zoomies Against Sexual Assault. I've learned even more about duty, honor, and patriotism, and I hold on to those values today. In spite of everything I experienced, it was the best mistake of my life.

Reflection Questions:

1. What would it take for you to "make peace" with the Academy if your experience was similar to hers?
2. To what extent should the Air Force Academy have provided remedial swimming lessons for those that did not have access to pools or lessons growing up?
3. To what extent was there a bias against those that did not have access to pools or swimming lessons before attending the Air Force Academy?
4. To what extent are you aware of other policies or rules that seem to be biased toward a particular group of people?

Group Discussion:

If two people are mistaken for each other (and in their own estimations do NOT look alike), what do you think must change in the environment to avoid this happening? List at least five things.

What are the responsibilities of the leader in an environment where this happens? What should an individual do to avoid mistaking one person for another (even after multiple interactions)?

How can taking action on this issue contribute to an environment where everyone can thrive?

Smith wrote, "Black and White kids didn't swim in the same pool—not unlawful, but not by customs or practice. There were no certified lifeguards and regular swim lessons on my side of Division Street." This was her reality. Yet there are negative stereotypes about Black people and their ability to swim. Now that you have read this story, who can you think of that you have stereotypes about? Are you curious about their story?

It may not be appropriate to ask, but where are opportunities to be authentically curious about people you know, who you see through your filters? What would be the benefits of curiosity and empathy toward your acquaintance relationships, friendships, colleagues, supervisees? (Note: this isn't intended that you probe into the privacy of others, but to consider being open to learning from what others are willing to share, and listening with generosity.)

Military culture has norms, rituals, and traditions (just like any other culture). When you consider the culture of firm boundaries across levels and ranks within the military, and the rituals that are afforded to one's superiors, what are the short-term and long-term impacts of the teasing of the type described by Smith? "She teased me about the haircut, she dared me to cry, and she called me ugly. I kept my chin in, and gave her the appropriate 'yes, ma'am' or 'no, ma'am' responses. I kept it together until she left and I could go to the converted latrine to cry. I was prepared for discipline and military rigor, but I wasn't prepared for cruelty." How does this kind of treatment impact a person's ability to thrive? What behaviors, initiated by superiors, would foster thriving?

Racism and sexism exist in the military. This is supported by quantitative and qualitative studies, as well as incidents that have been reported to authorities and highlighted in the media. At the same time, behaviors such as yelling, verbal aggression, suggestive comments, and even songs that poke fun at people are part of the traditions and rituals frequently employed and may be derogatory. Having read Smith's essay where she concludes that she made peace with her experiences, address the following: What causes a person to have to make peace with an experience? Have you ever had to make peace with an experience, and if so, how did you do it? What is the system's responsibility when it comes to creating or condoning experiences where people are impacted to the extent that they must "make peace" with it?

CHAPTER 29

THE CADET PFT

Kenneth L. Korpak, Lieutenant Colonel, USAF (ret.)
Former Athletic Director, US Air Force Academy Preparatory School
(2008–2013)

The US Air Force Academy Cadet PFT is the hardest physical fitness test I have ever taken or administered.

It is comprised of five events in sequence: pull-ups, 1-minute rest, standing broad jump, 1-minute rest, 2 minutes of sit-ups, 1-minute rest, 2 minutes of push-ups, 2-minute rest, followed by a 600-yard run. 100 points each for a max score of 500.

The strategy for the run?

Run.

There are trash cans at the end, and the "preppies" are briefed in advance that they are not to throw up on the field turf. Most of them comply.

As athletic director (AD), my only quantitative measure of recommending a kid for appointment to the United States Air Force Academy was their performance on this test.

A passing grade of 200 (equals a "D") earned my thumbs-up every year.

Why such a low bar? There are three reasons kids are at the prep school: math, science, and English.

Like USAFA, we give out "ropes" at the end of each grading period to recognize Cadet Candidates (C/C) who achieved top scores in each of the three mission elements: academics, military training, and athletics.

A prior enlisted C/C approached me one day and asked if I would be willing to administer him an out-of-cycle, one-on-one PFT so he could attempt to earn the athletic rope. He had scored in the mid-350s and would need to improve by roughly 80 points to qualify. I explained I was more than willing to administer the test—roughly forty-five minutes of my time—but wanted him to be realistic about his chances. Eighty points is a seismic improvement.

Nevertheless, if it was important to him, I made it important to me.

The next day, the young man brought two classmates to cheer him on. Once we started, I counted every rep aloud—long pull-ups, locking out each repetition, and deep push-ups, butt down, straightened back . . . no free chicken. The standard is the standard.

After four events, he posted four solid scores—maxing sit-ups and push-ups—but would need an above-average score on the 600-yard run. Over the decades, many dreams have died on the prep school's square, outdoor, wind-battered, beer budget track. After his first lap (of two) I could tell it was going to be close. Rounding the last turn, he gave it his best "Secretariat" and DOWN THE STRETCH HE CAME! He broke the tape at the finish line and collapsed in a heap of vomit and urine—again, perfectly normal for *any* kid who gives 100 percent on the PFT. His score easily earned him the athletic rope.

He inspired me that day.

It was not until the Ropes Ceremony a few weeks later, I realized the athletic rope was the last piece he needed to earn the coveted Commander's Rope for excellence in all three mission areas. A year or two later, I also learned that the cadet was gay and voluntarily disenrolling from USAFA. Every preppie who chooses disenrollment (or is disenrolled) from the Academy must schedule an exit interview with the prep school commander. We tried to talk him out of it, but to no avail. Thankfully, a year later he returned, and was ultimately commissioned a second lieutenant.

As an AD for roughly 1,200 preppies over the course of five years, he was the only one who ever asked to take another PFT.

No doubt he will continue to inspire the people he leads.

Reflection Questions:

1. What pressures do gay cadets face that might make them decide to disenroll from a service academy?
2. To what extent has the military culture embraced gay service members since the repeal of Don't Ask, Don't Tell?
3. To what extents have you helped to create an inclusive environment for gay service members?

Group Discussion:

Kurt Lewin, who is known as the father of social psychology, posited that the behavior of a person is a function of the person *and* his/her environment. If voluntary disenrollment from USAFA (behavior) is a function of the person and his/her environment, what are at least five environmental contributors you've seen that would lead to someone leaving the service or service academy (whichever is most relevant to your current role)? As a leader and/or manager, what are you called to do to rectify environmental factors under your control or influence?

When a person voluntarily leaves or disenrolls, what does the system lose when this happens? Explain how you think these losses impact the larger system.

Have you ever left a situation voluntarily because the environment was untenable? What made the environment untenable? What was the impact of leaving on you? What do you think was the impact your leaving had on the system (even if the system didn't or couldn't recognize this impact)? What do your responses tell you about the environments that must be fostered for the benefit of both the individual and the system?

Share the story of a time when you feel you made a positive difference in a teammate's or subordinate's professional life (not a friend or family member). Specify the behaviors you exhibited that you believe made a difference. What indicators do you have that you made a positive difference? What environment would be created if your behaviors and those of your colleagues who have also made a difference in a teammate's or subordinate's professional life were multiplied and normed within your organization's culture? What impact might that have?

CHAPTER 30

AM I GOING TO REGRET THIS?

Kim Beveridge, Lieutenant Colonel, USAF (ret.)
Program Manager, Scott Air Force Base

"No . . . you are kidding me . . . you can't be serious?"

Those were the words that I heard from my director as he literally fell out of his chair. I stood there, embarrassed, disappointed, doubting every decision that I had made. I was twenty-nine years old, a captain in the Air Force, operations director at a very fast-paced and exciting environment, at the top of my game. I was also married and carrying our first child. This was not the reaction I had expected when I announced that I was going to leave active duty to be a full-time mom. At his reaction, I wanted to step back and really ask myself: *Am I going to regret this decision?*

At that point I had had some amazing opportunities and been surrounded by family and friends that supported me. I was told that if I worked hard enough, I could achieve anything that I set my mind to. And I had worked hard; I received a BS in electrical engineering, graduating cum laude, distinguished graduate of my ROTC class, was just finishing a MS in industrial engineering, and had received numerous awards. I was now stepping away from all of that and was trying to ascertain if my past ten years had been a waste of time. After all, I was making a decision to "stay home" and "just be a mom." How could I reconcile everything that I had been working toward with this moment?

I couldn't speak and I tried my hardest not to show the range of emotions I was feeling. I had struggled with this decision, agonized over it. I LOVED what I did, and I had worked hard to get here. I had climbed the ladder one step at a time, and now I was leaping off of this ladder and into an unknown world. My husband and I had talked numerous times about it. He had even offered to be the stay-at-home parent. But I really appreciated having a stay-at-home mom for most of my childhood. I wanted to be able to offer that to my kids.

I suppose I needed to trace my steps back to the beginning to figure out how I got to this point. My mother was born in Mexico and my father was born in Germany, but I never really considered myself "first generation." Nor did I consider myself first to attend college. Although neither of our parents went to college, there was an expectation that each of us four siblings would go to college. My mom especially expressed her desire for us to be able to stand on our own, never to rely on someone else, and to push ourselves and realize our full potential. My dad, a construction worker for all of his life, was one of the hardest working people I will ever know. His lasting impression on me was his love of life and his belief that we could do anything we set our minds to. He took us hiking, exploring, and never slowed down, never allowed us to opt out. Anything he expected of my brother, he expected of his daughters.

When we realized that we were to fund our own college educations, I immediately started exploring scholarship opportunities. I did not have any close associations to anyone in the military, but it had always fascinated me. I lived in Ferguson, Missouri. Yes, that Ferguson. The airport was not far from my house. We used to drive to the end of the runway, park the car, and lie on our backs to watch the airplanes take off. If we were lucky, we would catch the F-4s screaming overhead. I suppose that this may have been the spark. However, admittedly, it was the scholarship money that really caught my attention. I figured that I didn't have anything to lose, and much to gain. Scholarship money, a great education, experience in the military, and only a four-year commitment. Sign me up!

What I had not realized during my four years in college as well as the subsequent years in the military was that *this* is where I belonged. These were "my people." It brought out the best in me. I was challenged, expectations were high, I was given opportunities that I would have never dreamed of. I was given responsibilities that most of my peers couldn't imagine. As a lieutenant I was charged with maneuvering DoD communications satellites to their correct positions. As a captain I was selected to a premier position as flight commander overseeing thirteen people on the operations floor during eight-hour shifts. As I moved to newer and more exciting missions, I was also given more responsibilities. People listened to me; I was making a difference. I did not have any problems being the only female "at the table" in many instances. I never doubted myself in circumstances where I had to reprimand a subordinate or question a leader's decision. In fact, I felt more comfortable among my military friends than I did with my female civilian acquaintances. In social situations I often drifted away from the "wives" and to my coworkers, talking shop talk, sharing work experiences, collaborating on issues.

What was I thinking?

I could hear the questions swirling all around me: but she has worked so hard to get to this point, and she is going to throw it all away? Why did she spend all of that time and effort on an education if she is just going to stay home? Doesn't she know that she can work and have kids? Doesn't she know about equal rights, and all of the work that women have done to get us here? At that moment, and in that room, announcing my decision to my director, I felt that the weight of everything that I had done, all of the efforts that others had done in support of me, and all of the work women before me had done, fighting for equal rights. How could I let everyone, including myself, down? Then it occurred to me. The answer came rushing to me.

"How did I get here?"

I got here because of who I am, the fortunate upbringing that I was given, and the efforts of so many women before me. I am a strong woman with strong convictions, and fortunate to live in an era that I was given the ability and freedom to make my own decision. My decision was to get an engineering degree, join the Air Force, serve my country, and now my decision was to step aside and put all of my efforts, talents, and abilities into the next generation.

I never looked back.

Well, perhaps once or twice. Being a mom is the most challenging, exhausting, and yet in its own way, rewarding experience that I have ever had, and continue to have. However, my Air Force career did not end there. What I once thought would be a four-year commitment turned into a twenty-eight year career in the Air Force. After leaving my seven-year active duty adventure, I transitioned to the Air Force Reserves, where I continued to serve as an admissions liaison officer for the US Air Force Academy, IMA at Air Force Materiel Command, and part-time reservist at Air Mobility Command until I retired as a lieutenant colonel in 2019. Still happily married, we have four children. One of them will be going to medical school in 2021, two are currently in ROTC, hoping to serve in the Air Force, and one of them is halfway through high school. In a way, I am still contributing to the Air Force, and to the next generation.

No, I definitely do not regret my decision.

Reflection Questions:

1. To what extent does the military offer flexibility for single parents or dual-income families?
2. To what extent is there room for the military to offer more work flexibility to its workforce?
3. To what extent do PCS moves over the last two to four years support dual-income families?

Group Discussion:

Who are "your people"—the people you resonate with and gravitate to? Describe their characteristics. When you think of "where you belong," how would you describe that environment? For both of your answers, what is the overlap between your answer and the attributes of an environment where everyone can thrive?

What are the disconnects? What have you discovered by exploring these questions?

What are your conscious and unconscious expectations related to being rewarded for working hard? Have these expectations panned out? Share your thoughts about this.

What in your environment supported your efforts? To what extent are these factors the same for everyone? If you asked someone who is very different from you (in any of your identities e.g. gender, sexual orientation, race, religion, political preference, etc.), how would they answer the question?

A person has needs, wants, and values. An organization has needs, wants, and values. When the needs, wants, and values of the individual part company with those of the organization, if the organization has created an environment where everyone can thrive, how would these differences be navigated? To what extent were they navigated in the manner Beveridge described in her essay? What message does this convey to the individual, organizational members, and stakeholders of the organization? What are the costs and benefits of the individual acting in the best interests of their wants, needs, and values? What are the costs and benefits of the organization acting in the best interests of its wants, needs, and values?

Describe the work or educational environment (depending on your current context) that brings out the best in you. Then, ask two colleagues who are very different from you, "Would you mind describing the work/school environment that brings out the best in you?" How would you and your colleague(s) explain the differences in your optimal environment? What do you think organizations can do to foster environments where a variety of people can each experience an environment that brings out their best? Or can they?

CHAPTER 31

FROM NEW YORK WITH LOVE

Luis Maldonado, Major, USAF
Defense Fellow, 117th Congress

The following is a story about a young man's journey from the urban landscape of New York City to the Air Force and the socioeconomic challenges associated with this endeavor. It touches upon some of the factors that led him to military service and how he persevered in an unfamiliar environment. It offers insight into some of the factors that lead minorities to serve and offers one perspective to highlight the diversity of the US Air Force. This story shows the strength in inclusion and diversity and how it helps to develop unique Airmen who contribute to our national security.

So there I was . . . Military Entrance and Processing Station (MEPS), Fort Hamilton, Brooklyn, New York, 1996: "Okay, young man, drop your drawers and cough." What did I just get myself into? Do I really want to do this? I don't know about this. What are my options at this point? I can go back to the streets and hang out with my knucklehead friends, who happen to be part-time entrepreneurs in the "pharmaceutical business." Or maybe I can join one of the other organizations in my neighborhoods like the "Bloods" or the "Latin Kings"; they have a "uniform," but although their morale is sky high, they won't necessarily provide the benefits and entitlements I need to pay the bills. After some deliberation, I chose to push through the invasive MEPS "inspection" and continue my journey to become a F-111 avionics apprentice. I'm not sure what that's all about, but I'll get to work on a jet and gain some great experience to help me once I'm done with my four-year stint in the Air Force. These were the options at my disposal. Body cavity inspection complete!

These were the cards that had been dealt. For a Puerto Rican kid growing up in 1990s New York City, there weren't very many options. College is great, but how was I going to pay the bills? I needed something in the near term; the long term could wait. Onward I went, as the first in my family to serve. For the time being, I would attend monthly meetings with the other "deppers" or entrants also on delayed enlistment just waiting to graduate high school and blow this joint. The priority was to stay out of trouble until July

1997 and I would be home free, off to a new, exciting journey. One day, out of the blue, I got a call from my recruiter, Staff Sergeant Ferreira: "Maldonado, based on your ASVAB score we want you to take the DLAB [Defense Language Aptitude Battery]. It's a test to measure your ability to learn a foreign language in a high-pressure fashion. If you pass, you can become a linguist and you'll get a nice bonus, plus some stripes." Hmmm, so I reply, "What's the catch, Sargento?" He replies, "Take the test first then we'll discuss the finer details." Here we go . . .

"Maldonado, you passed." So what does this mean? Staff Sergeant Ferreira replies: "So you asked about the catch . . . if you decide to become a linguist, your contract will go from four to six years but you will be promoted to Airman first class and receive a $4,000 bonus after tech school; sound good? Oh yeah, and tech school is almost two years." Wow, talk about a commitment! To a seventeen-year old, six years sounds like a lifetime! I'm going to need a moment to think about it, Sargento. At that moment, I glanced over to a stack of magazines and on the cover was a guy with headsets; the title of the magazine was "Linguists: a profession no one knows about" or something to that effect. Seemed like an omen to me. I guess I would never find out what avionics was all about because I was going to push with this option! At that very moment, I realized that life is all about opportunities, and you have to take them or be content with the status quo. Here we go . . . 1997, Presidio of Monterey, California: "Welcome to the Defense Language Institute (DLI). This program is not for the faint of heart. Our attrition rates are extremely high, and even officers with advanced degrees routinely wash out of the program. You will have hours of homework every evening, and if you can't keep up you will be retrained or separated from the Air Force. Good luck!" Wow, talk about intimidating. I had just graduated from one of the worst public school districts in the country at the time, and here I was, preparing to learn Russian. Let me start by saying it was rough. DLI is academically daunting even for the most well-educated students. My New York public education was going to have to do if I hoped to graduate at some point. If the first few months were any indication of my future success, I would be lucky to string together a few coherent sentences in Russian by the end of this endeavor.

Some might say that I was a "fish out of water," and it wouldn't be too far from the truth. My first plane ride ever was when I reported to basic training. I had never left the New York Metropolitan area; now I found myself as one of the few Hispanics at a tech school with few minorities or people with experiences similar to mine. The change of environment, people, and educational demands, compounded by military life, made it exceedingly difficult to make the adjustment. Grit and tenacity were critical to my success. There was no turning back. As an orphan who had never met his father, I had few options in my rearview mirror. My uncle Carlos, who had raised me, would always say, "Siempre pa'lante" or "Always move forward." Quitting was not an option.

In October 1998, we held our graduation ceremony; I had the distinct honor of being the top graduate and got to present graduation remarks in Russian. Never in my wildest dreams did I think I would be behind a lectern speaking a strange foreign language in front of my peers and their families. I was a world away from my humble beginnings and ready to seize this opportunity by the horns. It was the beginning of an incredible journey that I continue to this day. Despite all of the systemic adversity in our society and trials and tribulations I have endured, I was able to rise to the rank of senior master sergeant and earn a master's degree before pursuing a commission in 2009. Some food for thought: I grew up fifty minutes away from the Military Academy at West Point, but it might as well have been a world away. I would never see a service academy recruiter walk through the doors of Walton High School in the Bronx. Was the candidate pool less qualified? Did we not fit the "mold" expected of future officers? Had this option been available to me in 1996, I and many others like me might be wearing the eagles of a colonel right now. However, this was not the case, and I, along with many of my fellow Brown and Black peers took the "long way" by enlisting first, and only then, realizing that an officer's commission was a possibility available to all of us. With the dearth of minorities across the senior ranks, it is not hard to see that my experience is likely a major contributing factor to the lack of diversity in those very ranks. After many assignments, deployments, and family separation, I am now an Air Force major serving as a Legislative Fellow in our nation's capital.

Reflection Questions:

1. To what extent is it easier for some groups of people to "always move forward" than others, and is this a problem?
2. How similar has your experience been to that of the author?

Group Discussion:

Many people, from various backgrounds and with various identities, find themselves "fish out of water" when they arrive at a service academy or for basic training for a branch of the military.

In your opinion, how much of a person's survival should be about "grit and tenacity" and how much is about being in an environment that is supportive and inclusive? Share your rationale.

If quitting is not an option, and siempre pa'lante [always forward] is the person's mantra, what is your obligation as a leader, supervisor, or colleague who wants the best for both the person and the organization?

How does your obligation play out in terms of policies, cultural norms, and actions?

Mistreatment of persons and/or the inability of individuals to succeed is often at-tributed to systemic _____ (sexism, ageism, racism, homophobia, etc.). What does the term systemic ___(fill in the blank)_____ mean?

How do you identify it, if it exists?

What can be done about it?

CHAPTER 32

Reflections from History

Sue Hoppin
Social Entrepreneur and Advocate

My mom warned me that there would be people who would try to make me feel like I didn't belong, that I was somehow less than them. She said that I should always remember that I came from a good family background. My grandfather was a former prime minister of Laos. Our family was educated, Mom having gone to university in France and England, Dad attending school in the United States. She made sure I understood that regardless of what anyone said, I should hold my head up high and feel confident that I did belong.

This pep talk came as I was leaving home for boarding school, a prestigious all girls' school in the DC area that boasts philanthropists, journalists, sportswomen, and business leaders among its alumnae. It wasn't unusual to see Secret Service details on campus during parents' weekends, and you never knew who you were going to meet on the sidelines during sporting events. Despite all that, I was never made to feel lesser than. At least not while I was at school. It was a different story many years later when I married my Air Force husband. Navigating my new life, I would often think back to my mom's words when I was faced with comments like:

"You must be so grateful to your husband for saving you from that life."

"Your English is really good."

"I heard your people were really quiet and subservient, did you not get that memo?"

I quickly realized that in the military, the biases and preconceived notions ran deep. It didn't matter what kind of background I came from, these people who knew nothing about me other than the way I looked felt very comfortable making all sorts of assumptions and then treating me accordingly.

When we were stationed in Okinawa, Japan, our son split his chin open at a waterpark in town and I rushed him to the emergency room on base. The orderlies on duty were professional and handled the initial intake exam efficiently, explaining every step of the process to me. However, the physician's assistant who was later brought in for the consultation went about his business without addressing me at all. He would interact with the orderlies, get his information from them,

227

and ignore me altogether. I was starting to get frustrated at his lack of communication, but around the same time, my husband came rushing in to find us, dressed in his flight suit. That same physician's assistant who had pointedly ignored a distraught mother, could not run to my husband's side fast enough to explain the situation to him. Meanwhile, my husband only had eyes for my son and me and brushed the PA aside, saying, "Thanks, I'll get the update from my wife." I could see the flash of guilt and annoyance cross the PA's face, and it dawned on me that he wasn't a poor communicator, he had just judged and dismissed me as insignificant. Not the first or the last time that would happen.

Throughout my husband's Air Force career, I would be relegated to the role of the trailing spouse, an Asian one at that. Despite my background and what I would go on to accomplish in my own professional career, the assumption was that my husband had saved me from some unsavory life and afforded me the opportunity to live the American dream.

Being an Asian woman in America means that you are part of a model minority and marginalized. It's too easy to lump all Asians into one category, but a glance under the surface would tell you that Asian Americans are not a homogenous group. There is no universally shared language or experience. We come from different socioeconomic and educational backgrounds. Some of us come from families who have been in the United States for generations. If you've met one Asian person, you've met one Asian person.

Times are changing, but unfortunately not fast enough. People may still see themselves coming up against lingering biases and stereotypes. My advice to those in similar situations . . .

Don't get caught up in labels and breaking glass ceilings. During my first meeting of the USAFA Board of Visitors (BOV), the chairman congratulated me on being the first Asian American to be appointed to BOV. I also happened to be the youngest member of the board. If I had stopped to think about those labels, I probably would have felt the crushing weight of expectations on my shoulders. Instead, I relegated them to the back of my mind and set to doing the work.

Don't ever get discouraged because you can't see the impact you're having. You never know what difference you're making in someone else's life. Sometimes, just being there is enough. I once had a young military spouse find me at a conference to tell me that it meant so much to her to see that one of the leaders within the military family community was a fellow spouse of Asian heritage. Representation matters.

Don't let that chip on your shoulder keep you from recognizing the friends, allies, and opportunities in front of you.

Don't for a second, "Why me?" Instead, flip the dynamic and ask yourself, "Why not me?" You are no less worthy of an opportunity than anyone else. Why waste time trying to figure out why you've been afforded the opportunity. It's what you do with it that matters. At the end of the day, my being Asian had less to do with my work on the board than the skills and capabilities I brought to the position. My presence didn't generate any grand discussions of race or equity. However, I did realize that I approached the issues differently than my peers. My background gave me a different set of experiences that may not have otherwise been represented in those rooms where decisions were being made.

Don't let other people's biases and stereotypes define who you are and what you're able to achieve. Each one of us is more than a statistic.

Reflection Questions:

1. To what extent have you treated others like the author was treated above?
2. To what extent have you had a similar experience to the author?
3. Are there people in your organization who you tend to ignore? Why?

Group Discussion:

The author provides some excellent advice. What can organizational leaders do to create an environment where advice like this becomes unnecessary?

Many organizations provide environments where most people feel a sense of belonging. To what extent should leaders find "most" acceptable? Do leaders have a responsibility to create environments where all members feel a deep sense of belonging? Why?

CHAPTER 33

THE DOOR

Vicente Miguel R. Pamparo, Capt, USSF
Class of 2015, US Air Force Academy

When I first immigrated into the United States, my first memories were sounds: the ring of a flagpole, T-6 Texan engines roaring overhead, and my father's accent describing the boxy buildings along the flight line. At the time, the Air Force was foreign to me, yet it was the first to embrace our family in this new land.

I was ten years old when I first left what I thought was home. Truthfully, my memories of the Philippines were meager. I mostly remember myself in a constant blur of play and, naturally, trouble. I reckon that's probably why my father and mother, both stern disciplinarians, always made sure my jet black hair was scrupulously combed and my manners sharp. Our struggles in the Philippines ensured that my parents aspired more for our small family.

In high school, I was an unimposing five foot three and 115 pounds. In PE, I hated counting out loud in fear of mispronouncing a number. In class, I refrained from raising my hand to avoid pronouncing ambiguous words and embarrassing myself. At lunch, I didn't bring home-cooked meals to hide from my friends' aversion to food that did not look like a pizza. After school, I took an extra class—English Second Language—to help formulate coherent sentences and tone down my accent.

I internalized it all, but it did not matter to me; as my hero, Muhammad Ali once said, "Float like a butterfly, sting like a bee." I focused on developing myself and blurring out the noise. With grit, perseverance, and a little chip on my shoulder, I quietly worked. I worked until I earned varsity letters in three sports, followed by election to leadership positions for various clubs and eventually graduating as the valedictorian. The repetition of stoicism, hard work, and sheer determination lend well to the Air Force Academy prize. My father mentioned it once in passing; he talked of it as if it were a mythical mirage. I saw it as an opportunity to give back to the country that has given our family so much and also a way for me to selfishly continue molding myself.

The Academy challenged me in so many ways. The stifling mix of academics, military, athletics, and character development were difficult, and the solitary perseverance I'd relied on could no longer carry me. I felt a sense of unbelonging.

I was an impostor. I struggled through the different pillars of the Academy. I could barely string public speaking without the fear of my accent slipping out or using the wrong expression. I looked around at the portraits, instructors, commanders, and people who did not look a shade similar to me, let alone share the same cultural insecurities. We read and exchanged biographies, and I couldn't relate. Classmates joked and made comments about my home.

"No, as in where are you originally from?" People could not fathom that I considered US military bases in Japan, Texas, Maryland, and Portugal my home. I felt that I had to prove my family's loyalty to the US despite my father's service in the Air Force and our love for the country. On top of the struggles that we all experienced at the Academy, I along with others faced an invisible struggle. The struggle to belong not just to the Academy but to America itself.

During tough times, I found myself walking in hallways filled with painted portraits of Air Force heroes and their stories. I walked along with hopes that their words would nudge me out of my struggles. I peered into the doors of instructors and commanders who graciously opened their schedules.

How would they understand? I thought.

They say that the bonds you forge at the Academy and the Air Force are lifelong, and they are absolutely right. My friends, very much like the first base when I was ten years old, embraced me. I confided with them about my struggles and they helped me push through. It was tough love, and I owe them so much.

And yet, I yearned for mentorship. Mentorship from people who have an inkling of knowledge on the kaleidoscope of insecurities I felt on top of the Academy's rigors. As I raised my right hand and repeated the words of the oath of office, I dedicated my butter bars to my father and mother. In the back of my head, I thought of the few brash minority officers who unknowingly gave me a jolt of inspiration. They told me to embrace the diversity I brought to the Academy, the Air Force, and America. They told me that I'd done the work and proven myself time and time again. For once, I saw people that looked like me be successful in what I used to consider a mirage. The door was held for me, and it was now time for me to hold it for others.

My military experience cultivated many abilities—the opportunity to lead teams to solve complex problems, persistence to overcome adversities, and opportunity to make organizations and people better. But what I most hold dearly is the privilege to help shape the next generation of cadets and officers. Several individuals did the same for me, and I wish to repay them by passing the torch.

I realize that my personal satisfaction is not to be found in public recognition or personal success alone. Instead, it comes from knowing that I've made tangible contributions to the mosaic we call America. Nowadays, that's what satisfies me—being useful to the country that has given me so much, leaving behind a legacy that has made our country more secure even in the smallest increment. I wish to continue to be a part of that process. As an immigrant, this nation embraced me, and my heart is filled with love for its people, its institutions, and its ideals.

Reflection Questions:

1. Why do you think the author's "yearning for mentorship" was so strong?
2. Can you relate to the author's sense of "unbelonging"? Why or why not?

Group Discussion:

What can leaders do to create environments where everyone feels that they belong?

How important is it for leaders to create environments where everyone feels that they belong?

CHAPTER 34

OWN YOUR WORTH

Jazmin D. Furtado, Captain, USSF
Class of 2016, US Air Force Academy

I have always been one of the youngest people in my grade. That, combined with being just over five feet tall, made "cute" a common adjective for me in school. That did not bother me much in high school because it didn't stop me from doing anything I set my mind to. Other than being told, "You don't look Asian," I never really thought about my ethnicity as a factor in how people treated me, and I never felt discriminated against for my gender. I am extremely proud of my mixed Portuguese and Filipino immigrant heritages, and I grew up proud of how my parents, grandparents, and great-grandparents made new lives for themselves in America, and grateful that I have such strong female role models in my family.

When I started applying to colleges, my mixed heritage started to become more relevant in applications—if they only allowed me to put one ethnicity, did I say "Asian," "Pacific Islander," "Hispanic," "Latino," "White"? What would look better on the application? Did it matter? I always just considered myself of Portuguese and Filipino heritage. I never had to consider other labels. I remember when being nervous about my application to the Air Force Academy, I was told by a teacher, one of my only mentors at the time, "Don't worry about it—you'll get in because you're a female and a minority." And I remember not really understanding why that would make any difference. I just pushed the comment aside, thinking the belief I had in myself would withstand anything that came my way.

I applied to the Air Force Academy to serve the country that gave my family so much. When I got there, the first thing that hit me was that I did not have the upper body strength nor running speed to keep up with the majority of the other basics in exercises. I became aware that I was much smaller than I thought I was. Suddenly, I was conscious that other squad mates had to do more pull-ups to compensate for me because I could not complete the average of ten per person. I was quickly aware that one and a half of my own strides equaled one stride of my team members' and that carrying even just ten pounds of gear was 5 percent more of my weight than most others'. I felt smaller, weaker, less capable.

Many of my decisions at USAFA were attempts to combat that feeling. I worked out more, joined extracurriculars, tried really hard at academics, and got a couple of squadron positions I thought would help prove that I deserved to be there. My senior year, I was able to compete at USA Climbing Collegiate Nationals and even scored a graduate degree slot for MIT before I would start my job as an Air Force acquisitions officer. Still, some of my most vivid memories of that year are of being mocked in a high-pitched, sarcastic tone for my command voice and being told that I would not be a good leader because I wasn't aggressive enough.

In both situations, I was not directly confronted, and I was not sure how to appropriately respond. If I ignored it, was I communicating that behavior was acceptable? If I said anything, would I be seen as fragile and overly sensitive? Was I just overreacting? After all, we were a bunch of seventeen to twenty-two-year-olds learning just as much about each other as we were learning about ourselves.

I could not help but wonder how to move forward. If I were to speak in a lower pitch and be more aggressive, would I be taken more seriously? Why did I get negative feedback on those characteristics, with no mention of the actual content of my words and contributions in those situations?

I received similar feedback in grad school, where I was more publicly told that I had to be more aggressive when presenting my work. Why was "aggressive" always brought up? What did that even mean? If I were to start interrupting others or acquire a sharper tone, would I be taken seriously or have credibility? I did not see the same qualities being pushed as feedback for my male counterparts. While they were being judged on the content of their work, I was also being judged for my delivery. I had so many questions with no answers, instilling a consistent level of uncertainty over six years.

After completing my studies, I became a program manager in the Air Force. Thrust into this role as a lieutenant, I learned what it meant to truly rely on a team. As I grew into the roles with which I was entrusted, I started to understand what it meant to develop and empower my teammates. I was no longer studying for a test or competing for a grade, relying on my own hard work to get by. I was responsible for a program, and many people relied on my critical thinking and decision-making skills to provide direction and deliver products. The positive feedback I was getting from my leadership fueled my self-esteem.

In interacting with a more diverse group of people, I also received the most backhanded comments. "Princess," "Yes, Mom," "That's cute," "You're just so young," "My grandchildren are your age," "See here, young lady," "What's your ethnicity? . . . That's a good mix," "Could I give you a bit of advice? You need to be more aggressive." There is much that remains unspoken in these comments. Almost all were said in jest or lightheartedly, but they were all spoken at work, by men, and none were thought inappropriate to tell me at the time.

But they were inappropriate, and I was starting to realize my worth, what I contributed to the fight. Whether it be because I am a woman, I am short, I look "ambiguous," I am younger, or any other reason or combination of reasons, I could no longer tolerate demeaning behavior, because words have the ability to destroy a team's trust and respect for each other. I stopped dismissing the comments and instead pushed for explanations. I had spent much time trying to figure it out myself, trying to justify it myself, so instead of trying to answer for them, I held those individuals responsible for their words. Confronting them, I found they were just as much at a loss for justification as I had been, and in turn, they stopped bringing up comments that spoke down to me. What it took was a conversation and sharing that those comments were seen as more than a joke to me. I discovered that most people strive to be respectful and inclusive and are willing to make adjustments when they find they are not. Bringing awareness to how their comments are perceived is a first step to building a more inclusive culture.

My experiences with adversity are not extreme, by any means, but they were real to me and molded the person I am today. The Air Force provided me a space to truly grow and tap into my potential. I got to work on impactful, innovative projects with a diverse, skilled group of people. Most importantly, I found mentors that changed my perception of leadership and my own power to lead. They were commanders in my chain of command who respected my drive and potential, seeing my gender, age, rank, and ethnicities as assets, not setbacks. They fostered a culture of 360° feedback, mentored me without belittlement or disrespect, and listened to my input and insight. They empowered me to make my own calls and had my back if I was questioned because they trusted me and knew I would learn the most from my mistakes. It's interesting that I do not recall a particular phrase or inspirational quote—I just remember how they made me feel.

These few individuals have been role models for me, and it is their feedback that I truly internalized and grew from. I saw what it looked like to display confidence versus aggression, speak thoughtfully versus loudly, speak at the right time versus all of the time, encourage ideas versus dismiss them, admit mistakes and misunderstandings versus ignore them, and have a continuous learning mindset versus static knowledge. There is much that I have yet to learn, but with the mentorship and support I have received within the Air Force, I have been given the opportunities to lead innovation within the DoD, be a decision-maker at the table, and feel valued for my contributions.

Knowing the impact that forward-thinking servant leadership has had on my personal and professional growth, I work to share the same values, guidance, and assistance to those who also feel underestimated or hesitant. The Air Force's key to success has always been its people, and with an increasingly technological and fast-paced world, strong leadership that supports, encourages, and promotes diversity is paramount. We cannot afford to tolerate prejudice, intolerance, sexism, or racism of any degree, or else we squander our organic talent, lose our advantage, and fail the country we swore to protect. I believe the Air Force is changing and actively pursuing more diversity of thought. Its leaders recognize it, and I am seeing more conversations about it and actions to encourage and celebrate it in the workplace. It's a promising step to empower all Airmen, like myself, to stand in the door.

Reflection Questions:

1. What message is being sent when a person is told to be more aggressive?
2. Have you ever told a person they need to be more aggressive? If so, what impact did it have?

Group Discussion:

Being aggressive is often viewed as a positive quality. How true is this? What impact does "aggression" have on organizations?

How effective is the feedback system in your organization?

CHAPTER 35

JUST ANOTHER WHITE GUY IN THE ROOM: DIVERSITY FROM A DIFFERENT PERSPECTIVE

James T. Demarest, Brigadier General, Florida ANG
Class of 1982, US Air Force Academy

My mother was the third of five children born in Mexico City to a family of modest means who placed a great emphasis on education. She emigrated to the United States at age eighteen to live the American dream, working as a bilingual secretary. She met and married my father, an Irish American self-made man raised in New Jersey. I am the oldest of their three children, a blue-eyed, light-skinned Mexican American. I look like my father from the outside and mother from the inside. When my mother pushed me around the neighborhood in a baby carriage, people would ask her, "Are you the maid?" Since then I've always been just another White guy in the room.

My status as a "Mexican American" first came to light when I started applying to college. Up until that point nobody had ever asked, and I failed to see how my mother's country of birth mattered. The first application I filled out was to the United States Air Force Academy, as the Academy's long and arduous admissions process required an early start. When I got to the spot in the application about ethnicity, I asked my mother, "What should I mark?" I felt as though checking the box marked "Hispanic" was not really a true reflection of who I was. I was American, through and through. However, my mother was quick to answer, "Your mother is Mexican, you are Mexican; mark Hispanic." I did, and thought of myself as a "check-the-box Mexican."

The Air Force Academy was my first real experience with people who didn't look like me. The cadet wing, while mostly male and White, was made up of people from all over the country. It was a snapshot of the best and brightest from all the different races and ethnicities found across our land. And while I had learned not to see color growing up, now I was seeing color, and it made me realize something that is as true today as it was back in 1978.

Human beings are visual creatures. Ninety percent of information absorbed by the brain is visual. Like it or not, much of what we experience is from what we see, meaning that visual differences make an impression on us. This is not an excuse, nor a problem; just a fact. When we assess a situation, we say, "Look around the room." We don't say, "Listen around the room."

People see color and ethnicity because we are wired to do so. The more important question for me was and is, "What do we do with this information?" My upbringing in a Hispanic culture taught me to see difference as a gift not a problem. When I met someone who didn't look like me, I was wired to ask, "What do they know, and what have they seen that I have not?" I never thought they knew less than I did, and instead thought they knew something I did not. Maybe it was this simple view that allowed me to get along with pretty much everybody.

My approach to people and my jobs helped me to succeed in the Air Force. Academy class president, number one graduate in pilot training, distinguished graduate from the F-15 fighter weapons school, top graduate in JAG school, and now a brigadier general in the Florida Air National Guard. Perhaps I just figured out how to excel in Air Force training programs, but I like to think there is a bit more to it than that. As I reflect on my diversity experience, here are the lessons I've learned which have helped me navigate my unique military career.

Diversity is part of what we are as a country.

It doesn't take a history major to appreciate the fact that our country was occupied by a diverse native population, and colonized by a diverse group of people. Regardless of how our families ended up in the United States, America has rightly been called the "melting pot" or "salad bowl." I'm a sports fan, and one thing we could learn from professional soccer, football, baseball, basketball, or hockey is that performance is what really matters. Sports bring together talent regardless of where it comes from or what it looks like, and so should our Air Force. To me this means we must continue to recognize, celebrate, and embrace our differences as strengths. Anything less is un-American.

Immigrants and their children are motivated and driven.

Time and again I've encountered immigrants and the children of immigrants from all over the world, and I've noticed a pattern. First, they are thankful to be in America and driven to earn the American dream. Motivated by their circumstances elsewhere, they clearly see the opportunities many take for granted, and are not afraid to work for a better life. Doctors driving taxis, engineers cleaning houses, and countless others working jobs well beneath their education and experience, just for the chance at something more. Second, the children of immigrants seem especially committed to excel and succeed. Whether it is because of the stories their parents tell of a tougher life, or the desire for a better life than their parents had early on, the children of immigrants often rise to the top of their chosen fields. Finally, contrary to what others may believe, whenever I hear the sentiment that someone "got that opportunity because of their diversity," I often think instead, "They got that opportunity in spite of their diversity" because they likely had to outwork others just to get noticed.

A broader worldview is a strength to be celebrated.

My wider view of the world started with my Mexican family, but was later informed by travel. Lots of travel. While at the Academy, Operation Air Force sent me to Japan and Korea, and I went to Egypt one summer to visit Canadian relatives working in Cairo. My first F-15 assignment to Germany afforded me travel opportunities all across Europe, and I took every opportunity presented. As parents, my wife and I used travel to educate our children, with stops in Europe, Africa, Central and South America along the way. My military and civilian travels have helped me keep and indeed expand my worldview, which I continue to use to inform and drive my military service to this day. It helps and it matters.

Diversity is a military necessity.

My firsthand experience is that diversity is a force multiplier, but don't take my word on it. Here is what the Air Force has to say:

> Diversity is a military necessity. Air Force capabilities and warfighting skills are enhanced by diversity among its personnel. At its core, such diversity provides our Total Force an aggregation of strengths, perspectives, and capabilities that transcends individual contributions. Air Force personnel who work in a diverse environment learn to maximize individual strengths and to combine individual abilities and perspectives for the good of the mission. Our ability to attract a larger, highly talented, diverse pool of applicants for service with the Air Force, both military and civilian, and develop and retain our current personnel will impact our future Total Force. Diversity is about strengthening our force and ensuring our long-term viability to support our mission to Fly, Fight, and Win . . . in Air, Space, and Cyberspace.

Given this truth, it is up to all of us to recognize, celebrate, and embrace our differences as strengths. When we meet someone who doesn't look like us, think about what they've seen and what they know. When you add their perspective into the equation, you are likely to get a much better answer. And remember, diversity is more than what we look like, so don't forget to ask another White guy in the room. You never know what he's seen or done.

Reflection Questions:

1. Do you see difference as a gift? Why or why not?
2. To what extent do you see diversity as a force multiplier?

Group Discussion:

In what ways does your organization "celebrate diversity"? Share examples of how diversity has acted as a force multiplier in your organization.

CHAPTER 36

Through the Fire and Flames

Marae A. Kalian, First Lieutenant, USA
Platoon Leader, Explosive Ordnance Disposal (EOD)

My failure does not define me, nor does my race, gender, or sexuality.
Definition comes from within—the heart and soul.

Staring into my own eyes through the mirror, I ask myself, "Who are you?" I think of the people I love, the things that make or used to make me happy, and all my accomplishments and failures. And then I slowly fall apart before my own eyes. I break down and let it all out. Then when I am done, I look back up and stare at myself again and say, "I am Marae Anna Kalian, and I can do this." This is the exact thing I have done in every low moment of my life. I sit in front of the mirror and stare at myself until I am ready to pick myself back up. I am not sure why I do it, but I always do my best self-reflection during this time. I think of my core values, my purpose in life, and how I got to where I am today because I have not always been able to pick myself up off the floor and know who I am. I had to go through trials and tribulations, ups and downs, and darkness—a lot of darkness to become who I am today. And I think of my life as a sum of these moments.

The first major event that changed my life occurred when I was eighteen years old. It ultimately led me to leave the United States Air Force Academy Preparatory School (USAFA) and turn down my appointment to USAFA. Haunted houses are scary. Even though you know that nothing about them are realistic, you still fear them. You know in the back of your head that at the end of the frightening journey, reality is waiting for you after you flee the darkness. The year I spent at the prep school was my own personal haunted house. What scared me was the hardships of freshman year at USAFA. After being sick for about six months with mononucleosis, which resulted in the removal of my tonsils, I was unable to participate in physical activity for most of my prep school experience. I became scared of the physical hardships I would encounter during basic training and lost the confidence in myself to overcome the tasks. I also fell behind in academics, being on bed rest and medical leave for so long, that I feared I would not be able to succeed.

I was "that girl"—the one on profile all the time. I could not help it, though—I was legitimately sick. Nonetheless, I was still "that girl." But why is this even a thing? It is rare that someone cares if a male is on a profile—he is simply injured or sick. Yet, if a woman is injured or sick, she is weak— "that girl." Now, let it be known that I am not having a pity party, or even saying women have it worse than men. I am all about equal treatment/standards. Everyone needs to be able to keep up with training regardless of gender. However, I believe there are people, women AND men, out there who "milk" profiles. Still, women are almost always weaker (in this type of situation) than a man in the military, even if she has a genuine reason for her profile. That is just the reality of it all—women have to overperform, overcompensate, and constantly prove themselves just to be considered equal. The military is very fast-paced and unforgiving when it comes to setbacks, but often, women just become "that girl," and it can be very discouraging. You are expected to drive on no matter what—mission first, ALWAYS. Eighteen-year-old me struggled with that concept. I felt left behind and unworthy.

On top of that, I had my "coming-out" moment. I realized I was gay and I was terrified, because Don't Ask, Don't Tell had not been repealed yet. I did not come out publicly yet, but I had the "aha" moment, and I was afraid that I would get kicked out of the military if I could not "fix" myself. By "fix," I mean figure out how to be straight, because back in 2011 that seemed like the only option. With that fear, I also lost focus. I scared myself away from my own dream. Once the fear set in, I ran. I applied to UCLA and was set on leaving because I was just too scared of what was to come if I stayed at USAFA. In my head, I had lost who I was. In my heart, I knew I was capable of overcoming this struggle. In the end, fear won and I let my dream go—I left USAFA and attended UCLA.

Leaving USAFA is one of my biggest regrets and life lessons. At the time, leaving seemed like a good idea. I was running from my fears and looking for the easy way out. I was terrified that I did not have what it took to be in the military—I was just "that girl." I was looking at the smaller pictures rather than the larger picture, but once reality hit and those smaller pictures came to an end, I was left with nothing but regret.

I took my opportunity to attend the school I had worked my entire life to attend for granted and was extremely blessed to be afforded a second chance by West Point after I realized UCLA was not for me. I had to work ten times harder to get into a service academy the second time, and because of that I have become more resilient. It took me a year or so, but I realized I was not "that girl." I was determined to become an officer and attend a service academy no matter what. But I almost lost my opportunity to commission again during my time at West Point.

For me, love is life—it is everything and it is who I love that has caused me a lot of turmoil. Love is what motivates me to keep pushing in school, work, my relationships, and just life in general. Love is the glue to my being and fuels the fire inside me. When I was nineteen years old, right after I left USAFA, I came out to my parents. It was a terrible experience for me, and I thought everyone would react this way. I was convinced that even though Don't Ask, Don't Tell had been repealed at this point, that my military career would be hindered by my sexuality. I would love to say that my sexuality has never been an issue during my time in the military, but unfortunately, it has. There's a long story between my time at USAFA and my time at West Point, but my time at West Point is where I encountered my first real experiences where I felt "attacked" for being gay.

When I was a cow (junior) at West Point, I dated a plebe (freshman), which is considered fraternization in the cadet realm. I ended up getting in trouble for it, and I wholeheartedly believe I should have—I broke the rules. However, what happened during my disciplinary board is mind-blowing. The lieutenant colonel (LTC) running my board asked me, "So do you just pursue and prey on women and hope that they're like you, or how does that work?" like I was some type of predator. My jaw literally dropped and I was left speechless when he asked this. Upperclassman dating plebes is probably one of the more common disciplinary issues at West Point, but I doubt he asked a straight individual this kind of question. I tried not to let it bother me, though. I knew the truth, and I know the people who love and care for me know the truth as well.

Then, that following summer, during a twenty-one-day field exercise, a group of us cadets were talking and asking each other questions. Someone asked me how I planned on having children. I explained that I would like to do it via in vitro fertilization (IVF) or intrauterine insemination (IUI). One of the cadets in the group chimed in and said, "So, basically, you're going to create a zoo animal in a test tube." Again, I was left speechless. Luckily, I did not have to defend myself— other cadets did it for me. I did not know someone could be so ignorant. I am from Southern California originally, so homophobia, racism, etc. was not really something I had encountered before, since California is so diverse. It was 2017 at this point, and I was honestly surprised by the comment he made because of how much things had progressed. It just showed me that society had not progressed as much as I thought.

The last situation at West Point that really bothered me was when I was publicly shamed on an anonymous Twitter-type app called Jodel right before I graduated. The Jodel about me said, "Q: Why is MK 18 graduating on time? A: Because she is a minority homosexual woman." My punishment for getting in trouble was restriction for 310 days and a six-month delay in graduation, so I would graduate December of 2018 rather than May of 2018. I went through two character development programs, became a distinguished cadet (cumulative GPA of 3.67 or higher), genuinely developed myself, and decided to appeal the punishment; I was awarded the appeal and graduated on time. It is now over two years later, and I still think about the day I opened the app and saw what had been written about me. I actually still have the screenshot on my phone two and a half years later. My race was attacked, my gender was attacked, my sexuality was attacked—I was attacked. But why? Did this person know my whole story? Did they care to? Were they the perfect, ideal cadet, or just human in general? I highly doubt that. I will always admit that what I did was wrong and that I deserved the punishment I received, but I also know what I did to overcome that.

I am not an easily offended person, but these situations really have stuck with me. I know that being a minority, in multiple senses, will always leave me susceptible to judgment, but I have thick skin. And the way I see it is that all of these situations are part of that sum of moments that make me Marae Anna Kalian—a gay, Mexican/German/Armenian woman. Am I more than those things? Absolutely. Those attributes are only skin deep. My failure does not define me, nor does my race, gender, or sexuality. Definition comes from within—the heart and soul.

Reflection Questions:

1. Why do you think it took as long as it did for Don't Ask, Don't Tell to be repealed?
2. How do you treat members of the LGBTQ community?

Group Discussion:

To what extent have LGBTQ members been included in your organization?

Early opponents to the repeal of Don't Ask, Don't Tell argued that homosexuality was incompatible with military service. Do you see any evidence that this was the case?

CHAPTER 37

Attitude Adjustment from our
Southern Partners

Jaime P. Martinez, Maj, USAF
Exchange Officer to the Royal Netherlands Air Force

Finally.

After years of assimilating and navigating cultural challenges within the USAF, it was time for a familiar dynamic: I would be attending an international version of Squadron Officer School with instructors and officers from seven different South and Central American countries. Having grown up a Spanish speaker in the Caribbean, it was easy to feel more at home with people of similar backgrounds. It was an unlikely advantage that four hundred years of Spanish colonialism in the West would offer. I was looking forward to collaborating with officers of similar cultures in a learning environment that lends itself to openness. However, it served as the unlikely whistleblower that revealed that the same assumptions I and many others in the military make about each other can lead to misunderstanding and ineffective teams.

In the DoD, we all wear the same flag on our shoulder. Why then, does so much hang on our visible physical traits and the stripes, pins, and badges on our uniform? We see this play out daily in the military. The mischievous child in me snickered as I, out of uniform, allowed other Airmen to struggle guessing which crew position I held in the KC-10. Boom operator? Flight engineer? Crew chief? Few people would guess I was a pilot, I imagine because of how underrepresented my ethnicity was in the airframe. In stark contrast, while wearing bars on my shoulders, others made assumptions about what my values are or interests. And then, it's only fair to throw spears at myself: Why did I assume at a conference that the woman was there because of her husband, and not the other way around?

We would be insulated from all these privilege-driven sociocultural misconceptions at I-SOS, I thought. I could not have been more mistaken. Our initial willingness to create a collaborative environment was all too familiar, reminiscent of walking into a new USAF squadron and wanting to contribute to the team. We exchanged names, asked about where we come from, about our work experience. But in the back of our heads a different dialogue was taking place. *Flyer. Woman. Army guy. Presidential security. Fit. Well-spoken.* We quickly began to size each other up and figure out where they would fit in our team.

Day two came with our first academic assignment, along with the first failed assumption. *Everyone here is an officer, so there's a minimum level of writing skill we expect,* the student coordinating our academics later admitted. We quickly realized, and our instructor sternly pointed out, that being able to communicate effectively in a military environment does not always translate to equally effective academic and stylistic standards. It was a warning of other issues we would later experience, but we were too busy moving forward to extend our lesson learned to the rest of our interactions.

Another painfully relevant experience came during the Leadership Reaction Course. Although we were all communicating in the same language, misunderstandings led to frustration, apathy, and in almost all initial cases, failure to clear the objectives. Through an entire sequence of exercises and debriefs, we were too focused on the wrong causes to realize it was our assumptions about each other that were getting in the way. Only when an outsider pointed it out were we able to quickly recover. The days and challenges continued to pile on. From an officer struggling to stay awake because he, unbeknownst to his teammates, skipped meals with the goal of saving money, to foul play during the field leadership exercise that was simply blamed on the opponent. At every turn we faced obstacles driven by our own over- or underestimation of each other's abilities, intentions, and backgrounds.

The many evenings sitting around a barbecue pit throughout the program confirmed that I was not the only one making these assumptions. We expressed to each other how we had *thought* things run in our each other's worlds because we considered them similar, and we thought we understood the differences. It is important for me to make the connection between these assumptions and privilege. In many of these cases, to the detriment of the team. We benefited from the privilege of getting the benefit of the doubt because we are officers, which puts the many enlisted Airmen who are far smarter and have a better education than me at a disadvantage. The privilege of being American, and not being taken advantage of like some of our partners were during their time in the US. The privilege of 180-degree change in a police officer's behavior when as a young student, after pulled over for speeding, I presented my Puerto Rico driver's license. Subsequently asked for an *American* driver's license, I nervously offered my military ID, and to my relief was immediately deemed as American as apple pie.

On the other hand, the most relevant differences when it comes to our team were at the individual level. Finding out what motivates an individual and how to most effectively communicate with them does not happen in a classroom. It is earned through the irreplaceable hours putting ourselves at the same level, encouraging open communication, and getting to know them as a human being, leaving little to be assumed. This is perhaps the best cure to curbing the effects of privilege and reducing miscommunication. The rigid communication structure we have in the military, while effective in crisis, is a major obstacle for this. It requires an incredibly deliberate and persistent effort to truly open communication, especially in some of the large organizations present within DoD.

International SOS was a challenging program because of the preconceptions I had about my classmates, and how I convinced myself that I had calibrated my expectations to the new environment. As I reflect on it, I don't feel I made more assumptions than I would have in the traditional program. I was just wrong more often. However, it could not have been a more valuable experience in illustrating that the more I think I know, the more there is to discover. As a professional, I realize I can't walk onto a team and give everyone the feeling that I have no assumptions and have to learn everything from the ground up, but I feel I must overcompensate for what I *think* I know by constantly telling myself *I know nothing.*

Our Airmen, Soldiers, and Sailors deserve the best environment possible to continue giving so much of themselves to our nation. We cannot, however, provide them this environment if we are not all aware of the sociocultural obstacles in their way. I hope this collection of narratives and theory provide the ammunition for anyone with influence to help show at a deeper level what happens when you assume.

Reflection Questions:

1. What does the author mean by privilege?
2. How often do you question the assumptions you make?
3. To what extent do you think the author was trying to fulfill the need for belonging by attending the international version of Squadron Officer School?

Group Discussion:

Martinez talks primarily about misconceptions regarding race. What are some misconceptions officers have regarding the enlisted force, and what can be done to address these misconceptions?

ᴥ SECTION IV ᴥ

SOCIAL POLICY PERSPECTIVES

In *On War*, Clausewitz reminds military commanders that "war is merely a continuation of policy by other means." Ultimately, the Prussian, who has become a thought leader on classic military strategy, explicates the inextricable connection between politics and military service with policy as the nexus.

The final chapters in this section are academic papers that, by nature, use scientific principles and protocols to forward arguments that can be used by military leaders to shape future policies in hope that we can avoid unnecessary war, be it with our foreign adversaries or, as we are witnessing today, the culture war that continues to wage within American society as to what it means to be a "true American."

As the military continues to plot a course that promises to continually reshape the policies that will govern the behavior on the key topics covered within this volume in the years to come, we can only hope that some of the ideas in the following chapters can be useful in shaping the social policy perspective for the decades to come within the military.

Unlike the case study from Section I on the national political debate, or the essays in Section II that outline the institutional dialogues, or Section III authored by active duty and retired service members who have had to bear witness to the social policy issues of their day and were significantly affected by them, the following section is comprised of chapters written by professional scholars who all have a deep connection to the US Armed Forces because of who they are, what they choose to do, and ultimately, for the love of their country and for the service members in uniform who constantly strive to protect our way of life. Their proposals are not solutions. If they were, we could have already resolved all of our policy problems by now. To the contrary, the following chapters contain ideas—*because ideas matter*. The following ideas are brought to the forefront to conclude this volume in hopes of continuing to catalyze additional conversations about *action*: what we can each do as citizens, as military members, as leaders, as commanders, and most importantly, as decent human beings to make life for those in uniform a bit better. These service members honor their service commitments to us as they continually strive to protect the American way of life.

CHAPTER 38

DoD's Rationale for Reinstating the Transgender Ban Is Contradicted by Evidence

Vice Admiral Donald C. Arthur, MD, USN (ret.)
Former Surgeon General of the US Navy

Major General Gale Pollock, MD, USA (ret.)
Former Acting Surgeon General of the US Army

Rear Admiral Alan M. Steinman, MD, USPHS/USCG (ret.)
Former Director of Health and Safety (Surgeon General equivalent)
of the US Coast Guard

Nathaniel Frank, PhD
Director, What We Know Project, Cornell University

Professor Diane H. Mazur,
JDLegal Research Director, Palm Center

Professor Aaron Belkin, PhD
Director, Palm Center

This paper is a reprint of a 2018 white paper written for the Palm Center. Reprinted with permission.

Executive Summary

On March 23, 2018, the White House released a report, endorsed by Defense Secretary James Mattis, entitled, "Department of Defense Report and Recommendations on Military Service by Transgender Persons" ("Implementation Report"). The 44-page document contains recommendations that, if enacted into policy, would have the effect of banning many transgender individuals from military service. As of the writing of this study, inclusive policy for transgender individuals remains in effect because federal courts have enjoined the administration from reinstating the ban, and because the Report's recommendations have not yet been entered into the Federal Register or enacted into policy. The Justice Department, however, has asked the courts to allow the administration to reinstate the ban.

Given the possibility that the Implementation Report's recommendations could become policy, it is important to assess the plausibility of DoD's justification for reinstating the ban. This report undertakes that assessment and finds its rationale wholly unpersuasive.

The Implementation Report claims that inclusive policy would compromise medical fitness because there is "considerable scientific uncertainty" about the efficacy of medical care for gender dysphoria (incongruity between birth gender and gender identity), and because troops diagnosed with gender dysphoria are medically unfit and less available for deployment. Cohesion, privacy, fairness, and safety would be sacrificed because inclusive policy blurs the "clear lines that demarcate male and female standards and policies." Finally, according to the Report, financial costs would burden the military's health care system because the annual cost of medical care for service members diagnosed with gender dysphoria is three times higher than for other troops.

After carefully considering the recommendations and their justification in the Implementation Report, we have concluded that the case for reinstating the transgender ban is contradicted by ample evidence clearly demonstrating that transition-related care is effective, that transgender personnel diagnosed with gender dysphoria are deployable and medically fit, that inclusive policy has not compromised cohesion and instead promotes readiness, and that the financial costs of inclusion are not high. Specifically, we make the following eight findings:

1. **Scholars and experts agree that transition-related care is reliable, safe, and effective.** The Implementation Report makes a series of erroneous assertions and mischaracterizations about the scientific research on the mental health and fitness of individuals with gender dysphoria. Relying on a highly selective review of the evidence, and distorting the findings of the research it cites, the Report inaccurately claims there is "considerable scientific uncertainty" about the efficacy of transition-related care, ignoring an international consensus among medical experts that transition-related care is effective and allows transgender individuals to function well.

2. **The proposed ban would impose double standards on transgender service members, applying medical rules and expectations to them that do not apply to any other members.** The Implementation Report's claim that individuals who transition gender are unfit for service only appears tenable when applying this double standard. When service members diagnosed with gender dysphoria are held to the same standards as all other personnel, they meet medical, fitness, and deployability standards.

3. **Scholarly research and DoD's own data confirm that transgender personnel, even those with diagnoses of gender dysphoria, are deployable and medically fit.** Research shows that individuals who are diagnosed with gender dysphoria and receive adequate medical care are no less deployable than their peers. DoD's own data show that 40 percent of service members diagnosed with gender dysphoria deployed to the Middle East and only one of those individuals could not complete deployment for mental health reasons.

4. **The Implementation Report offers no evidence that inclusive policy has compromised or could compromise cohesion, privacy, fairness, or safety.** Despite the lack of evidence, DoD advances these implausible claims anyway, citing only hypothetical scenarios and "professional military judgment." Yet the military's top Admirals and Generals have explicitly stated that, while the impact on cohesion is being "monitored very closely," they have received "precisely zero reports of issues of cohesion, discipline, morale," and related concerns after two years of inclusive service.

5. **The Report's contention that inclusive policy could compromise cohesion, privacy, fairness, and safety echoes discredited rationales for historical prohibitions against African Americans, women, and gays and lesbians.** In each of these historical cases, military leaders advanced unsupported arguments about cohesion, privacy, fairness, and safety. In each case, evidence showed that inclusive policies did not bring about the harmful consequences that were predicted, suggesting the fears were misplaced and unfounded.

6. **Research shows that inclusive policy promotes readiness, while exclusion harms it.** A more rigorous and comprehensive assessment of the implications of transgender service shows that a policy of equal treatment improves readiness by promoting integrity, reinforcing equal standards, increasing morale for minorities, and expanding the talent pool available to the military, while banning transgender service or access to health care harms readiness through forced dishonesty, double standards, wasted talent, and barriers to adequate care.

7. **The Implementation Report fails to consider the readiness benefits of inclusive policy or the costs to readiness of the proposed ban.** All policy changes involve costs and benefits, yet DoD's research focuses solely on the costs of inclusion, entirely ignoring the readiness benefits of inclusion and the costs of exclusion.

8. **The Implementation Report's presentation of financial cost data inaccurately suggests that transition-related care is expensive.** The Report states that medical costs for troops with gender dysphoria are higher than average, but isolating any population for the presence of a health condition will raise the average cost of care for that population. In truth, DoD's total cost for transition-related care in FY2017 was just $2.2 million, less than one tenth

of one percent of its annual health care budget for the Active Component, amounting to just 9¢ (nine cents) per service member per month, or $12.47 per transgender service member per month.

Introduction[1]

On March 23, 2017, the White House released "Department of Defense Report and Recommendations on Military Service by Transgender Persons" ("Implementation Report"), a 44-page document whose recommendations would, if enacted into policy, have the effect of banning many transgender individuals from military service. Alongside the Implementation Report, the White House released a "Memorandum for the President" in which Defense Secretary James Mattis endorsed the Implementation Report's recommendations. As of the writing of this study, inclusive policy for transgender individuals remains in effect because federal courts have enjoined the administration from reinstating the ban, and because the Report's recommendations have not yet been entered into the Federal Register or enacted into policy. Although inclusive policy remains in effect at this time, the Justice Department has asked courts to dissolve the preliminary injunctions that prevent the administration from banning transgender service members. If courts grant the request, the administration will almost certainly reinstate the ban by implementing recommendations contained in the Implementation Report.

Given the possibility that the Implementation Report's recommendations could be enacted into policy, it is important to assess the plausibility of DoD's justification for the proposed reinstatement of the ban. According to DoD's Implementation Report, inclusive policy for transgender service members could compromise the medical fitness of the force; undermine unit cohesion, privacy, fairness, and safety; and impose burdensome financial costs. According to the Report, inclusive policy would compromise medical fitness because there is "considerable scientific uncertainty" about the efficacy of medical care for gender dysphoria (incongruity between birth gender and gender identity), and because troops diagnosed with gender dysphoria are medically unfit and less available for deployment. Cohesion, privacy, fairness, and safety would be sacrificed because inclusive policy "blur[s] the clear lines that demarcate male and female standards and policies."[2] Finally, according to the Report, financial costs would burden the military's health care system because the annual cost of medical care for service members diagnosed with gender dysphoria is three times higher than for other troops.

After carefully considering the recommendations and their justification in the Implementation Report, we have concluded that the case for reinstating the transgender ban is contradicted by the evidence: (1) Scholars and experts agree that transition-related care is, in fact, reliable, safe, and effective; (2) The proposed ban would impose double standards on transgender service members, in that DoD would apply medical rules and expectations to them that it does not apply to any other members; (3) Scholarly research as well as DoD's own data confirm that transgender personnel, even those with diagnoses of gender dysphoria, are deployable and medically fit; (4) The Report does not offer any evidence that inclusive policy has compromised or could compromise cohesion, privacy, fairness, and safety, and assertions and hypothetical scenarios offered in support of these concerns are implausible; (5) The Report's contention that inclusive policy could compromise cohesion, privacy, fairness, and safety echoes discredited rationales for historical prohibitions against African Americans, women, and gays and lesbians; (6) A more comprehensive assessment of costs and benefits indicates that inclusive policy promotes readiness, while the proposed ban would compromise it; (7) The Report fails to consider the benefits of inclusive policy or the costs of the proposed ban; and (8) The Report's presentation of financial cost data inaccurately suggests that transition-related care is expensive.

Gender Transition Is Effective

The Implementation Report relies on a series of erroneous assertions and mischaracterizations about the substantial scientific research on the mental health and fitness of transgender individuals with gender dysphoria. As a result, it draws unfounded conclusions about the efficacy of gender transition and related care in successfully treating gender dysphoria and the health conditions that are sometimes associated with it. The Implementation Report argues that there is "considerable scientific uncertainty" about the efficacy of transition-related care, and that the military cannot be burdened with a group of service members for whom medical treatment may not restore medical fitness and "fully remedy" symptoms. This assertion, however, relies on a highly selective review of the relevant scientific evidence. In truth, the data in this field show a clear scholarly consensus, rooted in decades of robust research, that transgender individuals who have equal access to health care can and do function effectively.[3]

Consensus about the Efficacy of Care

An international consensus among medical experts affirms the efficacy of transition-related health care. The consensus does not reflect advocacy positions or simple value judgments but is based on tens of thousands of hours of clinical observations and on decades of peer-reviewed scholarly studies. This scholarship was conducted using multiple methodologies, study designs, outcome measures, and population pools widely accepted as standard in the disciplinary fields in which they were published. In many cases, the studies evaluated the complete universe of a country or region's medically transitioning population, not a selection or a sample.

The American Medical Association (AMA) has stated that "an established body of medical research demonstrates the effectiveness and medical necessity of mental health care, hormone therapy and sex reassignment surgery as forms of therapeutic treatment" for those with gender dysphoria. In response to the publication of DoD's Implementation Report, the AMA reiterated its view that "there is no medically valid reason—including a diagnosis of gender dysphoria—to exclude transgender individuals from military service." The AMA stated that the Pentagon's rationale for banning transgender service "mischaracterized and rejected the wide body of peer-reviewed research on the effectiveness of transgender medical care."[4]

The American Psychological Association responded to the publication of the Implementation Report by stating that "substantial psychological research shows that gender dysphoria is a treatable condition, and does not, by itself, limit the ability of individuals to function well and excel in their work, including in military service." A statement released by six former U.S. Surgeons General cited "a global medical consensus" that transgender medical care "is reliable, safe, and effective." The American Psychiatric Association has recognized that "appropriately evaluated transgender and gender variant individuals can benefit greatly from medical and surgical gender transition treatments." The World Professional Association for Transgender Health has stated that gender transition, when "properly indicated and performed as provided by the Standards of Care, has proven to be beneficial and effective in the treatment of individuals with transsexualism, gender identity disorder, and/or gender dysphoria" and that "sex reassignment plays an undisputed role in contributing toward favorable outcomes" in transgender individuals.[5]

The global consensus reflected in this scholarship—that gender transition is an effective treatment for gender dysphoria—is made clear in numerous comprehensive literature reviews conducted across the last thirty years (which themselves confirm conclusions reached in earlier research). By conducting systematic, global literature searches and classifying the studies generated by the search, researchers and policymakers can avoid basing conclusions and policies on cherry-picked evidence that can distort the full range of what is known by scholars in the field.

Most recently, researchers at Cornell University's "What We Know Project" conducted a global search of peer-reviewed studies that addressed transgender health to assess the findings on the impact of transition-related care on the well-being of transgender people. The research team conducted a keyword search that returned 4,347 articles on transgender health published over the last 25 years. These were evaluated by reading titles, abstracts, and text to identify all those that directly address the impact of transition-related care on overall well-being of transgender individuals. Of the final 56 peer-reviewed studies that conducted primary research on outcomes of individuals who underwent gender transition, the team found that 52, or 93 percent, showed overall improvements, whereas only 4, or 7 percent, found mixed results or no change. No studies were found that showed harms. The research team concluded there was a "robust international consensus in the peer-reviewed literature that gender transition, including medical treatments such as hormone therapy and surgeries, improves the overall well-being of transgender individuals."[6]

The "What We Know" researchers assessed evidence from the last 25 years because it represents the most recent generation of scholarship. But the consensus

dates to well before this period. In 1992, one of the first comprehensive literature reviews on transitioning outcomes was published in Germany. It examined
76 follow-up studies from 12 countries published between 1961 and 1991, covering more than 2,000 individuals. The review concluded that overall outcomes
of gender transition were positive, stating that "sex reassignment, properly indicated and performed, has proven to be a valuable tool in the treatment of individuals with transgenderism."[7] A 1999 study notes that, throughout the 1990s,
comparative research found uniformly positive outcomes from gender transition
surgery, stating: "A review of postoperative cases [during this decade] concluded
that transsexuals who underwent such surgery were many times more likely to
have a satisfactory outcome than transsexuals who were denied this surgery."[8]

The positive results of research on transition-related care have only grown
more robust with time. For more detailed information on the global consensus
that transition-related care is effective, please see the Appendix.

DoD's Critique of Efficacy Literature Is Contradicted by Evidence

The Implementation Report claims that permitting service by transgender individuals treated for gender dysphoria poses an unacceptable risk to military
effectiveness because "the available scientific evidence on the extent to which
such treatments fully remedy all of the issues associated with gender dysphoria
is unclear." The Report argues that the evidence that does exist is insufficient
or of too poor quality to form a robust consensus. In support of that claim, the
Implementation Report cites one government report by the U.S. Centers for
Medicare and Medicaid Services (CMS) concluding that there is "not enough
high quality evidence to determine whether gender reassignment surgery improves health outcomes" for individuals with gender dysphoria. In addition, the
Implementation Report cites two literature reviews and one research study suggesting that the quality of efficacy evidence is low.

Yet DoD's findings rely on a selective reading of scholarship. Despite decades
of peer-reviewed research, the Implementation Report could identify only four
studies to sustain its conclusion. Critically, even these four studies, supposedly
representing the best evidence documenting the uncertainty about transition-related care's efficacy, all conclude that such care mitigates symptoms of gender dysphoria. As we show below, these four studies do not sustain the Implementation
Report's assertion about scientific uncertainty.

Before addressing each study that the Implementation Report relies on individually, several observations about standards of evidence require elaboration.
To begin, the Implementation Report's critique that efficacy studies are not
randomized controlled trials does not, in and of itself, impeach the quality
or the force of the evidence. The Implementation Report places considerable
weight on the absence of randomized controlled trials in the efficacy literature,
but it fails to acknowledge that there are many criteria for assessing the quality
of clinical research and many acceptable study designs. The CMS study that

the Implementation Report relies on to indict the efficacy literature explains that while "randomized controlled studies have been typically assigned the greatest strength, . . . a well-designed and conducted observational study with a large sample size may provide stronger evidence than a poorly designed and conducted randomized controlled trial." CMS concludes that "methodological strength is, therefore, a multidimensional concept that relates to the design, implementation, and analysis of a clinical study."[9]

Elsewhere, CMS explains that random trials are not the only preferred form of evidence, which can include "randomized clinical trials *or* other definitive studies."[10] CMS continues that other forms of evidence can support Medicare policy as well, including "scientific data or research studies published in peer-reviewed journals" and "consensus of expert medical opinion."[11] Finally, there is a good reason why the efficacy literature does not include randomized controlled trials of treatments for gender dysphoria: the condition is rare, and treatments need to be individually tailored. Given these circumstances, randomized controlled trials are unrealistic.[12]

The Implementation Report mentions four times that transition-related care does not "fully remedy" symptoms of gender dysphoria, but that is not a standard that the military or other public health entities apply to efficacy evaluation. Using this phrase falsely implies that the military enjoys a level of complete certainty about the medical evidence on which it relies in all other areas of health policy formulation. Yet as six former U.S. Surgeons General explain in a recent response to the Implementation Report, "An expectation of certainty is an unrealistic and counterproductive standard of evidence for health policy—whether civilian or military—because even the most well-established medical treatments could not satisfy that standard. Indeed, setting certainty as a standard suggests an inability to refute the research."[13] Many medical conditions are not categorically disqualifying for accession or retention, and none come with a guarantee that available treatments always "fully remedy" them, suggesting that a double standard is being applied to the transgender population. As documented above, decades of research confirm the efficacy of medical treatments for gender dysphoria, and recent research underscores that as treatments have improved and social stigma has decreased, transgender individuals who obtain the care that they need can achieve health parity with non-transgender individuals.

Parallel to its "fully remedy" double standard, the Implementation Report attempts to indict the efficacy literature because studies do not "account for the added stress of military life, deployments, and combat."[14] Given the historical transgender ban, it is unclear how efficacy literature could ever meet this standard, as DoD did not allow treatment for gender dysphoria while the ban was in effect, so service members could not have participated as subjects in efficacy studies. Generally, service members are not subjects in civilian research studies, and while service member medical and performance data, such as disability separation statistics, are studied to inform policy decisions about accession standards, civilian studies on the efficacy of medical treatments are not.[15]

CMS Study

The Implementation Report relies heavily on a 2016 CMS review of literature to sustain its claim about scientific uncertainty concerning the efficacy of gender transition surgery. According to the Implementation Report, CMS "conducted a comprehensive review of the relevant literature, [including] over 500 articles, studies, and reports, [and] identified 33 studies sufficiently rigorous to merit further review." It then cited CMS's conclusion that "the quality and strength of evidence were low."[16]

Yet the Implementation Report's interpretation and application of the CMS findings are highly misleading. By omitting a crucial point of context, the Implementation Report implies that CMS ultimately found insufficient evidence for the efficacy of gender reassignment surgery, when in fact it found the opposite. That point of context turns on the distinction between negative and affirmative National Coverage Determinations (NCDs). Negative NCDs are blanket denials of coverage that prohibit Medicare from reimbursing for the cost of medical treatment. Prior to 2014, a negative NCD prohibited Medicare from covering the cost of gender reassignment surgery, but a Department of Health and Human Services Appeals Board ("Board") overturned the NCD after a comprehensive review of the efficacy literature determined surgery to be safe, effective, and medically necessary. As a result, under Medicare policy the need for gender reassignment surgery is determined on a case-by-case basis after consultation between doctor and patient, and there is no surgical procedure that is required in every case.

An affirmative NCD, by contrast, is a blanket entitlement mandating reimbursement of a treatment, the mirror opposite of a negative NCD. Affirmative NCDs are rare. The CMS review that the Implementation Report relies on did not contradict the Board's 2014 conclusion that there is "a consensus among researchers and mainstream medical organizations that transsexual surgery is an effective, safe and medically necessary treatment for transsexualism."[17] Nor did it contradict the Board's 2014 findings that "concern about an alleged lack of controlled, long-term studies is not reasonable in light of the new evidence"[18] and that "nothing in the record puts into question the authoritativeness of the studies cited in new evidence based on methodology (or any other ground)." Rather, CMS concluded in 2016 that there was not enough evidence to sustain a blanket mandate that would automatically entitle *every* Medicare beneficiary diagnosed with gender dysphoria to surgery.

In addition, CMS only found that the evidence was "inconclusive *for the Medicare population*," not for all persons with gender dysphoria. CMS acknowledged that gender reassignment surgery "may be a reasonable and necessary service for certain beneficiaries with gender dysphoria," and confined its conclusions to the Medicare population, noting that "current scientific information is not complete for CMS to make a NCD that identifies *the precise patient population for whom the service would be reasonable and necessary*." CMS explained that the Medicare population "is different from the general population" and "due to the biology of aging, older adults may respond to health care treatments differently than younger adults. These differences can be due to, for example, multiple health conditions or co-morbidities, longer duration needed for healing, metabolic variances, and impact of reduced mobility. All of these factors can impact health outcomes."[19]

The Board's 2014 repeal of the negative NCD and CMS's 2016 decision not to establish an affirmative NCD means that, like most medical treatments, the need for gender reassignment surgery is determined on a case-by-case basis after consultation between doctor and patient under Medicare policy. The Implementation Report's depiction of the 2016 CMS review, however, obscures that point. In noting that CMS "decline[d] to require all Medicare insurers to cover sex reassignment surgeries," DoD mischaracterizes the CMS decision and erroneously states that its review "found insufficient scientific evidence to conclude that such surgeries improve health outcomes for persons with gender dysphoria." CMS did not bar transition-related coverage for the Medicare population, but determined that care should be offered on an individualized basis, which is the general standard applied to most medical care.

Perhaps the most misleading aspect of the Implementation Report's discussion is the suggestion that the 2016 CMS review undercuts the case for inclusive policy and the provision of medically necessary care. Quite to the contrary, both the 2014 Board review and the 2016 CMS review closely align Medicare policy with DoD's inclusive policy established by former Defense Secretary Ashton Carter. Under the Carter policy, treatment for gender dysphoria is determined on a case-by-case basis after consultation between doctor and patient, and there is no blanket entitlement to care for service members diagnosed with gender dysphoria. The 2016 CMS review may undercut the case for a blanket entitlement to gender reassignment surgery for Medicare beneficiaries. But it does not, as the Implementation Report insists, undercut the rationale for providing care to service members on an individualized basis as determined by doctor and patient.

According to Andrew M. Slavitt, Acting Administrator of CMS from March 2015 to January 2017, "It is dangerous and discriminatory to fire transgender service members and deny them the medical care they need. It is particularly disingenuous to justify it by a purposeful misreading of an unrelated 2016 CMS decision. Both the 2014 Board review and the 2016 CMS review closely align Medicare policy with DoD's inclusive policy established by former Secretary Carter. Under both Medicare and military policy, treatment for gender dysphoria is determined on a case-by-case basis after consultation between doctor and patient."[20]

Hayes Directory

DoD's Implementation Report cites the Hayes Directory in arguing that there is "considerable scientific uncertainty" about whether transition-related treatment fully remedies symptoms of gender dysphoria:

> According to the Hayes Directory, which conducted a review of 19 peer-reviewed studies on sex reassignment surgery, the "evidence

suggests positive benefits,"... but "because of serious limitations," these findings "permit only weak conclusions." It rated the quality of evidence as "very low" due to the numerous limitations in the studies . . . With respect to hormone therapy, the Hayes Directory examined 10 peer-reviewed studies and concluded that a "substantial number of studies of cross-sex hormone therapy each show some positive findings suggesting improvement in well-being after cross-sex hormone therapy." Yet again, it rated the quality of evidence as "very low" . . . Importantly, the Hayes Directory also found: "Hormone therapy and subsequent [gender transition surgery] failed to bring the overall mortality, suicide rates, or death from illicit drug use in [male-to-female] patients close to rates observed in the general male population."[21]

Hayes is not a scholarly organization and the Hayes Reports have not been published in a peer-reviewed journal, unlike the numerous literature reviews cited above. But Dr. Nick Gorton, a nationally recognized expert on transgender health, conducted a critical analysis of the report cited by DoD as well as a 2004 Hayes Report addressing related research, and he shared his findings with us in a memo. "The Hayes Reports evaluating transition-related care," writes Dr. Gorton, "make repeated substantive errors, evidence poor systematic review technique, are inconsistent in applying their criteria to the evidence, make conclusions not supported by the evidence they present, misrepresent the statements made by professional organizations treating transgender patients, and have a strong systematic negative bias." He concludes that "these problems fatally damage the credibility of their analysis, casting substantial doubt on their conclusions. The reports cannot be relied upon as a valid systematic clinical review of the evidence on transition-related health care."[22]

For example, Hayes claims that its reports are comprehensive, but its 2004 report omitted dozens of relevant studies from its analysis. Dr. Gorton identified 31 applicable scholarly articles that Hayes failed to include in its review.[23] Hayes labels 13 studies it chose for one analysis as consisting only of "chart reviews or case series studies" and concludes that the "studies selected for detailed review were considered to be very poor." But Hayes does not explain why it selected what it considered to be poor quality studies when numerous high quality studies were available. Furthermore, the 13 studies Hayes did choose to review were not, in fact, only chart reviews and case series studies, but included cohort studies, which are considered higher quality evidence. "By mislabeling all the studies as 'chart reviews or case series,'" Dr. Gorton observed, Hayes is "saying they are lower level evidence than what is actually found in that group of studies."[24] Finally, Hayes erroneously states that none of the 13 studies "assessed subjective outcome measures before treatment." Dr. Gorton's review of the studies, however, shows that three of the studies included such baseline measures.

Hayes also asserts that a 2012 Task Force report of the American Psychiatric Association "concluded that the available evidence for treatment of gender dysphoria was low for all populations and treatments, and in some cases insufficient for support of evidence-based practice guidelines." Yet Hayes misrepresents the conclusion of the Task Force by taking quotes out of context and omitting mention of the higher quality evidence the APA also cites—*and uses as a basis for recommending consensus-based treatment options that include gender transition.* The "insufficient" evidence conclusion that Hayes cites applied only to studies of children and adolescents. What the Task Force concluded about adults with gender dysphoria was that there is sufficient evidence to recommend that treatment including gender transition be made available.[25]

Quoting the APA fully on this matter illustrates Hayes's misrepresentation: "The quality of evidence pertaining to most aspects of treatment in all subgroups was determined to be low; however, areas of broad clinical consensus were identified and were deemed sufficient to support recommendations for treatment in all subgroups. With subjective improvement as the primary outcome measure, current evidence was judged sufficient to support recommendations for adults in the form of an evidence-based APA Practice Guideline with gaps in the empirical data supplemented by clinical consensus."[26]

Finally, Dr. Gorton observes that "Hayes writes reports that are aimed to please their customers who are all health care payers interested in being able to refuse to cover expensive or, in the case of transgender patients, politically controversial care. They obscure the nature of their systematically biased analysis by preventing scientists and clinicians from reading the reports and calling attention to their poor quality and systematic bias as would happen to any other evidence based review of health care treatments." Thus, clients of Hayes who may have paid for the meta-analyses could have a financial interest in declining to reimburse patients for transition-related care.[27]

Swedish Research

Of the four studies that the Implementation Report cited to sustain its claim that there is scientific uncertainty about the efficacy of transition-related care, only one, a 2011 study from Sweden co-authored by Cecilia Dhejne, offers original research. According to the Swedish study, individuals receiving gender transition surgery had higher mortality rates than a healthy control group.

Yet much of the data on which the 2011 Swedish study relied in assessing outcomes was collected decades prior, when life for transgender individuals was more grim, with many subjects in the study undergoing gender transition as long ago as 1973. Importantly, the Swedish study, which assessed health data across three decades, compared outcomes from the first 15 years to those from the more recent 15 years and found that individuals who underwent transition since 1989 fared far better. This "improvement over time" is elaborated on in a more recent study co-authored by the same Swedish scholar in 2016 that states, "Rates of psychiatric disorders and suicide became more similar to controls over time; for the period 1989–2003, there was *no difference* in the number of suicide attempts compared to controls."[28]

Dhejne's 2016 study reviewed more than three dozen cross-sectional and longitudinal studies of prevalence rates of psychiatric conditions among people with gender dysphoria. The authors found, contrary to research cited in the Implementation Report, that transgender individuals who obtain adequate care can be just as healthy as their peers. Among its study sample, most diagnoses were of the common variety (general anxiety and depression) whereas "major psychiatric disorders, such as schizophrenia and bipolar disorder, were rare and were no more prevalent than in the general population." They concluded that, even when individuals start out with heightened anxiety or depression, they "improve following gender-confirming medical intervention, in many cases reaching *normative values*."[29]

In a 2015 interview, Dhejne explained that anti-transgender advocates consistently "misuse the study" she published in 2011 "to support ridiculous claims," including that transition-related care is not efficacious, which is not what her study found. She said that "if we look at the literature, we find that several recent studies conclude that WPATH Standards of Care compliant treatment decrease[s] gender dysphoria and improves mental health."[30]

Mayo Clinic Research

Similar to the CMS study, the Hayes Directory, and the Swedish research, the Mayo Clinic study actually concludes that transition-related care mitigates the symptoms of gender dysphoria, with 80 percent of subjects reporting "significant improvement" in gender dysphoria and quality of life, and 78 percent reporting "significant improvement" in psychological symptoms. Moreover, data cited in the Mayo Clinic report reach as far back as 1966, more than 50 years ago, covering a period when the social and medical climates for gender transition were far less evolved than they are today. As we show in this report, more recent research demonstrates even more positive results.[31]

As we note above, the AMA responded to the release of the Implementation Report by stating that DoD "mischaracterized and rejected the wide body of peer-reviewed research on the effectiveness of transgender medical care," and six former U.S. Surgeons General responded to DoD by citing "a global medical consensus" that transgender medical care "is reliable, safe, and effective." Similar to AMA, both APAs, WPATH, and the former Surgeons General, we are wholly unpersuaded by the Implementation Report's contention that there is "considerable scientific uncertainty" about the efficacy of transition-related care. Such a conclusion relies on a selective reading of a much larger body of evidence that flatly contradicts these claims.

Ban Would Create Separate Standards for Transgender Personnel

DoD's current, inclusive regulations hold transgender personnel to the same medical, fitness, and deployability standards as all other personnel. Contrary to the Implementation Report's assertion that former Defense Secretary Carter "relaxed" standards for transgender personnel,[32] the policy that he established requires transgender service members to meet all general medical, fitness, and deployability requirements. There are no exceptions for transgender personnel or for gender transition. The proposed ban, in contrast, would impose double standards on transgender troops, as DoD would apply unique rules and expectations to them that it does not apply to any other members. The Implementation Report's recommendations are not about requiring transgender personnel to meet military standards, because they already do. Under the guise of maintaining standards, the recommendations are about establishing separate standards that target transgender people alone. Separate standards, in other words, are bans in disguise.

The Implementation Report frequently emphasizes the importance of military standards and the necessity that all service members be required to meet them. It refers to "standards" well over one hundred times in the course of the Report. In endorsing the Implementation Report, the Secretary of Defense also pointed to the importance of standards, writing the following with respect to accession and retention of individuals with a history of gender dysphoria:

> Furthermore, the Department also finds that exempting such persons from well-established mental health, physical health, and sex-based standards, which apply to all Service members, including transgender Service members without gender dysphoria, could undermine readiness, disrupt unit cohesion, and impose an unreasonable burden on the military that is not conducive to military effectiveness and lethality.[33]

No one objects to the fundamental principle that a single standard should apply equitably to all service members. But the Implementation Report redefines the usual military understanding of a "standard" in order to create what are in fact two separate standards, one for transgender service members and one for everyone else.

DoD's regulation on disability evaluation offers a pertinent example of a true single standard, applicable to all. It states that service members will be referred for medical evaluation possibly leading to separation if they have a medical condition that may "prevent the Service member from reasonably performing the duties of their office, grade, rank, or rating ... for more than 1 year after diagnosis"; or that "represents an obvious medical risk to the health of the member or to the health or safety of other members"; or that "imposes unreasonable requirements on the military to maintain or protect the Service member."[34]

A February 2018 memo from the Under Secretary of Defense, Personnel and Readiness, announced a stricter enforcement of this retention policy with respect to availability for deployment. It directed, consistent with the DoD regulation, that "Service members who have been non-deployable for more than 12 consecutive months, for any reason" will be processed for administrative or disability separation, absent a waiver at the service headquarters level.[35] Again, however, the standard that service members cannot remain non-deployable for more than 12 consecutive months is presumably a standard that applies across the board to all who are subject to the policy.

The Implementation Report on transgender policy turns the idea of a single standard on its head. Rather than determining whether transgender service members, who have been serving openly for almost two years now, have met this or other generally applicable standards, the Implementation Report recommends a behavior-based standard that only affects transgender personnel. Moreover, the only way to meet this targeted standard is to behave as if one is not transgender. The Implementation Report attempts to cast this as a single standard—that no one can behave as if they are transgender—but it obviously works as a ban targeted only at transgender personnel.

According to the Implementation Report, transgender individuals are eligible to serve if they can prove themselves indistinguishable from individuals who are not transgender. For example, at accession, transgender applicants with a history of gender dysphoria must submit medical documentation showing they are stable living in birth gender—not the gender in which they identify—for at least three years.[36] For transgender persons already in uniform (other than a specifically excepted registry of service members diagnosed with gender dysphoria prior to an effective date), retention is technically permitted but only if they serve in birth gender for the duration and receive no medical care in support of gender identity.[37]

In other words, transgender service members can be retained only if they suppress or conceal their identity as transgender. The Implementation Report characterized this as an equal treatment of, and a single standard for, all service members, whether transgender or not. Nominally, everyone must serve in birth gender, and no one can receive medical care in support of a gender identity that is inconsistent with birth gender:

> Service members who are diagnosed with gender dysphoria after entering military service may be retained without waiver, provided that they are *willing and able to adhere to all standards associated with their biological sex*, the Service member *does not require gender transition*, and the Service member is not otherwise non-deployable for more than 12 months or for a period of time in excess of that established by Service policy (which may be less than 12 months).[38]

This is the "standard" to which all service members will be held. According to the Implementation Report, this standard is necessary to maintain equity not only with colleagues who are not transgender, but also with transgender colleagues who, "like all other persons, satisfy all mental and physical health standards and are capable of adhering to the standards associated with their biological sex."[39] This incorrectly suggests that the problem with transgender personnel is that they cannot meet the standard, but the "standard" is drafted to target them by definition. The Implementation Report also casts those needing to transition gender as simply "unwilling" to meet standards, as in "unwilling to adhere to the standards associated with their biological sex."[40]

The Implementation Report carefully avoids any direct evaluation of transgender service members under a true single standard of fitness. It even misstates current accession standards in a way that makes it appear transgender individuals cannot meet them. For example, the Implementation Report incorrectly states that a history of chest surgery is disqualifying for enlistment.[41] The actual enlistment standard states that a history of chest surgery is only disqualifying for six months, assuming no persistent functional limitations.[42] The Implementation Report also incorrectly states that hormone therapy is specifically disqualifying.[43] It is not. The actual enlistment standard in fact permits enlistment by women who are prescribed hormones for medical management of gynecological conditions.[44]

The consistent theme of the Implementation Report is that transgender service members are so uniquely unfit and uniquely disruptive that they must be measured by unique and separate standards. But the strength of a traditional and single standard is that each service member is measured by the same expectation. Standards are no longer standards when they are not consistent across all members and are instead targeted narrowly to exclude or disqualify only one group.

This is why the current DoD regulation that governs gender transition in military service made clear that not only must transgender members be "subject to the same standards and procedures as other members with regard to their medical fitness," but also that command decisions and policies should ensure individuals in comparable circumstances are treated comparably. For example, the primary regulation governing gender transition directs as follows:

Any determination that a transgender Service member is non-deployable at any time will be consistent with established Military Department and Service standards, as applied to other Service members whose deployability is similarly affected in comparable circumstances unrelated to gender transition.[45]

The Implementation Report's recommendations are not about requiring transgender personnel to meet military standards because, as we show in the next section of this study, they already do. The recommendations are about establishing separate standards that target transgender people alone. Those separate standards are nothing less than bans in disguise.

Transgender Service Members Are Medically Fit

According to a statement by six former U.S. Surgeons General, "transgender troops are as medically fit as their non-transgender peers and there is no medically valid reason—including a diagnosis of gender dysphoria—to exclude them from military service or to limit their access to medically necessary care."[46] The Implementation Report concludes, however, that individuals who transition gender are uniquely unfit for service. As we demonstrate below, when service members diagnosed with gender dysphoria are held to the same standards as all other personnel, they meet medical, fitness, and deployability standards. The Implementation Report's characterization of unfitness depends on the application of standards that apply only to transgender service members, but not to anyone else.

DOD's Claim: Medically Unfit by Definition

The Implementation Report contends that service members with gender dysphoria who need to transition gender are, *by definition*, medically unfit. According to the Report, transgender service members may or may not be medically fit.

But any transgender service member with a medical need to transition gender is automatically unfit. The Report observes that, "Today, transsexualism is no longer considered by most mental health practitioners as a mental health condition . . . Gender dysphoria, by contrast, is a mental health condition that can require substantial medical treatment . . . According to the APA, the 'condition is associated with clinically significant distress or impairment in social, occupational, or other important areas of functioning.'"[47]

Although the Implementation Report is correct in noting that "clinically significant distress or impairment" is a criterion of the diagnosis, it failed to contextualize the observation in terms of the American Psychiatric Association's (APA) reasoning for defining gender dysphoria in this way. In creating the diagnosis, APA was well aware that many transgender individuals who need to transition are fully functional. In the American medical system, however, patients cannot obtain treatment without a diagnosis code. Insurance companies tend not to reimburse care for mental health conditions that do not include the "clinically significant distress or impairment" language.

At the same time, APA was mindful that defining gender dysphoria in terms of clinically significant symptoms could risk stigmatizing transgender individuals as mentally ill. According to Dr. Jack Drescher, who helped create the gender dysphoria diagnosis during his service on the APA's DSM-5 Workgroup on Sexual and Gender Identity Disorders, "One challenge has been to find a balance between concerns related to the stigmatization of mental disorders and the need for diagnostic categories that facilitate access to healthcare."[48] Dr. Drescher explained to us in a personal communication why a diagnosis of gender dysphoria should not be conflated with unfitness:

> Many transgender individuals who receive gender dysphoria diagnoses are fully functional in all aspects of their lives. When APA revised the diagnosis, words were chosen carefully. Thus, making a diagnosis requires the presence of distress *or* impairment, not distress *and* impairment. One cannot and should not conflate "clinically significant distress" with impairment, as many recipients of the diagnosis experience no impairment whatsoever. In addition, "clinically significant distress" is a purely subjective measure that is difficult to objectively quantify. Many fully functional individuals may have clinically significant distress, such as a soldier separated from his family during deployment. However, being distressed does not mean the individual is impaired.[49]

The fact that DoD's own data reveal, as we discuss below, that 40 percent of service members diagnosed with gender dysphoria have deployed in support of Operations Enduring Freedom, Iraqi Freedom, or New Dawn, and that after the ban was lifted only one individual deploying with a diagnosis of gender dysphoria was unable to complete the deployment for mental health reasons, underscores the inaccuracy of conflating a diagnosis of gender dysphoria with unfitness. In response to DoD's release of the Implementation Report, the American Psychiatric Association's CEO and Medical Director Saul Levin stated that "transgender people do not have a mental disorder; thus, they suffer no impairment whatsoever in their judgment or ability to work."[50]

Artificial Restrictions on Deployment Status

The Implementation Report's discussion of deployability illustrates how attributions of unfitness to transgender personnel depend on double standards. The Report overlooks that the small minority of transgender service members who are unfit, or who become unfit as a result of gender transition, can be managed under existing standards that apply to all service members. This includes the small minority of transgender personnel who, like other personnel, may be temporarily non-deployable. As with its recommendation for accession and retention policy, however, the Implementation Report avoids evaluating transgender members under existing deployability standards and instead assumes a separate standard that no one else will be required to meet. It assumes that transgender members are uniquely at risk of becoming non-deployable and then concludes—contrary to policy—that therefore they must be measured by unique standards.

The Implementation Report makes the uncontroversial observation that deployment is a universal military obligation. No one disagrees that all must take their fair share of the burden:

> Above all, whether they serve on the frontlines or in relative safety in non-combat positions, every Service member is important to mission accomplishment and must be available to perform their duties globally whenever called upon . . . To access recruits with higher rates of anticipated unavailability for deployment thrusts a heavier burden on those who would deploy more often.[51]

Determination of medical eligibility for deployment, however, requires an individual assessment of fitness. Army deployment standards, as a representative example, state: "Because of certain medical conditions, some Soldiers may require administrative consideration when assignment to combat areas or certain geographical areas is contemplated."[52] The Army guidance goes on in greater detail to describe considerations that should be taken into account when evaluating certain conditions, including mental health conditions. For example, most psychiatric disorders are not disqualifying, provided the individual can "demonstrate a pattern of stability without significant symptoms for at least 3 months prior to deployment."[53] Medications are also generally not disqualifying for deployment, although the regulation includes a list of medications "most likely to be used for serious and/or complex medical conditions that could likely result in adverse health consequences," and these medications should be reviewed as part of a complete medical evaluation. Hormones, however, are not on this list of medications most likely to be used for serious or complex medical conditions.[54]

Given that medical deployment standards would not appear to be a significant obstacle for service members who are *not* transgender but have been diagnosed with a mental health condition or may be taking prescription medication, the Implementation Report's conclusion that gender transition makes someone uniquely unfit for deployment is difficult to understand. The Implementation Report does not rely on general standards that apply to service members across the board. Instead, the Report shifts focus to what "could" happen to "render Service members with gender dysphoria non-deployable for a significant period of time—perhaps even a year" or longer.[55]

Neither does the Implementation Report take into account the prior DoD professional judgment that gender transition can often be planned in ways that do not interfere with deployment or pose a risk to service member health. Instead, the Implementation Report sets up a false choice between assuming the risk of treatment and assuming the risk of complete denial of treatment.[56] In contrast, the Commander's Handbook—a DoD document containing military judgment on best practices for managing gender transition—relies on planning a schedule of transition care "that meets the individual's medical requirements and unit readiness requirements."[57] The policy explicitly authorizes commanders to schedule gender transition so as not to interfere with deployment, and this balance is no different from the balance that commanders apply in managing deployment readiness for any other service member. Indeed, current military regulation requires that all service members be determined fit or unfit for deployment in accordance with established standards, "as applied to other Service members whose deployability is similarly affected in comparable circumstances unrelated to gender transition."[58]

The Implementation Report claims that "limited data" make it "difficult to predict with any precision the impact on readiness of allowing gender transition," but it cites the "potential" that individuals who transition gender will be "sent home from the deployment and render the deployed unit with less manpower."[59] But DoD's own data on deployment of service members diagnosed with gender dysphoria show these conclusions to be incorrect. Out of 994 service members diagnosed with gender dysphoria in FY2016 and the first half of 2017, 393 (40 percent) deployed in support of Operation Enduring Freedom, Operation Iraqi Freedom, or Operation New Dawn. *Exactly one* individual deploying with a diagnosis of gender dysphoria was unable to complete the deployment for mental health reasons since policy protecting transgender personnel from arbitrary dismissal was established in June 2016.[60] While the Implementation Report stated that "the Panel's analysis was informed by the Department's own data and experience obtained since the Carter policy took effect,"[61] the Panel's use of data is selective in nature. This information about actual deployment did not appear in the Implementation Report.

What did appear in the Implementation Report instead was a reference to service data showing that "cumulatively, transitioning Service members in the Army and Air Force have averaged 167 and 159 days of limited duty, respectively, over a one-year period."[62] This data was not connected to deployment and did not demonstrate any failure to meet a deployment obligation. What it did demonstrate, however, is the arbitrary way in which separate standards for fitness, targeted specifically against transgender personnel, can make them appear less medically fit and less deployable than their peers. Note that the Implementation Report's discussion of limited-duty status did not include the Navy. That is because, as the data source itself explains, the Navy does not automatically assign limited-duty status for gender transition without specific justification, which leads to a much smaller percentage of individuals on limited duty.[63] It stands to reason that average days of limited duty will be higher if the status is assigned arbitrarily without individual assessment, unlike the standard practice for personnel who are not transgender.

The Implementation Report cites the specific deployment guidelines[64] applicable to the U.S. Central Command (CENTCOM) combatant command in support of its contention that gender dysphoria limits ability to deploy and also presents risk to the service member and to others in a deployed environment.[65] First, as was the case with respect to accession standards, the Implementation Report mischaracterizes the content of CENTCOM deployment standards in order to buttress its case that service members who will transition gender cannot meet them. Second, the CENTCOM deployment standards supply another example of creating a separate standard that targets only transgender service members, rather than applying a single standard that evaluates fitness in comparable fashion to personnel who are not transgender.

It is correct, as the Implementation Report states, that diagnosed psychiatric conditions can, in some circumstances, require individual waiver prior to deployment. However, it is not correct that "most mental health conditions, as well as the medication used to treat them, limit Service members' ability to deploy."[66] Waivers are normally required only if the condition presents special risk: residual impairment of social and/or occupational performance, substantial risk of deterioration, or need for periodic counseling.[67] A judgment based on these factors would necessarily be individual and case-by-case. All other psychiatric concerns in the CENTCOM standard are tied to the use of particular psychiatric medication such as benzodiazepines, recent hospitalization or suicide ideation/attempt, or recent treatment for substance abuse.[68]

Gender dysphoria, however, stands apart as the only condition requiring waiver regardless of lack of impairment, regardless of lack of risk of deterioration, and regardless of need for counseling. The CENTCOM standard automatically designates gender dysphoria as a condition with "complex needs" that must be treated differently. Not only does the standard require waiver in every instance regardless of mental fitness and stability, it specifically recommends that waiver should *not* be granted ("generally disqualified") for the duration of gender transition, "until the process, including all necessary follow-up and stabilization, is completed."[69]

Standards that designate anyone as automatically unfit for indefinite periods of time, without consideration of individual fitness, are extremely rare. In fact, the only mental health diagnoses that CENTCOM designates as a greater risk than gender dysphoria are psychotic and bipolar disorders, which are "strictly" disqualifying rather than "generally" disqualifying. This is clearly a circumstance in which gender dysphoria and gender transition are being evaluated under a standard that is unique to transgender service members. No other service members with mental health diagnoses are so completely restricted from deployment, with extremely rare and justified exception. This artificial restriction on deployment is then used to justify a ban on transgender service members and gender transition.

Service members routinely deploy with medication requirements, including hormones, but a transgender person's use of hormones is again assessed in unique fashion. The CENTCOM standard states that hormone therapies for endocrine conditions must be stable, require no laboratory monitoring or specialty consultation, and be administered by oral or transdermal means.[70] Part of the justification for the Implementation Report's conclusion that gender transition is inconsistent with deployment is the assumption that hormone therapy requires quarterly lab monitoring for the first year of treatment.[71] The Implementation Report cited civilian Endocrine Society guidelines in support of that monitoring requirement. According to the Implementation Report:

> Endocrine Society guidelines for cross-sex hormone therapy recommend quarterly bloodwork and laboratory monitoring of hormone levels during the first year of treatment ... If the operational environment does not permit access to a lab for monitoring hormones (and there is certainly debate over how common this would be), then the Service member must be prepared to forego treatment, monitoring, or the deployment. Either outcome carries risks for readiness.[72]

While it is true that Endocrine Society standards of care recommend one year of monitoring after the commencement of hormone therapy, the Implementation Report did not disclose that the author of those guidelines communicated in writing to DoD to explain his medical judgment that monitoring hormone levels for three months prior to deployment, not twelve, was easily sufficient and that "there is no reason to designate individuals as non-deployable after the commencement of hormone replacement therapy."[73] Dr. Wylie C. Hembree, author of the Endocrine Society's standards of care, wrote the following in an October 2015 letter to the Pentagon's transgender policy group:

> (1) The recommendation for clinical monitoring was intended to cover a diverse, civilian population, including older, unreliable and/or unhealthy individuals who are not characteristic of the population of service members; (2) An initial monitoring at the 2–3 month mark is important to determine whether the initial prescribed hormone dose is appropriate for bringing an individual's hormone levels into the desired range. The initial dose will be accurate for approximately 80% of young, healthy individuals. Of the remaining 20% whose hormone levels will be discovered to be slightly too high or too low at the initial monitoring, adjusting the dose to bring levels into the desired clinical range is a simple matter; (3) Of the approximately 20% whose hormone levels will be discovered to be slightly too high or too low at initial monitoring, the health consequences of being slightly out of range are not significant; (4) The monitoring and, if necessary, re-adjustment of prescribed doses do not need to be performed by endocrinologists or specialists. Any physicians or nurses who have received a modest amount of training can perform these tasks; (5) Research is quite clear that hormone replacement therapy, especially for young, healthy individuals, is safe, with complication rates of less than 5%.

Hembree concluded that "there is no reason to designate individuals as non-deployable after the commencement of hormone replacement therapy. While individuals might be placed on limited duty (office work) until the initial monitoring at the 2–3 month mark, they can perform their jobs overseas in a wide range of deployed settings both before and after the initial monitoring."

The Hembree letter was provided directly to a Pentagon official who played a prominent role on the Transgender Service Review Working Group (TSRWG) that former Defense Secretary Carter created to study readiness implications of inclusive policy. The TSRWG, in turn, relied on the letter in determining how to implement inclusive policy without compromising readiness. That same official played a prominent role in Secretary Mattis's Panel of Experts, but the Implementation Report did not mention the Hembree letter. Instead, it inaccurately claimed that a need for long-term monitoring would preclude deployment. The Report then established a false choice in claiming that service members commencing hormone therapy would have to "forego treatment, monitoring, or the deployment."[74] The Report added that "some experts in endocrinology . . . found no harm in stopping or adjusting hormone therapy treatment to accommodate deployment during the first year of hormone use."[75] As the author of the Endocrine Society's standards of care explained, however, there is no need to forego deployment after the initial 2–3 month period of monitoring.

Nor is refrigeration an obstacle to deployment. The Implementation Report cites a RAND study observation that British service members taking hormones serve in deployed settings, but that "deployment to all areas may not be possible, depending on the needs associated with any medication (e.g. refrigeration)."[76] However, hormone medications do not require refrigeration.

More broadly, singling out transgender service members as warranting a downgrade in medical fitness or deployment status is at odds with the way that the Defense Department treats hormone therapy for non-transgender troops. In 2014, former U.S. Surgeon General Joycelyn Elders co-directed a commission with a co-author of this study (Steinman), and the commission published a peer-reviewed study addressing hormones, gender identity, deployability, and fitness. While the commission's discussion of hormones is lengthy, we quote it in full because it underscores the contrast between the Implementation Report's treatment of hormone therapy for transgender personnel and the way that non-transgender service members requiring hormones are managed. The commission conducted its research before the implementation of inclusive policy, yet its observations about the double standards of the historical ban are fully applicable to the Implementation Report's proposed ban:

> [T]he military consistently retains non-transgender men and women who have conditions that may require hormone replacement. For example, the military lists several gynecological conditions (dysmenorrhea, endometriosis, menopausal syndrome, chronic pelvic pain, hysterectomy, or oophorectomy) as requiring referral for evaluation only when they affect duty performance. And the only male genitourinary conditions that require referral for evaluation involve renal or voiding

dysfunctions. The need for cross-sex hormone treatment is not listed as a reason for referral for either men or women. The military also allows enlistment in some cases despite a need for hormone replacement. DoDI 6130.03, for example, does not disqualify all female applicants with hormonal imbalance. Polycystic ovarian syndrome is not disqualifying unless it causes metabolic complications of diabetes, obesity, hypertension, or hypercholesterolemia. Virilizing effects, which can be treated by hormone replacement, are expressly not disqualifying.

Hormonal conditions whose remedies are biologically similar to cross-sex hormone treatment are grounds neither for discharge nor even for referral for medical evaluation, if service members develop them once they join the armed forces. Male hypogonadism, for example, is a disqualifying condition for enlistment, but does not require referral for medical evaluation if a service member develops it after enlisting. Similarly, DoDI 6130.03 lists "current or history of pituitary dysfunction" and various disorders of menstruation as disqualifying enlistment conditions, but personnel who develop these conditions once in service are not necessarily referred for evaluation. Conditions directly related to gender dysphoria are the only gender-related conditions that carry over from enlistment disqualification and continue to disqualify members during military service, and gender dysphoria appears to be the only gender-related condition of any kind that requires discharge irrespective of ability to perform duty.

Military policy allows service members to take a range of medications, including hormones, while deployed in combat settings. According to a Defense Department study, 1.4 percent of all US service members (approximately 31,700 service members) reported prescription anabolic steroid use during the previous year, of whom 55.1 percent (approximately 17,500 service members) said that they obtained the medications from a military treatment facility. One percent of US service members exposed to high levels of combat reported using anabolic steroids during a deployment. According to Defense Department deployment policy, "There are few medications that are inherently disqualifying for deployment." And, Army deployment policy requires that "A minimum of a 180-day supply of medications for chronic conditions will be dispensed to all deploying Soldiers." A former primary behavioral health officer for brigade combat teams in Iraq and Afghanistan told Army Times that "Any soldier can deploy on anything." Although Tricare officials claimed not to have estimates of the amounts and types of medications distributed to combat personnel, Tricare data indicated that in 2008, "About 89,000 antipsychotic pills and 578,000 anti-convulsants [were] being issued to troops heading overseas." The Military Health Service maintains a sophisticated and effective system for distributing prescription medications to deployed service members worldwide.[77]

The Implementation Report's contention that transgender service members commencing hormone therapy must "forego treatment, monitoring, or the deployment" is inaccurate. Such therapy is not grounds for characterizing transgender service members as non-deployable or medically unfit beyond the initial 2–3 month monitoring period. Nor are such characterizations consistent with DoD's willingness to access, retain, and deploy tens of thousands of non-transgender service members who require hormones.

DoD's rationale for reinstating the ban cannot be about lost duty time during gender transition, because DoD's latest policy recommendation disqualifies from enlistment applicants who have already transitioned gender. The consistent theme across the Implementation Report is to create separate standards that target gender dysphoria and gender transition as uniquely disqualifying circumstances requiring uniquely disqualifying measures, but to disregard generally applicable standards that transgender members would in fact meet. This allows the Implementation Report to suggest that transgender service members must be seeking "special accommodations,"[78] when the only accommodation they seek is the opportunity to meet general standards that apply to all.

Mental Health Encounters Mandated by Policy

The Implementation Report observes that "Service members with gender dysphoria are also nine times more likely to have mental health encounters than the Service member population as a whole (28.1 average encounters per Service member versus 2.7 average encounters per Service member)."[79] [The encounters took place over 22 months, from October 2015 to July 2017.] However, the Implementation Report overlooked the main reason why service members diagnosed with gender dysphoria have high mental health utilization, leaving the incorrect impression that high usage is a reflection of medical unfitness or the difficulty of treating gender dysphoria.

In particular, the Implementation Report neglected to consider over-prescription of appointments for administrative rather than medical reasons. We determined in our research that service members with gender dysphoria diagnoses have high rates of utilization not because they are medically unfit, but because the military has over-prescribed visits as part of the process of providing transition-related care, requiring numerous medically unnecessary encounters for service members diagnosed with gender dysphoria, but not other medical conditions.

The over-prescription of appointments in the military has resulted from two distinct considerations, neither of which reflects medical unfitness. First, it has resulted from the medicalization of administrative matters, as aspects of care that would normally be handled administratively have been assigned to medical providers. As a result, the gender transition process can require a dozen or more mental health appointments regardless of the individual's actual mental health status and without regard to stability, fitness, or need for care. For example, a command decision to grant permission to wear a different uniform to work (exception to policy) requires a mental health workup and recommendation. Each step of the transition process, regardless of import or need, requires mental health workup and recommendation, and the medicalization of non-medical decisions inevitably increases usage.

The reason for the extra layer of administrative "ticket-punching" is not medical. It is the result, rather, of a military determination that it cannot allow transition-related medical care to occur without command supervision designed to ensure that changes in uniforms, grooming standards, facilities use, and the like do not undermine good order and discipline. And while these considerations are important and necessary to maintain operational readiness, they are not indicators of impaired mental health in the transgender member. The military, of course, follows standard professional guidelines for the diagnosis of gender dysphoria, the prescription of hormone therapy, and the authorization of surgery. The generation of unnecessary mental health visits comes not from these decisions directly, but from the fact that, in the military, mental health providers serve as emissaries between the medical system and commanders. Mental health providers need to sign off on various administrative decisions along the way that have no counterpart in the civilian system, and no counterpart in the military's treatment of other mental health conditions. The military adds on an extra layer of medical approval to what otherwise would be purely administrative or workplace decisions, and this necessarily affects the degree to which medical providers are involved.

We reviewed a range of documents that mandate or guide the steps taken by military medical teams responsible for the care of transgender service members. For example, the principal DoD regulation governing gender transition[80] expands a medical provider's responsibility beyond making medical diagnoses and determining medically necessary treatment. In addition to those traditional and necessary aspects of health care, medical providers are responsible for justifying those medical judgments "for submission to the commander."[81] Medical providers must "advise the commander" on matters of gender transition, and in turn commanders must "coordinate with the military medical provider regarding any medical care or treatment provided to the Service member, and any medical issues that arise in the course of a Service member's gender transition."[82] The commander must approve every step along the path of gender transition, including the timing of any medical treatment and the timing of gender transition itself. Even with respect to military matters such as an exception to policy to wear a different-gender uniform, a military medical provider is responsible for consultation as part of requesting a commander's approval. These extra administrative consultations cannot help but increase medical utilization, even though they are not medically necessary in a traditional sense and do not reflect any lack of medical fitness.

The Commander's Handbook similarly emphasizes the unusual dual layer of justification and approval for decisions affecting transgender service members: "The oversight and management of the gender transition process is a team effort with the commander, the Service member, and the military medical provider."[83] Our observations are not intended to suggest there is anything inappropriate or militarily unnecessary about regulatory requirements that medical providers serve as emissaries between the medical system and the command structure. The point is simply that these dual layers of consultation and approval cannot help but drive up utilization of mental health care, but for reasons that are unrelated to mental health or fitness for duty.

Service-specific regulations produce over-prescriptions as well. According to interim guidance contained in a Navy Bureau of Medicine and Surgery document, a mental health diagnosis of gender dysphoria, coupled with a provider's determination that gender transition is medically necessary to relieve gender dysphoria, is only the first step in a series of requirements for approval of that medical care. Once a diagnosis and a recommendation for treatment is made, that diagnosis and recommendation must be referred for another layer of medical approval from the Transgender Care Team (TGCT). The TGCT will either validate or revise those medical decisions and forward the plan back to the originating provider. These decisions must then be documented once again as part of the package prepared to obtain a commander's approval: "Once the . . . medical provider has received the validated medical treatment plan from the TGCT, the Service member and . . . medical provider should incorporate the validated medical treatment plan into the full gender transition plan for the Service member's commanding officer's review."[84]

Even at the end of the process of gender transition, the service member's "psychological stability" must be validated by a treating provider, validated a second time by the TGCT, and then validated a third time by a commander, all before an official gender marker change can occur. It might make sense to rely on a service member's duty performance as part of the judgment of whether he or she "consistently demonstrated psychological stability to transition to the preferred gender,"[85] but service-level procedures can instead substitute arbitrary numbers of mental-health visits over arbitrary minimums of time to satisfy a finding of "psychological stability." An "Individualized TGCT Care Plan" obtained from the Naval Medical Center in San Diego recommends that "at a minimum, the service member [undergoing transition] should follow up with a mental health provider or psychosocial support group on a monthly basis." These at-least-monthly visits are used to demonstrate a "6 month period of stability in real life experience documented by a mental health professional" and a "6 month period of emotional/psychosocial stability documented by a mental health professional."[86]

A senior military psychologist who has worked with transgender military members confirmed to us that in order to transition gender, a medical team must document several benchmarks of readiness for treatment and also for permission to change one's gender marker in the military identification system. As a result, he explained, many transgender service members may be required to attend multiple, inexpensive support group sessions that are essentially used as "ticket-punching" to verify administrative requirements. "It almost requires them to have those individual sessions on an ongoing basis," the psychologist said.[87] These requirements established by departments throughout the military health system are far more voluminous than anything required by the civilian medical system. Satisfying them necessitates extensive documentation, which creates incentives for over-prescribing health care appointments.

Lack of experience is the second reason for the over-prescribing of mental health visits, as well-intentioned medical providers inexperienced in transition-related care have been overly cautious in documenting gender stability. It is inevitable that an adjustment period would be needed for the military medical system, given how new it is to transgender health care. A survey of military medical providers found that even after the lifting of the ban, physicians were unprepared to treat transgender service members, as most respondents "did not receive any formal training on transgender care, most had not treated a patient with known gender dysphoria, and most had not received sufficient training" to oversee cross-hormone therapy.[88] This inevitable learning curve is closely connected to the over-prescribing of visits, in that overly cautious medical providers are requiring numerous, medically unnecessary appointments to document stability.

One social worker who is a clinical case manager for transgender service members explained that "the only way to verify that someone has been stable in their gender for six months is if they communicate with someone showing that they're stable. So they must be checking in at least once per month," and sometimes more. As a result of that requirement, he said his department put recommendations in their transition treatment plans that service members check in with either a primary care provider or mental health provider regularly, or that they attend one of the transgender support groups. "Most of the naval hospitals within our region have a weekly trans support group," he said, "and that tends to be provided through the mental health department. People may be attending those meetings every week and that would show up in their notes as going to a mental health appointment every week." In short, to establish required stability, individuals "have to be reporting that to someone so it's documented so we can point to it and say, 'See? They're stable,' so we can draft a memo verifying it."[89]

A Veterans Affairs psychiatrist familiar with the military's management of transgender personnel told us that doctors "could be requiring the person to go to a mental health provider to check on their stability, and they *have* to go. These are situations that would be absent any specific need for mental health on the part of the service member. They're either explicitly required to go or implicitly required: you can't demonstrate stability if you're not seen by someone." He estimated that "people may have four to seven appointments, *absent any particular need*, just to demonstrate that they're stable in the course of their in-service transition." He added that most military clinicians "are unfamiliar with the process, and they don't yet have capacity. They're trying to learn this as they go along, and so they're being cautious. There's a kind of learning curve. As the system becomes more adept at working with this population, it could be that the number of visits goes down because the clinicians don't need the comfort of seeing the people as often as they do now."[90]

Transgender service members confirm that most of their mental health encounters are the result of over-prescribing visits, not medical need. We assessed the experiences of ten Active Duty transgender troops who transitioned or started to transition over the past two years. Out of 81 total mental health visits reported, 97.5 percent (79 visits) were classified as obligatory. A large number of these visits were mandated monthly counseling sessions that helped provide administrators with ways to document readiness and stability of transitioning service members. An Army First Lieutenant told us that upon beginning hormone therapy, he had "monthly checkups with my behavioral health clinical social worker, monthly checkups with my nurse case manager." A sailor reported that "I have to go for a five-minute consultation for them just to say, 'this is when your surgery is.'"[91]

An analysis by the Veterans Health Administration demonstrates that when a system is not characterized by over-prescribing, mental health care utilization among transgender individuals is far lower than the rate reported by DoD, and also that utilization among transgender and non-transgender individuals is roughly equivalent (as suggested below by the California Health Interview Survey). VHA data reveal that from FY2011 to FY2016, transgender patients averaged between 2.3 and 4.4 mental health encounters per year, as compared to slightly lower utilization among non-transgender patients diagnosed with depression.[92] These data suggest that DoD's finding that service members diagnosed with gender dysphoria have an average of 15.3 mental health encounters per year is not a reflection of medical need.

Table 1. Incidence proportion of mental health utilization among VA patients by FY

	FY11	FY12	FY13	FY14	FY15	FY16
Transgender Group	n	n	n	n	n	n
Total unique patients	396	487	562	680	879	1089
Total # of mental health encounters	923	1454	1584	2653	2943	4806
Incidence of encounters/patient	2.3	3.0	2.8	3.9	3.3	4.4
Sample of Nontransgender Patients						
Total unique patients	1188	1461	1686	2040	2637	3267
Total patients with depression diagnosis	173	201	230	276	338	446
Total # of mental health encounters	248	274	432	438	745	1381
Incidence of encounters/patient	1.4	1.4	1.9	1.6	2.2	3.1

Research indicates that when health care delivery is not over-prescribed, utilization among transgender and non-transgender adults is roughly equivalent. A 2018 study drew on California Health Interview Survey (CHIS) data to assess "utilization rates in access to primary and specialty care among a large cohort of insured transgender and cisgender [i.e., not transgender] patients." The authors calculated the "percentage of patients accessing primary care providers or specialty care providers among patients who reported having insurance coverage" and categorized patients as low, medium, or high utilizers. The results were that transgender patients "accessed both primary and specialty care services at a lower frequency than cisgender individuals and were more likely to fall into the low and medium utilizer groups." Fully 72.9 percent of transgender individuals were low utilizers (0–3 annual visits) compared to 70.9 percent of non-transgender individuals. Just 0.8 percent of transgender individuals were high utilizers (13–25 annual visits) compared to 4.6 percent of non-transgender people. The authors concluded that "transgender individuals are less likely to utilize healthcare services" than the overall population.[93]

Table 2: Frequency of Doctor Visits by Gender Identity

Number of Doctor Visits In Past Year	Gender Identity					
	Not transgender (i.e., cisgender)		Transgender or gender non-conforming		All	
Low Utilizers (0–3 visits)	70.9%	15,117,000	72.9%	81,000	70.9%	15,197,000
Medium Utilizers (4–12 visits)	24.4%	5,203,000	26.3%	29,000	24.4%	5,232,000
High Utilizers (13–25 visits)	4.6%	990,000	0.8%	1,000	4.6%	991,000
Total	100%	21,310,000	100%	110,000	100%	21,421,000

High utilization is not evidence of unfitness, the burdensome needs of transgender troops, or the difficulty of treating gender dysphoria. To the extent that service members diagnosed with gender dysphoria log more mental health visits than average, it is because the system treats them differently and requires more engagement with mental health providers. It has little to do with need for care or fitness for duty. Military medical providers are taking extra steps, sometimes to comply with regulations, and other times out of excessive caution, to justify medical and administrative decisions during the transition process. DoD's failure to address this possibility in its research creates the misimpression that excessive utilization demonstrates the medical unfitness of transgender troops. But it is the military bureaucracy that creates elevated usage figures, not transgender service members.

Suicide Is a Military Problem, Not a Transgender Problem

Children of service members are more than 50 percent more likely to have attempted suicide than the general population, yet the military does not bar individuals in this high-risk group from entry.[94] The Implementation Report, however, attempts to invoke an analogous risk factor among transgender people in general as a basis for disqualification. The Implementation Report claims that "high rates of suicide ideation, attempts, and completion among people who are transgender are also well documented in the medical literature," and cites research indicating lifetime rates of suicide attempts among transgender civilians ranging from 41 percent to as high as 57 percent. But neither applicants for military service nor serving members in uniform are evaluated by characteristics of larger groups; they are measured by standards as individuals.

The Implementation Report also mischaracterizes and selectively cites DoD data on military personnel that, if accurately presented, would in fact demonstrate that rates of suicidal ideation among transgender and non-transgender service members are roughly equivalent. The Implementation Report claims that among military personnel, "Service members with gender dysphoria are eight times more likely to attempt suicide than Service members as a whole (12% versus 1.5%)" during a 22-month study window.[95] This is an inaccurate reading of DoD's own data as well as an inaccurate interpretation of what the data mean. First, the DoD data do not show that service members with gender dysphoria were eight times more likely to *attempt* suicide than other service members during the 22-month study period, but to *contemplate* suicide, a major distinction that the Implementation Report misconstrued.

Second, service members with gender dysphoria are not eight times more likely to contemplate suicide than other service members, because the data under-report the frequency of suicidal thoughts among service members as a whole. The reported 1.5 percent suicidal ideation rate among service members as a whole was based on a review of administrative records.[96] When DoD used more sophisticated methods to determine rates of suicidality among service members not being treated for behavioral health problems, military researchers determined that 14 percent of service members have had suicidal thoughts at some time in their lives, 11 percent had suicidal thoughts at some point during their military careers, and 6 percent had suicidal thoughts during the past year.[97] Suicide is a military problem. It is not a transgender problem.

Finally, while DoD data indicate that service members diagnosed with gender dysphoria are slightly more prone to suicidal ideation than other service members, the Implementation Report did not take the historical legacy of the transgender ban into account. Extensive research has confirmed that both stigma and the denial of medically necessary care can lead to suicidality.[98] The historical transgender ban, in other words, contributed to stigma and deprivation of health care, which exacerbates the problems the Implementation Report has deemed disqualifying.

The reaction of professional mental health providers to this circular reasoning—denying necessary health care to transgender troops and then citing suboptimal health as the reason for exclusion—is summed up by statements recently released by two of the largest mental health associations in America. The CEO of the American Psychological Association recently stated that he was "alarmed by the administration's misuse of psychological science to stigmatize transgender Americans and justify limiting their ability to serve in uniform and access medically necessary health care."[99] And the American Psychiatric Association stated that the Pentagon's anti-transgender "discrimination has a negative impact on the mental health of those targeted."[100] If inclusive policy remains in effect, DoD will continue to provide medically necessary care to transgender service members. As a result, we would expect the slightly elevated ideation rate among service members diagnosed with gender dysphoria to disappear over time.

Unit Cohesion Has Not Been Compromised

The Implementation Report concludes that inclusive policy for transgender personnel could compromise unit cohesion, privacy, fairness, and safety by allowing transgender men who retain some physiological characteristics of their birth sex and transgender women who retain some physiological characteristics of their birth sex to serve in the military, thus blurring the line that distinguishes male and female bodies:

> [B]y allowing a biological male who retains male anatomy to use female berthing, bathroom, and shower facilities, it [inclusive policy] undermines the reasonable expectations of privacy and dignity of female Service members. By allowing a biological male to meet the female physical fitness and body fat standards and to compete against females in gender-specific physical training and athletic competition, it undermines fairness (or perceptions of fairness) because males competing as females will likely score higher on the female test than on the male test and possibly compromise safety.[101]

According to the Implementation Report, "sex-based standards ensure fairness, equity, and safety; satisfy reasonable expectations of privacy; reflect common practice in society; and promote core military values of dignity and respect between men and women—all of which promote good order, discipline, steady leadership, unit cohesion, and ultimately military effectiveness and lethality."[102] Yet the Report does not include any evidence to support its contention that inclusive policy has had these effects. Three weeks after the Report's publication, Army Chief of Staff General Mark Milley responded to Senator Kirsten Gillibrand, who asked whether he had heard "anything about how transgender service members are harming unit cohesion," by testifying that "I have received precisely zero reports of issues of cohesion, discipline, morale and all those sorts of things."[103] Chief of Naval Operations Admiral John Richardson, Air Force Chief of Staff General David Goldfein, and Marine Corps Commandant General Robert Neller subsequently confirmed that inclusive policy has not compromised cohesion.[104]

The Implementation Report's explanation for failing to provide evidence is that cohesion "cannot be easily quantified" and that "not all standards . . . are capable of scientific validation or quantification. Instead, they are the product of professional military judgment acquired from hard-earned experience leading Service members in peace and war or otherwise arising from expertise in military affairs. Although necessarily subjective, this judgment is the best, if not only, way to assess the impact of any given military standard on the intangible ingredients of military effectiveness mentioned above—leadership, training, good order and discipline, and unit cohesion."[105]

This contention, however, does not withstand scrutiny. In response to Senator Gillibrand's question about whether transgender troops have harmed unit cohesion, General Milley testified that "it is monitored very closely because I am concerned about that."[106] In addition, many military experts have quantified cohesion and other dimensions of readiness, and have assessed cause-and-effect claims about those phenomena in their research.[107] In 2011 and 2012, for example, a group of Service Academy professors used multiple methods including surveys, interviews, field observations, and longitudinal analysis to assess whether the repeal of "don't ask, don't tell" (DADT) had impacted readiness and its component dimensions, including unit cohesion and morale, and results were published in a leading peer-reviewed military studies journal.[108]

In the case at hand, DoD could have studied the validity of its contentions about cohesion, privacy, fairness, and safety without difficulty. For example, DoD could have (1) assessed readiness by comparing the performance of units that include a service member diagnosed with gender dysphoria with units that do not include anyone with a diagnosis; (2) measured cohesion via interviews, surveys, and/or field observations and then compared results from units that include a service member diagnosed with gender dysphoria with units that do not include anyone with a diagnosis; (3) assessed privacy and fairness via interviews, surveys, and/or field observations and then compared results from units that include a service member diagnosed with gender dysphoria with units that do not include anyone with a diagnosis; and (4) assessed safety by comparing disciplinary records of units that include a service member diagnosed with gender dysphoria with units that do not include anyone with a diagnosis.

Instead, and in lieu of evidence, the Implementation Report offers three scenarios, two of which are hypothetical, to sustain its assertions. The scenarios, however, do not sustain the conclusion that inclusive policy has compromised or could compromise cohesion, privacy, fairness, or safety. Under the first hypothetical scenario, fairness and safety are compromised when transgender women compete with cisgender women in sporting events, for example boxing competitions.[109] The Report assumes incorrectly that "biologically-based standards will be applied uniformly to all Service members of the same biological sex," contrary to current practice in which gender-based presumptions are adjustable based on circumstances. At the U.S. Military Academy, for example, the Implementation Report observes that "matching men and women according to weight may not adequately account for gender differences regarding striking force." But the Report ignores that Cadets' skill level and aggression, not just weight, are factored into safety decisions, and West Point allows men and women to box each other during training.[110]

While sex-based standards are used in concert with other factors to promote fairness and safety, male-female segregation is not absolute—and it is not sufficient. Ensuring fairness and safety in combative training is always a command concern because of the wide variation in body size and weight within gender even when gender is defined by birth. Commanders at all levels are able to make judgments about how to conduct training in ways that adequately protect the participants, and they are able to do the same thing for transgender service members when and if needed. This hypothetical scenario does not lend any credence to the contention that inclusive policy has compromised or could compromise cohesion, privacy, fairness, or safety.

Under the second hypothetical scenario, a transgender man who has not had chest-reduction surgery wants to perform a swim test with no shirt and breasts exposed. It is farfetched to imagine a transgender service member making such a request, and the Implementation Report does not offer any actual examples to buttress this hypothetical concern despite almost two years of inclusive policy. Despite the low likelihood of such a scenario, the Commander's Handbook guides commanders in what to do, and the guidance is sufficient. The Handbook holds the transgender service member responsible for maintaining decorum: "It is courteous and respectful to consider social norms and mandatory to adhere to military standards of conduct."[111] Then, the Handbook advises commanders that they may counsel the service member on this responsibility, but also may consider other options such as having everyone wear a shirt. Ultimately, according to the Handbook, the fundamental principle for commanders is that "it is within your discretion to take measures ensuring good order and discipline."[112] Similar to the first hypothetical scenario, this scenario does not sustain a conclusion that inclusive policy has compromised or could compromise cohesion, privacy, fairness, or safety.

The third scenario, the only scenario that is not hypothetical, describes a cisgender female who claimed that the presence in shower facilities of a transgender female who retained some physiological characteristics of birth sex undermined her privacy, and the transgender service member claimed that her commander had not been supportive of her rights.[113] DoD guidance offers commanders tools that should have been sufficient for resolving the matter. The situation closely matches scenarios 11 and 15 in the Commander's Handbook, which emphasize that all members of the command should be treated with dignity and respect: "In every case, you may employ reasonable accommodations to respect the privacy interests of Service members."[114] Commanders are given the following guidance on reasonable accommodations: "If concerns are raised by Service members about their privacy in showers, bathrooms, or other shared spaces, you may employ reasonable accommodations, such as installing shower curtains and placing towel and clothing hooks inside individual shower stalls, to respect the privacy interests of Service members. In cases where accommodations are not practicable, you may authorize alternative measures to respect personal privacy, such as adjustments to timing of the use of shower or changing facilities."[115]

The Commander's Handbook also makes clear that the transgender service member has responsibility: "Maintaining dignity and respect for all is important. You will need to consider both your own privacy needs and the privacy needs of others. This includes, but is not limited to, maintaining personal privacy in locker rooms, showers, and living quarters. One strategy might include adjusting personal hygiene hours."[116]

Inclusive policy cannot be blamed if commanders fail to follow the guidance or to implement it properly, and this scenario does not lend any credibility to the Implementation Report's contention that inclusive policy has compromised or could compromise cohesion, privacy, fairness, or safety. Army training materials are even more straightforward, essentially reminding Soldiers that military life involves a loss of privacy and instructing them that it is not the Army's job to protect tender sensibilities: "Understand that you may encounter individuals in barracks, bathrooms, or shower facilities with physical characteristics of the opposite sex despite having the same gender marker in DEERS."[117]

Cohesion and Related Concerns Have Historically Proven Unfounded

The Implementation Report's contention that inclusive policy could compromise cohesion, privacy, fairness, and safety echoes discredited rationales for historical prohibitions against African Americans, women, and gays and lesbians. In each case, military leaders made arguments about cohesion, privacy, fairness, and safety.[118] In the case of "don't ask, don't tell," for example, leaders insisted that because heterosexual service members did not like or trust gay and lesbian peers, lifting the ban would undermine unit cohesion. One of the principal architects of the policy, the late professor Charles Moskos, insisted that allowing gay men and lesbians to shower with heterosexuals would compromise privacy, and a judge advocate general argued that a "privacy injury" would take place every time an openly gay or lesbian service member witnessed the naked body of a heterosexual peer.[119] Others argued that the repeal of DADT would lead to an increase in male-male sexual assault.[120] One year after the ban's repeal, military professors published a study repudiating these predictions, and the New York Times editorialized that "politicians and others who warned of disastrous consequences if gay people were allowed to serve openly in the military are looking pretty foolish."[121]

Inclusive Policy Promotes Readiness

Scholarly research has shown that inclusive policy for transgender personnel pro-motes military readiness. According to a comprehensive implementation analysis by retired General Officers and scholars writing before the 2016 lifting of the ban, "when the US military allows transgender personnel to serve, commanders will be better equipped to take care of the service members under their charge."[122] While scholars have explored the relationship between readiness and inclusive policy for transgender personnel from a variety of angles including medical fitness, imple-mentation, command climate, and deployability, all available research has reached the same conclusion: At worst, inclusive policy does not compromise readiness. At best, it enhances readiness by holding all service members to a single standard and promoting medical readiness.[123]

After a year of in-depth research, the Pentagon's Transgender Service Review Working Group (TSRWG) reached that very conclusion. Former Secretary of Defense Carter created the TSRWG on July 28, 2015, to study "the policy and readiness implications of welcoming transgender persons to serve openly."[124] The TSRWG included dozens of civilian and military policy analysts who engaged in extensive research, and who concluded that holding transgender service members "to the same standards and procedures as other members with regard to their medical fitness for duty, physical fitness, uniform and grooming, deployability, and retention, is consistent with military readiness."[125] DoD senior civilian leaders as well as the Service Chiefs signed off on the lifting of the transgender ban on June 30, 2016, because they concluded that inclusive policy would be "consistent with military readiness." The Office of the Secretary of Defense as well as the Services published 257 pages of implementing guidance spread across 14 documents and regulations.[126] These documents instruct commanders and service members how to implement inclusive policy without compromising readiness.

As part of the TSRWG's research, DoD commissioned the RAND Corpo-ration to study whether inclusive policy for transgender personnel would com-promise readiness. RAND studied the health care needs of transgender service members and estimated expected health care utilization rates as well as the expected financial cost of providing care following the lifting of the ban. In addition, RAND studied the impact of inclusive policy on unit cohesion and availability to deploy. Finally, RAND studied whether readiness had been com-promised in foreign militaries that allow transgender personnel to serve openly. RAND published a 91-page study concluding that the impact of inclusive pol-icy would be "negligible."[127]

Organizational experiences confirm the findings of the scholarly research. Eighteen foreign militaries allow transgender personnel to serve openly, and none has reported any compromise to readiness, cohesion, or any other indicator of military performance. A peer-reviewed study of 22 years of inclusive pol-icy for transgender personnel in the Canadian Forces concluded that "allowing transgender personnel to serve openly has not harmed the CF's effectiveness."[128]

According to RAND's analysis of foreign militaries that allow transgender personnel to serve openly, "In no case was there any evidence of an effect on the operational effectiveness, operational readiness, or cohesion of the force."[129]

In the U.S., transgender service members have been serving openly for almost two years and have been widely praised by commanders. We interviewed four former senior DoD officials who oversaw personnel policy for more than 6 months of inclusive policy, as well as one current senior DoD official who oversaw personnel policy for more than 9 months of inclusive policy. During their combined 35 months of collective responsibility for personnel policy, none of these senior officials was aware of any evidence that inclusive policy compromised readiness. According to one of the former officials, "As of the time we left office, we had not seen any evidence that the Department's new transgender policy had resulted in a negative impact on readiness." When we asked former Navy Secretary Ray Mabus if inclusive policy for transgender personnel promoted readiness, he observed, "Absolutely . . . A more diverse force enhances readiness and combat effectiveness."[130]

DoD's Critique of Prior Readiness Research Is Unsupported by Evidence

In recommending reinstatement of the ban, however, the Implementation Report takes aim at RAND's methodology as well as the validity of its conclusions. According to a memorandum from Secretary Mattis that accompanied the release of the Implementation Report, the RAND study "contained significant shortcomings. It referred to limited and heavily caveated data to support its conclusions, glossed over the impacts of healthcare costs, readiness, and unit cohesion, and erroneously relied on the selective experiences of foreign militaries with different operational requirements than our own."[131] The Implementation Report elaborated:

> The RAND report thus acknowledged that there will be an adverse impact on health care utilization, readiness, and unit cohesion, but concluded nonetheless that the impact will be "negligible" and "marginal" because of the small estimated number of transgender Service members . . . Because of the RAND report's macro focus, however, it failed to analyze the impact at the micro level of allowing gender transition by individuals with gender dysphoria. For example, . . . the report did not examine the potential impact on unit readiness, perceptions of fairness and equity, personnel safety, and reasonable expectations of privacy at the unit and sub-unit levels, all of which are critical to unit cohesion. Nor did the report meaningfully address the significant mental health problems that accompany gender dysphoria—from high rates of comorbidities and psychiatric hospitalizations to high rates of suicide ideation and suicidality—and the scope of the scientific uncertainty regarding whether gender transition treatment fully remedies those problems.[132]

Referring to both the TSRWG as well as the RAND study, the Implementation Report concludes that "the realities associated with service by transgender individuals are more complicated than the prior administration or RAND had assumed."[133]

The Implementation Report's critique of the RAND study is unsupported by evidence. Before addressing flaws in the critique, we underscore the depth of RAND's military expertise and trustworthiness. The RAND Corporation is perhaps the most distinguished and trusted research institute in the U.S. on matters of defense and national security, and RAND operates three federally funded research and development centers engaging in military research: RAND Arroyo Center, sponsored by the U.S. Army; RAND Project Air Force, sponsored by the U.S. Air Force; and RAND National Defense Research Institute, sponsored by the Office of the Secretary of Defense, the Joint Staff, the Unified Combatant Commands, the Department of the Navy, and other defense agencies.

While these centers are not government entities, they cooperate closely with their Defense Department sponsors. According to RAND Arroyo's 2015 annual report, for example, the Arroyo Center Policy Committee consisted of 17 General Officers (including the U.S. Army Vice Chief of Staff, the Chief of the National Guard Bureau, five Deputy Chiefs of Staff, and the Commanding General of U.S. Army Forces Command) and five Assistant Secretaries of the Army. RAND Arroyo's Director reported that "we collaborate closely with our Army sponsors not only as we develop our research agenda and design individual analysis, but also as we conduct our research."[134]

The Defense Department relies on RAND to provide nonpartisan, methodologically sophisticated research studies on strategy, doctrine, resources, personnel, training, health, logistics, weapons acquisition, intelligence, and other critically important topics. During the past several decades, RAND has published more than 2,500 military reports, and three of those reports concerned military service by LGBT individuals. In 1993, DoD commissioned RAND to do a $1.3 million study of whether allowing gays and lesbians to serve openly in the military would undermine readiness. RAND assembled a team of 53 researchers who studied foreign militaries, police and fire departments, prior experiences of minority integration into the military, and other aspects of the topic. RAND then published a 518-page report concluding that sexual orientation was "not germane" to military service and that lifting the ban would not undermine readiness. Military and political leaders disagreed with that conclusion, however, and the report was shelved. Seventeen years later, in 2010, DoD hired RAND to replicate its earlier study, and RAND again engaged in comprehensive research and again concluded that allowing gay men and lesbians to serve openly would not compromise readiness. DADT was repealed shortly after the publication of the second RAND study, and subsequent research confirmed the validity of RAND's 1993 and 2010 analyses, in that inclusion did not undermine any aspect of readiness including unit cohesion, morale, retention, and recruitment.[135]

The Implementation Report's critique of the 2016 RAND study on transgender military service is no more persuasive than earlier critiques of RAND's studies on gays and lesbians in the military. First, as argued throughout this study, and despite almost two years of inclusive policy, the Implementation Report has not produced any evidence showing that inclusive policy for transgender personnel has compromised any aspect of readiness, including medical fitness, unit cohesion, or good order and discipline. It is instructive that in its extensive analysis of the ways in which inclusive policy is expected to undermine cohesion, privacy, fairness, and safety, the Implementation Report did not offer any supporting data. The Implementation Report critiques RAND for failing to assess unit cohesion "at the unit and sub-unit levels," but as noted above, the Service Chiefs confirmed after the Report's publication that inclusive policy has not compromised unit cohesion, including Army Chief of Staff Milley's testimony that cohesion "is monitored very closely because I am concerned about that and want to make sure that they [transgender Soldiers] are in fact treated with dignity and respect and no, I have received precisely zero reports of issues of cohesion, discipline, morale, and all those sorts of things."

Second, DoD data validate most of RAND's statistical predictions. RAND estimated that between 1,320 and 6,630 transgender service members serve in the Active Component, and DoD data now show that there are 8,980 active duty transgender troops. RAND estimated that transgender service members in the Active Component would require an overall total of 45 surgeries per year, and DoD data indicate that the actual number was 34 surgeries during a 12-month window, from September 1, 2016, to August 31, 2017.[136] RAND estimated that transition-related health care would cost between $2.4 and $8.4 million per year, and DoD data indicate that the cost in FY2017 was $2.2 million.[137]

Third, the Implementation Report mischaracterized RAND's overall finding by drawing selectively from the study. According to the Implementation Report, RAND "acknowledged that there will be an adverse impact on health care utilization, readiness, and unit cohesion, but concluded nonetheless that the impact will be 'negligible' and 'marginal' because of the small estimated number of transgender Service members." But the Implementation Report misconstrues RAND's analysis. Any policy change yields some costs and some benefits, and RAND found that inclusive policy for transgender troops would have some negative effects, such as the financial cost of health care. But RAND found that inclusive policy would have some positive effects as well, and that continuing to ban transgender troops would entail some costs.[138] RAND did conclude that the effect of lifting the ban would be "negligible" because of the small number of transgender troops, but the Implementation Report fails to acknowledge the context of that conclusion, namely that RAND identified the benefits of inclusive policy and the costs of reinstating the ban, both of which would offset the minor downsides of the policy shift.

Fourth, while it is true that RAND did not address "perceptions of fairness and equity, personnel safety, and reasonable expectations of privacy at the unit and sub-unit levels, all of which are critical to unit cohesion," RAND had a good reason for restricting the scope of its analysis, in that available evidence indicated that cohesion was not compromised in any military force allowing transgender personnel to serve openly. Hence, there was no reason to focus on cohesion at a more granular level. Given that DoD has not offered any evidence to sustain any of its assertions about cohesion, privacy, fairness, and safety despite almost two years of inclusive policy, it seems unreasonable to critique RAND for neglecting to address a problem that does not exist.

Fifth and finally, the Implementation Report's critique of RAND's analysis of foreign militaries is unsupported by evidence. Neither RAND nor DoD has identified any evidence that any foreign military that allows transgender personnel to serve openly has experienced a decline in readiness or cohesion. But the Implementation Report mischaracterizes evidence in the RAND study to obscure that simple fact. An in-depth study of transgender military service in the Canadian Forces (CF) "found no evidence of any effect on unit or overall cohesion," but did find that the CF's failure to provide commanders with sufficient guidance and failure to train service members in inclusive policy led to implementation problems. But the CF's failure to provide implementation guidance does not mean that inclusive policy compromised readiness or cohesion. Rather, it means that the CF should have provided more guidance. Secretary Carter's TSRWG studied the Canadian example, learned from it, and issued extensive guidance and training materials, thus avoiding the CF's implementation challenges.

The Implementation Report claims that because the CF chain of command "has not fully earned the trust of the transgender personnel," there are "serious problems with unit cohesion." But according to the authors of the study, one of whom is a professor at the Canadian Forces College and one of the world's leading experts on personnel policy in the CF, the lack of trust is not evidence that inclusive policy has compromised unit cohesion. Rather, it is a reflection of the CF's failure to implement inclusive policy effectively, for the reasons discussed above.

The study of the CF that informed the RAND report was published in a leading, peer-reviewed military studies journal and was based on careful methodology, including an "extensive literature review, using 216 search permutations, to identity all relevant media stories, governmental reports, books, journal articles and chapters."[139] In addition, the authors received written, interview, and focus group data from 26 individuals, including 2 senior military leaders, 10 commanders, 2 non-transgender service members who served with transgender peers, 4 transgender service members and veterans, and 8 scholarly experts on readiness in the CF. By contrast, the Implementation Report presents exactly zero original research on the CF. If a professor in the Canadian Forces College concludes in a peer-reviewed study, and on the basis of extensive research, that inclusive policy, despite implementation problems, has not compromised readiness or cohesion, DoD cannot dismiss the weight of the conclusion by selectively relying on a handful of quotes.

The Implementation Report makes a similar attempt to dismiss RAND's conclusions about readiness and inclusive policy in the Israel Defense Forces (IDF). Available research on transgender service in the IDF is not as thorough as research on the CF, but RAND nonetheless analyzed a study that was based on several interviews, including interviews with two senior IDF leaders who confirmed that inclusive policy had not compromised readiness or cohesion. The Implementation Report dismisses these "sweeping and categorical claims," but offers no evidence to the contrary. If two senior leaders in a military organization confirm that a policy has a certain effect, that counts as data, especially absent contradictory evidence, and especially when the data line up with evidence from other military forces.

The Implementation Report is correct that operational and other differences distinguish the U.S. armed forces from other militaries. That does not detract, however, from the fact that RAND was unable to find any evidence that readiness or cohesion had declined as a result of inclusive policy in any of the 18 nations that allow transgender personnel to serve openly.

DoD Does Not Consider Benefits of Inclusive Policy or Costs of Ban

Every change of policy involves costs and benefits, and when analysts study whether or not to abandon the status quo in favor of an alternative policy option, typically they address the costs and benefits of both the status quo as well as the contemplated policy modification. DoD's research, however, was artificially narrowed at the outset to focus exclusively on the costs of inclusion, and the Implementation Report did not include any assessment of the benefits of inclusive policy or the costs of the proposed ban. DoD could have framed its research question broadly by asking, "What impact has inclusive policy for transgender troops had on military readiness?" Instead, the Implementation Report addressed only the costs of inclusive policy and failed to consider overall readiness implications. A more rigorous and comprehensive assessment of readiness indicates that inclusive policy for transgender personnel promotes readiness, while banning transgender personnel and denying them medically necessary care compromises it.

Failure to Consider Benefits of Inclusive Policy

If DoD researchers had studied benefits as well as costs, they could have assessed promotion rates, time-in-service, and commendations to determine whether transgender personnel have served successfully. They could have conducted case studies of transgender personnel who have completed gender transition to determine whether transitions have been effective. DoD researchers could have studied the experience of Lieutenant Colonel Bryan (Bree) Fram, an astronautical engineer currently serving as the Air Force's Iraq Country Director at the Pentagon, overseeing all Air Force security cooperation and assistance activity for operations in Iraq. They could have evaluated the experience of Air Force Staff Sergeant Logan Ireland, who deployed to Afghanistan after transitioning gender and was named "NCO of the Quarter." DoD could have studied the experience of Staff Sergeant Ashleigh Buch, whose commander said that "she means the world to this unit. She makes us better. And we would have done that [supported gender transition] for any airman but it made it really easy for one of your best." Or DoD could have assessed the experience of Lance Corporal Aaron Wixson, whose commander reported that "we are lucky to have such talent in our ranks and will benefit from his retention if he decides to undertake a subsequent tour of duty . . . Enabling LCpl Wixson to openly serve as a transgender Marine necessarily increases readiness and broadens the overall talent of the organization."[140]

The Implementation Report's explanation for failing to study the performance of transgender troops is that "limited data exists regarding the performance of transgender Service members due to policy restrictions . . . that prevent the Department from tracking individuals who may identify as transgender as a potentially unwarranted invasion of personal privacy."[141] But this excuse in unpersuasive, as DoD researchers could have asked data analysts to match medical records of service members diagnosed with gender dysphoria with administrative records concerning promotion rates, time-in-service, commendations, and other indicators of performance without revealing names or identifying details. Instead, DoD failed to consider any benefits of inclusive policy, and it focused exclusively on costs.

By omitting any analysis of benefits, the Implementation Report failed to address critical ways in which the accession and retention of transgender personnel promote readiness. To begin, inclusive policy for transgender service members promotes medical readiness by ensuring adequate health care to a population that would otherwise serve "underground." As we mention in our discussion of efficacy, a robust body of scholarly research shows that transgender people who receive the care they need are better off and function well at work and beyond.[142]

After the repeal of "don't ask, don't tell," gay and lesbian service members experienced a decline in harassment, because they could approach offending colleagues and politely point out that unprofessional behavior was no longer acceptable in the workplace, or could safely report inappropriate behavior if it persisted.[143] Inclusive policy for transgender personnel is expected to produce a similar effect, but the Implementation Report does not address this possibility.

Finally, the Implementation Report ignores the financial gains of retaining transgender personnel. DoD data indicate that the per-person cost of care in FY2017 was $18,000 for each service member diagnosed with gender dysphoria, but the Report does not mention that by DoD's own estimate, recruiting and training one service member costs $75,000.[144] It is much cheaper to provide medical care than to replace service members who need it.

Failure to Consider Costs of the Ban

In response to DoD's release of the Implementation Report, the American Psychiatric Association's CEO and Medical Director Saul Levin stated that the proposed transgender ban "not only harms those who have chosen to serve our country, but it also casts a pall over all transgender Americans. This discrimination has a negative impact on the mental health of those targeted." The Implementation Report, however, seems premised on the notion that the proposed ban would incur no costs. In addition to evidence that enables us to assess costs directly, scholars and experts have produced a great deal of evidence concerning the costs of "don't ask, don't tell," and it is not unreasonable to expect that some of the burdens associated with that failed policy could recur if the transgender ban were reinstated.

Research on transgender military service as well as DADT suggests that reinstating the ban could (1) undermine medical readiness by depriving 14,700 transgender service members of medically necessary care should they require it;[145] (2) increase harassment of transgender personnel, just as DADT promoted harassment of gay men and lesbians;[146] and (3) drain financial resources due to the cost of replacing transgender personnel and the cost of litigation.[147] In addition, the ban could (4) compromise unit cohesion by introducing divisiveness in the ranks; (5) discourage enlistment and re-enlistment by lesbians, gays, and bisexuals, who would be wary of serving in an anti-LGBT atmosphere; (6) discourage enlistment and re-enlistment by women, because this ban is based on discomfort with people who cross gender lines or otherwise violate traditional gender roles; and (7) promote policy instability. The ban would constitute the fifth policy on transgender military service over the past two years. As former U.S. Navy Judge Advocate General Admiral John D. Hutson observed, "Whatever one thinks about transgender service . . . , there is no question that careening personnel policy from one pole to the other is bad for the armed forces."[148]

Similar to DADT, the reinstatement of the ban would (8) force many transgender service members to hide their gender identity, given the stigma that the Implementation Report implicitly authorizes. Scholars have demonstrated that the requirement to serve in silence effectively forces troops to lie about their identity, leading to elevated incidence of depression and anxiety.[149] (9) When service members lie about their identity, peers suspect that they are not being forthcoming, and both social isolation and general distrust can result.[150] In turn, (10) forcing service members to lie about their identity compromises military integrity. Prior to the repeal of DADT, former Chairman of the Joint Chiefs of Staff Admiral Mike Mullen said that, "I cannot escape being troubled by the fact that we have in place a policy which forces young men and women to lie about who they are in order to defend their fellow citizens. For me, personally, it comes down to integrity—theirs as individuals and ours as an institution."[151]

Finally, (11) the ban would signal to the youth of America that the military is not a modern institution. Scholarly research established that DADT was an ongoing public relations embarrassment for the Pentagon and that ripple effects impacted recruitment. Every major editorial page in the U.S. opposed DADT, and anti-military activists used the policy to rally opposition.[152] Approximately three-quarters of the public opposed DADT.[153] According to one report, high schools denied military recruiters access to their campuses on 19,228 separate occasions in 1999 alone, in part as an effort "to challenge the Pentagon's policy on homosexuals in the military."[154] In the case of military service by transgender personnel, the Implementation Report cites one poll suggesting that service members oppose inclusive policy. Other polling, however, indicates that service members, veterans, retirees, and military family members favor inclusion, as does the public at large.[155] There is every reason to believe that the transgender ban would be just as unpopular as was DADT.

DoD Cites Misleading Figures on Financial Costs of Inclusion

The Implementation Report observed that "since the implementation of the Carter policy, the medical costs for Service members with gender dysphoria have increased nearly three times—or 300 percent—compared to Service members without gender dysphoria."[156] While the Implementation Report's claim is correct, the cost data are taken out of context and reported in a misleading way. DoD data indicate that the average annual per-person cost for service members diagnosed with gender dysphoria is approximately $18,000, as opposed to the $6,000 annual cost of care for other service members.[157] But the higher average per-person cost would appear any time a population is selected *for the presence of a specific health condition* and then compared to an average cohort of all other service members.

The Report's claim that medical costs for service members diagnosed with gender dysphoria are three times, or 300 percent, higher than for other troops implies that medical care for transgender personnel is expensive. But the Report does not mention that DoD's total cost for transition-related care in FY2017 was only $2.2 million, which is less than one tenth of one percent of DoD's annual health care budget for the Active Component.

Insurance actuaries sometimes calculate costs in terms of the cost of care per plan member per month of coverage. With financial costs of transition-related care distributed force-wide, the cost of providing transition-related care is 9¢ (nine cents) per service member per month.[158] Even if the per-member/per-month cost estimate were restricted to the cohort of transgender service members, the financial impact of providing care would be low, because very few of the currently serving 14,700 transgender troops required *any* transition-related care during FY2017: $2.2 million / 14,700 = $149.66 per transgender service member per year; $149.66 / 12 = $12.47 per transgender service member per month.

Higher average per-person costs would appear any time a population is selected for the presence of a specific condition and then compared to an average cohort of other service members. Even setting this qualification aside, reporting the cost of care for service members with gender dysphoria as 300 percent higher than the cost of care for other troops, without contextualizing the observation in terms of the low overall cost, could mislead readers into believing that transition-related care is expensive, which it is not.

Conclusion

Scholars and experts agree that transition-related care is reliable, safe, and effective, and medical research as well as DoD's own data confirm that transgender personnel, even those with diagnoses of gender dysphoria, are deployable and medically fit. In advancing its case for the reinstatement of the transgender ban, however, the Implementation Report mischaracterized the medical research that sustains these conclusions. The proposed transgender ban is based on double standards consisting of rules and expectations that DoD would apply only to transgender service members, but to no one else. The Report did not present any evidence showing that inclusive policy has compromised or could compromise cohesion, privacy, fairness, or safety. Finally, the Implementation Report's justification depends on partial and misleading assessments of costs and benefits, as DoD neglected to assess the benefits of inclusive policy or the costs of the ban.

The RAND study was correct in concluding that inclusive policy was unlikely to pose a meaningful risk to the readiness of the armed forces. If anything, the evidence suggests that inclusive policy for transgender service members has promoted readiness. Just like justifications for prohibitions against women and African Americans in the military as well as the failed DADT policy, the case for banning transgender individuals from the armed forces is not supported by evidence and is unpersuasive.

Appendix

Efficacy of Transition-Related Care

As we described earlier, an international consensus among medical experts affirms the efficacy of transition-related health care. This Appendix details that scholarship, showing that the DoD Report selected only a small slice of available evidence to reach its conclusions about the efficacy of transition-related care.

A large Dutch study published in 2007 reported follow-up data of 807 individuals who underwent surgical gender transition. Summarizing their results, the authors reaffirmed the conclusion of a much-cited 1990 study that gender transition dramatically reduces the symptoms of gender dysphoria, and hence "is the most appropriate treatment to alleviate the suffering of extremely gender dysphoric individuals." They found that, across 18 outcome studies published over two decades, 96 percent of subjects were satisfied with transitioning, and "regret was rare." The authors wrote that, even though there were "methodological shortcomings" to many of the studies they reviewed (lacking controls or randomized samples), "we conclude that SRS [sex reassignment surgery] is an effective treatment for transsexualism and the only treatment that has been evaluated empirically with large clinical case series." Gender transition, they stated, "is not strongly theory driven, but a pragmatic and effective way to strongly diminish the suffering of persons with gender dysphoria." It must be noted that not all studies of the efficacy of gender transition lack controls. The Dutch authors cite a controlled study from 1990 that compared a waiting-list condition with a treatment condition and found "strong evidence for the effectiveness" of surgical gender transition.[159]

In a 2010 meta-analysis noted by the Implementation Report, researchers at the Mayo Clinic conducted a systematic review of 28 scholarly studies enrolling 1,833 participants who underwent hormone therapy as part of gender transition. The reviewed studies were published between 1966 and February 2008. Results indicated that 80 percent of individuals reported "significant improvement" in gender dysphoria and in quality of life, and 78 percent reported "significant improvement" in psychological symptoms. The authors concluded that "sex reassignment that includes hormonal interventions . . . likely improves gender dysphoria, psychological functioning and comorbidities, sexual function and overall quality of life."[160]

A 2015 Harvard and University of Houston longitudinal study of testosterone treatment also reviewed prior literature and found that numerous recent cross-sectional studies "suggest that testosterone treatment among transgender men is associated with improved mental health and well-being," including improved quality of life, less anxiety, depression and social distress, and a reduction in overall mental stress.[161]

A 2016 literature review screened 647 studies to identify eleven longitudinal studies providing data on transgender individuals. Ten of them found "an improvement of psychiatric morbidity and psycho-pathology following" medical intervention (hormone therapy and/or gender-confirming surgery). Sizing up the overall research body on transgender psychiatric outcomes, Cecilia Dhejne and her co-authors wrote: "This review found that longitudinal studies investigating the same cohort of trans people pre- and post-interventions showed an overall improvement in psychopathology and psychiatric disorders post-treatment. In fact, the findings from *most studies showed that the scores of trans people following GCMI were similar to those of the general population.*"[162]

Another 2016 study, a systematic review of literature, identified numerous longitudinal studies finding that "depression, global psychopathology, and psychosocial functioning difficulties appear to reduce" in transgender individuals who get treatment for gender dysphoria, leading to "improved mental health."[163]

Copious studies reflecting a wide range of methodologies, population samples, and nationalities reached similarly positive conclusions to what was found by the researchers mentioned above, namely that individuals who obtain the care they need achieve health parity with non-transgender individuals. A 2009 study using a probability sample of 50 transgender Belgian women found "no significant differences" in overall health between subjects and the general population, which the study noted was "in accordance with a previous study in which no differences in psychological and physical complaints between transsexuals and the general Belgian population were found."[164] A 2012 study reported that "most transsexual patients attending a gender identity unit reported subclinical levels of social distress, anxiety, and depression" and did "not appear to notably differ from the normative sample in terms of mean levels of social distress, anxiety, and depression."

Patients who were not yet treated for gender dysphoria had "marginally higher distress scores than average, and treated subjects [were] *in the normal range.*"[165] An Italian study that assessed the impact of hormonal treatment on the mental health of transgender patients found that "the majority of transsexual patients have no psychiatric comorbidity, suggesting that transsexualism is not necessarily associated with severe comorbid psychiatric findings."[166] A Croatian study from the same year concluded that "despite the unfavorable circumstances in Croatian society, participants demonstrated stable mental, social, and professional functioning, as well as a relative resilience to minority stress."[167]

Efficacy of Hormone Therapy

Studies show clearly that hormone treatment is effective at treating gender dysphoria and improving well-being. In 2015, Harvard and University of Houston researchers published the first controlled longitudinal follow-up study to examine the immediate effects of testosterone treatment on the psychological functioning of transgender men. The study used the Minnesota Multiphasic Personality Inventory test (2nd ed.) to take an empirical measure of psychological well-being after hormone treatment, assessing outcomes before and after treatment. (The MMPI-2 is one of the oldest, most commonly used psychological tests and is considered so rigorous that it typically requires many years of intensive psychotherapy to generate notable improvements in outcomes.) The results showed marked change in just three months: Transgender subjects who presented with clinical distress and demonstrated "poorer psychological functioning than non-transgender males" prior to treatment functioned "as well as male and female controls and demonstrated positive gains in multiple clinical domains" after just three months of testosterone. "There were no longer statistically significant differences between transgender men and male controls" on a range of symptoms including hypochondria, hysteria, paranoia, and others after three months of treatment, the study concluded. "Overall findings here," concluded the study, "suggest significant, rapid, and positive effects of initiating testosterone treatment on the psychological functioning in transgender men."[168]

These findings echoed earlier research on the efficacy of hormone therapy for treating gender dysphoria. A 2006 U.S. study of 446 female-to-male (FTM) subjects found improvements when comparing those who had and had not received hormone treatment: "FTM transgender participants who received testosterone (67 percent) reported statistically significant higher quality of life scores (p<0.01) than those who had not received hormone therapy." The study concluded that providing transgender individuals "with the hormonal care they request is associated with improved quality of life."[169] A 2012 study assessed outcome differences between transgender patients who obtained hormone treatment and those who did not among 187 subjects. It found that "patients who have not yet initiated cross-sex hormonal treatment showed significantly higher levels of social distress and emotional disturbances than patients under this treatment."[170]

An Italian study published in 2014 that assessed hormone therapy found that "when treated, transsexual patients reported less anxiety, depression, psychological symptoms and functional impairment" with the improvements between baseline and one-year follow-up being "statistically significant." The study stated that "psychiatric distress and functional impairment were present in a significantly higher percentage of patients before starting the hormonal treatment than after 12 months."[171] Another study published in 2014 found that "participants who were receiving testosterone endorsed fewer symptoms of anxiety and depression as well as less anger than the untreated group."[172]

Efficacy of Surgery

A wide body of scholarly literature also demonstrates the effectiveness of gender-transition surgery. A 1999 follow-up study using multi-point questionnaires and rigorous qualitative methods including in-depth, blind follow-up interviews evaluated 28 MTF subjects who underwent transition surgery at Albert Einstein College of Medicine. The study was authored by four physicians who conducted transition surgeries at university centers in New York and Israel. *All* their subjects reported satisfaction in having transitioned, and they responded positively when asked if their lives were "becoming easier and more comfortable" following transition. Large majorities said that reassignment surgery "solved most of their emotional problems," adding in follow-up assessments comments such as: "I am now a complete person in every way," "I feel more self-confident and more socially adapted," "I am more confident and feel better about myself," and "I am happier." Summarizing their conclusions, the authors noted "a marked decrease of suicide attempts, criminal activity, and drug use in our postoperative population. This might indicate that there is a marked improvement in antisocial and self-destructive behavior, that was evident prior to sex reassignment surgery. Most patients were able to maintain their standard of living and to continue working, usually at the same jobs."[173]

A 2010 study of thirty patients found that "gender reassignment surgery improves the QoL [quality of life] for transsexuals in several different important areas: most are satisfied of their sexual reassignment (28/30), their social (21/30) and sexual QoL (25/30) are improved."[174] A long-term follow-up study of 62 Belgian patients who underwent gender transition surgery, published in 2006, found that, while transgender subjects remain a vulnerable population "in some respects" following treatment, the vast majority "proclaimed an overall positive change in their family and social life." The authors concluded that "SRS proves to be an effective therapy for transsexuals even after a longer period, mainly because of its positive effect on the gender dysphoria."[175]

Efficacy of the Combination of Hormone Therapy and Surgery

Some studies assessed global outcomes from a combination of hormone treatment and transition surgery, or they did not isolate one form of treatment from the other in reporting their overall results. They consistently found improved outcomes when transgender individuals obtained the specific care recommended by their doctor.

A 2011 Canadian study found that "the odds of depression were 2.8 times greater for FTMs not currently using hormones compared with current users" and that FTM subjects "who were planning to medically transition (hormones and/or surgery) but had not begun were five times more likely to be depressed than FTMs who had medically transitioned." The finding shows that gender transition is strongly correlated with improved well-being for transgender individuals.[176] An Australian study found that "the combination of current hormone use and having had some form of gender affirmative surgery provided a significant contribution to lower depressive symptoms over and above control variables."[177]

A 2015 study conducted in Germany with follow-up periods up to 24 years, with a mean of 13.8 years, tracked 71 transgender participants using a combination of quantitative and qualitative outcome measures that included structured interviews, standardized questionnaires, and validated psychological assessment tools. It found that "positive and desired changes were determined by all of the instruments." The improvements included that "participants showed significantly fewer psychological problems and interpersonal difficulties as well as a strongly increased life satisfaction at follow-up than at the time of the initial consultation." The authors cautioned that, notwithstanding the positive results, "the treatment of transsexualism is far from being perfect," but noted that, in addition to the positive result they found in the current study, "numerous studies with shorter follow-up times have already demonstrated positive outcomes after sex reassignment" and that this study added to that body of research the finding that "these positive outcomes persist even 10 or more years" beyond their legal gender transition.[178]

Regrets Low

A strong indicator of the efficacy of gender transition is the extremely low rate of regrets that studies have found across the board. A recent focus in popular culture on anecdotes by individuals who regretted their gender transition has served to obscure the overall statistics on regret rates. A 2014 study co-authored by Cecilia Dhejne evaluated the entirety of individuals who were granted a legal gender change in Sweden across the 50-year period from 1960 through 2010. Of the total number of 681 individuals, the number who sought a reversal was 15, a regret rate of 2.2 percent. The study also found a "significant decline of regrets over the time period." For the most recent decade covered by Dhejne's data, 2000 to 2010, the regret rate was just three tenths of 1 percent. Researchers attribute the improvements over time to advances in surgical technique and in social support for gender minorities, suggesting that today's transgender population is the most treatable in history, while also sounding a caution that institutional stigma and discrimination can themselves become barriers to adequate care.[179]

The low regret rate is consistent in the scholarly literature, and it is confirmed by qualitative studies and quantitative assessments. A 1992 study authored by one of the world's leading researchers on transgender health put the average regret rate at between 1 and 1.5 percent. This figure was based on cumulative numbers from 74 different follow-up studies conducted over three decades, as well as a separate clinical follow-up sample of more than 600 patients.[180] A 2002 literature review also put the figure at 1 percent.[181] A 1998 study put the figure as high as 3.8 percent, but attributed most regret to family rejection of the subjects' transgender identity.[182] The 1999 study of transition surgery outcomes at Albert Einstein College of Medicine found that "None of the patients regretted or had doubts about having undergone sex-reassignment surgery."[183] The 2006 Belgian study mentioned elsewhere followed 62 subjects who underwent transition surgery and "none of them showed any regrets" about their transition. "Even after several years, they feel happy, adapt well socially and feel no regrets," the authors concluded.[184] And the 2015 German follow-up study of adults with gender dysphoria found that none of its 71 participants expressed a wish to reverse their transition.[185]

Endnotes

[1] The authors wish to thank John Blosnich, Drew Cameron, Jack Drescher, Jesse Ehrenfeld, Nick Gorton, Evan Schofer, Andy Slavitt, Hugh Waddington, and the many medical experts and service members who provided feedback. We are grateful for their invaluable assistance in preparing this study.

[2] Department of Defense, "Department of Defense Report and Recommendations on Military Service by Transgender Persons" (February 2018), 5.

[3] Ibid., 32.

[4] American Medical Association (Resolution), "Removing Financial Barriers to Care for Transgender Patients" (2008); American Medical Association, Letter to James N. Mattis from James L. Madara, MD, April 3, 2018.

[5] American Psychological Association, "Statement Regarding Transgender Individuals Serving in Military," March 26, 2018; Palm Center (news release), "Former Surgeons General Debunk Pentagon Assertions about Medical Fitness of Transgender Troops," March 28, 2018; American Psychiatric Association, "APA Reiterates Its Strong Opposition to Ban of Transgender Americans from Serving in U.S. Military" (News Release), Mar. 24, 2018; World Professional Association for Transgender Health, "WPATH Policy Statements: Position Statement on Medical Necessity of Treatment, Sex Reassignment, and Insurance Coverage in the U.S.A.," December 21, 2016.

[6] What We Know Project, Center for the Study of Inequality, Cornell University (research analysis), "What does the scholarly research say about the effect of gender transition on transgender well-being?" 2018.

[7] Freidemann Pfäfflin and Astrid Junge (1998), "Sex Reassignment—Thirty Years of International Follow-up Studies after Sex Reassignment Surgery: A Comparison Review, 1961–1991" (translated from the German edition, 1992, into English, 1998).

[8] Jamil Rehman, Simcha Lazer, Alexandru Benet, Leah Schaefer, and Arnod Melman (1999), "The Reported Sex and Surgery Satisfactions of 28 Postoperative Male-to-Female Transsexual Patients," *Archives of Sexual Behavior*, 28(1): 71–89.

[9] Tamara Jensen, Joseph Chin, James Rollins, Elizabeth Koller, Linda Gousis, and Katherine Szarama. "Final Decision Memorandum on Gender Reassignment Surgery for Medicare Beneficiaries with Gender Dysphoria," Centers for Medicare and Medicaid Services (CMS), August 30, 2016, 71.

[10] CMS 100-08, Medicare Program Integrity Manual (2000), 13.7.1, https://www.cms.gov/Regulations-and-Guidance/Guidance/Manuals/Internet-Only-Manuals-IOMs-Items/CMS019033.html, accessed April 23, 2018.

[11] Ibid.

[12] Cecilia Dhejne, Paul Lichtenstein, Marcus Boman, Anna Johansson, Niklas Langstrom, and Mikael Landen (2011), "Long-Term Follow-up of Transsexual Persons Undergoing Sex Reassignment Surgery: Cohort Study in Sweden," *PLoS One*, 6(2).

[13] Palm Center (news release), "Former Surgeons General Debunk Pentagon Assertions about Medical Fitness of Transgender Troops," March 28, 2018. At the time of writing, the publicly released version of the statement has been signed by two former Surgeons General. Since the statement's release, however, four additional former Surgeons General have signed. The revised signatory list will be released soon.

[14] DoD Report, 24.

[15] Department of Defense Instruction 6130.03, Medical Standards for Appointment, Enlistment, or Induction in the Military Services (April 28, 2010, incorporating Change 1, September 13, 2011), 9. Also see http://www.amsara.amedd.army.mil/.

[16] DoD Report, 24, quoting Jensen, et al. "Final Decision Memorandum," 62.

[17] Department of Health and Human Services (HHS), Department Appeals Board Appellate Division, NCD 140.3, Transsexual Surgery Docket No. A-13-87 Decision No. 2576, May 30, 2014, 20.

[18] HHS, Transsexual Surgery Docket, 20.

[19] Jensen et al. "Final Decision Memorandum," 54, 57, emphasis added.

[20] Personal communication with the authors, April 21, 2018.

[21] DoD Report, 25–26.

[22] R. Nick Gorton, "Research Memo Evaluating the 2014 Hayes Report: 'Sex Reassignment Surgery for the Treatment of Gender Dysphoria' and the 2004 Hayes Report: 'Sex Reassignment Surgery and Associated Therapies for Treatment of GID,' April 2018."

[23] Ibid.

[24] Ibid.

[25] Ibid.

[26] William Byne et al. (2012), "Report of the American Psychiatric Association Task Force on Treatment of Gender Identity Disorder," *Archives of Sexual Behavior*, 41(4): 759–96.

[27] Gorton, "Research Memo."

[28] Dhejne et al., "Long-Term Follow-up"; Cecilia Dhejne, Roy Van Vlerken, Gunter Heylens, and Jon Arcelus (2016), "Mental Health and Gender Dysphoria: A Review of the Literature," *International Review of Psychiatry*, 28(1): 44–57, emphasis added.

[29] Dhejne et al., "Long-Term Follow-up"; Dhejne et al., "Review of the Literature," emphasis added.

[30] Cristan Williams, "Fact Check: Study Shows Transition Makes Trans People Suicidal," The TransAdvocate, November 2, 2015.

[31] M. Hassan Murad et al. (2010), "Hormonal Therapy and Sex Reassignment: A Systematic Review and Meta-Analysis of Quality of Life and Psychosocial Outcomes," *Clinical Endocrinology*, 72(2): 214–31.

[32] DoD Report, 19.

[33] Memorandum, Secretary of Defense, Military Service by Transgender Individuals (February 22, 2018), 2.

[34] Department of Defense Instruction 1322.18, Disability Evaluation System (August 5, 2014), 23.

[35] Memorandum, Under Secretary of Defense, Personnel and Readiness, DoD Retention Policy for Non-Deployable Service Members (February 14, 2018).

[36] DoD Report, 5

[37] Ibid., 5–6.

[38] Ibid., 5 (emphasis added).

[39] Ibid., 32.

[40] Ibid., 6, 32.

[41] Ibid., 10.

[42] DoDI 6130.03, 18.

[43] DoD Report, 11.

[44] DoDI 6130.03, 25.

[45] Department of Defense Instruction 1300.28, In-Service Transition for Transgender Service Members (October 1, 2016), 3.

[46] Palm Center, "Former Surgeons General."

[47] DoD Report, 20–21.

[48] Jack Drescher et al. (2012), "Minding the Body: Situation Gender Identity Diagnoses in the ICD-11," *International Review of Psychiatry*, 24(6): 568; See also Jack Drescher (2010), "Queer Diagnoses: Parallels and Contrasts in the History of Homosexuality, Gender Variance, and the Diagnostic and Statistical Manual," *Archives of Sexual Behavior*, 39(2): 427–60.

[49] Personal communication with the authors, April 10, 2018.

[50] American Psychiatric Association, "APA Reiterates Its Strong Opposition."

[51] DoD Report, 27.

[52] Army Regulation 40-501, Standards of Medical Fitness (December 22, 2016), 60.

[53] Ibid., 62.

[54] Ibid., 63.

[55] DoD Report, 33.

[56] Ibid., 34.

[57] Department of Defense, Transgender Service in the U.S. Military: An Implementation Handbook (September 30, 2016), 31 ("Commander's Handbook").

[58] DoDI 1300.28, 3.

[59] DoD Report, 34.

[60] Department of Defense, Health Data on Active Duty Service Members with Gender Dysphoria: Comparison Health Care Data with Statistical Analysis, Deployment, Treatment Plan, Surgical Recovery Times, Separation Data and Cost Data (December 13, 2017), 10–12.

[61] DoD Report, 18.

[62] Ibid., 33

[63] Department of Defense, Health Data on Active Duty Service Members with Gender Dysphoria, 17.

[64] Modification Thirteen to U.S. Central Command Individual Protection and Individual, Unit Deployment Policy, Tab A (March 2017).

[65] DoD Report, 34n130.

[66] Ibid., 34.

[67] Modification Thirteen, 8.

[68] Ibid., 9–10.

[69] Ibid., 8.

[70] Ibid., 4.

[71] DoD Report, 33.

[72] Ibid.; See also DoD Report, 22–23, 34 and 41n164.

[73] Letter from Dr. Wylie C. Hembree, M.D. (October 25, 2015).

[74] DoD Report, 33.

[75] Ibid., 34.

[76] Ibid., 33n123, citing Agnes Schaefer et al. (2016), "Assessing the Implications of Allowing Transgender Personnel to Serve Openly," RAND Corporation, 59.

[77] M. Joycelyn Elders, George R. Brown, Eli Coleman, Thomas A. Kolditz, and Alan M. Steinman (2014), "Medical Aspects of Transgender Military Service," *Armed Forces and Society*, 41(2): 206–207 (footnotes omitted).

[78] DoD Report, 2.

[79] Ibid., 22.

[80] DoDI 1300.28.

[81] Ibid., 9.

[82] Ibid.

[83] Commander's Handbook, 13.

[84] Department of the Navy, BUMED Notice 6000, Medical Treatment of Transgender Service Members—Interim Guidance (September 27, 2016), 3.

[85] Ibid.

[86] "Individualized TGCT Care Plan (n.d.)," NMW Transgender Care Team, Naval Medical Center San Diego.

[87] Personal communication with the authors, February 7, 2018.

[88] Natasha Schvey et al. (May 2017), "Military Family Physicians' Readiness for Treating Patients with Gender Dysphoria," *Journal of the American Medical Association, Internal Medicine*, 177(5): 727–29.

[89] Personal communication with the authors, February 6, 2018.

[90] Ibid., February 9, 2018.

[91] Surveys and follow-up emails between anonymous service members and Palm Center researchers, February 1–15, 2018; Telephone interview with authors, August 30, 2017. The 81 mental health visits were the total number reported by the seven of our subjects who completed written surveys.

[92] John Blosnich, Letter to the Editor (draft in preparation for peer-review submission, forthcoming, 2018). Unlike the military, VHA does not provide transition surgery. VHA mental health utilization among transgender individuals could increase if VHA provided surgery, because patients might need additional mental health approval to qualify. At the same time, mental health utilization might decrease if VHA provided surgery, because surgery can mitigate gender dysphoria, which would diminish the need for mental health care.

[93] Jesse M. Ehrenfeld, Del Ray Zimmerman and Gilbert Gonzales (March 16, 2018), "Healthcare Utilization Among Transgender Individuals in California," *Journal of Medical Systems*, 42(5): 77.

[94] Tamika Gilreath et al. (2015), "Suicidality among Military-Connected Adolescents in California Shools," *European Child & Adolescent Psychiatry*, 25(1): 61–66.

[95] DoD Report, 21.

[96] Ibid.

[97] Department of Defense, Defense Suicide Prevention Office, Military Suicide Data Surveillance: Baseline Results from Non-clinical Populations on Proximal Outcomes for Suicide Prevention (July 25, 2017), 5.

[98] See Schaefer et al., "Assessing the Implications," 9–10.

[99] American Psychological Association, "Statement Regarding Transgender Individuals."

[100] American Psychiatric Association, "APA Reiterates Its Strong Opposition."

[101] DoD Report, 31.

[102] Ibid., 28.

[103] Claudia Grisales, "Defense Chief Says He Is 'Prepared to Defend' New Transgender Military Policy," *Stars and Stripes*, April 12, 2018.

[104] Geoff Ziezulewicz, "No Reports of Transgender Troops Affecting Unit Cohesion, Marine Corps and Navy Leaders Say," *Military Times*, April 19, 2018; Rebecca Kheel, "Air Force Chief Not Aware of Cohesion, Morale Issues Due to Transgender Troops," *The Hill*, April 24, 2018.

[105] DoD Report, 3.

[106] Grisales, "Defense Chief Says."

[107] On the measurement of unit cohesion, see, for example, James Griffith (1988), "Measurement of Group Cohesion in U. S. Army Units," *Basic and Applied Social Psychology*, 9(2): 149–71.

[108] Aaron Belkin, Morten G. Ender, Nathaniel Frank, Stacie R. Furia, George Lucas, Gary Packard, Steven M. Samuels, Tammy Schultz, and David Segal (2013), "Readiness and DADT Repeal: Has the New Policy of Open Service Undermined the Military," *Armed Forces and Society*, 39(4): 587–601.

[109] DoD Report, 29.

[110] Alex Bedard, Robert Peterson, and Ray Barone, "Punching through Barriers: Female Cadets Integrated into Mandatory Boxing at West Point," Association of the United States Army, November 16, 2017.

[111] Commander's Handbook, 63.

[112] Ibid.

[113] Ibid., 37.

[114] Ibid., 65.

[115] Ibid., 29.

[116] Ibid., 22.

[117] Training Slides Tier III Training: Education and Training Plan for the Implementation of Army Policy on Military Service of Transgender Soldiers (September 16, 2016), 14.

[118] David Ari Bianco, "Echoes of Prejudice: The Debates Over Race and Sexuality in the Armed Forces," in Craig A. Rimmerman, ed. (2006), *Gay Rights, Military Wrongs: Political Perspectives on Lesbians and Gays in the Military* (New York: St. Martin's Press); Nathaniel Frank (2009), *Unfriendly Fire: How the Gay Ban Undermines the Military and Weakens America* (New York: St. Martin's); Brian Mitchell (1997), *Women in the Military: Flirting with Disaster* (Washington: Regency Publishing).

[119] Aaron Belkin and Melissa S. Embser-Herbert (2002), "A Modest Proposal: Privacy as a Rationale for Excluding Gays and Lesbians from the U.S. Military," *International Security*, 27(2): 178–97.

Melissa Wells-Petry (1993), *Exclusion: Homosexuals and the Right to Serve* (Washington: Regnery Gateway), 127–30.

[120] Peter Sprigg, "Homosexual Assault in the Military," Family Research Council, 2010.

[121] "A Military Success Story," *New York Times* (editorial), September 15, 2012.

[122] Gale S. Pollock and Shannon Minter (2014), "Report of the Planning Commission on Transgender Military Service," Palm Center, 21.

[123] Schaefer et al., "Assessing the Implications"; M. Joycelyn Elders, George R. Brown, Eli Coleman, Thomas A. Kolditz, and Alan M. Steinman (2014), "Medical Aspects of Transgender Military Service," *Armed Forces and Society*, 41(2): 199–220; Pollock and Minter, "Report of the Planning Commission"; Alan Okros and Denise Scott (2014), "Gender Identity in the Canadian Forces: A Review of Possible Impacts on Operational Effectiveness," *Armed Forces and Society*, 41(2): 243–56.

[124] Department of Defense, "Statement by Secretary of Defense Ash Carter on DoD Transgender Policy," (press release), July 13, 2015, Memorandum from Ashton Carter, Secretary of Defense, "Transgender Service Members" (July 28, 2015).

[125] DTM 16-005, Military Service of Transgender Service Members (June 30, 2016); DoDI 1300.28, In-Service Transition for Transgender Service Members (June 30, 2016), 2.

[126] This list does not include service-level training materials or Military Entrance Processing Command accession documents: DTM 16-005, Military Service of Transgender Service Members (June 30, 2016); DoDI 1300.28, In-Service Transition for Transgender Service Members (June 30, 2016); Department of Defense, Transgender Service in the U. S. Military: An Implementation Handbook (September 30, 2016); Assistant Secretary of Defense, Health Affairs, Guidance for Treatment of Gender Dysphoria for Active and Reserve Component Service Members (July 29, 2016); Interim Defense Health Agency Procedures for Reviewing Requests for Waivers to Allow Supplemental Health Care Program Coverage of Sex Reassignment Surgical Procedures (November 13, 2017); Army Directive 2016-30, Army Policy on Military Service of Transgender Soldiers (July 1, 2016); Army Directive 2016-35, Army Policy on Military Service of Transgender Soldiers (October 7, 2016); OTSG/MEDCOM Policy Memo 16-060, Interim AMEDD Guidance for Transgender Medical Care (August 3, 2016); SECNAV Instruction 1000.11, Service of

Transgender Sailors and Marines (November 4, 2016); U.S. Navy, Transgender and Gender Transition: Commanding Officer's Toolkit (2016); Department of the Navy, BUMED Notice 6000, Medical Treatment of Transgender Service Members–Interim Guidance (September 27, 2016); AFPM 2016-36-01, Air Force Policy Memorandum for In-Service Transition for Airmen Identifying as Transgender (October 6, 2016); Marine Corps Bulletin 1121, Transgender Service (November 22, 2016); U.S. Coast Guard, COMDTINST M1000.13, Military Transgender Service (December 22, 2016).

[127] Schaefer et al., "Assessing the Implications," 70.

[128] Okros and Scott, "Gender Identity in the Canadian Forces," 243.

[129] Schaefer et al., "Assessing the Implications," xiii.

[130] Correspondence with senior civilian DoD official, April 21, 2017; Telephone interview with former Navy Secretary Ray Mabus, April 20, 2017; Correspondence with former Air Force Secretary Deborah James, April 20, 2017; Correspondence with former Army Secretary Eric Fanning, April 24, 2017; Correspondence with former senior civilian DoD official, April 19, 2017.

[131] Memorandum, Secretary of Defense, Military Service by Transgender Individuals (February 22, 2018), 2.

[132] DoD Report, 14.

[133] Ibid., 44.

[134] Rand Arroyo Center Annual Report 2015, 1.

[135] Belkin et al., "Readiness and DADT Repeal."

[136] Department of Defense, Health Data on Active Duty Service Members with Gender Dysphoria, 21.

[137] Ibid., 31.

[138] For various benefits of inclusive policy and costs of the ban, see Schaefer et al., "Assessing the Implications," 8 (surgical skills); 45, 60–61 (diversity and readiness); and 10 (denial of care).

[139] Okros and Scott, "Gender Identity in the Canadian Forces," 246.

[140] John D. Hutson, "An Unwarranted Attack on Transgender Service," *Stars and Stripes*, February 6, 2018; Steve Liewer, "Transgender Offutt Airman – Finally 'Able to Live as My True Self' – Finds Support, Acceptance during Transition," *Omaha World-Herald*, April 22, 2017; Emanuella Grinberg, "A transgender Marine Comes Out, Tests Military's New Policy," *CNN*.com, November 19, 2016.

[141] DoD Report, 37, Note 143.

[142] Dhejne et. al, "Mental Health and Gender Dysphoria."

[143] Gay and lesbian service members reported an increase in morale after DADT repeal. See Belkin et al., "Readiness and DADT Repeal."

[144] According to a 2015 estimate by Accession Medical Standards Analysis and Research Activity (AMSARA), "Recruiting, screening and training costs are approximately $75,000 per enlistee." Accession Medical Standards Analysis & Research Activity, http://www.amsara.amedd.army.mil/Default.aspx, last modified date April 1, 2015, accessed August 3, 2017.

[145] See Schaefer et al., "Assessing the Implications," 9–10. For the estimate that 14,700 transgender personnel serve currently in the Active Component and Selected Reserve, see Palm Center, "Breaking Down the March 23, 2018 Transgender Military Ban," March 27, 2018.

[146] For extensive evidence on this point, see the ten annual reports of the Servicemembers Legal Defense Network that are posted at http://dont.law.stanford.edu/commentary/, accessed April 23, 2018. Sharon Terman argues that harassment cannot be regulated in institutions that allow formal discrimination. See Sharon Terman, "The Practical and Conceptual Problems with Regulating Harassment in a Discriminatory Institution," Center for the Study of Sexual Minorities in the Military, 2004.

[147] Aaron Belkin, Frank J. Barrett, Mark J. Eitelberg, and Marc J. Ventresca (2017), "Discharging Transgender Troops Would Cost $960 Million," Palm Center.

[148] Hutson, "An Unwarranted Attack."

[149] Tobias Barrington Wolff (1997), "Compelled Affirmations, Free Speech, and the U.S. Military's Don't Ask, Don't Tell Policy," *Brooklyn Law Review*, 63: 1141–1211.

[150] Frank, *Unfriendly Fire*, xix.

[151] "Top Military Officer: Gays Should Serve," *NBC News*, February 2, 2010.

[152] Aaron Belkin (2008), "'Don't Ask, Don't Tell': Does the Gay Ban Undermine the Military's Reputation?" *Armed Forces and Society*, 34(2): 276–91.

[153] Belkin, "'Don't Ask, Don't Tell.'"

[154] "Easier Access for Military Recruiters," *Tampa Tribune*, July 6, 2000, as cited in Belkin, "'Don't Ask, Don't Tell,'" 283, and David F. Burrelli and Jody Feder (2009), "Homosexuals in the U.S. Military: Current Issues," Congressional Research Service, 24.

[155] According to a poll that was administered to 5,650 service members, retirees, veterans, and their family members in October and November 2017, "Twice as many respondents support transgender individuals serving in the military as those who don't." See "Survey 2017 Results," Military Family Advisory Network, 31. According to an August 2017 Quinnipiac poll, 68 percent of voters support allowing transgender individuals to serve in the military, with 27 percent opposing. See Quinnipiac University, "U.S. Voters Say 68–27% Let Transgender People Serve," (press release), August 3, 2017.

[156] DoD Report, 41.

[157] Department of Defense, Health Data on Active Duty Service Members with Gender Dysphoria, 31-32.

[158] $2.2 million / 2.1 million service members / 12 months = 9 cents per member per month.

[159] Luk Gijs and Anne Brewaeys (2007), "Surgical Treatment of Gender Dysphoria in Adults and Adolescents: Recent Developments, Effectiveness, and Challenges," *Annual Review of Sex Research*, 18(1): 178–224. The 1990 study was Charles Mate-Kole, Maurizio Freschi, and Ashley Robin (1990), "A Controlled Study of Psychological and Social Change after Surgical Gender Reassignment in Selected Male Transsexuals," *The British Journal of Psychiatry*, 157(2): 261–64.

[160] Murad et al., "Hormonal Therapy." The DoD Report notes that the Murad study found the quality of most evidence to be "low," a claim we address elsewhere in this report.

[161] Colton Keo-Meier, Levi Herman, Sari Reisner, Seth Pardo, Carla Sharp, and Julia Babcock (2015), "Testosterone Treatment and MMPI-2 Improvement in Transgender Men: A Prospective Controlled Study," *Journal of Consulting and Clinical Psychology*, 83(1): 143–56.

[162] Dhejne et. al, "Mental Health and Gender Dysphoria."

[163] Rosalià Costa and Marco Colizzi (2016), "The Effect of Cross-Sex Hormonal Treatment on Gender Dysphoria Individuals' Mental Health: A Systematic Review," *Neuropsychiatric Disease and Treatment* 12: 1953–66.

[164] Steven Weyers et al. (2009), "Long-Term Assessment of the Physical, Mental, and Sexual Health among Transsexual Women," *The Journal of Sexual Medicine*, 6(3): 752–60.

[165] Ester Gomez-Gil et al. (2012), "Hormone-Treated Transsexuals Report Less Social Distress, Anxiety and Depression," *Psychoneuroendocrinology*, 37(5): 662–70.

[166] Marco Colizzi, Rosalià Costa, and Orlando Todarello (2014), "Transsexual Patients' Psychiatric Comorbidity and Positive Effect of Cross-Sex Hormonal Treatment on Mental Health: Results from a Longitudinal Study," *Psychoneuroendocrinology*, 39: 65–73.

[167] Nataša Jokic-Begic, Anita Lauri Korajlija, and Tanja Jurin (2014), "Psychosocial Adjustment to Sex Reassignment Surgery: A Qualitative Examination and Personal Experiences of Six Transsexual Persons in Croatia," *Scientific World Journal 2014*, 6.

[168] Keo-Meier et al., "Testosterone Treatment."

[169] Emily Newfield, Stacey Hart, Suzanne Dibble, and Lori Kohler (2006), "Female-to-Male Transgender Quality of Life," *Quality of Life Research*, 15(9): 1447–57.

[170] Gomez-Gil et al., "Hormone-Treated Transsexuals."

[171] Colizzi, Costa, and Todarello, "Transsexual Patients' Psychiatric Comorbidity."

[172] Samuel Davis and S. Colton Meier, (2014), "Effects of Testosterone Treatment and Chest Reconstruction Surgery on Mental Health and Sexuality in Female-to-Male Transgender People," *International Journal of Sexual Health*, 26(2): 113–28.

[173] Rehman et al., "The Reported Sex and Surgery Satisfactions."

[174] Nathalie Parola et al. (2010), "Study of Quality of Life for Transsexuals after Hormonal and Surgical Reassignment," *Sexologies*, 19(1): 24–28.

[175] Griet De Cuypere et al. (2006), "Long-Term Follow-up: Psychosocial Outcome of Belgian Transsexuals after Sex Reassignment Surgery," *Sexologies*, 15(2): 126–33.

[176] Nooshin Khobzi Rotondi et al. (2011), "Prevalence of and Risk and Protective Factors for Depression in Female-to-Male Transgender Ontarians: Trans PULSE Project," *Canadian Journal of Community Mental Health*, 30(2): 135–55.

[177] Crystal Boza and Kathryn Nicholson Perry (2014), "Gender-Related Victimization, Perceived Social Support, and Predictors of Depression among Transgender Australians," *International Journal of Transgenderism*, 15(1): 35–52.

[178] Ulrike Ruppin, and Freidemann Pfäfflin (2015), "Long-Term Follow-up of Adults with Gender Identity Disorder," *Archives of Sexual Behavior*, 44(5): 1321–29.

[179] Cecilia Dhejne, Katarina Öberg, Stefan Arver, and Mikael Landén (2014), "An Analysis of All Applications for Sex Reassignment Surgery in Sweden, 1960-2010: Prevalence, Incidence, and Regrets," *Archives of Sexual Behavior*, 43(8): 1535–45.

[180] Freidemann Pfäfflin (1992; sometimes listed as 1993), "Regrets after Sex Reassignment Surgery," *Journal of Psychology and Human Sexuality*, 5(4): 69–85.

[181] Aude Michel, Marc Ansseau, Jean-Jacques Legros, William Pitchot, and Christian Mormont (2002), "The Transsexual: What about the Future?" *European Psychiatry*, 17(6): 353–62.

[182] Mikael Landén, Jan Wålinder, Gunnar Hambert, and Bengt Lundström (1998), "Factors Predictive of Regret in Sex Reassignment," *Acta Psychiatrica Scandinavica*, 97(4): 284–89.

[183] Rehman et al., "The Reported Sex and Surgery Satisfactions."

[184] De Cuypere et al., "Long-Term Follow-up."

[185] Ruppin and Pfäfflin, "Long-Term Follow-up."

CHAPTER 39

AMERICAN ATTITUDES TOWARD MILITARY SERVICE OF TRANSGENDER PEOPLE[1]

Ryan Kelty, PhD
Associate Professor of Sociology, US Air Force Academy

Karin K. De Angelis, PhD
Associate Professor of Sociology, US Air Force Academy

Morten G. Ender, PhD
Professor of Sociology, US Military Academy at West Point

Michael D. Matthews, PhD
Professor of Engineering Psychology,
US Military Academy at West Point

Dean David E. Rohall, PhD
Dean of Campus and Community Relations, Ohio University Eastern

The service of openly transgender members in the United States military is a contested social issue with ongoing policy changes and challenges (Doyon & Hinton, 2020; Ender, 2017). A consequential shift occurred in June of 2016 when Secretary of Defense Ash Carter announced that the US military would change its policies and move incrementally toward allowing transgender people to serve openly (Department of Defense, 2016). This process was to be deliberate and grounded in research, as senior leaders recognized integration challenges including unit acceptance and cohesion, medical and personnel policies, and the

---

[1]The views of the authors are their own and do not purport to represent the views of the United States Air Force Academy, the United States Military Academy, the United States Air Force, the United States Army, the Department of Defense, or the United States Government.

financial obligations connected to transgender medical care (Dunlap et al., 2020; Schaefer et al., 2016). Though this move was considered appropriate and overdue by many, it was not without detractors concerned about impact on readiness and morale (Cooper, 2017a; Parco et al., 2015; Ender et al., 2016).

In accordance with the 2016 announcement, the US Department of Defense [DoD] worked for the next year on implementing the change. The initial focus was on retention or allowing transgender people already in the military to transition to their identified gender without fear of mandatory separation. The next step was to focus on accession standards, which are more stringent than those governing retention. On January 1, 2018, the DoD began accepting transgender recruits (Cooper, 2017b; Segal, 2018); however, they were doing so at the same time when the policy—once again—was being contested under the Trump presidency.

A few months into his first term, President Donald Trump called for a swift change in policy, with a tweet calling for a complete bar of transgender service members (Trump, 2017). Pivoting from their previous work, the Department of Defense spent many months translating President Trump's expressed intent into policy. In March 2018, the DoD ordered a "qualified ban" that requires separation of any service member diagnosed with gender dysphoria with a few "limited exceptions" such as exempting currently serving transgender personnel from the new policy (Gonzales & Raphelson, 2018). It has since codified the bar and exemptions in an instruction, "Military Service by Transgender Persons and Persons with Gender Dysphoria" (Department of Defense, 2020). Ongoing legal challenges are working through the system, but the Supreme Court in a 5–4 decision ruled that the bar could go into effect until the lower court decisions are complete (Liptak, 2019). Those currently serving remain in limbo and marginalized (Bishop et al., 2017; Embser-Herbert, 2019).

Estimates vary on the number of transgender service members in the US military. The two most cited numbers come from the Williams Institute, which estimates 15,500 transgender personnel in the military, and the RAND Corporation's 2016 estimate that between 2,150–10,790 transgender personnel currently serve (Gates & Herman, 2014; Schaefer et al., 2016). Because these numbers are only estimates—the Department of Defense does not collect data on gender identity—there is variability, but also overall agreement that transgender people make up roughly 0.5 percent of the active duty and reserve forces (Schaefer et al., 2016). The DoD potentially could be the country's largest employer of transgender people in the US, making this specific military personnel concern a national issue (Gates & Herman, 2014). Political battles at the national level, however, do not necessarily reflect what the general citizenry think and feel. This paper analyzes data from civilian and military college students in the US to examine the level of support for barring transgender Americans from military service.

A Conservative Institution That Aspires to Pluralism

The US military is an open system recruiting service members from among the general population. A central tenet of American civil-military relations is that the military's demographic composition should reflect the nation that it is sworn to serve and protect (excepting a significant under-representation of women) (Rohall et al., 2017a; Segal, 1989). The realization of this aspiration has been uneven and is not yet complete. Even before the all-volunteer force (AVF) was established in 1973, the US military was paying close attention to racial representation in the force. The AVF also increased an appreciation for and interest in recruiting and retaining women, although until recently with restrictions (Han, 2017; Segal, 1989). The Don't Ask, Don't Tell, Don't Pursue (DADT) policy of the early 1990s eased formal restrictions on service for lesbian/gay/bisexual people until the policy's September 20, 2011, repeal allowing for fully open service (Smith & De Angelis, 2017). Though the military arguably was an institutional leader in racial integration in America, the armed forces have been noticeably tardy in achieving full integration of lesbians/gays/bisexuals and women compared to civilian institutions (Han, 2017; Rohall et al., 2017b; Segal, 1989; Smith and De Angelis, 2017). Transgender people remain marginalized by the military (Rosenstein, 2017) and potentially excluded (again) if the courts uphold the Trump Administration's bar on transgender people from military service.

In a military that relies on voluntary enlistment with restrictions, one of the concerns is the development of a potential civil-military political gap. Studies over the last twenty years have systematically revealed a clear over-representation of people with conservative political ideologies serving in the US military, with corresponding under-representation of people with liberal political ideologies (Ender et al., 2013; Gronke & Feaver, 2001; Holsti, 2001; Ricks, 1997). This over-representation of conservative-leaning members also may influence support for the transgender military bar, with the majority of Republicans stating that someone's gender is determined by their sex at birth and that society is too accepting of transgender people, while the majority of Democrats state that a person's gender can be different than their sex assigned at birth and that society is not accommodating enough (Brown, 2017; Ender et al., 2016). Some contend this gap in political ideology represents a fundamental threat to civil-military relations due to a strong military that is out of alignment with the overall political views (or at least proportional views) of the population (Janowitz, 1960). Others argue that this skewed political representation is not necessarily problematic so long as there remains strong civilian control over the military through legislative and the executive branches (Huntington, 1957).

Identity theory suggests that the various identities we hold are linked to powerful normative expectations. These expectations, in turn, are important determinants of both attitudes and behaviors (Rohall et al., 2015). Rohall, Ender, and Matthews (2017a) argue that military status produces a strong social identity, which significantly impacts how one thinks about and acts in the world. The strength and commitment one has to a military identity will influence one's general attitudes and behaviors. For many, the normative expectations of the military serve to reinforce and amplify one's views. For people whose views do not align well with the informal norms and values of the military, the result could be either rejection of the institution or a realignment of individual views and institutional orientations to reduce the tension. In either case, the military is a powerful and conservative institution, and it intentionally exerts its power to instill a strong sense of military identity within its personnel. Given this, identity theory suggests that those affiliated with the military will be less likely than their civilian peers to accept open service by transgender people.

While there is strong evidence that members of the US military are more conservative in their political views on social and political issues than the US population in general (Ender et al., 2013; Feaver & Kohn, 2001; Ricks, 1997; Sondheimer et al., 2012), the military has made significant efforts to instill in its ranks and codify in its regulations and policies the core value of protecting the US Constitution and demonstrating respect for others, including the underlying premises of equality and justice. These values are expressly presented as and understood to refer to basic respect for the common humanity of others, but importantly respect for people of diverse characteristics. Support for basic civil rights is incorporated in the services' value statements under integrity and honor. The service branches systematically emphasize these core values,[2] though they continue to face challenges within their respective services. While there is undoubtedly room for improvement on issues of respect, diversity, inclusion, and equality, America's military has made historic strides on these core values in recent decades.

Adhering to policy does not always align with one's own socio-political views on these kinds of diversity and inclusion issues. The empirical question remains whether the conservative orientation of those who tend to be drawn to military service is stronger than the desire to orient oneself to the core values of respect and equality (i.e., pluralism) forcefully promoted by the institution with which one strongly identifies. The struggle for equality and respect within the military continues on all fronts, and the fight for full citizenship rights and inclusion of transgender people is the latest of these battles.

Brief Overview of Mainstream Cultural Oppression and Inclusion of Transgender People

While all marginalized groups had distinct experiences in pursuit of full equality, including in the military, the history of transgender people's struggle for equal access and equal treatment in the armed forces mirrors similar broad currents to that of other historically marginalized groups (e.g., racial/ethnic minorities, women, lesbians/gays/bisexuals, and the physically and mentally disabled). Both formal and informal means were (and continue to be) used to oppress transgender people. Informal mechanisms include *de facto* normative exclusion based on local/

---

[2]See core values statements for Army (https://www.army.mil/values/), Air Force (https://www.uc.edu/afrotc/future-cadets/media/jcr%3Acontent/MainContent/download_19/file.res/USAF%20Core%20Values.pdf), Navy (http://www.secnav.navy.mil/Ethics/Pages/corevaluescharter.aspx), and Marine Corps (https://www.hqmc.marines.mil/hrom/New-Employees/About-the-Marine-Corps/Values/).

institutional norms and cultural values; physical and psychological aggression; and gender-based discrimination and harassment in the workplace that limit opportunities, encourage separation, and in general create fear, anxiety, and stress through a hostile work environment (Harrison-Quintana & Herman, 2013; Lombardi et al., 2008).

Formal means of excluding transgender people take the form of official policies, regulations, and laws that restrict the rights of transgender people and their access to services. Examples of these include classification of transgender people as having "gender dysphoria" through the *Diagnostic and Statistical Manual* (DSM-V, 2013), legal rulings that fail to include transgender people as one of the protected classes under federal anti-discrimination law, prohibitions or restrictions in athletic participation (Jones et al., 2017), as well as the military's bar on openly serving as a transgender individual—including appropriate medical care for transgender-related health issues (Harrison-Quintana & Herman, 2013; Kosciw et al., 2012; Wright et al., 2006). Perhaps the best known of these formal exclusionary measures is the 2016 North Carolina House Bill 2—better known as "The Bathroom Bill"—in which people were required to use public bathrooms that corresponded with the sex listed on their birth certificate (Gordon et al., 2016). While this bill was eventually repealed (Silva, 2017), a related case in which a student sued his public high school to allow him to use restrooms appropriate for his gender identity found its way to the Supreme Court, but the refusal of the court to take up the case left the issues to local and state authorities without clear federal guidance (Brown & Balingit, 2017). The Trump Administration's policy to reverse the decision to allow transgender people to serve openly in the military is situated in this stridently contested socio-political gender climate.

Despite these formal and informal means of oppression, transgender people and their allies are increasingly advocating for equality; likewise, support for transgender rights are growing in the general population (Norton & Herek, 2012; Rosenstein, 2017). Increased media normalization from television to film to magazines and newspapers to music and sources of social media has increased awareness and support for transgender people. Bruce Jenner's well-publicized transition to Caitlyn Jenner in the summer of 2015 is perhaps the most well-known example of this positive media attention (Bissinger, 2015). Negative news stories focused on the social and economic sanctions against states and companies with anti-transgender laws and policies (Berman, 2017) have added to the media's impact on this issue.

The road toward equal treatment in the US military for transgender people has lagged behind that of African Americans, women, and lesbians/gays/bisexuals, but the process echoes that of these other groups (see Moskos et al., 2000; Rosenstein, 2017). Historically, each group was fully and formally excluded, although people of color and women had served in segregated units while gay/lesbian/bisexual people had to serve clandestinely. Eventually, due to both functional necessity and social pressures, members of these groups became included, but only in marginalized ways (e.g., racially segregated units, female auxiliary forces, and DADT).

Due in part to the quality contributions made by these marginalized service members, restraints on service eventually lifted, and open service in all branches across military specializations became normative. Despite LGBT openness, outing oneself varies from low to high openness among different constituent groups in the military such as chaplains, officers, unit leaders, helping professionals, and friends, suggesting culture change lags behind structural change (McNamara et al., 2020). In the past couple of years the status of transgender people has vacillated between these stages, which distinguishes their march toward equality apart from that of the previous groups.

This review of the literature motivates the question, to what degree does civilian versus military status affect support for allowing transgender people to serve in the armed forces? Drawing from decades of literature documenting socio-political gaps between service members and the general public, combined with expectations that social identities motivate attitudes and behaviors based on normative expectations for the groups associated with those identities, we would expect greater attitudinal support of civil rights of people (i.e., freedom, equality, respect of others) to be inversely related to support for a bar on transgender people serving in the military. Additionally, we would expect people with military affiliation to be more likely than civilians to support barring transgender people serving in the military.

A final question we pose is whether military affiliation (military vs. civilian) moderates the relationship between civil rights attitudes and support for barring transgender people from military service, such that civilians will demonstrate a significantly stronger relationship between civil rights attitudes and support for a bar on transgender individuals' military service than do their military peers.

Analytic Model Predicting Attitudes Toward Transgender Military Participation

To answer the questions above about civilian versus military attitudes on transgender military participation, we collected survey data from a convenience sample using web-based software. Data were collected from 1,359 military academy cadets, ROTC cadets at civilian colleges and universities, and civilian college and university students. Civilian institutions, including ROTC cadets and civilian students, included both larger public universities as well as small private colleges located primarily on the East Coast and Midwest of the United States.

The average age of respondents was just shy of twenty years old, with approximately three quarters of respondents being male—reflecting the highly skewed gender balance of military academy cadets. On average, respondents reported being slightly to the right politically, middle-to-upper social class, and White. When academy and ROTC cadets are combined in a single group of military affiliated students, they represent 87.3% of the sample.[3]

---

[3]See Appendix I for a table of full sample socio-demographic characteristics.

Model Variables

We use a civil rights scale comprised of three items to measure respondents' attitudes toward freedom, equality, and respect for others.[4] This civil rights variable is a key independent variable used to predict attitudes toward transgender military participation (our outcome variable). Higher values on the civil rights variable correspond to greater support for civil rights and respect of all people in society. Higher values on our outcome variable correspond with more tolerant attitudes—that is, disagreement that transgender people should be barred from military service. Finally, whether or not someone is affiliated with the military is used as the moderating variable in our model in order to determine whether the relationship between attitudes toward civil rights and support for transgender military participation differs between civilian and military respondents. Analytically, we test for this moderation effect by interacting the civil rights variable with the civ-mil variable to predict attitudes toward transgender military participation. Preliminary analysis indicated that the two military samples, ROTC and military academy cadets, did not differ significantly on the key independent or outcome variables tested, so they were combined into a single group (i.e., military). Students at civilian colleges and universities not enrolled in ROTC programs comprise the civilian group in our analysis.

Several control variables are included in our analytic model to more accurately specify the unique effects of attitudes toward civil rights and civ-mil status on attitudes toward barring transgender people from military service. These control variables include age, sex, race, political orientation, and family income. Without these control variables accounting for covariance in our model we risk over- or under-estimating the explanatory power of civil rights attitudes and civ-mil status.

In the following section we present the findings from both the descriptive analyses of the key predictor and outcome variables. Next, we will present the results of the multivariate regression model used to test for main effects of the civil rights attitudinal scale and military versus civilian status on support for barring transgender people from military service. In addition, we report the results of our moderation analysis to determine whether or not civilian versus military status affects the relationship between civil rights attitudes and support for barring transgender people from serving in the armed forces.

Civil-Military Attitudinal Differences on Transgender Military Participation

Descriptive analysis of attitudes toward barring transgender people from military service reveals a skewed distribution of attitudes across the various response categories for this variable, with more than two-thirds of civilians (69.2%) and nearly half of military respondents (49.7%) disagreeing strongly with a bar on transgender people serving in uniform. Respondents reported considerably less support for "agreeing somewhat" with a transgender bar (12–20%), "disagreeing

---

[4]See Appendix II for additional details on study methodology.

somewhat" with a bar (11–17%), and "disagreeing strongly" (7–13%). Overall, this pattern of responses indicates high levels of support for inclusion of transgender people in the US military.

Figure 1. Attitudes Toward Barring Transgender People from Military Service

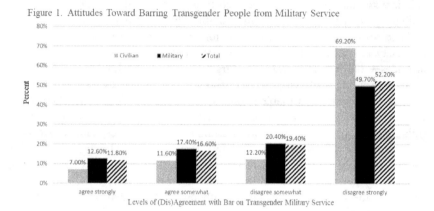

Levels of (Dis)Agreement with Bar on Transgender Military Service

Descriptive results for the civil rights attitudinal scale produced a mean of 3.80 and a standard deviation of 0.37 on this 4-point Likert scale (4 = very important). This indicates that on average, respondents report that freedom, equality, and respect for others are important characteristics of our society. In addition, preliminary correlation analyses demonstrated significant linear relationships among the study's three focal variables. Attitudes toward barring transgender people from military service was positively correlated with attitudes toward civil rights (r =.243, p<.01), and negatively correlated with civilian versus military status (r = -.114, p<01). Attitudes on the civil rights scale was negatively correlated with civilian versus military status (r =-.051, p<.05). As such, stronger support for civil rights and being civilian are associated with greater support for full inclusion of transgender people in the military, and civilian respondents are more supportive of civil rights than their military peers.

Results of the full model predicting support for transgender military service are presented in Table 1 and demonstrate mixed support for our hypotheses. Model 1 demonstrated regressed attitudes toward a bar on transgender military service on several socio-demographic control variables. Political ideology, sex, and household income are each significant predictors in this model. The more liberal an individual is, the more likely they are to support transgender people serving in the military (B= -0.182, p<.001). Women are significantly more likely than men to support transgender people in the armed forces (B=0.423, p<.001). Higher levels of household income are associated with greater support for military participation of transgender people (B=0.061, p<.05). Age and each of the dummy variables for race failed to reach significance. Younger people do not report significantly different attitudes than older people toward transgender military participation. The non-significant findings for the dummy variables on race/ethnicity indicate that Blacks, Asians, and Hispanics do not differ significantly from Whites on their attitudes toward military service of transgender people.

Model 2 includes the civil rights attitudinal scale and whether or not one is affiliated with the military as key independent variables predicting attitudes toward barring transgender people from military service. The civil rights scale reached significance in predicting attitudes toward barring transgender people from military service (B=0.487, p<.001). Greater support for civil rights issues of freedom, equality, and respect of others was associated with greater acceptance of transgender military service. These results support hypothesis 1. Military affiliated respondents were not significantly different than their civilian peers on their level of support for the inclusion of transgender people in the armed forces. This result fails to support hypothesis 2, which predicted civilians would have significantly more favorable attitudes than their military peers on military participation of transgender people. Results of the control variables in Model 1 were unchanged in the context of the new variables introduced in Model 2.

The interaction term (Civil Rights * Military vs. Civilian) included in Model 3 tests whether or not civilian versus military status moderates the relationship between civil rights attitudes (key independent variable) and support for transgender people serving in the military (dependent variable). In other words, it is assessing whether the relationship between one's attitudes on civil rights and one's support for transgender military participation differs depending on whether one is civilian or affiliated with the military. The coefficient for the interaction (B= -0.030, SE=.221) fails to reach significance, indicating that the relationship between civil rights attitudes and support for transgender military barring is essentially similar between civilians and military respondents. This result fails to support hypothesis 3, which predicted civilians would have a significantly stronger relationship between civil rights attitudes and attitudes toward military service of transgender people. All findings from Model 2 remain constant in Model 3 when the interaction is added.

To better visualize the importance of the results of the moderation analysis above, Figure 2 presents a graphic representation of the data. The figure plots the civil rights attitude scale along the x-axis, and attitudes toward barring transgender people from military service along the y-axis. Recall that higher numbers on the civil rights scale correspond with more supportive attitudes toward freedom, equality, and respect. Higher values on attitudes toward barring transgender military service represent more tolerant orientations—i.e., *rejecting* the bar on transgender service. The dashed line represents civilians' attitudes, and the solid line the attitudes of military respondents.

Table 2. Predictors of Attitudes toward Support for Barring Transgender People from Military Service

	Model 1			Model 2			Model 3		
	b	SE		b	SE		b	SE	
Control Variables									
Political Ideology	-0.182	0.017	***	-0.172	0.017	***	-0.172	0.017	***
Age	-0.019	0.013		-0.020	0.013		0.020	0.013	
Sex	0.423	0.065	***	0.358	0.068	***	0.358	0.068	***
Income (Family)	0.061	0.025	*	0.063	0.025	*	0.063	0.025	*
Black	-0.121	0.108		-0.124	0.106		-0.124	0.106	
Asian	-0.031	0.094		-0.001	0.093		-0.001	0.093	
Hispanic	0.098	0.108		-0.046	0.107		-0.047	0.107	
Focal Variables									
Civil Rights Scale				0.487	0.067	***	0.513	0.210	***
Military vs. Civilian				-0.073	0.088		0.040	0.849	
Civil Rights * Military vs. Civilian							-0.030	0.221	
$R^2 \Delta$	0.129***			0.033***			0.000		

N=1359. *p<.05, ***p<.001 (two tailed test)

Greater support for civil rights is associated with higher levels of support for transgender people serving in the military. Those affiliated with the military show similar levels of support as their civilian peers on transgender military participation. Those with more liberal political ideology, higher household income, and women are more supportive of people who are transgender serving in the military than are conservatives, men and those from households with lower income.

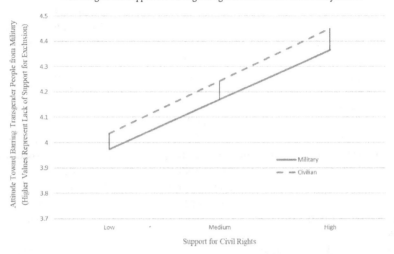

Figure 2. Moderation Effect of Civ-Mil Status on Relationship Between Attitudes on Civil Rights and Support for Barring Transgender Individuals from Military Service

The military and civilian lines plotted on the graph each show positive slopes, indicating that greater support on the civil rights scale corresponds with more favorable attitudes toward transgender people serving in the military. The military and civilian lines plotted on the graph show essentially the same significant positive slope, but with civilians at a slightly higher vertical level than their military peers. These virtually parallel lines represent the non-significant interaction coefficient, indicating that the relationship between civil rights attitudes and attitudes toward barring transgender military service are essentially similar for the two groups.

The civilian line is consistently higher than the military line in Figure 2, indicating that civilians show a higher level of support for allowing transgender people to serve in the military at each level of support on the civil rights scale. The fact that the test statistic is not significant for this moderation analysis tells us that, accounting for all other model variables, civilians and military affiliated people have similar relationships between attitudes toward civil rights and support for transgender military participation.

Discussion

The analyses presented in this chapter contribute to our understanding of attitudes toward transgender people serving in the military through use of a more robust sample than prior studies, inclusion of a measure of support for attitudes toward basic civil rights, and a test of whether military versus civilian status moderates the relationship between attitudes toward civil rights and support for military service of transgender people.

Results indicate that most civilian and military affiliated people support basic aspects of civil rights, and this variable is shown to be a significant predictor of support for military service of transgender people. Further, the relationship between civil rights attitudes and support for military service of transgender people is positive for both groups, and no significant difference by civilian-military status is observed. This result was contrary to the expected moderation effect of civilian-military status on the effects of civil rights support on attitudes toward military participation of transgender people.

On a practical level, the lack of both a main effect and moderation effect for civilian-military status observed in this study suggests that integration of openly serving transgender people could be successful. Civil rights are not viewed to relate differently to support for transgender people serving in the armed forces based on military versus civilian status of respondent. Given that the various service branches routinely and enthusiastically promote the values of respect and equality, it makes sense that an official policy that aligns with these values (e.g., full integration of transgender people) would be respected and complied with for reasons beyond the mere issuance of an order. This expectation is also in line with predictions from identity theory that suggest those who identify as service members will adopt the institution's values and behavioral expectations.

Indeed, leaders should leverage the alignment of service members' value of freedom, respect, and equality with that of the military as an institution valuing diversity, equity, and inclusion. Leaders should treat transgender military status—indeed, all marginal groups striving for full access to military participation—as a civil rights issue rather than a civilian imposed rule on the military institution and its members; it's something *done for* American citizens rather than something *done to* military members. In doing so, it can serve to amplify positive attitudes toward both civil rights and support for full inclusion of transgender service members. Explicit support for core civil rights as a foundational principle of the military and its members will also set the tone for the organizational climate across military units. In short, promoting core military values is likely to also increase support for service of transgender people.

Experiences from other Western democratic militaries such as Canada on the integration of transgender people into their respective militaries suggests it can be accomplished with minimal challenges (Crosbie & Posard, 2016; Okros & Scott, 2014; Rosenstein, 2017). In recent US history, the repeal of DADT in 2011, which allowed open service and full integration of LGB people in our military, did not produce significant issues socially or in terms of military effectiveness (Belkin et al., 2013; Bishop et al., 2017; Hix & MacCoun, 2010). To the extent that changes in military policy keep pace with broader civilian society, whether the DoD leads the change or follows the lead of the civilian population, the prevailing view of civil-military relations in the US suggests such concordance is good for the institution of the military and the nation broadly—i.e., with respect to civil-military relations, the military is a part of society rather than apart from it (Janowitz 1960).

As with the integration of women (Woodruff & Kelty, 2017; Schaefer, 2010) and lesbian/gay/bisexual service members (Schell et al., 2010), privacy concerns persist as a pragmatic issue for integration of transgender people (Rosenstein, 2017).

Research on the integration of lesbians/gays/bisexuals and women has shown that so long as basic privacy and personal safety issues are addressed, those from the group being integrated and those from the dominant group can be freed up to serve effectively in the military (Ender et al., 2016; Rostker, 2010). Moreover, the process used to refocus training and requirements for different jobs in the military on the functional necessities needed to perform various duties explicitly recognizes that the metric for military service should be a willingness to serve our country and the physical/cognitive ability to perform one's job—not secondary characteristics such as race/ethnicity, sex, sexual orientation, or gender identity. This set of issues involves both clear leadership, as discussed above, but also structural and regulatory considerations. Again, these are not insurmountable, and experiences from other Western democratic nations suggests that while these considerations need careful attention and may incur some costs, they are humane, manageable, and necessary for effective integration of transgender people in the armed forces.

In considering the results and implications of this research, a few caveats are in order. We note that data for this study were obtained from a convenience sample of college students. These results may not generalize to non–college educated populations, which includes most enlisted service members. Research has demonstrated that education has a liberalizing effect on socio-political attitudes (Loftus, 2001; Olhander et al., 2005; Weakliem, 2002). Moreover, relatively few of those in the ROTC and military academy cadet sample have substantial experience as full-time Soldiers, Sailors, Airmen, or Marines. To be admitted to a service academy or to receive a ROTC scholarship, they must have high scores on standardized aptitude tests like the SAT, and have excelled in academics, sports, and club activities in high school. These attributes may bias this sample to more liberal attitudes. The combination of these factors of the current sample indicate the importance of replicating this study in a more representative sample of enlisted and officer personnel serving on active duty and an education-matched civilian sample. Such a study would provide important evidence as to whether or not the effects reported in this chapter are further generalizable.

A more encouraging caveat is that our military sample represent the future leaders of the military. Those who advance to flag rank will serve into the 2050s. If they retain these inclusive attitudes, the future integration of transgender people into active duty will be eased. That said, once our military respondents are commissioned as officers, they will be subject to the (re)socialization processes and peer pressure inherent in a highly structured organization. Arguably, these forces could result in an attenuation of their current attitudes and beliefs. To test this possibility, when replicating this study with active duty officers, including years of service will be essential. This could begin to tease out whether attitudes are a cohort effect or change systematically and predictability over time. Given the considerations outlined here, the current study should be taken as an exploratory set of analyses that offers fruitful insight to guide future research in this area.

Works Cited

Belkin, A., Ender, M.G., Frank, N., Furia, S.R., Lucas, G.R., Packard, G., Samuels, S.M., Schultz, T. & Segal, D.R. (2013). Readiness and DADT repeal: has the new policy of open service undermined the military? *Armed Forces & Society, 39*(4), 587–601. https://doi.org/10.1177/0095327X12466248

Berman, M. (2017, March 27). North Carolina's bathroom bill cost the state at least $3.7 billion, new analysis finds. *The Washington Post.* Retrieved June 1, 2018, from https://www.washingtonpost.com/news/post-nation/wp/2017/03/27/north-carolinas-bathroom-bill-cost-the-state-at-least-3-7-billion-new-analysis-finds/?utm_term=.e9891a407d54

Bishop, A., Cook, M.L., Ficarrotta, J.C., Lucas, G.R., & Schultz, T.S. (2017). Understanding Trump's memo on transgender service members: what it means, and why it is so contrary to fact and law. *Palm Center.* http://www.palmcenter.org/wp-content/uploads/2017/08/Trumps-Transgender-Ban.pdf

Bissinger, B. (2015, June 25). Caitlyn Jenner: the full story. *Vanity Fair.* Retrieved June 5, 2018, from https://www.vanityfair.com/hollywood/2015/06/caitlyn-jenner-bruce-cover-annie-leibovitz

Brown, A. (2017, November 8). Republicans, Democrats have starkly different views on transgender issues. Pew Research Center. Retrieved June 25, 2018, from http://www.pewresearch.org/fact-tank/2017/11/08/transgender-issues-divide-republicans-and-democrats/

Brown, E. and Balingit, M. (2017, March 6). Supreme Court's decision to pass on transgender bathroom case leaves schools, parents without answers. *The Washington Post.* Retrieved June 5, 2018, from https://www.washingtonpost.com/news/education/wp/2017/03/06/supreme-courts-decision-to-pass-on-transgender-bathroom-case-leaves-schools-parents-without-answers/?utm_term=.021a22d14cbf

Cooper, H. (2017a, December 11). Transgender people will be allowed to enlist in the military as a court case advances. *The New York Times.* Retrieved June 26, 2018, from https://www.nytimes.com/2017/12/11/us/politics/transgender-military-pentagon.html

Cooper, H. (2017b, August 3). Trump cites familiar argument in ban on transgender troops. *The New York Times.* Retrieved June 25, 2018, from

https://www.nytimes.com/2017/08/03/us/politics/transgender-military-trump.html

Crosbie, T. and Posard, M. (2016). Barriers to serve: social policy and the transgendered military. *Journal of Sociology, 52*(3), 596–85. https://doi.org/10.1177/1440783316655632

Department of Defense. (2020, September 4). *Military Service by Transgender Persons and Persons with Gender Dysphoria.* https://www.esd.whs.mil/DD/

Department of Defense. (2016, June 30). Secretary of Defense Ash Carter announces policy for transgender service members. https://www.defense.gov/News/News-Releases/News-Release-View/Article/821675/secretary-of-defense-ash-carter-announces-policy-for-transgender-service-members/

Doyon, J. & Hinton, E. (2020). Dreams deferred: The battle for transgender military rights marches on. *NBCUniversal.* Video and article available on the LX website: https://www.lx.com/community/dreams-deferred-the-battle-for-transgender-military-rights-marches-on/14371/

DSM V—*Diagnostic and Statistical Manual of Mental Disorders*—5th edition TR. (2013). American Psychiatric Association.

Dunlap, S.L., Holloway, I.W., Pickering, C.E., Tzen, M. Goldbach, J.T., & Castro, C.A. (2020). Support for transgender military service from active duty United States military personnel. *Sexuality Research and Social Policy, 18*(1), 137–143. doi: 10.1007/s13178-020-00437-x. https://pubmed.ncbi.nlm.nih.gov/34276831/

Embser-Herbert. M. (2019). "Welcome! Oh, wait…" Transgender military service in a time of uncertainty. *Sociological Inquiry, 90*(2), 405–429. DOI : https://doi.org/10.1111/soin.12329

Ender, M.G. (2017, August 7). Tweets, trans, and the American military. *Just Security.* https://www.justsecurity.org/43912/tweets-trans-american-military/

Ender, M.G., Rohall, D.E., & Matthews, M.D. (2013). *The Millennial Generation and National Defense. Attitudes of Future Military and Civilian Leaders.* Palgrave.

Ender, M.G., Rohall, D.E., & Matthews, M.D. (2016). Cadet and civilian undergraduate attitudes toward transgender people: a research note. *Armed Forces & Society, 42*(2), 427–435. https://doi.org/10.1177/0095327X15575278

Feaver, P.D. & Kohn, R.H. (Eds.). (2001). *Soldiers and Civilians: The Civil-Military Gap and American National Security.* MIT Press.

Gates, G.J. & Herman, J.L. (2014). Transgender military service in the United States. Retrieved July 9, 2018, from https://williamsinstitute.law.ucla.edu/wp-content/uploads/Transgender-Military-Service-May-2014.pdf

Gonzales, R. & Raphelson, S. (2018, March 23). Trump memo disqualifies certain transgender people from military service. NPR. Retrieved July 9, 2018, from https://www.npr.org/sections/thetwo-way/2018/03/23/596594346/trump-memo-disqualifies-certain-transgender-people-from-military-service

Gordon, M., Price, M.S., & Perlata, K. (2016, March 26). Understanding HB2: North Carolina's newest law solidifies state's role in defining discrimination. *The Charlottesville Observer.* http://www.charlotteobserver.com/news/politics-government/article68401147.html

Gronke, P. & Feaver, P.D. (2001). Uncertain confidence: civilian and military attitudes about civil-military relations. In Feaver, P.D. & Kohn, R.H. (Eds.), *Soldiers and Civilians: The Civil-Military Gap and American National Security.* pp. 129–162. MIT Press.

Han, J. (2017). African-Americans in the US military. In Rohall, D.E., Ender, M.G., & Matthews, M.D. (Eds.), *Inclusion in the American Military: A Force for Diversity.* pp. 19–36. Lexington Books.

Harrison-Quintana, J. & Herman, J.L. (2013). Still serving in silence: transgender service members and veterans in the National Transgender Discrimination Survey. *LGBTQ Policy Journal.* https://docshare.tips/harrison-quintana-herman-lgbtq-policy-journal-2013_5871f7f7b6d87f716d8b4a11.html

Hix, W.M. & MacCoun, R.J. (2010). Cohesion and performance. In Rostker, B.D. (Ed.), *Sexual Orientation and US Military Personnel Policy: An Update of RAND's 1993 Study.* pp. 137–166. RAND Corp.

Holsti, O.R. (2001). Of chasms and convergences: attitudes and beliefs of civilians and military elites at the start of the new millennium. In Feaver, P.D. &. Kohn, R.H. (Eds.), *Soldiers and Civilians: The Civil-Military Gap and American National Security.* pp. 15–100. MIT Press.

Huntington, S.P. (1957), *The Soldier and the State: The Theory and Politics of Civil-Military Relations.* Vintage Books.

Janowitz, M. (1960). *The Professional Soldier: A Social and Political Portrait.* The Free Press.

Jones, B.A., Arcelus, J., Bouman, W.P. & Haycraft, E. (2017). Sport and transgender people: a systematic review of the literature relating to sport participation and competitive sport policies. *Sports Medicine, 47*(4), 701–716. https://doi.org/10.1007/s40279-016-0621-y

Kosciw, J.G., Greytak, E.A., Bartkiewicz, M.J., Boesen, M.J, & Palmer, N.A. (2012). The 2011 National School Climate Survey: the experiences of lesbian, gay, bisexual and transgender youth in our nation's schools. Gay Lesbian and Straight Network. https://www.glsen.org/sites/default/files/2011%20National%20School%20Climate%20Survey%20Full%20Report.pdf

Liptak, A. (2019, January 22). Supreme Court revives transgender ban for military service. *New York Times.* https://www.nytimes.com/2019/01/22/us/politics/transgender-ban-military-supreme-court.html

Loftus, J. (2001). America's liberalization in attitudes toward homosexuality, 1973–1998. *American Sociological Review, 66*(5), 762–782. https://doi.org/10.2307/3088957

Lombardi, E.L., Wilchins, R.A., Priesing, D. & Malouf, D. (2008). Gender violence: transgender experiences with violence and discrimination. *Journal of Homosexuality, 42*(1), 89–101. doi: 10.1300/j082v42n01_05

McNamara, K.A., Lucas, C.L., Goldbach, J.T., Castro, C.A., & Holloway, I.W. (2020). Even if the policy changes, the culture remains the same: a mixed methods analysis of LGBT service members' outness patterns. *Armed Forces & Society, 47*(3), https://doi.org/10.1177/0095327X20952136

Moskos, C. (2000). Toward a postmodern military: the United States. In Moskos, C., Williams, J.A. & Segal, D.R. (Eds.), *The Postmodern Military: Armed Forces After the Cold War*, pp. 14–31. Oxford University Press.

Norton, A.T. & Herek, G.M. (2012). Heterosexuals' attitudes toward transgender people: findings from a national probability sample of US adults. *Sex Roles, 68*(11–12), 738–753. http://dx.doi.org/10.1007/s11199-011-0110-6

Okros, A. & Scott, D. (2014). Gender identity in the Canadian forces: a review of possible impacts on operational effectiveness. *Armed Forces & Society, 41*(2), 243–256. https://doi.org/10.1177/0095327X14535371

Olhander, J., Batalova, J. & Treas, J. (2005). Explaining educational influences on attitudes toward homosexual relations. *Social Science Research, 34*(4), 781–799. https://doi.org/10.1016/J.SSRESEARCH.2004.12.004

Parco, J.E., Levy, D.A., & Spears, S.R. (2015). Transgender military personnel in the post-DADT repeal era: a phenomenological study. *Armed Forces & Society, 41*(2), 221–242. https://ssrn.com/abstract=2407710

Ricks, T. (1997, July). The widening gap between military and society. *The Atlantic.* Retrieved May 25, 2018, from https://www.theatlantic.com/magazine/archive/1997/07/the-widening-gap-between-military-and-society/306158/

Rohall, D.E., Ender, M.G., & Matthews, M.D. (2017a). Diversity in the military. In Rohall, D.E., Ender, M.G., & Matthews, M.D. (Eds.), *Inclusion in the American Military: A Force for Diversity.* pp.1–16. Lexington Books.

Rohall, D.E., Ender, M.G., & Matthews, M.D. (2017b). The intersection of race, class, gender, and sexuality in the military. In Rohall, D.E., Ender, M.G., & Matthews, M.D. (Eds.), *Inclusion in the American Military: A Force for Diversity.* pp. 191–209. Lexington Books.

Rohall, D. E., Milkie, M., & Lucas, J. (2015). *Social Psychology: Sociological Perspectives*, 3rd Edition. Pearson.

Rosenstein, J.E. (2017). The integration of trans people into the military. In Rohall, D.E., Ender, M.G., & Matthews, M.D. (Eds.), *Inclusion in the American Military: A Force for Diversity*. pp.149–168. Lexington Books.

Rostker, B.D. (2010). *Sexual Orientation and US Military Personnel Policy: An Update of RAND's 1993 Study*. RAND Corp.

Schaefer, A.G. (2010). Insights from the expanding role of women in the military. In Rostker, B.D. (Ed.), *Sexual Orientation and US Military Personnel Policy: An Update of RAND's 1993 Study*. pp. 389–410. RAND Corp.

Schaefer, A. G., Iyengar, R., Kadiyala, S., Kavanagh, J., Engel, C.C., Williams, K.M., & Kress, A.M. (2016). *The Implications of Allowing Transgender Personnel to Serve Openly in the US Military*. RAND Corp.

Schell, T. L., Berry, S.H., Bradly, M., Brown, R.A., Hosek, S., Huynh, A. & Miyashiro, L.S. (2010). Military focus groups In Rostker, B.D. (Ed.), *Sexual Orientation and US Military Personnel Policy: An Update of RAND's 1993 Study*. pp. 233–253. RAND Corp.

Segal, C. (2018, March 9). As Trump's ban plays out in court, America's first openly transgender recruits are joining the military. *PBS News Hour*. https://www.pbs.org/newshour/nation/as-trumps-ban-plays-out-in-court-americas-first-openly-transgender-recruits-are-joining-the-military

Segal, D.R. (1989). *Recruiting for Uncle Sam*. Kansas University Press.

Silva, D. (2017, April 2). HB2 Repeal: North Carolina overturns controversial "bathroom bill." *NBC News*. https://www.nbcnews.com/news/us-news/north-carolina-senate-votes-repeal-controversial-bathroom-bill-n740546

Smith, D.G. & De Angelis, K. (2017). Lesbian and gay service members and their families. In Rohall, D.E., Ender, M.G., & Matthews, M.D. (Eds.). *Inclusion in the American Military: A Force for Diversity*. pp. 129–147. Lexington Books.

Sondheimer, R. M., Toner, K., & Wilson III, I. (2012). Cadet perceptions of military and civilian ideology. *Armed Forces & Society*, *39*(1), 124–134. https://doi.org/10.1177/0095327X12442304

Trump, D.J. (@realDonaldTrump) (2017, 26 July, 0704 EST). "After consultation with my Generals and military experts, please be advised that the United States Government will not accept or allow . . .Transgender people to serve in any capacity in the US Military. Our military must be focused on decisive and overwhelming . . . victory and cannot be burdened with the tremendous medical costs and disruption that transgender in the military would entail. Thank you." Tweet.

Weakliem, D.L. (2002). The effects of education on political opinions: an international study. *International Journal of Public Opinion Research*, *14*(2), 141–157. https://doi.org/10.1093/ijpor/14.2.141

Woodruff, T. & Kelty, R. (2017). Gender and deployment effects on pro-organizational behaviors of US soldiers. *Armed Forces & Society*, *43*(2), 280–299. https://doi.org/10.1177/0095327X16687068

Wright, T., Colgan, F., Creegan, C., & McKearney, A. (2006). Lesbian, gay and bisexual workers: equality, diversity and inclusion in the workplace. *Equal Opportunities International*, *25*(6), 465–470. http://hr.fhda.edu/_downloads/Lesbian_Gay_and_Bisexual_Workers_Equalit.pdf

Appendix 1. Socio-Demographic Characteristics of Sample

	Freq. (%)	Mean	s.d.
Age		19.67	2.20
Political orientation*		5.79	1.67
Civil rights scale**		3.78	0.40
Military‡	1187, (87.3)		
Family income (family)			
LT 25K	52 (3.8)		
25K-50K	127 (9.3)		
51K-90K	314 (23.1)		
91K-145K	359 (26.4)		
150K+	507 (37.3)		
Males	1,029 (75.7)		
Race/Ethnicity			
Race			
American			
African American	99 (7.3)		
Caucasian	1,035 (76.1)		
Asian	129 (9.5)		
Hispanic	96 (7.1)		
n = 1,359			

* Measured using a 10-point scale where higher values represent more conservative political views
**Military includes military service academy and ROTC respondents
‡Military includes academy and ROTC respondents

Appendix II. Study Methodology

The study presented in this chapter uses data from web-based survey including a convenience sample of military academy cadets, ROTC cadets, and civilian college/university students (see Ender et al., 2013).

Analysis includes both descriptive data analysis and predictive modeling using hierarchical regression analysis in order to specify as accurately as possible the unique explanatory power of each of the model variables. Data analysis were performed on SPSS 15.0.

Focal study variables

Civil rights scale: Each item was preceded by a prompt to indicate "how important the following principles are for you." The first item asked respondents to rate "equality of people, regardless of gender race, religion, etc." The respect item asked respondents to rate "respect for individuals." The Freedom item prompted respondents to rate "basic freedoms of individuals" (i.e., freedom of assembly, ideas, speech, the press, etc.). All three items used the same Likert scale with 1 = very important, 2 = somewhat important, 3 = somewhat unimportant, 4 = very unimportant. These items were reverse coded before being combined in the scale so that higher values correspond to greater support for civil rights and dignity of all people in society.[5] The outcome variable for our model is a measure asking respondents whether or not it is all right to bar transgender people from serving in the military. Response categories were presented in a Likert scale ranging from 1 = strongly agree to 4 = strongly disagree. Higher values on this variable correspond with more tolerant attitudes—that is, disagreement that transgender people should be barred from military service. Finally, whether or not someone is affiliated with the military is used as the moderating variable in our model in order to determine whether the relationship between attitudes toward civil rights and support for transgender military participation differs between civilian and military respondents. A single item is used to measure this status. Preliminary analysis indicated that the two military samples, ROTC and military academy cadets, did not differ significantly on the key predictor or outcome variables tested, so they were combined and coded as "military" = 1. Students at civilian colleges and universities not enrolled in ROTC programs were coded as "civilian" = 0.

Control variables

Age is measured in years. Sex is coded as 0 = male and 1 = female.[6] Political orientation is measured on a 10-point Likert scale from 1 = extreme left to 10 = extreme right. Family income is measured by a question asking respondents to self-report "your family's yearly household income" and provides space to write in a dollar amount. Due to several extreme outliers at the top end of the distribution, household income was recoded into five categories to reduce the effects of these outliers (1 = LT 25K, 2 = 25–49.9K, 3 = 50–89.9K, 4 = 90–149.9K, 5 = 150K and greater). Finally, race/ethnicity was measured using a series of dummy variables for African Americans, Asians, and Hispanics, with Caucasians excluded as the comparison group. These dummy variables allow us to compare each racial/ethnic minority group to Caucasian respondents.

---

[5] The three-item scale demonstrated strong internal reliability (α = .73) suggesting that they have a significant shared underlying construct—what we are calling "attitude toward civil rights."

[6] Air Force regulations do not currently allow surveys to ask about non-binary sex/gender categories.

CHAPTER 40

DEVELOPING INCLUSIVE AND RESPECTFUL LEADERS: HOW TO INTENTIONALLY DESIGN MEANINGFUL FACE-TO-FACE EXPERIENCES WITH DIFFERENT TYPES OF "OTHERS"

Michelle A. Butler Samuels
US Air Force Academy, Colorado Springs, CO

Background

> One does not need to look far within our current, international community to observe evidence of prejudice, discrimination, stereotyping, civil unrest, and interpersonal/intercultural conflict toward many types of "others," individuals we may see as different from ourselves. These are practices that serve to divide, rather than unite, humanity. (Butler Samuels & Scharff, in press)

Sadly, the ubiquitous fear of "others" is at the core of many of these destructive behaviors (Palmer, 2007), and the US military is no exception (Department of Defense, 2018). Focused care and attention are required to ensure respect for others is at the core of all military-military and military-civilian relations (Department of Defense, 2018). In this chapter, I will describe an empirically validated strategy for developing inclusivity and respect (reducing prejudice) for groups of others that military leaders can adapt to develop troops in their command. This strategy allows leaders and followers to meaningfully contribute to solutions for developing respect between people that when multiplied, has the potential for impacting military organizations around the world. A good idea in the military can travel great distances; conversely, so can a bad idea.

In the preface to the 2010 edition of *Attitudes Are Not Free*, Parco and Levy state:

> Since World War II, the US military has emerged as an iconic example of diversity. In nearly every unit across the armed services, you will find men and women from every race, religion, and creed serving side by side in the defense of our nation. But the diversity evident in today's military

isn't the result of a deliberate strategy to create an inclusive organizational culture as much as the result of an emergent strategy where the
integration of minority groups has been resisted at every turn. Instead,
the military has periodically been directed to make changes at the direction of its civilian leadership to ensure the composition of the armed
forces is reflective of the larger society. (p. 10)

Unfortunately, the military's resistance to integrating minority groups persists today. This is acutely apparent in the military's resistance to fully including
individuals who identify as transgender. Instead, the military implemented an
intentional reversal of policy that had been previously inclusive of transgender
individuals (Department of Defense, 2019). It is deeply disturbing that the military is often not just neutral on issues of diversity or inclusivity—that would be
concerning enough—but is actively resistant to the inclusion of various types of
"others" (Department of Defense, 2019).

In former President Barack Obama's Nobel Peace Prize acceptance speech
(Obama, 2009), Mr. Obama unequivocally stated that a primary goal of military
leadership is to substitute war with peace when possible. For this peace to endure,
he asserted, it must be based on the inherent rights and dignity of every individual. He continued:

As the world grows smaller, you might think it would be easier for
human beings to recognize how similar we are . . . and yet somehow,
given the dizzying pace of globalization, it perhaps comes as no surprise
that people fear the loss of what they cherish in their particular identities—their race, their tribe . . . their religion. In some places, this fear has
led to conflict. At times, it even feels like we're moving backwards. (p. 20)

Many of us did not realize how foreboding these comments would be in
2020. Eleven years after Mr. Obama accepted the Nobel Peace Prize as Commander in Chief of the US Armed Forces, he reminded the American people
that the one constitutional office elected by all the people is the presidency. He
believed that at a minimum, we should expect a president to own a sense of
responsibility for the well-being of all 330 million of us—regardless of what we
look like, how we worship, who we love, how much money we have, or who we
voted for (Obama, 2020).

Over the past decade, my co-authors and I designed high-impact field trip
experiences to develop interpersonal respect. We drew from the literature on
prejudice reduction to develop interventions that involved face-to-face experiences with "others" who had sensory challenges, brain/spinal cord injuries, or
homelessness. We assessed individuals before and after the experiences on their
level of respect for others and compared this to a control group. Our observations and data confirm face-to-face experiences effectively develop respect for
diverse others (Butler Samuels & Scharff, 2021). Based on empirical research, this
chapter will provide guidance for intentionally designing face-to-face experiences

to help develop inclusive and respectful leaders. Discussion includes: 1) effectively selecting and partnering with collaborators, 2) co-creating and implementing intentional objectives for the experience, 3) adequately preparing the leadership team and the participants for the experience, 4) designing the experience based on empirical evidence and the objectives, 5) providing the necessary cognitive and emotional supports for the leadership team and participants, and 6) assessing if objectives were achieved, and revising and improving as necessary.

One of the factors related to the persistence of prejudice and discrimination is individuals have had no meaningful experience with the groups in question (Hewstone & Swart, 2011). They have not experienced their world, their environment, and have no sense of what it might be like to walk in their shoes. With limited information, individuals naturally construct stereotypes—mental shortcuts that often oversimplify what is true about a particular group of people (Kahneman, 2011). Hence, the difficulties between people persist. Certainly, there are computer-based trainings that simulate some of these interactions and may develop one's experience. What our work shows is by creating meaningful face-to-face interactions (in person) and conversations between different groups of individuals, stereotypes are often dismantled, allowing space for truth and opportunities for peace as opposed to conflict.

Before the face-to-face experience, many individuals report sadness or sympathy, difficulty relating, or a sense of foreignness and awkwardness or fear of offending toward the other group. (The response of sadness or sympathy was likely specific to the types of individuals with whom our participants were interacting, i.e., individuals who were experiencing sensory challenges, neurological conditions, or homelessness.) In addition, participants have less knowledge about the other group before the experience. After the experience, individuals commonly report hope or inspiration, empathy or sense of connection, and comfort or approach toward the other group. They also have more knowledge about the other group after the experience. Overall, individuals who have participated in these high-impact experiences start to appreciate they are more similar to the other group than they originally thought. Their mental models shift in the direction of greater respect for the other group (Butler Samuels & Scharff, 2021). These changes in perspective can offer a bridge between groups that fosters enhanced understanding of the "other" and can lead to positive growth and further interaction. Some of the most convincing evidence of this effect is that authentic cross-group friendships often have the highest levels of respect between groups (Hewstone & Swart, 2011).

Educating troops is a critical responsibility of the US military to ensure mission readiness. To this end, the military can benefit from the vast literature regarding how individuals best learn and remember information. One approach to teaching and learning discussed in the literature is integrative education. According to Palmer and Zajonc (2010, vii), "Transformational, or integrative, education involves educating the whole person by integrating the inner life and the outer life, by actualizing individual and global awakening, and by participating in compassionate communities." It is about combining all the meaningful parts of being human and the increasingly formidable challenge of how we live together in our time on earth (Palmer & Zajonc, 2010).

> As those who have done it know, an integrative approach to teaching and learning can get messy. But it gets no messier than life itself, and done well, can help bring order to chaotic raw experience, as in the case with any well-crafted cycle of action and reflection. The real question is whether we want … education to be about life. (p. 36)

By focusing on the development of the individual and how they view the world, the strategy offered here is one attempt to reverse the current resistance in today's military toward different groups of "others," and a way to orient military members in the direction of peace that Mr. Obama calls them to do. This technique for developing respect for others fits squarely within integrative education. It focuses on work that matters (i.e., affecting hearts and minds of people for the greater good) and the responsibility that goes along with doing work that matters. Studies confirm this strategy develops respect, but only if the experiences are intentionally and carefully considered and executed.

Our Previous Research

Over the past decade, my co-authors (Scharff and De Angelis) and I immersed US Air Force Academy cadets in high-impact field trip experiences with different types of "others," individuals they might see as quite different from themselves. We drew from the literature on prejudice reduction and intergroup contact theory specifically (e.g., Allport, 1954; Hewstone & Swart, 2011; Kuh, 2008; Pettigrew, 1997, 1998; Pettigrew & Tropp, 2006, 2008; etc.) to develop interventions that involved face-to-face experiences with "others" who had sensory challenges (deaf/hard of hearing or blind/low vision), neurological conditions (brain/spinal cord injuries), or homelessness. We assessed individuals before and after the experiences on their level of respect for others and compared this to a control group. Our observations and data confirm face-to-face experiences effectively develop respect for diverse others (Butler Samuels & Scharff, 2021).

In addition, we effectively adapted these principles to a senior cadet capstone project on developing inclusive leaders at the US Air Force Academy. Through this experience, we apply lessons learned to intercultural exchanges between cadets and students enrolled in a Buddhist-inspired university. The shared goal of this collaboration is to develop understanding and respect between groups to better meet each university's mission. Paralleling research-focused face-to-face experiences, informal feedback suggests cadets are developing respect through this application-focused experience as well (Butler Samuels & Scharff, 2021).

As an example of one of our high-impact, face-to-face experiences, students enrolled in the sensation and perception course visited a school for the deaf and the blind that included tours of the school led by high school students who were either deaf/hard of hearing or blind/low vision. The tour guides created an environment where our students felt comfortable asking questions about blindness or deafness. Students: (a) toured dorms; (b) navigated their environment with blindfolds, canes, and guides; (c) participated in a sign language class led by a deaf student and staff member; and (d) played goal ball against a team of students from the school for the blind while blindfolded (Butler Samuels & Scharff, 2021). (Note: "goal ball" is played by two blindfolded teams who attempt to roll a ball with a bell inside through the goal zone without it being blocked by the opposite team.)

As a second example, students enrolled in the biopsychology course visited a brain/spinal cord rehabilitation center. The trip included a tour of the state-of-the-art facility and an opportunity to ask questions of the staff. In various iterations of this experience, students engaged in deep interactive conversations with graduates of the program and participated in hands-on activities to better understand life after catastrophic injury. These activities included wheelchair navigation, painting with assistive technology, and virtual reality therapy (Butler Samuels & Scharff, 2021).

We assessed students on a variety of quantitative and qualitative measures before and after the field trip. Regardless of which experience students participated in (sensory challenges, neurological conditions, homelessness), several years of data reliably indicate positive and profound changes in students' thinking about "others." In the written comments, students often spoke about how their eyes were opened through the interactions and how they had more understanding and fewer unfair judgments about the group they recently met. They shared they were more comfortable interacting with these individuals than before and looked forward to interacting with them in the future. In short, they often said these individuals were more like them than they previously realized. These interventions had a positive impact on our students. Anecdotally, it was common for students to tell us several years later how much the experience meant to them and how it changed their perspectives about a particular group of "others" (Butler Samuels & Scharff, 2021).

As briefly referenced above, we began an inclusive leadership collaboration four years ago between our cadets and undergraduates from a Buddhist-inspired university to create powerful, real-world opportunities to *dialogue with difference*, a term that emerged through our work. Through this intercultural experience, we continue to apply lessons learned from the intergroup contact work referenced above. Our practices are taking hold in this new environment and are having a positive impact as evidenced by strong and reliable support from both institutions' administrative leadership, faculty, students, and staff (Butler Samuels & Scharff, 2021). By complementing the research agenda with application of this work to additional settings, we can greatly expand the circle of influence.

6 Steps for Intentionally Designing Face-to-Face Experiences to Develop Respect for Others

1) Effectively selecting and partnering with collaborators
   The leadership team's primary goal is to create a safe space for individuals from different perspectives to meaningfully interact and get to know each

other better. To do this, the team will need to determine which group of "others" to partner with for the greatest benefit and identify a collaborator with relevant expertise at an organization who will help them meet their objectives of developing respect. The team can consider collaborators who are internal to the military base or external in the surrounding community. These groups might include: individuals with sensory challenges, neurological conditions, homelessness, racial/ethnic differences, cultural differences, political differences, variations in sexual orientation or gender identity, or the elderly, etc. When ready, the leadership team can reach out to those organizations, share their idea, and see if they are interested in collaborating with their group toward the same goals (i.e., increased understanding and respect between people). It has worked well for us to create mutually beneficial partnerships, so the leadership team might consider the gains for each institution and openly discuss those with the collaborator. The team can tailor the design to its people and circumstances, and for what makes the most sense.

In our work, we brought military cadets together with individuals who were deaf/hard of hearing, blind/low vision, brain/spinal cord injured, who were experiencing homelessness, or who were of a different cultural background (Buddhist). Field trip planning involved collegial collaboration between us and the field trip site personnel with the ultimate goal of maximizing student learning as well as providing a beneficial experience for individuals at the sites. At each of our field trip sites, we partnered with administrators who shared our commitment for educating the community about its population and program for the greater good. Given our students will be Air Force officers after graduation with international careers, they are natural ambassadors to share information on a myriad of important social issues. Our site collaborators knew this as they invested time and energy in our students. It is plausible this was one of the reasons for our decade-long success with these organizations and something to consider if someone is seeking to build a collaboration with a different organization. That is, mutually beneficial partnerships and intrinsic motivation go a long way. Just like any good relationship, collaborations are an investment of time and energy that require care and attention, but the payoff can be huge.

Before engaging in any intergroup contact experience, I recommend the leadership team reach out to the Diversity and Inclusion Office on base to share their ideas and gather informed feedback. That office may also be willing to partner with the team through the process, serving as an additional expert collaborator. In addition, any plan would need to be communicated through the appropriate channels of command.

2) Co-creating and implementing intentional objectives for the experience
   Intentionality is fundamental to success. Before engaging in any experience, the leadership team and collaborating organization will need to decide on what they hope to achieve through this experience. In our case, we were

intentionally designing an interactive experience to develop interpersonal respect. Once the outcome is determined, the team can design an experience backward to reach that objective. Every decision the leadership team makes should refer back to the outcome and how it meets the mission. If, for any reason, the experience seems to diverge from the original outcome, it should be paused and re-evaluated before resuming.

3) Adequately preparing the leadership team and the participants for the experience

Preparing the leadership team: Intergroup contact experiences, although effective, are dependent on objective knowledge and informed processes. One can imagine casually bringing together two groups of individuals with very different worldviews, and respective emotional convictions may not result in enduring, positive learning and development, but unintentional tension and conflict. Therefore, the leadership team is responsible for learning about the "others." This means becoming well informed about the individuals their troops will be meeting, including reading objectives, scientifically grounded materials, and possibly partnering with an experienced mentor in this area to help answer questions and cross-check design. The mentor ideally would be someone who has intentionally and carefully designed these experiences before and has expertise in this area. In addition to learning about "others," the leadership team should also deeply consider their own relationship to the work and any preexisting schemas and worldviews that might be relevant. Ideally, the team would recognize any potential biases and enter the collaboration and the experience with open minds regarding learning something new. They should also think about how they or their troops might respond emotionally to the experience and be ready to activate supports as needed. Listening and attending to the details of how the experience is affecting participants is paramount.

Preparing participants: As the leadership team is reading objective materials to learn more about the group, they can also share some of those materials with troops before they interact with the other group. Generally, the leadership team may want to provide a short article or video clip with accurate information about the other individuals. For example, when cadets were interacting with individuals who were deaf, they read materials that better helped them understand the nature of being deaf. Again, the mentor or Office for Diversity and Inclusion may be able to help with selecting appropriate materials. In addition, the leadership team should assure participants they will be supported throughout the process.

4) Designing the experience based on empirical evidence and the objectives

Kuh (2008) reports impactful experiences designed to develop diversity and global learning often include explorations of "difficult differences" that expose students to "cultures, life experiences, and worldviews different from their own" (online source, no page number). By following the recommendations here, the leadership team and the collaborator will be co-designing the experience based on empirical evidence. They will need to decide on how to execute the interaction. They may decide a guest speaker, volunteer work, a shared project, or a social gathering would be more appropriate than a field trip. Regardless of the specific path chosen, often when embarking on something new, it is prudent to start small and pilot test the experience. The team may want to limit the number of participants until there is confirmation that the design is sound and effective.

Although there are numerous ways to achieve objectives, if possible, bringing individuals into the actual world of the other group creates powerful and nearly effortless learning. Think of the difference between visiting a school for the deaf and the blind, having that world instantly become apparent through interacting with numerous individuals in their "home" environment, versus meeting with one deaf individual on base. The learning can still be valuable from listening to that individual's story, but it is not the same, nor as vivid, as being in their world. However, a high-impact field trip is often not practical, and resources and logistics need to be considered. Fortunately, there are myriad ways to implement these strategies.

Reflection opportunities can lead to larger changes in personal, citizenship, and social learning outcomes than when they are not included (Bain, 2004). Given intergroup contact often generates emotional and cognitive tension, using reflection to raise student awareness could potentially reinforce and deepen their learning experience (Pettigrew & Tropp, 2008). In the military environment, this might mean providing time for the troops to discuss or write about their impressions from the experience privately or publicly. Ideally, the leadership team and collaborators would moderate such discussions and activities and provide informed feedback and insight.

5) Providing the necessary cognitive and emotional supports for the leadership team and participants

As individuals grapple with the messiness of life and confront their own potential biases, it is imperative their leadership team commits to providing intentional, structured support. Through this work, we have learned it is critical to be responsible, deliberate, sensitive, and supportive when designing experiences to bring diverse others together. Palmer and Zajonc (2010) remind us, "Those of us who want to host conversations that are generative . . . must be intentional about creating spaces that are hospitable to the human spirit as we make ourselves vulnerable to honest exchanges, new ideas, and hopes for change" (pp. 137–138). Individuals need to know they are safe and the leadership team will mentor and guide them through the experience as needed. Given the inherent challenges of intergroup contact, it needs to be sensitively approached with planned supports in place. Supports can include: 1) providing individuals with knowledge about the group they will interact with, 2) providing information about the site they will be visiting, and 3) letting them know that it is understandable to have feelings of concern or anxiety. The leadership team can also reassure them that they will be with them throughout the experience should they need anything then or at a later time.

6) Assessing if objectives were achieved and revising and improving as necessary
   As in any program designed toward continual improvement, it is helpful to acquire evidence of the experience. The leadership team can design objective or subjective questions that can be administered before or after the experience or schedule focus groups to discuss the experience. This data can help determine if outcomes were met and if any changes need to be made moving forward. In our ten years of using these strategies, we have made adjustments every year based on evidence to improve our effectiveness.

Summary

Having real face-to-face experiences and conversations with others whom we see as different from ourselves is not the path of least resistance. It can deeply challenge who we are and what we believe to be true about people and how the world works. Not surprisingly, it tugs at our hearts and minds as human beings. Intergroup contact is about getting comfortable with being uncomfortable, and not running away because it feels better. It requires remaining steadfast in the situation and working through emotions and thoughts so they can inform one's perspective. Just because the work is difficult or "messy," as noted above, does not mean it should not be done or it is not worth the effort. To the contrary, the fact that it is "messy" and calls into question who we are as human beings is an indicator that it is exactly the kind of work we need to be doing. Regarding the Department of Defense, this means generously and regularly funding high-quality endeavors that seek to meaningfully develop interpersonal respect. Our research shows there is significant reward: respect for others can be learned through intentionally designed experiences (Butler Samuels & Scharff, 2021). Through these findings, we are reminded how important perspective taking, characterized by humility and open-mindedness, is when interacting with others. Perspective taking challenges the individual: 1) to engage critical thinking to examine one's background and potential biases, 2) to seek objective and accurate information to inform perspectives, 3) to consider others' perspectives, and 4) to deeply reflect and apply this information when making decisions and/or interacting with others. Learning experiences, such as those described here, create real-world opportunities to practice prosocial thinking and acting in a supported environment. As this body of work is adapted to additional military settings, our hope is for individuals to energetically and regularly apply what they learn in an international, interdependent environment that will continue to demand compassion and respect for all people to promote peace (Butler Samuels & Scharff, 2021).

References

Allport, G. W. (1954). *The nature of prejudice*. Addison-Wesley.

Bain, K. (2004). *What the best colleges teachers do*. Harvard University Press.

Butler Samuels, M. A., & Scharff, F. V. (2021). Applying the scientist-educator model to develop and assess respect for human dignity. *Scholarship of Teaching and Learning in Psychology*. Department of Defense. (2018). *Diversity management and equal opportunity in the DoD*. DODD 1020.02.

Department of Defense. (2019). *Military service by transgender person and persons with gender dysphoria*. DTM-19-004.

Hewstone, M., & Swart, H. (2011). Fifty-odd years of inter-group contact: From hypothesis to integrated theory. *British Journal of Social Psychology, 50*, 374–386. https://doi.org/10.1111/j.2044-8309.2011.02047.x

Kahneman, D. (2011). *Thinking, fast and slow*. Farrar, Straus, & Giroux.

Kuh, G. D. (2008). *High-impact educational practices: What they are, who has access to them, and why they matter*. AAC&U.

Obama, B. H. (2009). A just and lasting peace. https://www.nobelprize.org/prizes/peace/2009/obama/26183-nobel-lecture-2009/

Obama, B. H. (2020). *Speech at the Democratic National Convention, August 20*. http://www.latimes.com

Palmer, P. J. (2007). *The courage to teach*, 10th Anniversary Edition. Jossey-Bass.

Palmer, P. J., & Zajonc, A. (2010). *The heart of higher education*. Jossey-Bass.

Parco J. E., & Levy, D. A. (2010). *Attitudes are not free*. Air University Press.

Pettigrew, T. F. (1997). Generalized intergroup contact effects on prejudice. *Personality and Social Psychology Bulletin, 23*, 173–185. https://psycnet.apa.org/doi/10.1177/0146167297232006

Pettigrew, T. F. (1998). Intergroup contact theory. *Annual Review of Psychology, 49*, 65–85. https://doi.org/10.1146/annurev.psych.49.1.65

Pettigrew, T. F., & Tropp, L. R. (2006). A meta-analytic test of intergroup contact theory. *Journal of Personality and Social Psychology, 90*(5), 751–783. https://doi.org/10.1037/0022-3514.90.5.751

Pettigrew, T. F., & Tropp, L. R. (2008). How does intergroup contact reduce prejudice? *European Journal of Social Psychology, 38*(6), 922–934. https://doi.org/10.1002/ejsp.504

Acknowledgements: I would like to extend my sincerest gratitude to my colleagues Dr. Lauren F. V. Scharff and Dr. Karin De Angelis, US Air Force Academy, Colorado Springs, CO, for partnering with me on this research and to Dr. Gary A. Packard, Jr., currently at the University of Arizona, for helping to inspire this work many years ago. Additionally, this work would not have been possible without the enthusiastic support from the Colorado School for the Deaf and the Blind, Colorado Springs, CO; Craig Hospital, Englewood, CO; Marian House, Colorado Springs, CO; and Naropa University, Boulder, CO.

CHAPTER 41

Leadership Implications of Inclusion as a Scale: Deeper Understanding and Greater Impact[1]

Steven M. Samuels, PhD
Professor, US Air Force Academy

Gary A. Packard Jr., PhD
Dean, College of Applied Science and Technology,
University of Arizona

Aaron M. Oats
Captain, USAF

The Problem

On 6 January 2021, we watched the insurrection in horror as rioters stormed the United States Capitol, literally carrying the banner of the current Commander in Chief who had been legally voted out of office. With a combined eighty years serving our country, we never could have predicted that citizens demonstrating in our nation's capital would be party to sedition. Earlier in the day, when the President of the United States of America appeared to have encouraged the soon-to-be-insurrectionists, there was almost no condemnation from the president's side of the aisle. It was over three hours after the violence started (at 4:17 p.m. Eastern Time; see for example Petras et al., 2021) before the president himself told the insurrectionists to "go home." Even then, many Republicans refused to publicly condemn the action.

This appalling event left five people dead and dozens injured. It is a tragic reminder of the danger of unfounded belief and dichotomous thinking. The insurrection was based on a belief that the 2020 presidential election was "stolen," despite the lack of any actual evidence introduced in nearly ninety legal

---

[1] The views of the authors are their own and do not purport to represent the views of the United States Air Force Academy, the United States Air Force, the Department of Defense, or the United States Government.

court losses (the only court victory concerned a few votes and was overturned at the state supreme court: Post-election lawsuits related to the 2020 United States presidential election, 2021). The polarizing rhetoric emerged from echo chambers created as like-minded people refused to talk with or listen to anyone with an opposing opinion. The result was a mentality that ignored reality, elevated fictitious accusations, and ended with violence and threats of murder, as evidenced by artifacts such as a hanging gallows erected outside the Capitol (see, for example, Mahbubani, 2021).

Over the next few weeks, investigations uncovered "that nearly 1 in 5 people charged over their alleged involvement in the attack on the U.S. Capitol appear to have a military history" (Dreisbach & Anderson, 2021). This despite the fact that all active duty and civilian members of the US military are required to annually attend training that would condemn such an attack. If you serve or have served in the military, we are certain that you sat through multiple required training events on the laws of armed conflict, diversity, sexual assault, suicide prevention, and many other difficult social and ethical issues. We are also certain that, post-training, little changed in your organization's culture.

Our experiences may mirror yours. Often the scenario plays out like the movie *Groundhog Day*, with the same result occurring over and over again. After your unit finishes their annually required training on diversity and inclusion, you are all walking back to the office together. You thought the information was appropriate and the trainer made some excellent points. You ask the group their thoughts. A talented young leader who seems to be respected by their peers says, "If I may be blunt, it was the same thing as last year. Why don't they just send us the PowerPoint to read so we can get back to work quicker?"

You know this isn't the only negative feedback you will hear. Some will see the training as unwelcome advocacy or political correctness that is ruining the organization they love. This was evident in the Trump administration memo stating the "Executive Branch agencies have spent millions of taxpayer dollars to date 'training' government workers to believe divisive, anti-American propaganda" (Vought, 2020). Others see the training as not enough: the time for words is past; we need action! You know that after the training, you will spend more time mediating disagreements than advancing policies and attitudes that genuinely create a more inclusive culture. You have no doubt that a year from now, you will go to a repeat of the training, hear the same complaints, and experience little if any change. You are desperate for better tools that will make a difference but don't know where to turn. Sadly, as the above events have demonstrated, our apathy to civilly and responsibly addressing the divides in our nation have deadly consequences. What we need is to move beyond black and white thinking about our differences and develop training tools that help create an inclusive culture that respects the human dignity of all.

Our goal in this chapter is to propose a tool to help leaders develop that culture. We don't have a magic training program or "easy button" solution. Instead, we turn to the science of socially embedded development to suggest improvements to the climate we so desperately need to cultivate. Instead of a simple dichotomy (inclusive vs. not inclusive), we believe leaders should approach inclusion as a spectrum. We propose a six-stage scale to help leaders create meaningful and sustainable improvements toward inclusive personnel and organizations. We start by clarifying common definitions of diversity and inclusion and use these definitions to propose a model of developing inclusiveness. Finally, we offer practical tips for leaders to leverage this information.

The Objectivity of Diversity vs. the Subjectivity of Inclusion

Before we discuss how to improve inclusion, we want to create a common understanding of the definitions of diversity and inclusion. Mostly, diversity and inclusion are treated synonymously. They are merged to form a catch-all phrase that can mean (depending on your predisposition) "social justice," "improved mission effectiveness," "make everyone feel better," or just "get over it . . . toughen up, buttercup!" Speaking in such generalities allows people to avoid difficult conversations by diluting down to the "correct answer" in a way that precludes thinking deeply about the concepts. Like most training designed to prevent bad outcomes (e.g., suicide prevention, cyber security, interpersonal violence prevention, etc.), the goal seems to be, "When a threat exists, we'll talk around the issue so we can all conclude that we can prevent bad stuff by simply increasing our awareness." Instead, we will choose *not* to simplify the conversation about diversity and inclusion.

We will start with diversity, the more objective of the two terms. Diversity is a demographic variable that describes an agreed-upon difference. In this way, diversity is a basic numerical count of who you have working for you. As a numerical count, diversity can be used as a metric for who is a member of an organization as well as their status. It can lead to rules, such as the Academy of Motion Picture Arts and Sciences (2020) requiring films wishing to be considered for the Oscars to meet specific standards. Another way to use diversity is to define the minimum representation in an organization. For example, US military service academies require that every congressional district is represented. This aspect of admissions is rarely brought up even though it is the *only* diversity quota that exists at any of these institutions.

Inclusion, on the other hand, is much more complex, mostly because it is a more subjective construct. Diversity is commonly defined by the organization, whereas inclusion is internal to individuals. Your unit can decide your placement in a category, but only you know if you feel included. If we think of diversity as who gets into the room, inclusion is how people feel once they're in the room. Just having a seat at the table doesn't mean people are valued for who they are and the skills and perspectives they bring. Notice that once categories are defined, anyone can figure out the diversity of an organization. It is much more difficult for a person from a majority group to tell you about how inclusive an organization is without some way to validate the perspectives of less representative groups.

This creates several problems. A notorious one is the assumption that when a person from a particular minority group speaks, they speak for all members of their group. In fact, asking one person to speak for their entire group by definition lacks inclusiveness; ask yourself, can you think of *any* person in the various groups you belong to that can effectively speak for *all* members? This assumption is nearly always made for minority but not majority groups. For example, the US is a majority Christian nation. A person who identifies as Christian is rarely asked to speak on behalf of all Christians, but a person who is Muslim is often asked to speak on behalf of all members of their faith (especially in areas where Muslims are extreme minorities). This is based on the belief that while my (dominant) group is quite diverse, your (less representative) group is all the same.[2] Of interest, outgroup homogeneity is an organizational problem that can solved by increasing inclusiveness (Mitchell et al., 2015).

These and other such behaviors not only tend to go unnoticed by the majorities, but also often make it difficult for a person in a minority group to explain *why* they don't feel included. When I am in the majority, I am more likely to feel included, making it difficult for me to understand why you don't. If you are part of a majority group, you can see diversity sitting in your unit, but you may not understand how marginalized people feel. Even with the best intentions and policies, it is nearly impossible to know their internal experiences and dialogue.

Framing Inclusion: Simple Dichotomies vs. Developmental Thinking

We realize the paradox above: how do you discover how people feel without asking them, but asking them how they feel as a group member can make them feel less included! To deal with the inclusion complexity described above, we need an organizational schema that is broader than simple dichotomies ("inclusive or not inclusive") but not so broad that it is unmanageable ("all humans are unique").

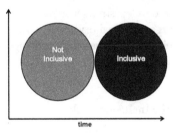

Dichotomies fail, as they create non-overlapping Venn diagrams. Organizations strive to be inclusive by assuming some of their people are in one group ("not inclusive") and thus need to be moved to the other ("inclusive"). This type of thinking necessitates conducting trainings with the goal of moving organizational members to the inclusive category. Such trainings are often based on assuming people are ignorant: if you knew the facts, you would become inclusive. People are clever enough to know what answers leadership wants, and can pass factual tests from such trainings, earning their certificates upon completion. Certified or not, focusing on the idea that people are generally exclusive, and thus need to be made inclusive, is not only bound to fail, but also can lead to more negative attitudes from the people involved (Bezrukova, Jehn, & Spell, 2012; Dobbin & Kalev, 2016; Samuels, 2014, and others).

---

[2] If during this paragraph, you thought, "what kind of Christian? There are so many types!" You are probably in the majority. We don't think about the number of sub-groups for minority religions. How many people thought, "what type of Muslim? There are so many types!"

So how do we create a way to understand inclusion effectively? One approach is to understand how developmental psychologists think. To capture this complexity, they commonly create categories to represent "stages." They assume one stage evolves from an earlier stage in a sequential pattern (e.g., Kohlberg, 1969; Piaget, 1932; etc.). While these categories are not perfect, they are useful in designing programs appropriate for most members of a group who share that stage. Good leaders recognize they cannot move on to more complicated knowledge, skills, or activities until simpler ones are mastered. Whether you are in charge of a special ops team or a middle school math class, the process is the same. Ensure you have a solid assessment to know what your people are capable of at any point, and then add a series of small achievable steps to advance them to the ultimate desired goal (e.g., Bandura, 1977; Vygotsky, 1932; etc.).

Our scale is a tool that leaders can use to develop inclusion in such a manner by defining stages where people and organizations may reside, and in turn, what the next step could be. The scale starts by simply identifying a transition from unacceptable (Intolerance) to barely acceptable (Tolerance). It then increases in complexity and nuance as it moves through intermediate levels (Acceptance and Accommodation) to more advanced ones (Respect and Embodiment).

This scale allows leaders to realize that their people are more than simply inclusive or not inclusive. It then suggests what follow-on steps can be taken to develop stronger inclusion. We must understand both the individual and the organizational readiness of an audience if we hope to effectively develop our people and lead measurable change in our organizational culture. The use of a scale also allows training to be tailored appropriately to an audience: not making it so complex or so simple that it becomes ineffective.

The Inclusion Scale

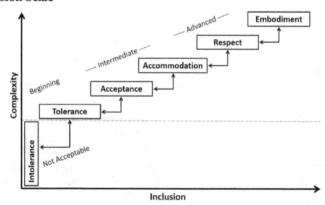

Stage 1—Intolerance: "You can't come in"

Perhaps the simplest definition for intolerance is discrimination: actively not allowing an individual into an organization due to their group status. This is usually overtly stated and agreed upon for either rational or (more often) partisan reasons. One example is women not being allowed to attend US military academies. Before the summer of 1976, the policy was clear, "Women need not apply." Intolerance is often challenged in increments. In 1976, women were also allowed to attend Air Force pilot training with male students for the first time (Tolerance). However, women were not allowed to fly combat aircraft until 1993. Why not? If anything, their smaller size should allow them to handle more *g* force. Intolerance, unless bounded by absolute organizational need[3], inevitably causes harm to the organization, and immediately causes harm to the group not tolerated. It is also the only "not inclusive" stage of the scale, and probably why most people think they are inclusive. If there are only two choices, and you know you are not actively discriminating, you become by definition inclusive. Therefore, you do not need training nor personal development.

Stage 2—Tolerance: "You can come in, but you have to be like us"

If Intolerance is unacceptable for inclusion, the lowest form of acceptable levels would be "Tolerance." As mentioned above, the policy of "Intolerance" based on sex as a criterion to attend a US military service academy legally ended in 1976, when the first classes with women started training. However, Tolerance does not mean acceptance, as it is barely inclusive. One of our authors (Packard) was a cadet at the US Air Force Academy (USAFA) from 1978–1982 as part of the third class with women. When he was a first-year cadet, he clearly remembers faculty members stating publicly in class that they didn't personally believe women belonged. They tolerated their presence but clearly didn't accept it.

Another author (Oats) entered the Academy in 2011 at a time when public statements about women were rarely made by officers. At this point, the inclusion of women in the Academy had clearly advanced, as women were (at least) widely accepted as cadets by their peers and faculty.[4] However, 2011 was significant in that it marked the repeal of the Don't Ask, Don't Tell policy, allowing lesbians, gays, and bisexuals (LGB) to serve openly in the military. Because openly serving LGB cadets were now simply Tolerated as a fact of Academy life, disparaging comments toward them were actively shared by faculty and other commanders. As you can see, Tolerance allows Intolerance to easily slip in.

Those who Tolerate others, perhaps due to this lack of understanding, tend to make "color-blind" (or other-blind, like gender) mistakes. A leader who announces, "I don't see color, I just see Airmen," immediately devalues the identity of all

---

[3] An example of permissible intolerance could be the fitness standards required to enter a military academy, which do not allow service by individuals with a variety of physical disabilities.

[4] Of interest, the third author (Samuels) arrived on faculty in 1993, between the other two authors, as the institution was transitioning between these two states. He clearly remembers the English department holding debates about whether women belonged at USAFA. He asked the dean if it would be appropriate to hold debates asking if African Americans belonged. The practice was stopped shortly thereafter.

military members of color. Like other attempts to develop inclusion at a more complex level, such Tolerant environments often respond with fierce resistance. This may again be because people who are part of such organizations know they are not Intolerant. The classic Tolerant question that follows this logic is, "Why don't we have White male history month?"[5] If the inclusion bar is set by the statement, "I am not a racist," then even Tolerant people don't have much motivation to pursue anti-racist activity leading to more equitable social structures.

Stage 3—Acceptance: "We want you and your differences because of external factors"

Acceptance is the first of the intermediate levels, and it occurs when people and organizations recognize that diversity can make us more effective. An example would be that a diverse group of recruits are needed because the military should represent the people who they are fighting for. The focus here is on the external reasons: it is a part of duty. There can also be a moral component: "It's the right thing to do." While more advanced than the previous two levels of inclusion, Acceptance also comes with problems.

Acceptance often lauds minimal levels of inclusion. Organizations that sponsor "diversity & inclusion events" focused solely around food fall into this category. While food is a wonderful way to share cultures, if the extent of your multi-ethnic endeavors is to have a taco salad, you are probably in the Acceptance level of inclusion. That may be the result of diversity being merely policy and inclusion being a duty. Because of this, confusion can set in with diversity versus inclusion. This may be where many of the problems with using the two words interchangeably starts (see above: "diversity & inclusion events" doesn't actually mean anything). Perhaps the most public Acceptance blunder came when presidential-hopeful Mitt Romney was pushed on why his potential cabinet choices were all men. His response that he obtained "binders full of women" reduced women to a numerical status that were only brought in to fit the diversity need (Binders Full of Women, 2012, among other places). Hiring or promoting anyone for the sole reason that they belong to a certain group is certainly Acceptance's greatest flaw.

Stage 4—Accommodation: "We welcome you because you benefit us"

More than any reason (other than legal, perhaps), organizations seek diversity and inclusion changes in order to improve. There is a large research literature showing that diversity and inclusion benefit decision-making and outcomes in team settings. While they are not as efficient (as fast) as homogenous groups, they are more likely to come up with unique solutions and deal much better with novel situations (e.g., Siebold, 2006 for the military). You don't need to be a behavioral scientist to realize this must be true: multiple perspectives inevitably yield more creative solutions, crucial in novel situations (see Samuels & Samuels, 2010 for benefits in wartime). If you recognize that diversity is good for your organization,

---

[5] The classic answer is, "Every month is White male history month."

you are probably in the Accommodation level of inclusion: the focus on productivity, the basic fact that your organization is better off when it is diverse, and when those diverse people feel included.

While Accommodation creates value for members of marginalized groups, the problem is that the need is still outcome-focused: if members feel included, then organizational productivity increases. That's a step in the right direction, but it still does not place human value on the member as a person. This oversimplification can lead to several potential mistakes. The first clear one is labeling. This can lead to recruiting anyone who fits a certain group, regardless of whether they represent that group well. It is often easier to try and diversify an organization by finding someone who fits a desired category in one area but is exactly the same in every other category. Perhaps this is what Senator Lindsey Graham was thinking when he said, "I care about everybody. If you're a young African American [or] an immigrant, you can go anywhere in [South Carolina], you just need to be conservative not liberal" (Dzhanova, 2020, among others). This undermines the benefits of diversity, and creates problems with inclusion for others in the same category: "Why can't you act like that person? S/He is one of the 'good ones'" (Johnson, 2001).

Stage 5—Respect: "Your personal unique perspective is crucial"

As we move into the more advanced stages of inclusion, complexity goes up and problems go down. By the time people and organizations reach Respect, they show value for each diverse member as an individual. In this stage, members are more than just organizational assets, not simply anonymous representatives of their group. Now they are valued for skills as well as the categories they inhabit. Once leaders and organizations realize their people are more than just their most visually obvious identity, they can take the time to get to know them and their individual needs.

While the problems are not at the same levels as those mentioned earlier, there are some complications. Respect for diverse members tends to be internal. Two-way, trusting conversations between marginalized and privileged group members are, by definition, private. Even if it is an institutional norm, active role-modeling still needs to occur. Thus, learning can be incidental, and respect can sometimes be reactive. It often takes a major divisive issue to bring matters to a forefront. In many departments at USAFA, the events of 2020 and the Black Lives Matter movement, coupled with the reaction of the Trump administration, has caused great pain for members. Working through these issues at both private and public levels is necessary for healing to occur. Thus, Respect is easier for individuals to practice, but harder for organizations to reach.

Stage 6—Embodiment: The culmination of personal internalizing and organizational normalizing belongingness

With regard to nearly all developmental scales, the uppermost stage tends to be the least well-defined. Our scale is no different, and we have struggled with conceptually defining a stage that seems to defy description. Perhaps this is because there is no endpoint to any aspect of human development short of the end of life.

As a result, the last stage of most developmental theories is frequently described as a process whereby individuals continue to refine what is learned earlier in life rather than acquiring a new way of thinking: for example, Piaget's formal operations (1932) or Kohlberg's post-conventional reasoning (1969). The highest stage of one of the most well-known theories in psychology, Maslow's (1943) hierarchy of needs, is self-actualization, a similarly abstract concept described as becoming "everything one is capable of becoming" (p. 382).[6] For our end stage, Embodiment best describes a continuous journey of improving one's perspective taking and empathy toward others. Embodiment is a drive to genuinely and fully embrace the goal of vicariously experiencing events through the lives of others in our community. For example, in a recent Zoom faculty meeting, one author (Packard) listened as a faculty member expressed genuine sorrow when one of her students shared that he had just lost his pet hedgehog. She put aside any preconceptions of hedgehogs and personally experienced her student's grief as if it were her own. She saw the loss of the student's pet through his eyes, not her own. This is the essence of embodying another person's live experience and leads to a profound sense of empathy of that person's reality.

When applied to inclusion, we embody a person's perspective when we experience a phenomenon such as the #MeToo movement through the eyes of a survivor and not through the eyes of a bystander, or the Black Lives Matter movement through the eyes of a person of color and not (for two of the authors) our own White experiences. Embodiment is an intrinsic drive to take on the perspectives of *all* others. Operating at this level of inclusion is proactive, transparent, empathic, and internal. Respect is public and defines the community culture. For an organization, Embodiment is normalized in the culture when inclusion becomes the water in which we swim.[7] We don't always see or notice it, but it supports the organization's efforts to ensure all members have a sense of belonging equally shared throughout the community.

Leadership Implications and Applications

First Things First: Leaders Must Set the Example

Before we offer leadership suggestions, there is a fundamental issue that needs to be addressed. In order to effectively leverage the model, leaders must first look in the mirror and assess their own inclusive readiness. Earlier in this chapter, we described an example of the color-blindness common to the Tolerance stage of our model: "I don't see color, I just see Airmen." We would love to say that this incident happened many years ago, said by a person in lower or middle

---

[6] Maslow's theory is technically not a developmental theory. However, the hierarchical nature of his theory is complimentary to the developmental theories mentioned above.

[7] From David Foster Wallace's inspiring 2005 Kenyon College graduation address, *This Is Water*, for the concept of the water in which we swim (see https://fs.blog/2012/04/david-foster-wallace-this-is-water/). Foster Wallace, in turn, almost certainly obtained the story from traditional Zen Japanese lore.

management. Unfortunately, it was a very recent and public event, said by an Air Force brigadier general. Two of the authors sitting in the audience watched the chilling effect of that general's words on the body language of officers and enlisted of color. Leaders set the culture for their organizations (Schein, 2010). Thus, we would expect Tolerant leaders to set Tolerant organizational cultures. Even if the leaders parrot more inclusive guidance from above, their bias is certain to be revealed in their personal rhetoric and behavior.

Thus, our first and most important suggestion is that if leaders want to significantly improve inclusion in their organization, they must start by acknowledging their own privilege and work to remedy their own explicit and implicit biases. They must do the difficult work of honestly identifying their weaknesses, and then strive to improve. To this end, if your organization is dominated by a majority of White males (e.g., most of the US military), understand that this status holds a positive form of privilege. Therefore, a leader must be intentional about constructively confronting privilege as a vital part of the inclusion conversation.

Working with the Scale

At this date, our scale has not been psychometrically assessed. However, that does not prevent its use as a tool to assist leaders in building more inclusive cultures in their organizations. The statistician George Box is noted for coining the aphorism, "All models are wrong, but some are useful." While we are currently in the testing phase of the model, we are still quite confident of several things. Most importantly, we know inclusion is not dichotomous. We also know that not everyone will go through every stage in a set order. And we do know that people are at different stages for different groups of people. One person could be Respectful of race, Tolerant of gender, Intolerant of sexual orientation, etc. Thus, to support development in their people and organizations, leaders should think carefully about the scale.

While our scale would be useful for trainers to better understand their audiences, we believe it is most effective for leaders seeking to improve their unit culture. Again, when leaders think about inclusion as a static dichotomy of inclusive or not inclusive, they are unable to take advantage of the processes that help create environments for helpful dialogue. When operating from a dichotomous world view, it is almost impossible to counter the claim, "I am not a racist." However, when leaders use the scale as a tool, they can acknowledge a person's perspective that they are not a racist and also thoughtfully bring in the perspectives of people in the organization who do not feel included.

For example, when one of the authors (Packard) was conducting a briefing on changes to transgender service policy, he was asked by an audience member to not spend the hour politically correct bashing of his beliefs. Rather than challenging the belief (what Legault et al., 2007, calls an "internal locus of causality"), Packard acknowledged the emotional concern of the audience member and asked for his participation to support the policy as stated by the organization out of his sense of duty (Acceptance). By not engaging in a conversation about the value of Respect or Embodiment, Packard lowered the emotionality of the conversation for everyone in the room. The use of the scale in this matter creates space for contemplation and processing of new information instead of engaging in a likely ineffective passionate debate. Leaders can now be more likely to create productive rather than destructive conversations.

The crux of the issue is that dichotomies highlight the stark, stereotypical divides between groups and often lead to the majority defending their privilege rather than trying to understand marginalized perspectives. Without the active participation of the better-represented group, lasting positive change has little chance of occurring (Dover et al., 2015). The use of a scale versus a dichotomy provides an opportunity to address important inclusion issues without coming off as accusatory, aggressive, or politically correct.

Conversations at the Cusps

Meaningful interpersonal contact does not come in the form of PowerPoints that present factual information in a one-size-fits-all manner. Inclusion is advanced by leaders who regularly engage in productive conversations that allow people to understand diverse perspectives without defensiveness. Our goal in conceptualizing inclusion as a scale is to provide leaders with a tool that will allow them to invite people to the conversation rather than requiring them to listen to why they are wrong. Therefore, it would be disingenuous to provide a laundry list of approved solutions to these types of conversations. However, we do want to highlight that conversations should target transitions from one stage to the next (Samuels, Packard, & Butler, 2019). We hope these ideas spark your creativity as you design useful conversations in your organizations.

- Intolerance → Tolerance: There is only one position for a leader hoping to move people from intolerance to tolerance: clear messaging that intolerance is unacceptable. President Trump's refusal to condemn White supremacy groups during the first presidential debate on 29 Sep 2020 (Gabbatt, 2020, among others) was met with surprise, and members of his party immediately afterward stood up and said it was unacceptable not to condemn them (Wu, 2020, among others). In contrast, USAFA's Superintendent, Lt Gen Jay Silveria (2017) sent a clear message to the Cadet Wing after a racist incident at the USAFA Preparatory School: "If you can't treat someone with dignity and respect, you need to get out."

- Tolerance → Acceptance: Strong leaders should be active when experiencing color- (and other-) blindness. Sometimes, merely asking a question as to why that can seem hurtful to some people can start a deep conversation. Meyerson (2008) suggests that "Verbal Jujitsu" can be helpful. The idea is to ask a question that doesn't challenge the speaker's personal beliefs but seeks clarification in a way that pulls the conversation in a more productive direction. The above example of Packard addressing a resistant Airman during a transgender policy brief is a perfect example of this.

- Acceptance → Accommodation: Finding examples of how diversity increases effectiveness can be useful in this transition. Our USAFA students find a particularly powerful example occurred during recent conflicts in Muslim countries. Soldiers and Marines would enter villages and search for weapon caches. They discovered local women knew where such caches were hidden and wanted them removed (as they posed a danger to families). However, culturally, these women could not speak to male service members. Reports from those deployed in Iraq and Afghanistan soon came flooding back that any military woman, regardless of her job, was immediately recruited by such combat units and brought into villages to speak with the local women.

- Accommodation → Respect: We have often heard "respect needs to be earned," but in this case, we would argue, "respect needs to be modeled." Again, as a leader, you set the tone for your unit. Leaders at the Accommodation level recognize that different group members have different needs and are able to give exemptions when their people ask for them. Leaders at the Respect level are aware of those diversities and actively *educate themselves* to their people's needs (e.g., know ahead of time when their Jewish members may be fasting for Yom Kippur or their Muslim members fasting for Ramadan).

- Respect → Embodiment: All we can say is if you and your organization are here, congratulations! One of the best things you can do is continue to create opportunities that sustain and nurture your inclusive culture and educate others with your successes (and failures). This might include stepping outside of your comfort zone by attending artistic performances that deal with complexities of diversity, building panels that further educate on marginalized groups, combining social activities with interpersonal growth, and finding ways for people to share their own journeys toward self-development.

Conclusion

In his book *How to Be an Antiracist* (2019), Ibram Kendi states, "When policies fail, do not blame the people. Start over and seek out new and more effective antiracist treatments until they work" (p. 232). The goal of this chapter is to acknowledge that our current approach to improving inclusion within organizations is not working. Year after year (including an "Extremism Stand Down" just announced by the SECAF, 11 February 2021) we perpetuate the status quo with well-intentioned training that often causes more harm than good. People are left defensive or wanting, then they return back to their work convinced they are not racist, sexist, or homophobic because they certainly aren't a part of the Intolerant group defined in the training. Our goal with our inclusion scale is to stop blaming people for failed policy and seek out a new and better approach to sustained improvements to inclusive cultures.

If we truly believe military strength depends on genuine inclusion, and we further believe people have the right to be included simply by the fact they are a part of the human race, then dichotomous thinking that allows for mere toleration is insufficient. Strength requires at least Acceptance and, ultimately, Respect on the path toward Embodiment for all who volunteer to serve. At a minimum, we must at least embrace the reality that when the bullets are flying, what matters is the training and ability of the person fighting alongside you. That ability will be positively or negatively impacted by how honestly we respect the human dignity of *all* people in our organizations. By focusing on their needs, and recognizing them for who they are, we know that we can count on them and they, in turn, can count on us (Samuels & Packard, 2012).

Works Cited

Academy of Motion Picture Arts and Sciences. (2020, September 8). Academy established representation and inclusion standards for Oscars® eligibility. https://www.oscars.org/news/academy-establishes-representation-and-inclusion-standards-oscarsr-eligibility.

Bandura, A. (1977). *Social learning theory*. Prentice-Hall.

Bezrukova, K. Jehn, K. A., & Spell, C. S. (2012). Reviewing diversity training: Where we have been and where we should go, *Academy of Management Learning & Education, 11*(2), 207–227. http://dx.doi.org/10.5465/amle.2008.0090

Binders Full of Women (2012, October 16). Mitt Romney discusses how he found women for his cabinet at the second presidential debate [Video]. YouTube. https://www.youtube.com/watch?v=g2MeJYPL_ow

Dobbin, F. & Kalev, A. (2016, Jul–Aug). Why diversity programs fail. *Harvard Business Review, 94*(7), 52–60. https://hbr.org/2016/07/why-diversity-programs-fail

Dover, T. L., Major, B., & Kaiser, C. R. (2015). Members of high-status groups are threatened by pro-diversity organizational messages. *Journal of Experimental Social Psychology, 62*, 58–67. http://dx.doi.org/10.1016/j.jesp.2015.10.006

Dzhanova, Y. (2020, October 10). Sen. Lindsey Graham says Black people are free to "go anywhere" in South Carolina so long as they're conservative, *Business Insider*. https://www.businessinsider.com/graham-black-people-go-anywhere-in-south-carolina-if-conservative-2020-10

Gabbatt, A. (2020, September 30). Trump's refusal to condemn white supremacy fits pattern of extremist rhetoric, *The Guardian*. https://www.theguardian.com/us-news/2020/sep/30/trump-white-supremacy-extremist-rhetoric

Johnson, A. G. (2001) *Privilege, power, and difference*. Mayfield Publishing Company.

Kendi, I. X. (2019). *How to be an antiracist.* One World.

Kohlberg, L. (1969). Stage and sequence: The cognitive developmental approach to socialization. In D. A. Goslin (Ed.), *Handbook of socialization theory and research* (pp. 347–480). Rand McNally.

Legault, L., Green-Demers, I., Grant, P., & Chung, J. (2007). On the self-regulation of implicit and explicit prejudice: A self-determination theory perspective. *Personality and Social Psychology Bulletin, 33*(5), 732–749. https://doi.org/10.1177/0146167206298564

Meyerson, D. E. (2008). *Rocking the boat: How tempered radicals effect change without making trouble*. Harvard Business Press.

Mitchell, R., Boyle, B., Parker, V., Giles, M., Chiang, V., & Joyce, P. (2015). Managing inclusiveness and diversity in teams: How leader inclusiveness affects performance through status and team identity. *Human Resource Management, 54*(2), 217–239. https://doi.org/10.1097/hmr.0000000000000088

Piaget, J. (1932). *The moral judgment of the child*. Kegan, Paul, Trench, Trubner & Co.

Samuels, D. R. (2014). *The culturally inclusive educator: Preparing for a multicultural world*. Teachers College Press.

Samuels, S. M. & Packard, G. A., Jr. (2012, February 6). Repeal of DADT makes military stronger, *Air Force Times*, p. 24.

Samuels, S. M., Packard, G. A. Jr., & Butler, M. A. (2019, November). *Deconstructing the inclusion dichotomy: Deeper understanding from a nuanced scale*. Poster presented at the 2019 ACMHE Annual Convention, Amherst, MA.

Samuels, S. M., & Samuels, D. R. (2010). Incorporating the concept of privilege into policy and practice: Guidance for leaders who strive to create sustainable change. In J. E. Parco, D. A. Levy, & F. R. Blass (Eds.) *Attitudes aren't free: Thinking deeply about diversity in the U.S. Armed Forces* (pp. 321–341). AU Press.

Silveria, J. (2017, September 29). *Hear Lt. Gen. Jay Silveria's full speech about racism at the Air Force Academy*. https://www.youtube.com/watch?v=mU0RfhvYN8s

Vought, R. (2020, September 4). Memorandum M-20-34: Training in the Federal Government. https://www.whitehouse.gov/wp-content/uploads/2020/09/M-20-34.pdf.

Vygotsky, L. S. (1929). The problem of the cultural development of the child, *Journal of Genetic Psychology, 36*, 415–434.

Wu, N. (2020, September 30). Republicans in Congress say Trump should have directly condemned white supremacists at presidential debate, *USA Today*. https://www.usatoday.com/story/news/politics/elections/2020/09/30/gop-senators-trump-should-have-directly-condemned-white-supremacists/3571277001/

CHAPTER 42

A CALL TO ACTION: THE THRIVE PROJECT AT USAFA

The powerful contributions in the first four sections of this book collectively send a strong message: *It is imperative that we create and sustain organizations that both support each individual's thriving and support the achievement of organizational missions.*

To this end, over the past three years, a team of scholars at the US Air Force Academy (USAFA) has embarked upon a systematic exploration of the construct *thriving*. We have defined thriving as *a positive and energizing state that emerges when individual and system needs are fulfilled within a symbiotic relationship.* We propose that *thriving* is at the heart of organizations that meet the core human needs of the members as well as the organization's imperative for effectiveness.

> People in the Air Force are busy: we fly, teach, lead, and have families, but when you offend others because you're ignorant, that's entirely on you. People might not value diversity for the beautiful thing that it is, but when you ostracize a team member, willingly or unwillingly, the entire team suffers. (Acevedo)

Suffice it to say that thriving likely exists to some degree when we point to those rare individuals in our organizations and say, "That person is on fire." They wake up excited to come to work, are energized by their work and those around them, and perform brilliantly. We think the average organization has a small percentage of its population in the "thriving" category. Imagine what an organization would look like, what it could accomplish, if 80 or 90 percent of the members of the organization experienced thriving. We have to use our imaginations to visualize this, because it simply doesn't exist. At least we haven't found it yet.

Developing a comprehensive understanding of thriving and how to enable it is still in its early stages. In this section we present our conceptual understanding of *thriving*—elaborating on our conceptualization of what thriving means and what we propose are critical considerations for leaders who wish to enable thriving within their organizations. First, let us recap the first four sections of this book to underscore why the notion of thriving is so important. Section I presented publicly available excerpts from some of our country's current and past leaders, a sampling of the rhetoric that contributed to our collective thinking about diversity, inclusion, and equity as reflected by events and experiences that occurred during this recent period in history. In Section II, past and present military leaders shared their perspectives about how the military has handled various aspects of diversity, for better or worse. Section III showcased the experiences of military personnel in ways that might help us better understand how the treatment the contributors experienced shaped their lives and careers. In Section III, we also asked readers to reflect upon and discuss critical questions intended to bring each of us into the mindset of processing how the stories of others intercept with our current reality and to reflect upon how we want to *be*, how we *need to be* both personally and institutionally to foster environments where the members of the organization and the organization itself are *thriving*. In Section IV, scholars presented their research, bringing to the forefront some of the theory, tools, and conceptual contributions to the body of knowledge needed to support our efforts to enable thriving.

The Way Forward

We invite you to join the members of the Project Thrive Team at USAFA as we consider two questions:

- How do we more deeply understand thriving as a positive and energizing state that is evidenced when individual and system needs are fulfilled within a symbiotic relationship?
- Given your understanding, how do you enable and sustain thriving environments within your organization?

As we share our thinking about thriving and articulate a way forward, it is important to discuss the precursors that support thriving and must be incorporated when fostering environments where thriving occurs. The Project Thrive team searched for existing theory that might shed light on our early conceptualizations of thriving; self-determination theory (Deci & Ryan, 1980) struck us as relevant. Self-determination theory (SDT), which has been empirically studied for over forty years, suggests that human beings have three innate psychological needs that must be met in order for them to experience subjective well-being (Ryan & Deci, 2000). These needs are *autonomy, competence,* and *relatedness.*

It became clear that SDT explained the criticality of individual needs satisfaction. However, to focus solely on the individuals' needs seemed woefully inadequate in the context of a larger system. The individual exists within an environment, and the environment (e.g. organization or other human system) has its own desired ends. The following question arose: what are the precursors that enable thriving in the symbiotic relationship between individual and organization? This led to the transmutation of our original conceptualization of thriving to include explicit reference to the role organizations play in creating environments where individuals can experience thriving *and* the organizational goals are attended to.

As Chuck Bush (see chapter 25) was fond of saying, "Diversity is a leadership issue," and we broadened this statement to include diversity as embedded within the thriving construct; autonomy, competence, and relatedness have diverse expressions depending on the individual. The satisfaction of these core needs is aided by a variety of variables, unique to some extent for each person.

Through experience, we noticed that organizations often operate without adequate consideration for the universal human needs of autonomy, competence, and relatedness. Take the experience of a maintenance officer who utilizes standard operating procedures to repair an airplane. The SOPs are there for good purpose: to be able to diagnose a problem and resolve it. We also know that the interrelated triad of autonomy, competence, and relatedness can be brought to bear in critical situations, enabling system members to think and act outside of the stated parameters to achieve desirable ends. Yet systems often create and reify rigidity in order to control what happens, thwarting not only individual needs but disabling the realization of system requirements. We propose that there is a dynamic flow inherent in the relationship between individual and system, which demands the application of periodic assessment by both elements lest the symbiotic state be thrust into an unproductive imbalance. This imbalance can manifest as stifling, unwelcome, or unjust treatment of individuals and/or non-optimal system production and output. When considering the interdependence between the individual and larger system, the satisfaction of the needs for autonomy, competence, and relatedness were essential but did not paint the full picture of an effective system, of which the individuals are an integral part. We proposed that thriving requires individual agency, self-efficacy, and belonging.

As you reconsider the chapters in Section III, you will notice that the precursors required for thriving (agency, self-efficacy, and belonging) within the larger system were often lacking. The authors may not have used the terms agency, self-efficacy, and belonging in their discussions, but if you revisit the essays from the vantage point of thriving, we're sure you will identify the connections. To actualize thriving, the message is clear to us that leaders must create organizations with cultures that enable agency, self-efficacy, and belonging in abundance. Let's take a brief look at these three components:

Agency

"I told myself it was time to crawl back under my rock if I was going to succeed at this base." (France)

Autonomy as experienced by an individual, when considering the relationship between individual and system, must translate into agency. Agency is a perceived ability of the person to influence their environment in addition to experiencing a sense of freedom within it (Bandura, 1989). Given the symbiotic relationship between the individual and the system, it is clear that the individual must have the agency within the social and technical aspects of a given system in order to utilize his or her autonomy to make decisions and undertake tasks utilizing his or her skills, talents, and strengths.

Self-efficacy

"I fought this battle for over ten years, complaining at every single developmental team meeting and, on at least two occasions, to the commander of the Air Force Personnel Center." (France)
"The commandant's staff assigned me to give tours to VIP guests of the superintendent from Harmon Hall for three weeks. I had little guidance and no supervision or aptitude retraining. Next, I worked as an Element Leader for BCT. Again, no real review of my performance." (Smith)

Competence, or the sense that one has the skills and training required to accomplish a task, connects with the belief that an individual can influence their environment through the application of their skills and training. This dovetails with self-efficacy (Bandura, 1982), which considers the extent to which an individual can exercise their competence within the larger environment in order to impact system outputs.

Belonging

"I had lost my sense of belonging until I entered my teenage years, when I started to develop physically and became more involved in athletics. The fact that I was different began to fade away because the people I began to associate with had one thing in common: we all wanted to win." (Clark)
"The whole 'never leave a man behind' attitude didn't exist—at least not for me." (Grant)
"Silence. What keeps us silent whether witnessing someone being harmed, or being harmed yourself? Fear keeps you silent, fear of your boss or coworker's retribution, fear of ending up in the out group. Fear keeps us where we're at and silence, silence is the face of that fear." (Grant)

The next logical transformation from SDT involved expanding relatedness to belonging, where the individual experiences "community, support, membership and acceptance" within the larger system (Strayhorn, p. 6, 2019). The individual must not only have functional relationships at the local level within the system, but must experience belonging—not simply inclusion, but full membership in the system and all that entails, without question. Only when there is a constant attention to enabling a thriving environment can the system reach its highest potential. This perspective highlights what Kurt Lewin posited: behavior is a function of the person and their environment (citation). The two are interdependent.

The Critical Role of Leaders

"What gets emphasized by leadership gets results." (Barrientes)
"I joined the Air Force to serve a greater purpose, so if I am
going to lead change, I want to do so in partnership with everyone
around me who took an oath to defend our Constitution." (Levy)
"Finally, on October 13, 2010, Secretary of the Air Force
Michael Donley promulgated Air Force Policy Directive 36-70,
Personnel: Diversity, which commences with the statement:
'Diversity is a military necessity.' Diversity is a leadership issue."
(Bush)

As you read the stories in Sections II and III, there is a duality. Each person could be deemed successful in terms of rank or accomplishment, how they were/are regarded by their peers, and how they are rewarded. This might lead us to the thinking, "If you suck it up, if you push through, if you work hard enough, anyone can make it. See, they did!" The accounts contradict this assertion by showing us time and time again that the stories were told by wounded warriors. They may not have been wounded in the way we think of the combat wounded. But they, in ways often unseen, have had parts of themselves hobbled, incapacitated, or destroyed. By friendly fire.

Martinez's story exemplified the need for a coordinating, facilitating, support-ive role leaders must assume within the thriving process:

> Although we were all communicating in the same language, misunder-standings led to frustration, apathy, and in almost all initial cases, fail-ure to clear the objectives. Through an entire sequence of exercises and debriefs we were too focused on the wrong causes to realize it was our assumptions about each other that were getting in the way. Only when an outsider pointed it out were we able to quickly recover. The days and challenges continued to pile on. From an officer struggling to stay awake because he, unbeknownst to his teammates, skipped meals with the goal of saving money, to foul play during the field leadership exercise that was simply blamed on the opponent. At every turn we faced obstacles driven by our own over or underestimation of each other's abilities, intentions, and backgrounds.

The scenario depicted by Martinez is all too common. In it we see that neither the individuals nor the system has its needs met, limping from task to task in a tangled maze of faulty assumptions and weak structures. The USAFA Thrive Team proposes that the fulcrum of the thriving process is owned by leaders who see and transmit the big picture, and who guide and facilitate the processes using their positional power to ensure both individual need achievement as well as organizational effectiveness. This proposition pointedly layers additional obliga-tions onto a leader's plate. This may seem overwhelming at first. However, as indi-viduals increase their agency, self-efficacy, and increasingly experience belonging, we hypothesize that some, if not many, of the day-to-day burdens currently on the shoulders of a single leader may be taken on by the talented and skilled individuals who ache to more fully achieve their needs, which in this symbiotic relationship plays a vital role in driving organizational success.

Where do we go from here?

The Project Thrive team has examined a number of existing methods and interventions for organizational change and effectiveness. One of the most promising is a method we call B.A.R, which stands for baseline, action, results (DePorres et al., 2018). B.A.R. is a form of action research and has several properties that align closely with helping systems enable thriving. Users of B.A.R. identify the context in which thriving is not optimal and undertake a collaborative data-gathering process to determine the baseline, or initial state, conditions, and variables involved. With this baseline, and a picture of the desired state shared across the stakeholders of the issue, the group transitions to taking action. When taking action, B.A.R. departs from common approaches and hones in on the micro-actions that can be quickly and easily executed that will ideally help the system move toward the desired state, but more importantly help the system generate knowledge about itself and the problem at hand.

The B.A.R. process quickly gives rise to new knowledge, and is seen by those engaged in it as generative and "value-added." This accomplishes a number of (things): the knowledge generated is experienced as positive. While the barriers to enabling thriving will not be resolved with one action, those engaged in the process definitely experience progress and renewal, as the knowledge generated can be applied immediately. Another benefit of engaging in the B.A.R. approach is that it can be done in perpetuity, addressing issues and taking advantage of opportunities to enable thriving.

The beauty of the B.A.R process is that there is no claim to having correct answers before the journey begins, which is fortunate since the answers regarding how best to create environments where every member can thrive are likely quite complex. What we can say definitively is that we feel strongly that this journey toward thriving is one that must be taken if we are to address the pressing issues discussed in this book. You know you're successful when you are creating environments where more and more people are experiencing agency, efficacy, and belonging. We wish you luck on this important journey.

References

Bandura, A. (1982). Self-efficacy mechanism in human agency. *American Psychologist*, *37*(2), 122–147. https://psycnet.apa.org/doi/10.1037/0003-066X.37.2.122

Bandura, A. (1989). Human agency in social cognitive theory. *American Psychologist*, *44*(9), 1175–1184. https://doi.org/10.1037/0003-066x.44.9.1175

Deci, E.L., & Ryan, R. M. (1980). The empirical exploration of intrinsic motivational processes. In L. Berkowitz (Ed.), *Advances in experimental social psychology* (Vol. 13, pp 33–80). Academic.

DePorres, D., Ferrante, C., Levy, D., Preston, J., & Tucker, E. (Fall 2018). Raising the bar: a call to action. *Organization Development Journal, 36*(3), 45. https://www.researchgate.net/publication/328626998_Raising_the_bar_A_call_to_action

Ryan, R.M., & Deci, E.L. (2000). Self-determination theory and the facilitation of intrinsic motivation, social development, and well-being. *American Psychologist, 55*(1), 68–78. https://psycnet.apa.org/doi/10.1037/0003-066X.55.1.68

Strayhorn, T.L. (2019). College students' sense of belonging; a key to educational success for all students. Routledge.

Epilogue
The Coming Federal Divide in America[1]

Amit Gupta, PhD

Over the next twenty-five years, spatial and demographic shifts will create major changes within the American political system: by 2040, it is estimated that eight states will have 50 percent of the population, and another seven states will have an additional 25 percent of the populace; second, by 2045, the minorities in the United States become a majority, making it the first Western nation to have moved to this status. The United States, therefore, is going through a major spatial and demographic transition that will reshape the relations between the fifty states. The conservative political scientist Norman Ornstein has argued that as a result of this spatial realignment of the population, the presidency will be determined by older white voters living in sparsely populated states (because the American system of the Electoral College will give these states a continued advantage in determining the election results).[2] This report argues that while institutional power may remain in the hands of the demographically older, sparsely populated, and conservative states, the states with the largest populations will have the demographic resources and be at the center of the knowledge economy that the United States is fast becoming. The rich, educated, multicultural, and multiethnic states, therefore, are going to rewrite the terms of their relationship with the poorer, more homogenous, and educationally backward states—most likely to the disadvantage of the poorer states. Further, the more populated states may be able to bring out some significant changes in the social and economic policies of the less populated states, for if the latter seek investments and work forces from these more populated states, they will have to adapt their policies to satisfy investors.

Additionally, this spatial and demographic shift will be influenced by a gender transition, which sees more women in positions of power and influence, and the transition from the baby boomers to the millennials in the economy. Such

---

[1] This manuscript has been authorized for republication by the Forum of Federations (Occasional Paper Series, Number 64, 2022). For more information about the Forum of Federations and its publications, please visit www.forumfed.org

[2] Ornstein's interview on the subject was cited in Phillip Bump, "In about 20 years, half the population will live in eight states," *The Washington Post*, July 12, 2018.

shifts will shape the domestic clash of civilizations as some religious and alt-right groups continue to push back against progressive values.

Demographic Transition

The US Census Bureau has calculated that by 2045, more than half of all Americans are projected to belong to a minority group; thus the United States will be the first Western nation that sees a significant racial shift in its composition as the minority becomes the majority.[3] Despite the best efforts of Stephen Miller (senior advisor to the Trump White House) and the Trump Administration to halt immigration and to try and reverse this demographic shift, it seems that the transformation of America may happen sooner than later. Recently released statistics show how rapidly this shift is taking place in the youngest demographic cohort of Americans: while in 1997, over 63 percent of the 46.1 million US public school students were White, now White students comprise just 49.7 percent of the 50 million students enrolled.[4] The significance of this shift cannot be underestimated even though in the United States it is seen largely in terms of electoral politics and voting calculations. The real significance lies in the fact that we will see cultural and foreign policy shifts that will have far-reaching consequences for public policy within the United States and in how the country views its role in world affairs.

The demographic shift has already led to a cultural change in terms of the representation of Americans on television shows, in advertisements, in cuisine, and in university courses. Joe Biden repeatedly referred to this shift in a speech commemorating the 100th anniversary of the Tulsa Massacre:

> And although I have no scientific basis of what I'm about to say, but those of you who are over fifty—how often did you ever see—how often did you ever see advertisements on television with Black and White couples? Not a joke. I challenge you—find today, when you turn on the stations—sit on one station for two hours. And I don't know how many commercials you'll see— eight to five—two to three out of five have mixed-race couples in them. That's not by accident. They're selling soap, man. (Laughter.) Not a joke.[5]

This change in the demographic composition of the United States will only accelerate because, as the Pew Foundation points out, the most common age for a White person in the United States is fifty-eight while the most common age for a Hispanic is eleven; for a Black it is twenty-seven, and for an Asian it is twenty-nine.[6] The minorities, therefore, will have the bulk of the young people in

---

[3] Sandra L. Colby and Jennifer M. Ortman, Projections of the Size and Composition of the U.S. Population: 2014 to 2060, United States Census Bureau, Issued March 2015, p. 1.

[4] Grace Chen, White Students are Now the Minority in U.S. Public Schools, Public School Review, October 14, 2019.

[5] Remarks by President Biden Commemorating the 100th Anniversary of the Tulsa Race Massacre, The White House, Speeches and Remarks, June 1, 2021, Washington, DC.

[6] Katherine Schaeffer, The most common age among whites in U.S. is 58 – more than double that of racial and ethnic minorities, Pew Research Center, July 30, 2019.

the country who are going to dominate the workforce and, more importantly, this will be the cohort from which innovations will most likely come to bring about transformations in America's knowledge economy.

The role of minorities in America's knowledge economy cannot be underestimated since after the pandemic hit, the top five tech companies accounted for 20 percent of the value of the stock market, and in each of these companies the number of minority employees, particularly Asians, was high.[7] As the table below shows, Asians have an outsized role in America's biggest tech industries:

Percentage of Asians in Major Tech Companies (Figures in parentheses give the date of the company's diversity report from which the data was retrieved)

Company	Percentage of Asians
Microsoft	33.3% (2019)
Alphabet/Google	42.3% (2021)
Facebook	44.4% (2020)
Apple	27% (2020)
Amazon	13.6% (2020)

For those energized by Trumpian populism, it is important to understand that what we are seeing is not a shift from the American work ethic—migrants tend to exemplify the Protestant work ethic—but rather a move away from the idea of a White Anglo-Saxon Protestant culture, and the foreign and economic policies that have gone hand in hand with it, to one which is more globalized and focusing on the non-Western parts of the world. Second, the bulk of the minorities are in the major states since those are the regions where the maximum jobs are likely to be located, especially for reasons discussed below. Thus, we are likely to see a shift in relations between Europe and the US to a greater focus in the United States' foreign and economic relations with Asia, which is the fastest-growing economic region in the world, and with Central and South America—where a large percent of the minority-majority population will have its roots. European politicians are beginning to accept this change as being inevitable, for, as French President Emmanuel Macron warned, Europe has focused too much on growing as a market and that the United States now pays more attention to the Pacific rather than to Europe.[8] Further, Latinos support the UN and multilateralism, are less interested in waging foreign wars and intervention, and are more supportive of the Palestinians in the Arab-Israeli dispute.[9]

---

[7] Paul Eavis and Steve Lohr, "Big Tech's Domination of Business Reaches New Heights," *The New York Times*, August 19, 2020.

[8] "Macron criticized by US and Germany over NATO 'brain death' claims," *The Guardian*, November 7, 2019.

[9] For a discussion see Amit Gupta, Demographic Shifts and US Foreign Policy, Orbis, Summer 2016, p. 363.

Demographics, the Generational Shift

In the next ten years, millennials are estimated to become about 75 percent of the American workforce by most reports, and their values and ideology will shape the nature of the American workforce and of American society. What is coming after the millennials is generation Z, also known as the zoomers, who were born, depending on varying studies, between 1997 and 2016.

The political attitudes of these generations are significantly different from those of the baby boomers and Generation X in areas of social justice, the environment, inclusiveness, and the role of government. The Pew Center, which has done some of the most comprehensive research on the political attitudes of the millennials and Generation Z, in a report states that "similar to Millennials, Gen Z'ers are progressive and pro-government, most see the country's growing racial and ethnic diversity as a good thing, and they're less likely than older generations to see the United States as superior to other nations."[10] While millennials do have different political ideologies, with many calling themselves libertarian and being in favor of small government, their social attitudes and their workplace requirements tend to be similar. One may describe their approach, tongue in cheek, as Libertarianism with Socialist characteristics.

As Charlotte Alter (national correspondent for *Time* magazine) has written, millennials tend to favor government-run health care, student debt relief, cannabis legalization, and criminal-justice reform, and they demand urgent government action on climate change.[11] They are also more likely to be openly LGBTQ. So, diversity in the workplace and a social safety net are societal aspects that millennials tend to agree on, and they want to live in areas where their value system is respected. Further, given the emphasis on education in this generation, there will be a natural tendency to move to the states that are the basis of America's knowledge economy.

Time Is on Their Side

The millennials and zoomers have an added advantage that conservatives will find impossible to counter—they are young and time is on their side. For other generations, the aging process is rapidly catching up with them and they will be leaving the workforce or dying. In 2020, the youngest World War II veteran (who was eighteen in 1945) is ninety-three, the youngest Korean War veteran is eighty-five, and the youngest Vietnam War veteran is sixty-six. These generations have long left or are soon to leave the workforce, and their place is being taken by the millennials who, by 2025, are expected to be 75 percent of the workforce.[12] Moreover, those espousing the political agenda of the millennials and zoomers will be living for a very long time. If we assume eighty-five is the American life expectancy, then Alexandria Ocasio-Cortez may live till 2075 while Pete Buttigieg will live till

---

[10] Kim Parker and Ruth Igielnik, "On the Cusp of Adulthood and Facing and Uncertain Future: What we know about Gen Z so far," *Pew Research Center*, May 14, 2020.

[11] Charlotte Alter, "How millennial leaders will change America," *Time*, January 23, 2020.

[12] Big demands and high expectations, *The Deloitte Millennial Survey*, January 2014, p. 2.

at least 2065. In that year, to go into the realm of fantasy, Donald Trump would be 119 and Mike Pence would be 106, and conservative icons like Addison Mitchell McConnell would be 123 while Lindsay Olin Graham would be 110. It is safe to say that all of them will likely be deceased or infirm by then. In the interregnum, the Ocasio-Cortez and Buttigieg generation will leave its mark on public policy.

Even more progressive than the millennials may be the zoomers and the generation that comes after them, as best seen in the influence of a teenager named Greta Thunberg and *Time* magazine's new "Kid of the Year" Gitanjali Rao. Thunberg, at age sixteen, addressed both Houses of Congress and the United Nations General Assembly on climate issues, while Gitanjali Rao, an Indian-American, has spoken about "her astonishing work using technology to tackle issues ranging from contaminated drinking water to addiction and cyberbullying, and about her mission to create a global community of young innovators to solve problems the world over."[13] Given current life-expectancies, both teenagers could live till 2090 (when they would be eighty-five) and Donald John Trump would be 144, Ivanka Trump would be 109, and Addison Mitchell McConnell would be 148. Let us face facts: time is running out for the older generation and its ideas, and states clinging to such ideas and attitudes will not be attractive to the coming generation. Youth flight is likely to follow in even greater numbers from these states.

The Spatial Divide

Norm Ornstein's comments on elderly White populations determining the presidency come from a report of the Weldon Cooper Institute at the University of Virginia that ran the data to come up with the conclusion about the spatial distribution of population in America. The eight states were:

State/Country	Estimated Population in 2040
USA	379,392,729
California	46,467,701
Texas	40,015,913
Florida	20,873,488
New York	20,873,488
Georgia	12,820,271
Pennsylvania	12,809,150
North Carolina	12,658,927
Illinois	12,397,564

Source: Weldon Cooper Center, University of Virginia, Population Projections for the 50 States and D.C., Available at: https://demographics.coopercenter.org/national-population-projections

---

[13] Angelina Jolie, "Kid of the Year: Gitanjali Rao, 15," *Time*, December 3, 2020.

Additionally, the next seven most populated states will have another 25 percent of the population.

State	Population in 2040
Ohio	11,751,540
Virginia	9,876,728
Washington	9,776,728
New Jersey	9,470,012
Arizona	9,166,279
Colorado	7,692,907
Indiana	7,095,000

Source: Weldon Cooper Center, University of Virginia, Population Projections
for the 50 States and D.C., Available at: https://demographics.coopercenter.org/
national-population-projections

These fifteen states will also have a strong correlation with the demographic
shifts in America as minorities flock for employment to them. Therefore, Florida
requires large-scale immigrant labor to maintain its agricultural programs while
states like California, Texas, and Washington will need knowledge economy–
based employees who will come both from within America and from around the
world. The numbers in the future populous states are already quite revealing for,
as the Migration Policy Institute data has shown, in the last two decades, Georgia
has seen an 84 percent growth in its foreign-born population, Florida 67.6 percent, and Texas 70 percent.[14] This influx is particularly apparent in the knowledge
economy companies as can be seen from the data in Table 3 showing how many
Asians (both foreign born and native) are in their workforce:

Table 3

Corporation	Asians as Percentage of Workforce
Apple	21%
Facebook	41.4%
Google	36.3%
Microsoft	38.2%
Twitter	25.8%

Source: Diversity Reports of each corporation, 2018

---

[14] Migration Policy Institute, State Demographics Data | migrationpolicy.org

The tech companies are the sunrise industries of America, and for them to attract world-class labor, they have to ensure that their workforce lives and carries out its professional duties in an environment that is not racist, sexist, homophobic, or demeaning to women (although the argument can be made that tech companies have problems with gender issues, which they are now seeking to address). States that cannot provide such an environment will lose out on attracting new investments in cutting-edge industries.

The counterargument is made that the conservative states offer non-union labor forces and cheaper wages. In the medium to long term, this factor will become far less relevant because of the rapid advent of 5G, artificial intelligence, and robotics into the forces of production. Such technological innovations will dramatically reduce the demand for unskilled labor while having a growing need for small numbers of highly educated labor.

Along with the spatial shift has come a clear division of wealth in the nation with the liberal areas accounting for an overwhelming proportion of the wealth. In a study published shortly after Trump's 2016 win, the Brookings Institute presented some startling figures on the division of wealth in the country by county. As the authors pointed out, Hillary Clinton won 472 American counties, thus winning 2.9 million more votes than Trump but, more importantly, her counties accounted for 64 percent of American GDP. In contrast, Trump won 2,584 counties, but these areas only accounted for 36 percent of American GDP.15 In the 2020 election, the wealth divide and electoral divide was even more striking, as Joe Biden won 477 counties, which gave him 7 million more votes than Trump but, again, these 477 counties generate 70 percent of American GDP. In contrast, Trump won 2,497 counties, which account for only 29 percent of American GDP.16 The data graphically illustrates that there is a concentration of wealth and population taking place in America, and this divide will only be exacerbated by the coming demographic and spatial divides. Added to the demographic and spatial shifts will be three factors: the feminization of America, the rise of knowledge economies, and the urbanization of America.

Feminization

For the past four decades, more women than men have obtained college degrees and, in fact, the number of men getting college degrees continues to decline. According to the data of the National Council of Education Statistics, by 1980, 54 percent of all college degrees were being awarded to women, and by 2019–2020 the percentage had gone up to 61.3 percent.17 Traditionally, women have been poorly represented in the sciences, but even there the number of degrees awarded

---

15 Mark Muro and Sifan Liu, Another Clinton-Trump divide: High-output America vs low-output America, Brookings Institution, November 29, 2016.

16 Mark Muro, Eli Byerly Duke, Yang You, and Robert Maxim, Biden-voting counties equal 70% of America's economy. What does this mean for the nation's political-economic divide? Brookings Institution, November 10, 2020.

17 Degrees conferred by postsecondary institutions, by level of degree and sex of student: Selected years, 1869-70 through 2027-28, National Center for Education Statistics, Available at: https://nces.ed.gov/programs/digest/d17/tables/dt17_318.10.asp?current=yes

to women are going up. The National Center for Science and Engineering Statistics data shows that in the hard sciences the number of women, which used to be low, is now quite impressive.

Table 4

Field of Study	Bachelors	Masters	Doctoral
Computer Science	18.7%	30.8%	20.1%
Engineering	20.9%	25%	23.5%
Mathematics & Statistics	42.4%	41.6%	28.5%
Physical Sciences	19.3%	22.1%	19.3%

Source: Women, Minorities, and Persons with Disabilities in Science and Engineering, National Center for Science and Engineering Statistics. Available at: https://ncses.nsf. gov/pubs/nsf19304/digest/field-of-degree-women#physical-sciences

With more women getting advanced college degrees, particularly graduate degrees, they will have greater economic and professional independence and will be making decisions in their households about where to locate in the United States; one may argue that given the shift in the political and social views of the millennials and the zoomers, they are not likely to want to go to states with conservative ideologies and instead prefer to stay in the urban, cosmopolitan states that are densely populated and are more gender friendly.

Education and Innovation

The gap between the educated and the less educated—those with college degrees versus those that do not have them—will also grow as the nature of the American economy changes to one that increasingly relies on innovation and services. Coupled with the pull toward the knowledge economy, which is high reward but also employs lower numbers, is the fact that manufacturing in America will be increasingly dependent on automation; therefore, the jobs that existed for unskilled and semi-skilled labor, in sectors such as automobile manufacturing, will shrink as corporations taking advantage of the Industrial Internet of Things created by 5G will move toward robots that are high performance, that can interact with each other, and that have low latency rates. This will most likely accelerate the movement out of the less populated states, as they will find it increasingly difficult to provide lucrative employment to younger populations. Along with the fact that employment with good wages may be hard to come by is the fact that the move to the more populated states will come because of a demand for a lifestyle imperative.

The Lifestyle Imperative

The 2018 edition of the United Nations World Urbanization Prospects report highlighted the advantages of an urban lifestyle:

"Urban areas also serve as hubs for development, where the proximity of commerce, government and transportation provide the infrastructure necessary for sharing knowledge and information. Urban dwellers are often younger, more literate and more highly educated, are more likely to have access to decent work, adequate housing and social services, and can enjoy enhanced opportunities for cultural and political participation as well as gender equality."[18] The lure of urbanization and the impact it could have on shaping corporate decisions was perhaps best seen in the competition for Amazon's HQ2—its second headquarters in the United States.

Amazon's HQ2 competition laid out the requirements for the second campus as follows: "In choosing the location for HQ2, Amazon has a preference for:

- Metropolitan areas with more than one million people.
- A stable and business-friendly environment.
- Urban or suburban locations with the potential to attract and retain strong technical talent."[19]

Among the additional requirements for the locating of the second headquarters were proximity to a major international airport and a major urban center, but then the requirements became more precise and demanded what overly conservative states could not provide. The report stated that the headquarters would require a highly educated workforce, so a strong university system would be required. Also, "The Project requires a compatible cultural and community environment for its long-term success. This includes the presence and support of a diverse population, excellent institutions of higher education, local government structure and elected officials eager and willing to work with the company, among other attributes."[20] The report concluded its requirements by stating that "we want to invest in a community where our employees will enjoy living, recreational opportunities, educational opportunities, and an overall high quality of life."[21]

Two-hundred thirty-eight cities in the United States, Canada, and Mexico applied for hosting the headquarters, and New York and Northern Virginia were eventually chosen. What Amazon was calling for was a location that was hip, urban, multicultural, educated, and racially diverse, and this is likely to become the template for any major corporation that is seeking to invest in the United States since it means moving their skilled and educated workforce to such a location.

Yet while the economic trends are suggesting that the new economy of the United States will be highly skilled, highly educated, multicultural, and requiring social, cultural, and educational stimulation, political power in the United States will continue to rest with the aging states with declining population. This then raises an important question for the future: Will the United States, because of its

---

[18] World Urbanization Prospects, The 2018 Revision, (United Nations, Department of Economic and Social Affairs, New York, 2019), pp. 1–2.

[19] Amazon HQ2 RPF, p.1, RFP_3._V516043504_.pdf (ssl-images-amazon.com)

[20] Ibid., p. 5.

[21] Ibid., p. 5.

antiquated version of contestation and representation (an electoral college that does not reflect the realities of population and a Senate system where a Wyoming with a population of roughly half a million gets two senators as does California with a population of over 39 million) become the country that Norm Ornstein says it will—one where less populated states full of elderly White people decide the presidency and, because of representation in the Senate, public policy? Or will the concentration of wealth, educational attainment, innovation, and youth give the more populated states an advantage in shaping public policy?

The Left Strikes Back?

The 2020 elections saw 74 million Americans vote for Donald Trump and the agenda of Make America Great Again. The media and politicians call for dialogue with disaffected Trump supporters, and the common refrain is to not talk down to them.

The American federal system was constructed to give an equal voice to all states, to prevent a monarchical type leader imposing their will, and to have slow, measured debate with resulting policy being based on compromise. Instead, in an age of advanced communications and demographic and spatial shifts, we are witnessing increasing polarization and routine gridlock. In this situation, public policy is not a reflection of debate and compromise but, instead, the ability of one party to garner enough votes in the Senate to push through bills that may not be endorsed by the majority of the population. Thus, in the past few years, the United States Senate has successfully appointed three conservative judges to the Supreme Court even though their judicial philosophies may not reflect the social and political values of the bulk of the population—of the big eight states of the future, the senators from California, New York, and Illinois did not vote for the most recent Supreme Court nominee, while in Pennsylvania the vote was split. Is such a state of affairs likely to continue?

The 2020 elections would suggest a mixed record since, with the exception of Arizona, most Republican senators managed to retain their seats despite pollsters projecting a blue wave that would see Democrats winning a majority in the senate. On the other hand, in Georgia, Jon Ossoff and Raphael Warnock won by handy margins and turned the state blue in the Senate.

Also, it was clear that despite the Democrats' long-standing affiliation with labor and minorities, in a number of regions Trump overperformed with the minorities to the extent that he handily won the election in Florida and Texas— both states, because of their sizable minority populations, were considered possible pick-ups by the Democrats.[22] While such shifts within minority populations may aid the conservative movement and the Republican party, it will not change the overall concentration of wealth in the progressive suburbs of America where

[22] For an analysis see Jack Herrera, "Trump Didn't Win the Latino Vote in Texas. He Won the Tejano Vote," Politico, November 17, 2020, https://www.politico.com/news/magazine/2020/11/17/trump-latinos-south-texas-tejanos-437027

Joe Biden found his vote bank (also, despite making a dent in the minority vote in both Texas and Florida, the majority of non-White votes in these states still went to the Democrats). With such a concentration of wealth, based as it is around sunrise industries and financial services, these blue states will be able to exercise a considerable degree of leverage over the aging and less populated conservative states by using the financial lever to demand a softening of social and economic positions that at present are inimical to the richer blue states. Such a strategy has been described as one of embedding environmental, social institutions but instead to use investments to bring about definitive social and economic changes incrementally.[23] Two examples come to mind of such a trend becoming prevalent in America. One is the possible response to the overturning of America's pro-choice law.

On June 24, 2022, the Supreme Court of the United States overturned *Roe vs. Wade, the decision that had kept abortion legal in the United States for* forty-nine years. The division among American states was predictable, as the liberal states mobilized to try and protect the right to choice while the conservative states rapidly imposed the trigger laws they had in place to immediately ban abortions in their jurisdiction (trigger laws were meant to come into place immediately after the Supreme Court gave a decision against Rowe).[24]

Liberal groups sought to influence corporations since it would be difficult to change the composition of legislatures in red states and impossible to change the membership of the Supreme Court unless vacancies occurred. While fewer than 10 percent of corporations commented publicly on the verdict, a number of prominent firms like Uber, Microsoft, and Disney vowed to help give employees access to abortions.[25] While employers have not as yet taken more proactive measures to help their workforce, observers believe that "given the widespread implications for half the workforce in anti-abortion states, experts have said companies based in jurisdictions with abortion bans will face repercussions around recruitment and retention and even possible legal jeopardy."[26] Although it is too early to say how this will play out in the American workforce, the corporate response to Georgia's attempt to pass a stringent abortion law was met with a vigorous counter from corporations.

In 2019, Georgia passed a restrictive abortion law that banned all abortions after six weeks of pregnancy had elapsed. The law was met with criticism and threats from Hollywood corporations like Disney, Warner Media, and Netflix, who threatened to pull film and television series production from the state. Atlanta and the surrounding areas have been dubbed the Hollywood of the South because of the extensive film and TV shooting that takes place in the area, and a

---

[23] Tensie Whalen, "Making a Better Business Case for ESG" Stanford Social Innovation Review, August 17, 2020. Making a Better Business Case for ESG (ssir.org)

[24] 19-1392 Dobbs v. Jackson Women's Health Organization (06/24/2022) (supremecourt.gov)

[25] Aine Cain, Avery Hartmans, and Marguerite Ward, "Uber, Nike, Lyft, Disney, JP Morgan and others vow to help employees access abortions after Supreme Court overturns Roe v. Wade: "We must keep up the fight." Business Insider, June 30, 2022.

[26] Ibid.

boycott of Georgia would have had considerable impact on the state's economy as well as potentially leading to pressure on other major Atlanta-based corporations like Delta, Home Depot, and Coca-Cola to consider relocation of their corporate headquarters. The controversy was resolved because a federal judge struck down the law as unconstitutional, but it gives an indication of the potential power of major industries in America that have progressive values in shaping political decisions in otherwise conservative states.

In 2021, in reaction to a new law passed by the Georgia legislature, which restricts voting rights in the state and is seen as being targeted at minorities, both Delta and Coca-Cola came out against the new voting law, as did a group of other corporations, which saw the impending demographic shift as their future market.

This battle is far from over since Georgia has some leverage over these companies. Coca-Cola could make a symbolic gesture and move its corporate headquarters out of Atlanta, but it would be impossible for Delta to shift its major hub of operations from Atlanta airport to another city. Georgia also decided to play hard ball with Delta by stripping it of the jet fuel tax break it enjoyed courtesy of the state.

Texas Abortion Law

Another issue that will see a clash between progressives and conservatives is the recent Texas abortion law that makes medical terminations of pregnancy illegal after six weeks and also permits the novel approach of allowing vigilantes or bounty hunters to turn in suspected abortion receivers for a reward. The law is draconian, as it leads to "a near-total ban on abortions, includes several provisions that experts say tilt the scale toward plaintiffs, including protecting serial plaintiffs who could file dozens or hundreds of cases, incentivizing civilians to sue with a $10,000 cash reward if successful and removing defendants' ability to recoup their legal fees. If survivors of rape become pregnant and seek an abortion, those procedures could become the object of lawsuits."[27] Conservative states across America are looking to adopt versions of the Texas law, especially since the US Supreme Court has overturned *Roe v. Wade*.

Unlike the Texas voting law, corporate response to the new abortion law has been mixed, with smaller companies like Uber, Lyft, dating sites like Match and Bumble, and the website provider Go Daddy providing relief measures.[28] The largest companies in Texas like Dell, Pizza Hut, ATT, ExxonMobil, Hewlett-Packard, and American Airlines have remained silent, as have the major defense corporations like Lockheed that have a sizable physical presence in the state.[29] The reason the major companies have remained silent is the favorable business environment in Texas, which is difficult to replicate in other conservative states that do not have as diversified economies as Texas, which combines energy,

---

[27] Erin Douglas and Carla Astudillo, "We annotated Texas' near-total abortion ban. Here's what the law says about enforcement," Texas Tribune, September 10, 2021.

[28] Karl-Evers Hillstrom, "Texas abortion law roils businesses," *The Hill*, September 7, 2021.

[29] Lauren Aratani, Texas's largest companies stay silent on state abortion ban despite outrage, *The Guardian*, September 15, 2021

defense production, and high technology, making it an impressive industrial hub for which it is not easy to find an alternative.

Yet time is on the side of the progressives since they are unlikely to shift future investments to states that are socially and politically backward looking. More importantly, conservative states that are unwilling to change may find it hard to attract people to work in the knowledge economy sectors of their state—doctors, engineers, and university faculty to name a few.

Pressure is even beginning to come from apolitical institutions like the military to bring about reform in the conservative states, particularly when it comes to issues like the provision of quality education. At Maxwell Air Force Base in Montgomery, Alabama, for instance, the poor education system has become a critical issue since Airmen are leaving their families behind when being assigned to the base because of the poor educational institutions in the city and the fact that employment opportunities for well-educated spouses are limited. As the former commander of the base, General Anthony Michael Cotton publicly lamented, "I'm having a hard time getting folks to apply to be faculty members here as I'm trying to lure them away from schools in the Northeast, schools in Washington, DC, schools in the Midwest, schools from San Jose—Silicon Valley—and once again the feedback I get is pretty simple: It's about the school system."[30] When institutions like the Air Force, which traditionally do not engage in political or social controversy, begin to take a position on such issues it means that the old ways of business as usual cannot continue.

Another serious problem that is likely to strike home in the coming decades, with the aging of the population, is the willingness of doctors and medical personnel to go to states where education is poor, economic opportunities are less, and social values are different from those of the affluent states. Obviously three of the heavily populated states of the future are Texas, Georgia, and Florida, and all of them have traditionally been conservative, red states. But in 2020, Georgia flipped because of the influx of liberal professionals into the Atlanta area and Texas, while having a traditional oil and gas sector and a ranching economy, continues to see an influx of skilled professionals from other states and they come with a different set of political and social values.

One could go further and ask if the present level of industrialization in states with an aging workforce, which ranges from automobile manufacturing to aircraft and other high technologies, can continue to survive if these states do not bring about serious political and social changes? Companies like BMW in South Carolina and Mercedes in Alabama may well have to reassess their positions on investing in these areas.

The Rise of Economic Progressivism

Last, while there may be deep social and cultural divides in America, one issue that may bring the country together is economic progressivism and the quest for wage equality. Florida gave Trump a solid victory but at the same time passed a

---

[30] Christi Ham, "Quality education for children is a military readiness issue," *Military Times*, March 31, 2019.

referendum to have a $15 minimum wage. According to academic and pollster Stanley Greenberg, such a trend is not surprising because we are seeing the rise of "Biden Republicans." He argues: "I don't think the Republicans are as disillusioned with Trump as polls suggest, but I do think there's huge support for the relief package. Trump voters, a large portion of them, want a welfare state that is dependable for working people. The Reagan Democrats and these White working-class voters are incredibly pro-Medicaid expansion. Look at what happened in any of these Senate races in '18 in states [with initiatives on] on the minimum wage or Medicaid expansion. The minimum wage and Medicaid expansion won by much bigger numbers [than the incumbents]. I mean, it won in *Utah*."[31] If the demand for economic progressivism resonates in the conservative states, the demand for other types of workers' rights may follow. One should add a cautionary note here that it will be hard to break the patterns of the past as the failed attempt to unionize Amazon workers at the warehouse in Bessemer, Alabama, showed. There, the wages that Amazon paid were attractive enough to stave off the demand for unionization.

To sum up, America's election system may be archaic for political functioning in the twenty-first-century economy and polity, and it may well lead to political outcomes where the skewing of the electoral college leads to less populated states choosing the president, but this is, at best, a pyrrhic   victory. As wealth and talent continue to spatially concentrate in America, it is the centers of such dynamism that will have considerable leverage in shaping their relationship with the political power centers of the country. Economics will determine federalism.

What the Federal Divide Means for the Military's Quest for Diversity

In light of the broad spatial, demographic, gender-based, and educational changes that are going to emerge in American society and how that may actually empower progressives in the country, the implications these shifts will have on the US military will continue to impact the racial, ethnic, religious, and gender diversity to be reflective of the coming demographic change in America. Put simply, a new policy that encourages and protects diversity is needed, for otherwise the military will have difficulty in getting the best people to go to many of the locations where it is located. Instead, we may well see flight from these jobs as people are unwilling to live in states with laws that are perceived as being hostile to gender and minority rights. Further, if the gap between the states that are knowledge economies and those that lag educationally continues to grow, then this problem with recruitment and staffing will only be accelerated.

Table 5 shows the states that have one or a combination of the following problems for the emerging multicultural workforce and the number of military installations they host. These problems include regressive anti-abortion laws, lower standards of education, the fact that the lifestyle may not be conducive to younger generations (as discussed above), and that minorities—ethnic, racial, and LGBTQ plus—may not feel comfortable in them.

---

[31] Zack Stanton, "The Rise of the Biden Republicans," *Politico Magazine*, March 4, 2021.

Table 5

State	Number of Military Installations
Alabama	6
Alaska	9
Arkansas	4
Florida	22
Georgia	13
Indiana	3
Iowa	3
Kentucky	3
Louisiana	6
Mississippi	7
North Dakota	2
Oklahoma	7
South Carolina	8
South Dakota	1
Tennessee	4
Texas	24
West Virginia	2

Source: Military Bases By State – ID, IL, IN, KS, KY, LA, ME, MD, MA, MI, MS, MO

In some of these states, the anti-abortion laws will pose challenges for women serving both in the military and as civilians in these military installations, for while the military will have, for now, the protection of a federal base with its own clinic, the civilians will have to go to the local hospitals, and doctors will be subject to state laws. Women will likely be reluctant to go work in such installations, fearing the legal- and health-related consequences that might ensue.

Similarly, if the push in some of these states is against LGBTQ-plus personnel, it will be difficult to get people from those groups to accept jobs there either. At least one justice of the Supreme Court, Clarence Thomas, has called for repealing the laws that permit contraception and gay marriage, which should both be considered to be settled law in the United States but, if the Dobbs decision is any indication, could be easily reversed by the Supreme Court if a legal challenge was mounted by conservative groups against these rights.[32]

The other crucial factor will be education or, more precisely, the lack of it. While rankings of education systems have their obvious flaws, this one by

---

[32] Oriana Gonzalez, "Clarence Thomas wants SCOTUS to reconsider decisions on gay marriage, contraceptives," *Axios*, June 24, 2022.

WalletHub underlines the problem of lower standards of education in a knowledge economy of the future. Of the states listed above, Indiana is 29th in school level education, South Dakota 34th, Tennessee 41st, Oklahoma 44th,, Kentucky 45th, Alabama 46th, Arkansas 47th, Louisiana 48th, South Carolina 49th, and Mississippi was 50th.[33] States like Texas, Georgia, and Florida, while not making the top-ten school systems in the country, were high enough to not deter workers—military and civilian—from bringing their children to reside in the state.

Texas, of course, will be an interesting outlier, for while its social policies and laws are becoming increasingly conservative, it has a large enough knowledge economy and a substantial presence of the defense industry that it may still be able to recruit twenty-first-century knowledge workers in significant numbers. Others, however, may be less lucky—the above discussion about Alabama is a case in point where the general in charge of Maxwell Air Force Base publicly bemoaned the consequences of the state's poor educational levels. The question then arises, if the US Armed Forces needs an increasingly skilled and educated military and civilian personnel, what needs to be done to make sure such a workforce feels comfortable working in all fifty states of the country?

While military personnel will have protections under military law and through the armed forces health care system, civilian personnel will be vulnerable to state laws. The administration as a first step, therefore, needs to pass an executive order granting protections to civilians employed by the federal government on military installations in states with current laws that are anti-abortion and possible future laws that adversely impact the rights to contraception and gay marriage. Once such an order is passed, the branches of Congress need to attempt to pass a law that protects the rights of federal workers. Some of these states may not like such measures and see it as interference, but if they see personnel leaving their state or refusing to come to it, they will recognize the future potential problems for their economies and educational systems.

In the case of education, the military has to create guidelines on what it considers acceptable levels of education at the K-12 level and suggest to states that if they do not take immediate steps to implement reforms, they may find some of the military installations in their state being put on the next list for base closures. While that decision may be difficult to bring to fruition, it will make states pause since they recognize the enormous boost to their economies that comes from basing in remote and less economically vibrant areas.

In conclusion, the US military of the future must reflect the changing demographics of the nation, and to do so it has to encourage social equality, improved education, and reproductive rights at the state level. Not doing so will make the military even less representative of the nation than it already is and it will lose the skilled workforce needed for a twenty-first-century high-tech military to succeed.

---

[33] Ann Schmidt, "The most, least educated US states in 2022: report," For its report, WalletHub compared all 50 US states based on eighteen measurements such as share of adults aged twenty-five and older with at least a high school diploma, quality of school system, blue ribbon schools per capita, public high school graduation rate, and NAEP Math & Reading test scores. Available at, The most, least educated US states in 2022: report | Fox Business

CONTRIBUTORS
(listed alphabetically by last name)

Donald C Arthur Jr., MD, Vice Admiral, USN, Retired, is a retired Navy medical corps officer who entered the Navy in 1974, qualified as both a naval flight surgeon and a submarine medical officer, and served as the thirty-fifth surgeon general of the Navy from 2004 to 2007. VADM Arthur is a board-certified preventive medicine physician, and he commanded Naval Hospital Camp Lejeune and National Naval Medical Center Bethesda. VADM Arthur is a past president of the Aerospace Medical Association and recipient of many civilian and military leadership awards. He is a summa cum laude graduate of the University of Massachusetts School of Law, where he was first in his graduating class.

Abel Barrientes, Major General, USAF, Retired, is a native of San Antonio, Texas. Barrientes graduated from the US Air Force Academy in 1982. While on active duty he flew the T-39, C-21, and C-5 before entering the Air Force Reserve program at Travis Air Force Base, California. During his thirty-six-year USAF career he held command positions at the squadron, wing, and numbered Air Force levels. Barrientes was mobilized for operations Desert Shield and Desert Storm in 1990, and for operations Enduring Freedom and Iraqi Freedom in 2003. In 2006, he deployed as the senior military advisor to the Iraqi Air Force. He retired in 2018.

Aaron Belkin, PhD, is a scholar and advocate who has written and edited more than thirty scholarly articles, chapters, and books, the most recent of which is a study of contradictions in American warrior masculinity. Since 1999, Belkin has served as founding director of the Palm Center, which the *Advocate* named as one of the most effective LGBT rights organizations in the nation. Harvard Law Professor Janet Halley said of Belkin, "Probably no single person deserves more credit for the repeal of Don't Ask, Don't Tell." He earned his BA in international relations at Brown University in 1988 and his PhD in political science at the University of California, Berkeley, in 1998.

Ashan M. Benedict began serving as the special agent in charge of the Washington Field Division of the Bureau of Alcohol, Tobacco, Firearms and Explosives (ATF) in January 2019. He holds a bachelor of science degree in accounting from Fordham University and is a graduate of the Asian American Government Executive Network's Senior Executive Service Development Program. He is responsible for ATF operations throughout Washington, DC, the Commonwealth of Virginia, and the eastern panhandle of West Virginia. Benedict is a New York City native and grew up in the Bronx and Yonkers. In 2017, Benedict received the Federal Drug Agent Foundation's (FDAF) Lifetime Achievement Award. He and his wife, ATF Special Agent Katherine Benedict, have three children.

David H. Berger, General, USMC, assumed the duties of commandant of the Marine Corps on July 11, 2019. A native of Woodbine, Maryland, General Berger graduated from Tulane University and was commissioned in 1981. He commanded at every level—including a Reconnaissance Company; 3d Battalion, 8th Marines in Haiti during Operation SECURE TOMORROW; Regimental Combat Team 8 in Fallujah, Iraq, during Operation IRAQI FREEDOM. As a general officer, he commanded 1st Marine Division (Forward) in Afghanistan during Operation ENDURING FREEDOM; I Marine Expeditionary Force; US Marine Corps Forces Pacific/Fleet Marine Forces Pacific; and Marine Corps Combat Development Command. General Berger's staff and joint assignments include serving as assistant division commander of 2d Marine Division; policy planner in the Strategic Plans and Policy Directorate, J-5; chief of staff for Kosovo Force (KFOR) Headquarters in Pristina, Kosovo; director of operations in Plans, Policies, and Operations, Headquarters, US Marine Corps; and deputy commandant for Combat Development and Integration. General Berger's formal military education includes the US Army Infantry Officer Advanced Course, US Marine Corps Command and Staff College, and US Marine Corps School of Advanced Warfighting. He holds multiple advanced degrees including a master of international public policy from Johns Hopkins University School of Advanced International Studies.

Kim Beveridge, Lieutenant Colonel, USAF, Retired, retired from the Air Force in 2019 after twenty-eight years of active duty and reserve service. She earned degrees with honors in electrical engineering and industrial engineering. Her USAF experiences varied from space operations to program management. Her proudest, most challenging, and rewarding experiences have been as a mom to Jordan (22), Colin (21), Owen (19) and Luke (16). Married to her biggest supporter for twenty-six years, Brian, Kim lives in St. Louis, Missouri, and continues to serve as a civilian in the Department of the Air Force.

Joseph Robinette Biden Jr. is currently serving as the forty-sixth president of the United States of America. He was born in Scranton, Pennsylvania, the first of four children of Catherine Eugenia Finnegan Biden and Joseph Robinette Biden Sr. In 1953, the Biden family moved to Claymont, Delaware. President Biden graduated from the University of Delaware and Syracuse Law School and served on the New Castle County Council. At age twenty-nine, President Biden became one of the youngest people ever elected to the United States Senate. Just weeks after his Senate election, tragedy struck the Biden family when his wife Neilia and daughter Naomi were killed, and sons Hunter and Beau were critically injured in an auto accident. Biden was sworn into the US Senate at his sons' hospital bedsides and began commuting from Wilmington to Washington every day, first by car, and then by train, in order to be with his family. He would continue to do so throughout his time in the Senate. Biden married Jill Jacobs in 1977, and in 1980, their family was complete with the birth of Ashley Blazer Biden. A lifelong educator, Jill earned her doctorate in education and returned to teaching as an English professor at a community college in Virginia. Beau Biden, attorney general of Delaware and Joe Biden's eldest son, passed away in 2015 after battling brain cancer with the same integrity, courage, and strength he demonstrated every day of his life. Beau's fight with cancer inspires the mission of President Biden's life—ending cancer as we know it. As a senator from Delaware for thirty-six years, President Biden established himself as a leader in facing some of our nation's most important domestic and international challenges. As chairman or ranking member of the Senate Judiciary Committee for sixteen years, Biden is widely recognized for his work writing and spearheading the Violence Against Women Act—the landmark legislation that strengthens penalties for violence against women, creates unprecedented resources for survivors of assault, and changes the national dialogue on domestic and sexual assault. As chairman or ranking member of the Senate Foreign Relations Committee for twelve years, Biden played a pivotal role in shaping US foreign policy. He was at the forefront of issues and legislation related to terrorism, weapons of mass destruction, post–Cold War Europe, the Middle East, Southwest Asia, and ending apartheid. He was elected the forty-seventh vice president of the United States in 2008. As vice president, Biden continued his leadership on important issues facing the nation and represented our country abroad. Vice President Biden convened sessions of the president's cabinet, led interagency efforts, and worked with Congress in his fight to raise the living standards of middle-class Americans, reduce gun violence, address violence against women, and end cancer as we know it. Biden helped President Obama pass and then oversaw the implementation of the Recovery Act—the biggest economic recovery plan in the history of the nation and our biggest and strongest commitment to clean energy. The president's plan prevented another Great Depression, created and saved millions of jobs, and led to seventy-five uninterrupted months of job growth by the end of the administration. And Biden did it all with less than 1 percent in waste, abuse, or fraud—the most efficient government program in our country's history. President Obama and Vice President Biden also secured the passage of the Affordable Care Act, which reduced the number of uninsured Americans by twenty million by the time they left office and banned insurance companies from denying coverage due to preexisting conditions. He served as the point person for US diplomacy throughout the Western Hemisphere, strengthened relationships with our allies both in Europe and the Asia-Pacific, and led the effort to bring 150,000 troops home from Iraq. In a ceremony at the White House, President Obama awarded Biden the Presidential Medal of Freedom with Distinction—the nation's highest civilian honor. After leaving the White House, the Bidens continued their efforts to expand opportunity for every American with the creation of the Biden Foundation, the Biden Cancer Initiative, the Penn Biden Center for Diplomacy and Global Engagement, and the Biden Institute at the University of Delaware. On April 25, 2019, Biden announced his candidacy for president of the United States. Biden's candidacy was built from the beginning around three pillars: the battle for the soul of our nation, the need to rebuild our middle class—the backbone of our country, and a call for unity, to act as one America. It was a message that would only gain more resonance in 2020 as our nation confronted a pandemic, an economic crisis, urgent calls for racial justice, and the existential threat of climate change.

Aryemis C. Brown, Cadet First Class, USAFA, commanded the Air Force Cadet Wing during the fall 2020 semester where he was responsible for the welfare of 4,400 cadets as a member of the class of 2021. He majored in legal studies and humanities, and minored in religion studies and philosophy. Brown's research interests are in space and cyberspace law, technology, policy, and philosophy. His overall order of merit, combining athletic, military, and academic performance is 2 of 1059. He was named a Truman Scholar and Rhodes Scholar-elect in 2020.

Kristine Brands, PhD, is an assistant professor of management at the US Air Force Academy. She is a member of the Institute of Certified Management Accountants Board of Regents and the Institute of Management Accountants Technology Solutions and Practices Committee. She is past president of the Colorado Society of CPAs Educational Foundation and is a member of its board of directors. Her research interests include business analytics, accounting ethics, XBRL, accounting for sustainability, organizational development for accounting course quality, and the integration of technology in accounting courses. She is also a contributing member of the Project Thrive Team at USAFA.

Charles Q. Brown Jr., General, USAF, is the chief of staff of the Air Force. As chief, he serves as the senior uniformed Air Force officer responsible for the organization, training, and equipping 689,000 active-duty, Guard, Reserve, and civilian forces serving in the United States and overseas. As a member of the Joint Chiefs of Staff, the general and other service chiefs function as military advisers to the Secretary of Defense, National Security Council, and the president. Gen. Brown was commissioned in 1984 as a distinguished graduate of the ROTC program at Texas Tech University. He has served in a variety of positions at the squadron and wing levels, including an assignment to the US Air Force Weapons School as an F-16 Fighting Falcon instructor. His notable staff tours include aide-de-camp to the chief of staff of the Air Force; director, Secretary of the Air Force and Chief of Staff Executive Action Group; and deputy commander, US Central Command. He also served as a National Defense Fellow at the Institute for Defense Analyses, Alexandria, Virginia. Gen. Brown has commanded a fighter squadron, the US Air Force Weapons School, two fighter wings, and US

Air Forces Central Command. Prior to serving as the Air Force Chief of Staff, Gen. Brown was the commander of Pacific Air Forces, Air Component Commander for US Indo-Pacific Command. Gen. Brown is a command pilot with more than 2,900 flying hours, including 130 combat hours.

Bettina Bush, a respected voice in parenting, multiculturalism, and gender equality, started her lifelong career in media at age seven, voicing pop culture icons such as Rainbow Brite. Bush became editor-at-large for *Working Mother* magazine after serving as CEO of a telecommunications company formed to bridge the digital divide in underserved communities. She has hosted and produced national radio shows, podcasts, and video series, and regularly appears as an advocate on television and in various media. Inspired by her trailblazing father and schoolteacher mother of multicultural descent, Bush has devoted much of her career to educating on issues of diversity.

Jeff Butler, PhD, Brigadier General, USAF, Retired, is a professor emeritus at the US Air Force Academy (USAFA) and former chair of the USAFA Engineering Division consisting of six world-class academic departments. Brig Gen Butler retired after thirty+ years in the Air Force serving in a range of assignments in acquisition, space, cybersecurity, intelligence, and education. He holds undergraduate degrees in electrical engineering and mathematics, master's degrees in military studies and engineering, and a doctorate in computer engineering. He is also a contributing member of the Project Thrive Team at USAFA.

Edward Cabrera, Colonel, USAF, Retired. Prior to his current program manager position at the Jet Propulsion Laboratory, Eddie was a senior program manager at Lockheed Martin Skunk Works. As a program manager, he led a classified portfolio of advanced technology programs where he helped deliver game-changing capabilities enhancing America's national security strategy. As an Air Force Colonel, he served as the vice commander of the 46th Test Wing, a world-class group of four thousand experts conducting conventional weapons, electronic warfare, and command & control development and testing. He managed an annual budget of $480M and unique range infrastructure valued at $12.5 billion. During his military career, Eddie served as a combat-proven F-16 fighter pilot and experimental test pilot. He has nearly four thousand hours in sixty-five different aircraft types. As a test pilot, he led the Joint Strike Fighter Test Force at Edwards AFB, CA, and Patuxent River, MD, which set world records for X-aircraft testing in the X-32 and X-35 concept demonstrators (the X-35 subsequently won the national Collier Trophy). He was the Air Force's sole X-32 test pilot and became the only Air Force pilot in history to fly both the X-32 and F-22 Raptor. He earned four national-level awards for his contributions leading the nation's most advanced aircraft development programs. Eddie is a 1982 graduate from the United States Air Force Academy, where he earned a BS in astronautical engineering. He also holds an MS in mechanical engineering from California State University-Fresno, an

MA in strategic studies from the Air University, and an MBA from Pepperdine University. He is a distinguished graduate of the US Air Force Test Pilot School.

Nancy C. Chavez, Major, USAF, is currently serving at the Air Force Academy as an instructor and course director in the Department of Management. She is a mentor, academic advisor-in-charge, and officer representative for cadets across various intercollegiate and affinity clubs. Prior to her current position, she served at the US Embassy in Bogota, Colombia, where she focused on strengthening our international partnerships. Additionally she is a career linguist and airborne intelligence officer with over seven hundred combat flight hours. Her research interests include self-determination theory and how it can be fostered for the benefit of large organizations. She is also a contributing member of the Project Thrive Team at USAFA.

Steven M. D'Antuono is the assistant director in charge of the Federal Bureau of Investigation's Washington Field Office. D'Antuono joined the FBI as a forensic accountant in 1996 and was assigned to the Providence Resident Agency in Rhode Island, under the Boston Field Office. He supported criminal investigations into financial crimes, public corruption, organized crime, drugs, and counterintelligence. In 1998, D'Antuono was appointed a special agent. In 2019, D'Antuono was named special agent in charge of the Detroit Field Office. Prior to joining the FBI, D'Antuono was a certified public accountant focused on auditing, forensic accounting, and taxation. He earned a bachelor's degree in accounting from the University of Rhode Island.

Kevin J. Davis, DBA, Colonel, USAF, Retired, is a professor of management at the United States Air Force Academy. He earned his MBA and DBA from Harvard University. Dr. Davis has published in a variety of journals including the *Journal of Investments, Financial Services Review, Information and Management, Human Factors,* and the *Journal of Leadership Studies.* He previously served as an Air Force pilot, completing twenty-eight years of Air Force service. He is also a contributing member of the Project Thrive Team at USAFA.

Karin De Angelis, PhD, is an associate professor of sociology in the Department of Behavioral Sciences & Leadership at the US Air Force Academy (USAFA). She joined the USAFA faculty in 2011 and serves as the department's socio-cultural discipline lead. Her research interests include race/ethnicity in the US military, with a focus on Hispanic service members; the intersection of gender, work, and family; military families; sexual assault prevention; diversity in organizations; and Gen Z and millennial attitudes toward social issues.

Jim Demarest, Brigadier General, Florida Air National Guard, spent ten years as an active-duty F-15 pilot and was a distinguished graduate of the Air Force Fighter Weapons School. He served in Desert Storm as an F-15 pilot and chief of the

Combat Mission Planning Cell. Following his active-duty service, Jim graduated from Cornell Law School where he served as managing editor of the *Cornell Law Review* while specializing in advocacy and international law. He returned to military service when he joined the Florida Air National Guard as a JAG and was promoted into a leadership position as chief of staff and deputy commanding general.

Daphne DePorres, EdD, is an assistant professor of management at the US Air Force Academy. She is a senior organization development practitioner, scholar, and educator. Dr. DePorres has dedicated her career to the pursuit of organizational excellence and individual agency within large complex systems. Her research interests are intently focused on the intersection of, and symbiotic relationship between, organizational effectiveness and individual agency, efficacy, and belonging. Dr. DePorres has assisted numerous organizations in the pursuit of quality, productivity, equity, and supportive cultures. She is also a contributing member of the Project Thrive Team at USAFA.

Edith A. "Edie" Disler, PhD, Lieutenant Colonel, USAF, Retired, received her commission via Air Force ROTC at the University of Michigan in 1984. Edie spent the next twenty-five years as an Air Force officer in various operational, support, and educational assignments. Today Edie is an artist specializing in metal sculpture, embracing the expressive and therapeutic value of work as an artisan. Edie has earned several degrees, including a PhD in linguistics from Georgetown University. She is the author of the book *Language and Gender in the Military: Honorifics, Narrative and Ideology in Air Force Talk* from Cambria Press, as well as several articles and book chapters regarding gender, language, and the military.

Morten G. Ender, PhD, is a professor of sociology at the US Military Academy at West Point, New York, USA. He writes about the military, war, and teaching. His articles have appeared in *Teaching Sociology; Journal of Adolescence; Death Studies; Military Psychology; Journal of Homosexuality; War & Society;* and *Armed Forces & Society*, among others. He is the book review editor for *Res Militaris: The European Journal of Military Studies*. His latest book is titled *Teaching and Learning the West Point Way* (Routledge, in press).

Sonia Esquivel, PhD, is a faculty academic advisor, professor of Spanish, and the officer-in-charge of the Hispanic Heritage Club at the US Air Force Academy. In this position, she advises, mentors, and teaches fourth-class cadets. She most notably assisted in building the Academy's first innovative hybrid academic advising model. Dr. Esquivel leads research on sense of belonging of cadets at USAFA, providing a centric research/information/analysis to guide the institution. The Air Force Academy awarded Dr. Esquivel one of the Outstanding Academy Educators in 2020. *Latina Style* awarded Dr. Esquivel the Distinguished Military Service Award in 2018. She is also a contributing member of the Project Thrive Team at USAFA.

Claudia Ferrante, PhD, is a professor of management at the US Air Force Academy. She earned her BS in biology from Bucknell University, MBA and master of health administration from the University of Pittsburgh, master of public policy and management from Carnegie Mellon University, and doctorate in organizational behavior from Carnegie Mellon University. Her teaching and research interests focus on the intersection of organizational behavior, human resource management, nonprofit management, and service learning. She has published numerous peer-reviewed journal articles and book chapters and is the recipient of several awards for her teaching, research, and service efforts. She is also a contributing member of the Project Thrive Team at USAFA.

Martin E. France, Brigadier General, USAF, Retired, served as the permanent professor and head of the USAF Academy Astronautics Department (2005–2018), supervising the astronautics and space operations curriculum and research program programs. His assignments include the AF Research Lab, as the AF exchange engineer to France, DARPA program manager, and in staff and leadership roles at AF Space Command, HQ USAF, and on the Joint Chiefs of Staff. His education includes a BS from USAFA, MS from Stanford University and The National War College, and PhD from Virginia Tech. He was also a Fulbright Scholar to Nanyang Technological University (Singapore).

Nathaniel Frank, PhD, is an author, historian, and advocate whose latest book is *Awakening: How Gays and Lesbians Brought Marriage Equality to America* (Harvard University Press). He is a senior research consultant at the Palm Center and director of the What We Know Project, a research initiative at Cornell University. He has written for the *New York Times, Washington Post,* the *Atlantic, New York Magazine,* and others, and appeared on *The Daily Show* and other major media outlets. His first book was the critically acclaimed *Unfriendly Fire: How the Gay Ban Undermines the Military and Weakens America.* He graduated from Northwestern University and earned a PhD in history from Brown University.

Jazmin Furtado, Captain, USSF, is an acquisitions officer in the United States Space Force. In addition to her degree from the US Air Force Academy, she holds a master's degree from the Massachusetts Institute of Technology (MIT). She has served at the forefront of innovation in the Air Force, created data-driven software systems to enable AI, and she has represented the Air Force as a Fellow at SpaceX. She is also the cofounder of the education nonprofit VESPERE, is an advocate/speaker for women in technology, and is the author of various tech publications.

Michael Gilday, Admiral, USN, is the son of a Navy Sailor. A surface warfare officer, he is a native of Lowell, Massachusetts, and a graduate of the US Naval Academy. He holds master's degrees from the Harvard Kennedy School and the National War College. At sea, he deployed with USS Chandler (DDG 996), USS

Princeton (CG 59), and USS Gettysburg (CG 64). He commanded destroyers USS Higgins (DDG 76) and USS Benfold (DDG 65) and subsequently, commanded Destroyer Squadron 7, serving as sea combat commander for the Ronald Reagan Carrier Strike Group. As a flag officer, he served as commander Carrier Strike Group 8 embarked aboard USS Dwight D. Eisenhower (CVN 69), and as commander, US Fleet Cyber Command and US 10th Fleet. His staff assignments include the Bureau of Naval Personnel; staff of the Chief of Naval Operations, and staff of the Vice Chief of Naval Operations. Joint assignments include executive assistant to the chairman of the Joint Chiefs of Staff and naval aide to the president. As a flag officer, he served in joint positions as director of operations for NATO's Joint Force Command Lisbon; as chief of staff for Naval Striking and Support Forces NATO; director of operations, J3, for US Cyber Command; and as director of operations, J3, for the Joint Staff. He recently served as director, Joint Staff. He has served on teams that have been recognized with numerous awards and is the recipient of the Defense Distinguished Service Medal, Distinguished Service Medal, Defense Superior Service Medal (four awards), Legion of Merit (three awards), Bronze Star, Navy and Marine Corps Commendation Medal with Combat "V," and the Combat Action Ribbon. Gilday began serving as the 32nd Chief of Naval Operations August 22, 2019.

Amit Gupta, PhD, is a senior advisor to the Forum of Federations. His recent writings have focused on diaspora politics, popular culture and politics, the US-China rivalry, and the impact of demography on US foreign and domestic policy. His articles have appeared in *Orbis, Asian Survey, Security Dialogue, The Round Table, Mediterranean Quarterly, The International Journal of the History of Sport,* and *Sport in Society.* He is also the author or editor of eight books. He retired from Air War College in 2022.

Kamala D. Harris is currently serving as the forty-ninth vice president of the United States of America. She was elected vice president after a lifetime of public service, having been elected district attorney of San Francisco, California, attorney general, and United States Senator. Vice President Harris was born in Oakland, California, to parents who emigrated from India and Jamaica. She graduated from Howard University and the University of California, Hastings College of Law. Vice President Harris and her sister, Maya Harris, were primarily raised and inspired by their mother, Shyamala Gopalan. Gopalan, a breast cancer scientist and pioneer in her own right, received her doctorate the same year Vice President Harris was born. Her parents were activists, instilling Vice President Harris with a strong sense of justice. They brought her to civil rights demonstrations and introduced role models—ranging from Supreme Court Justice Thurgood Marshall to civil rights leader Constance Baker Motley—whose work motivated her to become a prosecutor. Growing up, Vice President Harris was surrounded by a diverse community and extended family. In 2014, she married Doug Emhoff. They have a large blended family that includes their children, Ella and Cole. Throughout her career, the vice president has been guided by the words she spoke the first time she stood up in court: Kamala Harris, for the people. In 1990, Vice President Harris joined the Alameda County District Attorney's Office where she specialized in prosecuting child sexual assault cases. She then served as a managing attorney in the San Francisco District Attorney's Office and later was chief of the Division on Children and Families for the San Francisco City Attorney's Office. She was elected district attorney of San Francisco in 2003. In that role, Vice President Harris created a groundbreaking program to provide first-time drug offenders with the opportunity to earn a high school degree and find employment. The program was designated as a national model of innovation for law enforcement by the United States Department of Justice. In 2010, Vice President Harris was elected California's attorney general and oversaw the largest state justice department in the United States. She established the state's first Bureau of Children's Justice and instituted several first-of-their-kind reforms that ensured greater transparency and accountability in the criminal justice system. As attorney general, Vice President Harris won a $20 billion settlement for Californians whose homes had been foreclosed on, as well as a $1.1 billion settlement for students and veterans who were taken advantage of by a for-profit education company. She defended the Affordable Care Act in court, enforced environmental law, and was a national leader in the movement for marriage equality. In 2017, Vice President Harris was sworn into the United States Senate. In her first speech, she spoke out on behalf of immigrants and refugees who were then under attack. As a member of the Senate Homeland Security and Governmental Affairs Committee, she fought for better protections for DREAMers and called for better oversight of substandard conditions at immigrant detention facilities. On the Senate Select Committee on Intelligence, she worked with members of both parties to keep the American people safe from foreign threats and crafted bipartisan legislation to assist in securing American elections. She visited Iraq, Jordan, and Afghanistan to meet with service members and assess the situation on the ground. She also served on the Senate Judiciary Committee. During her tenure on the committee, she participated in hearings for two Supreme Court nominees. As senator, Vice President Harris championed legislation to reform cash bail, combat hunger, provide rent relief, improve maternal health care, and address the climate crisis as a member of the Senate Committee on Environment and Public Works. Her bipartisan anti-lynching bill passed the Senate in 2018. Her legislation to preserve historically Black colleges and universities was signed into law, as was her effort to infuse much-needed capital into low-income communities during the COVID-19 pandemic. On August 11, 2020, Vice President Harris accepted President Joe Biden's invitation to become his running mate and help unite the nation. She is the first woman, the first Black American, and the first South Asian American to be elected vice president, as was the case with other offices she has held. She is, however, determined not to be the last.

Troy Harting, PhD, Colonel, USAF, is the permanent professor and head of the Department of Management at the US Air Force Academy, leading a department of thirty-nine faculty and responsible for all curriculum, personnel, budget, research, and long-range planning associated with the management major, as well as interfaces with the operations research, data science, and systems engineering majors. He has also served as vice provost for USAFA's 650-member faculty, delivering the curricula in thirty-two academic disciplines to over four thousand undergraduates. He earned his PhD in business administration from the University of Virginia's Darden School of Business. He is also a contributing member of the Project Thrive Team at USAFA.

Tonya Henderson, DM, is an organization development scholar-practitioner and aerospace industry professional. She was the 2019 chair for the Academy of Management's Management Consulting Division and the 2016 Organizer and Curator of TEDx Colorado Springs. Tonya has provided complexity and OD-informed consulting and problem-solving to a wide range of industry clients and currently works for Torch Technologies developing future system requirements. As a doctor of management, a graduate of the US Naval Academy, and a veteran of the consulting and aerospace industries, her work is informed by multi-disciplinary experience, education, and scholarship. She is also a contributing member of the Project Thrive Team at USAFA.

Scott G. Heyler, PhD, Colonel, USAF, Retired, is an assistant professor in the Department of Management at the US Air Force Academy. He recently retired from the Air Force after twenty-six years of service. He served in leadership positions at all levels of the Air Force and in the joint arena. In particular, he served as an Air Officer Commanding at USAFA where he was responsible for the mentoring and military training of 110+ cadets. Dr. Heyler completed his doctorate at Auburn University where his research focused on ethical decision making and character development. He is a husband and father to three children. He is also a contributing member of the Project Thrive Team at USAFA.

Daniel Robert Hokanson, General, USNGB, is a four-star general in the United States Army who currently serves as the twenty-ninth chief of the National Guard Bureau. He previously served as the twenty-first director of the Army National Guard. His previous military assignments include vice chief of the National Guard Bureau, deputy commander of United States Northern Command, adjutant general of the Oregon National Guard, and commander of the 41st Infantry Brigade Combat Team. He is a veteran of Operation Iraqi Freedom, Operation Enduring Freedom, and Operation Just Cause. Hokanson assumed his current assignment on August 3, 2020. Gen. Hokanson was born in Happy Camp, California, on June 27, 1963, the son of Bob and Diann (Kieffer) Hokanson. He graduated from Happy Camp High School in 1980 and attended the College of the Siskiyous before being accepted to the United States Military

Academy at West Point, New York. Gen. Hokanson graduated from West Point in 1986 and was commissioned as a second lieutenant in the aviation branch. He is also a graduate of the United States Army Airborne School. Gen. Hokanson then served for several years as an aviator with the 7th Infantry Division at Fort Ord, California, including deployment to Panama for Operation Just Cause in 1989–90. In 1991 he completed the Aviation Officer Advanced Course and AH-64 (Apache) Combat Aircraft Qualification Course. He subsequently served with 1st Battalion, 229th Aviation Regiment at Fort Hood, including command of the battalion's Company B, and then served as a project engineer for the Aircraft Armament Test Division at Yuma Proving Ground in Arizona. Army National Guard Hokanson left the Regular Army in July 1995 and was a member of the Army Reserve Control Group until October. Gen. Hokanson then began his career as a member of the Army National Guard, assigned initially as aide-de-camp in the office of Oregon's adjutant general. His later assignments included: operations officer, 641st Medical Battalion (Helicopter Evacuation); aviation operations officer, Oregon Army National Guard; plans analyst, Program Analysis and Evaluation Division, National Guard Bureau; executive officer, 641st Medical Battalion (Evacuation Helicopter), Oregon Army National Guard; deputy director, Army Aviation, Oregon Army National Guard; commander, 641st Medical Battalion (Helicopter Evacuation), Oregon Army National Guard; chief of staff, Combined Joint Task Force Phoenix V, Afghanistan; deputy commander, 41st Infantry Brigade Combat Team, Oregon Army National Guard; and commander, 41st Infantry Brigade Combat Team, including deployment as part of Multi-National Corps—Iraq.

John D. Hopper, Jr., Lt Gen, USAF, Retired, received his commission from the United States Air Force Academy (USAFA) in 1969. He served on active duty for more than thirty-five years, accumulating over four thousand flying hours including combat missions in Vietnam and Desert Shield/Storm. He commanded at every level to include command of 21st Air Force and as USAFA Commandant of Cadets. Post retirement he served as CEO of the not-for-profit Air Force Aid Society, member/chair of the Civil Air Patrol Board of Governors, trustee of the Falcon Foundation, and as a member of one federal commission and chair of another.

Sue Hoppin is a nationally recognized expert on military spouse and family issues working to bridge the cultural gap between government, private and public groups, and military communities. She is an advocate, published author, and consultant with more than twenty years of experience and expertise in military community programs. She is also a trusted advisor. In addition to serving on multiple nonprofit boards, Sue was appointed by President Obama to the board of visitors of the United States Air Force Academy; she completed her tenure in 2018 as the board's vice chairman. In 2020 she was appointed to the VA's Veterans' Advisory Committee on Education.

Steny H. Hoyer is the US House Majority Leader for the 117th Congress. Congressman Hoyer is the second-ranking member of the House Democratic leadership. He is charged with mobilizing the party vote on important legislation, acting as a liaison between members and the Democratic leadership, and coordinating strategy within the caucus. He also plays a key role in shaping House Democrats' legislative priorities and in delivering the Democratic message. Congressman Hoyer's experience, know-how, and strong work ethic have led to increasing responsibilities within the House Democratic leadership. He has served as House Majority Leader since 2019—making him the highest-ranking member of Congress from Maryland in history. Previously he served as the House Majority Leader from 2007 to 2011 and as House Democratic Whip from 2003 to 2007 and from 2011 to 2019. Prior to serving in his first term as whip, Congressman Hoyer served as chair of the Democratic Caucus—the fourth-ranking position among House Democrats—from 1989 to 1995. He is the former co-chair (and a current member) of the Democratic Steering Committee and served as the chief candidate recruiter for House Democrats from 1995 to 2000. Congressman Hoyer also served as Deputy Majority Whip from 1987 to 1989. Now in his twenty-first term in Congress, he also became the longest-serving member of the US House of Representatives from Maryland in history on June 4, 2007. Congressman Hoyer currently serves on the St. Mary's College board of trustees. He also is a former member of the board of regents of the University System of Maryland and the United States Naval Academy board of visitors. Congressman Hoyer and his wife, the late Judith Pickett Hoyer, have three daughters: Susan, Stefany, and Anne; son-in-law Loren Taylor; grandchildren Judy, James Cleveland, and Alexa; and great-grandchildren Ava, Braedon, and Brooklyn.

John E. Hyten, General, USAF, serves as the eleventh vice chairman of the Joint Chiefs of Staff. In this capacity, he is the nation's second-highest-ranking military officer and a member of the Joint Chiefs of Staff. Gen. Hyten attended Harvard University on an Air Force Reserve Officer Training Corps scholarship, graduated in 1981 with a bachelor's degree in engineering and applied sciences, and was commissioned a second lieutenant. The general's career began in engineering and acquisition before transitioning to space operations. He has commanded at the squadron, group, wing, and major command levels. In 2006, he deployed to Southwest Asia as director of Space Forces for operations Enduring Freedom and Iraqi Freedom. He commanded Air Force Space Command, and prior to his current assignment, was the commander of US Strategic Command, one of eleven combatant commands under the Department of Defense.

Marae A. Travis, Captain, US Army, graduated from the United States Military Academy at West Point with a business management degree in 2018. Her achievements include winning first place in the Mid-Hudson Business Plan Competition (Clean-Tech category), receiving the Margaret Chase Smith Leadership Excellence award, and earning the Honor Graduate title for her class in the

Logistics Basic Officer Leader Course. She is currently an Explosive Ordnance Disposal (EOD) officer, serving as a platoon leader at Fort Carson, Colorado, in the 749th EOD Company.

Ryan Kelty, PhD, is an associate professor of sociology at the US Air Force Academy. He is an award-winning teacher and scholar whose research focuses on diversity and social psychology issues in military organizations. Dr. Kelty has consulted with numerous national and international defense organizations. He is co-editor of *Private Military and Security Contractors: Controlling the Corporate Warrior* (2016) and *Risk-Taking in Higher Education: The Importance of Negotiating Intellectual Challenge in the College Classroom* (2017). He earned his BA from Middlebury College and PhD from the University of Maryland. Dr. Kelty previously served on the faculty at West Point and Washington College.

Kenneth L. Korpak, Lieutenant Colonel, USAF, Retired, is a graduate of the US Air Force Academy Prep School. He has advanced degrees from Johnson & Wales University (culinary arts), University of Northern Colorado (education, sports administration), and the US Air Force Academy. A career space operations officer, he authored National Space Policy while assigned to the National Reconnaissance Office, Chantilly, Virginia. Following his Air Force career, he served a culinary internship at The Broadmoor, Colorado Springs, Colorado, under Chef De Cuisine, Mario Viguie. He is currently a laboratory manager performing supercritical fluid extraction, refinement, and R&D for Purplebee's, a Schwazze company.

Charles E. Lewis III, Captain, USAF, is an instructor of management at the US Air Force Academy from where he also graduated in 2014. Lewis received his MBA from Duke University Fuqua School of Business with a dual concentration in leadership/ethics and marketing. Prior to becoming an instructor, he served as a financial management officer and deputy cost chief at Hanscom Air Force Base, MA. He is also a contributing member of the Project Thrive Team at USAFA.

David A. Levy, PhD, is a professor of management at the United States Air Force Academy and has been teaching courses on leadership, power, organization development, and change there since 2002. He graduated from the US Air Force Academy in 1988 with a bachelor's degree in psychology and served as a security forces officer and as an internal consultant for ten years on active duty. After leaving the military, he worked as an organizational change consultant for Grant-Thornton and KPMG, now Bearing Point. Dr. Levy received his doctorate in organizational behavior from Cornell University applying principles from cognitive psychology to organizational theory. He is currently focusing his efforts in two areas. First, he is attempting to bridge the gap between action research and effective leadership, arguing that effective leadership looks like good action research. Second, as co-leader of the Thrive Project at USAFA, he is working toward creating environments where all members can maximize their potential and thrive. Dr. Levy is a co-author of five books with Dr. Parco including *The 52nd Floor: Thinking Deeply about Leadership*, *Attitudes Aren't Free: Thinking Deeply about Diversity in the US Armed Forces*, *Echoes of Mind: Thinking Deeply about Humanship*, *The Rise and Fall of DADT: Evolution of Government Policy Toward Homosexuality in the US Military*, and *The Line: A Very Short, Short Story*. He is also a contributing member of the Project Thrive Team at USAFA.

Hila Levy, Major, USAF Reserve, has previously served in a variety of roles as an active duty and reserve Air Force intelligence and foreign area officer at tactical, operational, and headquarters-level assignments in the Republic of Korea, Japan, the United Kingdom, and the Pentagon. She is a top graduate of the US Air Force Academy, where she became the first Puerto Rican resident to be awarded a Rhodes Scholarship. She holds an MPhil from the School of Advanced Air and Space Studies; MS from Johns Hopkins University; and MSt, MSc with Distinction, and DPhil from the University of Oxford. Dr. Levy served as a White House Fellow in the Office of Science and Technology Policy.

Luis Maldonado, Major, USAF, is a Defense Fellow for Congressman Don Bacon, Brig Gen (ret.), of Nebraska. Major Maldonado hails from the Bronx, New York. He entered the Air Force as a Russian linguist in July 1997. He has served as an interpreter implementing arms control treaties in Russia and other former Soviet states. In 2009, after earning senior master sergeant stripes, he commissioned as a distinguished graduate of Officer Training School and serves as an intelligence officer. He has a bachelor's degree in Russian from Excelsior College, New York, and a master's degree in international relations from Troy University, Alabama.

Jaime Martinez, Major, USAF, (he/his/him) is a US exchange officer integrated into the Royal Netherlands Air Force. As chief instructor and flight examiner of a foreign unit, he is responsible for integrating Dutch air refueling assets into coalition operations at a tactical level. He has over 3,400 hours in military aircraft including 1,100 combat hours providing in-flight refueling support to US and coalition aircraft. Jaime earned a bachelor's degree in behavioral science from the US Air Force Academy, where he conducted independent research focused on overcoming resistance to the concept of privilege. After graduating he co-authored a peer-reviewed article on the subject in the journal *Reflections*. He is currently an MLA student of international relations at the Harvard University Extension School, where he continues to study how to transform the social differences that create conflict into opportunities for cooperation.

Michael D. Matthews, PhD, is a professor of engineering psychology at the United States Military Academy. He is a Templeton Foundation Senior Positive

Psychology Fellow, a Fellow of the Army Chief of Staff's Strategic Studies Group
(2014–2015), and author of *Head Strong: How Psychology is Revolutionizing War*
(Oxford University Press, 2014) and numerous other books, chapters, and scientific articles. Dr. Matthews is a founding member of the Military Child Education
Coalition's Science Advisory Board and a leadership consultant to governmental
agencies.

Diane Mazur, JD, is a retired University of Florida law professor and expert
on military regulation and personnel policy, especially on issues related to inclusion, equal opportunity, and gender. She is the author of *A More Perfect
Military: How the Constitution Can Make Our Military Stronger*, a book on why
the military is at its best when it embraces civilian constitutional values among
its core military values. Before attending law school, Professor Mazur served as
an aircraft and munitions maintenance officer in the United States Air Force.

A. Mitchell "Mitch" McConnell Jr. is the US Senate Minority Leader for
the 117th Congress. He is the longest-serving Senate Republican Leader in
American history, unanimously elected to lead the conference eight times since
2006. From 2015 to 2021, McConnell served as Senate Majority Leader. He is
only the second Kentuckian to ever be Majority Leader of the US Senate. The
first, Senator Alben Barkley, led the Democrats from 1937 to 1949. McConnell
previously served in leadership as the Majority Whip in the 108th and 109th
Congresses and as chairman of the National Republican Senatorial Committee
during the 1998 and 2000 election cycles. McConnell has been praised in numerous media outlets for his consequential Senate leadership. He's been called
"the most important Republican since Ronald Reagan" and "the most conservative leader of either party in the history of the Senate." A veteran political
commentator titled him as the "most effective floor leader in either party I've
ever seen." In 2015 and 2019, *TIME* magazine named McConnell one of the
100 Most Influential People in the World. McConnell led a transformation
of the federal judiciary in a victory for the rule of law and the Constitution.
His consequential decision to follow precedent and keep a Supreme Court va-
cancy open during the 2016 presidential election gave him the opportunity
to confirm three justices as Majority Leader. In four years, he also prioritized
the confirmation of 30 percent of circuit court judges nationwide and a total
of 234 lifetime appointments to the federal bench. First elected to the Senate
in 1984, McConnell is Kentucky's longest-serving senator. He made history
that year as the only Republican challenger in the country to defeat an incumbent Democrat and as the first Republican to win a statewide Kentucky race
since 1968. On November 3, 2020, he was elected to a record seventh term,
winning 117 of the Commonwealth's 120 counties. McConnell graduated with
honors from the University of Louisville College of Arts and Sciences, where
he served as student body president. He also is a graduate of the University
of Kentucky College of Law, where he was elected president of the Student

Bar Association. McConnell worked as an intern on Capitol Hill for Senator John Sherman Cooper before serving as chief legislative assistant to Senator Marlow Cook and as deputy assistant attorney general to President Gerald Ford. Before his election to the Senate, he served as judge-executive of Jefferson County, Kentucky, from 1978 until he commenced his Senate term on January 3, 1985. McConnell currently serves as a senior member of the Appropriations, Agriculture, and Rules Committees. He is the proud father of three daughters. McConnell is married to Secretary Elaine L. Chao, the eighteenth US Secretary of Transportation. Previously, Secretary Chao served for eight years as President George W. Bush's Secretary of Labor. She is also a former president of the United Way of America and director of the Peace Corps.

James C. McConville, General, USA, assumed duties as the fortieth chief of staff of the US Army, Aug. 9, 2019, after most recently serving as the thirty-sixth vice chief of staff of the US Army. He is a native of Quincy, Massachusetts, and a graduate of the US Military Academy at West Point, New York. He holds a master of science in aerospace engineering from Georgia Institute of Technology and was a National Security Fellow at Harvard University in 2002. McConville's command assignments include commanding general of the 101st Airborne Division (Air Assault), where he also served as the commanding general of Combined Joint Task Force-101, Operation Enduring Freedom; deputy commanding general (Support) of the 101st Airborne Division (Air Assault), where he also served as the deputy commanding general (Support) of Combined Joint Task Force-101, Operation Enduring Freedom; commander of 4th Brigade, 1st Cavalry Division, Operation Iraqi Freedom; commander of 2nd Squadron, 17th Cavalry Regiment, 101st Airborne Division (Air Assault); and commander of C Troop, 2nd Squadron, 9th Cavalry Regiment, 7th Infantry Division (Light). His key staff assignments include the US Army deputy chief of staff, G-1; chief of Legislative Liaison; executive officer to the vice chief of staff of the Army; G-3 for 101st Airborne Division (Air Assault); J5 strategic planner for US Special Operations Command; S-3 for 25th Combat Aviation Brigade; S-3 for 5th Squadron, 9th Cavalry; and S-3 for Flight Concepts Division. McConville is a senior Army aviator qualified in the AH-64D Longbow Apache, OH-58 Kiowa Warrior, AH-6, AH-1 Cobra, and other aircraft. His awards and decorations include two Distinguished Service Medals, three Legions of Merit, three Bronze Star Medals, two Defense Meritorious Service Medals, three Meritorious Service Medals, two Air Medals, the Joint Service Commendation Medal, two Army Commendation Medals, four Army Achievement Medals, the Combat Action Badge, the Expert Infantryman's Badge, the Master Army Aviator Badge, the Air Assault Badge, the Parachutist Badge, and the Army Staff Identification Badge.

Amanda Metcalfe, PhD, has spent twenty years serving the Colorado Springs community as a community and military counselor and consultant. She is currently an assistant professor in behavioral science and leadership at the US Air Force Academy, and an adjunct instructor of counseling and human services at University of Colorado at Colorado Springs.

Metcalfe has extensive experience with trauma treatment for which she has utilized for recovery and support of veterans, soldiers, civilians, and numerous survivors of sexual trauma. She applies further specialization of mindfulness for performance in support of warriors, athletes, and students to hone mindfulness skills to improve resiliency and performance. She is also a contributing member of the Project Thrive Team at USAFA.

Mark A. Milley, General, USA, is the twentieth chairman of the Joint Chiefs of Staff, the nation's highest-ranking military officer, and the principal military advisor to the president, Secretary of Defense, and National Security Council. Prior to becoming chairman on October 1, 2019, General Milley served as the thirty-ninth chief of staff of the US Army. A native of Massachusetts, General Milley graduated from Princeton University in 1980, where he received his commission from Army ROTC. General Milley has had multiple command and staff positions in eight divisions and Special Forces throughout the last thirty-nine years to include command of the 1st Battalion, 506th Infantry, 2nd Infantry Division; the 2nd Brigade, 10th Mountain Division; Deputy Commanding General, 101st Airborne Division (Air Assault); Commanding General, 10th Mountain Division; Commanding General, III Corps; and Commanding General, US Army Forces Command. While serving as the Commanding General, III Corps, General Milley deployed as the Commanding General, International Security Assistance Force Joint Command and Deputy Commanding General, US Forces Afghanistan. General Milley's joint assignments also include the Joint Staff operations directorate and as a military assistant to the Secretary of Defense. General Milley's operational deployments include the Multi-National Force and Observers, Sinai, Egypt; Operation Just Cause, Panama; Operation Uphold Democracy, Haiti; Operation Joint Endeavor, Bosnia-Herzegovina; Operation Iraqi Freedom, Iraq; and three tours during Operation Enduring Freedom, Afghanistan. He also deployed to Somalia and Colombia. In addition to his bachelor's degree in political science from Princeton University, General Milley has a master's degree in international relations from Columbia University and one from the US Naval War College in national security and strategic studies. He is also a graduate of the MIT Seminar XXI National Security Studies Program. General Milley and his wife, Hollyanne, have been married for more than thirty-four years and have two children.

Aaron M. Oats, Captain, USAF, (he/his/him) is a KC-10 Tanker Pilot in the US Air Force, stationed in Travis Air Force Base California. He has over 1,100 hours in military aircraft including 400 combat hours providing in-flight refueling support to US and coalition aircraft. Aaron earned a bachelor's degree in behavioral science from the US Air Force Academy. Aaron also conducted independent research focused on privilege and organizational inclusion. In his extracurricular time, he competed as an intercollegiate boxer and rugby player. Aaron is currently pursuing a master's degree in industrial and organizational psychology at Liberty University.

Barack H. Obama was the forty-fourth president of the United States of America. He was elected president in 2008 and became the first African American to hold the office. Obama faced major challenges during his two-term tenure in office. His primary policy achievements included health care reform, economic stimulus, banking reform and consumer protections, and a repeal of the Don't Ask, Don't Tell policy preventing lesbian and gay Americans from serving openly in the military. Obama's father, Barack Sr., a Kenyan economist, met his mother, Stanley Ann Dunham, when both were students in Hawaii, where Barack was born on August 4, 1961. They later divorced, and Barack's mother married a man from Indonesia, where he spent his early childhood. Before fifth grade, he returned to Honolulu to live with his maternal grandparents and attend a private prep school on scholarship. In his memoir *Dreams from My Father* (1995), Obama describes the complexities of discovering his identity in adolescence. After two years at Occidental College in Los Angeles, he transferred to Columbia University, where he studied political science and international relations. Following graduation in 1983, Obama worked in New York City, then became a community organizer on the South Side of Chicago, coordinating with churches to improve housing conditions and create job-training programs in a community hit hard by steel mill closures. In 1988, he went to Harvard Law School, where he attracted national attention as the first African American president of the *Harvard Law Review*. Returning to Chicago, he joined a small law firm specializing in civil rights. In 1992, Obama married Michelle Robinson, a lawyer who had also excelled at Harvard Law. Their daughters, Malia and Sasha, were born in 1998 and 2001. Obama was elected to the Illinois Senate in 1996, and then to the US Senate in 2004. At the Democratic National Convention that summer, he delivered an acclaimed keynote address. In 2008, after winning the Democratic nomination after a hard-fought primary race with Hillary Clinton, he defeated Arizona Senator John McCain by 365 to 173 electoral votes in the general election. As an incoming president, Obama faced many challenges including the 2008 financial crisis, wars in Iraq and Afghanistan, and the continuing global war on terrorism. Inaugurated before an estimated crowd of 1.8 million people, Obama proposed unprecedented federal spending to revive the economy and a renewal of America's stature in the world. During his first term he signed three signature bills: economic stimulus, health care reform, and legislation reforming the nation's financial institutions. Obama also pressed for a fair pay act for women and new safeguards for consumer protection. In 2009, Obama became the fourth president to receive the Nobel Peace Prize. However, in the 2010 midterm elections, the Democrats lost control of the House of Representatives, thus affecting Obama's future domestic policy agenda. In 2012, he was reelected over former Massachusetts Governor Mitt Romney by 332 to 206 electoral votes. The Middle East remained a key foreign policy challenge. Obama directed the military and intelligence operation that led to the killing of Osama bin Laden, the head of Al-Qaeda and the terrorist responsible for the September 11, 2001, attacks on the United States. However, a new self-proclaimed Islamic State arose during a civil war in Syria and began inciting terrorist attacks. Obama sought to manage a hostile Iran with a treaty that hindered its development of nuclear weapons. The Obama administration also adopted the Paris Climate Agreement signed by 174 states and the European Union in 2015 to reduce greenhouse gas emissions and slow global warming. In the last year of his second term, Obama spoke at two events that clearly moved him—the fiftieth anniversary of the civil rights march from Selma to Montgomery and the dedication of the National Museum of African American History and Culture. "Our union is not yet perfect, but we are getting closer," he said in Selma. "And that's why we celebrate," he told those attending the museum opening in Washington, "mindful that our work is not yet done."

Matthew Orlowsky is the deputy department head for management at the United States Air Force Academy and a PhD candidate at the University of Denver. Matt has twenty-three years' experience as a military officer with assignments in the United States, Korea, Germany, Iraq, and three deployments. He graduated from the US Air Force Academy. Matt has masters' degrees from both Troy State University and the Naval War College. His research interests include how corporate governance, autonomy, and leadership development contribute to thriving in an organization and leadership as a system. He is also a contributing member of the Project Thrive Team at USAFA.

Gary Packard Jr., Brigadier General, USAF, Retired, (he/his/him) is dean of the College of Applied Science and Technology at the University of Arizona (azcast.arizona.edu). Gary's military career spanned thirty-seven+ years with various assignments and 3,900 flying hours. He served twenty+ years at the US Air Force Academy retiring as a vice dean. Gary served on the 2010 DoD study leading to the repeal of Don't Ask, Don't Tell. Gary earned his doctorate in developmental psychology from North Carolina at Chapel Hill, masters' degrees in counseling from Michigan State and aeronautical science from Embry Riddle, and a bachelor's degree in behavioral science from the Air Force Academy.

Vicente Miguel Pamparo, Captain, USSF, is an acquisitions officer in the United States Space Force. In addition to his acquisition experience, he is also a language enabled Airman and served at his alma mater, the US Air Force Academy, as an admissions advisor and continues to mentor cadet candidates as an admissions liaison officer. He is a degree candidate at Harvard's Extension School (international relations). Finally, he is the executive director and cofounder of the education nonprofit VESPERE.

James E. Parco, Lieutenant Colonel, USAF, Retired, graduated from the US Air Force Academy in 1991. While on active duty, he served on the National Security Council at the White House and in a diplomatic capacity overseas with the American embassy in Tel Aviv. He went on to earn an MBA from the College of William & Mary and a PhD from the University of Arizona. He later served on the faculties of the US Air Force Academy (1996–1999; 2003–2007), Air Command & Staff College (2007–2011), and Colorado College (2011–2020). In 2008, he received both the top teaching and top research awards at USAFA. In 2009, Parco received the Military Officers' Association of America's top teaching award at Air Command & Staff College, and in 2010, he was named educator of the year for the US Air Force's Education and Training Command. Parco was the first active-duty instructor ever promoted to the rank of full professor at Air University. In 2017, he was named the Lloyd Worner Outstanding Teacher of the Year at Colorado College. He retired from academia in 2020.

Michael R. Pence was the forty-eighth vice president of the United States of America. He was born in Columbus, Indiana, on June 7, 1959, one of six children born to Edward and Nancy Pence. He attended Indiana University School of Law and met the love of his life, Second Lady Karen Pence. After graduating, Vice President Pence practiced law, led the Indiana Policy Review Foundation, and began hosting *The Mike Pence Show*, a syndicated talk radio show and a weekly television public affairs program in Indiana. Along the way he became the proud father to three children, Michael, Charlotte, and Audrey. In 2000, he launched a successful bid for his local congressional seat, entering the United States House of Representatives at the age of forty. On Capitol Hill he established himself as a champion of limited government, fiscal responsibility, economic development, educational opportunity, and the US Constitution. His colleagues quickly recognized his leadership ability and unanimously elected him to serve as chairman of the House Republican Study Committee and House Republican Conference Chairman. In 2013, Vice President Pence left the nation's capital when Hoosiers elected him the fiftieth governor of Indiana. As governor of Indiana, Vice President Pence increased school funding, expanded school choice, and created the first state-funded Pre-K plan in Indiana history. Vice President Pence's record of legislative and executive experience, as well as his strong family values prompted President Donald Trump to select Mike Pence as his running mate in July 2016. Unlike President Trump, Pence was said to have fostered strong relationships with the men who preceded him in the executive branch. In November 2017, a news story revealed that Pence conversed with Obama's VP, Joe Biden, at least once per month, and also met with Bush's former second-in-command, Dick Cheney. Their discussions were said to involve the exchange of ideas and advice, with the former VPs relaying valuable lessons learned during their administrations. In August 2018, Pence delivered a speech at the Pentagon in which he outlined the administration's plans to create a sixth branch of the US military, the "Space Force." Declaring, "We must have American dominance in space, and so we will," he noted that President Trump would request $8 billion over the next five years to support military operations in that arena. The following year, Pence was dragged into the House impeachment inquiry of President Trump after the *Washington Post* reported that the vice president was involved in efforts to pressure Ukraine into investigating 2020 presidential candidate Joe Biden. On February 26, 2020, President Trump announced that Vice President Pence would lead the administration's response to the coronavirus, which originated in China and was spreading around the world. While his regularly scheduled press briefings were soon dominated by the presence of Trump, Pence focused on delivering measured versions of the president's fluctuating pronouncements, coordinating efforts with governors and addressing matters of supply shortages. On Monday, March 9, he announced that testing capabilities had increased to the point where five million tests would be distributed by the end of the week. With the administration looking to find ways to reopen businesses and schools by April, the vice president raised eyebrows by visiting the Mayo Clinic in Minnesota without a face mask late in the month, saying he wanted to be able to look workers in the eye and thank them without being obstructed. On October 2, 2020, President Trump revealed that he and wife Melania had both tested positive for COVID-19. Pence and wife Karen were also tested, but their results came back negative. Although Pence expressed confidence in a reelection victory, the days-long effort to count the ballots brought increasingly grim news for the incumbents, until Biden was declared as the president-elect on November 7, 2020. While Trump raged against the "illegal" voting and launched a flurry of lawsuits to challenge the results, Pence offered a more grounded perspective of the proceedings, urging supporters to "remain vigilant" as the litigation played out. On December 14, 2020, all 538 electors in the Electoral College cast their vote, formalizing Biden's victory over President Trump in the 2020 presidential election. Biden received 306 votes and Trump received 232. Trump continued to insist that he won the election, and he called on Pence, as president of the Senate, to reject the results of contested states when Congress convened to formalize the Electoral College vote on January 6, 2021. However, Pence publicly broke with Trump just before the start of the congressional meeting by issuing a letter which read: "It is my considered judgment that my oath to support and defend the Constitution constrains me from claiming unilateral authority to determine which electoral votes should be counted and which should not." That afternoon, after the president held a rally in which he criticized his vice president who refused to join his cause, Pence was among the lawmakers who were whisked to safety when an unruly mob broke into the Capitol and clashed with police, resulting in four deaths and the declaration of a public emergency by Washington, DC, Mayor Muriel Bowser. "To those who wreaked havoc in our Capitol today, you did not win," the vice president said when order was restored, and he went on to formally declare Biden's victory just after 3:40 a.m. on January 7, 2021.

Gale S. Pollock, MD, Major General, USA, Retired, served as acting surgeon general of the Army and commander of the Army Medical Command, and is the first woman and first non-physician to hold those positions. Previously she served as deputy surgeon general of the Army and twenty-second chief of the Army Nurse Corps. Other assignments in her thirty-six-year military career included serving as commanding general, Tripler Army Medical Center, Pacific Regional Medical Command; special assistant to the surgeon general for information management and health policy; and commander, Martin Army Community Hospital, Fort Benning, GA.

John W. "Jay" Raymond, General, USSF, is the chief of Space Operations, United States Space Force. As chief, he serves as the senior uniformed Space Force officer responsible for the organization, training, and equipping of all organic and assigned space forces serving in the United States and overseas. Gen. Raymond was commissioned through the ROTC program at Clemson University in 1984. He has commanded at squadron, group, wing, numbered air force, major command, and combatant command levels. Notable staff assignments include serving in the Office of Force Transformation, Office of the Secretary of Defense; the director of plans, programs and analyses at Air Force Space Command; the director of plans and policy (J5), US Strategic Command; and the deputy chief of staff for operations, Headquarters US Air Force. Gen. Raymond deployed to Southwest Asia as director of Space Forces in support of operations Enduring Freedom and Iraqi Freedom. Prior to leading establishment of the US Space Force and serving as the first chief of Space Operations, Gen. Raymond led the re-establishment of US Space Command as the eleventh US combatant command.

Chris Rodda is a writer and researcher who has worked for the Military Religious Freedom Foundation (MRFF) as senior research director since 2007. She is the author of several books on the history of religion and religious liberty in America, the most recent being *From Theocracy To Religious Liberty: Connecticut's Journey from Thomas Jefferson's "Wall of Separation" Letter to a State Constitution, as Told Through the Newspapers of the Time.*

William D. Rodriguez, Rear Admiral, USN, Retired, spent thirty-two years in the Navy as a surface warfare officer and as an engineering duty officer. Tours of duty included OIC of a Naval Electronics Engineering Center; program manager for a number of C4ISR Systems; acting commander and chief engineer for SPAWARSYSCOM; and PEO for the Navy's Enterprise Information Services. Upon retirement, he served in a number of leadership positions including CEO, San Ysidro Education Vanguard Foundation; national president of ANSO; board member of HVLA; Vocational Solutions board of directors; and executive consultant for Suss Consulting.

David Rohall, PhD, is a professor of sociology and department head of the Department of Sociology & Anthropology at Missouri State University. He has studied trends in American society generally and the military services specifically for almost twenty years. His most recent works include *Symbolic Interaction in Society* (2019, Rowman & Littlefield) and *Inclusion in the American Military: A Force for Diversity* (2017, Lexington Press).

Jaime Sampayo, JD, DM, is currently the employee management & relations officer at Schriever AFB, CO; and part owner of the mediation firm—Sampayo & Prescott Mediation Group, and the law firm—Sampayo & Sampayo, Attorneys at Law. He has thirty+ years of experience in business, law, and teaching. Dr. Sampayo served overseas and in the continental US as an attorney (USAF JAG) and Foreign Area Officer (FAO). He has taught for several universities and at the US Air Force Academy, where he taught law, management, and Spanish. His research interests are in HR leadership models and conflict resolution. He is also a contributing member of the Project Thrive Team at USAFA.

Michelle A. Butler Samuels, PhD, is on faculty (experimental psychologist) at the US Air Force Academy (USAFA). Her inclusion research focuses on resilience, employability, respect for individuals with disabilities, and face-to-face experiences with different types of others. She developed high-impact long-term collaborations with community partners including Colorado School for the Deaf and the Blind (CSDB), Craig Hospital-Brain/Spinal Cord Rehabilitation, and most recently (Buddhist-inspired) Naropa University. She served as a USAFA committee member for the Development of Respect for Human Dignity, is serving her second term as a board of trustee of CSDB, and served as a visiting scholar at Naropa.

Steven M. Samuels, PhD, (he/his/him) is a professor of behavioral sciences and leadership at USAFA. He was one of the original twelve civilians to integrate the institution in 1993 and has been active publishing and working internally on issues of psychology, inclusive leadership, and pedagogy. He has also worked leadership and inclusion topics at USNA's Stockdale Center, the Citadel (South Carolina), the University of Colorado, and the Pentagon's DADT Repeal task force. Steve received his bachelor's from Brandeis University, and his doctorate from Stanford University. He is the first, and so far, only civilian to earn Jump Wings from USAFA.

Alfredo Sandoval, Lieutenant Colonel, USAFR, Retired, served as chairman of the US Air Force Academy Board of Visitors (2012–2017), a position that was appointed to him by the president and nominated by the speaker of the House. As chairperson, he directed the board in providing independent advice and recommendations on matters relating to the Air Force Academy, such as the morale, discipline, curriculum, instruction, physical equipment, fiscal affairs, and academic methods. Sandoval also recently served as chairman for the US Air Force Academy's Diversity Advisory Panel, consulting senior leadership on diversity recruiting, retention, and accessions. He is a recipient of AFA's Outstanding Diversity Officer award. As an Air Liaison Officer, he mentored scores of candidates to become cadets, and later officers. Mr. Sandoval also serves as the chairman of the Congressional Nomination Committee for California Congressman Raul Ruiz. During his career, he has helped many congressional members and their staff improve their nomination processes. Sandoval is a managing partner of the Private Investment Group, which focuses on portfolio management and wealth transfer. He is a former senior vice president at Merrill Lynch and a co-founder of Creosote Partners, bringing real estate development and renewable energy projects to tribal reservation lands in the Coachella Valley, Calif. A 1982 graduate from the United States Air Force Academy, Sandoval earned a master of finance and a masters of marketing degree from Wright State University. He is a graduate of the Air Force's Air Command and Staff and Air War Colleges and holds an international relations certificate from the University of Pennsylvania, Wharton School.

Charles Ellis "Chuck" Schumer is the US Senate Majority Leader for the 117th Congress. He was born and raised in Brooklyn, NY, where his dad owned a small exterminating business, and his mom was a housewife. He attended public school and graduated from James Madison High School before heading to Harvard University, and then Harvard Law School. Chuck has two daughters, Jessica and Alison, and he still resides in Brooklyn with his wife, Iris Weinshall. After graduating from Harvard Law School in 1974, Chuck was elected to the New York State Assembly, where he soon made his mark with his trademark vigor and relentless advocacy. In 1980, at twenty-nine, Chuck was elected as a congressman from the 9th Congressional District. In 1998, Chuck was elected to the US Senate; he became New York's senior senator when Senator Daniel Patrick Moynihan retired in 2000. After New Yorkers reelected him in 2004, Chuck secured two powerful posts: a seat on the Senate Finance Committee, which oversees the nation's tax, trade, social security, and healthcare legislation, and the chairmanship of the Democratic Senatorial Campaign Committee (DSCC). Chuck successfully led the DSCC for two consecutive cycles and greatly expanded the number of seats in his conference. Following the elections of 2006, then Majority Leader

Harry Reid (D-NV) appointed Chuck to serve as vice chair of the Democratic Conference, the number three position on the Democratic leadership team. In 2016, Chuck was once again reelected by the people of New York, and at the same time, his colleagues elected him to serve as leader of the Democratic Caucus, the first time a New York senator has held the position.

Michael Rafi Sherwin served as the interim United States Attorney for the District of Columbia from 2020 to 2021. Raised in Cleveland, Ohio, Sherwin earned his BA in political science and liberal arts at the Ohio State University in 1994 and his JD at the University of Notre Dame in 1998. Sherwin served as a naval intelligence officer from 1999 to 2004, participating in Operation Southern Watch, Operation Northern Watch, Operation Enduring Freedom, and Operation Iraqi Freedom. He also served as an assistant US attorney for the Southern District of Florida. Sherwin was named interim US attorney in May 2020 when Shea, after three months as US attorney, was appointed to lead the Drug Enforcement Administration. Trump nominated Justin Herdman to be Shea's permanent successor. Some high-profile investigations the US attorney's office handles are related to special counsel Robert Mueller's Russia investigation. On March 3, 2021, he was replaced by Channing D. Phillips.

Kathryn L. Smith, Esq., earned her law degree from Notre Dame and practiced law for almost twenty-five years before she retired in 2016. Kate's last position was an assistant general counsel at Verizon where she drafted and negotiated contracts and provided legal advice to the sales and marketing staff. She also practiced commercial litigation at two major law firms, and led a contracts division at Motorola. She is also a veteran, having served her country as an acquisition officer after graduating from the United States Air Force Academy in 1982 with a bachelor of science degree in engineering management. She lettered in volleyball at the Academy. She serves on two boards of directors, and volunteers with charitable organizations. Recently, she consulted on DEI and justice efforts with Common Defense, a grassroots veterans organization, and graduated with a master's degree in public leadership at the University of San Francisco.

Rod Smith, PhD, Lieutenant Colonel, USAF, is an assistant professor in the Department of Behavioral Sciences and Leadership at the US Air Force Academy. He has worked in operational, testing, executive, strategic planning, and academic settings. His work focuses on the use of love in the development of inclusive leaders of character who can innovate solutions to adaptive challenges. His efforts support gendered and racial leadership development efforts. He is a contributing member of AK Rice Institute, Group Relations International, International Leadership Association, and Adaptive Leadership Network. He is also a contributing member of the Project Thrive Team at USAFA.

Alan M. Steinman, MD, Rear Admiral, US Coast Guard, Retired, was commissioned in the Public Health Service as a lieutenant in July 1972, commencing a military career of over twenty-five years in the Coast Guard and the Public Health Service. He was selected for promotion to flag officer in August 1993 for the position of director of health and safety at USCG Headquarters (equivalent to both the surgeon general and chief of safety programs for the other service branches). He retired in September 1997. RADM Steinman is the most senior military officer to self-identify as gay after his retirement, and lives with his adopted son and his husband in Olympia, WA.

Donald John Trump was the forty-fifth president of the United States of America. He was born in Queens, New York, on June 14, 1946. His father, Fred Trump, was a successful real estate developer. Trump was educated at the New York Military Academy and the Wharton School of Finance and Commerce at the University of Pennsylvania. In 1971, he took over his father's real estate company, renaming it the Trump Organization. The business soon became involved in a variety of projects, including hotels, resorts, residential and commercial building, casinos, and golf courses. His first of many books was *The Art of the Deal*, published in 1987. In 2004, he launched the reality television show *The Apprentice*. In 2005, Donald Trump married Melania Knauss. They have one son, Barron. Trump also has four adult children from previous marriages: Donald Jr., Ivanka, Eric, and Tiffany. During the 2016 primary, Trump defeated more than a dozen rivals to win the Republican nomination. While he lost the popular vote, Trump defeated former Secretary of State Hillary Clinton in the general election by winning a majority of Electoral College votes. His campaign slogan was "Make America Great Again." Without previous elected political experience, President Trump used unconventional methods to communicate his priorities. Most notably, he used the social media platform Twitter as a primary mechanism for direct communication with the American public, other politicians, and the press corps. As president, he signed a major tax reform bill into law and oversaw a reduction of federal regulations. His protectionist trade policies included tariffs in foreign aluminum, steel, and other products. The Trump administration also renegotiated trade agreements with Mexico, Canada, China, Japan, and South Korea. Other domestic priorities included Supreme Court and federal judiciary appointments, increased military budgets, aggressive border and immigration control, criminal justice reform, and the reduction of prescription drug prices. In foreign policy, the Trump administration moved the US embassy in Israel from Tel Aviv to Jerusalem and brokered normalization agreements between Israel and a number of countries. In 2018, President Trump attended a summit with Kim Jong Un, marking the first time a sitting president met with a North Korean leader. In 2018, there was a partial government shutdown as Trump disagreed with Congress over funding for a border wall between the United States and Mexico. The funding lapse lasted thirty-five days before it was resolved. In 2019, a federal whistleblower filed a complaint that Trump had pressured Ukrainian President Volodymyr Zelensky to investigate former Vice President Joe Biden's son Hunter, who had served on the board of Bursima Holdings, a natural gas company in Ukraine. Later that year, the House of Representatives impeached President Trump based upon allegations of obstruction of Congress and abuse of power. In 2020, the Senate acquitted Trump on both articles of impeachment. The first confirmed case of COVID-19 was reported in the United States on January 20, 2020. The remainder of Trump's presidency was consumed with the coronavirus pandemic. Critics argued that Trump's response to the pandemic was delayed and did not sufficiently encourage public health practices to reduce the spread of the virus. However, the Trump administration's program "Operation Warp Speed" assisted in the private sector development of two approved vaccines. Nonetheless, by the time Trump left office, more than 400,000 Americans had died of COVID-19. Trump lost reelection to Democratic candidate Joe Biden, but publicly claimed widespread voter fraud had affected the outcome. Supporters of President Trump traveled to Washington, DC, for a "Save America" rally on January 6, 2020. Trump spoke to the large crowd on the Ellipse near the White House and encouraged attendees to protest the counting of the Electoral College votes in Congress. The rally turned violent when the president's supporters overwhelmed law enforcement, breaching the United States Capitol and disrupting the vote count. Five people died as a result of the violence, and the Capitol complex suffered millions of dollars in damage. On January 13, 2021, Trump's actions resulted in the House of Representatives approving another article of impeachment: the incitement of insurrection. He is the only president in American history to be impeached twice by Congress.

Eric Tucker, PhD, Lieutenant Colonel, USAF, Retired, is an assistant professor in the Management Department at the Air Force Academy. He received his PhD in industrial engineering and management systems from the University of Central Florida. He received a BS in aeronautical engineering from the Air Force Academy, MS in engineering and technology management from Oklahoma State University, and a MA in national defense and strategic studies from the Naval War College. Eric is a retired Air Force Lieutenant Colonel and has been at the Air Force Academy for ten years. His current research involves the improvement of organizational performance management systems using analytics. He is also a contributing member of the Project Thrive Team at USAFA.

Michael L. "Mikey" Weinstein is the founder and president of the Military Religious Freedom Foundation. The MRFF is the undisputed leader of the national movement to restore the obliterated wall separating church and state in the United States Armed Forces. Described by *Harper's Magazine* as "the constitutional conscience of the US military, a man determined to force accountability," Mikey is a 1977 Honor Graduate of the United States Air Force Academy, served for more than ten years with the Judge Advocate General (JAG) Corps, and spent over three years working in, and for, the West Wing of the Reagan Administration as legal counsel in the White House.

Fletcher H. "Flash" Wiley graduated from the United States Air Force Academy in 1965, and continued his studies as a Fulbright Scholar in Paris, France, at L'Institut Des Etudes Politiques. Following service as a captain in the US Air Force, Mr. Wiley resigned his commission to pursue graduate studies. In 1974, he received his master's in public policy from Harvard's Kennedy School of Government and his law degree from Harvard Law School. For more than two decades, Mr. Wiley worked as a practicing attorney concentrating in the areas of corporate and commercial law, small business development, entertainment law, and real estate. On September 1, 1996, Mr. Wiley resigned as a senior partner with the Boston Law firm of Goldstein & Manello, P.C. to join PRWT Services, Inc., a Philadelphia-based products and services company, as a principal of the company and its executive vice president and general counsel. On September 30, 2008, Mr. Wiley retired from employment with PRWT after playing a key role in building it into one of the nation's largest minority-owned businesses and *Black Enterprise* magazine's 2009 "Company of the Year." He remains a principal in the company, and is the chairman of the PRWT Advisory Board. Mr. Wiley has served as a director of several for-profit business organizations, including three public companies. He recently retired after two decades as a director of The TJX Companies, Inc. (NYSE). He is also "of counsel" to Morgan Lewis & Bockius, LLP, one of the nation's largest law firms, where he specializes in corporate and commercial law. Additionally, as chairman and CEO of The Centaurus Group, LLC, Mr. Wiley is an investor and principal in several commercial, real estate development, and management consulting ventures. Mr. Wiley is extensively involved in civic and charitable activities. In 1984, he founded and chaired until 1990 the Governor's Commission on Minority Business Development. He also served as a director of the Economic Development and Industrial Corporation of Boston from 1980 to 1993. In 1994, he stepped down from a seven-year involvement as president, and then national chairman of the Black Entertainment and Sports Lawyers Association, Inc., to assume a two-year term as chairman of the board of the Greater Boston Chamber of Commerce "GBCC"). He is a benefactor of Crispus Attucks Children's Center, Inc.; a founding member of the Harvard Law School and the Harvard Kennedy School Black Alumni Organizations; a former director of the New England Legal Foundation; overseer of the New England Region Anti-Defamation League; and chairman of the board of The Dimock Center, Inc. He is also the recipient of numerous civic and professional awards, including induction in 2010 into the GBCC's "Academy of Distinguished Bostonians." In 2011, he was named by US Secretary of Defense Gates to the board of visitors of The Air University; and in 2012, President Obama appointed him to the board of visitors of the US Air

Force Academy. In 2012 he also received an honorary doctorate in human letters from Cambridge College and an honorary doctorate in law from New England School of Law. In 2019, Mr. Wiley was named a distinguished graduate of the US Air Force Academy. Mr. Wiley is a member of the bars of the Commonwealth of Massachusetts and District of Columbia, and belongs to the American, National, and Massachusetts Bar Associations.

The Inspector General
Department of
the Air Force

Report of Inquiry (S8918P)
Independent Racial Disparity Review
December 2020

This page intentionally blank

TABLE OF CONTENTS

REPORT OF INQUIRY (Case S8918P)

CONCERNING

INDEPENDENT RACIAL DISPARITY REVIEW

PREPARED BY
THE SAF/IGS IRDR TEAM
December 2020

I. INTRODUCTION

The Secretary of the Air Force (SecAF), Chief of Staff of the Air Force (CSAF), and Chief of Space Operations (CSO) directed the Department of the Air Force Inspector General (DAF IG) to assess racial disparity in military discipline processes and personnel development and career opportunity as they pertain to black Airmen and Space Professionals. For purposes of this review, "racial disparity" refers to a noted data difference between races. Specifically, this Review defines racial disparity as existing when the proportion of a racial/ethnic group within a subset of the population is different from the proportion of such groups in the general population. While the presence of a disparity alone is not evidence of racism,[1] discrimination, or disparate treatment, it presents a concern that requires more in depth analysis.[2] Guided by the disparities identified and concerns raised in this report, the root cause analyses and systemic action plan phase will follow as outlined in the "Highlights" section below.

The DAF recognizes other disparities across a range of minority groups are equally deserving of such a review. However, this Review was intentionally surgically-focused on discipline and opportunity regarding black service members to permit a timely yet thorough review that should lead to systemic and lasting change, as appropriate. Nonetheless, lessons learned and insights gained from this Review should benefit broader minority initiatives.

It is worth noting this Review and resulting actions are a subset of, and will feed into, broader and more comprehensive Department of Defense and Department of the Air Force Diversity & Inclusion initiatives directed by the Secretary of Defense and the Secretary of the Air Force.

METHODOLOGY

It is important for the reader to understand the scoping and methodology of this Review. A key element of the effort was timeliness, which in turn required a careful focus to ensure

---

[1] Racism--1: a belief that race is a fundamental determinant of human traits and capacities and that racial differences produce an inherent superiority of a particular race; 2: the systemic oppression of a racial group to the social, economic, and political advantage of another. *Merriam-Webster.com Dictionary*, https://www.merriam-webster.com/dictionary/racism. Accessed 9 Nov, 2020.

[2] Importantly, this Review was not chartered to determine whether or not racial bias or discrimination is present. Such an examination would require considerable social sciences expertise, a broader look at American society in general, and was outside the defined scope.

thoroughness without delaying the report. The initial goal was to complete the Review in 120 days. Root cause analyses of the disparities found during the Review were not conducted as that would have taken considerably more time. The intent was that root cause analyses would follow completion of the DAF IG report, as necessary.

Most crucially, this Review was designed to not only analyze existing information, but also to hear directly from our Airmen and Space Professionals through five lines of effort: (a) anonymous surveys, (b) written feedback to DAF IG, (c) feedback through the DAF IG telephone and email hotline, (d) individual interviews of senior leaders, subject matter experts (SMEs), and service members, and (e) in-person group discussions with Airmen and Space Professionals across all MAJCOMs and the USSF.

While the Review team fully appreciates limitations of surveys, this tool was deliberately chosen and included to capture the voice of our Airmen and Space Professionals. The response we received was strong and the substance was detailed. Over 123,000 members of the DAF chose to share their views through the survey in just a two week period. Another 1300 plus Airmen and Space Professionals offered their inputs in small-group discussions with DAF IG. Our service members and civilians also provided their experiences and thoughts in the form of more than 27,000 single-spaced pages of free text comments. The voice of our Airmen and Space Professionals was an important element of this Review and its intended purpose to ensure commanders at all levels heard the perspectives and concerns of all our DAF members.

Key themes from the surveys, individual feedback from Airmen and Space Professionals, and interviews were further explored in 138 in-person group discussions with members from across all MAJCOMs and the USSF as well as meetings with wing commanders, vice commanders, command chiefs, Staff Judge Advocates, and Area Defense Counsels across 20 installations. Importantly, the Review found that all feedback conduits consistently reinforced common themes, providing confidence in the overall findings.

Next, the Review assessed the feedback received as it related to Air Force demographic data in the areas of military discipline as well as career development and opportunities. Specifically, this Review included an examination of the DAF military justice data dating back to 2012; an examination of career development and opportunity data involving civilian, enlisted, and officer ranks; a review of all pertinent 36-series (personnel) and 51-series (legal) Air Force Instructions and related publications; a re-examination of 23 past studies and reports involving race and demographics in the military; and an examination of other information and data culled from thousands of Airmen, Space Professionals, and civilian employees, DAF and third-party subject matter experts, retired senior military officers, and Air Force MAJCOM as well as Space Force representatives.

Finally, please note that the identification of racial disparity does not automatically mean racial bias or racism is present. This Review focused on the existence of racial disparity, but it did not specifically assess racial bias or individual acts of racism within the DAF, which may cumulatively contribute to racial disparity overall. Thousands of black service members and civilians reported experiencing issues ranging from bias to outright racial discrimination. These experiences indicate bias and isolated individual acts of racism may contribute to the racial disparities identified in this report.

HIGHLIGHTS

This Independent Review confirmed racial disparity exists for black service members in the following areas: law enforcement apprehensions, criminal investigations, military justice, administrative separations, placement into occupational career fields, certain promotion rates, professional military educational development, and leadership opportunities. While the data show racial disparity, it does not indicate causality. Data alone do not address why racial disparity exists in these areas. Examples of disparities identified include:

Military Justice and Discipline – enlisted black service members were 72% more likely than enlisted white service members to receive Uniform Code of Military Justice (UCMJ), Article 15, commanding officer's non-judicial punishment (NJP), and 57% more likely than white service members to face courts-martial.

Administrative Disciplinary Actions and Discharges – young black enlisted members are almost twice as likely as white enlisted members to be involuntarily discharged based on misconduct.

Investigations – black service members are 1.64 times more likely to be suspects in Office of Special Investigations (OSI) criminal cases, and twice as likely to be apprehended by Security Forces. Based on limited data, black service members are investigated and substantiated for Military Equal Opportunity (MEO) sexual harassment cases at a higher rate than white members. No racial disparity was identified in IG reprisal and restriction investigations, and the DAF does not maintain demographic data on Commander Directed Investigations.

Accessions – enlisted black service members are overrepresented[3] in accessions when compared to their proportion of the eligible U.S. population. Black service members are underrepresented[4] in operational career fields and overrepresented in support career fields, which may affect their promotion opportunities.

Professional Military Education (PME) – since 2015, black officers have been overrepresented in PME nominations but underrepresented in designations to attend. The gap between nomination percentages and designation percentages is larger in Senior Developmental Education (SDE) than Intermediate Developmental Education (IDE). Enlisted PME are all "must attend" courses based on rank and promotion date.

Promotions – black service members are underrepresented in promotions to E5-E7 and O4-O6. Additionally, black officers are underrepresented in Definitely Promote (DP)

---

[3] Overrepresentation is defined as including a disproportionately large number of (a particular category or type of person), as in a statistical study.
[4] Underrepresentation is defined as including a disproportionately small number of (a particular category or type of person), as in a statistical study.

allocations for O5 and O6. Black, permanent, full-time civilians are underrepresented in GS-13 through Senior Executive Service (SES) grades.

Retention – across the enlisted population, the data revealed no consistent disparity in retention rates by race. Within the officer population, the data revealed black officers were slightly overrepresented in separations at 5-15 years of service and underrepresented in separations at 16-20 years of service.

AFI Review – no inherent, systemic, or procedural biases were found in the twenty 36-series (personnel) guidance documents or the 51-series (legal) publications pertaining to discipline. Edits to enhance clarity were recommended.

The Voice of the Airmen and Space Professionals – black service members voiced a consistent lack of confidence in DAF discipline processes and developmental opportunities compared to their white peers. For example, of the 123,000+ DAF IG Survey respondents:

- 2 out of every 5 black enlisted, civilians, and officers do not trust their chain of command to address racism, bias, and unequal opportunities

- 1 out of every 3 black service members said they believe the military discipline system is biased against them

- 3 out of every 5 black service members believe they do not and will not receive the same benefit of the doubt as their white peers if they get in trouble

- 1 out of every 3 black officers do not believe the Air Force and Space Force provide them the same opportunities to advance as their white peers, and

- 2 out of every 5 black civilians have seen racial bias in the services' promotion system

History – What we've known, what we've done, what has worked, what has not? – The Review Team examined 23 previous reports and studies related to diversity and racial disparities dating back to 1973. The findings of these studies and associated proposed recommendations often did not identify root causes, often did not compel follow-through, often lacked mechanisms to measure effectiveness over time, and broadly lacked accountability for progress.

This report is designed to address racial disparities as noted across the "life of an Airman or Space Professional." First, the report examines military justice processes and development and opportunities afforded to Airmen and Space Professionals. Second, the report reviews all DAF policies and guidance related to military discipline and personnel development matters. Next, is a compelling discussion of the insightful input and substance received in over 27,000 pages of feedback, 123,000 surveys, and 138 sessions with members across the DAF. Finally, the report takes an historical look at the wide array of past investigations, inquiries, and reviews on the same or similar issues and provides an assessment of the results of those efforts.

Due to the complex nature of the issues addressed herein and their wide-ranging impact on the force, this report provides broad recommendations. SecAF, CSAF, and CSO tasked key stakeholders in the DAF to thoroughly review this report, conduct a root cause analysis for the disparity areas within their responsibility, and develop substantive recommendations and plans that will systemically address the highlighted issues. DAF Stakeholder's initial assessment/action plans are summarized in Appendix A of this report. We recommend DAF stakeholders begin root cause analysis and provide updated action plans, as appropriate, to SecAF, CSAF, and CSO within 60 days. Once approved, we recommend any updated initial action plans be publicly released to all Airmen and Space Professionals. DAF IG will conduct and publicly release a "progress report" six months after this report's publication, followed by full reviews annually. The progress report and subsequent annual reviews will assess the stakeholders' root cause analyses, the development of substantive recommendations to address the highlighted issues, and most importantly, the effectiveness of any changes.

The 60-day updates to SecAF, CSAF, and CSO must, as a minimum, specifically address the issues listed below which are identified in this report, as well as propose appropriate action plans, as warranted:

Military Discipline Processes
- The racial disparity in military justice actions, including Article 15s and courts-martial (p. 6-15)
- The disparity in marijuana use among our youngest enlisted members as evidenced by the random drug testing program (p. 10-15)
- The racial disparity in administrative discipline as evidenced by administrative discharges as well as substantive feedback from a large number of Airmen and Space Professionals (p. 16-20)
- The racial disparity in Security Forces (SF) apprehensions (p. 27-30)
- The racial disparity in substantiated Military Equality Opportunity (MEO) sexual harassment complaints (p. 32-34)

Personnel Development & Career Opportunities
- The disparity in Air Force Specialty Codes (AFSCs), especially as it relates to operational versus support career fields (p. 34-45)
- The disparity in Undergraduate Pilot Training (UPT) accession and graduation rates by race, gender, and ethnicity (p. 40-42)
- The disparity in the officer IDE and SDE process, given that analysis shows black officers are being nominated for PME at higher than the overall nomination rate but designated to attend at a lower rate (p. 52-57)
- The disparity in the civilian Intermediate Developmental Education (IDE) and Senior Developmental Education (SDE) selection process given black civilians are identified to meet the Civilian Developmental Education Board (CDEB) at a consistently lower rate than white civilians (p. 57-59)
- The racial disparities in promotions to E5-E7 and O4-O6 (p. 59-74)
- The racial disparities in civilian leadership representation from GS-13 to SES (p. 75-78)

- The lack of thorough Barrier Analysis among some Developmental Teams[5] (p. 79-86)
- The racial disparity in wing command and equivalent positions (p. 84-86)

Other Department-wide Concerns
- The lack of satisfaction service members expressed regarding IG and EO, with special emphasis on the process of referring cases back to the chain of command (p. 106-107)
- The lack of trust black DAF members expressed in their chain of command to address racism, bias, and unequal opportunities (p.91, 104-116)
- The sentiment expressed by a majority of black DAF members that they are not given the benefit of the doubt by their chain of command (p. 99, 104-116)

II. MAGNITUDE OF THE PROBLEM

MILITARY JUSTICE AND DISCIPLINE DATA

Measured in Rates Per Thousand (RPT), black Airmen are more likely to face formal disciplinary action than their white peers. Specifically, black service members were 74% more likely to receive Article 15s and 60% more likely to face courts-martial than white service members. The primary offenses where the difference could be seen were: willful dereliction, failure to go to/leaving from appointed place of duty, making a false official statement, and drug-related offenses. Data alone cannot provide insight on the cause of the racial disparity in Air Force discipline, and further analysis is required.

RATE PER THOUSAND (RPT) DATA

The percentage of personnel facing courts-martial or Article 15 (NJP) represents a small fraction of the total service population, 2.39% from 2012 to 2016. However, a close examination of demographics based on RPT methodology shows a persistent disparity between white and black service members. For example, the 2017 to 2019 RPT data show racial disparity in courts-martial and Article 15s, with substantial gaps between black and white Active Duty enlisted members in the ranks of E1-E4. Since 2017, the number of courts-martial and Article 15s has decreased overall; however, the RPT gap between white and black service members in the ranks has increased.

---

[5] AFI 36-205, *Affirmative Employment Program (AEP), Special Emphasis Programs (SEPS) and Reasonable Accommodation Policy*, dated 15 Dec 16, defines barrier analysis as "an investigation of anomalies found in workplace policies, procedures, and practices that limit or tend to limit employment opportunities for members of any race or national origin, either sex, or based on an individual's disability status. Barrier analysis identifies the root causes of those anomalies, and if necessary, eliminates them." (Ex 62) A barrier analysis includes the following steps: identify triggers (trends, disparities, or anomalies), explore root causes of triggers, develop an action plan, implement the action plan, and assess the action plan result. A detailed explanation of the barrier analysis process may be found in AFI 36-205 and EEOC MD-175. (Ex 62; Ex 63)

Fig 1: Enlisted Courts-Martial and Article 15s (FY12-FY16 and FY17-FY19)

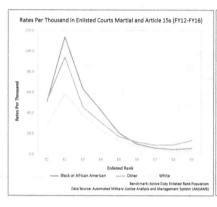 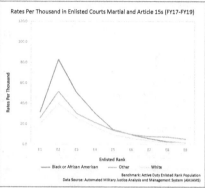

Due to the small number of Article 15s and courts-martial involving officers, the overall data did not change much when including officer information. Further analysis of the officer data separate from the enlisted numbers revealed a similar racial disparity in officer NJP. Note: both the enlisted and officer data highlight the importance of continuing efforts like this Review to examine disparities between other races and groups.

Fig 2: Officer Courts-Martial and Article 15s (FY12-16 and FY17-19)

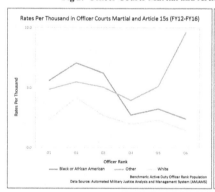 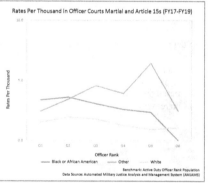

The RPT data demonstrate disparity in the proportional number of military justice cases by race, but it does not indicate the root cause of the disparity. Evidence indicates factors other than race impact the RPT disparity. For example, data indicates socio-economic factors may contribute to the disparity. While further study is required, AF/A1 data indicates a link between the quality of education prior to joining the service and behavior while in the military. Objective investigation data from OSI and Security Forces indicate some of the disparity in NJP results from a disparity in behavior rather than race. Accessions data show that members who joined the service with moral waivers are more likely to receive military discipline during their time in service. (Ex 56:10) Finally, the disparity in population numbers between demographic groups disproportionally impacts the RPT data. Because there are fewer black service members than white service members (ratio of about 1:5 overall and 1:13 for officers), even one additional individual disciplinary action will have a far greater impact on the RPT for black service members.

To accurately assess and better understand the magnitude of racial disparity in military discipline, DAF IG examined additional quantitative data:

Racial Disparity in Military Justice (Further Data Analysis)

Racial disparities in military justice actions against black service members is a complex issue that has been reviewed in-depth by the Air Force Judge Advocate General's Corps (AFJAG). A 20-year analysis of Air Force NJP data and courts-martial revealed the following:

- For every single year between 1999 and 2019, black Airmen were more likely to receive NJP than white service members, in terms of RPT. Black service members were 1.74 times more likely than white service members to receive NJP and 1.60 times more likely than white service members to be court-martialed.

- For every single year, black service members were more likely to face courts-martial than white service members. Black service members were court-martialed at an average RPT of 3.39, compared with white service members at an average RPT of 2.12. This data reveals that black Airmen were 60% more likely to face court-martial than white service members.

In 2016, an AFJAG analysis revealed the racial disparity in NJP for black service members primarily involved two offenses: marijuana use/possession and absent without leave (AWOL) – which includes reporting late, leaving early, or generally being absent from unit, organization, or place of duty without authorization. An AFJAG-led review of data from the Air Force Automated Military Justice and Analysis Management System (AMJAMS) from 2006-2016 showed black service members receive NJP at a much higher rate for wrongful use, possession, etc., of controlled substances (Article 112a, UCMJ). Specifically, black service members received NJP for Article 112a offenses at a rate of approximately 2.6 to 1 (average RPT of 2.72 for black service members compared to 1.03 for white service members) for all controlled substances; and approximately 3.9 to 1 (average RPT of 2.15 for black service members compared to 0.55 for white service members) for use or possession of marijuana.

This Review's analysis of AMJAMS data confirmed the disparity AFJAG identified. Our data review provided further details focused on total specifications (or allegations of misconduct under the UCMJ) and enlisted members from FY12 to FY19.

Fig 3: Total Article 15 Specifications (E1-E9) RPT and Disparity Ratio

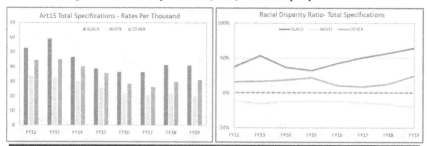

This Review identified the eight specifications with the highest disparity in RPT for black and white service members. Analysis identified substantial racial disparity in drug-related offenses as well as willful dereliction, failure to go to or going from appointed place of duty, and making a false official statement.

Fig 4: Article 15 Rates Per Thousand by Race and Top Offenses

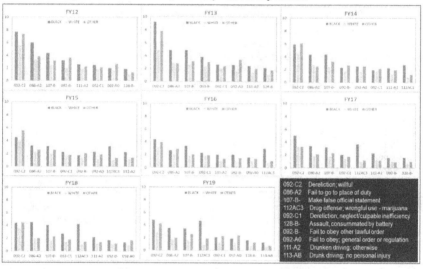

Both the AFJAG data and this Review's data analysis clearly show racial disparity, and the offenses most likely to involve disparity, but the data does not reveal "why" there is a disparity.

Accessions data of new recruits indicates that certain service members are more prone to disciplinary action than others, regardless of race. The data show black and white male recruits who enter the Air Force or Space Force with moral waivers due to previous criminal convictions (such as those involving assault, DUI, grand theft, marijuana use/possession, and vehicular infractions, among a host of other categories) are more likely to receive an Article 15 at some point during their time in the service. Note: Whether a recruit enters the service with a "moral waiver" for misconduct depends on the severity, frequency, and category of the crime.

The RAND Corporation found recruits who entered the Air Force with moral waivers receive Article 15s more often than those who do not. Among those with moral waivers, black males receive Article 15s at higher rates than white males with the same waivers. While this data sheds light on why some service members are more likely to receive Article 15s, it still does not fully explain the disparity in the rate at which service members who had moral waivers receive Article 15s.

The DAF military justice process ensures sufficient grounds exist for taking action in every case. Prior to a commander imposing an Article 15, a military attorney reviews witness testimony and documentary evidence to determine whether a UCMJ violation may have occurred. Commanders have discretion on whether to impose disciplinary action and which level of action to utilize--including no action, administrative action, Article 15, or court-martial. Without interviewing a representative sample of commanders who imposed punishments and probing all potential reasons for punishment decisions, it is difficult to determine conclusively why black service members were punished more frequently for offenses such as AWOL or dereliction of duty. Further, there are many variables to consider, such as whether it was a first-time offense or repeated offenses. In contrast, Article 15s for marijuana use are usually the result of a positive urinalysis test, and there is less commander discretion in this offense category. More study is needed to understand why black service members are punished disproportionately for some offenses.

Drug Use Cases

The DAF does not tolerate the illegal or improper use of drugs and employs a random urinalysis program to test all service members. If an Airman or Space Professional tests positive for marijuana use, the usual course of action is to impose Article 15 punishment and then administratively separate those personnel from the service. Use of other illegal drugs – such as cocaine and heroin – will typically result in a court-martial. The various charts below show black service members are overrepresented when it comes to positive drug tests, including by rank and drug class.

Fig 5: Drug Offenses: Positive Test Rate

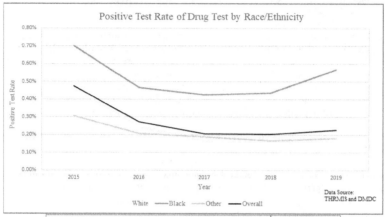

Year	Black	Other	White	All Airmen
2015	0.70%	0.31%	0.46%	0.48%
2016	0.47%	0.21%	0.25%	0.27%
2017	0.43%	0.19%	0.16%	0.20%
2018	0.44%	0.17%	0.16%	0.20%
2019	0.57%	0.18%	0.16%	0.23%
2020	0.64%	0.18%	0.14%	0.22%

Fig 6: Racial Disparity in Positive Random Drug Tests

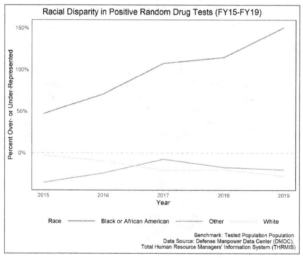

Fig 7: Racial Disparity in Positive Random Drug Tests by Rank

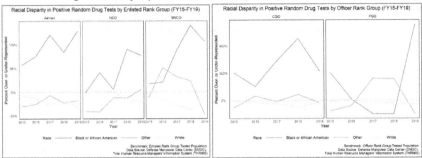

Fig 8: Drug Offenses: Trends in % of Positive Drug Tests by Drug Class and Race

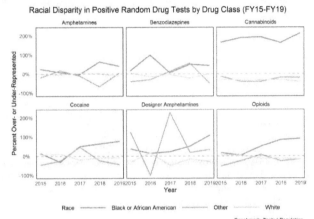

An initial review of random urinalysis data found that black service members appear to be consistently overrepresented in testing by approximately 1% to 2% from 2015 to 2019. Although the percentages are small, data analysts consider this anomaly to be statistically significant, considering several hundred thousand Airmen comprise the sample set. However, this anomaly does not mean the testing is not random. The overrepresentation could result from a confluence of factors such as differences in availability for testing after random selection.

Furthermore, racial disparities in rank combined with testing rate differences by rank could influence the overrepresentation.

Fig 9: Racial Disparity in Random Drug Test Selection

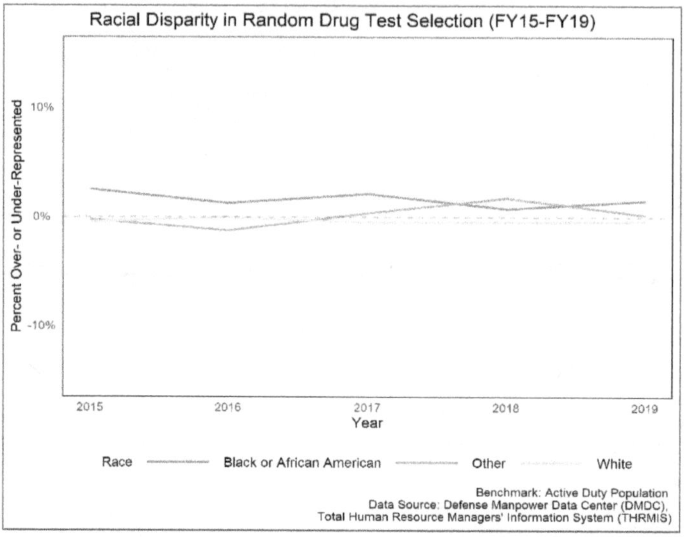

Although there is an up to 2% racial disparity in overall testing rate for black service members from 2015 to 2019, when broken down by rank, the numbers show black E1-E4s are actually underrepresented in random testing when compared to their white peers, which indicates there was no inappropriate targeting of young black enlisted members for drug testing. Overall, this report revealed enlisted members were tested at a higher rate than officers consistently from 2015 to 2019, as depicted below.

Fig 10: Random Drug Test Selection by Rank

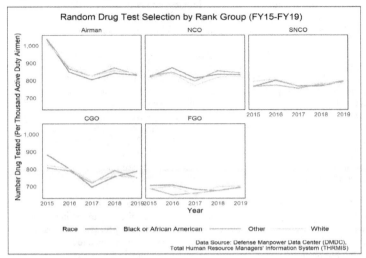

Fig 11: Racial Disparity in Random Drug Testing by Rank

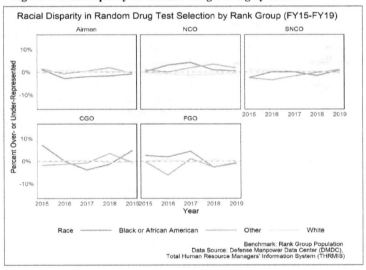

Given this Review's data analysis and the fact that random test selections are based on social security numbers, the IG concluded black E1s to E4s are not being singled out based on their race to disproportionally provide urinalysis samples leading to positive test results.

As the data show, black E1-E4s are not overrepresented in random testing rates. As the standard disciplinary action for a positive drug test for marijuana is an Article 15, the disparity between the numbers of Article 15s for drug use between white and black Active Duty Airmen E1s to E4s appears to be the result of a disparity in behavior rather than racial bias.

Conclusion on Military Justice Data

As early as 1974, the DAF identified racial disparity in military justice actions. AFJAG is aware of the racial disparity in Article 15 actions and courts-martial and informs leadership at all levels of this disparity. Also, AFJAG analyzed the military judicial process to address the potential of racial bias. In 2016, the DAF determined there was no evidence of selective prosecution in courts-martial based on a review of courts-martial records under the guidelines set in the Supreme Court case *Batson v. Kentucky*[6] The DAF also found no disparity among conviction rates between black and white service members. Based on the available data, this Review found no instances of intentional racial bias or discrimination after an accused entered the court-martial process.

While the DAF has taken some action to address potential bias in the judicial process, it has not answered that next-level question of "why" racial disparity exists in military justice actions. AFJAG provides training to commanders highlighting that racial disparity exists; however, no training is provided on what causes the racial disparity and how to address the disparity. For more subjective cases such as AWOL or dereliction of duty, where the commander has discretion to impose disciplinary action and the severity of that disciplinary action, the DAF has not analyzed why racial disparity is present. This Review included interviews with members of the Disciplinary Actions Analysis Team (DAAT), which was established in 2017 to address racial disparity in military justice actions. These interviews revealed the DAAT, after meeting more than three years, was unable to ascertain the reason for such disparity. For more objective cases, such as marijuana drug use cases arising from random testing, this Review determined behavioral disparity accounts for at least some disparity indicated. However, the DAF must conduct further review to understand why there may be behavioral disparity among racial groups and how to address that behavioral disparity. Multiple studies show certain racial and age groups view marijuana use differently resulting in disparate use among those groups. (Ex 57) As of this Review, it appears the DAF has not examined these studies and considered how this behavioral disparity among its youngest enlisted members might be addressed.

---

[6] As a note, the Air Force did receive criticism for relying on a case involving discretionary juror removal which was not germane to selective prosecution.

Young black service members are almost twice as likely to be involuntarily discharged from the DAF with misconduct as the basis. The DAF will soon require commanders to report the type of administrative action, rank, age, gender, race, and ethnicity of the person imposing the administrative disciplinary action, along with the same information for the recipient of the disciplinary action.

Outside of non-judicial punishment and courts-martial under the UCMJ, service members may also receive administrative disciplinary action to correct and punish bad behavior. Administrative disciplinary actions consist of Letters of Reprimand, Letters of Admonishment, and Letters of Counseling (LORs, LOAs, LOCs), with the LOR being the most severe rebuke and the LOC the least. The DAF has not historically tracked racial demographics in administrative disciplinary actions. However, a review of administrative separation actions shows there is racial disparity in the percentage of black enlisted members in the rank of E1 to E4 whom the DAF involuntarily discharges with misconduct as a basis, which is generally and largely based upon a record of LORs, LOAs, and LOCs. Thus, young black service members as a whole may be receiving more administrative disciplinary actions than their peers, based on the frequency with which they are being administratively discharged for misconduct.

Administrative disciplinary actions

First-line supervisors and commanders have wide latitude and the discretion to issue administrative disciplinary actions to service members. An Airman or Space Professional who reports late to work for the first time could receive no punishment, verbal counseling, or an LOC that, depending on the circumstances, could serve as part of the basis for an administrative discharge later on. Similarly, a service member consistently late to work for a week could receive no punishment, or a verbal counseling, or a combination of LOCs, LOAs, and LORs. The last of these might establish the basis that the service member committed several minor disciplinary infractions or engaged in a pattern of misconduct that could result in administrative discharge, when coupled with other instances of misconduct.

Unlike Article 15s and courts-martial, there is no requirement for supervisors, First Sergeants, or commanders to consult with the base legal office on administrative disciplinary actions. There is no tracking of whether supervisors and commanders issue LORs, LOAs, and LOCs in a similar manner, magnitude, and frequency to enlisted members, regardless of race, gender, or ethnicity. The service relies on the judgment and training of supervisors and commanders on these matters. The DAF trusts relatively young and inexperienced service members with significant supervisory responsibilities at the beginning of their careers, with 25-year-old staff sergeants and 22-year-old second lieutenants in supervisory roles. As such, oversight and mentorship by commanders and senior non-commissioned officers (SNCOs) is needed to ensure supervisors are guided through administrative disciplinary actions and aware of the role bias may play in decision making. To this end, within the past several years, the Air

Force has incorporated bias training[7] for commanders and non-commissioned officers (NCOs) at various points in their career to help address the racial disparity the DAF faces in the disciplinary realm.

Next year, the DAF will begin computerized tracking of administrative disciplinary actions. New policies will require commanders to report the type of administrative action, rank, age, gender, race, and ethnicity of the person issuing the paperwork, along with the same information for the recipient of the disciplinary action.

Administrative discharges

Overall, black enlisted members were consistently overrepresented by about 50% in administrative discharge cases versus the rest of the Active Duty enlisted corps, as shown below. That means black enlisted members received 50% more discharges than we would have expected based on their population proportion. For black enlisted personnel, the top three bases for administrative discharges were: discharge in lieu of courts-martial, unsatisfactory performance, and misconduct.

---

[7] This Review recognizes the direction promulgated by Executive Order 13950: Combating Race and Sex Stereotyping, as well as Office of Management and Budget (OMB) memo M-20-34 (4 Sep 20), *Training in the Federal Government*, and OMB memo M-20-37 (28 Sep 20), *Ending Employee Trainings that Use Divisive Propaganda to Undermine the Principle of Fair and Equal Treatment for All.* Nothing in this Review is intended to imply or endorse sentiments or recommendations other than that which would be fully consistent with this guidance.

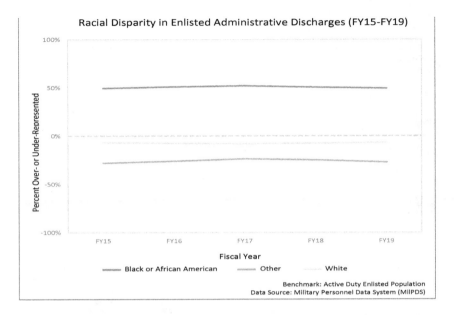

Similar to courts-martial and Article 15s, administrative discharges contained the most significant racial disparity in black enlisted members in the E1-E4 category. These service members were disproportionately discharged with misconduct as a basis. In FY15 black service members overrepresented by 52% in administrative discharges. That number steadily increased to 86% in FY19, as shown in the chart below. That means in FY15, black service members received 1.5 times the rate of administrative discharges expected based on their proportion of all E1 through E4, and, in FY19, they received almost twice the rate expected.[8]

---

[8] This Review also looked at administrative discharges for misconduct involving non-commissioned and senior non-commissioned officers, but there were not enough cases to provide statistical analysis.

Fig 13: Racial Disparity in Administrative Discharges: Misconduct

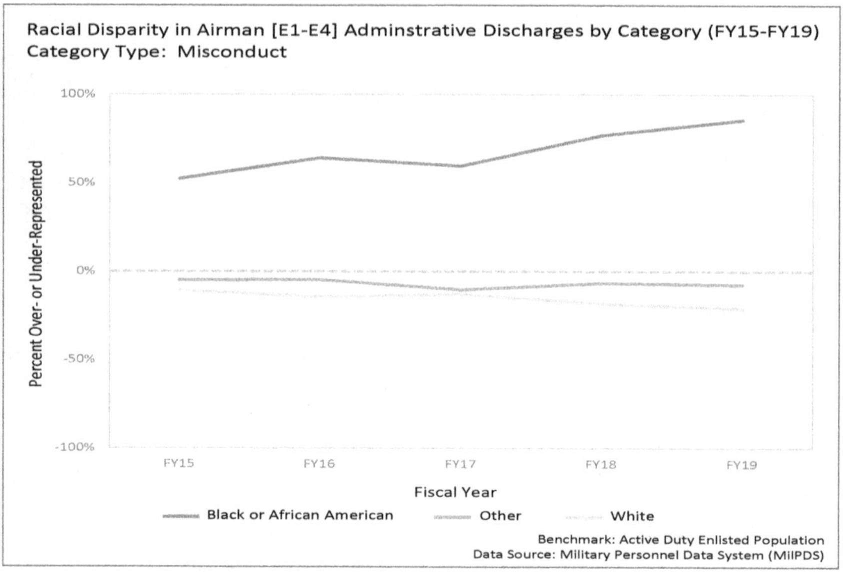

Racial Disparity in Airman [E1-E4] Adminstrative Discharges by Category (FY15-FY19)
Category Type: Misconduct

Benchmark: Active Duty Enlisted Population
Data Source: Military Personnel Data System (MilPDS)

Fig 14: Administrative Discharge (E1-E4) for Misconduct

Administrative Discharge of Airman (E1-E4) for Misconduct FY15-19

FY	Black	White	Other	Total
2015	456	1,206	214	1,876
2016	460	1,019	196	1,675
2017	501	1,103	200	1,804
2018	583	1,068	214	1,865
2019	619	1,013	212	1,844

Airman (E1-E4) Population, FY15-19

FY	Black	White	Other	Total
2015	18,563	83,829	13,957	116,349
2016	20,358	86,385	14,946	121,689
2017	21,407	86,476	15,228	123,111
2018	22,007	87,270	15,326	124,603
2019	23,184	89,146	15,922	128,252

Source: MilPDS

  When a commander recommends an enlisted member for administrative discharge, the base legal office plays a larger role. Military attorneys review the proposed discharge action to determine whether it is legally sufficient before passing the case onto higher-level commanders for review, concurrence, and approval. In other words, military attorneys help determine whether an enlisted member's misconduct supports a basis for discharge.

Military attorneys review the LORs, LOAs, and LOCs to ensure the misconduct is recorded properly in form and substance, and they review the proposed discharge action to determine whether the documented misconduct is sufficient for involuntary separation (for example, discharge based on a pattern of misconduct would require more than one LOC). This legal review process serves as a check and balance for the commander, supervisor, and the enlisted member. However, what is typically not checked and balanced is whether the commander and supervisor have given similar administrative disciplinary actions and discharge recommendations for other unit members of other races for similar misconduct. If there is a disparity in this area, it may contribute to the belief that black service members are not getting the benefit of the doubt in disciplinary actions, as discussed later in this report.

Data show there is racial disparity among young black service members as they are almost twice as likely to be discharged with misconduct as a basis. (Ex 2:61) The DAF is aware of this racial disparity but has not formally analyzed why the racial disparity exists. As noted above, individual supervisors and commanders may make these decisions and discharge recommendations with little, if any, oversight over the LORs, LOAs, and LOCs on which they are based.

INVESTIGATIONS

Upon a thorough review of case and investigative records and data, this Review found no evidence of racial bias on the part of law enforcement. It found, however, black service members are 1.64 times more likely to be suspects in OSI criminal cases, and twice as likely to be apprehended by Security Forces. Based on limited data, black service members are investigated and substantiated for MEO sexual harassment cases at a higher rate than white service members. No racial disparity was identified in IG reprisal and restriction investigations, and the DAF does not maintain demographic data on Commander Directed Investigations. Further analysis by the DAF enterprise is warranted to determine why there is racial disparity among suspects in investigations and apprehensions.

OSI Investigations

OSI provided the following criminal investigations data. Fig 15 shows OSI case percentages by types of offenses from CY16 to May 2020. Sexual offenses (51%) and drug offenses (33%) are the two largest case categories, collectively comprising 84% of OSI investigations. Sexual offenses include child and adult victim cases.

Fig 15: OSI Criminal Cases

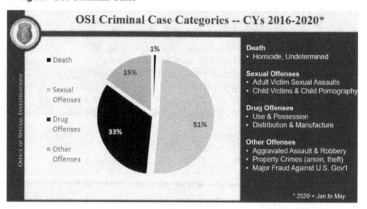

Additional data from OSI showed black Active Duty suspects are overrepresented in OSI criminal cases compared to the population of black Active Duty service members. Specifically, from CY 2016 to May 2020, 25.6% of suspects were black, while black service members only account for 15% of the total Active Duty population based on January 2020 data.

Fig 16: OSI Investigations Race Demographics

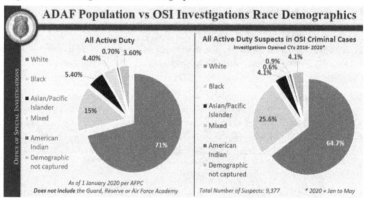

Independent analysis of the raw data correlates with the information provided by OSI.

Fig 17: OSI Investigations: Overall

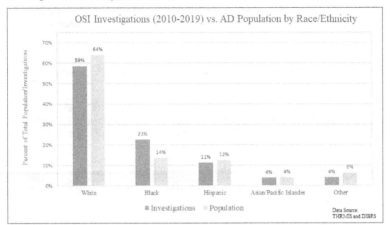

Among all closed OSI criminal investigations from 2010 to 2019, black service members are the only race overrepresented compared to their population. The magnitude of this overrepresentation is approximately nine percentage points (black service members represent 23% of the OSI investigations, but only 14% of the population), which means they are 64% overrepresented (disparity index[9] = 1.64).

Fig 18: OSI Investigations: Offense Type

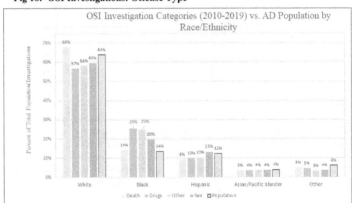

---

[9] In this report, the term "Disparity Index" is defined as the Rate Per Thousand (RPT) of black service members in a particular category divided by the white RPT for the same category. RPT black/RPT white.

Breaking down the OSI investigations by category and making the same comparison as the previous chart, black service members are specifically overrepresented in Drugs, Sex, and Other investigations. White service members are consistently underrepresented except in the category of Death investigations.

The charts below break the categories out to observe their trends over time while displaying the percent difference of OSI investigations in relation to the population of the race.

Drug Investigations

Looking at OSI investigations involving drug-related offenses, black service members were overrepresented by a substantial amount compared to other races. Drug-related offenses include use, possession, distribution, and manufacturing.

Fig 19: OSI Drug Investigations

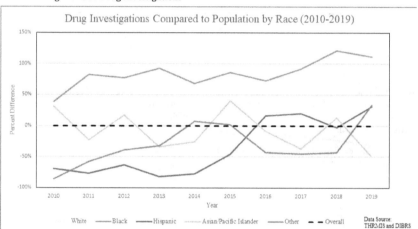

Approximately 85% of OSI drug cases stem from positive urinalysis reports from the DAF Drug Demand Reduction Program (DDRP). These cases are considered "reactive" drug cases because they did not result from OSI-initiated actions. In these instances, OSI agents must either open an investigation or refer the matter to Security Forces to open a case. Regardless of agency, it is mandatory to open a criminal investigation on a service member with a positive urinalysis result. OSI is not informed of the race of service members who test positive for illicit substances. That data is acquired during the investigation.

Approximately 15% of OSI drug cases are "proactive," in that the cases resulted from OSI-initiated activities, including information from informants. Of note, many OSI drug informants arise from positive urinalyses cases. The person testing positive may confess to illegal drug involvement and agree to provide information on others and/or make drug "buys" under OSI's control and direction. OSI officials have some discretion concerning opening proactive cases. According to OSI officials, all proactive drug investigations are based on evidence, and the majority of that evidence is gathered during reactive drug investigations.

Fig 20 compares reactive drug cases versus proactive drug cases conducted by OSI over the past five years by race. The data show a direct correlation between reactive and proactive cases and supports OSI's assertion that subjective (proactive) cases are based on evidence gathered during objective (reactive) drug investigations.

Fig 20: OSI Reactive versus Proactive Drug Cases

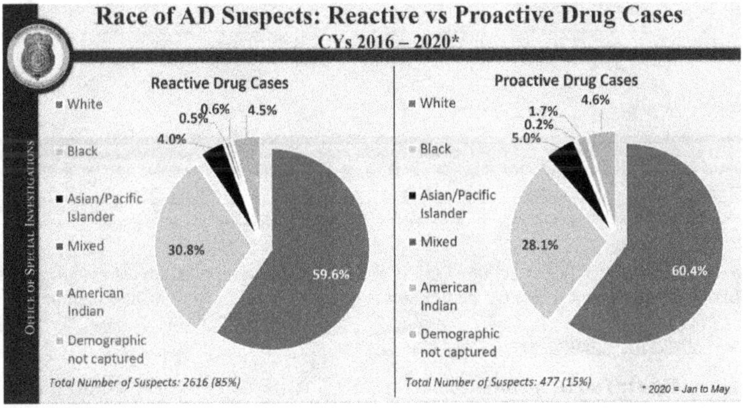
Race of AD Suspects: Reactive vs Proactive Drug Cases
CYs 2016 – 2020*
Office of Special Investigations
Reactive Drug Cases
White
Black
Asian/Pacific Islander
Mixed
American Indian
Demographic not captured
0.6%
0.5%
4.5%
4.0%
30.8%
59.6%
Total Number of Suspects: 2616 (85%)
Proactive Drug Cases
White
Black
Asian/Pacific Islander
Mixed
American Indian
Demographic not captured
4.6%
1.7%
0.2%
5.0%
28.1%
60.4%
Total Number of Suspects: 477 (15%)
* 2020 = Jan to May

Sex Crime Investigations

OSI investigations involving sex-related offenses also indicate an overrepresentation of black service members as suspects by 50%. Further analysis in this category showed that white service members are overrepresented in one subcategory of sex crimes, Child Sex Offenses. (Ex 2)

Fig 21: OSI Sex Investigations

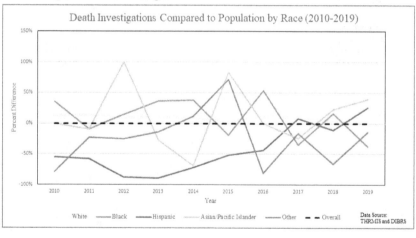

DoD and DAF policy require OSI to open investigations on all sexual assault allegations involving adult victims where the perpetrator is reported to be an Active Duty member.

Death Investigations

Fig 22: OSI Death Investigations

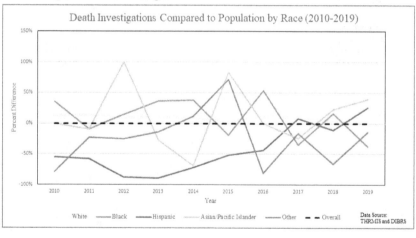

OSI investigations for deaths comprise approximately 3% of all cases since 2010 and 1% since 2016. Due to the smaller sample size, all races have fluctuated within this category. The only predominant trend is that white service members are overrepresented.

OSI runs full investigations into Active Duty deaths when the manner of death is ruled homicide or an unknown manner. Deaths due to suicide, natural causes, and accidents are only investigated so far as is necessary to support the manner of death is not a homicide.

Other Investigations

Fig 23: Other OSI Investigations

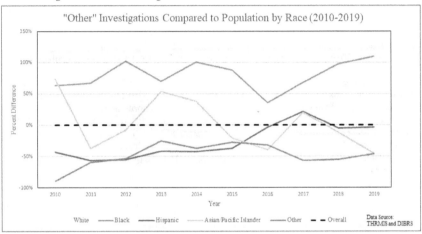

The "Other" category of OSI investigations includes crimes such as assault, fraud, robbery, and any crime not included in the previous three categories. Black service members are consistently overrepresented, varying from about 40% to over 100%. The other races are generally underrepresented (except for FY17).

Conclusion on OSI investigations

The significant majority, approximately 94%, of OSI cases are "reactive," in that offenses are reported/referred to OSI by command officials, DDRP, Sexual Assault Response Coordinators (SARCs), local law enforcement, victims, or witnesses. OSI agents do not have discretion regarding opening these investigations. The remaining 6% of OSI investigations are "proactive" investigations into drug-related offenses and "other" offenses. Although OSI agents have some discretion in these investigations, the evidence indicates proactive drug investigations are primarily the result of information gathered during reactive drug cases and "other" investigations are based on evidence of criminal activity.

The latest OSI data show black service members make up 15% of the Active Duty population but account for 25.6% of the subjects in OSI investigations. OSI's preliminary analysis indicates that the racial disparity observed in the number of case openings is consistent with the racial disparity in sexual assaults reported to OSI, victim and witness statements, command referrals, and referrals from the DDRP.

OSI leadership is aware of the racial disparity in OSI investigations and assesses proactive versus reactive investigations to monitor for potential racial bias in the OSI investigation process. OSI believes further analysis by the DAF enterprise on causation of the overrepresentation is warranted.

Security Forces Apprehensions

Review of Security Forces (SF) apprehensions was limited to the timeframe of 1 October 2019 to June 2020. The Security Forces Management Information System (SFMIS) was replaced in late 2019 and, as such, historical information prior to Oct 19 was not available.

In the apprehension process, an SF member consults with a military attorney on whether probable cause exists for an apprehension, and the SF member (also called a "defender") makes the final call. After being apprehended, service members[10] are normally returned to their commander or First Sergeant. The types of offenses most often listed in apprehensions include violations of federal and local laws, false official statement, assault, DUI/drunkenness/wrongful use, domestic violence, failure to obey a lawful order, and miscellaneous/multiple offenses. The data available included 3,094 apprehensions, of which 115 were officers and 2,979 were enlisted. (Ex 39:2-4)

---

[10] SF personnel are only authorized to apprehend Active Duty military members.

Fig 24: SF Apprehensions - Officers

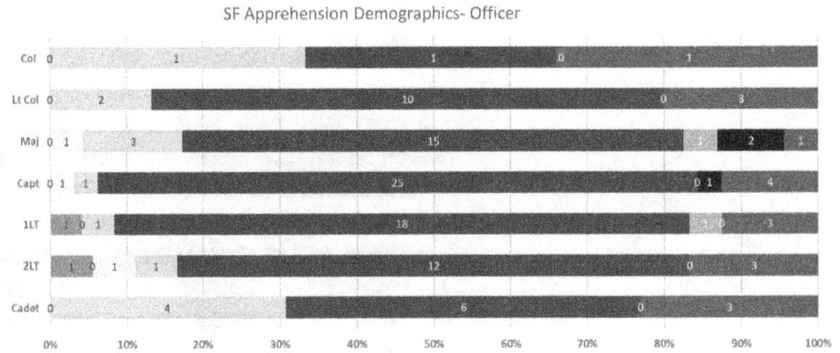

SF Apprehension Demographics- Officer

	Cadet	2LT	1LT	Capt	Maj	Lt Col	Col
Asian	0	1	1	0	0	0	0
American Indian/Alaskan	0	0	0	0	0	0	0
Latino/Hispanic	0	1	0	1	1	0	0
Black	4	1	1	1	3	2	1
White	6	12	18	25	15	10	1
More than 1	0	0	1	0	1	0	0
Other	0	0	0	1	2	0	0
UNK	3	3	3	4	1	3	1

Data Source: HAF/A4S (Air Force Justice Information System (AFJIS)

The officer apprehension data broken down by rank and race show black officers are slightly overrepresented, and white officers are slightly underrepresented compared to their population size. Officers account for only 3.7% of all apprehensions.

Fig 25: SF Apprehensions - Enlisted

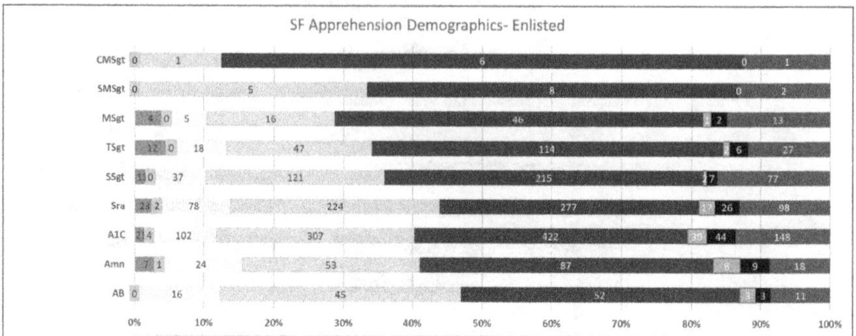

	AB	Amn	A1C	Sra	SSgt	TSgt	MSgt	SMSgt	CMSgt
Asian	0	7	21	23	11	12	4	0	0
American Indian/Alaskan	0	1	4	2	0	0	0	0	0
Latino/Hispanic	16	24	102	78	37	18	5	0	0
Black	45	53	307	224	121	47	16	5	1
White	52	87	422	277	215	114	46	8	6
More than 1	3	8	30	17	2	2	1	0	0
Other	3	9	44	26	7	6	2	0	0
UNK	11	18	148	98	77	27	13	2	1

Data Source: HAF/A4S AFJIS

Black enlisted service members are overrepresented in enlisted apprehension rates, with a disparity ratio of 1.76, while white enlisted service members are underrepresented with a disparity ratio of 0.72. (Ex 39:4) In addition, black E1 to E5 service members account for 91.9% of black service member apprehensions. White E1 to E5 service members account for 85.8% of white apprehensions. (Ex 39:4)

Fig 26: Airman Apprehensions: Rank RPT and Disparity Index

RANK	Black RPT	White RPT	Disparity Index
AMN (E1-E4)	29.3	13.0	2.25
SSGT (E5)	12.1	6.0	2.01
TSGT (E6)	8.2	4.48	1.83
MSGT (E7)	4.0	2.75	1.45
SMSGT (E8)	5.2	2.4	2.16
CMSGT (E9)	2.4	3.4	0.71

Data Source: HAF/A4S AFJIS

Conclusions about Security Forces Apprehensions

The reviewed data show racial disparity in Active Duty enlisted apprehensions. Black enlisted members are twice as likely as white enlisted members to be apprehended by Security Forces and are the only race overrepresented when compared to their population.. The magnitude of this overrepresentation is approximately 13% (black service members represent 27.7% of SF apprehensions, but only about 15% of the population), which means they are 76%

overrepresented (disparity index = 1.76). Black enlisted service members were apprehended at 19.7 RPT, other enlisted service members apprehended at 11.2 RPT, and white enlisted service members were apprehended at an 8.1 RPT. According to a SF representative, SF does not actively monitor the demographics associated with apprehensions and was not aware of the racial disparity prior to this data call.

Additional data show that black enlisted service members were overrepresented in drug usage apprehensions. The data show that the apprehension rate for black service members is 3.5 times higher than white service members. This rate includes apprehensions resulting from the DAF random drug test program. In accordance with AFI 71-101 Volume 1, *Criminal Investigations Program*, SF is directed to handle most positive random drug tests for the DAF except when the Joint Drug Enforcement Team, a combined OSI and SF team, takes the lead.

Complaints System Investigations (IG and EO)

The DAF has a robust complaints system that provides service members with several avenues to voice concerns. While using the chain of command for solving administrative issues is the primary method in the majority of circumstances, other agencies, including OSI, Security Forces, the Inspector General (IG), and Military Equal Opportunity (MEO) can take complaints and may conduct investigations. This Review analyzed data from IG and MEO as well as Commander Directed Investigations (CDI) to determine if any racial disparity exists in these investigations.

IG Investigations

This Review analyzed more than 1,036 IG reprisal and restriction investigations completed in the past five years. The data show no racial disparity between black and white subjects. The IG investigation process for reprisal and restriction investigations is defined in AFI 90-301, *Inspector General Complaints Resolution*. The number of subjects from these investigations was consistent with racial demographic statistics.

Fig 27: IG Reprisal and Restriction Investigations

RANK	WHITE INVEST	BLACK INVEST	OTHER INVEST	WHITE SUB	BLACK SUB	OTHER SUB
LIEUTENANT (O1-O2)	12	5	0	2	1	0
CAPTAIN (O3)	39	3	9	3	0	1
MAJOR (O4)	81	17	16	7	1	2
LT COL (O5)	190	8	24	28	0	6
COLONEL (O6)	195	14	6	23	3	0
SSGT (E5)	8	5	3	0	1	2
TSGT (E6)	27	8	6	4	1	2
MSGT (E7)	77	35	23	12	10	5
SMSGT (E8)	55	34	16	12	3	4
CMSGT (E9)	71	12	8	6	0	2
TOTAL	755	141	112	97	20	24
	RPT 2.38	RPT 2.1	RPT 1.08	RPT .31	RPT .30	RPT .23

*INVEST = INVESTIGATION; SUB = SUBSTANTIATED
*INCLUDES 5 YEARS OF REPRISAL AND RESTRICTION INVESTIGATIONS
*INCLUDES TOTAL FORCE, AD, AFR, ANG
* POPULATION AVERAGE USED: WHITE: 317,686; BLACK: 66,161; OTHER 103,974
* TOTAL INVESTIGATIONS 1,008   Data Source: SAF/IG Automated Case Tracking System (ACTS)

Fig 28: IG Investigations: Command Action

RANK	WHITE CA No Action	WHITE CA Verbal Counsel	WHITE CA LOC	WHITE CA RIC	WHITE CA LOA	WHITE CA LOR	BLACK CA No Action	BLACK CA Verbal Counsel	BLACK CA LOC	BLACK CA RIC	BLACK CA LOA	BLACK CA LOR
LT(O1-O2)	0	2	0	0	0	0	0	0	0	0	1	0
CAPTAIN (O3)	0	2	1	0	0	0	0	0	0	0	0	0
MAJOR (O4)	1	4	1	0	1	0	0	1	0	0	0	0
LT COL (O5)	5	6	7	0	3	7	0	0	0	0	0	0
COLONEL (O6)	12	7	2	0	2	0	0	2	0	0	1	0
SSGT (E5)	0	0	0	0	0	0	0	0	1	0	0	0
TSGT (E6)	0	2	2	0	0	0	0	0	0	0	0	1
MSGT (E7)	1	4	1	0	0	3	0	4	1	1	0	4
SMSGT (E8)	2	0	1	1	3	5	1	2	0	0	0	0
CMSGT (E9)	1	2	2	0	0	0	0	0	0	0	0	0
TOTAL	22	29	17	1	9	15	1	9	2	1	2	5

* CA = Command Action   Data Source: SAF/IG ACTS

Overall, the number of investigations of white subjects was slightly above their population percentage, 73% versus 71%. IG investigations with black subjects were slightly below their population percentage, 13% versus 15%. When using Rate Per Thousand (RPT) analysis, investigations on white subjects had a 2.38 RPT. Investigations on black subjects were slightly lower at 2.1 RPT. Additionally, the substantiation rate of investigations was 12% for black subjects and 13% for white subjects. The RPT shows that white subjects were substantiated at .31 RPT, and black subjects were substantiated at .30 RPT. (Ex 41: Chart 1) Additionally, command action resultant from these substantiated investigations shows the range of actions taken included no action, verbal counseling, LOC, LOA, LOR, Record of Individual Counseling (RIC), Unfavorable Information File (UIF), or removal from command/position. (Ex 43: Chart 2) The IG Review found no racial disparity in command actions arising from IG investigations, and the severity of the violation drove the command action.

Conclusions on racial disparity of IG investigations

The data do not indicate a racial disparity in Higher Headquarters (HHQ)-reviewed reprisal or restriction investigations. However, in accordance with AFI 90-301, *Inspector General Complaints Resolution,* many types of complaints are referred back to command for action and thus are not reviewed by HHQ.

MEO Investigations

Limited data were available regarding racial disparity in MEO actions because of a change in their data administration and other IT limitations. From November 2016 to February 2018, DAF MEO handled 97 formal discrimination complaints; 9 were substantiated (2 incidents based on race, 5 subjects were white). During the same period, after completing intakes on complaints, MEO referred 101 informal complaints to command; 58 were substantiated (38 incidents based on race, 48 subjects were white). AFI 36-2706, *Equal Opportunity Program, Military and Civilian,* directs MEO to conduct investigations when there is a formal complaint and the resultant report requires a legal review. For informal complaints, the MEO specialist takes the complaint, does an intake, and then returns it to command for action. The commander reviews the matter and is required to get a legal review. According to the MEO statistics from 2016 to 2018, the service had 40 substantiated race-based incidents in that time period.

The EO office also conducts sexual harassment investigations in the same manner as discrimination investigations. Because of legal reporting requirements, EO had three years of data on those complaints.

Fig 29: Sexual Harassment Complaints

YEAR	FORMAL INVEST	FORMAL SUB	INFORMAL INVEST	INFORMAL SUB	TOTAL	% OF SUB
2017	15	14	145	102	160	64%
2018	20	7	134	98	154	64%
2019	14	7	139	96	153	63%

INVEST = INVESTIGATIONS; SUB = SUBSTANTIATIONS   Data Source: DAF/A1Q

Fig 30: Sexual Harassment Substantiations

RACE	FORMAL SUB*	INFORMAL SUB	TOTAL SUB	PERCENTAGE of SUB	RPT**
2017 Black	4	18	22	20.4%	0.33
2017 White	9	15	59	54.6%	0.19
2017 Other	1	26	27	25.0%	0.26
2018 Black	3	21	24	22.8%	0.36
2018 White	4	49	53	50.5%	0.17
2018 Other	0	28	28	26.7%	0.27
2019 Black	1	23	24	23.3%	0.36
2019 White	3	44	47	45.6%	0.15
2019 Other	3	29	32	31.3%	0.31

SUB = SUBSTANTIATED
RPT = RATE PER THOUSAND
INCLUDES TOTAL FORCE: AD, AFR, ANG
POPULATION AVERAGE USED   Data Source: DAF/A1Q

The data in Fig 30 shows racial disparity in substantiated MEO sexual harassment complaints. According to the RPT, black service members are the subject of substantiated sexual harassment allegations slightly over twice as often as white service members.

The EO career field is composed of civilians, SNCOs and a few Technical Sergeants (TSgts), with a racial breakdown of 37.5% white, 47.5% black, and 15% other. The Director of DAF Equal Opportunity and Senior Program Manager (EEO/MEO) stated they believe the EO career field is understaffed. For example, they do not have time to analyze EO data and spend a disproportionate amount of their time reacting to HHQ's requests for information. AF/A1 explained that for years, there have been competing priorities for EO funding and resources. As such, the EO program has not necessarily been a high priority or received necessary senior leader focus from the DAF to the wing level. AF/A1 stated that recent events have appropriately increased the priority and focus on the EO program.

Conclusions on racial disparity of MEO investigations

The majority of substantiated EO cases involved white subjects. However, the EO sexual harassment investigation data show that black service members were more likely to be investigated for sexual harassment. Based on RPT, black service members are twice as likely to be the subject of a substantiated sexual harassment complaint. AF/A1Q was not aware of this disparity as they do not currently have the resources to analyze data. As such, AF/A1 was not made aware of this disparity. Further review of these issues is recommended to understand the causes of existing disparities.

Commander Directed Investigations (CDIs)

The Air Force does not centrally track CDIs. CDIs are directed by commanders at various levels to investigate issues occurring within their command. Due to the lack of centralized recordkeeping, there was not enough data to reach any conclusions. The DAF IG is in the final coordination process of formalizing a CDI Air Force Manual (AFMAN) to replace the Department's current CDI Guide. This CDI AFMAN, coupled with current guidance in AFI 90-301, *Inspector General Complaints Resolution*, will drive more centralized recordkeeping and allow for data analysis in the future.

SUMMARY OF DISCIPLINE DATA

Empirical data directly shows racial disparity in military discipline between black and white service members in the following areas:

- Article 15s and courts-martial
- OSI investigations
- Security Forces apprehensions
- Positive drug test results
- Administrative discharges

No data is tracked or recorded to assess whether racial disparity exists in administrative disciplinary actions involving LOCs, LOAs, and LORs. Plans and funding are in place to build a database to capture and track administrative disciplinary command actions in the future.

OPPORTUNITIES DATA

This Review next assessed whether racial disparity exists in leadership development opportunities throughout a service member's career, from accessions to exit surveys.

OFFICER ACCESSIONS

Officer accessions roughly meet the applicant pool goals, and there does not appear to be disparity in accessing black officers from the eligible population. However, black officers are consistently overrepresented in the support, medical, and acquisition fields and are underrepresented in the rated[11] operations Air Force Specialty Codes (AFSCs).

Recruitment of officers

Black officers represent six percent of the DAF Active Duty population. There are currently 64,500 Active Duty DAF officers, roughly 3,800 are black, and 47,000 are white.

---

[11] Paragraph 1.2 of AFI 11-412, Aircrew Management, 15 January 2019 identifies rated officers as pilots, Combat Systems Officers (CSOs), Air Battle Managers (ABMs), Remotely Piloted Aircraft (RPA) Pilots, and Flight Surgeons.

Air Force and Space Force Officers receive their commissions from four possible sources: the United States Air Force Academy (USAFA); Air Force Reserve Officer Training Corps (AFROTC); Officer Training School (OTS); and direct accession for specialized professions such as doctors, lawyers, pharmacists, and chaplains. For black officers, roughly 37% were commissioned via ROTC, 21.5% went through OTS, 17% graduated from USAFA, and 24% received their commission through another route, such as direct accession.

There are prerequisites to becoming a line officer: age (under 35), U.S. citizenship, health, and a college (bachelor's) degree. As such, the pool from which to select qualified candidates for the Officer Corps is narrower than the general U.S. population, regardless of race.

In 2014, RAND Corporation published a study on *Improving Demographic Diversity in the U.S. Air Force Officer Corps.* (Ex 21) At the time, given education, age, citizenship, and medical requirements, RAND calculated that of the U.S. population eligible to be commissioned 6% were black Americans.

Between 2015 and 2019, the Air Force commissioned about 1,500 black Active Duty officers, representing about 6% of all commissions. Thus, there does not appear to be disparity in accessing black officers from the eligible population using RAND's determination that black Americans made up 6% of the U.S. population eligible to become officers.

Qualifying Entrance Exam

The Air Force uses the Air Force Officer Qualifying Test (AFOQT) as an eligibility requirement for individuals to commission via OTS and to determine in which career field entry-level officers will serve. The AFOQT is a multiple-choice test measuring verbal and quantitative aptitudes to predict performance in the service, including for selection into specific jobs such as pilots and aircrew members. (Ex 58) A 2010 RAND study, *The Air Force Qualifying Test: Validity, Fairness, and Bias,* looked at demographic test scores and found moderate to large differences in test results among white and black test-takers. (Ex 58) For example, white test-takers earned a mean score of 59.67 in academics and 61.31 in pilot subtests, compared with mean scores of 30.91 and 25.42 respectively for black test-takers. However, the RAND study found the Air Force AFOQT is a "good selection test" that "is not biased against minorities or women" and may even be slightly skewed in favor of Hispanic and female applicants.

The RAND study noted "the differences in AFOQT scores observed, on average, across race and gender groups, provide no insight into the scores of any one individual who is a member of a given race or gender group. Even though minorities and women tend to score lower than white or male applicants, respectively, there are still many high-scoring individuals who are minorities and women. These high-scoring individuals would be predicted to do well as officers regardless of their race and gender." (Ex 58:33) The study concluded the use of the AFOQT "would result in a smaller proportion of minority individuals and women being selected into the officer corps than exists in the officer applicant pool" but that "such a reduction in the diversity of selectees does not negate its importance as a valid selection tool for the Air Force," since the test is an "unbiased predictor of who will succeed in officer training without regard to race and gender." (Ex 58)

ROTC

As of June 2020, the ROTC program produced the largest percentage of officers serving in the Air Force (40.4%, or about 26,000). Of those who received their commission through ROTC, 5.5% were black, compared with roughly 5% Asian, 8% Hispanic, and 75% white (the remainder were officers who had multiple or unknown racial/ethnic background).

Those racial demographic percentages roughly mirror the number of ROTC accessions from fiscal years 2015 to 2019:

Fig 31: ROTC Accessions by Racial Demographic

	FY15	FY16	FY17	FY18	FY19
Black/African American	6%	4%	4%	6%	6%
American Indian/Alaskan Native	0%	1%	0%	1%	1%
Asian	5%	6%	5%	8%	7%
Hispanic/Latino	8%	10%	10%	11%	10%
2 or More Races	3%	3%	4%	3%	3%
Native Hawaiian/Pacific Islander	0%	0%	0%	1%	1%
Unknown	2%	3%	3%	3%	3%

Source: Holm Center

The ROTC program relies on Program Guidance Letters that list career/occupational requirements by AFSC for rated and non-rated officers as overall targets. ROTC representatives say there are no racial demographic goals regarding recruitment of ROTC applicants. The ROTC program, however, does use analytics to determine locations and areas to recruit qualified minority students. In August 2020, the DAF added 100 new scholarships to award to students attending historically black colleges and universities (HBCUs) in order to increase interest from that demographic in the Air Force and Space Force.

USAFA

As of June 2020, there are roughly 14,600 USAFA graduates in the Air Force and Space Force. They comprise 23% of all DAF officers. 4.4% of USAFA graduates are black officers, while 76% are white.

In 2014, the Air Force established USAFA applicant pool goals to reflect America's eligible population based on information at the time. The overall goal was to have 30% of the applicants be either minority or female. The applicant pool goals were as follows:

Fig 32: USAFA Applicant Pool Goals

RACE	APPLICANT POOL GOAL
American Indian/Native Alaskan	1%
Asian American	8%
Black	10%
Native Hawaiian/Other Pacific Islander	1%
White	80%
ETHNICITY	
Hispanic/Latino	10%

A review of data for the class of 2020 to 2024 applicants shows USAFA met or exceeded goals for recruiting black students and other minorities to apply for admission in the last five years:

Fig 33: USAFA Applicant Pool (Class of 2020-2024)

RACE	USAF GOAL	APPLICANT POOL FOR CLASS OF:				
		2020	2021	2022	2023	2024
American Indian/Native Alaskan	1%	1.3%	1.3%	1.3%	1.2%	1.2%
Asian American	8%	8.5%	9.1%	9.6%	9.8%	10.4%
Black	10%	15.0%	15.3%	13.5%	13.3%	12.9%
Native Hawaiian/Other Pacific Islander	1%	1.8%	1.3%	1.6%	1.8%	2.1%
ETHNICITY						
Hispanic/Latino	10%	12.7%	12.9%	13.1%	13.4%	13.9%

**Excludes Internationals   Source: USAFA

For that five-year period, the Academy's percentage of black applicants ranged from 12.9% to 15.3%, exceeding the Air Force goal of 10%. Black applicants selected and chosen to attend the Academy during those years ranged from 8.5% to 11.3% of the overall cadet population. The percentage of black and other minority students who entered USAFA closely match the Academy's initial applicant pool goals. The racial demographics of each entering class is below. For the Class of 2020, 72 black cadets graduated, representing 7.4% of the graduating class.

Fig 34: USAFA Enrollment (Class of 2020-2024)

Race	2020	2021	2022	2023	2024
Asian	8.9%	8.1%	9.3%	9.2%	13.6%
Black	8.5%	10%	11.3%	10.5%	9%
Hispanic	9.4%	9.6%	9.9%	10.5%	13.6%
White	69.6%	63.7%	66.7%	67.9%	62.7%

OTS

As of June 2020, about 13,200 officers in the Active Duty Air Force commissioned through OTS, representing 20% of the officer corps. . Black officers comprised about 6% of the OTS commissionees. OTS has as an applicant pool target that changes annually, depending on the number of individuals who earn a bachelor's degree for that year. The figure below shows that in 2019, black college graduates represented 10% of the population who received a bachelor's degree (without regard for other eligibility requirements to enter the Air Force, such as age or citizenship). In FY19, about 8% of OTS applicants were black college graduates, which is less than what the DAF hoped it would attract to apply. Black college graduates represented 7.5% of those selected to attend OTS in FY19. In FY 20, a year when the DAF requirements for OTS accessions were drastically reduced, OTS held one board composed of Active Duty enlisted Airmen seeking to become officers. OTS selected 24 candidates, none of them were black.

Female	58.0%	17.3%	23.9%	21.0%	20.2%	16.3% ▼	18.0%	21.9%	22.9%	21.1%	20.8% ▼
Total	100.0%	503	2046	1493	1771	980 Count	473	921	415	616	24 Count
Caucasion	59.9%	67.0%	63.0%	65.9%	66.7%	73.2% △	67.2%	67.4%	71.8%	69.0%	95.8% △
Hispanic	14.4%	9.3%	12.6%	9.2%	14.1%	4.1% ▼	9.3%	10.5%	7.2%	13.1%	0.0% ▼
Asian	7.6%	6.6%	5.1%	5.6%	7.4%	4.3% ▼	6.1%	6.1%	8.0%	8.1%	4.2% ▼
African American	10.0%	10.1%	11.5%	11.5%	8.1%	13.3% △	10.1%	9.1%	6.7%	7.5%	0.0% ▼
Other (AI, PI, 2+, Unknown)	8.1%	7.0%	7.8%	7.8%	3.7%	5.2% △	7.2%	6.8%	6.3%	2.3%	0.0% ▼
Total	100.0%	100.0%	100.0%	100.0%	100.0%	100.0%	100.0%	100.0%	100.0%	100.0%	100.0%

YELLOW: Observed Data Lower Than Applicant Pool. GREEN: Observed Data Higher Than Applicant Pool.
*Applicant Pool Determined From JAMRS Data Indicating "First Major Bachelor's Degree" Awarded In 2019

Whether OTS selects an applicant for commissioning depends on several factors, one of which is whether the individual's major/college degree meets the Air Force's mission requirements, which may change each year based on the Air Force's need for certain AFSCs. Because an interview is required, OTS has incorporated bias training into its board selection process. In 2018, OTS restructured the interview process to standardize its applicant assessment to mitigate potential interviewer's bias. Additionally, selection boards are comprised of both genders from diverse backgrounds, including rated and non-rated officers.

Black Officers Overrepresented in Support Roles

Black officers are overrepresented in the acquisition, support, medical, and logistics/maintenance fields and are underrepresented in the operations AFSCs, as shown in the chart below. The disparity of black officers in the pilot career field could be a factor that translates to fewer promotion and career development opportunities, as discussed later in this report.

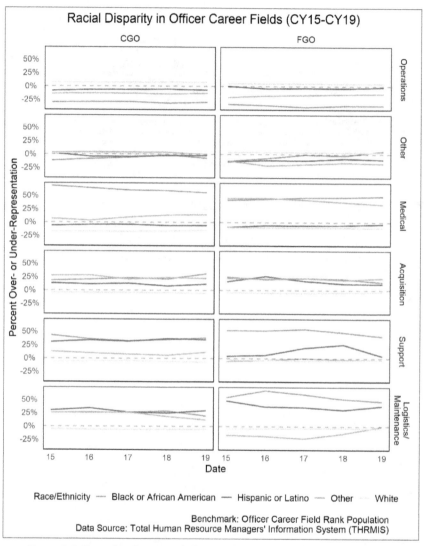

Racial Disparity in Officer Career Fields (CY15-CY19)

Personal choice and socio-economic factors affecting education may impact a black student's desire to select the Air Force or Space Force as a career path or choose a science, technology, engineering, and mathematics (STEM) based career in the DAF.

Lack of mentoring or guidance early on also come into play. One black officer we interviewed stated that had she been advised officers in the rated career fields are more likely to be promoted to higher ranks and senior positions, she would have chosen a rated path. The rated career field requires neither a STEM degree nor any other specific educational degree.

Pilot Accession

As of May 2020, there were 305 black pilots (about 2%) out of the roughly 15,000 Active Duty pilots in the Air Force. As will be discussed later, rated officers have an advantage when competing to become General Officers. There are four categories of rated officers: air battle managers, navigators, pilots, and remotely piloted aircraft pilots. According to those in Air Force recruiting, one of the most influential criteria in becoming an Air Force pilot is possessing the interest and desire. With less black pilots in the Air Force, black applicants may not have realized it was a viable option because they are less likely to have seen someone like them doing so. The second criteria is whether the individual is physically and medically qualified. These qualifications include no history of hay fever, asthma, or allergies after age 12, and visual acuity, such as normal color vision with near visual acuity of 20/30 without correction, among other criteria.[12] There are also height requirements, depending on the airframe, age (under 33), and education (a bachelor's degree, any major, with a grade point average of at least 2.5). Finally, an applicant's ability – or inability – to earn flying hours before selection for pilot training will also impact an applicant's competitiveness. Applicants from lower socio-economic groups may not compete as well when compared to those who might more easily afford flying lessons. The more flying hours a pilot applicant earns, the higher the applicant's score will be on the Pilot Candidate Selection Method (PCSM), which the Air Force uses to not only determine who is best qualified, but also as a predictor of how well an applicant will fare in the rigorous Undergraduate Pilot Training (UPT) program.

USAFA and ROTC each receive a little more than 40% of the pilot slots, with about 10% going to OTS. The final approximately 10% is for other types of accessions, such as Active Duty Airmen who cross-train. USAFA, ROTC, and OTS do not consider gender or race in making selections for pilot training. The Air Force recognizes, however, there is a disparity in the number of pilots and rated officers from underrepresented groups (minorities and women). As of July 2020, there were about 19,000 rated officers in the rank of O5 and below. About 3% of those rated officers are black, compared with 86% white. (Ex 59) UPT graduation and attrition rates by race, gender, and ethnicity require further study.

USAFA

Each USAFA cadet learns how to fly gliders as part of their course of study. Successful completion at USAFA confers a benefit: roughly half of the cadets who graduate go on to become pilots, representing about 400 to 500 of the pilot training slots each year. To become an

---

[12] https://www.airforce.com/frequently-asked-questions/officer-path/what-are-the-general-qualifications-to-fly-including-
height#:~:text=Meet%20Air%20Force%20weight%20and%20physical%20conditioning%20requirements.&text=Ha
ve%20no%20history%20of%20hay,or%20allergies%20after%20age%2012.&text=Have%20normal%20color%20vi
sion%20with,%2C%20correctable%20to%2020%2F20.

Air Force pilot, cadets must show an interest in and explicitly volunteer for the career field, earn a bachelor's degree in any field, and be medically qualified. USAFA selects cadets for pilot training based on their order of merit, a ranking system comprising how students fared in military training, academics, and athletic training. Additionally, USAFA considers a cadet's PCSM score, a combination of flying hours, AFOQT results, and Test of Basic Aviation Skills[13] (TBAS) results. The higher the cadet's order of merit and PCSM score, the better cadet's chance to be selected for pilot training.

ROTC

ROTC holds two digital boards each year to select cadets for pilot training. The board is not composed of people but rather a computer, which ranks cadets based on a combination of factors, in descending order: PCSM score, commander's ranking, field training, and academics and physical fitness (weighted equally). Only after the computer program has racked and stacked candidates does ROTC see the pilot selection board's results, including demographics. According to an ROTC representative who visited HBCUs to recruit black cadets to fly for the Air Force, black cadets are less interested in the pilot field. Some black cadets stated they were the first to go to college in their family and have no interest in serving long-term in the Air Force (a pilot incurs a 10-year service commitment). These cadets stated they intend to complete their four-year Active Duty service commitment then leave the Air Force for higher-paying jobs in the civilian world, which the cadets told the ROTC representative is a measure of success for their families. Not all black cadets feel this way, as many go on to serve long pilot careers, but such circumstances may partly help explain why there may be less interest among black ROTC cadets to become pilots.

OTS

OTS has the fewest number of allocated pilot training slots, about 10% a year. Everyone who commissions through OTS must already have a college degree, in addition to taking the AFOQT and meeting age and medical requirements. To become a pilot through this program, OTS considers a candidate's aptitude (education, PCSM score), leadership, and adaptability (statement of intent, letter of recommendation, experience). OTS holds one to two boards a year, manned by three to four O6s. Although there is no explicit guidance requiring diversity on the boards, OTS strives to have diverse representation on each board (i.e., a female officer and/or a minority officer). These board members have discretion and may weigh STEM degrees more preferentially among candidates vying for pilot training slots.

Initiatives to decrease racial disparity

Air Force recruiters have cited a lack of role models and lack of exposure to the pilot career field as reasons there may be less interest among black applicants to become pilots. Recognizing there is a disparity in the number of minority and women pilots, the Air Force initiated a task force to study barriers hindering these groups from becoming pilots, and the Air Force has begun different programs to increase diversity in its pilot corps. In 2018, the Air Force stood up Air Force Recruiting Service Detachment 1 (Det 1), whose explicit purpose is to

---

[13] The TBAS is a computerized psychomotor, spatial ability, and multi-tasking test.

increase interest in flying among underrepresented groups (minority/female students). Det 1 serves as the Chief of Staff of the Air Force's Rated Diversity Improvement initiative to publicize opportunities at USAFA, ROTC, and OTS.

One barrier to becoming an Air Force pilot is the PCSM score, which is partly based on the number of flying hours a candidate has earned. Candidates who do not have the financial means for, or access to private lessons to earn flight hours, are disadvantaged. Thus, their PCSM score will be lower than those who could pay for and take private flying lessons. One initiative of Det 1 is to hold summer flight camps for underrepresented youths to teach them to fly and earn hours to improve their PCSM scores. Additionally, with an eye at increasing interest among minority and women officers, the Air Force also started the Rated Preparatory Program to cross-train officers into the rated career fields by providing them basic aviation experience and up to 10 hours of flying hours to raise their PCSM score. Students are then required to apply for that year's Undergraduate Pilot Training board.

ENLISTED ACCESSIONS

Black Americans represent 8% of the total population eligible to enlist. However, black service members make up 15% of the DAF total enlisted force. There is racial disparity in enlisted entrance exam scores and enlisted career fields. On average, black applicants score lower on the AFQT, and black enlisted service members are overrepresented in support, medical, and acquisitions career fields and underrepresented in operations and logistics/maintenance career fields.

Fig 37: Enlisted Racial Demographics (Eligible Population and DAF Enlisted Force)

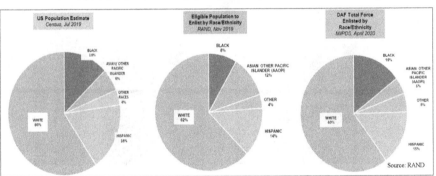

Entrance Exam

Like the rest of the Department of Defense, the Air Force uses the multiple-choice Armed Services Vocational Aptitude Battery (ASVAB) test as an entrance exam for high school (and equivalent) graduates interested in the enlisted corps.[14] Four subject areas of the ASVAB (Arithmetic Reasoning, Math Knowledge, Word Knowledge, and Paragraph Comprehension) comprise the bases for an applicant's Armed Forces Qualification Test (AFQT) score. Both score results are used to determine eligibility for enlistment as well as potential military occupational specialties.

Across the Department of Defense, black applicants score lower on the AFQT. According to the Office of the Under Secretary of Defense for Personnel and Readiness's 2020 *Report on the Armed Services Vocational Aptitude Battery (ASVAB)*, black applicants' mean AFQT scores were about 44, compared with roughly 58 and 60 for Asian American and white applicants respectively. (Ex 60 and Figure 38)

Fig 38: Mean AFQT Scores by Race

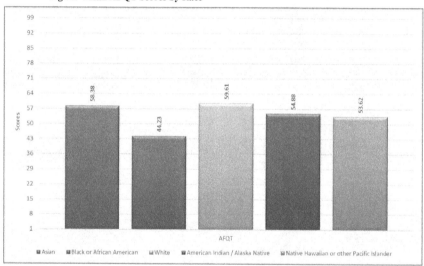

---

[14] The ASVAB tests General Science, Arithmetic Reasoning, Word Knowledge, Paragraph Comprehension, Math Knowledge, Electronics Information, Auto Information, Shop Information, Mechanical Comprehension, and Assembling Objects.

Enlisted Service Member Career Fields

More than 86% of DAF enlisted positions are in support career fields. Roughly 4% are n medical, 3% each are in operations and logistics, and the remainder are in special duty ositions or acquisition. ASVAB and AFQT test scores are the main factor in determining an nlisted service member's career field. Personal choice and the needs of the services at the time person enlists are also factors.

Compared to the proportion of race and ethnic groups in the Active Duty Air Force and pace Force enlisted rank groups, black enlisted service members are concentrated in support, nedical, and acquisitions AFSCs. They are underrepresented by 20 to 30% in logistics and perations career fields in all rank groups. Similarly, Hispanic and other minority enlisted ervice members are underrepresented by 5 to 20% in logistics and operations career fields. By ontrast, white enlisted service members are underrepresented by 5 to 30% in medical and upport career fields, and they are overrepresented in operations and logistics career fields.

The fact that black enlisted service members are concentrated in specific fields may dversely affect their promotion chances. Enlisted promotion rates are set to fill vacancies vithin an AFSC at a higher grade using factors in the Weighted Airmen Promotion System WAPS), like test scores. Certain career fields, like pararescue (where black enlisted service nembers are underrepresented) have higher promotion rates, given the field's higher turnover ate and larger number of vacancies that need to be filled.

Several factors may explain why black enlisted service members are overrepresented in upport fields. Interviews with those in the Air Force recruiting field, along with anecdotal vidence, suggest black enlisted service members choose to pursue career tracks for reasons such s: advice from veterans or family members; the career field is perceived to be more ransferrable in the civilian world; the individual may not have been exposed to operational-type obs; or their ASVAB and AFQT scores did not qualify them for other fields. Further, some jobs mpose stricter medical standards, which further restricts the candidate pool, and this may limit he number of enlisted service members, regardless of race, who select these career fields.

Fig 39: Racial Disparity in Enlisted Career Fields by Rank Groups

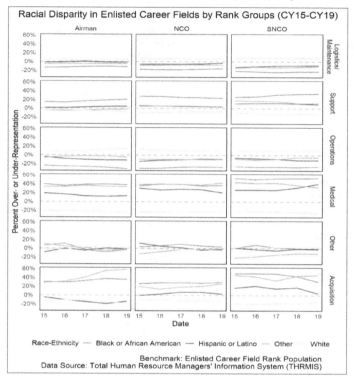

AIR FORCE RETENTION

Within the enlisted population, the data show no consistent racial disparity in retention rates. Black service members were slightly overrepresented in separations at 11-20 years of service and underrepresented in separations at 5 and 10 years of service. Within the officer population, the data show that black officers were slightly overrepresented in separations at 5-15 years of service and underrepresented in separations at 16-20 years of service.

The Review considered Air Force separation data from the Military Personnel Data System (MILPDS) broken down by officer and enlisted service members. The data covers 2015 through 2019 and showed disparity in separation rates relative to Race and Ethnicity and years of service. Fig 40 shows the racial disparity percent and number of over or underrepresented.

Fig 40: Racial Disparity in Enlisted Separations Rates

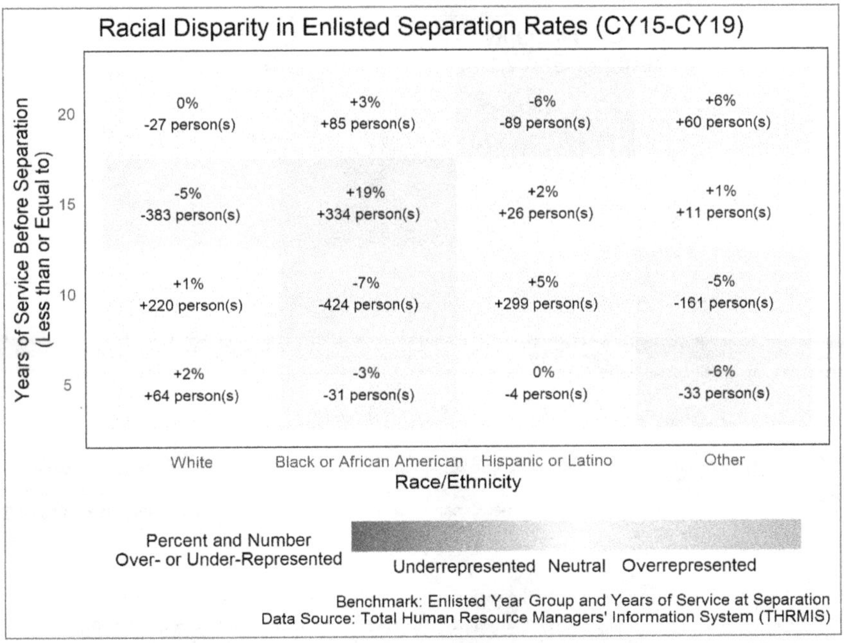

Racial Disparity in Enlisted Separation Rates (CY15-CY19)

Years of Service Before Separation (Less than or Equal to)	White	Black or African American	Hispanic or Latino	Other
20	0% / -27 person(s)	+3% / +85 person(s)	-6% / -89 person(s)	+6% / +60 person(s)
15	-5% / -383 person(s)	+19% / +334 person(s)	+2% / +26 person(s)	+1% / +11 person(s)
10	+1% / +220 person(s)	-7% / -424 person(s)	+5% / +299 person(s)	-5% / -161 person(s)
5	+2% / +64 person(s)	-3% / -31 person(s)	0% / -4 person(s)	-6% / -33 person(s)

Race/Ethnicity

Percent and Number
Over- or Under-Represented

Underrepresented Neutral Overrepresented

Benchmark: Enlisted Year Group and Years of Service at Separation
Data Source: Total Human Resource Managers' Information System (THRMIS)

Enlisted retention rates over the past five years show black enlisted service members were overrepresented in separations at 11-20 years of service and underrepresented in separations at 5-10 years of service. White enlisted service members were underrepresented in separations at 11-15 years of service. Hispanic and Latino enlisted service members were overrepresented in separations at 5-15 years of service, but underrepresented in separations at 16-20 years of service.[15]

---

[15] The number of Airmen over or underrepresented is rounded to the nearest whole number.

Fig 41: Air Force Racial Disparity Enlisted Separations: Relative to years of service

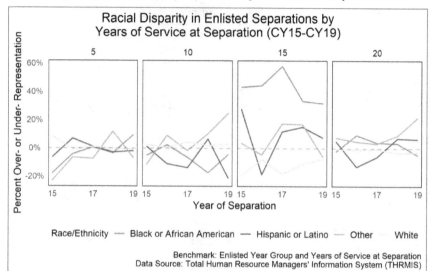

Enlisted retention rates over the past five years also show black enlisted service members were underrepresented in separations at 5 and 10 years of service but were overrepresented in separations at 15 years of service. Hispanic or Latino enlisted service members and enlisted service members of other races were approximately evenly represented in separations, but with substantial variation, limiting how informative the relative racial disparity metric is for these groups. White enlisted service members were slightly overrepresented in separations at 5 and 10 years of service, but underrepresented in separations at 15 years of service.

Note: The separations line charts only include separations at exactly the respective year of service, while the heatmaps (see Fig 42) include ranges (6-10, 11-15, 16-20) for years of service. A similar overrepresentation for black enlisted service members exists for both the 15 years of service group and the 11 to 15 years of service group.

Fig 42: Air Force Officer Retention Rate: Relative to Race/Ethnicity

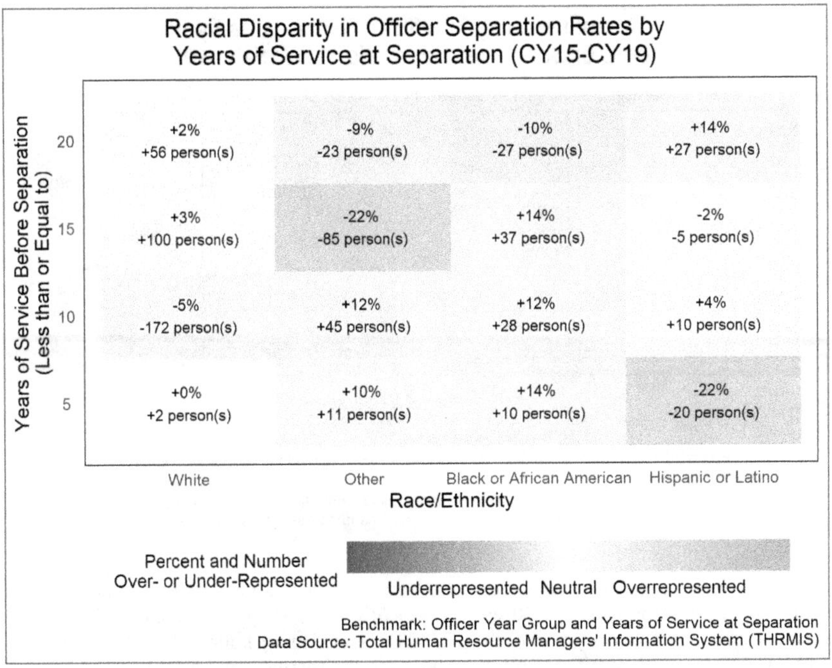

Racial Disparity in Officer Separation Rates by Years of Service at Separation (CY15-CY19)

Years of Service Before Separation (Less than or Equal to)	White	Other	Black or African American	Hispanic or Latino
20	+2% +56 person(s)	-9% -23 person(s)	-10% -27 person(s)	+14% +27 person(s)
15	+3% +100 person(s)	-22% -85 person(s)	+14% +37 person(s)	-2% -5 person(s)
10	-5% -172 person(s)	+12% +45 person(s)	+12% +28 person(s)	+4% +10 person(s)
5	+0% +2 person(s)	+10% +11 person(s)	+14% +10 person(s)	-22% -20 person(s)

Race/Ethnicity

Percent and Number
Over- or Under-Represented

Underrepresented   Neutral   Overrepresented

Benchmark: Officer Year Group and Years of Service at Separation
Data Source: Total Human Resource Managers' Information System (THRMIS)

When looking at officer retention rates over the past five years, the data show black officers were overrepresented in separations at 5-15 years of service and underrepresented in separations at 16-20 years of service. White officers were underrepresented in separations at 5-10 years of service, and overrepresented in separations from 11-20 years of service. Hispanic and Latino officers were overrepresented in separations at 16-20 years of service, but underrepresented in separations at 5 years of service.

Fig 43: **Racial Disparity in DAF Officer Separations: Relative to years of service**

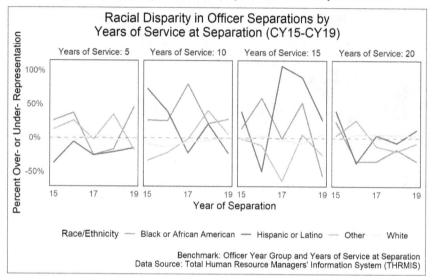

Officer retention rates over the past five years show black officers were generally overrepresented in separations at 5, 10, and 15 years of service. Hispanic or Latino officers and officers of other races were approximately evenly represented in separations, but with substantial variation, which limits how informative the relative racial disparity metric is for these groups. White officers were approximately evenly represented in separations at all years of service.

Note: The separations line charts only include separations at exactly the respective year of service, while the heatmaps include ranges (6-10, 11-15, 16-20) for years of service.

Fig 44: Racial Disparity in Officer Separations by Career Field

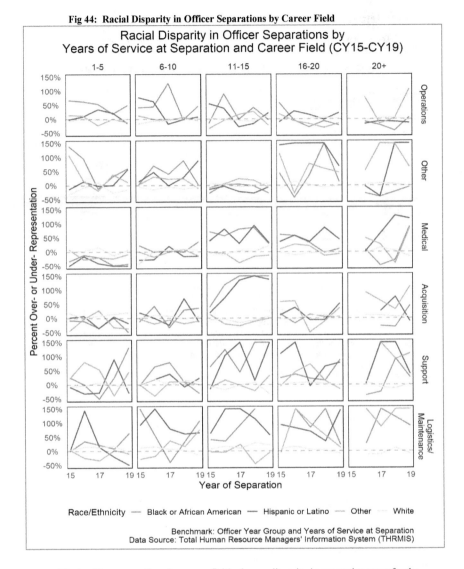

Black officer separations by career fields show a disparity in separation rates for the operations career fields during years one through ten and a disparity in the support career fields for most years.

Air Force Exit Survey Data

The Review team examined service members' responses to exit surveys completed during the separation process.

Fig 45: Air Force Exit Survey: Programs/Policies that influenced a service member's decision to separate

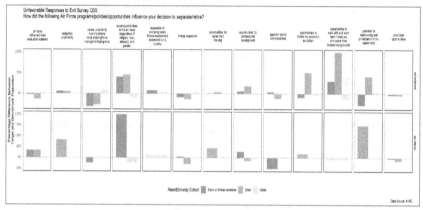

Fig 45 illustrates that black enlisted and officers were more likely to separate/retire than white service members based on Equal Opportunities in the Air Force and Opportunities for Professional Development. Black enlisted members are also more likely to separate/retire due to "opportunities to work with and learn from individuals who come from diverse backgrounds." Finally, the data show black officers are more likely to separate/retire due to the Air Force Officer Evaluation System.

Conclusions about Retention Issues

The enlisted population data show no consistent disparity in retention rates by race. While black service members were overrepresented in separations at 11-20 years of service, white service members were overrepresented in separations at 5 and 10 years of service. The exit survey responses from enlisted for both races are similar. However, exit survey responses should be reviewed thoroughly to help improve overall retention in the future.

The officer population data show that black officers were overrepresented in separations at 5-15 years of service and underrepresented in separations at 16-20 years of service. White officers were underrepresented in separations at 5-10 years of service and overrepresented in separations from 11-20 years. When looking at officer retention rates over the past five years, the data show that black officers are consistently overrepresented in separations at 5, 10, and 15 years of service. Hispanic or Latino officers are overrepresented in separations at 20 years of service and are underrepresented in separations at 5 years of service. Officers of other race-ethnicity groups are overrepresented in separations at 5 and 10 years of service but underrepresented in separations at 15 years of service. White officers are consistently underrepresented in separations.

The data also indicates black enlisted and officers are more likely to separate/retire due to Equal Opportunities in the Air Force and Opportunities for Professional Development. Black enlisted service members are also more likely to separate/retire due to "opportunities to work with and learn from individuals who come from diverse backgrounds." Black Officers are more likely to separate/retire due to the Air Force Officer Evaluation System.

PROFESSIONAL MILITARY EDUCATION (PME)

Since 2015, black officers have been overrepresented in PME nominations but underrepresented in designations to attend. The gap between nomination percentages and designation percentages is more significant in SDE than IDE. Enlisted PME programs are all "must attend" courses based on rank and promotion date. All individuals are scheduled to attend based on when they were promoted.

Officer PME

Officer PME is structured to provide continuous development opportunities across a career. It consists of Primary Developmental Education (PDE) for captains, Intermediate Developmental Education (IDE) for majors/major selects, and Senior Developmental Education (SDE) for lieutenant colonels (O5s), colonel selects (O6 select), and colonels (O6). (Ex 43:95, 96) Officers complete PME programs either in-residence or by distance learning. The DAF does not provide opportunities for all officers to attend all levels of PME in-residence.

PDE primarily consists of Squadron Officer School but also includes some advanced degree and other special programs. All eligible officers in the grade of captain within the following competitive categories are required to attend in-resident Squadron Officer School: line of the Air Force, LAF-J (judge advocates), and the non-line of the Air Force Chaplain Corps, Medical Services Corps, Biomedical Science Corps, Nurse Corps, Medical Corps, and Dental

Corps. Medical Corps and Dental Corps officers are not eligible to attend SOS in-residence during Graduate Medical/Dental Education (GME/GDE) nor in the nine months following GME/GDE completion. (Ex 43:94)

IDE programs include graduate education, fellowships, and PME at military command and staff colleges. Intermediate developmental education denotes a period of development during which, for example, officers typically earn Joint Professional Military Education Phase I credit. (Ex 43:95)

SDE programs include graduate education, fellowships, and PME at military war colleges. Senior developmental education denotes a period of development during which, for example, officers typically earn Joint Professional Military Education Phase II credit. (Ex 43:95)

For IDE and SDE in-residence programs, officers are nominated by their Senior Rater (SR) and meet a Central Developmental Education (DE) Board. Officers are designated once they meet the Central DE Board, are vectored by the Developmental Team (DT), matched to a program, and approved at the Developmental Education Designation Board (DEDB) to attend a specific in-resident DE program. Senior Raters must nominate selects and candidates in accordance with annual guidance. Lieutenant colonel promotion boards are no longer identifying officers as "selects" for SDE, and starting with the 2004 year group, all lieutenant colonels will be candidates and must be nominated by their SR for SDE. [16] IDE seats are allocated using field grade requirements above the wing level and squadron commander or equivalent billets for each AFSC (LAF). SDE seats are currently distributed using a fair share methodology on the eligible pool's size for SDE. For Academic Year (AY) 21-22, the AF/A1D guidance was 70% of SDE seats would go to selects (e.g., identified at the O5 board) and 30% of seats would go to candidates across all AFSCs. According to A1, SDE seats will soon go to a requirements-based allocation similar to IDE. (Ex 44:3, 6)

AF/A1 provided IDE/SDE nomination/designation data for 2015-2019. Except for 2015 IDE, black officers exceeded the average nomination rate for all officers. Black officers, however, are designated at a lower rate than average for all officers in both IDE and SDE (except for 2019 IDE where the black officer designation rate exceeded the average by 1.5%). As seen in the figure below, the number of additional black officers that would have been necessary to meet the average designation rate for all races ranged from a low of 2 for 2018 IDE to a high of 10 for 2019 SDE. The data show that black officers are consistently below the average designation rate for IDE and SDE compared to their white counterparts.

---

[16] The term "select" refers to officers formerly chosen during their respective promotion boards to attend school in-residence; the term "candidate" applies to all other officers while they remain within their respective windows of eligibility; the term "designee" refers to Selects or Candidates designated for school through the Developmental Education Designation Board process. Currently there are still some SDE selects who were selected at their lieutenant colonel promotion board to slated attend SDE (Ex 43:92)

Fig 46: 2015-2020 IDE/SDE Nomination/Designation Rates

IDE	2015						2016					
	Eligible	Nominated	Designee	Nom Rate	Des Rate	Des Delta	Eligible	Nominated	Designee	Nom Rate	Des Rate	Des Delta
White	4238	1281	440	30.2%	34.3%	2.1%	4266	1207	449	28.3%	37.2%	1.8%
Black	270	79	21	29.3%	26.6%	-5.7%	248	80	19	32.3%	23.8%	-11.7%
Total	5231	1583	511	30.3%	32.3%	5	5190	1498	531	28.9%	35.4%	9
						# needed to meet rate						# needed to meet rate

SDE	2015						2016					
	Eligible	Nominated	Designee	Nom Rate	Des Rate	Des Delta	Eligible	Nominated	Designee	Nom Rate	Des Rate	Des Delta
White	3062	964	204	31.5%	21.2%	1.5%	3071	936	207	30.5%	22.1%	1.3%
Black	207	82	9	39.6%	11.0%	-8.7%	205	74	11	36.1%	14.9%	-5.9%
Total	3621	1150	226	31.8%	19.7%	7	3659	1134	236	31.0%	20.8%	4
						# needed to meet rate						# needed to meet rate

IDE	2017						2018					
	Eligible	Nominated	Designee	Nom Rate	Des Rate	Des Delta	Eligible	Nominated	Designee	Nom Rate	Des Rate	Des Delta
White	4080	1190	451	29.2%	37.9%	1.2%	4026	1324	476	32.9%	36.0%	1.4%
Black	201	69	21	34.3%	30.4%	-6.2%	181	57	18	31.5%	31.6%	-3.0%
Total	4942	1454	533	29.4%	36.7%	4	4845	1579	546	32.6%	34.6%	2
						# needed to meet rate						# needed to meet rate

SDE	2017						2018					
	Eligible	Nominated	Designee	Nom Rate	Des Rate	Des Delta	Eligible	Nominated	Designee	Nom Rate	Des Rate	Des Delta
White	2966	874	209	29.5%	23.9%	1.6%	3032	936	217	30.9%	23.2%	1.4%
Black	207	82	9	39.6%	11.0%	-11.3%	196	69	9	35.2%	13.0%	-8.7%
Total	3571	1076	240	30.1%	22.3%	9	3664	1134	247	30.9%	21.8%	6
						# needed to meet rate						# needed to meet rate

IDE	2019						2020					
	Eligible	Nominated	Designee	Nom Rate	Des Rate	Des Delta	Eligible	Nominated	Designee	Nom Rate	Des Rate	Des Delta
White	4294	1331	466	31.0%	35.0%	1.4%	4468	1438	422	32.2%	29.3%	-1.0%
Black	225	74	26	32.9%	35.1%	1.5%	274	87	32	31.8%	36.8%	6.4%
Total	5233	1634	550	31.2%	33.7%	-1	5545	1788	543	32.2%	30.4%	-6
						# needed to meet rate						# needed to meet rate

SDE	2019						2020					
	Eligible	Nominated	Designee	Nom Rate	Des Rate	Des Delta	Eligible	Nominated	Designee	Nom Rate	Des Rate	Des Delta
White	4031	1171	221	29.0%	18.9%	1.5%	4031	1155	218	28.7%	18.9%	1.1%
Black	232	84	5	36.2%	6.0%	-11.4%	231	76	4	32.9%	5.3%	-12.5%
Total	4910	1422	247	29.0%	17.4%	10	4908	1410	250	28.7%	17.7%	9
						# needed to meet rate						# needed to meet rate

Source: AF/A1

In 2019, CSAF implemented a Definitely Attend (DA) process that gave every wing CC/ Senior Materiel Leader (SML) and a few additional SRs direct input into which officers are guaranteed IDE. 194 DAs were awarded for AY20-21 IDE and 275 were awarded for AY21-22.

According to AF/A1, the intent of the DA was to allow SRs, who are closest and most familiar with the talent of their officers, to select a small number of officers to attend IDE without having to be selected by the central board. This would allow SRs to use a DA for an officer who is a strong performer now, but may not have a strong record from earlier in their career, which would lower their order of merit at the DE board. AF/A1 provided the following demographic data for DAs. (Ex 44:14)

Fig 47: AY20-22 DA Demographics

AY 20-21 IDE DA			AY 21-22 IDE DA		
White	162	83.5%	White	211	76.7%
Black	11	5.7%	Black	17	6.2%
Other	21	10.8%	Other	47	17.1%
Total	194	100.0%	Total	275	100.0%

Source: AF/A1

AF/A1 indicated the DA process has given more minorities the opportunity to attend IDE. Black officers comprised 5.7% of the 194 DAs Awarded in 2019 and 6.2% of the 275 DAs awarded in 2020, which is higher than their percentage of the O4 population. AF/A1 correlated black officers meeting the average designation rates in 2019/2020 with the DA process, but said they had not done the analysis to see if the success was a direct result of the DA process. AF/A1 is building on a plan similar to DAs for IDE, wherein SRs will be able to designate an officer to attend SDE using a DA. AF/A1 is still working on the details, but intends to start allowing SDE DAs in approximately two years.

According to AF/A1, eligible officer records are ranked 1 to N at the Central DE board and the primary nominees are sent to the DTs. The DTs vector nominees to specific programs. After the DTs are complete, officers are matched to a specific DE program followed by a review/validation at the DEDB. (Ex 44:4)

It does not appear the Air Force Personnel Center (AFPC) or AF/A1 analyzes designation rates to determine if there are disparities in the nomination/designation process. The charts above indicate that IDE designation rates for black officers met or exceeded the average for 2019 and 2020. However, SDE designation rates are lower than the average designation rate for 2015 through 2020. AF/A1 is aware of the disparities, especially for SDE. Diversity slides briefed to the DEDB simply show what percentage of each race makes up the total IDE/SDE designees, which may have limited utility for comparing across races.

AF/A1 acknowledged the disparity and offered several points related to the issue. First, the DE board is a diverse group that is shown videos on bias and the records are masked for demographics. The board process is similar to promotion boards in that the records are scored on performance indicated by their performance reports, and any splits are resolved during the board process. AF/A1 senior leadership believes the board process is fair and has no reason to believe bias exists within the board process. Although this Review found no evidence of racial bias, the potential for racial bias exists when SRs have discretion to decide which officers they will nominate for DE and control the comments they include in the nomination.

Second, AF/A1 also published guidance stating the criticality of DTs identifying potential barriers that inhibit any group of Air and Space Professionals from key developmental milestones. According to AF/A1, there have been a number of good examples of DTs performing analyses, but many do not conduct analyses, citing time limitations based on mission requirements.

Enlisted PME Attendance

Enlisted PME is composed of Airman Leadership School (ALS), Noncommissioned Officer Academy (NCOA), Senior Noncommissioned Officer Academy (SNCOA), and the Chief Leadership Course. All programs are "must attend" courses based on rank and promotion date.

ALS is a primary level in-residence force development opportunity that meets all enlisted professional military education requirements for the service's most junior service members. Airmen and Space Professionals participate beginning at the three-year time-in-service mark. Completion of ALS is required for senior airmen selected for staff sergeant before their promotion increment month. (Ex 43:101)

NCOA is a primary level in-residence force development opportunity and completion is required prior to promotion to Master Sergeant (MSgt) based on grade, priority, and eligibility. Technical sergeants (TSgt) must attend NCOA before two years' time-in-grade. (Ex 43:101)

SNCOA is an intermediate and senior-level in-residence force development opportunity and is required for promotion to Senior Master Sergeant (SMSgt). Senior noncommissioned officers who complete a resident sister service equivalent course or Joint Special Operations Forces Senior Enlisted Academy receive enlisted professional military education credit for completing resident SNCOA. (Ex 43:101)

Chief Leadership Course is a senior-level in-residence force development opportunity and is required for all newly-selected Chief Master Sergeants (CMSgts/E9). CMSgts must attend Chief Leadership Course before one year time-in-grade. (Ex 43:101)

According to AF/A1DL, there are approximately 75-80 SNCOs who attend sister service Joint Professional Military Education (JPME) per year. These SNCOs are nominated by their respective MAJCOMs. Each MAJCOM is allowed to nominate SNCOs based on the number of slots allocated. For example, if the DAF were offered two slots at the U.S. Army Sergeants Major Academy, each MAJCOM would be allowed to nominate two SNCOs. The nominees are then sent to the MAJCOM Command Chiefs, sanitized of demographics, to score.

Except for the small number of JPME courses that use a nomination process, attendance at Enlisted PME is required for all Airmen and Space Professionals based on rank and promotion dates. Because all enlisted members attend PME, this Review found no racial disparities for the enlisted PME courses. As for the JPME courses, AF/A1 does not keep a database or analyze for racial disparities in nominees or selectees. AF/A1 was able to produce some data for FY19 JPME courses. AF/A1 filled 83 JPME slots with 54% white service members, 13% black service members, and 22% other races. AF/A1 did not have any data on the number and demographics of nominees. Demographics were not masked for scoring. This Review notes the potential for racial bias in both the nomination and scoring processes. The diversity of the chiefs scoring the packages depends on the diversity of the MAJCOM Command Chiefs. Since AF/A1 does not track the demographic data needed to allow analysis for potential racial disparity, there is no way to know if there is a disparity in the selection of JPME candidates.

Civilian PME Attendance

As demonstrated in the AFPC data in Figs 48 and 49, black civilians met the DT at a higher rate than the average rate of all civilians meeting the DT, for both IDE and SDE for AYs 2018-2021. However, black civilians met the Civilian Developmental Education Board (CDEB) at a lower rate than the average across the same AYs. Despite being below the average rate that met the CDEB, black civilians met or exceeded the average select rate for IDE AY18 and 19 and were above the average select rate for AY18 and AY20. In addition, AF/A1 indicated they had not analyzed the data in this manner, and therefore, were not aware of the racial disparity for black civilians meeting the CDEB.

Fig 48: 2018-2021 Civilian IDE Selection Rates

IDE AY 18	Inventory	Eligible	# Met DT	Rate Met DT	# Met CDEB	Rate Met CDEB	# Selected	Rate Selected
All	48307	45207	262	0.58%	88	33.6%	50	56.8%
Black/AA	5452	5133	36	0.70%	11	30.6%	6	54.5%
White	37740	35239	187	0.53%	64	34.2%	34	53.1%

IDE AY 19	Inventory	Eligible	# Met DT	Rate Met DT	# Met CDEB	Rate Met CDEB	# Selected	Rate Selected
All	48701	45947	195	0.42%	72	36.9%	48	66.7%
Black/AA	5659	5369	28	0.52%	7	25.0%	4	57.1%
White	37785	35570	140	0.39%	57	40.7%	37	64.9%

IDE AY 20	Inventory	Eligible	# Met DT	Rate Met DT	# Met CDEB	Rate Met CDEB	# Selected	Rate Selected
All	50979	47477	225	0.47%	88	39.1%	48	54.5%
Black/AA	6066	5738	30	0.52%	7	23.3%	4	57.1%
White	39259	36471	161	0.44%	68	42.2%	38	55.9%

IDE AY 21	Inventory	Eligible	# Met DT	Rate Met DT	# Met CDEB	Rate Met CDEB	# Selected	Rate Selected
All	53232	48559	257	0.53%	85	33.1%	43	50.6%
Black/AA	6437	6020	46	0.76%	12	26.1%	6	50.0%
White	40586	37021	172	0.46%	62	36.0%	31	50.0%

Fig 49: 2018-2021 Civilian SDE Rates

SDE AY 18	Inventory	Eligible	# Met DT	Rate Met DT	# Met CDEB	Rate Met CDEB	# Selected	Rate Selected
All	10570	10229	248	2.42%	154	62.1%	133	86.4%
Black/AA	663	648	18	2.78%	9	50.0%	9	100.0%
White	9077	8783	201	2.29%	129	64.2%	113	87.6%

SDE AY 19	Inventory	Eligible	# Met DT	Rate Met DT	# Met CDEB	Rate Met CDEB	# Selected	Rate Selected
All	11013	10715	294	2.74%	162	55.1%	135	83.3%
Black/AA	707	690	19	2.75%	10	52.6%	4	40.0%
White	9450	9185	248	2.70%	133	53.6%	118	88.7%

SDE AY 20	Inventory	Eligible	# Met DT	Rate Met DT	# Met CDEB	Rate Met CDEB	# Selected	Rate Selected
All	11605	11261	338	3.00%	195	57.7%	126	64.6%
Black/AA	767	740	31	4.19%	11	35.5%	6	54.5%
White	9902	9612	276	2.87%	166	60.1%	109	65.7%

SDE AY 21	Inventory	Eligible	# Met DT	Rate Met DT	# Met CDEB	Rate Met CDEB	# Selected	Rate Selected
All	12647	12176	362	2.97%	220	60.8%	134	60.9%
Black/AA	883	850	35	4.12%	13	37.1%	9	69.2%
White	10685	10311	295	2.86%	184	62.4%	111	60.3%

Civilian PME follows a process similar to the military IDE/SDE process. First, there is a call for nominations, followed by a Civilian DT, and then a Civilian DE board. Civilian personnel have to apply for IDE/SDE opportunities. Once they apply, they need an endorsement by their supervisor, and the endorsement must be from at least a GS-15 or SES. Unlike the military DE process, there is no cap on the number of civilians the supervisor (GS-15 or above) may endorse. The civilian DTs then evaluate the endorsed candidates to verify their eligibility, assess the candidate's performance, and determine which candidates meet the Civilian Developmental Education Board (CDEB). The CDEB then designates who will attend PME.

According to AF/A1, the CDEB is a diverse board and the school designations are merit based. Based on the data received from Civilian DE personnel in AFPC/A1, it does not appear designation rates are analyzed. Similar to the military IDE/SDE brief, the AF/A1 civilian diversity slides only show the percentages of the designees by race. They provide a comparison to the previous year by highlighting differences of plus or minus 3%. (Ex 45) Since the data only compares individual race groups to the same race group from the previous year, there is no way to identify potential racial disparity. This Review used the raw numbers to create Figures 48 and 49, which show the different rates black civilians and their white counterparts met the DT, were nominated by the DT for the CDEB, and were ultimately designated by the CDEB.

This Review found black civilians were nominated to the CDEB at a rate lower than the average rate and lower than the rate for white civilians for IDE and SDE AY18-21. Likewise, the selection rate for black civilians was below the average selection rate for half of the eight IDE/SDE AYs. This Review was unable to determine if racial bias contributed to the disparity. Points in the process susceptible to racial bias include the endorsement comments by supervisors and senior leadership and the DTs who review the applicants and decide who meets the CDEB. According to AF/A1, racial demographics are discussed during the CDEB outbrief to AF/A1 leadership. AF/A1 should consider conducting a more detailed analysis to determine why these disparities exist.

PROMOTIONS

The IG Review found that black service members are underrepresented in promotions to E5-E7 and O4-O6. Additionally, black officers are underrepresented in Definitely Promote (DP) allocations for O5 and O6. Black, permanent, full-time civilians are underrepresented in GS-13 to SES grades.

Demographics

The July 2019 Census estimated the U.S. population is 60% white, 18% Hispanic, 13% black, 6% Asian or Other Pacific Islander, and 4% other races. An April 2020 snapshot of enlisted and officer ranks show 16.9% of enlisted Airmen (E1-E4) are black, which is overrepresented compared to the U.S. population (13%) and the eligible population (8%). On the other hand, Air Force O1s are 6.3% black, which is underrepresented compared to the 7% eligible population and 13% of the total population. (Ex 42)

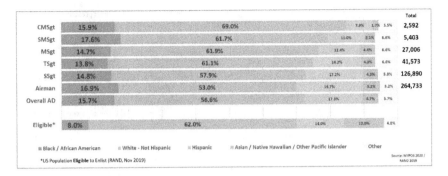

*US Population **Eligible** to Enlist (RAND, Nov 2019)

Source: MilPDS 2020 / RAND 2019

Fig 51: AD Officer Demographic by Rank

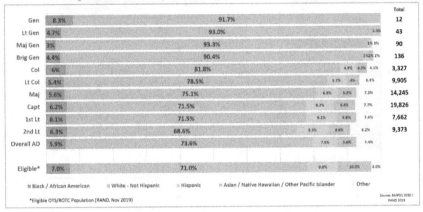

*Eligible OTS/ROTC Population (RAND, Nov 2019)

Source: MilPDS 2020 / RAND 2019

The representation of civilian leadership is challenging to assess because, unlike the military promotion system, there is no standardized central promotion system for civilian members. For DAF civilians, hiring actions and promotions are individual actions taken by individual hiring officials. Hiring officials can promote from within an organization, or they can select a candidate from outside of the organization or DAF. Furthermore, hiring priorities established by the Office of Personnel Management (OPM) must be observed. Nevertheless, the April 2020 snapshot of civilian representation by grade shows black civilians are overrepresented compared to the U.S. population in the lower grades (GS-1 through GS-11) and underrepresented in higher GS grades (GS-12 through SES). The disparity in black civilian representation increases as the grade increases.

Fig 52: Civilian Workforce Grade by Demographic Group

						Total
SES	5.0%	81.9%	8.9%	5.3%	3.9%	282
GS-15	6.1%	83.4%	4.8%	3.0% 2.9%		1,278
GS-14	9.1%	79.3%	5.8%	2.4% 3.4%		4,827
GS-12 - GS-13	12.7%	72.4%	7.5%	3.6% 3.8%		28,444
GS-9 - GS-11	15.7%	67.3%	9.0%	3.8% 4.4%		29,785
GS-1 - GS-8	19.3%	58.9%	12.0%	4.7% 5.1%		17,721
Overall USPFT	12.8%	70.3%	8.6%	4.1% 4.3%		
US Population*	13.0%	60.0%	18.0%	6.0% 4.0%		

■ Black / African American   ■ White - Not Hispanic   ■ Hispanic   ■ Asian / Native Hawaiian / Other Pacific Islander   ■ Other

*US Population Estimate (Census, Jul 2019)

Source: MilPDS 2020 / RAND 2019

Enlisted Promotions

Enlisted promotion data from 2015 through 2019 provided by AFPC and AF/A1 reveals disparities among some ranks and demographics. During these five years, black enlisted service members were underrepresented in promotion rates for all promotion categories and ranks except E8 and E9. White enlisted service members were overrepresented in all ranks. Enlisted service members of other races were underrepresented in all ranks except for E7. The most substantial disparity for promotion is evident in E5. Black service members promoted below the average by 5.7% in 2015 to 9.1% in 2019. After comparing the proportion of race groups in Active Duty enlisted year groups with their proportion in promotions, black enlisted service members are underrepresented by 10 to 20% in E5, E6, and E7 promotions. White enlisted service members are overrepresented by up to 10% in E5, E6, and E7 promotions. Small group sizes introduce more variability in the higher ranks.

Enlisted service members in the grades of E4, E5, and E6, who are eligible for promotion, are given a promotion recommendation through the Forced Distribution process.[17] Members' performance reports are reviewed, and their chain of command either advocates for or decides on the recommendation. While race, gender, and ethnicity are published in post-board statistics, SNCO selection boards are not provided this information and do not consider it during

---

[17]Per AFI 36-2406, *Officer and Enlisted Evaluations Systems,* Forced Distribution is "The allocation of the top two promotion recommendations, "Promote Now" and "Must Promote", from a force distributor...or promotion eligible SrA, SSgts, and TSgts." Large units receive their own forced distribution promotion allocations and allocations are awarded at the unit level. Promotion allocations for small units roll-up to compete at and received promotion recommendations allocations by the Senior Rater or Management Level Enlisted Forced Distribution Panel (EFDP). Large units are any organizational structure with 11 or more eligible Airmen, and small units are organizational structures with ten or less eligible Airmen. (Ex 53:115-118)

the selection process. However, board members may deduce a member's gender, race, or ethnicity based on the name of the individual.

Fig 53: Enlisted Promotion Rates

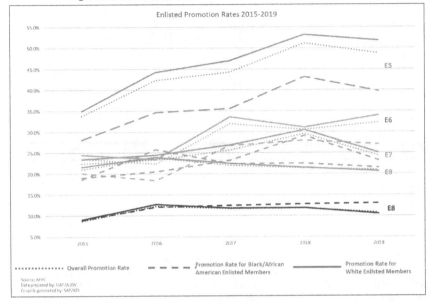

Fig 54: Racial Disparity in Enlisted Promotion Rates

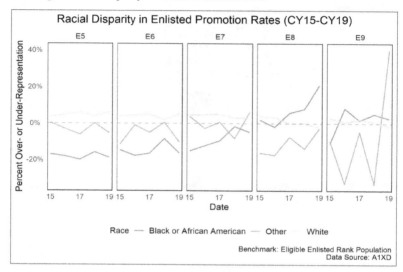

With the exception of the acquisition career field, black enlisted service members consistently take longer to promote to E5, E6, and E7. Figure 54 is based on total time in service, not the time to achieve each rank. Thus, delays in promotion to E5 contribute to the time to achieve the ranks of E6 through E9. Additionally, the following disparities are present in enlisted promotions (See Ex 2:87 for detailed graphics):

- Compared to the average years in service before promotion for each Active Duty enlisted year group from 2008 to 2012, black enlisted service members consistently take longer to promote to E5 across operations, logistics, support, and medical career fields.

- Compared to the average years in service before promotion for each Active Duty enlisted year group from 2004 to 2008, black enlisted service members consistently take longer to promote to E6 across operations, logistics, support, and medical career fields.

- Compared to the average years in service before promotion for each Active Duty enlisted year group from 2001 to 2005, black enlisted service members consistently take longer to promote to E7 across operations and support career fields.

- Compared to the average years in service before promotion for each Active Duty enlisted year group from 2001 to 2005, there seems to be no disparity in time to promote to E8 across race-ethnicity groups.

In order to understand E5 and E6 promotion disparities, it is necessary to understand how Weighted Airman Promotion System (WAPS) points are allocated. Promotion factors include Specialty Knowledge Test (SKT) score (if applicable), Promotion Fitness Examination (PFE) score, decorations, and EPRs (promotion recommendations increase points, referral evaluations[18] reduce points). Promotion eligibility requires members to earn a minimum score on the SKT and PFE.

Promotion recommendations are strong predictors of promotion and may largely explain promotion rates to E5 and E6. For E5 between 2017 and 2019, a "Promote Now" (PN) rating resulted in a 99% promotion rate, and a "Must Promote" (MP) resulted in an 86 to 90% promotion rate. The average promotion rate was around 50%. Between 2017 and 2019, E6s with a PN recommendation promoted at a 96-98% rate, and 71-76% rate with an MP recommendation. The average promotion rate was around 30%.

Data for the 2019 E5 promotion cycle provide some insight into the disparity in black enlisted promotions. Black airmen received a PN or MP recommendation at a slightly lower rate than the average rate. Black males received a PN or MP recommendation at a rate of 19%, which is below the 21% service average for males. Black females received a PN or MP recommendation at a rate of 26%, which was below the Air Force 30% average for females, but 5% above the service average for males and 7% above the average for black males. The overall average PN and MP recommendation rate for 2019 promotion to E5 was 23%, and the overall for black service members was 21%. Hispanic service members were above the average at 24%, and white service members met the average rate at 23%.

Lower test scores and increased quality force indicators also contributed to the lower promotion recommendation and promotion rates for black service members.[19] For enlisted members under 25 years old and have less than 5 years of service, black Airmen have an increased likelihood of having quality force indicators, including an Unfavorable Information File (UIF), Article 15s, and demotions.

In 2019, E6 promotion rates, promotion recommendations, and test scores for black males were below the service average. Black males averaged the lowest test scores of race/ethnic and gender groups. Black males promoted at 27%, which was 5% below the Air Force average, and at a lower rate than other racial and ethnic groups. A 2008 RAND study on WAPS standardized test scores found black enlisted service members' PFE and SKT scores

---

[18] Per AFI 36-2406, *Officer and Enlisted Evaluations Systems*, performance evaluations must be "Referred" when "[c]omments in any OPR, EPR, LOE, or TR (to include attachments), regardless of the ratings, that are derogatory in nature, imply or refer to behavior incompatible with or not meeting AF standards, and/or refer to disciplinary actions," "[w]hen an officer fails to meet standards in any one of the listed performance factors, in Section III or Section IX of the OPR," which "drives the overall evaluation to be marked "Does Not Meet Standards" and/or "an evaluator marks "Does Not Meet Standards" in Section III of AF Form 707 [Officer Performance Report (Lt thru Col)] or "Do Not Retain" in Section IV of AF Form 912 [Enlisted Performance Report (CMSgt)]." (Ex 53:34-35)
[19] Per AFI 36-2907, *Adverse Administrative Actions*, quality indicators include UIF, Control Roster, and Article 15s. The UIF is an "official record of unfavorable information about an individual. It documents administrative, judicial, and nonjudicial actions." The Control Roster "is a rehabilitative tool that commanders may use to establish a 6-month observation period," and Article 15, UCMJ is "nonjudicial punishment that allows commanders to administratively discipline Airmen without a court-martial."(Ex 54:19)

tended to be below average, and low test scores were consistent with lower AFQT test scores at accession. (Ex 15:102)

Starting in 2015, the Air Force removed time-in-grade (TIG) and time-in-service (TIS) points from WAPS scores, removing one-third of the point value each year until completely eliminating this point category in 2017. This Air Force decision was focused on driving and rewarding better performance by removing points based solely on seniority. With the removal of TIG and TIS points, a greater premium is placed on testing and performance with an opportunity to earn additional performance points through the award of PN or MP recommendations, as previously discussed. In addition, given known disparities in testing and the inability to centrally board the large number of E5s and E6s for promotion, greater emphasis was placed on performance and lower point values were placed on testing. Service members who have difficulty with SKT and PFE testing and whose performance does not earn them the additional points through a PN or MP will have a lower chance of promotion. E4 and E5 promotions rates in 2019 and 2020 also reveal service members who test well and often have fewer years of service tend to earn higher PN and MP promotion recommendation rates. Enlisted members who, over time, overcome their testing challenges may still promote at a lower rate as their TIG increases unless they earn the higher performance recommendations of PN and MP.

Black enlisted members are underrepresented in promotions to E7, whereas they are overrepresented in E8 and E9 promotions. In the past, SNCO promotion scoring was similar to NCOs. However, in 2019, the Air Force removed the WAPS testing requirement and decoration scores for E7 through E9 promotions. After these changes took effect in 2020, black service members were promoted to E7 near the service average. Analysis of E7, E8, and E9 promotions reveals the most recent promotion recommendation ("on-top" recommendation) and EPR ratings reflecting the most recent performance primarily explain promotion board scores. It is important to note that the enlisted evaluation board at AFPC (SNCO promotions) evaluates the last five years of performance reports, while Force Distributors (NCO promotions) evaluate the last three EPRs (including the "on top" year). In this manner, the emphasis is placed on recent performance and accomplishments since their last promotion. This ensures early discrepancies in performance or negative quality indicators from a younger portion of a career can be overcome and will not cause a continued negative impact for high performing Airmen. Coupled with removing testing, AF/A1 believes these changes are expected to help underrepresented groups – at the E7 level in particular.

Other factors drive promotion rates. Data indicate authorization structures impact promotion rates thus promotion rates vary by AFSC. Promotion rates are used as force shaping tools in overmanned and undermanned AFSCs. Career fields with higher turnover rates also tend to have higher promotion rates. Furthermore, for E5 and E6 promotions, testing and EPR scores do not have the same impact in every AFSC. In some career fields, test scores have a higher impact on promotion rates. More difficult SKTs for select career fields result in higher promotion disqualification rates. Finally, decorations could have an amplified impact for E5 promotions because enlisted service members earn points for decorations, and E5s with more medals are more likely to be awarded PNs and MPs.

AF/A1 is aware of the disparities in enlisted promotions by race and believes promotion board members appropriately score records. According to AF/A1, promotion disparities have three causes:

- Higher rate of quality force indicator issues for black E4s and E5s

- Lower test scores for black E4s, E5s, and E6s

- Overrepresentation of black service members in AFSCs that have lower promotion rates and lower turnover

AFPC and RAND research data support these points. AF/A1 believes bias may play a role as well. This Review's survey comments and group sessions also reveal black service members feel they are not given the benefit of the doubt, lack mentoring, and do not have equal opportunity for development.

Officer Promotions

According to AFPC and AF/A1 data, black officers were promoted below the average rates during the last five years. Between 2015 and 2019, black officers were promoted below the overall average rate and below white officers' rate in every IPZ board to O4, O5, and O6, except in the 2018 O6 board. Furthermore, black officers were consistently underrepresented from 2015 to 2019 APZ to O4. Also, black officers were underrepresented for both O5 and O6 BPZ. It is important to note, however, that small sample sizes introduce more variability in the higher ranks and smaller race/ethnic groups.

Over the past five years, compared to the proportion of other races, black officers were underrepresented in O4 Above Primary Zone (APZ) promotions, O5 and O6 Below Primary Zone (BPZ) promotions, and for all three grades for In Primary Zone (IPZ) promotion rates. Officers in the category of "other" races were underrepresented in all promotion categories and ranks except for O4 APZ. White officers were consistently overrepresented at every rank and in every promotion category. There is no BPZ data for O4 from 2015 to 2019 and no APZ data for O4 2018 to 2019. Group size for O6 APZ is not sufficient to calculate the relative racial disparity.

Fig 55: Officer Promotion Rates

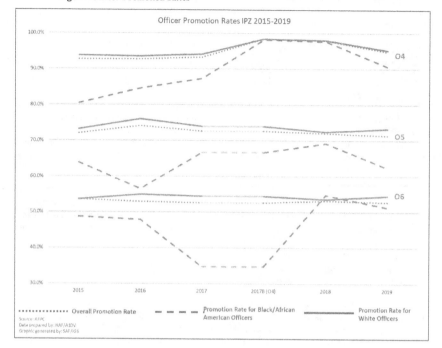

Fig 56: Racial Disparity in Officer Promotion Rates

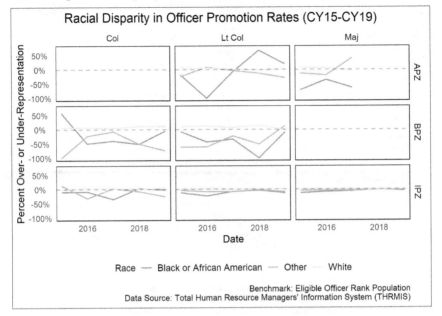

Pilots historically have a higher rate of BPZ selection than other AFSCs. Black officers' underrepresentation in the pilot AFSCs (2% of pilots) likely contributes to the disparity in black representation at higher officer ranks.[20]

---

[20] As of May 2020, 77.9% of the total AD officer force is white, but makes up 86.7% of the pilot force (11Xs). By comparison, 5.3% of the AD officer force is black, but only 2.0% of AF pilots are black. (Source MilPDS, HAF/A1DV).

Fig 57: O5 and O6 Below the Promotion Zone (BPZ) Selection Rates

O5 BPZ Rate By Occupation	Below Primary Zone (Selection Rate)					O6 BPZ Rate By Occupation	Below Primary Zone (Selection Rate)				
	2015	2016	2017	2018	2019		2015	2016	2017	2018	2019
Pilot	5.5%	5.5%	4.9%	6.7%	4.3%	Pilot	3.3%	4.3%	2.6%	2.3%	2.0%
Combat Systems Officer/Nav (2015-16)	2.1%	3.7%	1.8%	2.0%	2.1%	Combat Systems Officer	1.7%	0.0%	0.0%	1.1%	1.6%
Air Battle Manager	2.5%	2.4%	6.5%	1.1%	4.6%	Air Battle Manager	2.0%	0.0%	0.0%	0.0%	1.1%
Non Rated Ops	4.2%	2.4%	3.4%	2.3%	4.6%	Non Rated Ops	1.5%	1.0%	1.6%	2.0%	3.2%
Mission Support	3.8%	1.6%	2.1%	2.3%	3.5%	Mission Support	1.7%	1.0%	1.2%	2.3%	1.2%
Overall Rate	4.3%	3.4%	3.4%	3.9%	3.9%	Overall Rate	2.2%	2.1%	1.7%	2.0%	1.9%

In a 2016 interview, former Air Force Vice Chief of Staff, Gen (Ret) Larry Spencer, addressed the importance of BPZ selection rates in shaping the future of the Air Force's top leadership. He said, "[b]elow-the-zone is where, probably 99.9% of the time, General Officers come from…[T]hose are your future General Officers. That's when the Air Force as a system starts breaking out superstars who have the greatest potential. There's a lot that goes into that. Obviously, potential and talent goes into it, but also mentoring and the ratings you get and those types of things." (Ex 32:8) In 2019, the Air Force announced the transition from the below-the-zone system to a more merit-based system that allows for further development and advancement among later-blooming, superior performing officers.

Promotion recommendations largely explain promotion rates. Between 2015 and 2019, a "Definitely Promote" (DP) recommendation resulted in over a 99% selection rate for IPZ and a 100% selection rate for APZ to O4. For promotion to O5 from 2015 to 2019, 98.8 to 99.8% of DPs were selected IPZ. A DP BPZ increased the promotion rate to O5 from the average rate of 3.4 to 4.3% to the DP rate of 24.8 to 32.5%. 2015 to 2019 IPZ selection rate for O6 with a DP was 94.2 to 99.4%.

A closer look at the DP data by race shows from 2015 to 2019, black officers and other races consistently received DP recommendations to O5 below the average rate, while white officers were recommended for DP above the average rate. Black officers received DP recommendations to O6 from 2016 to 2019 below the average rate. In 2015, black officers received DP recommendations above the average rate – the same year, black officers were above the average for BPZ rates.

Fig 58: Racial Disparity O5 and O6 Definitely Promote (DP) Recommendation Rates

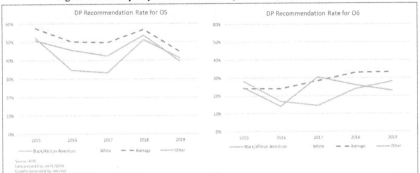

According to data provided by HAF/A1 and AFPC, there is a disparity in DP recommendations within AFSC categories. For instance, operational AFSCs (1XXX) appear to have a DP recommendation rate near the overall average. However, upon closer examination, it is apparent that pilots (11X) received DP recommendations well above the average rate, and all other 1XXX AFSCs combined receive DP recommendations well below the average rate. Pilots are the largest AFSC in the Air Force and the least diverse: only 2% of the pilot force is black. For operational AFSCs, black officers comprise 5.6% of intelligence officers and 10.1% of cyber officers. The AFSCs with higher percentages of black officers receive DP recommendations at a below-average rate. A similar trend is present with 2XXX Logistics AFSCs, which includes Aircraft Maintenance (21A), Munitions and Missile Maintenance (21M), and Logistics Readiness (21R). Logistics Readiness (21R) has the highest percentage of black officers (9.6% in 2019). Aircraft Maintenance (21A) and Munitions and Maintenance (21M) have lower percentages of black officers at approximately 6.5%. However, Aircraft Maintenance officers (21A) consistently received higher DP recommendations for O5 than the other 2XXX AFSCs, and well above the average. The higher rate of DPs for AFSCs with lower populations of black officers contributes to the racial disparity in officer promotions.

Fig 59: O5 and O6 Definitely Promote (DP) Recommendation Rates by AFSC

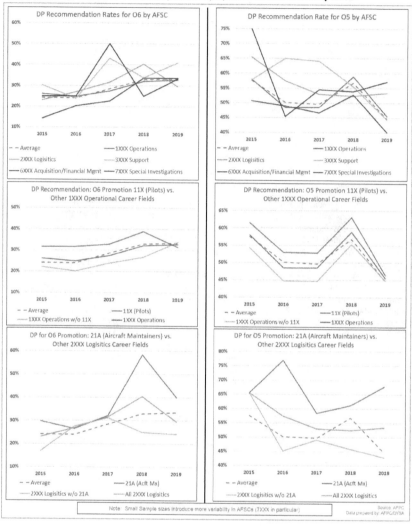

Fig 60: Select Officer AFSCs by Demographic Group

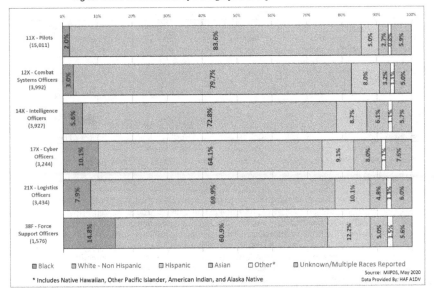

AF/A1 is aware of the racial disparities in officer promotions and assesses that the officer promotion boards appropriately score records. In 2014, RAND published a study on *Improving Officer Diversity*, which supported AF/A1's position. The study found "no evidence of differential promotion outcomes, suggesting that systematic bias is not present the Air Force's [officer] promotion system." (Ex 21:40) However, the study found unexplained gaps in the "Definitely Promote" (DP) and selection for black line officers' promotion as shown in the figure below. RAND's model for this gap analysis did not include other essential factors, such as stratification given to officers by their senior rater, enthusiastic endorsements for future positions or PME opportunities in performance reports, or positional opportunities and advantages such as working directly for a General Officer. Accordingly, RAND could not infer that DP and select gaps for minority groups were indicators of discriminatory practices.

Fig 61: Gaps in Definitely Promote (DP) and Promotion Selection for Line Officers

Outcome	Zone	Group	Rank	Source	Unexplained Gap
Selected (P)	IPZ	Women	Major	USAFA	Favors Women
Selected (All)	BPZ	Women	Colonel	USAFA	Favors Men
DP Award	IPZ	African Americans	Major	Non- USAFA	Favors Whites
DP Award	IPZ	African Americans	Lt. Colonel	USAFA	Favors Whites
DP Award	IPZ	African Americans	Lt. Colonel	HBCU	Favors Whites
Selected (All)	IPZ	African Americans	Colonel	Non- USAFA, Non-HBCU	Favors Whites
DP Award	IPZ	Hispanics	Colonel	USAFA	Favors Whites
Selected (All)	BPZ	Hispanics	Colonel	Non- USAFA	Favors Whites

NOTE: Selected (P) outcomes exclude DP awardees.   Source: RAND, Ex 21:41

RAND's 2014 study also found several variables established early in an officer's career, such as AFSC, are strong predictors of promotion to senior levels. The report said, "[t]he importance of these characteristics grows over time because promotion prospects at each level take into account an officer's entire career; they are not reset at each pay grade. For minority groups, who are less likely to have at least some of these vital characteristics, promotion prospects diminish as their career moves forward." (Ex 21: xviii) Furthermore, minorities are generally less represented in operational AFSCs that tend to have higher promotion rates. As career paths are generally selected at accession, any analysis of promotion must circle back to recruiting and accession. The RAND study concluded, "if improving promotion prospects for minorities is a policy goal, the Air Force likely needs to begin with recruiting." (Ex 21:28)

AF/A1's position is that bias in the system may cause black officers to be underexposed to career-broadening opportunities, less aware of or not pushed for key developmental positions, and less afforded mentorship engagements. This perspective is supported by black senior leaders' perspectives, service member responses in the Racial Disparity Review survey, and Racial Disparity Review group sessions. As such, on 8 September 2020, AF/A1 published a memorandum addressing bias and released the "Unconscious Bias Mitigation Training Architecture." If funded, training will be fully implemented by FY22 and embedded in every formal training and education touchpoint for officers, enlisted, and civilians. (Ex 33; Ex 34; Ex 35)

Although AF/A1 did not believe there was bias in the formal promotion board process, the training architecture includes a "just-in-time" tailored bias presentation for use before "Talent Evaluation." (Ex 35) Research shows that adequately crafted bias training can provide positive outcomes for a limited time. (Ex 36)

Bias training alone will not reduce promotion disparities. More research is needed to understand the disparities in DP allocation and promotion rates. Although AF/A1 requires functional Developmental Teams (DTs) to complete barrier analyses, there is little accountability for DTs who do not take this type of analysis seriously and do not fully comply with AF/A1's mandate. More oversight should be considered to ensure DTs are complying with AF/A1 direction to complete barrier analyses.

In 2020, the Air Force overhauled its Line of the Air Force (LAF) promotion system by creating six new promotion categories: air operations and special warfare, space operations, nuclear and missile operations, information warfare, combat support, and force modernization. This new system allows officers in each specialty category to compete against a standard that is more applicable to their respective career fields. By introducing specialty categories, AF/A1 expects promotions rates for minorities to improve. Based on data analyzed, the Review team concurs with AF/A1's prediction. The largest two AFSCs are pilots (15,011) and combat system officers (CSOs) (3,992). These AFSCs also have a low representation of minorities at 2% for black pilots and 3% for black CSOs; and pilots are consistently given DP recommendations above the average rate.

Under the new system, pilots and CSOs will compete in the air operations and special warfare category. AFSCs that have a higher representation of minorities, such as cyber officers and force support officers, will be assessed in separate categories allowing them to compete against officers of similar qualifications and experience. For example, acquisition AFSCs traditionally are given DP recommendations for promotion at a rate below the average, at least partly because officers in these fields have non-traditional, career-specific milestones they must meet, and they have fewer command opportunities, making them less competitive for promotion as compared to other AFSCs. According to May 2020 MilPDS data, the acquisition manager AFSC (63A) is composed of 2,692 officers, 9.2% of which are black, while the contracting officer AFSC (64P), with 825 officers, has 13.5% black officers. Under the new system, these officers will compete with officers in similar paths, increasing their overall promotion chances.

As mentioned previously, the 2020 overhaul of the officer promotion system also removed the BPZ system in favor of a more merit-based system. This change will increase the IPZ and APZ rates and is expected to reduce disparities in the promotion rates among AFSCs and minority officers over time. In May 2020, the Air Force conducted its first promotion board that included the changes mentioned above. Once the board results are released, AF/A1 plans to review the results to determine the impact of these changes. It is recommended that promotion disparities be examined after each promotion board to determine the long-term effects of these changes.

Civilian Leadership Representation

The DAF draws from the U.S. labor market to capitalize on available civilian talent.[21] As with the military service members, the DAF has not maintained a demographically diverse civilian workforce. (Ex 26:vii) Black civilians are underrepresented in Air Force civilian senior

---

[21] Due to "Veteran's Preference," the largest labor market for the DAF is military veterans. Veterans' Preference "gives eligible veterans preference in appointment over many other applicants. Veterans' preference applies to all new appointments in the competitive service and many in the excepted service. Veterans' preference does not guarantee veterans a job, and it does not apply to internal agency actions such as promotions, transfers, reassignments, and reinstatements." There are three types of preference eligibility: sole survivorship, non-disable, and disabled. (https://www.fedshirevets.gov/job-seekers/veterans-preference/)

leadership positions. Approximately 13% of the DAF permanent, full-time civilian workforce is composed of black service members. Yet, between 2015 and 2019, black civilians represented 8% to 8.8% of the GS-13/15 grades and 4.4% to 5.1% of the Senior Executive Service (SES) grades. Conversely, white civilians make up approximately 74.5% of the workforce. Their representation increases to approximately 82% of the grades of GS-13/15 and above 85% of SESs. All remaining race, ethnic, and gender groups are underrepresented in GS-13 through SES compared to the entire permanent workforce.

Fig 62: DAF Permenant Full-Time Civilians by Demographic Group

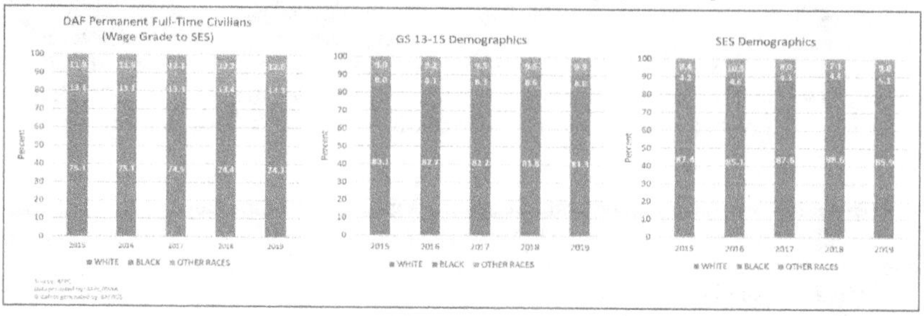

A 2020 RAND study on *Advancement and Retention Barriers in the U.S. Air Force Civilian White Collar Workforce* found that women, black men, and Hispanic men start at lower entry grades than white men. RAND's quantitative model found civilian employees who start at a lower grade cannot "catch up," limiting their opportunity to qualify for senior leadership positions. (Ex 31:viii, x)

Fig 63: Grade Level of Employees at Entry by Demographic Group

Table 3.1. Grade Levels of Employees at Entry by Demographic Group

	Average Grade at Entry	Average Grade at 2 YOS	Percentage Entering Grade 11 or Higher	Percentage Entering Grade 14 or Higher
Race/Ethnicity and Gender				
All male	10.2	10.7	55.3	4.5
All female	8.9	9.7	31.3	1.2
White male	10.4	10.9	58.2	5.1
White female	9.0	9.8	33.2	1.4
Black male	9.5	10.0	43.4	2.0
Black female	8.6	9.3	26.0	0.7
Hispanic male	9.5	10.1	43.4	2.0
Hispanic female	8.6	9.4	25.3	0.7
Asian male	9.8	10.7	48.1	2.6
Asian female	8.9	9.9	30.9	1.1
AI/AN male	10.0	10.5	51.2	3.5
AI/AN female	8.9	9.5	31.1	0.8
Self-Reported Disability Status				
No disability	9.8	10.4	48.6	3.6
Targeted disability	9.3	10.3	38.5	2.2
Other disability	9.9	10.4	50.1	3.0
Unidentified/not listed	10.0	10.6	53.0	4.3
VA Disability Rating				
Nonveteran	9.0	10.4	32.1	1.5
Retired enlisted (No disability)	10.0	10.3	54.4	0.8
Retired enlisted (30% disability)	9.7	10.1	49.1	0.6
Retired officer (No disability)	12.7	12.8	95.2	23.2
Retired officer (30% disability)	12.3	12.5	91.0	17.0
Other veteran (No disability)	9.5	9.9	44.1	1.9
Other veteran (30% disability)	9.2	9.7	38.8	1.1

SOURCE: Authors' calculations from Air Force personnel data.   Source: RAND, Ex 31:26
NOTE: YOS: years of civilian service.

The 2020 RAND study also found women and racial and ethnic minorities expressed slightly less awareness of promotion opportunities than white men. Many surveyed groups, regardless of race, ethnicity, or gender, reported that feedback, mentoring, and career development support are limited or lacking. Furthermore, several participants indicated their supervisors do not feel responsible for providing feedback, and some reported a lack of transparency surrounding selections for training opportunities. (Ex 34:xii) Finally, the RAND study found four factors that are important to promotion: (Ex 34:xi)

- Individuals' social networks (the survey population reported this as the most important factor)

- Individual qualifications, such as education and strong prior performance or experience

- Individual characteristics, such as initiative and drive

- Mobility or the willingness to move for a higher pay grade position

A promotion system where social networks play an important role in hiring decisions leaves room for bias in the selection process.

The 2020 RAND study provided three recommendations to overcome barriers to recruitment and retention in the civilian workforce: (Ex 34:xv)

- Identify root causes for the entry-level gap for women and other minority groups

- Ensure that supervisors and managers take responsibility for the career development and disability management of their staff

- Monitor the advancement and retention of civilian demographic groups that have lower-than-expected advancement or retention rates

Between 2015 and 2019, the representation for black GS-13/15s increased from 8.0% to 8.8%, and other races increased from 9.0% to 9.9%. Similarly, black SES representation increased from 4.2% to 5.1%, and other races increased from 8.4% to 9%. The improvements in minority and women representation may result from targeted efforts to increase diversity in civilian leadership positions. In 2015, the Air Force adopted significant policy changes after the Air Force Barrier Analysis Working Group (AFBAWG) identified several barriers to recruitment and selection. These barriers included using a "military lens" during the selection process, preferential hiring of retired military members, and geographic mobility expectations for development opportunities and promotions, limiting opportunities for women and minorities. (Ex 37:10) An April 2015 memorandum from the Secretary of the Air Force and Chief of the Staff of the Air Force on *2015 Diversity and Inclusion (D&I) Initiatives* outlined changes to hiring and selection of DAF civilians: (Ex 37; Ex 38)

- Diverse hiring panels for GS-14 and GS-15 positions are required. The panel must include one civilian with no prior military experience.

- External-only recruitment is prohibited.

- Use of specific military job requirements and attributes that may only be attained through uniformed service are prohibited unless absolutely required for the position.

- External, non-competitive, by-name requests for hiring into GS-14 and GS-15 positions are limited to mission-critical reasons

- All civilian jobs must be posted for a minimum of five business days. For GS-13 positions and above, 10 days is recommended.

The Review team was unable to obtain more data on civilian leadership representation between 2015 and 2019. DAF civilian leadership can only be as diverse as the representation of people who apply for positions and are minimally qualified for the job. A factor to consider is the role of "Veteran's Preference" in the hiring process. A qualified veteran is given hiring priority over other candidates, which could limit the hiring authority's ability to hire diverse applicants. Regardless, it is unknown if there is racial disparity in applicants for civilian leadership positions, a disparity in applicants' qualifications, or disparity in selection rates for those positions based on race, ethnicity, or gender. More data and study are suggested to understand why, despite incremental progress, there continue to be disparities in women and minority representation in DAF civilian leadership.

Interim Conclusion

The Air Force and Space Force promote officer and enlisted members from within the service. As such, representation across minority groups is influenced by the representation of these groups at accession. If promotion and retention are equivalent across race, ethnic, and gender groups, senior leaders will not be any more diverse than their cohort representation at accessions.(Ex 21:4) According to the Military Leadership Diversity Commission (MLDC), increases in the representation of minorities or women in the higher ranks are not possible "unless DoD implements systematic changes in how the services outreach, recruit, develop, retain, and promote their members." (Ex 21:1) Without policy intervention, the gap in minorities and women among senior leaders will not be closed. Furthermore, it is unclear why there is a disparity in women and minorities in civilian leadership position representation; additional study is suggested.

OFFICER ASSIGNMENTS

Officer and Civilian Development Teams

A critical component of officer and civilian development is Development Teams (DT). Under AFI 36-2670, *Total Force Management*, paragraph 1.4.1. Development Team Establishment, force development for officers and DAF civilians "is managed by development teams. Development teams should develop an understanding of both officer and civilian resources and requirements, and ensure all career field members are provided with appropriate development opportunities. Functional managers should integrate officer and civilian development teams to the maximum extent possible." (Ex 43:20, 21) Although the AFI does not specifically state DTs must be diverse, additional AF/A1 guidance states, "[i]t is incumbent upon the DT Chair to ensure their DT has diversity amongst voting and non-voting members as defined in AFI 36-7001, *Diversity and Inclusion*, paragraph 1.3., Air Force diversity includes but is not limited to: personal life experiences, cultural knowledge, philosophical/spiritual perspectives, geographic, socioeconomic, educational, and work background, language and physical abilities, age, race, ethnicity, and gender." (Ex 55:2; Ex 61:3)

Each DT is chaired by an O-6/GS-15 (or equivalent) or higher. For a development education DT, the chair must be a General Officer or member of the senior executive service. DT membership consists of the development team chair, career field manager, and key force development stakeholders (must be O-6/GS-15 or higher (e.g., Air Staff Directors/Deputy Directors, Air Staff-level subject matter experts, Major Command-level functional leadership). The overall responsibility of the DT is to identify education, training, and experiences appropriate for officers and civilians within each functional community based on current and future requirements. The AFI lists over 40 DT responsibilities, but for the purpose of this Review, the following related responsibilities are highlighted: (Ex 43:21)

- DTs provide developmental vectors to officers at five mandatory trigger points starting at promotion to major (O4): IDE outplacement, squadron commander outplacement, promotion to lieutenant colonel, and SDE outplacement. DTs validate and endorse self-nominated GS-14/15 candidates for the Civilian Strategic Leadership Program, and they determine Developmental Education Designation Board nominations (civilian) and vectors (military), squadron command and squadron director candidate lists, Advanced Studies Group nominations, and AF/A1-approved, functionally-sponsored development programs. (Ex 43:23-25)

- In addition, DTs are responsible for identifying and providing special attention to high-potential officers (HPO). Senior rater inputs are given primary consideration in making HPO determinations. HPOs demonstrate depth and expertise through exceptional performance in functional skills, and they excel in managing resources, leading people, improving the unit, and executing the mission. The AFI adds specific guidance regarding HPOs. To prevent unintended effects to both those identified and not identified, the specific outcomes of high-potential officer decision processes/tracking (e.g., names and targeted high-potential officer positions) will not be publicly shared or released. (Ex 43:22)

- Lastly, DTs are responsible for reviewing the functional community's demographic makeup and identifying potential barriers to all Airmen and Space Professionals reaching their highest potential. DTs conduct gap and barrier analyses to address any negative trends. AF/A1 provides DTs with diversity statistics by career field, and DTs analyze the data to determine if the career field lacks diversity. If a lack of diversity is found due to barriers identified, then DTs conduct barrier analyses, provide action plans, and/or recommended diversity discussion topics. (Ex 43:22) AF/A1 officer DT guidance states, "[i]t is critical that DTs identify potential barriers that inhibit any group of Air and Space Professionals from key developmental milestones, and the Office of the General Counsel (SAF/GC) will provide DTs with specific guidance and support on conducting the Barrier Analysis process."

DTs are a key component to ensuring officers and civilians are vectored to the appropriate developmental opportunities during their careers. Although AFI 36-2670, *Total Force Management*, does not direct diverse DTs, AF/A1 provides additional guidance placing responsibility on the DT chair to ensure diversity of its members. Since there is less diversity among the O-6 and GS-15 population, it is likely harder for DT chairs to ensure their DT's diversity. Because DTs have significant input on career development opportunities, there is a greater potential to introduce racial bias in the process. For example, the type of vectors DT members provide, which officers are identified as HPOs, and how closely they manage those HPOs, could all be influenced by bias. Both AFI and AF/A1 guidance call on DTs to identify barriers, conduct analyses, and provide action plans or discussion topics to address the barriers. However, this Review found the 2019 Barrier Analysis report provided to AF/A1DV was lacking in specifics. AF/A1 acknowledged not all DTs provide the required effort and analysis to identify and track diversity and potential barriers.

Executive Officer and Aide-De-Camp Positions

Fig 64: Executive Officer and Aide De Camp Positions by Race

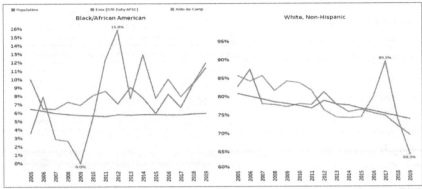

Source: AF/A1

AF/A1 found black officers are overrepresented in Executive Officer 97E and Aide-De-Camp 88A selection compared to the overall officer population. These data refer just to the 97E and 88A positions. However, executive officer positions at the squadron, group, and wing levels are not usually 97E positions. Typically, wing and group commanders hire strong performers from the wing's squadrons to fill key executive officer positions. Executive officer positions are key officer development opportunities, and officers selected over their peers for executive officer positions, particularly at the group and wing level, are typically considered high performers. In addition, officers whose performance reports are rated by a group or wing commander rather than a squadron commander could be a differentiator among officers with otherwise similar records. To analyze the demographics of wing level and below executive officer positions, AF/A1 should consider conducting a comprehensive review to identify officer performance reports with executive officer duty titles.

LEADERSHIP

Black officers are underrepresented in wing command and group command positions. Black enlisted service members are underrepresented at the group superintendent positions.

Squadron, group, and wing commander selection processes are important in the life cycle of an officer. An officer's performance as a squadron commander is a key indicator of whether the officer can successfully serve in the next higher grade. Similarly, strong performance as a wing commander would make it more likely the officer is promoted into General Officer ranks.

Officer Leadership

Squadron Commanders

The selection process begins with the Air Force Personnel Center (AFPC) issuing a Personnel Services Delivery Memorandum (PSDM) to announce the schedule of events for the Consolidated Squadron Commander, Mission Support Group, and Air Base Group Deputy Commander Candidate selection process. According to PSDM 20-17 for the CY21 Squadron Commander and Deputy Group Commander Candidate selection process, Development Teams from 29 different career fields met to consider candidates for available positions. (Ex 46)

Most communities have an "all in" policy where eligible officers are required to submit a Statement of Intent (SOI). Nominating authorities are Senior Raters (SR), such as wing commanders or equivalent and directors. There is no limit on the number of officers a nominating authority may nominate. However, SRs should only nominate those who possess the qualities required for command, such as exceptional leadership skills, set the example through unquestioned integrity and professional competence, can motivate others, demonstrate concern and interest in subordinates, show excellent mentoring skills, and possess a drive to take the initiative. Most career fields require the SRs to endorse, provide comments, and sometimes rank order their squadron commander nominations. (Ex 46)

AF-level DTs are typically held at AFPC and led by a GO or SES. The DTs consist of career field managers and senior officers and civilians from the HAF and MAJCOM staffs. For the larger flying category DTs such as Combat Air Forces (CAF), Mobility Air Forces (MAF), and Special Operations Forces (SOF), the leads are typically from the MAJCOMs. Under AFI 36-2670, DT membership will consist of the DT Chair, Career Field Manager (CFM), and key stakeholders representing the functional community. DTs are used to identify squadron commander candidates and identify career field-specific primary squadron commander lists from SR nominations. (Ex 43:21)

The data in the next figure shows, except for 2018, the percentage of black squadron commanders from 2012-2019 has been above 5.4%.

Fig 65: 2012-2019 Squadron Commander Demographics

RACE/ETHNICITY	SQUADRON COMMANDER							
	2012	2013	2014	2015	2016	2017	2018	2019
American Indian	0.35%	0.48%	0.41%	0.46%	0.34%	0.48%	0.36%	0.27%
Asian	1.82%	2.13%	2.03%	1.79%	2.36%	2.51%	2.93%	2.60%
Black/African American	6.94%	6.77%	6.44%	7.64%	7.48%	6.95%	5.33%	5.83%
Declined to Respond	3.73%	4.51%	4.46%	5.43%	5.26%	5.45%	6.27%	6.41%
Hispanic	2.73%	2.52%	2.30%	2.90%	3.04%	2.95%	2.71%	2.38%
Native Hawaiian/Pacific Islander	0.22%	0.17%	0.18%	0.09%	0.24%	0.44%	0.44%	0.40%
Two or More	1.13%	0.91%	1.40%	1.38%	1.40%	1.27%	1.38%	1.88%
White Non-Hispanic	83.09%	82.51%	82.79%	80.31%	79.87%	79.96%	80.58%	80.22%

Source: MiPDS
Provided by: HAF/A1XD, HAF/A1DV

The data do not indicate racial disparity in selection for squadron command. Most DTs use a promotion board-like scoring process to produce a merit-based list of candidates. CAF, MAF, and SOF boards are primarily made up of sitting wing commanders as their functional experts, whereas the support AFSCs usually have functional representation from each MAJCOM. Inputs to the process include SR comments, endorsements, and sometimes the SR's rank order, which could introduce biases into the process. (Of note, this is not unique to this process as reports, such as OPRs and EPRs, include subjective input controlled by a rater or SR.) As SRs and DTs do influence the identification and selection of squadron commander candidates, however, the process may be vulnerable to bias. The barrier analysis requirements discussed above, if given serious consideration and include a thorough analysis by the DTs, should provide good information for MAJCOMs and DTs to address any identified disparities or barriers.

Command Screening Board (CSB) Process

The Air Force has a command selection process to identify the most qualified colonels (O6) for the limited number of group, vice, and wing commander positions. Approximately 24% of all O6 positions are command billets. About half of the approximately 780 group, vice wing, wing command, and equivalent positions become vacant each year. (Ex 47:6)

AF/A1 identifies all Colonels and Colonel-selects who meet the published CSB eligibility criteria. The CSB is not a promotion board. All Colonels have access to their senior officer personnel briefs (SOPBs) that will be reviewed by the board electronically at any time. The memorandum of instruction provided to the board members includes a statement on the importance of diversity and inclusion and directs the board members to afford fair and equitable consideration for all potential command candidates. A board consisting of a panel of General Officers, chaired by a 4-Star General, reviews the Master Selection Folder (e-Record) consisting of performance reports, decorations, promotion recommendations, and SOPB for each eligible officer and scores the record. When the board is complete, and a cut line is established, the board conducts a diversity review for each category. According to AF/A1, the board reviews the list for diversity, and the board president has the option to adjust the candidate cut line and increase the number of candidates on the list if it would increase diversity without compromising the quality level of the list. CSAF approves the list of candidates, and AF/A1 publishes the Command Candidate List (CCL). (Ex 48)

Hiring authorities (typically MAJCOM/CCs) bid for candidates from the CCL for their projected command vacancies. The CSB is complete after AF/A1 deconflicts all bids, CSAF approves the projected matches, and the Command Selection List (CSL) is released. The remaining CCL candidates who are not matched with an assignment could be matched to un-projected command vacancies that may occur during the following year.

In addition to the diversity review during the board, AF/A1 also reviews the demographics of the officers on the CCL and provides an outbrief to the CSAF. This Review requested demographic data and AF/A1 provided the CCL data below. The CSL data, which is not presently tracked, would be useful to analyze if there were any racial disparities in the demographics of colonel who were actually matched to valid command positions.

The Review team noted that for 2017-2018, black group commanders were underrepresented by four and five candidates respectively for the CCL. With the small numbers of black officers, it only takes a difference of one or two officers to match the candidate select rate for all races. The Review noted there did not appear to be racial disparity in the number of black candidates for 2019-2020, and for all years, black candidates matched the overall select rates for the Health Profession and overrepresented in the Senior Materiel Leader positions. The "number to meet rate" in the figure below is the number of additional officers needed to match the overall select rate for the category.

Fig 66: 2017-2020 CCL Select Rates

2017 CCL Select Rates			# to Meet Rate
	Overall	White	Black	
Wing/CC	19%	20%	15%	1
SML	48%	45%	71%	
Group/CC	52%	54%	41%	4
HP	12%	13%	12%	

2018 CCL Select Rates			# to Meet Rate
	Overall	White	Black	
Wing/CC	19%	20%	13%	1
SML	78%	76%	88%	
Group/CC	57%	59%	45%	5
HP	13%	13%	16%	

2019 CCL Select Rates			# to Meet Rate
	Overall	White	Black	
Wing/CC	32%	33%	25%	2
SML	89%	89%	86%	1
Group/CC	64%	66%	67%	
HP	12%	12%	12%	

2020 CCL Select Rates			# to Meet Rate
	Overall	White	Black	
Wing/CC	37%	38%	32%	1
SML	84%	84%	100%	
Group/CC	69%	71%	65%	1
HP	31%	32%	29%	1

Source: HAF/A1LO

Group Commanders

When this data was compared to the 6% black Colonel population, there did not appear to be racial disparity in the percentage of black group commanders.

Fig 67: 2012-2019 Group Commander Demographics

RACE/ETHNICITY	SQUADRON COMMANDER							
	2012	2013	2014	2015	2016	2017	2018	2019
American Indian	0.35%	0.48%	0.41%	0.46%	0.34%	0.48%	0.36%	0.27%
Asian	1.82%	2.13%	2.03%	1.79%	2.36%	2.51%	2.93%	2.60%
Black/African American	6.94%	6.77%	6.44%	7.64%	7.48%	6.95%	5.33%	5.83%
Declined to Respond	3.73%	4.51%	4.46%	5.43%	5.26%	5.45%	6.27%	6.41%
Hispanic	2.73%	2.52%	2.30%	2.90%	3.04%	2.95%	2.71%	2.38%
Native Hawaiian/Pacific Islander	0.22%	0.17%	0.18%	0.09%	0.24%	0.44%	0.44%	0.40%
Two or More	1.13%	0.91%	1.40%	1.38%	1.40%	1.27%	1.38%	1.88%
White Non-Hispanic	83.09%	82.51%	82.79%	80.31%	79.87%	79.96%	80.58%	80.22%

Source: MilPDS
Provided by: HAF/A1XD, HAF/A1DV

Wing Commanders

When this data was compared to the 6% black colonel population, black officers were underrepresented in wing commander positions.

Fig 68: 2012-2019 Wing Commander Demographics

RACE/ETHNICITY	WING COMMANDER							
	2012	2013	2014	2015	2016	2017	2018	2019
American Indian/Native Alaskan								
Asian	0.86%	0.92%	0.99%		0.85%	0.90%	1.77%	2.59%
Black/African American	2.59%	2.75%	1.98%	5.61%	5.13%	4.50%	3.54%	4.31%
Declined to Respond	0.86%	0.92%	0.99%	3.74%	3.42%	2.70%	3.54%	2.59%
Hispanic	0.86%		1.98%	1.87%	1.71%	0.90%	0.88%	0.86%
Native Hawaiian/Pacific Islander							0.88%	0.86%
Two or More						1.80%	2.65%	2.59%
White Non-Hispanic	94.83%	95.41%	94.06%	88.79%	88.89%	89.19%	86.73%	86.21%

Source: MilPDS
Provided by: HAF/A1XD, HAF/A1DV

This Review's analysis found that compared to the proportion of race and ethnicity groups in the Active Duty Air Force O6 population, black, Hispanic, and Latino Colonels were generally underrepresented by between 10 and 50% respectively in wing commander positions. White Colonels were consistently overrepresented in wing commander positions. (Ex 2:68)

Fig 69: Racial Disparity in Wing Commanders

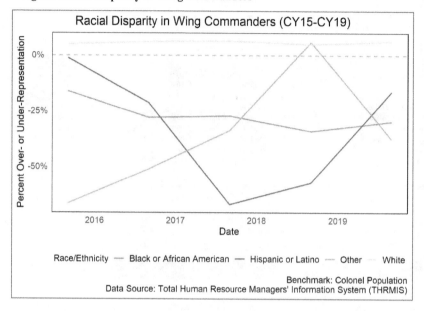

Fig 70: Career Field Disparity in Wing Commanders

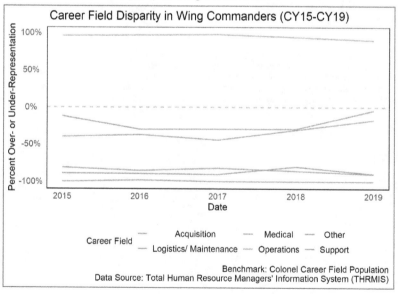

The Review's analysis also found that although 40 to 50% of Company Grade Officers (CGOs) and Field Grade Officers (FGOs) were in operations career fields, more than 80% of wing commanders come from an operations background. Furthermore, at the O6-level, operations career fields were overrepresented by close to 100% compared to the O6 population as a whole. As stated earlier in this report, black officers are underrepresented in the operations career fields, which then leads to underrepresentation in wing commander positions. (Ex 2:69) This racial underrepresentation is important because when there is a smaller pool at the lower ranks, it translates into a smaller pool at the O6 level, particularly when one accounts for attrition.

Leadership positions are key milestones in an officer's career. Officers who perform well in junior leadership roles increase their chances of promotion and serving in more senior group and wing leadership positions. The Review found DTs play a large role in determining command candidates. The Review also found, and AF/A1 acknowledged, that many DTs do not conduct a thorough review or a thorough barrier analysis as required by AFI 36-2670, *Total Force Management*. Although, the overall CSB process was found to be thorough and included diversity reviews, SR and DT comments and vectors are potential areas where bias could be introduced into the process.

Based on data provided by AF/A1, this Review found racial disparity in the CCL selection rates for wing commanders. AF/A1 does not capture the actual CSL or match rates, so this Review was unable to assess racial disparities in that process. AF/A1 acknowledged the racial disparity in wing commanders, but comprehensive analysis on the root cause of this disparity has not been conducted. AF/A1 advised that the low representation of black officers in operational career fields (2-10%), with the high percentage of commanders coming from those career fields (80%) is likely a substantial factor.

Enlisted Leadership

According to this Review's analysis of AF/A1 data, black enlisted members were underrepresented in group superintendent positions, overrepresented in command chief positions over the past five years, and evenly represented in First Sergeants. White enlisted service members were overrepresented in First Sergeants and group superintendent positions, and evenly represented in command chief positions. Hispanic or Latino enlisted service members and enlisted service members of other race-ethnicity groups were consistently underrepresented in all enlisted leadership positions. (Ex 2:70)

Fig 71: 2015-2019 Racial Disparity in Enlisted Leadership Roles

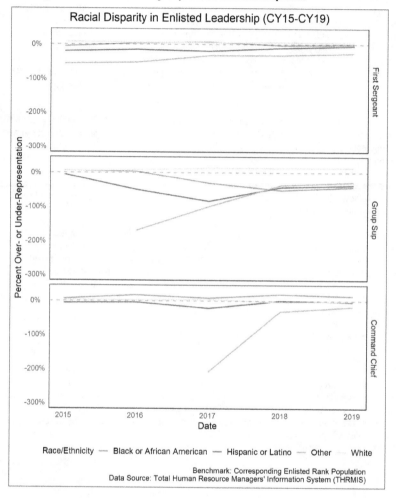

Group commanders typically interview and hire group superintendents from the pool of Chief Master Sergeants in the group's squadrons. Depending on the demographics of the squadron chiefs, there may not be an opportunity to hire a black chief. Not enough data exists for further analysis. This Review recommends AF/A1 consider further analysis into the group superintendent racial disparity.

SUMMARY OF OPPORTUNITIES DATA

Empirical data show racial disparities exist between black and white service members in several areas directly impacting a black service member's progression and advancement in the service:

- Accessions
- Test results – ASVAB, AFQT, AFOQT
- AFSC demographics
- Promotions
- Leadership Assignments
- PME Selections

The empirical data do not provide insight into why racial disparities in opportunities afforded to black and white service members exist. An AFI review of all personnel-related instructions outlined in the next section of this report did not identify any policy-driven or structural racial bias in the military leadership development and promotion process.

AIR FORCE INSTRUCTION (AFI) REVIEW

As part of the Racial Disparity Review, Air Force Manpower, Personnel and Services (AF/A1), AFJAG, and Air Force, Manpower and Reserve Affairs (SAF/MR) reviewed Air Force Instructions and guidance to determine if any guidance or policy could have disparate impact on any group or population. AF/A1 review found "no identifiable instances of applying policy which would discriminate against any group or population." Additionally, the AFJAG review determined "[n]o inherent/systemic/procedural bias found." Finally, the SAF/MR review stated, "[w]e found no policies that were overtly discriminatory. Rather, the policies normally provided an objective standard framework for executing military programs in an equitable fashion."

The following AFIs/AFPDs/AFHs/AFMANs were reviewed:

1. AFPD 36-26, *Total Force Development and Management*
2. AFI 36-2670, *Total Force Development*
3. AFH 36-2618, *The Enlisted Force Structure*
4. AFMAN 36-2643, *Air Force Mentoring Program*
5. AFPD 36-25, *Military Promotion and Demotion*
6. AFI 36-2501, *Officer Promotions and Selective Continuation*
7. AFI 36-2502, *Airman Promotion/Demotion Programs*
8. AFI 36-2504, *Officer Promotion, Continuation and Selective Early Removal in the Reserve of the Air Force*
9. AFPD 36-24, *Military Evaluations*
10. AFPD 36-26, *Total Force Development*
11. AFI 36-2110, *Assignments*
12. AFI 36-2406, *Officer and Enlisted Evaluation Systems*
13. AFI 36-2670, *Total Force Development*

14. AFH 36-2643, *Air Force Mentoring Program*
15. AFMAN 36-2806, *Awards*
16. AFI 36-808, *Pay Administration*
17. AFI 36-116, *Civilian Faculty Personnel Management*
18. AFI 36-128, *Pay Setting and Allowances*
19. AFI 36-130, *Civilian Career Programs and Development*
20. AFI 36-202, *Civilian Mobility*
21. All 51-Series AFIs

This Review found no inherent, systemic, or procedural bias in the publications listed.

While no procedural biases or discrimination were found, some recommendations were made by AFJAG and SAF/MR. AFJAG made proposals for AFI 51-202, *Nonjudicial Punishment,* and AFI 51-1201, *Negotiation and Dispute Resolution Program,* which were designed to be a proactive effort to avoid a perception of bias and ensure gender equality. SAF/MR recommendations included policies to add diversity requirements (diverse membership requirements on boards and requirements to review diversity demographics) to help ensure equitable development and promotion. Additionally, SAF/MR noted concerns with the execution of policies at the lowest levels, citing "mentoring" as an example.

THE VOICE OF THE AIRMEN AND SPACE PROFESSIONALS

A consistent and substantial disparity exists in the confidence black service members have in the DAF discipline and developmental opportunity processes compared to their white peers. Survey responses from 123,758 Total Force personnel, 138 DAF IG sessions with Airmen across all MAJCOMs, 27,000 pages of feedback, and targeted interviews show a substantial percentage of black DAF members believe racial bias exists in the DAF discipline and developmental opportunity processes.

SURVEYS

This Review was focused on hearing directly from the Airmen and Space Professionals regarding racial disparities in military discipline and developmental opportunities. The Review team developed a narrowly focused survey targeted at racial disparities between black and white service members in military discipline and developmental opportunities. The anonymous survey collected from a wide range of demographics and consisted of standard Likert scale questions.[22] Depending on how respondents answered specific questions, the survey presented an option to include write-in text responses. The write-in responses were included for respondents to share their personal experiences and recommendations. The write-in responses resulted in more than

---

[22] Various rating scales have been developed to measure attitudes directly (i.e., the person knows their attitude is being studied). The most widely used is the Likert Scale. The Likert Scale is named for American social scientist Rensis Likert, who devised the approach in 1932. Likert developed the principle of measuring attitudes by asking people to respond to a series of statements about a topic, in terms of the extent to which they agree with them, and so tapping into the cognitive and affective components of attitudes. (McLeod, S. A. (2008). Likert scale. Retrieved from https://www.simplypsychology.org/likert-scale.html)

27,000 pages of written comments. The survey was launched on 28 June 20 and closed on 12 July 20. More than 123,700 Total Force personnel responded to the survey. The component breakdown, including civilians as aligned with the component they most directly support, was 70% Active Duty, 18% Air National Guard, and 11% Air Force Reserves.[23]

Likert Question Data

The Likert response data was broken down by race, officer, enlisted, and civilian ranks. The data was analyzed comparing just the percentages of Agree and Disagree responses for each question to see respondent attitudes about the questions. The N/A, Neither Agree nor Disagree, and Don't Know responses are not included in the figures below. This Review analyzed the data to determine the magnitude of the issues as they relate to racial disparities in military justice and opportunities and gain insight into areas where service members believe there are racial concerns. The Review first analyzed the data, broken down by rank and race (white, black, and other), to compare the percent of responses for Agree and Disagree for each Likert question.

---

[23] No survey involving human response can be completely free of bias. To minimize its effect, the Independent Racial Disparity Review team ensured respondents knew their respective submissions were anonymous and made the survey widely accessible to all DAF members. For the Independent Racial Disparity Review survey, the DAF population was defined as 663,000 and more than 123,000 Airmen completed the survey.

Trust in Leadership, Opportunities for Mentorship, and Role Models

Fig 72: RDR Survey Question 7   **Source: RDR Survey**

I trust my chain of command to address racism, bias, and unequal opportunities regarding all enlisted, officers, and civilians.

	Agree	Disagree
Black Enlisted	46%	40%
White Enlisted	82%	10%
Other Enlisted	73%	16%
E7 - E9 Black	50%	39%
E7 - E9 White	87%	7%
Black Officers	49%	40%
White Officers	88%	7%
Other	76%	16%
O7-O10 Black	55%	45%
O7-O10 White	95%	3%
Black Civilians	47%	39%
White Civilians	83%	9%
Other Civilians	72%	16%

A service member's chain of command is one of the first lines of defense against racism, bias, and unequal opportunity.[24] The survey asked, "I trust my chain of command to address racism, bias, and unequal opportunities regarding all enlisted, officer, and civilian Airmen and Space Professionals." 40% of black officer, enlisted, and civilian respondents disagreed, indicating they did not trust their chain of command to address those issues. Whereas 7%, 10%, and 9% of white officer, enlisted, and civilian respondents respectively disagreed. In the more senior leadership enlisted ranks, 39% black E7-E9s and 45% black O7-O10s disagreed, and just 7% white E7-E9s and 3% white O7-O10s disagreed. The magnitude becomes clearer when the perspective gap is viewed across the Total Force.

---

[24] The survey did not define the term "bias," or make a distinction between "unconscious" or "conscious bias."

Black Airmen and Space Professionals have the same opportunities for mentorship, feedback, and role models as others in my organization.

	Agree	Disagree
Black Enlisted	46%	39%
White Enlisted	84%	5%
Other Enlisted	74%	11%
E7 - E9 Black	45%	43%
E7 - E9 White	88%	4%
Black Officers	37%	54%
White Officers	82%	7%
Other	69%	17%
O7-O10 Black	27%	73%
O7-O10 White	82%	13%
Black Civilians	41%	41%
White Civilians	79%	4%
Other Civilians	69%	11%

Mentorship, feedback, and role models are crucial to ensuring service members perform up to their full potential. The team surveyed the respondents with the question, "Enlisted, officer, and civilian black Airmen and Space Professionals have the same opportunities for mentorship, feedback, and role models as others in my organization." Black members, as they increased in rank, did not agree: 39% of enlisted, 54% of officers, and 73% of black general officers did not feel they had the same opportunities as their counterparts, nor did 41 percent of black civilian employees. Among white respondents, only a small percentage (between 4-7%) of white officer, enlisted, and civilian respondents did not believe black service members had the same opportunities, as did 13 percent of white general officers.

Military Justice

The Review team used specifically targeted survey questions to gain insight into disciplinary actions across the spectrum of administrative and non-judicial punishment. The survey asked the question, "I believe racial bias (including potential unconscious bias) exists when my leadership takes the following actions." There were five sub-questions:

1. Informal feedback, mentoring, and formal verbal counseling
2. Letters of Counseling, Letters of Admonishment, Letters of Reprimand
3. Referral performance reports, unfavorable information files, and control roster
4. Separations and discharges
5. Article 15s and Courts-Martial

I believe racial bias exists in the way my leadership provides informal feedback, mentoring, and formal verbal couseling.	Agree	Disagree
Black Enlisted	46%	27%
White Enlisted	11%	63%
Other Enlisted	23%	46%
E7 - E9 Black	49%	28%
E7 - E9 White	9%	73%
Black Officers	54%	25%
White Officers	14%	66%
Other	28%	49%
O7-O10 Black	64%	27%
O7-O10 White	18%	71%
Black Civilians (USPFT)	31%	18%
White Civilians (USPFT)	7%	52%
Other Civilians (USPFT)	15%	38%

Roughly half of all black service members and a third of black civilian employees believe there is racial bias when their leadership conducts informal feedback, mentoring, and formal verbal counseling (54%, 46%, and 31% of black officer, enlisted, and civilian respondents agreeing). That belief was even higher among black general officers, where 64 percent felt leadership engaged in racial bias in those activities (compared with 18 percent of their white general officer counterparts). In contrast, 14%, 11%, and 7% of white officer, enlisted, and civilian respondents felt the same way.

Fig 75: RDR Survey Question 10b   Source: RDR Survey

I believe racial bias exists when my leadership makes decisions concerning Letters of Counseling, Letters of Admonishment, and Letters of Reprimand.

	Agree	Disagree
Black Enlisted	45%	26%
White Enlisted	10%	64%
Other Enlisted	20%	47%
E7 - E9 Black	45%	28%
E7 - E9 White	7%	74%
Black Officers	54%	25%
White Officers	14%	66%
Other	28%	49%
O7-O10 Black	55%	27%
O7-O10 White	13%	72%
Black Civilians (USPFT)	28%	17%
White Civilians (USPFT)	5%	50%
Other Civilians (USPFT)	13%	36%

Half of all black service members and almost a third of black civilian employees felt racial bias played a part in administrative disciplinary actions (45% enlisted, 54% officers, and 28% civilian), while only between 5-14% of white officer, enlisted, and civilian respondents felt the same way.

I believe racial bias exists when my leadership makes decisions concerning referral performance reports, unfavorable information files, and the control roster.

	Agree	Disagree
Black Enlisted	41%	26%
White Enlisted	9%	64%
Other Enlisted	18%	47%
E7 - E9 Black	42%	29%
E7 - E9 White	6%	75%
Black Officers	43%	25%
White Officers	9%	68%
Other	19%	51%
O7-O10 Black	55%	27%
O7-O10 White	9%	74%
Black Civilians	28%	17%
White Civilians	5%	50%
Other Civilians	13%	37%

Roughly half (41-55%) of black enlisted and officers believe racial bias exists in their leadership's decisions concerning referral performance reports, unfavorable information files, and control rosters, while between 6-9% of their white peers responded similarly.

Fig 77: RDR Survey Question 10d   Source: RDR Survey

I believe racial bias exists when my leadership makes decisions regarding separations and discharges.

	Agree	Disagree
Black Enlisted	39%	25%
White Enlisted	7%	63%
Other Enlisted	16%	46%
E7 - E9 Black	40%	28%
E7 - E9 White	6%	74%
Black Officers	41%	24%
White Officers	8%	62%
Other	16%	45%
O7-O10 Black	64%	27%
O7-O10 White	9%	74%
Black Civilians	24%	15%
White Civilians	4%	47%
Other Civilians	10%	34%

Over a third of black enlisted and officers (39% and 41%, respectively) believe racial bias exists when their leadership makes administrative separation and discharge decisions. Among DAF senior leadership however, 64% of black general officers believe racial bias exists when leadership makes those decisions, compared with only 9% of their white counterparts.

Fig 78: RDR Survey Question 10e   Source: RDR Survey

I believe racial bias exists when my leadership makes decisions on Article 15s and courts-martial.

	Agree	Disagree
Black Enlisted	36%	24%
White Enlisted	7%	62%
Other Enlisted	15%	15%
E7 - E9 Black	37%	27%
E7 - E9 White	5%	72%
Black Officers	54%	25%
White Officers	14%	66%
Other	28%	49%
O7-O10 Black	73%	27%
O7-O10 White	9%	72%
Black Civilians	21%	14%
White Civilians	3%	44%
Other Civilians	8%	31%

The survey responses show 36% of black enlisted, 54% of black officers, and 73% of black general officers felt racial bias exists when leadership makes decisions on UCMJ disciplinary actions. In contrast, 7% of white enlisted, 14% of white officers, and 9% of white general officers felt the same way.

Fig 79: RDR Survey Question 11   **Source: RDR Survey**

I believe racial bias (including potential unconscious bias) exists in the conduct of investigations (e.g., CDI, EEO, IG, OSI, etc).		
	Agree	Disagree
Black Enlisted	39%	16%
White Enlisted	12%	52%
Other Enlisted	20%	35%
E7 - E9 Black	43%	17%
E7 - E9 White	10%	61%
Black Officers	48%	16%
White Officers	16%	55%
Other	26%	39%
O7-O10 Black	64%	18%
O7-O10 White	17%	67%
Black Civilians	36%	14%
White Civilians	9%	47%
Other Civilians	17%	33%

Investigations are often conducted prior to military justice decisions. When asked if respondents believe racial bias exists in the conduct of investigations (CDE, EEO, IG, and OSI), 48%, 39%, and 36% of black officer, enlisted, and civilian respondents agreed. White officer, enlisted, and civilian respondents agreed at 16%, 12%, and 9% respectively. 43% of black E7-E9s and 64% of black O7-O10s agreed.

Fig 80: RDR Survey Question 14   Source: RDR Survey

I believe black service members are less likely to receive the benefit of the doubt in AF discipline.		
	Agree	Disagree
Black Enlisted	59%	16%
White Enlisted	10%	63%
Other Enlisted	19%	45%
E7 - E9 Black	63%	18%
E7 - E9 White	8%	74%
Black Officers	64%	14%
White Officers	12%	63%
Other	22%	48%
O7-O10 Black	82%	9%
O7-O10 White	12%	66%
Black Civilians	39%	14%
White Civilians	5%	56%
Other Civilians	10%	42%

Respondents were asked whether, "black service members are less likely to receive the benefit of the doubt in Air Force discipline." A high percentage, 64%, 59%, and 39% of black officer, enlisted, and civilian respondents agreed, whereas white officer, enlisted, and civilian respondents agreed at substantially lower percentage of 12%, 10%, and 5% respectively. 63% of black E7-E9s and 82% of black O7-O10s agreed.

Based on the survey responses of black service members, roughly 50% or more believe racial bias exists when leadership executes the full range of administrative, non-judicial punishment, and courts-martial actions. Quantitative data shows that black enlisted Airmen in the ranks of E1-E4 are almost twice as likely to receive Article 15s and face courts-martial as their white counterparts. Survey results also revealed that 31% of black officers and 31% of black enlisted respondents believe black service members receive administrative disciplinary actions (LOCs, LOAs, and LORs) more frequently than other Airmen for the same behavior. Lastly, three out of five black officer and enlisted respondents believe black Airmen do not receive the benefit of the doubt when it comes to military discipline.

Developmental Opportunities

Along with examining racial disparities in military justice, this Review was charged with identifying racial disparities in developmental opportunities for black service members. The survey included four targeted questions regarding developmental opportunities. Two questions asked respondents if their organization provided recognition and opportunities for promotion and advancement on an equal and fair basis. The first question asked if all members had the same opportunities for competitive assignments, training, career-broadening experience, and education. The second question asked if respondents had seen bias as it relates to career development opportunities for black enlisted, civilians, and officers.

Fig 81: RDR Survey Question 17   **Source: RDR Survey**

All civilians, enlisted members, and officers have the same opportunity for competitive assignments, training, career broadening experience, and education in my organization.

	Agree	Disagree
Black Enlisted	**47%**	**27%**
White Enlisted	**80%**	**5%**
Other Enlisted	**68%**	**10%**
E7 - E9 Black	49%	31%
E7 - E9 White	88%	4%
Black Officers	**43%**	**38%**
White Officers	**82%**	**6%**
Other Officers	**69%**	**15%**
O7-O10 Black	45%	45%
O7-O10 White	92%	4%
Black Civilians	**42%**	**28%**
White Civilians	**76%**	**4%**
Other Civilians	**65%**	**9%**

Roughly half of black officers, enlisted, and civilian respondents believe they have the same opportunity for competitive assignments, training (e.g., advanced technical training, specialty schools), career broadening experience (e.g., exercises, deployments, career broadening assignments), and education (e.g., PME, advanced academic educations, self-development). In comparison, a substantial majority of white respondents (76-82%) felt they had the same opportunities for career enhancing assignments, training, education, and experiences. Notably, only 45% of black general officers believe everyone receives similar opportunities for advancement, compared with 92% of white general officers.

I have seen bias as it relates to career development
opportunities for enlisted, civilian, and officer black Airmen
and Space Professionals.

	Agree	Disagree
Black Enlisted	41%	26%
White Enlisted	11%	67%
Other Enlisted	18%	46%
E7 - E9 Black	50%	26%
E7 - E9 White	10%	77%
Black Officers	50%	25%
White Officers	11%	74%
Other Officers	21%	52%
O7-O10 Black	64%	27%
O7-O10 White	14%	80%
Black Civilians	40%	28%
White Civilians	8%	70%
Other Civilians	14%	48%

Almost half to more than half (41-64%) of black respondents had seen bias as it relates to career development opportunities for black service members and civilian employees. Only 8-14% of white respondents said the same. The vast majority of white respondents (67-80%) had not seen bias related to opportunities for black service members.

Overall, a large percentage of black service members believe they did not have the same career development opportunities as their white counterparts. Notably, 50% of black officer and 64% of black General Officer responded that they had observed bias related to career development.

Discrimination

The survey included two questions regarding racial discrimination. One question asked respondents if they ever experienced racial discrimination by another DAF member. The second question asked respondents if they had witnessed an act of racial discrimination by another DAF member.

Fig 83: RDR Survey Question 19   **Source: RDR Survey**

(Y/N) Have you ever been discriminated against by a member of the Department of the Air Force, because of your race or ethnicity?		
	Yes	No
Black Enlisted	50%	50%
White Enlisted	14%	86%
Other Enlisted	26%	74%
E7 - E9 Black	42%	58%
E7 - E9 White	15%	85%
Black Officers	48%	52%
White Officers	8%	92%
Other Officers	28%	72%
O7-O10 Black	45%	55%
O7-O10 White	6%	94%
Black Civilians	45%	55%
White Civilians	9%	91%
Other Civilians	21%	79%

Between 45-50% of black respondents said a DAF member had discriminated against them because of their race or ethnicity. A smaller percentage of white respondents (8-14%) also said they faced discrimination based on their race/ethnicity by a DAF member. Among senior leaders, 45% of black general officers said they have experienced discrimination, while 94% of white general officers did not face any discrimination based on race/ethnicity from a member in the DAF.

Fig 84: RDR Survey Question 20   **Source: RDR Survey**

(Y/N) Have you ever witnessed an act of discrimination based upon race or ethnicity by a member of the Department of the Air Force?		
	Yes	No
Black Enlisted	46%	54%
White Enlisted	17%	83%
Other Enlisted	24%	76%
E7 - E9 Black	49%	51%
E7 - E9 White	17%	83%
Black Officers	44%	56%
White Officers	12%	88%
Other Officers	22%	78%
O7-O10 Black	45%	55%
O7-O10 White	12%	88%
Black Civilians	41%	59%
White Civilians	11%	89%
Other Civilians	19%	81%

Almost half of black respondents have witnessed a DAF member engage in discrimination because of race or ethnicity. For white respondents, that number dropped to roughly 20%. According the survey, 45% of black general officers have witnessed racial/ethnic discrimination, while only 12% of white general officers have done so.

Of black service members who experienced or witnessed racial discrimination, about 80% said a supervisor or commander initiated the discrimination. Only about 35% of those black service members reported the incidents to leadership. 70% of black Airmen who reported the incident to their commander were not satisfied with the leadership response. Only 18% said they reported the incident to EO or IG, and of those, over 50% were not satisfied with the response from EO/IG.

The percentages of white Airmen who experienced or witnessed racial discrimination were lower (10% and 12% respectively). Nearly one third of those respondents reported the incidents to their leadership. Over half of those who reported to leadership were not satisfied with their leadership's response. Only 10% of the white service members who experienced or witnessed racial discrimination reported the incidents to IG or EO, and 60% of those said they were not satisfied with the response from EO/IG.

The survey write-in responses indicate many survey respondents did not go to their commanders because they believed their commanders and leadership lacked integrity, were dishonest, self-serving, and would abuse their authority. Some respondents believed leadership lied and covered up for themselves; and, instead of being protected, the complainant received additional disciplinary actions by leadership for reporting an issue. 44% of black service members and 33% of white service members who experienced racial discrimination and reported the incident or incidents to their commander, reported experiencing some form of reprisal for contacting their commander.

The survey and interview responses indicate service members have concerns about using the IG and EO because they believe complaints will be referred back to their chain of command. 45% of black service members and 37% of white members who went to EO or IG said they were reprised against by leadership as a result.

Overall, respondents thought IG and EO investigations were ineffective. Some members indicated the perpetrator was never held accountable or action was not taken at the conclusion of the investigation. Participants reported several instances of the IG refusing to take on their cases. Other times, they indicated their cases were not properly investigated, or their concerns were completely disregarded.

Finally, some white respondents indicated the IG or EO office would not consider their case because they were white and held the perception they could not be discriminated against due to being white.

Survey Response Conclusion

Survey responses revealed that black service members generally lacked trust in their chain of command to address racism, bias, and unequal opportunities. The perspective gap between black and white members was large. 40% of the black respondents indicated they did not trust their leadership in these areas, while only 10% of white respondents expressed doubt. This gap is more prominent when looking at officers, wherein 49% of black officers indicated they did not trust leadership compared to only 7% of white officers. A similarly large perspective gap was revealed in whether black Airmen had the same opportunities for mentorship, feedback, and role models as others in their organization. 43% of the black officer respondents indicated that all Airmen had the same developmental opportunities, while 82% of white officers believed everyone had the same opportunities. Of particular concern, approximately 50% of black officer, enlisted, and civilian respondents have either experienced and/or witnessed racial discrimination by another DAF member.

This Review found black survey respondents overwhelmingly believe racial bias exists in DAF disciplinary actions. In addition, the survey responses highlighted that black members believed racial disparities extend beyond the disparity in Article 15s and courts-martial. In particular, responses reveal a large perspective gap on whether racial bias exists when leadership issues Letters of Counseling, Admonishment, and Reprimand. Almost half (45%) of black enlisted and more than half (54%) of black officers believe racial bias exists when their leadership issues administrative disciplinary action, compared with less than 15% of white enlisted and white officers. The survey also reveals that black respondents believe they do not receive the same benefit of the doubt as white Airmen for the same infractions, which may play a role in the racial disparities in both military justice and administrative separation actions. The Review found that racial disparity in military justice actions likely extends beyond Article 15s, courts-martial and discharges to include lessor disciplinary actions such as LORs, LOC, and LOAs.

Survey Text Responses

In addition to the Likert scale questions, respondents were prompted to elaborate with written responses if they answered with a negative sentiment. Through this process, the survey recorded over 27,000 pages of write-in comments. A computer-based analysis of the comments was conducted to identify the most common themes. These themes, organized by their associated survey question, are listed below.[25] Of note, because the survey was anonymous, we could not validate individual text feedback. However, when many Airmen identified the same issue(s), and a consistent theme emerged, the Review team captured that consistent theme.

Please explain why your organization does not value contributions and ideas of black Airmen and Space Professionals?

The top themes were contributions, promotions, exclusion, or camaraderie. The comments on contributions included black members' ideas not being understood or disregarded because of their race. Others indicated black members are not included in planning and decision processes and are passed over for promotion because of a "good old boy" system. Some Airmen said they had to identify a white ally in order to get their views heard.

Please explain why you do not trust your chain of command to address racism, bias, and unequal opportunities?

Comments from this question focused on the presence of both bias and inequality when leadership makes decisions. Many respondents indicated they believe the bias is unconscious. Respondents report that leaders seem to avoid discussing race or seem to think that racism does not exist in the Air Force or Space Force. Some participants discussed behavior that ignores, minimalizes, or hides racial incidents.

Another theme identified was respondents' belief that black service members are not given equal career development opportunities. Many respondents said leaders do not ask for their input while they see others being asked for input. Some respondents said they are not given recognition for their ideas.

The respondents indicated they cannot trust one or more members in their chain of command regarding racism or bias in making decisions. Many respondents said they do not trust their chain of command on this issue based on past experiences within their chain and watching how their leadership has treated others in similar situations.

---

[25] The responses of individual Airmen and Space Professionals are provided for context and to illustrate themes identified by in-depth data analysis conducted by the Air Force Survey Office and the Air Force Inspection Agency. These responses, as representative of themes, are supported by corroborating inputs, but, as anonymous and/or protected communications to the IG they could not be independently validated. Specific complaints registered during the course of this Review were or are in the process of being handled in accordance with AFI 90-301.

Please explain why you believe racial bias (including potential unconscious bias) exists when your leadership takes any of the actions mentioned previously that are related to military personnel?

This question was offered when respondents agreed that racial bias existed when their leadership executed administrative and non-judicial punishment as well as Article 15 and courts-martial actions. Most respondents provided personal experiences as evidence of racial bias. The personal stories focused on issues of bias, injustice, and inequality. In addition, comments highlighted either experiencing or witnessing first-hand intolerance towards black service members compared to their white counterparts when facing the same level of infraction.

Please explain why you believe racial bias (including potential unconscious bias) exists in the conduct of investigations (e.g., CDI, EO/EEO, IG, OSI, etc.)?

The most prevailing theme in the responses to this question was the belief that since racism and bias exist in people, it must also exist in the conduct of investigations. The majority of responses in this category did not cite any particular incident or evidence related to bias in investigations, but instead were more general about the biases inherent in people. Some of these comments also suggested that investigators should be trained to recognize and work through their own biases.

Survey respondents also indicated a belief that investigations may be impacted by racially biased assumptions. The main concern was that black service members are presumed guilty until proven innocent, and thus black service members are not provided the benefit of the doubt before or during investigations.

Some respondents shared personal experiences of racial bias or of witnessing investigations in which race seemed to play a role. This included instances where they suspected the treatment during the investigation was based on race, where they observed people of different races receiving unequal punishments, or where they filed complaints about racism that were not resolved in a satisfactory manner.

Was there a particular reason why you didn't contact EO/EEO or IG?

The survey asked if respondents had been discriminated against or if they had witnessed someone being discriminated against. If the respondents agreed, they were then asked if they had contacted EO/EEO or IG. If they answered that they had not, respondents were then asked why they did not contact EO/EEO or IG. Survey respondents reported various reasons, but the most common ones were: lack of knowledge about the EO/EEO or IG processes, concerns with their chain of command or leadership, lack of proof/evidence, fear of reprisal, and negative impact on a member's career.

Many survey respondents indicated they did not contact the EO/EEO or IG because of the relationship between both offices and their chain of command. Expressly, survey respondents indicated they feared reprisal, retribution, or retaliation from their chain of command, peers, or other members in their organization.

Because the question asked why respondents did not contact "EO/EEO or the IG" combined, the Review team conducted subsequent analysis that revealed additional themes and comments that were attributable to EO and IG separately.

Three themes were specific to IG. First, some survey participants believed IG personnel protected the commander and/or leadership during investigations. Members also indicated that other commanders or leadership usually protected the commanders who were under investigation. Respondents identified a lack of objectivity amongst IG personnel and leadership and emphasized concern that those tasked with investigating complaints were not impartial. Furthermore, some members indicated the commander and IG personnel were often friends or part of "the good ole boys club."

Second, several participants reported instances of the IG refusing to take on their case. Other times, they indicated their cases were not properly investigated, or their concerns were completely disregarded.

Third, some participants indicated the IG would not consider their case because they were white. These members indicated they were not given the benefit of the doubt and that IG personnel automatically took the minority individual's side.

The Review also found themes that were somewhat unique to EO. First, members reported a lack of objectivity amongst EO/EEO personnel. Specifically, they felt EO/EEO personnel were not impartial in their decision making or while conducting an investigation. Members also indicated that EO/EEO personnel automatically leaned in favor of the minority complainant.

Second, participants who were white indicated the EO/EEO would not consider their case because they could not be victims of racial bias. Members indicated they were not given the benefit of the doubt and that EO/EEO automatically took the minority individual's side.

Third, some members reported that individuals sometimes abused the EO/EEO system. Members also claimed that individuals used the "race card" to their advantage, making false allegations to avoid working or if they felt slighted due to a missed promotion or job opportunity.

Lastly, participants indicated that leadership sometimes treated service members differently to avoid an EO/EEO complaint. Often, a member was given preferential treatment in the form of a hiring action, promotion, or positive performance appraisal because leadership wanted to avoid receiving an EO/EEO complaint against them.

If you would like to describe the discriminatory behavior you experienced, please do so below?

Respondents who indicated they experienced discrimination were asked to describe the discrimination they experienced. Common themes involved denial of promotion or advancement opportunities or receipt of punitive/disciplinary actions.

Many survey respondents identified racial slurs, and comments regarding dress and personal appearance as forms of discrimination against black service members. Specifically, survey participants, the majority of them military members, indicated they were targeted because of their hair and grooming standards, such as shaving. Under this question, survey participants indicated they experienced discrimination primarily from their immediate supervisors and/or leadership. For example, members described being assigned extra work, picked on, harassed, isolated, or humiliated based on their race.

What changes would you recommend to ensure a fair and equitable military discipline process for all uniformed Airmen and Space Professionals?

The following themes were identified as top recommendations:

- Treat every Air Force and Space Force member fairly by holding everyone to the same standards. Setting specific standards for infractions could set the tone across the Total Force and remove subjectivity from the process.

- Require a diverse, independent panel to review disciplinary actions for legal sufficiency and proportionality in a completely transparent process. Convene diverse juries in courts-martial.

- Document all disciplinary actions (both UCMJ and administrative) in a database. Some respondents also indicated that the Automated Military Justice Analysis and Management System (AMJAMS) should include race categories beyond black, white, and other to allow more transparency and analysis of overall statistics and the proportionality of disciplinary actions across demographic groups.

- Require cultural and bias training. A typical comment was:

   Cultural training for all members working in a supervisory or leadership role. Each ethnic group has a different culture that may lead leaders to feel as though they are disrespected due to actions/reactions of individuals. We must fully understand WHY people act/react the way they do and it is often a result of their community or culture.

"What changes would you recommend to ensure a fair and equitable career development system for all enlisted, officer, and civilian Airmen and Space Professionals?"

Top recommendations were:

- Increase diversity through accession and recruitment programs. Typical comments included:

   Change recruiting and accession methods to ensure minorities are provided job lists that include opportunities to operations and other high aptitude career fields. There is a disparity in recruiting African Americans in support AFSCs. Give more opportunities across all specialties.

   Recruiters should go into communities and schools and target minorities, encouraging them and inspiring them to believe in themselves and what they can aspire to be. I've seen too many people, of all races, but frequently minorities, who have developed the belief that they will only make it so far, that there exists a ceiling preventing them from accomplishing what their white counterparts can (promoting to higher ranks, becoming commanders, entering the USAFA or ROTC). There are far too few minorities who believe they can achieve these things. They also don't see enough Airmen in those roles who look like they do.

- Increase and expand mentorship opportunities. Enhance career development for service members of all ranks. Typical themes included:

Fund a group or commission to develop a mentorship and sponsorship program that involves crossover in racial background. A goal of this would be to inform existing white officers, NCOs and executives how to be better leaders of diverse military organizations. This, in turn, could increase the likelihood of more minorities being exposed to opportunities for faster promotions, real mentorship (and possibly sponsorship) from commanders and military influencers who shape our Force and PME opportunities.

I think mandating mentors across the board should occur. Cross utilize and mandate all Airmen have mentors and carve out mentoring sessions at FTAC, ALS, NCOA and any other session that is feasible. Create a platform that you can connect to a mentor virtually and have roundtable sessions that discuss what is impacting them, limiting them to reach their full potential and what they need to do to expand in their career. I think there is value in grooming our junior Airmen and officers but the stats on who is getting the opportunities will still be disproportionate if we are not advertising and mentoring all in the same manner and fashion.

The mentoring program is broken. There needs to be a way for minority officers to get the same mentoring and developmental opportunities as their white peers. There needs to be a conscious effort to mentor minorities and women better.

- Increase transparency over the application/selection processes for PME and special duty assignments. Ensure personnel are aware of career development opportunities and better understand why candidates for these opportunities were selected. Common statements included:

Make career development information widely available. Find ways to expose everyone to good information equally. It seems like most career development information is received by those lucky enough to have a mentor or small tight knit groups of individuals. Maybe an annual CBT tailored towards each rank. 'Congratulations on making E-5, this is what you should be working on over the next year. You commissioned in 2012, this is what you can expect in 2020 and what you should be doing to prepare. This is when your boards will be meeting.' Things like that would extremely helpful.

- Ensure diversity for selection boards/panels

- Provide the same opportunities to all service members

- Remove or mask all identifying elements from records or applications for career development and advancement, including promotion records, professional military education, and awards.

Summary: In their responses, black service members very clearly expressed their frustration with bias and race-related obstacles and barriers throughout their careers. They consistently commented they do not trust their leadership to address racism and bias, leadership does not value their contributions to the organization, and favoritism exists among leadership and supervisors because of the "good old boy" system.

With regard to military justice, the written comments supported strong beliefs about the lack of fairness and existence of racial bias in the military justice system. Although service members may not always have the full context for differences in levels of punishment, comments suggested the inequalities were more than just perceptions. Respondents commented they have personally seen harsher penalties for black service members for the same infractions as white service members and provided examples. Respondents also provided examples of black service members who did not receive the same benefit of the doubt as their white counterparts.

Written comments also included examples of racial bias in IG, EO, and other investigations. Airmen and Space Professionals pointed to a lack of trust in their leadership to objectively conduct investigations and to properly hold people accountable. They strongly believed IG and EO offices worked for and were too friendly with commanders and therefore protected commanders during investigations. Black service members also indicated a strong fear of reprisal or retaliation for raising complaints to either the IG or EO.

In both the survey and written comments, black service members identified obstacles and barriers that have led to an overall lack of confidence and trust in the system. Many comments pointed to a lack of trust in leadership to address racial bias and racism in the organization.

Base Visits and Group Discussions

The Review team interviewed personnel at all levels of the Department seeking experiences regarding disparity in military discipline processes and career development opportunities for black service members. Over a three-week period, the Review team executed 138 boots-on-the-ground and remote (virtual) sessions with Department members across all MAJCOMs. To gain a perspective from the Airmen themselves, the team interviewed more than 1,400 service members in small, diverse, anonymous group sessions of 8-10 people. These small group sessions were organized by rank/position: E1-E4s, NCOs and Civilian Equivalent First-Line Supervisors, First Sergeants, CGOs and Civilian Equivalents, and Squadron Commanders and Civilian Equivalents. Additionally, the Review team interviewed twenty wing command teams (commander, vice commander, and command chief), Staff Judge Advocates, and Area Defense Counsels. General session themes and specific group observations as well as comments from the command team sessions are discussed below:

General Group Session Observations

A notable portion of black service members felt they received harsher punishments than white service members when it came to lower-level disciplinary actions, such as documented verbal counseling, LOCs, LOAs, and LORs. Some NCOs and first-line supervisors shared that they felt pressured by leadership to issue punishment to black service members for very minor infractions. Several, first-line supervisors stated when black service members came into work late, leadership would not give them the benefit of the doubt and "go hard" on them. In contrast, if white service members came in late they would ask if the person is ok and give them the benefit of the doubt.

A large majority of service members believe they were not denied basic developmental opportunities based on their race or sex, and some stated these areas were never a factor in selection. However, some stated access to these opportunities depended heavily on the first-line supervisors, who set the tone for expectations within the flight. If black service members were viewed as "disagreeable," it reduced their chances for developmental opportunities. Some opined that black service members had to work "ten times harder" to be viewed as worthy of developmental opportunities, and if they had any type of discipline in their records, they were rarely afforded the opportunity for rehabilitation or development. Lack of diversity at many units led service members to believe they did not have someone to aspire to be like or see that getting to such roles was truly attainable for them. Some commented, "[p]eople of color are not seen as leaders in my unit."

The Review team found that organizational climate had a strong influence on young service members' attitudes regarding their sense of belonging, personal relationships, loyalty, and even work performance. These experiences could result in negative feelings towards job satisfaction, need for achievement, affiliation, overall effectiveness, performance, and commitment. However, black service members noted their strength, tenacity, tolerance, and resiliency helped them through all the negativity.

E1-E4

Very few participants felt their organizations initiated investigations fairly or implemented corrective and disciplinary measures without bias or favoritism. Some service members believed discrimination occurred in some organizations across the base, and black service members received harsher punishments at a higher rate than white service members with similar infractions. Many indicated their experiences were related to punishment in violation of the Air Force drug use policy, underage drinking, driving under the influence, dress and appearance standards, and weapons control. Some service members perceived the corrective and disciplinary measures for each of these instances were warranted, but also perceived that the level of punishment for black service members versus their white counterparts was not administered fairly.

Service members with personal experiences of being treated unfairly due to race or ethnic background described racial profiling, bias, and favoritism as reasons why black service members disproportionally received corrective or disciplinary actions. Others cited upbringing, poor communication, and being junior in rank as contributing factors. A majority of black service members felt they are constantly under the microscope and singled out by their unit and expected to do more than others.

Additionally, black service members believed they were repeatedly labeled the "angry black person." Black respondents believed that, at all levels of supervision and leadership, discipline was often administered to black service members for having an attitude or coming across as angry. Many black service members felt once they were on the radar, recovery was impossible. They also believed leadership continuously issued administrative paperwork in order to ultimately discharge black service members.

As for opportunities, some believed the more selective developmental opportunities were awarded to white co-workers more often because of favoritism. Many black service members stated that if they did not "hang out" or develop a common bond with their first-line supervisors, they were typically not awarded developmental opportunities.

NCOs and Civilian Equivalent First-Line Supervisors

Some NCOs stated that punishment for black service members and other races seemed to be inconsistent. Black service members felt they were singled out because of their appearance (for example, having hairstyles that were within regulations, but not favored by supervisors of a different race), and this often resulted in what they say as the beginning of a "paperwork trail," which negatively impacted career development opportunities for black service members. They also felt service members from other races or ethnic backgrounds were consistently given a second chance, while black service members were not. Additionally, NCOs felt the service hindered black service members' ability to be rehabilitated after one mistake.

A large number of NCOs interviewed expressed that in some cases, supervisors of a particular race appeared to favor service members who were of the same race and tended to give them available developmental opportunities. The NCOs also stated that the favoritism could involve any race or gender. Numerous black NCOs brought up that it is typical for them to have to "work 2-3 times as hard as any other race (particularly white NCOs) for the same level of recognition" within their squadron or higher.

First Sergeants

The majority of First Sergeant interviewees said they had not witnessed any difference in the treatment of service members based on race or ethnicity, but also said by the time they saw the paperwork based on a negative infraction, most fact-finding had been accomplished. In contrast, several First Sergeants noted when a black service member and a white service member committed the same infraction, either together or separately, the black service member's punishment was typically harsher than the punishment the white member received.

Many First Sergeants agreed that supervisors often do not take the time to get to know their subordinates. They also believe many supervisors see black service members as "having an attitude or cannot conform." This perception results in a paperwork trail of corrective actions, which often culminates in discharge.

When it came to opportunities, the First Sergeants consistently indicated first-line supervisors invested in subordinates to whom they could relate. Also, many of the First Sergeants said PME needs to teach young supervisors how to better interact in uncomfortable situations, address issues with those of other cultures and differing mindsets, and spend more time on how to better manage people. They also noted that many junior supervisors are not afforded the time to mentor and counsel their Airmen and Space Professionals appropriately.

Most First Sergeants agreed promotions and recognition were fair and based on performance. Many complained, however, about unqualified white service members being placed in positions where qualified black service members should have been placed. Additionally, they claimed information about opportunities was not equally disseminated to the entire organization. Job positions were not advertised, and organizations relied on the "good old boy" network to make hiring decisions. Some black First Sergeants mentioned that they felt they needed to work harder than their peers, not just to get recognized, but to be viewed as equal.

CGOs and Civilian Equivalents

With regard to military discipline, many CGOs said they had little to no experience with disciplinary actions against black service members. CGOs also mentioned that they believed everything followed the same process, was fair across the board, took biases into account, and was based on facts. Many CGOs said supervisors try to look at the situation for what the member had done, not on their physical appearance.

As for opportunities, many CGOs said they believe service members who worked to better themselves, whether by pursuing educational opportunities or by working hard at their assigned duties, would tend to have more favorable outcomes in terms of development. Some CGOs also said they thought individuals' race played no part in decisions regarding who was nominated for certain opportunities.

Some rated officers mentioned favoritism or the perception of individuals being predetermined for special or advanced opportunities, and members who developed close relationships to the senior staff were more likely to be chosen for unique TDY opportunities. While this observation was not based on race, one could see where a lack of black mentors in the senior ranks could have a greater impact on black officers. Some CGOs also mentioned recognition for the same work was different for people of different races.

Squadron Commanders and Civilian Equivalents

Despite half of the squadron commanders having seen or experienced racial disparity earlier in their careers, they had not seen anything unfair occurring in their units. Nonetheless, they opined that commanders need better training to properly administer the disciplinary actions they are empowered to give. Commanders recognized they have different internal and external tools, and the discipline process was designed with checks and balances. However, they also recognized it was hard to maintain consistency throughout the base and other levels of supervision. There were some specific occasions noted where black service members were not given the benefit of the doubt when not all of the evidence of an infraction was presented.

Squadron commanders and civilian equivalents generally believed everyone had a fair chance at developmental opportunities. They highlighted they used merit and work-ethic-based approach when sending people forward for certain opportunities. Some squadron commanders also rely on their first-line supervisors' inputs when developing people, and it was largely agreed that these first-line supervisors had the potential of being personally biased. Squadron commanders stated there are times when there was perceived pressure to send up certain individuals for specific awards, and they were not necessarily merit-based approaches. "Sometimes there are unspoken criteria to pick a certain person (based on race), no matter the award." Some commanders admitted the "good ole boy" club exist, and that it can create a perception of favoritism regarding opportunities, although this was not always necessarily racially motivated.

One black squadron commander commented on opportunity versus outcome and mentorship. The only mentorship he received throughout his career was from other black leaders. "You might get left behind if you don't have someone that looks like you helping to propel you. Black service members need to work twice as hard and you can't mess up." He went on to say that some of his black service members had made one mistake and that their military careers were over.

Overall, the team found the installation group session comments had similar themes and were consistent with how participants responded to the survey questions discussed earlier. The enlisted members generally felt that black service members received harsher punishment than white service members for similar offenses and were less likely to receive the benefit of the doubt for minor infractions compared to white service members. Officers also raised the issue of benefit of the doubt and the difficulty in maintaining consistency for punishment throughout the lower levels of supervision. Both enlisted and officers indicated a lack of diversity, favoritism, and "good ole boy" networks were likely barriers to career developmental opportunities for black service members.

Wing Command Teams

Most members of wing command teams said they received little to no diversity or bias training during their careers. Only a few of the Active Duty senior leaders were aware of either AFI 36-7001, *Diversity and Inclusion*, or its requirements. The Air Force Reserve Command (AFRC) members had more annual training and education on diversity and bias. In addition, AFRC designated all vice wing commanders as Diversity and Inclusion (D&I) program managers for their respective installations. Despite the overall lack of training on bias, nearly all respondents understood the concept of bias and provided an accurate definition of bias as well as various examples where it could manifest itself.

As for mentorship, the wing command teams overwhelmingly indicated they had mentored every racial, age, gender, and other identifying demographic, but acknowledged the mentees may not receive the mentorship the same way depending on trust or demographic differences between mentor and mentee.

With regard to racial bias or racial barriers in DAF processes, few on the command teams felt that racial disparities existed in the processes, and were race-neutral as written. However, most interviewees admitted that problems could arise when biased or subjective inputs were placed into the otherwise objective processes.

Wing command teams also believed there were minority bias trends in certain career fields, with many minorities being assigned to support career fields rather than operations career fields. The teams felt that under-recruiting and under-promoting minorities led to a small pool of members in high-ranking positions ("if I can't see it, I can't be it"). One wing command team member said, "[f]uture General Officers come only from operational career fields, who are primarily (if not exclusively) comprised of Caucasian males."

When asked about disparities in military justice, nearly all the teams were aware that black service members received disciplinary actions on a far more frequent basis than other demographic groups. The leaders believed the DAF had not done an in-depth look to determine the cause of these disparities. The leadership teams believed immediate supervisors were often rushed in making discipline decisions due to workload. Many said tracking lower-level administrative punishments would allow commanders to monitor for disparities. Leadership teams also believed first-line supervisors lacked adequate military discipline training, which leads to unequal application of disciplinary and rehabilitation standards.

Command teams said they could envision situations where one service member may be given a second chance or the benefit of the doubt, while another may be subjected to disciplinary paperwork on the first occurrence. This disparity may be especially true at the first-level supervisor level, where many supervisors are relatively inexperienced, untrained to recognize potential biases, and generally may be unprepared for the complexities of administration and mentorship of racially diverse groups.

When asked about racial disparities in promotion and advancement opportunities for Airmen, Space Professionals, and civilian employees, most interviewees had little input into whether there was a problem or not. All wings had both formal and informal professional development courses, but none of those courses covered diversity and inclusion, or bias.

Trends from Interviews / DAF-IG Hotline

At the end of the survey, Airmen and Space Professionals were directed to call or email the DAF IG Hotline if they wanted to provide additional feedback or needed help. As of 1 September 2020, DAF IG processed 338 hotline calls and emails.

The Review team assessed racial disparity concerns submitted by Airmen to the DAF IG Hotline dedicated to this Review, and we connected with 158 service members who identified themselves and provided contact information. Additionally, the Review team conducted targeted interviews based on the responses. We captured major trends that supported the findings from the survey responses and are worth highlighting.

- Many first-line supervisors did not have the experience to handle some of the cultural differences and racial issues that may arise at the lower levels of the organization. According to First Sergeants, first-line supervisors need more experience, better training, and more time to be able to learn about their subordinates personally.

- Black service members believed their leadership did not value their ideas and contributions.

- Black service members feared reprisal or being targeted for bringing up issues, and many would not raise issues because they did not believe it was worth the potential adverse effects on their careers,

- The majority of white service members, from enlisted to the General Officer ranks, do not believe racial bias and racial issues are a big problem in the Air Force.

SUMMARY – VOICE OF THE AIRMEN AND SPACE PROFESSIONALS

The Review team developed the Racial Disparity Review survey to encourage respondents to write in their personal experiences. This Review has incorporated their stories, thoughts, and recommendations throughout the report. The survey data, interviews, and discussion responses show a substantial disconnect between how black and white service members perceive DAF discipline and opportunities. The survey responses were consistent with the empirical data and highlighted that black service members believe the racial problem extends beyond data. In particular, the responses revealed a large perspective gap on whether racial bias exists in LOCs, LOAs, and LORs. The survey responses also revealed three out of five black service members believe they do not receive the same benefit of the doubt as white service members for the same infractions. The Likert scale responses revealed 40% of black service members do not trust their chain of command to address racism, bias and unequal opportunities, while the yes/no responses indicated that 50% of black service members have experienced or witnessed racial discrimination.

The installation group sessions, targeted interviews, and text responses in the surveys supported the Likert scale and yes/no survey responses. Specifically, the interviews and installation group discussions confirmed that black service members believe they receive harsher punishment for similar offenses and do not receive the benefit of the doubt for minor infractions compared to their white counterparts. Additionally, officers in the group discussions highlighted the difficulty in maintaining consistency at lower levels of supervision. As for developmental opportunities, enlisted, officers, and civilians indicated lack of diversity and favoritism were likely barriers for black service members.

III. HISTORY: WHAT WE'VE KNOWN, WHAT WE'VE DONE, WHAT HAS WORKED, WHAT HAS NOT?

This Review analyzed 23 previous reports and studies related to diversity and racial disparities in the military services, some dating back to 1973. The Review team's analysis determined the findings of these studies and associated proposed recommendations often did not identify root causes, did not compel follow-through, lacked meaningful measures to allow effectiveness to be assessed over time, and broadly lacked accountability for progress. This Review will focus on the most recent and pertinent reports, the 2011 MLDC, the 2014 MLDC update, and the 2019 GAO report, as well as objectives from the AF Disciplinary Action Analysis Team (DAAT).

CHRONOLOGY

DATE	EVENT
1973	Government Accountability Office (GAO) published the report, *Status of Equal Opportunity in the Military Departments*. (Ex 4)
1980	GAO published the report, *Military Discharge Policies And Practices Result In Wide Disparities: Congressional Review Is Needed*. (Ex 5)
Apr 95	GAO published the report, *Equal Opportunity, DoD Studies on Discrimination in the Military*. (Ex 7)
Mar 11	The Military Leadership Diversity Commission (MLDC) published the report, *From Representation to Inclusion: Diversity Leadership for the 21st Century Military*. (Ex 3)
Mar 14	DoD published the report, *Implementation of the Recommendations Made by the Military Leadership Diversity Commission*, updating the progress of implementing the MLDC's twenty recommendations. (Ex 20)
25 Apr 16	SAF/MR directed "deep dive" by AF/A1 and AFJAG. The working group convened and met over the next 90 days. (Ex 28:1)
6 Jun 17	Protect Our Defenders (POD)[26] released report, *Racial Disparities in Military Justice*.
26 Sept 17	SAF/MR established the Disciplinary Actions Analysis Team (DAAT). (Ex 26)
19 Oct 17	DAAT conducted first meeting to address the POD report and upcoming GAO report on military justice. (Ex 27)
May 19	The GAO released the report, *Military Justice, DOD and the Coast Guard Need to Improve Their Capabilities to Assess Racial and Gender Disparities*. (Ex 6)
May 20	POD published the report, *Federal Lawsuit Reveals Air Force Cover Up: Racial Disparities in Military Justice Part II*.
2 Jun 20	The Air Force Inspector General was directed to conduct an independent review of racial disparity in the Department of the Air Force. (Ex 1)

---

[26] Protect Our Defenders is an advocacy group "dedicated to addressing the epidemic of rape and sexual assault in the military" and an "impartially administered system of justice." (Ex 4:3)

2011 MLDC REPORT, RECOMMENDATIONS AND DOD PROGRESS UPDATE

In the National Defense Authorization Act (NDAA) for Fiscal Year 2009, Section 596, Congress asked the MLDC to "conduct a comprehensive evaluation and assessment of policies that provide opportunities for the promotion and advancement of the minority members of the Armed Forces, including minority members who are senior officers." The MLDC's report examines policies affecting the career life cycles of military personnel from the fives Services: Army, Navy, Air Force, Marine Corps, and Coast Guard, as well as the National Guard and Reserve. The report outlines a vision, strategy, and action plan for improving the inclusiveness of military leadership. (Ex 3:3)

The MLDC determined that its final recommendations should serve three interrelated goals:

- Establish the foundation for effective diversity leadership with a definition of diversity congruent with DoD's core values and vision of its future.

- Develop future leaders who represent the face of America and are able to effectively lead a diverse workforce to maximize mission effectiveness.

- Implement policies and practices that will make leaders accountable for instilling diversity leadership as a core competency of the Armed Forces. (Ex 3:8)

The MLDC proposed 20 recommendations to address the three interrelated goals. (Ex 3:125-130) Of the 20 recommendations, the following 12 are considered relevant to this Review:

- Recommendation 1 – The Department of Defense (DoD) should adopt a new definition of diversity.

- Recommendation 2 – To enhance readiness and mission accomplishment, effectively leading diverse groups must become a core competency across the DoD and services.

- Recommendation 3 – Leadership of the DoD and services must be personally committed to diversity becoming an institutional priority.

- Recommendation 4 – Diversity needs to become an integral part of the DoD culture.

- Recommendation 7 – Improve recruiting from the currently available pool of qualified candidates.

- Recommendation 8 – The services should optimize the ability of service members to make informed career choices from accession to retirement – with special emphasis on mentoring.

- Recommendation 10 – Improve transparency so that service members understand performance, expectations, promotion criteria, and processes.

- Recommendation 11 – Ensure that promotion board precepts provide guidance on how to value service-directed special assignments outside normal career paths or fields.

- Recommendation 16 – DoD and services must resource and institute clear, consistent, and robust diversity management policies with emphasis on roles, responsibilities, authorities, and accountability.

- Recommendation 18 – The services should conduct annual barrier analyses.

- Recommendation 19 – Institute mechanisms for accountability and internal and external monitoring for both active and reserve components.

- Recommendation 20 – Include an assessment of qualified minority and female candidates for top leadership positions in the annual diversity report to Congress.

2014 MLDC Progress Update

In 2014, DoD reported that 12 of the 20 original MLDC recommendations were fully implemented at the time of the update, and no further actions were required on these recommendations. The Office of the Secretary of Defense (OSD) and the services will continue to monitor the recommendations on a recurring basis for sustainment. The remaining eight recommendations were partially implemented at the time of this progress update. (Ex 20:2) The following is a brief summary of each of the 12 MLDC recommendations considered relevant to this Review and the corresponding progress updates from the DoD.

The first recommendation in the MLDC report was the DoD and services should adopt the following definition for diversity, "Diversity is all the different characteristics and attributes of individuals that are consistent with Department of Defense core values, integral to overall readiness and mission accomplishment, and reflective of the Nation we serve." (Ex 3:34) DoD used the MLDC's recommendation as the foundation of its definition, but revised it slightly to include the Total Force. As part of the *2012-2017 Department of Defense Diversity and Inclusion Strategic Plan*, diversity is defined as, "Diversity is all the different characteristics and attributes of the DoD's Total Force, which are consistent with our core values, integral to overall readiness and mission accomplishment, and reflective of the best of the Nation we serve." (Ex 20:6) The Air Force adopted a similar definition as part of AFI 36-7001, *Diversity and Inclusion*, which says, "Air Force broadly defines diversity as a composite of individual characteristics, experiences, and abilities consistent with the Air Force Core Values and the Air Force Mission." (Ex 61:3) DoD considered Recommendation 1 of the MLDC report fully implemented, and no further action was necessary.

For recommendation 2, diversity leadership refers to how leaders influence the way in which people and groups under their command relate to one another. The commission recommended two strategies to inculcate diversity leadership. The first focuses on leadership training at all levels to include education in diversity dynamics and training. The second strategy involves DoD and services developing a framework for implementation and assessing diversity leadership development. (Ex 3:44-45) The 2014 DoD progress update referenced the Air Force Doctrine Document 1.1, *Leadership and Force Development*, designating diversity as an institutional sub-competency under the *"Leading People"* competency.

Additionally, the Air Force Diversity Strategic Roadmap, published in March 2013, lays out a game plan to "promote diversity and inclusion through training, leadership development, and employee engagement programs." (Ex 20:34) Finally, AFI 36-7001, *Diversity and Inclusion*, identifies required training courses affiliated with diversity and inclusion education. (Ex 62:13) The Air Force Diversity and Inclusion (D&I) Task Force is currently reviewing Air Education and Training Command's (AETC's) implementation of these requirements (the AFI with these new requirements was released in February 19). DoD determined Recommendation 2 was only partially implemented, but a workable plan was in place or being developed to ensure full implementation.

Regarding Recommendation 3, the commission specifically noted, "It is important to remember how critical strong leadership is to service members' performance and morale. When change comes into view, there can be strong resistance. Changes that address people's racial/ethnic, religious, and other differences can prove to be especially challenging because these topics can be emotionally charged for many people." (Ex 3:46) According to the commission, it would take top-level leadership involvement to develop, implement, and maintain change. DoD's progress update states, "[s]enior leaders from all Services have demonstrated their personal commitment to making diversity an institutional priority." Specifically, the update noted the Secretary of the Air Force, Chief of Staff of the Air Force, and the Chief Master Sergeant of the Air Force all signed a Declaration on Diversity, reinforcing their commitment to the principles of diversity and inclusion in recruiting, retaining and developing Airmen representative of America's broadest landscape. (Ex 20:8) DoD considered Recommendation 3 of the MLDC report fully implemented, and no further action is necessary.

Recommendation 4 proposed DoD and the services make respect for diversity a core value, identifying and rewarding the skills needed to meet the operational challenges of the 21st century, and using strategic communications plans to communicate their diversity vision and values. (Ex 3:47) DoD concluded this recommendation was fully implemented based on the notion that diversity is inherent in leadership and built into the Armed Service's existing core values. Also, the consensus is that service members are better served by integrating diversity and inclusion into how people lead, think and act – with dignity, honor, and respect being paramount in all they do. According to the update, the Air Force and Air National Guard had published a diversity strategic plan or roadmap with a communication plan. (Ex 20:10) DoD considered Recommendation 4 of the MLDC report fully implemented, and no further action is necessary.

In Recommendation 7, the MLDC stated DoD and services should engage in activities to improve recruiting from the currently available pool of candidates by creating, implementing, and evaluating a strategic plan for outreach, and recruiting from untapped locations and underrepresented demographic groups. (Ex 3:79) According to the progress update, the Air Force Diversity Strategic Roadmap institutes goals, actions and performance measures to both attract and recruit "high-quality, talented, diverse individuals to consider service in the United States Air Force." Additionally, the Air Force Recruiting Service (AFRS) had a comprehensive strategy geared towards strengthening its position in the minority markets, including strategic marketing to targeted audiences and influencers. (Ex 20:17) The DoD considered Recommendation 7 of the MLDC report fully implemented, and no further action is necessary.

Recommendation 8 of the MLDC proposed the services ensure their career development programs and resources enhance service members' knowledge of career choices to optimize service members' ability to make informed career choices from accession to retirement. To achieve this, the MLDC further recommended mentoring and career counseling should start prior to the initial career field decision point and continue throughout the service member's career. (Ex 3:91) In response to this recommendation, DoD stated that each service had a strong mentoring program currently in place. According to the commission update, the Air Force charges its Airmen to actively mentor officer candidates, as well as enlisted and civilian recruits, before career field selection and throughout their careers. Air Force Manual 36-2643, *Air Force Mentoring Program*, provides specific guidance on Air Force Mentoring. Additionally, the DAF mentoring policy directive and development instruction provide effective mentoring guidelines, principles, and strategies to enhance communication between mentor and mentee. (Ex 20:20) The DoD considered Recommendation 8 of the MLDC report fully implemented, and no further action is necessary.

In Recommendation 10, the MLDC calls for the DoD, the services, and the National Guard Bureau to ensure transparency throughout their promotion systems so service members may better understand performance expectations, promotion criteria, and processes. To accomplish this, the commission recommended the services specify the knowledge, skills, abilities, and potential to be an effective General Officer or senior noncommissioned officer. (Ex 3:101) In response to this recommendation, DoD stated each of the services should ensure transparency throughout their promotion systems through a deliberate, continuous, and progressive relationship of education, training, performance, and career counseling. Specifically noted, the Air Force provides transparency to its officer promotion system by publishing legally required board convening notification prior to every board and by publishing the Air Force Pamphlet 36-2506, *You and Your Promotions – The Air Force Officer Promotion Program*. This pamphlet explains how officer promotions are made, how boards are comprised and operated, and what officers should do to ensure their records are accurate before meeting a board. Additionally, in September 2013, the Air Force introduced the Officer Continuum of Learning. The Continuum guides institutional competency development and provides a roadmap for development through education, training, and experiential opportunities. (Ex 20:24) DoD considered Recommendation 10 of the MLDC report fully implemented, and no further action is necessary.

According to Recommendation 11 of the MLDC report, the services should ensure promotion board precepts provide guidance regarding service-related special assignments outside normal career paths. Additionally, senior raters' evaluations shall acknowledge when a service member has deviated from their career path at the specific request of his or her leadership. The main motivation for this recommendation was to eliminate institutional bias that might contribute to the promotion gap between racial/ethnic minority and white officers. (Ex 3:104) DoD stated all the services update board precepts annually and include guidance regarding special assignments specific to their service's varying needs. The update noted the Air Force has developmental teams that work with senior raters to provide service members vectors on special duty or follow on assignments. These developmental teams identify the education, training, and experience appropriate for officers, enlisted, and DAF civilians within each functional community based on current and future requirements. (Ex 20:28) The DoD considered Recommendation 11 of the MLDC report fully implemented, and no further action is necessary.

In Recommendation 16, the MLDC called on DoD and the services to resource and institute clear, consistent, and robust diversity management policies, emphasizing roles, responsibilities, authorities, and accountability. Specifically, DoD and the services should implement strategic diversity plans that address all stages of a service member's life cycle. Another subset of Recommendation 16 is the establishment of a standard set of metrics and benchmarks that enable the Secretary of Defense (SecDef) to measure progress. Specifically, this requires developing a new set of metrics to capture the inclusion and capability aspects of DoD's broader diversity goals. One metric specifically noted for an inclusive environment is provided by discipline data: court-martial cases and non-judicial punishment. (Ex 3:101-104) The department developed the Diversity and Inclusion Strategic Plan 2012-2017 to address both military and civilian issues. The plan is supported by five goals and 39 initiatives and provides an overarching construct that encourages commitment and creates alignment across the department with the latitude for the Services and DoD. (Ex 20:41) DoD determined Recommendation 16 only partially implemented, but a workable plan is in place or under development to ensure full implementation.

Recommendation 18 stated the services should conduct annual barrier analyses to review demographic diversity patterns across the military life cycle, starting with accessions. Additionally, DoD should establish a universal data collection system, and the analyses of the data should be based on common definitions of demographic groups, a common methodology, and a common reporting structure. The annual analyses should include:

- Accession demographics

- Retention, command selection, and promotion rates by race/ethnicity and gender

- Analysis of assignment patterns by race/ethnicity and gender

- Analysis of attitudinal survey data by race/ethnicity and gender

- Identification of persistent, group-specific deviations from overall averages and plans to investigate underlying causes

- Summaries of progress made on previous actions (Ex 3:131)

In the commission update, DoD states that the current diversity accountability review construct process will allow the department to conduct barrier analyses based on data gathered for the accountability review. Specifically, analysis of how racial, ethnic, gender minorities are progressing along their notional career path. At a minimum, the construct will address, recruiting, assignments to key billets, education, retention and promotion. Since each service has its own career structures and career progression patterns, which it understands best, there is a need to develop service-specific actions to address concerns. The overall objective is to have a way ahead, mandating barrier analysis actions that each service must take to address their diversity health. Each year the services will reassess their barrier analysis progress and course correct as needed. (Ex 20:43) DoD determined Recommendation 18 only partially implemented, but a workable plan is in place or being developed to ensure full implementation.

Recommendation 19 calls for DoD to institute accountability and internal and external monitoring mechanisms for both active and reserve components. Accordingly, the services must embed diversity leadership in performance assessments throughout careers. Additionally, DoD should establish diversity leadership as a criterion for nomination and appointment to senior enlisted leadership positions and General Officers, including 3- and 4-star positions and service chief. (Ex 3:133) In addition to a few initiatives responding to previous MLDC recommendations, DoD developed an initial list of focus areas to assess and address barriers/gaps in diversity. Potential mechanisms being investigated for embedding diversity leadership into the core competencies expected of a service member include the following:

- Documentation of one's diversity leadership in a self-statement
- Incorporating diversity perspectives into leadership assessments
- 360-degree evaluations
- Utilizing relevant indicators such as climate survey trends, discipline, and EO data, and retention rates

Additionally, the Secretary of Defense (SecDef) directed unit climate assessment results be used as a mentoring tool by a commander's supervisor. To facilitate this directive, the climate survey results will be sent to the commander and the commander's supervisor simultaneously. This mandate ensures that dialogue will occur between commanders and their supervisors and is intended to put accountability into the climate assessment process. The requirement to forward the results to the commander's supervisor only applies to the annual climate survey, not the 120-day assessment. (Ex 20:44-45) DoD determined Recommendation 19 only partially implemented, but a workable plan is in place or being developed to ensure full implementation.

Finally, in Recommendation 20, the MLDC stated Congress should require SecDef to report an assessment of the available pool of qualified racial/ethnic minority and female candidates for the 3- and 4-star General Officer positions annually. Additionally, SecDef must ensure all qualified candidates have been considered for every 3- and 4-star position nomination. If there were no qualified racial/ethnic minority and/or female candidates, a statement of explanation should be made in the package submitted to the Senate for the confirmation hearings. (Ex 3:137) Regarding this final recommendation, the DoD progress update responded that the Department's senior leadership already considers recommendations for 3- and 4- star generals/flag officers from the entire pool of qualified candidates. Including diversity language in Title 10 increases the potential for nominations to become a search for quotas and the selection process of 3- and 4- star general/flag officers to become stagnated. (Ex 20:46) DoD determined Recommendation 20 is only partially implemented, but a workable plan is in place or being developed to ensure full implementation.

In the Strategic Way Ahead of the DoD's progress update to the MLDC, the report states OSD will continue working with key stakeholders to implement the DoD Diversity and Inclusion Strategic Plan 2012-2017. Additionally, an oversight framework was established to collaboratively review, discuss, guide, recommend, and act on DoD military and civilian workforce diversity and inclusion matters as well as an instrument for continued implementation of MLDC recommendations. (Ex 20:47) As noted later in this report, accountability for implementation and follow on measurements of success have faltered.

2019 GAO REPORT AND RECOMMENDATIONS

In 2019 the Government Accountability Office (GAO) released *Military Justice: DoD and the Coast Guard Need to Improve Their Capabilities to Assess Racial and Gender Disparities* in response to a provision in the FY 2018 NDAA that directed a study of the extent that disparities may exist in the military justice system. This report assessed the extent to which (1) the military services collect and maintain consistent race, ethnicity, and gender information for service members investigated and disciplined for UCMJ violations that can be used to assess disparities, and (2) there are racial and gender disparities in the military justice system, and whether DoD has studied disparities. GAO analyzed data from the investigations, military justice, and personnel databases from the military services, including the Coast Guard, from fiscal years 2013-2017, and interviewed agency officials.[27] (Ex 6:1-2)

The study found racial and gender disparities exist in investigations, disciplinary actions, and punishment of service members in the military justice system. GAO's analysis of available data from fiscal years 2013 through 2017, which controlled for attributes such as race, gender, rank, education, and years of service, found racial and gender disparities were more likely in actions that first brought service members into the military justice system. Specifically, GAO found that:

- Black, Hispanic, and male service members were more likely than white and female service members to be the subjects of recorded investigations in all of the military services, and were more likely to be tried in general and special courts-martial in the Army, the Navy, the Marine Corps, and the Air Force.

- There were fewer statistically significant racial and gender disparities in most military services in general and special courts-martial that were preceded by a recorded investigation than in general and special courts-martial overall. The study also found that statistically significant racial and gender disparities in general and special courts-martial that did not follow a recorded investigation were similar to those identified for general and special courts-martial overall.

- Black and male service members were more likely than white and female service members to be tried in summary courts-martial and to be subjects of NJP in the Air Force and the Marine Corps. The Army and the Navy did not maintain complete data, and the Coast Guard had too few summary courts-martial for us to analyze, and did not maintain complete NJP data. (Ex 6:38-39)

The report identified fewer statistically significant racial or gender disparities in case outcomes—convictions and punishment severity. Specifically:

- Race was not a statistically significant factor in the likelihood of conviction in general and special courts-martial in the Army, the Navy, the Marine Corps, and the Air Force, but gender was a statistically significant factor in the Marine Corps.

---

[27] In preparation for this report, in 2017, the Air Force assembled a working group called the Disciplinary Actions Analysis Team (DAAT) to examine the barriers certain demographic groups face to career success, including barriers to training opportunities, promotion, and retention. As of the 2019 GAO report, the working group was in the early stages of organizing and had not yet published any findings or recommendations for service leadership. (Ex 6:65)

- Black service members were less likely to receive a more severe punishment in general and special courts-martial compared to white service members in the Navy but there was no statistically significant difference for black service members in the Marine Corps, the Army, and the Air Force. Additionally, there were no statistically significant differences for Hispanic service members in the Navy, the Marine Corps, the Army, or the Air Force; and males were more likely than females to receive a more severe punishment in the Marine Corps, the Army, and the Air Force. (Ex 6:39)

According to the GAO report, the military services have some initiatives to examine and address disparities in military justice. In May 2016, the DAF conducted a service-wide data call to solicit information about cases involving challenges to a member of a courts-martial based on race or a motion for selective prosecution. A thorough review revealed no evidence of selective prosecution in Air Force courts-martial. In addition, the DAF conducted analyses of its military justice data. Specifically, the DAF routinely analyzed military justice data using a Rates Per Thousand analysis to identify whether certain demographic groups are tried by courts-martial or subject to NJP at higher rates than others.[28] These Air Force analyses found that black and male service members were more likely than white and female service members to be subject to courts-martial and NJP from fiscal years 2013 through 2017, which is consistent with what the GAO report found. (Ex 6:64-65)

The GAO made eleven recommendations, including three to the Secretary of Homeland Security, three to the SecDef, two to the Secretary of the Army, two to the Secretary of the Navy, and one to the Secretary of the Air Force. One of the recommendations to the SecDef was that the military services conduct an evaluation to identify the causes of any disparities in the military justice system, and then take steps to address the causes of these disparities. (Ex 6:70)

The GAO recommended SecAF develop the capability in the DAF to present service members' race and ethnicity data in its investigations and personnel databases using the same categories of race and ethnicity established in the December 2018 uniform standards for the military justice databases. According to GAO, this could be accomplished by either: (1) modifying the Air Force's investigations and personnel databases to collect and maintain the data in accordance with the uniform standards, (2) developing the capability to aggregate the data into the race and ethnicity categories included in the uniform standards, or (3) implementing another method identified by the Air Force. (Ex 6:69) The DAF has met this requirement.

AF DAAT OBJECTIVES

In September 2017, SAF/MR convened a meeting of the Military Justice Executive Steering Group to discuss the way forward in preparation for the upcoming GAO Report on military justice. The meeting resulted in the formation of the Disciplinary Action Analysis Team (DAAT). (Ex 26) The DAAT was charged with reviewing "policies, procedures, practices, and conditions regarding administrative and disciplinary actions served to Total Force Airmen across all demographics of the workforce with an eye toward identifying any problems, the root cause(s) of any problems identified, and, if there are barriers, to devise plans to eliminate them."

---

[28] A Rates Per Thousand analysis computes the number of service members within a demographic group that are subject to a particular military justice action, divided by the total number of service members of that demographic group, and multiplied by 1,000. (Ex 6:64)

(Ex 26:2) The DAAT membership included more than 40 members from a range of different offices, including AFJAG, SAF/GC AF/A1, SAF/MR, Medical Groups, AFPC, AFRC, and Total Force components, including Active Duty, reserve, guard, and civilian. (Ex 29:1)

The DAAT considered four aspects in approaching reform:

Education: Quality, research-based training can (1) help increase understanding of core concepts, (2) increase awareness about one's own behavior, and (3) contribute to setting or changing a tone about the subject. According to the 2019 DAAT Roadmap, the following objectives would address the training portion of reform:

- *Unconscious bias training*: Unconscious bias training is a well-established best practice among those addressing racial disparity in the civilian criminal justice system.

- *Cultural competency training*: The DAF defines cross-cultural competence as, "[t]he ability to quickly and accurately comprehend, then act appropriately and effectively in a culturally complex environment to achieve the desired effect – without necessarily having prior exposure to a particular group, region, or language."

- *General leadership training*: Leadership training at all levels, for enlisted and officers, should highlight the issue of racial disparity in the military justice system and educate leaders about their role that may contribute to it and actions to take to reduce it. (Ex 29:6)

Priming: Priming tools are reminders or other means of prompting individuals to apply their learning at the appropriate time. The DAF regularly uses priming tools, such as checklists and scripts, for everything such as aircraft operations to promotion ceremonies to courts-martial. The use of these tools has been institutionalized to ensure Total Force Airmen, once trained, complete tasks effectively and efficiently. Similarly, in this case, checklists could be used to ensure anyone administering an LOC, LOA, or LOR is prompted to exercise their cultural competence or be aware of their potential biases. (Ex 29:7-8)

Structures and Systems: Structures and systems drive individual behavior within a culture. The DAF is a highly structured organization designed to drive specific behavior and promote certain aspects of culture. For example, throughout of the Air Force's history, the Wingman concept has fostered a culture of support, comradery, and safety. To reinforce the concept, the Air Force has endorsed Wingman Day involving team sports and other team-building events to promote better relations among its members. The Air Force has extended the Wingman concept in its recent efforts to prevent sexual assault. For example, Airmen at Basic Military Training (BMT) are required to carry a Wingman card that includes the name of their wingman, as well as an emergency phone number. The established practice of participating in Wingman Day and developing the new Wingman card requirement help reinforce the Wingman concept and overall Air Force culture.

Objectives focused on structures and systems in the 2019 DAAT Roadmap included:

- Develop a tracking system modeled after the Automated Military Justice Analysis and Management System (AMJAMS) to track administrative disciplinary action such as LOCs, LOAs, and LORs.

- Develop a more accurate metric to measure racial disparity; perhaps one that is percentage-based rather than Rates Per Thousand.

- Develop a mentoring program (pairings or groups) at each base, where SNCOs are proactively matched with black E1-E5s in BMT or in the First Term Airman Center (FTAC). Mentors should be trained and equipped to discuss prevention of Article 112a and Article 86 offenses.

- Create SNCO-led affinity groups for black E1-E5 at each base.

- Evaluate and strengthen efforts to increase overall racial, ethnic, and gender diversity of Air Force members and leadership. Continue to determine and address barriers to recruitment, retention, and promotion of diverse Airmen. (Ex 29:8-9)

Accountability and Transparency: The DAF highly values the principle of accountability. The DAF charges its leaders to set standards, consistently uphold them, and hold the individuals accountable when they are not met. Additionally, transparency is critical, particularly given formal and informal oversight from Congress, the media, the Air Force community, and the general public. (Ex 29:5-6)

Objectives for accountability and transparency in the 2019 DAAT Roadmap included:

- In conjunction with developing a tracking mechanism for administrative actions, squadrons across the DAF should host regular Status of Discipline briefings for LOCs, LOAs, and LORs. The focus should be at the squadron level and attended by the group commander, squadron commander, flight commanders, Noncommissioned Officers in Charge (NCOICs), and First Sergeants.

- Leadership, from the senior DAF levels to the wing commander level, should issue regular communication about this issue to underscore the seriousness of it, lay out how it will be address, and celebrate accomplishments. (Ex 29:9)

In April 2020, the DAAT was renamed the Black/African American Team (BAAT) and has since been renamed again to the Black/African American Employment Strategy Team (BEST). The BEST is tasked to review and analyze guidelines, programs, data and other information for barriers to employment, advancement, and retention of black employees, applicants, and military members. (Ex 30)

ANALYSIS OF PREVIOUS REPORTS AND RECOMMENDATIONS

The 2011 MLDC report, *From Representation to Inclusion: Diversity Leadership for the 21st Century Military,* provided the DoD with a thorough assessment of policies that provide opportunities for the promotion and advancement of minority members of the Armed Forces. This report effectively put DoD and military services on notice that attention was required to address a gap in diversity at the leadership level. The three interrelated goals identified by the MLDC provided a clear sight picture for DoD to hold its leadership accountable for improving diversity and creating a culture where future leaders are able to effectively lead a diverse workforce to maximize mission effectiveness.

In 2014, DoD and military services provided an update to the implementation of recommendations made by the MLDC. The update provided the actions and plans the DoD and military services had taken to comply with all 20 recommendations. Although the progress update did provide context to the initiatives and actions the DoD and services proposed, it did not provide measurable results from these actions. Given the lack of measurable results, this Review could not assess the positive or negative impacts of implementing the MLDC's recommendations. There appeared to be a relaxed standard for what passed for implementation, and the accountability and follow up were not robust. As one senior DAF official put it, "[t]he assessment of what is considered implemented and closed is overly generous and leaves accountability for DoD and Service senior leaders at the cursory level. If these items were implemented as stated, you would expect to see different results from what the data collected [in this Review] shows. I believe this highlights the lack of senior leader follow up, determination, and accountability over time." Follow-up to the 2014 DoD progress update to the Commission's recommendations may be warranted and may enhance any recommendations made in this DAF IG Review.

The 2019 GAO report, *Military Justice, DoD and the Coast Guard Need to Improve Their Capabilities to Assess Racial and Gender Disparities,* provided the military services with an assessment of how they collect and maintain investigative and disciplinary data with regards to race, ethnicity, and gender. These data could then be used to assess the associated racial and gender disparities in the military justice system, and whether disparities have been studied by DoD. Again, this report provided a clear sight picture for the Air Force to acknowledge the deficiencies associated with capturing these data and conduct root cause analysis to the reasons why disparities exist.

The DAF's preemptive plan to address the findings in the 2019 GAO report and address issues involving administrative and disciplinary actions involving service members was the creation of the DAAT in September of 2017. After several years of attempting to stand-up and organize the DAAT, a 2019 DAAT Roadmap was produced to layout the priority objectives the team would attempt to implement. According to several past and current members of the DAAT, as well as current members of the BEST, the DAAT was ineffective at executing its charter and its objectives. When asked if the DAAT determined why there was racial disparity in military justice actions, one former member stated, "No... from my understanding we have not determined why there's a disparity. I think we developed some ideas and, like I said, one of those ideas is that supervisors may be, I guess having bias against certain members, you know, unconsciously and where they may be more patient and understand with people that look like them or remind them of themselves."

As the DAAT transitions to the BEST, the initial charter will focus on the barriers black service members face in all aspects of their military and civilian life cycle. This broader scope potentially impacts more service members and civilian employees than the previously limited focus of the disciplinary system. However, as the scope has increased, so too has team's necessity to have adequate resources and senior-level support to ensure success, something lacking in the DAAT.

INTERIM CONCLUSION

Past reports and studies addressing racial disparity in the DoD and military services focused on the quantitative data and made recommendations, but the disparities have persisted over time. This Review concluded the common theme in past initiatives is the lack of a root cause analysis to explain the racial disparities. Although the DAF has actively collected data to assess whether racial disparities exist, it has not attempted to answer the question of "why" they exist. In order to craft effective devise recommendations to resolve racial disparities, one must first identify the root cause of the disparities. A thorough root cause analysis of the disparities is necessary for targeted actions to bring about meaningful change.

The DAF attempted to address administrative and disciplinary practices by establishing the DAAT, which, although well-intentioned, was ineffectively executed and not adequately supported. As pointed out in previous studies and reports, involvement at all levels of leadership is critical. The 2011 MLDC report and 2019 GAO report both placed a premium on the importance of leadership in the majority of their conclusions and recommendations.

WHY DO WE CONTINUE TO SEE DISPARITIES?

DAF actions in response to recommendations in previous reports were focused on systemic or process-related solutions. After reviewing these reports and conducting interviews with people involved in these reports, SMEs, and other DAF members, the Review team identified two primary factors contributing to the persistence of these disparities: (1) the DAF did not systematically conduct an analysis to determine the cause of the disparities previously identified in the reports; and (2) lack of follow-through with measurable outcomes.

MLDC RESPONSE

The MLDC recommendations focused on the human aspects of the racial disparity such as leadership, understanding, and expectations. Yet, the DAF solutions focused on systemic fixes with no way to measure the impact on the human aspects and no direct tie to an identified racial disparity. For example, Recommendation 3 of the MLDC stated "Leadership of the DoD and services must be personally committed to diversity becoming an institutional priority." In the report, the commission linked strong, personal leadership to performance and morale. According to the 2014 MLCD Update, the Chief of Staff of the Air Force and the Chief Master Sergeant of the Air Force implemented this recommendation by signing a Declaration on Diversity, reinforcing their commitment to the principles of diversity and inclusion in recruiting, retaining, and developing Airmen representative of America's broadest landscape. DoD subsequently closed out the recommendation as fully implemented. There is no indication, however, that the DAF gathered data to determine the extent leadership became personally involved in making diversity a priority. The survey, interview, and discussion data gathered during this Review indicates increased personal involvement by senior leadership remains crucial.

DAAT RECOMMENDATIONS

In 2020, the DAAT team made several recommendations related to the human aspects of the racial disparity issue in military discipline. The DAF is assessing actions to implement recommendations, but it is not yet clear how many will focus on the human factors. This Review confirmed that, to be effective, any implemented solutions must involve commanders and be measurably linked to the racial disparity gaps.

The DAAT team's focus on unconscious bias training illustrates the importance of measures of effectiveness. At this point, the DAF has no concrete link between unconscious bias and the racial disparity in military discipline, therefore there is no way to measure the effectiveness of the proposed training. This Review provides information on personal experiences, perceptions, and beliefs that may be a good starting point for measuring training effectiveness. Without an effective means to measure success, bias training could easily fall into the category of additional training that drives additional duties but does not improve military capability and ultimately does not have lasting or meaningful impact on the racial disparity gaps. Furthermore, studies show poorly organized or inadequately led diversity training may make race relations worse. As such, the DAF must define meaningful measures of quality and effectiveness prior to implementing any proposed training program.

As articulated above, lack of leadership involvement and high membership turnover decreased the effectiveness of the DAAT. Three years after its inception, AF/A1 determined the DAAT was ineffective and the implementation of its recommendations was lacking. AF/A1 acknowledged senior DAF leadership changeover was a factor that contributed to the team's lack of effectiveness. The transition to the Black/African American Employment Strategy Team (BEST) with General Officer and SES leadership is likely a step in the right direction.

INTERIM CONCLUSION

Based on the evidence in this report, this Review concludes, past solutions implemented by the DAF were too focused on systems and processes. These solutions were not measurable or sustainable. Furthermore, these solutions were racially neutral and did not adequately involve commanders or account for the daily experiences of Airmen and Space Professionals.

IV. UNDERSTANDING THE MAGNITUDE

The survey data, interviews, and group discussions confirm that racial disparity in DAF discipline and developmental opportunities is deeper than the quantitative disparity numbers indicate. Analysis of DAF data shows racial disparity exists across the life-cycle of an Airman. The Racial Disparity Review survey analysis shows a significant percentage of black service members lack confidence in DAF discipline and developmental opportunity systems. In contrast, the majority of white service members have confidence in the AF systems. The write-in comments to the survey, discussions, and interviews clearly communicate that this disparity is significant, consistent, and personal to our Airmen and Space Professionals. The quantitative disparity numbers are indicators, symptoms, or cues of how the AF discipline system works and how opportunities to succeed are distributed. When combined with personal experiences, that often begin before members join the AF, these cues act as amplifiers resulting in a significant percentage of all DAF service members believing black service members are unfairly treated in the military discipline process and not given the same opportunities to succeed as white service members.

The magnitude of racial disparity in military discipline and development opportunities is substantial. Military justice data concerning Article 15s and courts-martial rates, OSI investigations, Security Forces investigations, and administrative discharge data provide empirical information showing racial disparity. Similarly, disparities between black and white Total Force service members in accessions and recruiting, promotions, leadership assignments, and PME selections indicate racial disparities impact a black service member's opportunity to succeed throughout their time in service. The DAF has known and monitored many of these indications for years, and previous attempts to close the disparity gap have not been uniformly successful. As such, well documented racial disparities persist. Further study must be conducted to determine and understand the root causes of these disparities.

Commanders and leaders at all levels must actively engage with Airmen and Space Professionals to foster an environment of inclusivity. They must also take necessary steps to build trust and confidence in military justice and developmental systems. In addition, DAF process owners must conduct further study to determine and understand root causes of each racial disparity identified in this report.

V. SUMMARY AND RECOMMENDATIONS

This Independent Review confirmed racial disparity exists for black service members in apprehensions, criminal investigations, military justice, administrative separations, placement into occupational career fields, certain promotion rates, professional military educational development, and leadership opportunities. While the data show race is a correlating factor, it does not necessarily indicate causality, and the data do not address why racial disparities exist in these areas.

It is important the reader appreciate the identification of racial disparity does not necessarily equate to either racial bias or racism. This report's primary focus is on identifying areas of racial disparity. During the course of this Review the team received a large volume of first-hand examples of bias, as well as individual acts of racism. While it is impossible to individually validate each example, the themes that emerged from an overwhelming volume of feedback make it reasonable to conclude individual acts of racism occur in the DAF and that racial bias contributes to the disparities found by the Review team.

Secretary of the Air Force, Barbara Barrett, former Air Force Chief of Staff, Gen David Goldfein, current Air Force Chief of Staff, Gen Charles Brown, and Chief of Space Operations, Gen John Raymond have repeatedly emphasized the importance of fair and equitable discipline, development, and opportunities for all our service members. They are committed to promoting an environment free from personal, social, and institutional barriers that might prevent our service members from rising to their highest potential. It is clear from the interviews, group discussions, and surveys that a substantial number of black service members believe there is racial bias in military discipline and developmental opportunities. The racial disparities identified, combined with the personal experiences of our service members, require attention to ensure fair and equitable treatment for all of our Airmen and Space Professionals. Past studies and initiatives failed to effectively address the racial disparities, in part, due to lack of follow-through, long-term commitment, accountability, and consistent involvement by leaders.

RECOMMENDATIONS

Systemic, effective, and lasting solutions to the disparities highlighted in this report will require relentless follow-through by all stakeholders, dogged emphasis by senior leaders, and most importantly, accountability.

- For each identified disparity or deficiency in this report, DAF IG recommends SecAF task the respective DAF stakeholders to, as warranted and appropriate, develop within 60 days systemic action plans, including plans and milestones to address the identified disparities. DAF stakeholders provided initial action plans which are summarized in Appendix A and will be further refined and finalized within 60 days. We also recommend releasing the details of the specific action plans to all Airmen and Space Professionals.

- DAF IG will establish a recurring assessment of the recommendations borne of this Review. DAF IG will provide a "progress report" six months after this report's publication and a full review and assessment of effectiveness of improvement measures annually. The assessments of DAF IG will be publicly released and provided to all Airmen and Space Professionals.

- The Diversity and Inclusion Task-Force should review this report to assess applicability to broader D&I initiatives.

Military Discipline Processes
- The racial disparity in military justice actions, including Article 15s and courts-martial (p. 5-10)
- The disparity in marijuana use among our youngest enlisted members as evidenced by the random drug testing program (p. 10-15)
- The racial disparity in administrative discipline as evidenced by administrative discharges as well as substantive feedback from a large number of Airmen and Space Professionals (p. 16-20)
- The racial disparity in Security Forces (SF) apprehensions (p. 27-30)
- The racial disparity in substantiated Military Equality Opportunity (MEO) sexual harassment complaints (p. 31-33)

Personnel Development & Career Opportunities
- The disparity in Air Force Specialty Codes (AFSCs), especially as it relates to operational versus support career fields (p. 34-45)
- The disparity in Undergraduate Pilot Training (UPT) accession and graduation rates by race, gender, and ethnicity (p. 40)
- The disparity in the officer IDE and SDE process, given that analysis shows black officers are being nominated for PME at higher than the overall nomination rate but designated to attend at a lower rate (p. 52-57)

- The disparity in the civilian Intermediate Developmental Education (IDE) and Senior Developmental Education (SDE) selection process given black civilians are identified to meet the Civilian Developmental Education Board (CDEB) at a consistently lower rate than white civilians (p. 57-59)
- The racial disparities in promotions to E5-E7 and O4-O6 (p. 59-74)
- The racial disparities in civilian leadership representation from GS-13 to SES (p. 75-78)
- The lack of thorough Barrier Analysis among some Developmental Teams[1] (p. 79, 86)
- The racial disparity in wing command and equivalent positions (p. 84-86)

Other Department-wide Concerns
- The lack of satisfaction service members expressed regarding IG and EO, with special emphasis on the process of referring cases back to the chain of command (p. 106-107)
- The lack of trust black DAF members expressed in their chain of command to address racism, bias, and unequal opportunities (p. 90-91, 104-105)
- The sentiment expressed by a majority of black DAF members that they are not given the benefit of the doubt by their chain of command (p. 99, 104-116)

VI. ACKNOWLEDGMENTS

The Review team would like to recognize all our partners who were invaluable in the completion of this Review. The Air Force Survey Office was crucial in helping to craft and execute one of the central elements of this effort, the Independent Racial Disparity Review survey. The Air Force Office of Studies, Analysis, and Assessments (AF/A9) provided exceptional support, guidance, and data analytics capability to assess multiple sources of raw data and built the majority of the graphics used in the report. The Office of the Deputy Chief of Staff of the Air Force for Manpower, Personnel, and Services (AF/A1) provided subject matter experts (SMEs) who contributed keen knowledge and guidance on programs involving Air Force Equal Opportunity, Air Force Diversity and Inclusion, Promotions, Evaluation, Fitness, Recognition, and Enlisted Force policies. Additionally, the Office of the Judge Advocate General of the Air Force (AFJAG), the Office of the Assistant Secretary of the Air Force for Manpower and Reserve Affairs (SAF/MR) and the Air Force Personnel Center (AFPC) provided critical input. The Review team also relied upon the experience and knowledge of a senior leader advisory group made up of more than 20 current and retired black Generals, Admirals, SESs, and CMSgts as well as a diverse team of Major Command (MAJCOM) advisors selected by their commanders. These two groups provided invaluable insight and perspective throughout the Review. Finally, prior to completing the analysis and publishing the report, the Review team consulted with experts from the RAND Corporation, who have years of experience working on and studying racial relations in the U.S. military.

---

[1] AFI 36-205, *Affirmative Employment Program (AEP), Special Emphasis Programs (SEPS) and Reasonable Accommodation Policy*, dated 15 Dec 16, defines barrier analysis as "an investigation of anomalies found in workplace policies, procedures, and practices that limit or tend to limit employment opportunities for members of any race or national origin, either sex, or based on an individual's disability status. Barrier analysis identifies the root causes of those anomalies, and if necessary, eliminates them." (Ex 62) A barrier analysis includes the following steps: identify triggers (trends, disparities, or anomalies), explore root causes of triggers, develop an action plan, implement the action plan, and assess the action plan result. A detailed explanation of the barrier analysis process may be found in AFI 36-205 and EEOC MD-175. (Ex 62; Ex 63)

TABLE OF FIGURES

LIST OF EXHIBITS

Exhibit

APPENDIX A: DAF-DIRECTED ACTION PLANS

Upon initial review of the IG Racial Disparity Review Report, SecAF directed the appropriate agencies to develop action plans to address RDR recommendations. These plans include designating Offices of Primary Responsibility (OPR) and Offices of Collateral Responsibility (OCR) for each of the main recommendations. In addition, the plans propose specific changes to policy, processes, and procedures, how the changes will address the specific racial disparities identified in each recommendation, and timelines for implementation. The action plans are summarized below. Separately, the agencies were also provided additional recommended actions included in Appendix B.

DAF IG will establish a recurring assessment of the recommendations borne of this Review. DAF IG will provide a "progress report" six months after this report's publication and a full review and assessment of effectiveness of improvement measures annually.

It is worth noting this Review and resulting actions are a subset of, and will feed into, broader and more comprehensive Department of Defense and Department of the Air Force Diversity & Inclusion initiatives directed by the Secretary of Defense and the Secretary of the Air Force.

MILITARY DISCIPLINE PROCESSES

IG Finding	Primary POC(s)	Secondary OCRs	Lines Of Effort	Related LOEs	Actions Visible	Impacts Visible	Expected Delivery Date	Measures of Merit
The racial disparity in military justice actions, including Article 15s and courts martial (p.6-15)	JA, Chain of Command	A1	1. Track adverse administrative actions prior to Art 15s or court-martial action. 2. Greater officer involvement in adverse administrative actions.	1. Review AF policy on moral waivers for misconduct. 2. Bias training for legal professionals, commanders, and front line supervisors.	1. Update Automated Military Justice Analysis and Management System (AMJAMS) to require tracking of prior administrative/judicial actions for Amn subject to Art 15 or court-martial action. 2. Update AFI 36-2907, *Adverse Administrative Actions*, and AFI 36-3208, *Administrative Separation of Airmen*, to require officer involvement in progressive adverse administrative actions, before establishing a pattern of misconduct.	1. Enhance racial disparity data we already possess, to narrow the focus to at risk units, locations, and career fields, allowing for concentration of effort. 2. Effect of earlier administrative involvement in adverse administrative actions on the number of Art 15 and court-martial actions overall, and by race.	1 Jan 2023 (FY21-FY22 analysis)	1. Average number of prior administrative actions prior to Art 15 or court-martial, by race. 2. Rates per thousand (RPT), by race, for Art 15s and courts-martial, compared to historical data.

IG Finding	Primary POC(s)	Secondary OCRs	Lines Of Effort	Related LOEs	Actions Visible	Impacts Visible	Expected Delivery Date	Measures of Merit
The racial disparity in administrative discipline as evidenced by administrative discharges as well as substantive feedback from a large number of Airmen and Space Professionals (p. 16-20)	A1, Chain of Command, JA		1. Track adverse administrative actions by race/rank. 2. Greater officer involvement in adverse administrative actions.	1. Review AF policy on moral waivers for misconduct. 2. Bias training for legal professionals, commanders, and front line supervisors.	1. Create a centralized system to track adverse administrative actions by the race/rank. 2. Update JA's Web-based Administrative Separation Program (WASP) to provide RPT (by race, gender, and rank) at the NAF, MAJCOM, and AF levels. 3. Update AFI 36-2907, *Adverse Administrative Actions*, and AFI 36-3208, *Administrative Separation of Airmen*, to require officer involvement in progressive adverse administrative actions, before establishing a pattern of misconduct.	1. Enhance racial disparity data we already possess, to narrow the focus to at risk units, locations, and career fields, allowing for concentration of effort. 2. Effect of earlier officer involvement in adverse administrative actions on the progressive discipline and administrative separations.	1 Jan 2023 (FY21-FY22 Analysis)	1. RPT (by race, gender, and rank) for administrative actions less than administrative separation, to determine racial disparity in adverse administrative actions. 2. Average grade of Amn giving administrative action, for those areas where racial disparity is identified. 3. RPT (by race, gender, and rank) for administrative separations for minor disciplinary infractions and a pattern of misconduct, compared to historical data.

IG Finding	LOEs	OPR / OCRs	Expected Delivery Date	Measures of Merit
The disparity in marijuana use among our youngest enlisted members as evidenced by the random drug testing program (p. 10-15)	1. Educate junior Airmen on medical/mission consequences of illegal drug use.	SG/A1	1 Jan 2023 (FY21-FY22 analysis)	RPT of black Airmen using marijuana, as measured by the random urinalysis program, compared to historical data.
	2. Educate junior Airmen on legal consequences of illegal drug use.	SG/JA		
	3. Review AF policy on moral waivers for drug use.	SG/A1, JA		RPT of Airmen using marijuana in states where marijuana use legalized vs states where not legalized. If correlation exists, assess whether focused training helps address the issue.
	4. Assess whether correlation exists between members with positive drug test results and their respective duty locations and/or homes of record to determine if relationship exists between members testing positive and whether marijuana use has been legalized where they are stationed or in their home state. If correlation exists, focus education and training accordingly.	SG/A1		

IG Finding	Primary POC(s)	Secondary OCRs	Lines Of Effort	Related LOEs	Actions Visible	Impacts Visible	Expected Delivery Date	Measures of Merit
The racial disparity in Security Forces (SF) apprehensions (p. 27 - 30)	A4S	HQ/AFSFC	1) Begin including specific disparity topics during SF Executive Board session, along with SF CC/SFM symposiums.		Y - short and long	Y - long	1) Dec 20	Determine root cause of identified disparities and highlight longitudinal evaluation of enterprise wide apprehensions.
			2) Commission and fund independent "deep dive" review and root cause analysis of identified disparities.				2) Sep 21	

IG Finding	LOE	OPR/OCR	Actions Visible	Impacts Visible	Expected Delivery Date	Measures of Merit
The racial disparity in substantiated Military Equal Opportunity (MEO) sexual harassment complaints (p. 32 - 34)	Conduct analysis to determine and eliminate root causes for disparate MEO sexual harassment complaints	A1	Y - Short (0-6 months)	Y - Mid (6-24 months)	21-Apr	Reduction over time of disparity in MEO sexual harassment complaints
	Implement training interventions to reduce disparity	A1	Y - Mid (6-24 months)	Y - Mid (6-24 months)	21-May	Reduction over time of disparity in MEO sexual harassment complaints

PERSONNEL DEVELOPMENT & CAREER OPPORTUNITIES

IG Finding	LOE	OPR/OCR	Actions Visible	Impacts Visible	Expected Delivery Date	Measures of Merit
The racial disparities in promotions to E5-E7 and O-4-O-6 (p. 59 - 74)	Review and rework EES to align with National Defense Strategy, with focus on removing disparate testing outcomes	A1/CMSAF	Y - Short & Mid	Y – Long (>2 years)	21-Jun	Longitudinal promotion rates by REG, grade, and AFSC
	Infuse OES with more emphasis on what we value (add emphasis to measure inclusive leadership)	A1	Y - Mid (6-24 months)	Y - Mid & Long	21-Jun	Longitudinal promotion demographics
	Implement developmental categories to allow greater development agility and evaluation among closer cohorts	A1	Y - complete	Y - complete	Complete	Longitudinal promotion demographics
	Expand mentorship matches and emphasis for minorities (with emphasis on key developmental experiences that are often promotion discriminators)	A1/MAJCOMs	Y - Short (0-6 months)	Y - Mid (6-24 months)	21-Mar	Longitudinal promotion demographics

IG Finding	LOE	OPR/OCR	Actions Visible	Impacts Visible	Expected Delivery Date	Measures of Merit
	Implement Bias Training for the force, with emphasis on supervisors and commanders	ODI	Y - Short (0-6 months)	Y - Mid & Long	21-Mar	Longitudinal promotion demographics
	**Actions tied to finding 3 are also critical to positive outcomes on finding 1	AETC/USAFA/A1	Y - Mid (6-24 months)	Y - Mid & Long	21-Mar	Increased accessions of minorities to underrepresented AFSCs
The racial disparities in civilian leadership representation from GS-13 to SES (p. 75-78)	Evaluate barriers to diversity in selection process	A1	Y - Short (0-6 months)	Y - Mid (6-24 months)	21-Mar	Longitudinal demographics of GS-13 and above
	Consistent with the law and merit selection principles, increase number of GS-13 and above positions filled through recruitment (vs processing applications)	A1/MAJCOMs	Y - Mid (6-24 months)	Y - Mid (6-24 months)	21-Jun	Longitudinal demographics of GS-13 and above
	Increase diversity of those serving on selection boards for GS13 +	A1	Y - Short (0-6 months)	Y - Mid (6-24 months)	21-Jun	Longitudinal demographics of GS-13 and above
The disparity in Air Force Specialty Codes (AFSCs), especially as it relates to operational versus support career fields (p. 34 - 45)	Implement Bias Training for the force, with emphasis on supervisors and commanders	ODI	Y - Short (0-6 months)	Y - Mid & Long	21-Mar	Longitudinal demographics
	Review AFS selection criteria for minority barriers to entry	AETC/A1	Y - Mid (6-24 months)	Y - Mid & Long	21-Mar	Increased accessions of minorities to underrepresented AFSCs
	Review rated officer selection processes and barriers to selection	AETC/USAFA/A1	Y - Mid (6-24 months)	Y - Mid & Long	21-Mar	Increased accessions of minorities to rated AFSCs
The disparity in the civilian Intermediate developmental Education (IDE) and Senior Developmental Education (SDE) selection process given black civilians are identified to meet the Civilian DEDB at a consistently lower rate than white civilians (p. 57 - 59)	Identify and address impact of "what we value" criteria on diversity of civilian IDE and SDE selections	A1	Y - Mid (6-24 months)	Y - Mid (6-24 months)	21-Jun	Longitudinal demographics of civilians recommended by DTs to meet the board; longitudinal Civilian DE demographics

IG Finding	LOE	OPR/OCR	Actions Visible	Impacts Visible	Expected Delivery Date	Measures of Merit
	Implement Bias Training for the force, with emphasis on supervisors and commanders	ODI	Y - Short (0-6 months)	Y - Mid & Long	21-Mar	Longitudinal demographics
The disparity in the officer IDE and SDE process, given that analysis shows black officers are being nominated for PME at higher than the overall nomination rate but designated to attend at a lower rate (p. 52-57)	Expand mentorship programs towards minorities (with emphasis on key development milestones)	A1	Y - Short (0-6 months)	Y - Mid & Long	21-Mar	Longitudinal trends of DE selection among minorities
	Implement "Definitely Attend" program targeting IDE	A1	Y - Complete	Y - Complete	Complete	DEDB board reports on D&I demographics; longitudinal selection among minorities
	Expand "Definitely Attend" program targeting SDE	A1	Y - Mid (6-24 months)	Y - Mid (6-24 months)	21-Mar	DEDB board reports on D&I demographics; longitudinal selection among minorities
	Ensure non-statutory selection boards (DTs and DEDBs) have a diverse board composition and review/scoring process	A1	Y - Mid (6-24 months)	Y - Long (>2 yrs)	21-Jun	Longitudinal trends of DE selection among minorities
	Implement Bias Training for the force, with emphasis on supervisors and commanders	ODI	Y - Short (0-6 months)	Y - Mid & Long	21-Mar	Longitudinal demographics
The racial disparity in wing command and equivalent positions (p. 84 - 86)	Strengthen minority representation and visibility throughout command selection and matching process (i.e. board composition, MOI, etc.)	A1	Y - Mid (6-24 months)	Y - Long (>2 yrs)	21-Jun	CSB selection demographics
	Expand mentorship programs towards minorities (with emphasis on key development milestones)	A1	Y - Mid (6-24 months)	Y - Long (>2 yrs)	21-Mar	Longitudinal demographics for Wing/CCs
	Implement Bias Training for the force, with emphasis on supervisors and commanders	ODI	Y - Short (0-6 months)	Y - Mid & Long	21-Mar	Longitudinal demographics
The lack of thorough Barrier Analysis among some Developmental Teams (p. 79 - 86)	Publish DT guidance that mandates barrier analysis and reporting requirements	A1	Y - Short (0-6 months)	Y - Mid (6-24 months)	21-Mar	Longitudinal demographics

IG Finding	OPR	OCR(s)	Lines Of Effort	Related LOEs	Actions Visible	Impacts Visible	Expected Delivery Date	Measures of Merit
The disparity in UPT accession and graduation rates by race, gender, and ethnicity (p. 40 - 42)	AETC/A3	AFRS/Det 1, AFJROTC	LOE 1: Inspire and attract talented and diverse youth: Increase awareness of rated careers with multi-layered outreach	LOE 2, 3	• Short term o Increased aviation early exposure to diverse youth: — Inspire Ops — Aim High Virtual Flight Academy — Aim High Flight Academy — Pathways to Wing events — AFJROTC Flight Academy o Increased Mentorship and guidance for accession process • Medium/Long term — AIM HIGH Outreach • Medium/Long term o Build upon existing networks and forge new relationships with organizations serving youth from underrepresented groups to promote awareness and interest in Air Force rated career fields o Conduct data analysis to continually inform additional initiatives to increase minority accession to UPT	Yes, Short term Increased diversity in applicant pool at source of commission	Currently ongoing	• Measures of effectiveness o Demographics of applicant pool at accession sources (showing increase until matching the demographics of the recruitable population) • Measures of performance o Number of underrepresented group youth outreach events o Demographics of participants in early exposure events o Growth and expansion of successful programs that increase demographics of applicant pool
General Response: Addressing the disparity in UPT accession and graduation rates by race, gender, and ethnicity requires a comprehensive solution. The Draft Rated Diversity Improvement (RDI) strategy targets this problem through three goals: 1) attract and recruit the best talent from diverse backgrounds to cultivate a high performing and innovative competitiveness for Air Force reflective of the best of our nation; 2) develop and retain the Air Force's best rated aircrew by harnessing diversity as a force multiplier and fostering a culture of inclusion; 3) optimize diversity advancement efforts by leveraging data driven approaches. UPT accession and graduation are one facet of overall RDI but are heavily influenced by the pre- and post-UPT RDI efforts. Early exposure initiatives heavily impact the diversity and qualifications of UPT candidates. Likewise, developing and retaining diverse rated officers and fostering a culture	Disparity in UPT Accession Causal Factors: Lack of early aviation exposure to generate interest Socio-economic barriers reduce barriers • Barriers within pilot selection process • Barriers in accession sources unique to each accession source	USAFA, AFROTC, AETC/A3, AFPC	LOE 2: Recruit and access diverse and talented candidates: expand to include various untapped geographic regions, academic sources, and increased emphasis on minorities and females.	LOE 1, 3	• Short term o Increased recruiting focus in underserved areas to increase underrepresented groups — USAFA First Year Lieutenant (FYL) program — AFROTC Gold Bar Recruiters (GBR) o Increased aviation early exposure within accession sources — AFROTC You Can Fly — USAFA Airmanship course battery o Increased Mentorship and guidance for UPT selection process — Aviation Inspiration Mentorship (AIM) Team o Pilot Selection Process Working Group — 12 comprehensive recommendations to identify and remove barriers in pilot selection process — Reduce impact of flying hours beyond where there is no statistical difference in the probability of successfully graduating pilot training —reduce socio-economic barriers — Increase early exposure	• Short term o Increased diversity at accession sources o Increased diversity in pilot applicant pool at sources of commission o Increased diversity in pilot selects — ROTC produces the highest number of diverse officers but the lowest percentage of diverse pilot selects	Currently ongoing	• Measures of effectiveness o Demographics of pilot selects o Demographics of pilot applicant pool o Demographics of cadets at sources of commission o Adverse impact of AFOQT and subgroup differences of TBAS — measured by comparing the selection rate and performance of underrepresented groups to the majority group Measures of performance o Number of mentorship engagements and feedback from mentees o PCSM scores by demographics at the various accession sources o Demographics and completion rates of participants in early exposure events o Number of recruiting engagements at minority serving institutions

IG Finding	OPR	OCR(s)	Lines Of Effort	Related LOEs	Actions Visible	Impacts Visible	Expected Delivery Date	Measures of Merit
		19 AF, HAF/A3TF, AFPC	LOE 3: Develop Rated Force (AETC, AFPC, 19 AF)	LOE 1, 2	• Short term o Identify and eliminate barriers in flying training based on race, gender, religion or sexual orientation — Create and maintain attrition database to aid in root cause attrition analysis — Cluster students from underrepresented groups to increase mutual support — Students provide real-time feedback on instructors — Student advocate embedded into the human performance team — Created a Profession of Arms class to teach diversity and inclusion basics in 19 AF processes and syllabi o Foster an environment of dignity, respect, and inclusion through improved dialogue, training, and professional development o Assess and streamline UFT medical requirements and waiver	• Medium term: Similar levels of attrition irrespective of race, gender, ethnicity.	Currently ongoing	• Measures of effectiveness o Demographics of pilot graduates – should reflect similar percentages to demographics of entrants o Attrition rates by race, gender, and ethnicity • Measures of performance o Demographics, completion rates, and performance at UFT crossflow boards of Rated Preparation Program o Student feedback during and at end of flying training

OTHER DEPARTMENT-WIDE CONCERNS

IG Finding	LOE	OPR/OCR	Actions Visible	Impacts Visible	Expected Delivery Date	Measures of Merit
The lack of satisfaction service members expressed regarding EO, with special emphasis on the process of referring cases back to the chain of command (p. 106 - 107)	Review and update EO processes for fairness and inclusion	A1	Y - Mid (6-24 months)	Y - Mid (6-24 months)	21-May	DEOCS trends over time
	Monitor customer satisfaction with EO	A1	Y - Short (0-6 months)	Y - Mid (6-24 months)	21-Mar	Over time, increase Airmen's level of reported satisfaction; Understand concerns via anonymous surveys
	Improve ability of Airmen and Space Professionals to resolve interpersonal conflicts	AETC/A1	Y - Mid (6-24 months)	Y - Mid (6-24 months)	21-Jun	Measurable increase in the # of complaints resolved; Increased use of ADR program
	Re concern about referring matters about "command" back to command: reeducate EOs, when get complaint, must carefully assess which must be "upchannelled" to the next level versus back to the same commander	A1	Y - Mid (6-24 months)	Y - Mid (6-24 months)	21-Jun	Over time, increase Airmen's level of reported satisfaction; Understand concerns via anonymous surveys

IG Finding	LOEs	OPR/OCR	Expected Delivery Date	Measures of Merit
The lack of satisfaction service members expressed regarding IG, with special emphasis on the process of referring cases back to the chain of command (p. 106 - 107)	1. Related to concern regarding referring matters about "command" back to command: Re-emphasize/Re-educate all IGs immediately: chain of command complaints must be carefully assessed to determine which complaints may be "upchannelled" to the next level in the chain versus back to the same commander — complaints against the chain of command are never referred to that same level of command IAW AFI 90-301 Table 3.12, "For all complaints, refer the complaint, in writing, to the appropriate agency, grievance channel or commander (Note 1) at least one level above the highest ranking responsible management official (RMO), to ensure an independent review." For appeals or reconsideration requests for referred command matters, the office referred should be the appropriate office to resolve the appeal, as long as no misconduct has been alleged against that RMO or Office.	IGQ	15-Nov-20	Collect and Analyze data via Surveys and IG Automated Case Tracking System (ACTS) // Over time, increase Airmen's level of reported satisfaction; Understand concerns via anonymous surveys // Measurable increase in the # of complaints resolved; Increased use of Alternate Dispute Resolution (ADR) program
	2. Related to concern regarding matters being taken to the IG and the IG does not investigate all of them: Reeducate all IGs immediately, during intake, clearly explain what IG will do and what will be referred to another agency or to command, and why, so complainant understands process not frustrated or surprised		15-Nov-20	
	3. Incorporate racial disparity report results into IGTC, quarterly telecons and the annual worldwide IGQ training		20 Nov 20	
	4. Robust AFI 90-301 para 1.50.1 – 1.50.2.5 by incorporating into agenda for 90-301 rewrite		21 Dec 20	
	5. Wing level IGQs will incorporate concerns identified in the racial disparity report to update the complaint resolution process (CRP) education; SAF/IGQ is preparing a standardized PP presentation with talking points to more clearly educate all Airmen on the USAF CRP — specifically "IG Matters" vs "Command Matters" so all Airmen understand when a complaint filed with the IG may be referred to Command or the appropriate office/agency for resolution.		20 Nov 20	

APPENDIX B: FUTURE ANALYSIS

The Department should consider implementing the following to allow for additional analysis and further progress in the future:

- Further assess the lack of trust black DAF members expressed in their chain of command to address racism, bias, and unequal opportunities (p. 91, 104-116) (IG)

- Further assess the sentiment expressed by a majority of black DAF members that they are not given the benefit of the doubt by their chain of command (p. 99, 104-116) (IG)

- Complete a comprehensive analysis on the Drug Demand Reduction Program to: determine the factors as to how military members are randomly selected for drug testing; examine the effectiveness of the computer program used for random selection; analyze how AF Installations execute the program; and explain the disparities identified in Fig 9 and Fig 10 of this report. (p. 12-15) (SG, JA)

- Start tracking CDIs to assess whether racial disparities exist, and if so, identify whether corrective or improvement actions are necessary (p. 34) (IG)

- Assess whether current black officer accession goals, which are based upon the eligible population, should be adjusted to a goal closer to that of the representative demographic population (p. 34-35) (A1)

- Start collecting data to assess whether the officer PME Definitely Attend (DA) process introduces disparities, and if so, identify whether corrective or improvement actions are necessary (p. 54-56) (A1)

- Start tracking the demographics of enlisted JPME nominations and selections to determine whether there are disparities, and if so, identify whether corrective or improvement actions are necessary (p. 56-57) (A1)

- Start collecting data to allow for analysis of civilian leadership position hiring processes to determine if there is a disparity in applicants for civilian leadership positions, a disparity in applicants' qualifications, and/or disparity in selection rates for those positions based on race, ethnicity, or gender, and if so, identify whether corrective or improvement actions are necessary (p. 75-78) (A1)

- Conduct a comprehensive review of key developmental positions, to include "executive officers," "aides," or "special assistants" to allow for analysis of the demographics of wing-level and below key positions (p. 80) (A1)

- Start collecting data to allow for analysis of racial disparities in Group Superintendent positions, and if they exist, identify whether corrective or improvement actions are necessary (p. 86-87) (A1)

- Start collecting data to allow for analysis of Command Selection List (CSL) data to assess whether there are racial disparities in command matches at the squadron, group, and wing levels and, if they exist, identify whether corrective or improvement actions are necessary (p. 82-83) (A1)

- Revisit previous reports covered herein--including primarily the 2011 Military Leadership Diversity Commission (MLDC) Report--to assess whether previously closed recommendations should be readdressed (p. 118-123, 129) (all appropriate stakeholders)

CPSIA information can be obtained
at www.ICGtesting.com
Printed in the USA
JSHW011157260623
43263JS00001B/1

.